Chris Webb

The Sobibór Death Camp
History, Biographies, Remembrance

Revised and Updated

Chris Webb

THE SOBIBÓR DEATH CAMP
History, Biographies, Remembrance

Revised and Updated

Bibliographic information published by the Deutsche Nationalbibliothek
Die Deutsche Nationalbibliothek lists this publication in the Deutsche Nationalbibliografie; detailed bibliographic data are available in the Internet at http://dnb.d-nb.de.

Bibliografische Information der Deutschen Nationalbibliothek
Die Deutsche Nationalbibliothek verzeichnet diese Publikation in der Deutschen Nationalbibliografie; detaillierte bibliografische Daten sind im Internet über http://dnb.d-nb.de abrufbar.

Cover picture: Sobibór Camp 1943 from the Johann Niemann photo album (USHMM)

This book is the revised and updated 2nd edition of the 2017 original edition.

ISBN-13: 978-3-8382-1860-1
© *ibidem*-Verlag, Stuttgart 2023
All rights reserved.

No part of this publication may be reproduced, stored in or introduced into a retrieval system, or transmitted, in any form, or by any means (electronic, mechanical, photocopying, recording or otherwise) without the prior written permission of the publisher. Any person who does any unauthorized act in relation to this publication may be liable to criminal prosecution and civil claims for damages.

Alle Rechte vorbehalten. Das Werk einschließlich aller seiner Teile ist urheberrechtlich geschützt. Jede Verwertung außerhalb der engen Grenzen des Urheberrechtsgesetzes ist ohne Zustimmung des Verlages unzulässig und strafbar. Dies gilt insbesondere für Vervielfältigungen, Übersetzungen, Mikroverfilmungen und elektronische Speicherformen sowie die Einspeicherung und Verarbeitung in elektronischen Systemen.

Printed in the United States of America

For Freya, Cora, and Otto

Dedicated to Jules Schelvis and Thomas (Toivi) Blatt'
In loving memory of
Rita Beard

Taken from us too soon.

Table of Contents

Foreword 9
About the Author 13
Author's Introduction 15

Chapter I *'Aktion Reinhardt'* An Overview 19
Chapter II History of the Sobibór Death Camp 31
Chapter III The *Arbeitsjuden* Remember 129
Chapter IV The Jewish Survivors, Escapees and Victims—
Roll of Remembrance 165

    Survivors and Escapees A–Z 167
    Roll of Remembrance—Poland and Other Countries A–Z ... 196
    Roll of Remembrance—Holland A–Z 211
    Roll of Remembrance—Greater German Reich A–Z 262
    Selected to work at Sobibór for Outside Labor Camps A–Z . 336

Chapter V The Perpetrators 351
    Aktion Reinhardt—Leading Personalities 355
    Sobibór Death Camp—Commandants 372
    SOBIBÓR DEATH CAMP. Garrison Listed in Alphabetical Order 378
    SUPPORT STAFF 424

Chapter VI Post War Testimonies by *SS*-Men 425
    Former *SS* Men Testimonies 426

Chapter VII Testimonies by Former *Trawnikimänner* 585

Chapter VIII The Author's Visits to Sobibór 605

    Trip to Poland 2002 605

    Trip to Poland 2004 607

Illustrations and Sources 611

Drawings, Maps and Sources 638

Documents and Sources 640

Appendix 1 Alphabetical List of Ukrainian Guards—Sobibór 657

Appendix 2 Glossary of Nazi Terms 661

Appendix 3 Table of Equivalent Ranks 666

Appendix 4 Transports from Holland 667

Appendix 5 Transports from Slovakia 678

Appendix 6 Transports from the Greater German Reich 685

Appendix 7 The Sobibór Area Labor Camps 690

Selected Bibliography 699

Index of Names 709

Foreword

The Final Solution needed a number of converging elements to afford it the opportunity to come to fruition. Excuse the term 'perfect storm', a rather ironic term in this situation, but it is defined as a critical or disastrous event created by a powerful and unlikely concurrence or confluence of factors. With respect to the Holocaust, some of these major factors include the following:

1. Successive stages of discrimination, oppression, marginalization, and ghettoization, culminating in mass genocide of unimaginable proportions.
2. A megalomaniacal tyrant with obvious issues of unresolved rageful hatred, combined with a need to scapegoat, as well as a tremendous appetite for greed, power, and conquest. A strangely charismatic character totally bereft of any conscience or humanity.
3. A propaganda campaign that was enormous in scope and one in which all forms of resistance or even dissenting opinion were blocked, prevented, silenced and/or punished—most often by death. Paving the way were the Anti-Semitic influences and indoctrinations of the bogus 'Protocols of the Learned Elders of Zion,' and the perversion of evolutionary theory known as Social Darwinism, the schooling of German children, and the writings and orations of many other influences of the years before Nazism and during its heyday. All of these were aimed at breeding hatred and amplifying prejudice.
4. A collective low morale among the German people following Germany's defeat in the First World War, aggravated by the crippling reparations it was forced to pay, the significant territorial concessions, as well as other terms

of the Versailles Treaty. This led to bitter resentment which powered the rise of the Nazi Party.
5. A severe economic collapse with extraordinarily high levels of unemployment.
6. In line with the point above, is an often overlooked or minimized motivation for the 'Final Solution'—that of avarice, grand theft, and opportunisms. There was an unprecedented confiscation of homes, land, businesses, and assets of every kind imaginable—including artificial limbs, gold teeth, hair and anything else that could be repurposed or otherwise utilized. The purpose, to finance their war effort, keep the military-industrial complex going, and enrich themselves. This illustrates that desperate people will often sacrifice their moral and ethical code when there are benefits and rewards to serve their selfish interests.

Like the parable of the blind men and the elephant—each examining the parts of it by feeling around and describing what seem to be quite disparate perspectives on the same animal—so too even among Holocaust scholars and researchers. They approach the subject from a wide variety of unique perspectives, and tend to narrow their focus because the Holocaust has so many facets. For example, some present biographical information about Hitler and his henchmen as their focus; some look at opportunisms the Holocaust within the context of geopolitics or social sciences. Some are concerned with demographics and the aggregation of statistics involving the numbers of those murdered. Some spend their time recording and documenting survivor testimonies, while others create timelines and deportation lists. Yet others compile databases and spreadsheets of victims. Some focus on the forensic investigation of extermination camps, while others study the Jewish resistance groups. And the list goes on!

Not surprisingly, and yet still surprisingly, there are those who focus on trying to deny or minimize the enormity of the

Holocaust. My particular niche is leading the way, primarily on social media platforms and other online venues to combat Holocaust denial. In order to effectively achieve this I engage in extensive research to refute all of the highly regurgitated so called 'challenges' to the historicity of the Holocaust.

Imagine my joy and pleasure when my path crossed with that of Chris Webb, since his niche ties into my speciality in the sense that he pulls together a vast array of elements that all converge to create an amazingly accurate portrait of the Nazi extermination camps—their conceptualizations, planning, construction, organizing, staffing, operations, policies and procedures, and portraits of many perpetrators, as well as biographies of countless captives, victims and survivors. His works are truly a Holocaust denier's nightmare.

All of this is meticulously compiled from a wide variety of highly trusted primary, secondary and tertiary sources from every perspective. Chris Webb fact-checks up front, so that you don't have to. He proactively points out even minor inconsistencies in testimonies, dates and numbers to obviate the need for anyone else to ever had the need to do so. Anyone would be hard pressed to legitimately question anything. All too often we read different accounts of the same historical events and the narratives compete with each other for dominance. It is comforting to find none of that in Chris Webb's books.

He even provides the reader with a collection of SS testimonies, wherein they attest to the crimes against humanity in which they had direct involvement. What could be more compelling and powerful than that? This begs the question of how we can possibly have people denying the Holocaust, when so many of the perpetrators not only confess to it, but spell things out in excruciating detail.

This truth-based reporting and writing, is sadly-enough—and all too often—giving way to a growing tendency to spin historical events and commentary to meet the presenter's need to influence, persuade, and peddle their biases and agenda, rather than to impart fact-based, objective historical information. Even the presentation of nightly news is essentially becoming more and more opinion-based these days.

The subtleties in choosing certain words and phrases; the deliberate misuse of statistics, revising history, whitewashing or glorifying on the one hand, and demonizing on the other have become more commonplace than people realize.

Nowadays we see an incredibly fast-growing proliferation of all manner of propaganda videos and comments on social media by social influencers using these venues to shape public opinion—as the Nazis started to do in the 1930's. To immerse oneself in that world is to see just how pernicious this is in inciting hatred through revisionism, widespread use of fallacious reasoning, inversions of truth, demonizing buzzwords, and intolerance of minority groups taken to its extreme—again reminiscent of what was done by the Nazis.

All that said, the reader of this book, as well as every other book by Chris Webb, will find it refreshing to be provided by the facts—the entirety of what is known about Sobibór in this case—and nothing but the facts.

There is no room for speculation or denial. This book is backed by converging evidence. Nothing is filled in, nothing is interpreted, nothing is meant to distort, mischaracterize, misinterpretat, or embellish. The only persuasion is that which is justified as a consequence of simply reading this book, it demands that people know it is a book of solid evidence, unbiased research and undeniable facts, and that they feel the compassion, empathy, outrage, and disgust over that was perpetrated at Sobibór, and that they use this as a lesson to caution all societies against any tendency to go down the dangerous steps that culminate in such massive crimes against humanity.

Jerry Steinberg
New Jersey, USA
November 2022

About the Author

Chris Webb was born on November 20, 1954, in Hillingdon, Middlesex, the youngest of three children. It was his father, Frederick John Webb, who started his passion for the Holocaust, during 1971 presenting him with the book by Gerald Reitlinger, *'The Final Solution.'*

Chris worked for the Post Office which later became Royal Mail from 1971, until 2011. He rose through the ranks starting as a Postal and Telegraph Officer on Windsor Counter, and ended his 39 year service as a Senior Manager. He worked at a number of places, mostly in the South East, and London Headquarters.

On his retirement from Royal Mail, he started working on his first book 'The Treblinka Death Camp', which was published in 2014. Chris Webb has now written a number of books on the *Aktion Reinhardt* death camps, as well as books on Auschwitz and Chelmno, all published by ibidem-Verlag in Germany.

In addition to his writing, and lecturing at a number of universities on the Holocaust, he has founded the Holocaust Historical Society website. He co-founded both the ARC website and the H.E.A.R.T. websites. He has also contributed to a number of television programmes by the BBC on the Holocaust such as *Auschwitz: 'The Final Solution'* and a number of programs for the *'Who Do you Think You Are'* series. He has also contributed to the French Tv documentary *'Annihilation.'* He has also participated in worldwide podcasts for the Ghetto Fighters House in Israel. He is also a member of the Treblinka Extermination Camp online group, and Tiergartenstrasse 4 Association

Chris is married to Shirley, and they have a daughter Heather, who is married to Mark. They have two beautiful daughters, Freya and Cora, cherished and much loved granddaughters of Chris and Shirley Webb.

Author's Introduction

Sobibor 2004—The Author far left

This book is an important contribution to the history of *Aktion Reinhardt* and the Holocaust.

This publication follows in the footsteps of the outstanding book *'Fotos Aus Sobibor,'* the collection of unique photographs taken in Sobibór from the private photograph album of Johann Niemann, the deputy commandant, published in 2020. They say a picture is worth a thousand words, and that saying has never been more apt.

Thanks to the album we can now see what the death camp looked like, and the *SS* men who ran it. We can put names to faces we have read about for years. This book exposes the stark reality of *Aktion Reinhardt*, through carefully screened and selected photographs.

This book records some of the results of the police investigations about the camp. The English translations of the statements made by the former *SS-Sonderkommando* Sobibór personnel, many appearing in this setting for the first time. Indeed these statements are at the heart of this book, and the reader will learn a host of new things about Sobibór in great detail; about the layout of the camp, how it operated on a day to day basis, and descriptions by the former guards on their fellow partners in crime.

One major improvement over the first edition, is that sources are now provided. Both the Jewish Roll of Remembrance and the Perpetrators chapters are expanded and updated with new biographies and information. This publication marks the anniversary of eighty years since the revolt took place. This is an important milestone.

I must pay tribute here to the fantastic and dedicated work of Ena Pflanz, who has translated the bulk of the post-war statements, from German to English. I cannot thank her enough. Also worthy of mention is Georg Biemann, who also translated statements from German to English, as well as conducting painstaking research into a number of individuals such as Rudolf Beckmann, Franz Stangl, Richard Thomalla, and Josef Wolf.

Georg's tireless research ended decades long of frustrating and often fruitless searches, in respect of Rudolf Beckmann. Indeed the uncovering of this complex and shrouded in mystery figure, is worthy of a book in its own right. We thought that we had tracked Beckmann down, only to find he was not born in Osnabruck as many eminent historians claimed, and that we had to search again. Thanks to the *Bundesarchiv* we were able to locate the real Rudolf Beckmann, who hailed from Buer, Gelsenkirchen. Without doubt Georg has considerably enriched this book, and I thank him for that from the bottom of my heart.

Regarding the post-war interrogation documents I must thank Rene Pottkamp from the NIOD—Institute for War, Holocaust and Genocide studies in Amsterdam, Holland, for allowing me to use these post-war testimonies. This was crucial in providing the basis for this book, indeed the whole *raison d'etre*, for the second edition.

I am also very much in debt to my friends Jerry Steinberg, who has once again written the Foreword to this book and Anne-Marie Hoppitt who has taken on the role as editor. She has performed this role with enormous skill and dedication. I cannot thank her enough for all her brilliant efforts, in making this book the best it could be. She is a treasure. I must also thank Peggy Scolaro for starting to edit this work, but had to give it up due to personal reasons. She was very supportive and I wish her all the best.

I want to pay a special tribute to Sandy H. Straus. She has constantly pushed me to provide the best possible writings and research that I could manage. This has been achieved through our great friendship and her sharp understanding of the subject matter and technical details. I cannot thank her enough for all that she has done to support and review this book, and my other Holocaust research in general. She is 'simply the best', borrowing the title of a well-known song.

The testimonies, and indeed much of the content of the history of Sobibór death camp, owes much to the late Jules Schelvis, who was a survivor of Sobibór, deported there from Westerbork camp in Holland, during June 1943. Jules was selected to work in a Jewish Labor camp, whilst his wife Rachel and other members of her family were murdered in the gas chambers on arrival. I was fortunate to correspond with Jules Schelvis many times, but sadly never met him in person. Another Sobibór survivor I made contact with was Thomas Blatt. He was most helpful and I am indebted to him for his contributions.

I am extremely grateful to Aline Pennewaard who supplied me with a number of research material, which has aided my writings; particularly in respect of solving the true identity of Luka, and attempting to trace Inge, and her twin sister, as mentioned by Thomas Blatt, who was deported to Sobibór from Holland in May 1943. Despite our very best efforts we have been unable to trace her. Aline is without doubt a real jewel in the crown, and I cannot thank her enough.

It goes without saying that I want to thank everyone who has supported this work, especially my family who quietly let me pursue my research. I must thank my wife Shirley, our wonderful daughter Heather, her husband Mark, and our two lovely grandchildren Freya and Cora, and Otto the son of Ena.

Chris Webb
Whitehill,
October 14, 2022

Chapter I
'Aktion Reinhardt'
An Overview

Aktion Reinhardt—also known as *Einsatz Reinhardt*—was the code name for the extermination of primarily Polish Jewry from the former *Generalgouvernement* and the Białystok area. The term was used in remembrance of *SS-Obergruppenführer* Reinhard Heydrich, the co-ordinator of the 'Final Solution of the Jewish Question' (*Endlösung der Judenfrage*)—the extermination of the Jews living in the European countries occupied by German forces during the Second World War.

On May 27, 1942, in a suburb of Prague, Jozef Gabčík and Jan Kubiš, members of the Czech resistance, ambushed Heydrich in his car while he was en-route to his office in Prague from his home at Panenské Březany. Heydrich died from his wounds at Bulovka Hospital on 4 June 1942.[1]

Four days after his death approximately 1,000 Jews left Prague in a single train which was designated AaH (*Attentat aus Heydrich*). This transport was officially destined for Ujazdów, in the Lublin district of Poland, but the deportees were gassed at the Bełżec death camp in the far south-eastern corner of the Lublin District. The members of Odilo Globocnik's resettlement staff henceforward dedicated the murder program to Heydrich's memory, under the code name *Einsatz Reinhardt*.[2]

The head of *Aktion Reinhardt* was *SS-Brigadeführer* Odilo Globocnik; the *SS* and Police Leader of the Lublin District, who had

---

[1] R. Cowdery, & P. Vodenka, *Reinhard Heydrich Assassination*. USM, Inc., Lakeville 1994, pp. 49 & 63.
[2] G. Reitlinger, *The Final Solution*. Vallentine, Mitchell, London 1953, pp. 105-106.

been appointed to this task by *Reichsführer-SS* Heinrich Himmler. At the *Führer's* Headquarters in Rastenburg (a town in present day Poland known as Kętrzyn), Heinrich Himmler, Friedrich-Wilhelm Krüger; *Höhere SS- und Polizeiführer Ost*, and Odilo Globocnik met at a conference on October 13, 1941, during which Globocnik was authorized to build a death camp at Bełżec. This was the first death camp built using static gas chambers. the first mass extermination camp in the East, which was *Kulmhof* (a town in present day Poland known as Chełmno) used gas vans from early December 1941.[3]

On January 20, 1942, at a villa in Wannsee, a suburb of Berlin, Heydrich organized a conference on the 'Final Solution to the Jewish Question in Europe'. The conference had been postponed from December 8, 1941, as Heydrich wrote to one of the participants Otto Hoffman, it had been necessary to postpone the conference 'on account of events in which some of the invited gentlemen were concerned'.[4] This was an allusion to the massacres that had taken place in the East. Dr. Rudolf Lange, for example, had overseen the murder of Jews at Riga; these executions were notable as this was the first time German Jews from the Reich had been executed en-masse—in this case the Jews were from Berlin. Those who attended the Wannsee Conference included the leading officials of the relevant ministries, senior representatives of the German authorities in the occupied countries, and senior members of the *SS*, including Heinrich Müller, head of the *Gestapo*, and Adolf Eichmann, head of Department IV B4, the subsection of the *Gestapo* dealing with Jewish affairs. Dr. Josef Bühler, *Staatssekretär*—who was representing Dr. Hans Frank, from the *Generalgouvernement*—demanded that the 'Final Solution' should be first applied to the Jews of the *Generalgouvernement*. This request was granted thus setting in train the mass

---

[3] P. Longerich, *The Unwritten Order—Hiter's Role in the Final Solution*. Tempus, Stroud 2001, p. 85.
[4] G. Reitlinger, *The Final Solution...*, op. cit., p. 101.

murder program, which was later to be named as '*Aktion Reinhardt*.'

Odilo Lothario Globocnik was born on April 21, 1904, in Trieste, the son of an Austro-Slovene family, and was a construction engineer by trade. In 1930, he joined the Nazi party in Carinthia, Austria and after the banning of the Nazi Party in Austria in 1934, earned a reputation as one of the most radical leaders of its underground cells. In 1933, Globocnik joined the *SS*, which also became a prohibited organization in Austria in 1934, and was appointed deputy Party District Leader (*Stellvertretender Gauleiter*).[5]

After serving several short terms of imprisonment for illegal activities on behalf of the Nazis, he emerged as a key figure in the pre-*Anschluss* plans for Austria, serving as a key liaison figure between Adolf Hitler and the leading pro-Nazi Austrians.[6]

After the *Anschluss* of March 1938, Globocnik's star continued to rise and on May 24, he was appointed to the coveted key position of Party District Leader (*Gauleiter*) of Vienna.

His tenure was short-lived, however, and on January 30, 1939, he was dismissed from this lofty position for corruption, illegal speculation in foreign exchange and tax evasion—all on a grand scale.[7]

After demotion to a lowly *SS* rank and undergoing basic military training with an *SS-Standarte*, he took part with his unit in the invasion of Poland. Eventually pardoned by Himmler, who needed such unscrupulous characters for future 'unsavoury plans', Globocnik was appointed to the post of *SS- und Polizeiführer* Lublin on November 9, 1939. Globocnik had been chosen by the *Reichsführer-SS* as the central figure in *Aktion Reinhardt*, not only because of his ruthlessness, but also because of his virulent anti-Semitism.

---

[5] J. Poprzeczny, *Hitler's Man in the East—Odilo Globocnik*. McFarland, Jefferson, 2004, p. 10.
[6] G. Reitlinger, *The Final Solution...*, op. cit., p. 262.
[7] J. Poprzeczny, *Hitler's Man ...*, op. cit., p. 76.

In Lublin, Globocnik surrounded himself with a number of his fellow Austrians, SS-Officers like Herman Julius Höfle, born in Salzburg on June 19, 1911. Höfle became Gobocnik's deputy in *Aktion Reinhardt*; responsible for personnel and the organization of Jewish deportations, the extermination camps and the re-utilization of the victim's possessions and valuables. Höfle was later to play a significant role in mass deportation *Aktionen* in Warsaw and Białystok. Ernst Lerch from Klagenfurt became Globocnik's closest confidante and adjutant. Georg Michalsen, a Silesian from Oppeln, was another adjutant and he, too, participated with Höfle in the deportation of Jews from the ghettos in Warsaw and Białystok. Another, early member of this group was Amon Göth, who cleared the Tarnów, Kraków and Zamość ghettos, and later became the notorious commander of Płaszów *Arbeitslager* in *Krakau*.[8]

The headquarters of *Aktion Reinhardt* was located in the *Julius Schreck Kaserne* at *Litauer Srasse 11*, in a former Polish school close to the city centre in Lublin, where Höfle not only worked but lived in a small apartment. Julius Schreck was Adolf Hitler's private chauffer; who had died of meningitis on May 16, 1936, and was given a state funeral.

Also located in Lublin were the buildings in which the belongings and valuables seized from the Jews were stored: the former Catholic Action (*Katholische Aktion*) building on *Chopin Strasse*, and in pre-war aircraft hangers on the Old Airfield (*Alter Flugplatz*) on Chelmska Street (Fabryczna Street in Polish) in the south-eastern outskirts of Lublin.[9]

Artificial limbs and medicines taken from the murdered Jews in the death camps were sent to the *SS-Polizeiführerkommando Sportplatz* in Lublin, which was under the control of Dr. Kurt Sickel. He was put on trial after the war for war crimes concerning the murders of American Prisoners of War at Malmedy, in the Ardennes, during the so-called 'Battle of the Bulge' in late 1944. He

---

8   J. Poprzeczny, *Hitler's Man* ..., op. cit., p. 95.
9   G. Reitlinger, *The Final Solution*..., op. cit., p. 314.

was found guilty and sentenced to death. His sentence was commuted and upon his release, he resumed his family practice in Cologne.[10]

The most notorious and fearsome member of *Aktion Reinhardt* was *SS-Obersturmführer/Kriminalinspektor* Christian Wirth, the first commandant of Bełżec death camp and later Inspector of the *SS-Sonderkommandos* of *Aktion Reinhardt*. Before his transfer to Poland, Wirth had been a leading figure in '*Aktion T4*,' the extermination of the mentally and physically disabled in six so-called 'euthanasia' killing centres in the Third Reich.

The role of the 'T4' euthanasia program was fundamental to the execution of *Aktion Reinhardt*, the great majority of the staff in the death camps served their 'apprenticeships' in mass murder at the Euthanasia Institutes of Bernburg, Brandenburg, Grafeneck, Hadamar, Hartheim and Pirna-Sonnenstein, where the victims had been murdered in gas chambers using CO gas from steel cylinders.

The T4 organization took its name from its Headquarters address at *Tiergartenstrasse4* in Berlin. This villa had been owned by the Jewish impressionist painter Max Liebermann. His wife Martha, aged 85, committed suicide on March 10, 1943. She was just about to be deported to the *Theresienstadt* transit ghetto, near Prague. Max Liebermann had passed away on February 8, 1935, in Berlin. Erwin Hermann Lambert, who went onto to build the gas chambers at Treblinka and Sobibór death camps, stated that his first job in T4 was to renovate this villa.

The senior officers in both *Aktion T4* and *Aktion Reinhardt* were all police officers with equivalent *SS* ranks, and with Himmler's approval *SS*-Non Commissioned Officers had emptied the gas chambers and cremated the bodies of the victims in portable furnaces. The *SS*-men performed this work wearing civilian clothes because Himmler did not want the possibility to arise of the public becoming aware of the participation of the *SS* in the killing. During *Aktion Reinhardt* the *SS* authorities also

---

[10] Correspondence between Georg Biemann and the author, November 2020.

supplemented the forces guarding the death camps, by employing former Red Army troops who had been captured or had surrendered to the Germans, mostly ethnic Germans (*Volksdeutsche*) from the Ukraine, the Baltic States and the Volga region of Russia. These were trained in an SS camp in the village of Trawniki, 25 km south-east of Lublin. The majority were already anti-Semitic—equating Bolsheviks with Jews—and were ideally suited to the persecution and extermination of Jews.

On November 1, 1941, construction of the first *Aktion Reinhardt* death camp began near the village of Bełżec, 125 kilometres south-east of Lublin, under the stewardship of Josef Oberhauser. The Bełżec death camp became operational in mid-March 1942, and was very much seen as the 'testing ground' for all the *Aktion Reinhardt* death camps. Franz Suchomel, in a post-war interview with Claude Lanzmann, described Bełżec 'was the laboratory.'

Construction of the second camp, at Sobibór, between the town of Włodawa and the city of Chełm on the River Bug, north-east of Lublin, came into operation at the end of April 1942. The third and last of these camps was located near the village train station of Treblinka[11], approximately 100 kilometres north-east of Warsaw. The construction of these two death camps was under the stewardship of Richard Thomalla who worked for the *SS-Zentralbauleitung* in Zamość.

All three camps shared some common vital facts: they were all situated on or close to main railway lines for the speedy delivery of the victims to their deaths, and they were located in sparsely—populated regions. The true fate of the Jews was initially hidden from them by announcing that they were being 'transported to the east for resettlement and work'. The *Aktion Reinhardt* death camps were very similar in layout, each camp being an improvement on its predecessor, and the 'conveyor-belt' extermination

---

[11] The village of Treblinka was in fact situated further from the camp than village of Poniatowo, which was the closest village to the extermination camp.

process developed at Bełżec by Christian Wirth was implemented, improved and refined at the other two camps.

The personnel assigned to *Aktion Reinhardt* came from a number of sources; SS and policemen who served under Globocnik's command in the Lublin district, other SS men and civilians drafted into the *Aktion* and members of the T4 Euthanasia program.[12] Yitzhak Arad quotes in his book *Belzec, Sobibor, Treblinka* that a total of 450 men were assigned to *Aktion Reinhardt* included 92 men from the T4 Euthanasia program,[13] more recent research by the authors has identified a slightly higher total of 98 men, of whom, 89 are known to have served at Sobibór at one time or another.

The Old Lublin Airfield on Chelmska Street was also used throughout *Aktion Reinhardt* as a mustering centre for personnel transferred from the T4 'euthanasia' institutions in the *Reich*, to the extermination of the Jews in the *Generalgouvernement*. The SS-men, police and civilians thus transferred were usually met at the airfield by Wirth personally, on occasions accompanied by the death camp commandants; Reichleitner from Sobibór and Stangl from Treblinka. According to witnesses, at these selections of personnel, all three wore *Schutzpolizei* uniforms and none of them mentioned anything about their future employment or where they would be based. At the airfield depot the newcomers received *Waffen-SS* uniforms, provided by the SS-Garrison Administration (*SS-Standortverwaltung*) in Lublin, but without the SS runes on the right-hand collar patches. The civilian employees from T4, especially the male psychiatric nurses among them were sent first to the SS training camp at Trawniki, for a two-week basic military training course.[14]

The men selected in Lublin and distributed to the three *Aktion Reinhardt* death camps were augmented by a company-sized unit

---

[12] Y. Arad, *Belzec, Sobibor, Treblinka—The Aktion Reinhard Death Camps*, Indiana University Press, Bloomington and Indianapolis 1987, p. 17.

[13] Ibid p. 17.

[14] M. Tregenza, Private Report Altoting 1972-Michael Tregenza Lublin Collection.

of about 120 black-uniformed auxiliary guards who had also been trained at the SS training camp in Trawniki—the so-called *Trawnikimänner*, usually referred to as 'Ukrainians' because they were the majority.

Those who spoke fluent German were appointed platoon or senior platoon leaders—*Zugführers* or *Oberzugführers*. The rest were known as *Wachmänner*. A select few of the *Trawnikimänner* were given other, special duties, including the maintenance and operation of the engines that pumped their poisonous exhaust fumes into the gas chambers. Among them at the Treblinka death camp were the infamous Ivan Marchenko (Ivan the Terrible) and Nikolay Shalayev.[15] In Sobibór another was Ivan Demjanjuk, who eventually faced justice in Germany, and who passed away before his appeal could be heard.

In the course of *Aktion Reinhardt* approximately 1.6 million Jews were murdered in the death camps at Bełżec, Sobibór and Treblinka. Jewish property to the value of 178, 045, 960 *Reichsmark* (*RM*) was seized by the SS, which represents the minimum known amount. Due to the theft of large amounts of cash and valuables by Globocnik, SS-men, policemen and guards, the true total will never be known.

The *Aktion Reinhardt* extermination operation ended officially in November 1943, and Himmler ordered Globocnik, who was by then the Higher SS and Police Leader for the Adriatic Coastal Region based in Trieste, to produce a detailed 'Balance Sheet' for the murder program. Globocnik produced the requested financial accounts and suggested that certain SS-officers should be suitably rewarded for their 'invaluable contribution' to *Aktion Reinhardt*. Globocnik received Himmler's thanks 'for his services to the German people', but made no mention of medals for any of Globocnik's subordinates.[16]

---

[15] Y. Arad, *Belzec, Sobibor, Treblinka—The Aktion Reinhard Death Camps*, Indiana University Press, Bloomington and Indianapolis 1987, p. 22.
[16] Ibid.op. cit., p. 375.

After completion of the extermination work in the *Generalgouvernement*, most of the men who had served in *Aktion Reinhardt* were transferred to northern Italy; where their headquarters was in a disused rice mill in the San Sabba suburb of the Adriatic port of Trieste (*Risiera di San Sabba*). Divided into three SS-units: R-I, R-II and R-III, they operated under the code designation 'Operation R' (*Einsatz R*), still under the command of Christian Wirth. Their primary task was the round-up and deportation to Auschwitz-Birkenau of the surviving Italian Jews, and confiscation of their property and valuables. *Einsatz R* was simply a smaller version of *Aktion Reinhardt*. Additionally, Italian-Jewish mental patients were removed from their hospitals and sent to the T4 'Euthanasia' institution at *Schloss Hartheim* in Austria for gassing. The units not engaged in these operations were assigned to security and anti-partisan patrols on the Istrian peninsula.

Wirth turned San Sabba into an interrogation and execution centre where not only Jews but also Italian and Yugoslav partisans were tortured, beaten to death, or simply shot, and their bodies cremated in a specially installed furnace in the courtyard.[17] The human ashes were dumped in the Adriatic Sea. There is also evidence that a gas-van was used in San Sabba.

The key members of *Aktion Reinhardt* mostly escaped justice; Globocnik and Höfle both committed suicide, whilst Wirth and Reichleitner (the second commandant of Sobibór death camp) were killed by partisans in northern Italy in 1944. Both Christian Wirth and Franz Reichleitner's graves can be found at the German Military Cemetery in Costermano, near Lake Garda, in Italy.

Amon Göth was tried and sentenced to death for crimes committed in the Płaszów concentration camp (today a suburb of Kraków). He was executed in the former Płaszów Camp during September 1946. Dr. Irmfried Eberl, the first Commandant of Treblinka death camp committed suicide in a West German prison

---

[17]   Ibid.,op. cit., p 399.

in 1948, while awaiting trial. Only Franz Stangl[18] (the first Commandant of Sobibór and second Commandant of Treblinka) and Kurt Franz (the final Commandant of Treblinka) were brought to trial. Both were found guilty of crimes against humanity and sentenced to life imprisonment. Gottlieb Hering the second Commandant of Bełżec death camp and Commandant of Poniatowa Jewish Labor camp died on October 9, 1945, in unknown circumstances in the waiting room at the *Katherinen* Hospital in Stetten im Remstal, Württemberg, Germany.

As for members of the *SS*-Garrisons at the three death camps a number of major figures; like Karl Frenzel, from Sobibór, and Heinrich Arthur Matthes, August Miete, Willy Mentz, and Kurt Franz from Treblinka, received life sentences, whilst many others received prison terms of less than ten years, but the vast majority of the *SS* men and Ukrainians who served within the framework of *Aktion Reinhardt* were never brought to justice.

At Hagen, West Germany during 1965-66, 12, former members of the *SS*-Garrison went on trial for murdering Jews at the Sobibór death camp. Some received sentences of life imprisonment, some were given only a few years in prison, and some were acquitted.

Former Ukrainian Ivan Demjanjuk, who was brought to trial in the mid-1980's in Israel, accused of being Ivan the Terrible at Treblinka, was found guilty and sentenced to death, but was later freed following a successful appeal. At the trial a *Trawnikimänner* identification card showed an entry stating he was posted to Sobibór.

He returned to the United States of America, to his family, but was pursued by the authorities. He was eventually extradited to Germany, and faced justice in a court in Bonn, for alleged war crimes committed at Sobibór. In May 2011, he was convicted of 28,060 counts of being an accessory to murder and was sentenced

---

[18] It should be noted that many of the key members in the death camps' staffing in the three death camps were of Austrian nationality! Eberl was Austrian as well as Reichleitner, Stangl, Wagner, Vallaster etc, and that Globocnik surrounded himself with his countrymen, such as Höfle, Lerch, Nemec, Helmut Pohl and others.

to five years imprisonment. He died on March 17, 2012, a free man in a nursing home in the southern Bavarian town of Bad Feilnbach, after being released pending his appeal.

Chapter II
History of the
Sobibór Death Camp

Odilo Globocnik (Second from Left), Vienna
(Chris Webb Private Archive)

The Sobibór Death Camp was located near the village of Sobibór in the eastern part of the Lublin District of Poland, close to the Chelm-Włodawa railway line. The camp was 5 kilometres away from the River Bug, which today forms the border between Poland and the Ukraine.

In 1942, the area around Sobibór was part of the border between the *Generalgouvernement* and the *Reichskommissariat* Ukraine, the terrain was swampy, densely wooded and sparsely populated. Sobibór was the second death camp to be constructed as part of the *Aktion Reinhardt* mass murder program, and was built on similar lines to Bełżec, incorporating the lessons learned from the first death camp to be constructed between late 1941 and early 1942.[19]

According to Polish railway worker Jan Piwonski who testified on April 29, 1975, in Lublin, he stated that:

> In the autumn of 1941, German officers arrived at the station of Sobibór on three occasions. It was in the days after the Germans had started the war against the Soviet Union. The Germans came to Sobibór station on one of those handcarts. During their visit to the station they took measurements of the platform, and the siding leading away from the platform, and then went into the woods nearby. I have no idea what they were doing there. The Germans were in SS uniform and had the skull and crossbones symbol on their caps.
>
> Some time later some very thick doors, which had rubber strips around them, arrived by train. We speculated on what purpose the doors might be serving, and it dawned on us that perhaps the Germans were building something here, especially when trainloads of bricks were also being delivered, and they started to bring Jews over as well. They were doing something or other over there, but none of us Poles dared to follow them to take a look.
>
> Early that winter—in January or February 1942—the Germans arrived at the station from the direction of the Chelm—Włodawa road, bringing Jews with them. They would go off and disappear into the woods. I think these people were living in barracks that had already been put up in the woods. I mean, the barracks in which the Jews were living had already been built by the edge of the woods, next to the railway line. There were around 120 Jews in all.[20]

In March 1942, following a reconnaissance visit by a small aircraft that circled over the village, a train arrived at Sobibór station, and two SS officers disembarked. They were Richard Thomalla, who worked in the *SS-Zentralbauleitung* in Zamość, and *Baurat* Bruno Moser from Chelm. They walked around the railway station, took

---

[19] Y. Arad, *Belzec, Sobibor, Treblinka*, Indiana University Press, Bloomington and Indianapolis, 1987, p.30.
[20] J. Schelvis, *Sobibor*, Berg, Oxford and New York, 2007, p.27.

measurements and made their way into the forest opposite the railway station.[21]

Jan Piwonski remembered the construction activity starting at Sobibór:

> The next morning the Jews had to dig holes, and the farmers from the villages brought poles, which were used to make a fence. The poles were about 3 meters high. After the poles had been put in place, barbed-wire was put up around them and pine branches were woven through the wires. The Jews put up the barbed-wire, while the farmers put the pine branches in place.
>
> The next day a German *SS* soldier, who spoke very good Polish came to the station cafeteria. He came from Poznan or Silesia.[22] When the woman behind the counter asked him what was being built there, he replied that she would find out soon enough, it was going to be a good laugh.[23]

Another source of information regarding the construction of the death camp in Sobibór came from Z. Krawczak, who had been a prisoner in the Jewish Labor Camp at Krychow, since June 1941. He escaped from Krychow and made his way to Switzerland, where he wrote an account of his experiences during the occupation.

Krawczak wrote that a few SS-men, under the command of Strumph, who was formerly the commandant of the Jewish Labor Camp in Sawin, near Chelm, arrived from another Jewish Labor Camp in Osowa, some 7 kilometres west of Sobibór. They arrived with a group of 120 Jews from Chelm to construct the death camp.

The building material was organized by the *Deutsch Horst* company, and was transported from the camp in Krychow and from the railway station in Chelm. The management of these supplies came under the authority of the Water Management Inspector, Engineer Franz Holzheimer, who originated from Hannover,

---

[21] T. Blatt, *Sobibor—The Forgotten Revolt*, H.E.P, Issaquah, 1998, p.13.
[22] This was probably Richard Thomalla, who originated from Annahof, in Upper Silesia.
[23] J. Schelvis, *Sobibor*, Berg, Oxford and New York, 2007, p.33-34.

and was based in Chelm. The overall construction of the camp was supervised by Moser, an architect, also based in Chelm, who was at a later date transferred to the *Technische Hauptamt* in Krakau.[24]

In March 1942, a new railroad spur was built, which ended at an earthen ramp with a buffer opposite the railway station. The camp fence with interwoven branches was built in a manner which ensured that the railway spur and the ramp were located inside the camp, thus preventing passengers at the station from observing what happened in the camp. The deportation trains entered the ramp through a gate and disappeared behind the 'green wall.' In the station area three large buildings already existed; the station, the Forester's House, a two-storey Post Office, which became the Commandant's living quarter, and a tiny isolated Catholic chapel, of approximately 16 square yards, which was built in 1926. Additionally there was a large Forester's iron observation tower, built before the war, 30 meters high which stood between *Lager I* and *Lager II*.

Jan Piwonski, who worked for the *Ostbahn* (Eastern Railways) at the Sobibór village station, as an assistant switch-man, recalled the shunting operations connected with the arrival of Jewish transports, in an interview with Claude Lanzmann, in the film '*Shoah.*'

> Yes. On German orders, Polish railmen split up the trains. So the locomotive took twenty cars and headed towards Chelm. When it reached a switch, it pushed the cars into the camp on the other track we see there. Unlike Treblinka, the station here is part of the camp.[25]

There appears to be some conflict here with the number of freight cars the ramp could accommodate, was it 11 or 20? According to a number of testimonies, the ramp at the Treblinka death camp was 200 meters long and could accommodate 20 wagons and the

---

[24] M. Bem, *Sobibor Extermination Camp 1942-1943*, Stichting Sobibor 2015, pp. 49-50.
[25] C. Lanzmann, *Shoah*, Pantheon Books, New York 1985, p.39.

locomotive. Given that the ramp at Sobibór was only 120 meters long, it is more probable that only 11 freight cars and the locomotive could be accommodated at Sobibór.

There was also a sawmill, and several houses for workers. As construction work progressed, undertaken by 80 Jews from nearby ghettos, such as Włodawa and Wola Uhruska—the site was inspected by a commission led by *SS-Hauptsturmführer* Naumann, head of the Central Construction Office of the *Waffen-SS* in Lublin. Once the Jews had completed the initial construction phase, they were gassed during an experimental gassing trial. Two or three of them escaped at that time to Włodawa, and informed the Hassidic rabbi there about what was happening in Sobibór. The rabbi even proclaimed a fasting in memory of the first victims, and also as a sign of resistance. Both the escapees and the rabbi were denounced by a Jewish policeman and all of them were executed.[26]

The camp was in the form of a 400 by 600 meter rectangle, surrounded by a 3 meter high double barbed-wire fence, partially interwoven with pine branches to prevent observation from the outside. Along the fence and in the corners of the camp were wooden watchtowers. Each of the four camp areas was individually fenced in, the *SS* Administration area (*Vorlager*), the housing and workshops of the Jewish working prisoners. *Lager II* was the reception area, and the extermination camp was in *Lager III*. During 1943, a munitions supply area, *Lager IV*, was added.

The administration area, which was in the southeast of the camp, was divided into two sub-camps: the Forward Camp (*Vorlager*) and *Lager I*. The Forward Camp included the entrance gate, with its sign that read *SS Sonderkommando*, in gothic letters, the railway ramp, which held 11 cattle cars, and the living quarters of the *SS* men and the Ukrainians. Eda Lichtman recalled that:

> Karl Frenzel, Gustav Wagner, Hermann Michel, Getzinger, Otto Weiss, Bredow, Steubl, Paul Groth, and Hubert Gomerski lived in

---

[26] R. Kuwalek, *Extermination Camp in Sobibor*, Zeszyty Majdanka, Vol XXI, 2001.

a villa called *Schwalbennest* (Swallow's Nest) Adolf Muller, Richter, Johann Klier, Nowak, the two Wolf brothers, Borner, Graetschus, Schutt, Vallaster, Unverhau Erich Bauer, named their villa *Am Lustigen Floh* (The Happy Flea)[27]

Another of the SS living quarters was known as *'Gottes Heimat'* (Gods Home), they all looked like Tyrolean style houses, designed to camouflage the camp's true purpose.

Unlike Bełżec, all the SS men lived inside the camp. The Jewish prisoners who worked in Sobibór were kept in *Lager I*. This area included their living quarters and workshops, where some of them worked as shoemakers, tailors, blacksmiths etc.

The reception area was called *Lager II*. The Jews who arrived with the transports were, after, disembarking, driven inside this area. It included the undressing barracks of the victims and the barracks where clothes and belongings were stored.

The former Forester's house, located in this area, was used for camp offices and living quarters for some of the SS men, and the place where gold and valuables were sorted and stored. A high wooden fence, which presented observation, separated the main part of the Forester's house from the area where the victims passed. At the northeast corner of the fence began the 'Tube.' This *'Schluch,'* which connected *Lager II* with the extermination area, was a narrow passageway, about 3 to 4 meters wide and 150 meters long. It was closed on both sides by barbed-wire intertwined with tree branches. Through here the victims were driven into the gas chambers located at the end of the 'Tube.' Close to the entrance of the 'Tube' was a stable, a pigpen, and a poultry coop. Halfway through the 'Tube' was the barber shop, a barrack where the hair of the Jewish women was cut, before they entered the gas chambers.

The extermination area, called *Lager III*, was on the northwest side of the camp. It included the gas chambers, burial pits, a barrack for the Jewish prisoners employed there, and a guard barrack. The burial pits were 50 to 60 meters long, 10 to 15 meters wide, and 5 to 7 meters deep. For easier absorption of the corpses into the pits, the sandy sidewalls were made oblique. A narrow-

---

[27] Miriam Novitch, *Sobibor*, Holocaust Library, New York, 1980, p.56.

gauge railway with a trolley led from the railway station up to the burial pits, by-passing the gas chambers. People who had died in the trains, or those who were unable to walk from the platform to the gas chambers were taken there by the trolley.[28]

Before the narrow-gauge railway was established Kurt Bolender recalled:

> Upon reflection I can now say that in the extermination camp Sobibór, handicapped or sick Jews who arrived at the camp were taken by horse-drawn cart—it was one of those twin-axled hay carts, like the ones used on the land—and transported from the siding to the wooded area of what was later to become *Lager IV*. In this wooded area of the camp there was also a grave. I did not see it. I know about it only from hearsay. The pit was not visible from *Lager III*. Whenever the transports arrived, shots were fired in that part of the camp. I heard those shots.[29]

Hubert Gomerski, who arrived in Sobibór at the end of April 1942, described the narrow-gauge railway in a post-war testimony:

> As regards the narrow-gauge rail track, I can say that it existed until the camp ceased to be operational. It was a small, narrow-gauge track, which led away from the siding at Sobibor station, through the camp into *Lager III*.
>
> In my estimation, the narrow-gauge track was about 300-400 meters long. Initially, when the camp first became operational, the groups of people who had been selected to go to *Lager III* had to march there on foot, from the siding: later they were taken there by horse-drawn carts.
>
> Sepp Vallaster was the main person dealing with the rail operation. When Jewish transports arrived, he drove the diesel engine. The railway track was principally used to move incapacitated people from the Jewish transports that arrived. This included the old and the sick, as well as injured Jews.[30]

---

[28] Y. Arad, *Belzec, Sobibor, Treblinka*, Indiana University Press, Bloomington and Indianapolis, 1987, pp 32-33.
[29] J. Schelvis, *Sobibor*, Berg, Oxford and New York, 2007, p. 64.
[30] J. Schelvis, *Sobibor*, Berg, Oxford and New York, 2007, p. 65.

SS-Oberscharführer Erich Bauer testified about his arrival at Sobibór and he described *Lager III*:

> When we arrived *Lager III* had not been completely fenced off yet, certainly not on the right-hand side, and I am not sure whether any fence had been put up through the woods. The gas chamber was already there, a wooden building on a concrete base, about the same size as this courtroom, though much lower, as low as a normal house.
>
> There were two or three chambers, in front of which there was a corridor that, from the outside, you accessed via a bridge. The doors were indeed wooden, they were changed later, when the gas chamber was completely rebuilt. The airtight doors arrived only later. I collected them myself from Warsaw, but that was not until the new building went up.[31]

During the court case against Karl Frenzel, the jury in Hagen prepared a description of the gas chamber facility, which is regarded as one of the best descriptions of the gas chambers:

> About 500 meters west of that chapel, the preliminary works squad put up a building with a gas chamber inside it, a small massive construction on a concrete foundation. Inside the building were three separate gastight chambers of 4 meters by 4 meters, parallel with each other. Each chamber had an insulated door in the opposite empty walls, with one door serving as the entrance, and the other as the exit—for taking corpses out.
>
> The building team had had all fittings installed and a special annexe built by the back gable wall. In the annexe, there was an engine which fed exhaust fumes to kill the Jews. The gas chamber building was situated in the so-called *Lager III*, which was a fenced yard. It had its own separate fence made of barbed wire.
>
> The building with the gas chambers in it was located in the southernmost part of that area. The annexe with the engine was beside the building with the gas chambers. The exhaust pipe of the huge engine, 'Otto', was connected to the system of cables, which ended in the shower nozzles on the ceilings of the particular gas chambers. The engine received specifically calculated settings for

---

[31] Ibid, p.101.

the carburettor, and the number of revolutions. With the gas chamber doors locked, it was possible to create such a high degree of concentration of poisonous exhaust fumes from the engine inside the chambers that the people trapped inside suffocated in agony for about 20-30 minutes.

In time the gas chambers turned out to be too small, and the efficiency of the Sobibór camp proved to be too low. The old building with the gas chambers was partially torn down by the Lublin headquarters building crew under Lambert's technical guidance. It was replaced by a new massive building with twice as many chambers. Each of them had an area of 4 meters by 4 meters, and a height of 2.20 meters. They were positioned on both sides of the corridor. Each of the chambers could hold about 80 people, if they were tightly squeezed.

Since then, after the buildings work that lasted only for a few weeks, in the six chambers about 480 people could be killed at the same time. The old chambers proved to be impractical also due to too small an exit door, which was used for taking corpses out of the chamber. During the renovation, the door was replaced by a broader 'pendular' one. Since then, the working squad of *Lager III* could more easily get out of the chambers tightly huddled corpses, often extremely dirty, standing next to each other or twisted together, and then transport them to the pits along the narrow-gauge tracks. A special squad of prisoners in *Lager III* was to clear the chambers of blood and excrement as quickly as possible, before the next group of victims went inside.[32]

While the basic installations were being made ready to exterminate the Jews, the organization of the *SS* Garrison and Ukrainians was also taking shape. In April 1942, *SS-Obersturmführer* Franz Paul Stangl was appointed by Odilo Globocnik, to the post of Commandant of Sobibór, and he arrived in Sobibór on April 28, 1942.

Franz Stangl recalled to Gitta Sereny how he was recruited into the *Aktion Reinhardt* mass murder program, during a meeting with Odilo Globocnik in Lublin:

---

[32] M. Bem, *Sobibor Extermination Camp 1942-1943*, Stichting Sobibor 2015, pp. 59-60.

> I came upon Globocnik sitting by himself on a bench about ten meters away from—and with his back to—the building. There was a lovely view across lawns and trees to buildings far away.... It had been decided, he told me, to open a number of supply camps from which the troops at the Front could be re-equipped. He said that he intended confiding to me the construction of a camp called Sobibór. He called an adjutant—who must have lurked somewhere nearby—and told him to bring the plans.
>
> The plans arrived and he spread them out on the bench between us and on the ground in front of us. They showed a design for the camp: barracks, railway tracks, fences, gates. Some of the buildings—bunkers they were—were crossed out with red ink. 'Do not worry about those,' he said, concentrate on getting the rest done first. It has been started but they've got Poles working there. It's going so slowly they must be asleep. What the place needs is someone to organize it properly and I think you are the man to do it. And then he said he would arrange for me to leave for Sobibór the next day-that was all.[33]

Stangl, after settling in at Sobibór, visited Christian Wirth, the Commandant of the Bełżec death camp, to obtain guidance and experience. Stangl recalled his visit to Bełżec in an interview with Gitta Sereny during 1971:

> I went there by car. As one arrived, one first reached Bełżec railway station, on the left side of the road. The camp was on the same side, but up a hill. The Kommandantur was 200 meters away, on the other side of the road. It was a one storey building.
>
> The smell .... He said, 'Oh God, the smell. It was everywhere. Wirth wasn't in his office. I remember, they took me to him... he was standing on a hill, next to the pits.. the pits... full... they were full. I can't tell you; not hundreds, thousands, thousands of corpses... oh God. That's where Wirth told me—he said, that was what Sobibór was for. And that he was putting me officially in charge.[34]

After his visit to Bełżec, the pace of construction speeded up. Franz Stangl, an Austrian who had served in the T4 euthanasia

---

[33] Gitta Sereny, *Into That Darkness*, Pimlico. London 1974, pp. 102-103.
[34] Ibid, p.111.

program at Hartheim and Bernburg, had as his deputy, another *SS* man with experience of the euthanasia program, *SS-Oberscharführer* Hermann Michel, although he was replaced a few months later by *SS-Oberscharführer* Gustav Wagner.

The initial commander of *Lager I* was *SS-Oberscharführer* Bruno Weiss, who was replaced by *SS-Oberscharführer* Karl Frenzel. Frenzel had previously supervised the prisoners in *Lager II*. *SS-Oberscharführer* Kurt Bolender served as commander of *Lager III*, from April 1942, until the autumn of the same year, when he was replaced by *SS-Oberscharführer* Erich Bauer. Alfred Ittner was in charge of the camp's administration, but was later transferred to *Lager III*. The Ukrainian guards at Sobibór came from the Trawniki *Ausbildungs-Lager,* located some 27 kilometres south of Lublin. These were led by *SS-Scharführer* Erich Lachmann up until the autumn of 1942, when Bolender took over this responsibility. The *Trawnikimänner* were organized into three platoons, led by Ukrainian *Volksdeutsche.*

In early April 1942, when the camp was nearly completed, further experimental gassings took place—about 250 Jews from the forced labor camp at Krychow were brought to Sobibór for this purpose. *SS-Unterscharführer* Erich Fuchs recalled this time at Sobibór:

> Sometime in the spring of 1942, I received instructions from Wirth to fetch new camp staff from Lublin by lorry. One of these was Erich Bauer (also Stangl and one or two other people).
>
> On Wirth's instructions I left by lorry for *Lemberg* and collected a gassing engine there which I then took to Sobibór. Upon arriving in Sobibór I discovered a piece of open ground close to the station on which there was a concrete building and several other permanent buildings. The *Sonderkommando* at Sobibór was led by Thomalla. Amongst the *SS* personnel there was Floss, Bauer, Stangl, Friedl, Schwarz, Barbl and others.
>
> We unloaded the motor. It was a heavy, Russian petrol engine (presumably a tank or tractor engine) of at least 200HP (carburettor engine, eight-cylinder, water-cooled). We put the engine on a concrete plinth and attached a pipe to the exhaust outlet.

> Then we tried out the engine. At first it did not work. I repaired the ignition and the valve and suddenly the engine started. The chemist whom I already knew from Bełżec went into the gas chamber with a measuring device, in order to measure the gas concentration.
>
> After this a test gassing was carried out. I seem to remember that thirty to forty women were gassed in a gas chamber. The Jewesses had to undress in a clearing in the wood which had been roofed over, near the gas chamber. They were herded into the gas chamber by the above mentioned SS members and Ukrainian volunteers.
>
> When the women had been shut up in the gas chamber I attended to the engine together with Bauer. The engine immediately started ticking over. We both stood next to the engine and switched it up to 'release exhaust to chamber' so that the gases were channelled into the chamber. On the instigation of the chemist I revved up the engine, which meant that no extra gas had to be added later. After about ten minutes the thirty to forty women were dead. The chemist and the SS gave the signal to turn off the engine.
>
> I packed up my tools and saw the bodies being taken away. A small wagon on rails was used to take them away from near the gas chamber to a stretch of ground some distance away. Sobibór was the only place where a wagon was used.[35]

Franz Stangl also recalled another trial gassing, this time conducted by Christian Wirth:

> And then one afternoon, Wirth's adjutant, Oberhauser, came to get me. I was to come to the gas chamber. When I got there, Wirth stood in front of the building wiping the sweat off his camp and fuming. Michel told me later that he had suddenly appeared, looked around the gas chambers on which they were still working and said, 'Right, we will try it out right now with those twenty-five work-Jews; get them up here.'
>
> They marched our twenty-five Jews up there and just pushed them in, and gassed them. Michel said Wirth behaved like a

---

[35] Ernst Klee, Willi Dressen, Volker Riess, *Those Were The Days*, Hamish Hamilton London 1991, p. 231.

> lunatic, hit out at his own staff with his whip to drive them on. And then he was livid because the doors had not worked properly. Oh he just screamed and raved and said the doors had to be changed. After that he left.[36]

By mid-April 1942, the death camp was ready to receive the first transport. It is probable the first transport came from Rejowiec near Chelm, where more than 2,000 Jews were deported to Sobibór. This transport from Rejowiec arrived in Sobibór on April 7, 1942, although it is possible that the first transport to Sobibór was from Kazimierz Dolny, via Opole Lubelski. Wartime sources state that people on the transport from Kazimierz Dolny threw letters, in which they wrote stating they were deported in the direction of Włodawa, out of the train.[37]

In his book *'To Survive Sobibor,'* Dov Freiberg recalled the horrors of the train transport to Sobibór in May 1942, and this provides an example of the journeys the deportees took. He made the journey with his uncle Michael, his aunt Esther and his cousin Mirale:

> By the time we reached the regional city of Krasnystaw, evening had fallen. The entire crowd was led into a large yard besides some railway tracks. People didn't know what to do and ran back and forth, looking for water, a place to relieve themselves, a place to sit, to eat something, to rest and to sleep. People lost each other in the dark, and it took a long time until everyone managed to get themselves organized somehow beneath the dark sky. We also found ourselves a place and my uncle gave everyone a piece of bread........
>
> The whistle of a locomotive engine that was manoeuvring along the nearby train tracks woke us with the dawn, while the mists were still dissipating. It was freezing cold. In the light of day I could see the crowd scattered around the area, with one side bordered by high buildings and the other side by railway tracks.......
>
> While I was pondering this, a troop of soldiers in black uniforms approached us, armed with bayonet rifles and led by a German

---

[36] Gitta Sereny, *Into That Darkness*, Pimlico. London 1974, pp. 113-114.
[37] Robert Kuwalek in correspondence with Chris Webb.

officer. They stopped not far from us, and after performing some drills, spread themselves out along the railway tracks. Apparently these were Ukrainians serving in the *SS*.

Afterward, a group of *SS* officers arrived. The locomotive engine, which manoeuvred incessantly among the freight cars, finally attached itself to a long line of freight cars along the tracks at the edge of the big yard. The Germans ran back and forth along this train, and we realized it was meant for us. Everyone packed their bundles and readied themselves for travel; the people were anxious to set out, if only to get to wherever we were headed.

Sudden orders were shouted: 'Get up! Get on the train! Quickly, Quickly!' The Germans and the Ukrainians pushed and prodded us with shouts and blows. The freight cars were high, without steps, and it was difficult to climb into them. People helped each other, many getting injured, and the Germans pushed more and more people into the boxcars, endlessly. I walked together with my aunt, my uncle and Mirale to the freight car, climbed inside quickly with my uncle and helped my aunt and Mirale climb up.

For a few moments we were all together, pleased that we were all together, pleased that we were already inside, but the car filled up quickly, and the Germans pushed more and more people inside, as many as possible and with it, the fear and the shouts, until finally the heavy door was slid to shut us in.

Dov Freiberg then described the conditions with the freight car:

> Gloom was all around us. There was only a tiny knothole at the corner of the car, near the ceiling. It was hot and suffocating in the car and a terrible odor washed over us. I felt nauseated and I was sure that I was going to throw up........
>
> Suddenly we felt a strong push, which toppled us all on top of each other at one end of the car, like a pile of rags, and then we immediately fell back to the other side, where there was a little space. The train lurched forward. We had begun to travel. Fresh air seeped into the boxcar and the travellers thanked God that they could breathe.........

The ordeal was nearly over:

> The journey in the boxcars continued, with all of us horribly packed together, hungry but mostly thirsty, surrounded by

suffocation and stench, close to losing consciousness. I don't know how long we travelled, probably hours. It seemed to me that this torturous journey would never end.

The shouting had died down, the children had stopped crying, and silence prevailed. Everyone had either grown used to it, or grown tired. Somewhere the train slowed down and stopped, as if in the middle of its journey, in a spot that was completely silent. We tried to hear what was happening outside and the sounds that reached us were of cows, chickens, the barking of dogs, and especially the chirping of birds. It wasn't difficult to guess that we were in a rural area. The man who peeped through the knothole said that he saw only fields and forest. The smell of greenery and pine trees wafted into the car.

Our locomotive moved to and fro, each time pushing more boxcars, until finally our car, as well went through a gate into a closed camp. The door of the boxcar opened noisily and we were greeted by shouting in German: 'Out, out, Quickly, Quickly.'[38]

The mass exterminations began in earnest during the first days of May 1942. The arrival process which Dov Freiberg outlined was that the deportation trains usually consisting of 60 wagons stopped at the Sobibór station. Then a locomotive pushed 11 freight cars through the railway gate into the camp. When these had been unloaded on the ramp, the next part of the train was pushed into the camp. The train escort and railway workers had to stay outside the fencing, only a specialized team of trusted *Reichsbahn* employees was allowed to enter the camp. Once inside, the wagons stopped alongside the ramp and the cars were opened by the Ukrainian guards. Those who were still alive were ordered to disembark from the wagons onto the ramp, and then the *SS* men and Ukrainians, quickly and brutally accepted them into the camp itself.

Dov Freiberg, gave a detailed description of Sobibór:

> Opposite the branch of railroad tracks stood *Lager I*, a group of wooden country houses serving as lodgings for the Germans, the

---

[38] Dov Freiberg, *To Survive Sobibor*, Gefen Publishing House, Jerusalem, 2007, pp. 183–189.

kitchen and their canteen. The site was well tended. The fronts of the houses had rows of flowers, low wooden fences and paved paths... further on stood the workshops where the Jews now worked—sewing suits and making shoes for the Germans and their wives.

Between *Lager I* and *Lager II*, the Germans had set up an animal farm, where the Jews raised pigs, fattened geese, and tended horses—all for the *SS* in the camp. Near the railway tracks, not far from the Germans lodgings and the Jewish barracks, a big barracks was built to house the Ukrainians and next to it, a smaller building—the Ukrainian kitchen.

Opposite the barracks stood a small building that served as a guard-house, where *Oberscharführer* Graetschus sat, in charge of the Ukrainian guards, and on the other side, towards the German lodgings, stood the weapons warehouse.

In *Lager II*, stood a lovely, big wooden building with a porch extending along its entire front facade. The building faced the yard where the people undressed, and in it were secretaries and the warehouse for money, gold and valuables. The Jewish goldsmith worked there, sorting the valuables and packing them for transport. In the same building, there was a medical storehouse as well, where the pharmacist, a Jew, sorted medicines, drugs, perfumes and cosmetics and packed them for transport. On the other side of the building stood barracks filled with clothing and possessions that had belonged to the people in the transports, and from there was a path to the forest, the path to *Lager III*.[39]

Thomas 'Toivi' Blatt, who arrived in Sobibór from Izbica, in late April 1943, described the main entrances:

> The only camp entrances were at the right corner of the front fence, and consisted of two gates: a main gate[40] opened onto the central road in the camp; to its right, a smaller gate opened onto the siding from the main railway line outside of the camps area.

---

[39] Ibid. p.202.
[40] Thomas Blatt confirmed the main entrance gate was a single large gate, in a telephone conversation with Chris Webb during June 2010.

Above the main gate was a wooden sign, about two feet by eight, with the words '*SS-Sonderkommando*' painted in Gothic letters.[41]

Jan Piwonski recalls one of the early transports to Sobibór:

> Early in June[42] the first convoy arrived. I would say there were over forty cars. With the convoy were SS men in black uniforms. It happened one afternoon, I had just finished work. But I got on my bicycle and went home.
>
> I merely thought that these people had come to build the camp, as the others had before them. That convoy—there was no way of knowing that it was the first earmarked for extermination—and besides, one could not have known that Sobibór would be used for the mass extermination of the Jewish people.
>
> The next morning when I came here to work, the station was absolutely silent, and we realized after talking with the other railwaymen who worked at the station here, that something utterly incomprehensible had happened. First of all, when the camp was being built, there were orders shouted in German, there were screams. Jews were working at a run, there were shots, and here there was that silence, no work crews, a really total silence.
>
> Forty cars had arrived and then nothing. It was all very strange. It was a silence... a standstill in the camp. You heard and saw nothing, nothing moved. So then they began to wonder, 'where have they put those Jews.'[43]

Stephan Stelmaszuk who was born in 1928, and lived in Osowa, which was 4 kilometres from Sobibór, described the outside of the camp during an interview in 1983:

> First I saw nothing. All you could see was a fence around it. There was a railway line that ran along the camp. The railway track was like this: Chelm was here, Włodawa was there. Very close to the camp. You couldn't see much from the tracks. It was closed off with planks.
>
> I rode past it once on the train. The train had low windows and high windows. I stood on something so I could see through the

---

[41] T. Blatt, *Sobibor—The Forgotten Revolt*, H.E.P, Issaquah, 1998, p.15.
[42] The first transport of Jews to Sobibor took place in May 1942, not June 1942.
[43] C. Lanzmann, Shoah, Pantheon Books, New York, 1985, pp. 66-67.

high windows to look over the fence. But unfortunately there was nothing to see apart from the roofs. You couldn't see the houses at all. Only the roofs. There were a lot of houses.[44]

Tadeus Syczuk was born in Dorohucza, but lived in Osowa from an early age. He worked for the Railway company from 1941. He worked at Włodawa, Sobibór, and Uhrusk. In an interview in 1983, he described what he saw at the Sobibór railway station:

> In Sobibór you could see through the gate, how they had the Jews come out of the wagons. That was on the side of the grinding. There you could see how they got off the train. You saw the trains arrive. You could only see it for a moment, because they didn't let you watch. You could only see something when you walked past. There were no other obstacles blocking the view.
>
> And there was only barbed wire. And the branches of the trees. Thin branches, thick branches that became bare after the leaves had fallen off. So there was nothing blocking your view. The building went on as usual. They brought Jews to work there. They built a fence, houses. They converted the buildings of the Foresters that were there. I don't know if the sawmill was converted, because people worked there.[45]

Erich Bauer gave a very detailed account of how the Jews were murdered in Sobibór:

> When the first transport that I was involved with arrived, I was already stationed in *Lager III*, along with Fuchs and *Askaris* (Ukrainian volunteers). The Jews were separated by gender; the women had to undress first and were led through the *Schlauch* (Tube) into *Lager III* and the gas chambers. I took the transport from *Lager II* through the Tube to the back of the chambers and opened the doors.
>
> The *Askaris* and the Jewish labor commando of *Lager III* then pushed the Jews into the chambers and closed the doors once they were full. Then either Vallaster or Getzinger or Hödl and the *Hiwis* (sometimes Bodessa, also someone by the name of Iwan [sic], called the 'Terrible') would start the engine in the engine

---

[44] Stephan Stelmaszuk Interview: Sobibor Interviews NL 1983.
[45] Tadeus Syczuk Interview: Sobibor Interviews NL 1983.

room. The pipe connecting the engine to the gas chamber was already in place. Fuchs left the fitting of the peg (open exhaust) until later.

In my opinion it was a petrol engine, a big engine, I think a Renault. At a later stage the engine was started earlier on, but to begin with not until the people were already in the chamber, because the open-exhaust was not available at first. It always took two men to start the engine, the battery alone was not sufficient. Fuchs had built a special contraption. There was an old magnet. One man turned the crank which started up the engine. The flywheel had some sort of crowbar, which was used to start it, while at the same time someone else had to operate the magnetic ignition; that is why two men were required to start it.

I cannot exactly remember where the petrol supply tank was situated, I think it was on the wall. I am not sure how the gas was regulated. I think it was somehow fixed in position with a screw. I think it was similar to the way the gas handle was positioned in motor vehicles. It was not necessary for one person constantly to press down on the lever to keep the engine running.

The chambers were permanently connected to the engine; the way it worked was that if a wooden plug was pulled out, the fumes went outside; if the plug was pushed into the pipe, the fumes went into the chambers. The gassing took about half an hour. I assume that about 50 to 60 people went into each chamber, but I am not sure of the exact number.

Jewish laborers supervised by the Germans took the bodies out. The supervision was carried out mainly by Vallaster, who was later killed in the uprising, right at the start, he was a very good friend of mine.

It is quite amazing how oblivious the Jews were that they were going to die. There was hardly ever any resistance. The Jews became suspicious only after they had already entered the gas chamber. But at that point there was no way back. The chambers were packed. There was a lack of oxygen. The doors were sealed airtight and the gassing procedure was started immediately. After about twenty to thirty minutes there was complete silence in the chamber, the people had been gassed and were dead.

> I remember quite clearly that a camouflage net had been draped over the gas chamber. I collected this net myself from the ammunition warehouse in Warsaw. It was thrown over the top of the roof and fixed onto it. When this was, I can no longer say. To start with, we had fir and pine trees covering the roof. In front of the *Lager* we had also planted some fir trees. That was at the time when German aviation units were flying to Russia. The German pilots were not able to see inside. The camouflage net was torn off the roof when the gas chamber was rebuilt. The camouflage net was acquired when the old wooden barracks were still in use, because such a lot of steam was generated.[46]

SS-Oberscharführer Kurt Bolender also testified how the extermination process took place:

> Before the Jews undressed, *Oberscharführer* Hermann Michel made a speech to them. On these occasions, he used to wear a white coat to give the impression he was a physician. Michel announced to the Jews that they would be sent to work. But before this they would have to take baths and undergo disinfection, so as to prevent the spread of diseases.
>
> After undressing, the Jews were taken through the 'Tube,' by an SS man leading the way, with five or six Ukrainians at the back hastening the Jews along. After the Jews had entered the gas chambers, the Ukrainians closed the doors, the motor was switched on by the Ukrainian Emil Kostenko and by the German driver Erich Bauer from Berlin. After the gassing, the doors were opened and the corpses were removed by a group of Jewish slave workers.
>
> After the first few weeks, during which the undressing took place on the open square of *Lager II*, a barrack for this purpose was erected. Inside this barrack were signs indicating the direction of the cashier and the baths. At the cashier the Jews were ordered to surrender their money and valuables.
>
> In the *Forsthaus* was a room which overlooked the path where the naked people had to pass on their way to the *Schlauch* (Tube) and the gas chambers, and the victims handed over their money and valuables through the window of this room. The cashier was

---

[46] J. Schelvis, *Sobibor*, Berg-Oxford, New York, 2007, pp. 101-102.

SS-Oberscharführer Alfred Ittner, who was the accountant of the camp. Later he was replaced by *SS-Schar* Hans Schutt and *SS-Scharführer* Erich Herbert Floss.

A limited number of skilled workers, among them carpenters, tailors, shoemakers and a few dozen strong men and women were selected from some of the transports. It was their duty to carry out the physical work. Every day some of them were shot and their ranks were filled by arrivals from new transports. Some of the Jews selected to work were taken to *Lager III*, where they were ordered to remove the bodies of those murdered in the gas chambers and bury them. Others were employed in *Lager II*, engaged in the collecting and sorting out of clothes and personal belongings of the victims, which were sent to the *Alter Flugplatz* (Old Airfield) in Lublin, for disinfection and distribution throughout the Reich.

The 200-300 Jewish prisoners who were incarcerated in *Lager III*, who removed the bodies from the gas chambers and buried them, had no contact with the other Jewish prisoners in other parts of the camp. Their food was cooked in Lager I and taken by Jewish prisoners to the gate of *Lager III*.[47]

Kurt Bolender also testified in post-war interrogations about those early days in *Lager III* in Sobibór:

> The first grave had been covered with a layer of sand. As this grave was completely full, the other bodies had to be taken elsewhere, even though the new grave was not yet ready. I still clearly remember arriving for work at the second grave one morning, to find that the bodies which had already been piled up along one side had decomposed to such an extent that in the sweltering heat, blood and body fluids had run all along the bottom of the unfinished grave.
>
> It was clear that we could not continue working under such circumstances. I remember giving directions to build a kind of bank, about 30cm high perhaps, right across the bottom of the grave. Ittner was there as well. I spoke to him about it.
>
> In this context I can also give an impression of the extent of deterioration of the bodies in the first grave. The layer of the sand

---

[47] J. Schelvis, *Sobibor*, Berg-Oxford, New York, 2007, pp. 52-53.

covering the grave cracked and rose up to the point where some of the bloated bodies were being pushed up to the surface, rolling out sideways. So I had the *Arbeitsjuden* build a proper sand bank all around the grave. The sight of it was intolerable, and the stench also unbearable.[48]

Hans-Heinz Schutt described how the process was supervised by the camp staff, and how the victims reacted:

> Getting the detainees into the gas chambers did not always proceed smoothly. The detainees would shout and weep and they often refused to get inside. The guards helped them on by violence. These guards were Ukrainian volunteers, who were under the authority of members of the *SS Kommando*.
>
> Members of the *SS* held key positions in the camp, i.e. one *SS* man oversaw the unloading, a further *SS* man led the detainees into the reception camp, a further *SS*-man was responsible for leading the detainees to the undressing area, a further *SS*-man oversaw the confiscation of valuables, and a further member of the *Kommando* had to drive the detainees into the so-called 'Tube,' which led to the extermination camp. Once they were inside the so-called 'Tube,' which led from the hut to the extermination camp, there was no longer any escape.[49]

SS-Unterscharführer Hubert Gomerski testified in Hagen on November 30, 1965:

> There was a Jewish commando in *Lager III*, they slept there. How many times this commando was gassed I do not know. It was changed from time to time, i.e. killed and replaced by other people. I do not think that people knew exactly was going on in *Lager III*.
>
> In *Lager III* there was a permanent watch. When the Germans went off duty, the Ukrainians were left to guard the posts by themselves. In the tower there were always two men, each with an S.M.G (heavy machine-gun).

---

[48] Ibid pp. 110-111.
[49] E. Klee, W. Dressen, V. Reiss, *Those Were the Days*, Hamish Hamilton, London, p.240.

> At night an electric light shone from the tower. The electricity came from *Lager I*, there was no generator in *Lager III*. The light was always switched on. At night there were also ground patrols in *Lager III*. The camp was surrounded by two barbed wire fences, with a path in between. The guards patrolled along this path day and night. At the front of *Lager III* there was a single gate, which was also guarded day and night. The guards went up and down the path, usually there were three. In the tower there were two others. Every day new passwords were given out. The *Arbeitsjuden* were able to sleep at night. I do not know of any nighttime gassings. In the gas chamber there was a light, which was powered by the engine.[50]

After the first few weeks of undressing in the open air square of *Lager II*, an undressing barrack was erected. Inside the barrack were signs indicating directions 'To the Cashier,' and 'To the Baths.' The Jews handed over their money and valuables through the window of the cashier's room. The cashier was *SS-Oberscharführer* Alfred Ittner, who was the camp's accountant, until he was replaced by *SS-Scharführer* Erich Herbert Floss.

Elderly people, the sick, and invalids were told they would receive medical treatment, and they were put in carts, although later small gauge railway tippers were used, and taken to the *Lazarett* in *Lager III*, directly to open pits behind the pre-war Catholic Chapel[51], with a cross on its roof, where they were shot by a detachment of Ukrainians led by *SS-Unterscharführer* Paul Bredow.

Moshe Bahir testified at the Adolf Eichmann Trial on June 5, 1961, about the *Lazarett:*

> The *Lazarett*, it was a pit, not far from the camp, five hundred meters away from the camp and from where we were working. When we were running two hundred meters with the bundles, there was a pit and when someone was injured or had his sexual organs bitten by the dog Barry, *SS-Unterscharführer* Paul Groth would say to him, 'What happened to you, my poor man? You

---

[50] J. Schelvis, *Sobibor*, Berg-Oxford, New York, 2007, pp. 112-113.
[51] The wooden chapel was built in 1926, but was abandoned from 1942-1943, when Sobibór was in operation.

can't carry on like that. Who did that to you? Come with me to the *Lazarett'*. And he went with him. A few minutes later, we would hear a shot.[52]

The slave workers who had to carry out these duties in the extermination process were selected from the transports, a few dozen strong young men and women who were spared for a few days, before being murdered. Their ranks were filled by arrivals from new transports. Some deportees were taken to *Lager III*, where they had to remove the gassed bodies and bury them in mass graves.

Probably from June 1942, the groups of prisoners selected to live; such as Carpenters, Tailors, and Shoemakers, as well as other prisoners, were engaged in collecting and sorting out the victims property, which was sent to the Reich. The 200 to 300 prisoners who were kept in the Extermination Area, (*Lager III*) had virtually no contact with those prisoners in the other parts of the camp. Their food was cooked in *Lager I* and taken by Jewish prisoners to the gate of *Lager III*.

Sholmo Szmajzner described his arrival at the Sobibór Death Camp on May 12, 1942, in a transport from Opole:

> It was late afternoon when we noticed that the noise made by the train wheels on the rails had slowly lessened its speed. Next we heard the squeak of metal caused by the brakes and the train stopped. We soon noticed they were manoeuvring the engine and suddenly the wagons started to be pushed instead of pulled. A few seconds later we stopped again. We were all silent, since we were worried at the continuous comings and goings of the engine. We felt it was finally separated from the rest of the convoy and was going fast away from the place we thought should be a railroad yard. Some more minutes went by while we waited for the result of all of the fluster. We were all filled with intense anxiety and only whispers were heard, broken at times by the cry of a child, immediately silenced by its mother. All of a sudden the door was opened.

---

[52] The Adolf Eichmann Trial Transcripts, June 5, 1961. Session 65. Nizkor—online resource.

> All the other wagons were opened at the same time and we saw dozens of SS soldiers, whom we already knew very well, waiting for us along the whole long convoy. Scattered among them were approximately as many soldiers. They wore special uniforms of which the most remarkable element was a black cap, with a skull emblem right in front. They carried wooden truncheons, whips, and their guns were in their hands. Their uniform was different from that of the Germans, and it was forest green in colour. They had been recruited in Ukraine, among who were those of German descent and many of them spoke German. We immediately heard violent shouts and curses, followed by an incisive command, 'Outside quickly!'

The horror of the arrival in hell continued:

> This was the reception the bandits gave us making the hopes of the most optimistic turn to pessimism, which was already latent. The Ukrainians and their German masters, using the whips in an indiscriminate way, instigated the great human cargo to make us leave the crowded wagons hurriedly and violently. We hardly had time to breath and we were forced to hurl ourselves disorderly out, like an excited herd. We stepped on each other and pressed against one another, walking over the bodies that hampered our way and slipping on the foul slippery paste that covered the whole floor of the freight car.
>
> As soon as the wagons were emptied, we were impelled towards a long corridor flanked by two fences made of barbed-wire. There were guards all around us, urging us to walk as fast as possible, in spite of the state we were in. At the end of that passage there was an arrogant Nazi officer accompanied by two Ukrainian soldiers holding their truncheons. The corridor was the stage of an unforgettable scene for the sophisticated cruelty which was practiced there. The three criminals stood at the end of the corridor positioned to form a triangle, with the higher ranking officer, a little behind the two guards who stood on either side of him. Both of them had a menacing posture, with their fearful truncheons, and their vicious faces.

The separation of the men from the women and children was about to take place:

Meanwhile the mass of Jews was coming by fits and starts and, when they came within reach of the morons, they were violently separated—the men to the right and the women to the left, with the beast-like sectarians fiercely wielding their cudgels and hitting everyone pitilessly. The picture we saw was very painful, with whole families being separated: mothers were separated from their children and husbands in tears: young people were driven away from their parents and siblings: babies were deprived of their mothers love. As we were being separated according to our sex, we were thrown into a larger yard located at the end of the corridor.

This area could not hold us all and we had to be pushed and pressed to one another until it became totally saturated with people, because about two thousand of us had come in our transport. The cursed SS were waiting for us at the entrance to the yard, which looked like a football field. They did not intend to waste any time, since they immediately aligned the women into four rows and made them start walking towards a gate, behind which lay the unknown.

Stanislaw Szmajzner continued:

As soon as they had disappeared behind the gate, which was noisily shut, the Nazis focused their attention on the men. They put us also in rows of four and we waited for the command to march. This did not come immediately though and we had to stand where we were. In the commotion generated by the disorderly exit from the train—when no one could understand anything amidst the running and shouting. I had been close to my brother, to my nephew and to my cousin Nojech. From that moment onwards we never separated for a single minute and now we were together. The same did not happen to my father, with whom we lost all contact during the bedlam resulting from the human avalanche, which had been hurled out of the wagon. If we had not been able to find him then, we thought it impossible, now, to try to locate him, since we were all grouped and under the strict surveillance of the Germans.

With all the men in formation, there suddenly appeared a giant German officer, with a disdainful look in his eyes and whom I thought to be the leader there. Actually roaring, he started to select us according to our aptitudes. Thus the farmers were selected first, then the physically stronger, as well as those who seemed to be most able to resist. Next the carpenters, the mechanics, the tailors, and then other professionals, until all of us had been subdivided into diverse groups, according to the most useful professions.

As no goldsmiths were called I was very surprised and daringly left the files of those who had not been called and addressed the officer. When I got close enough to him, without waiting for him to say a word, I tried to be very courteous and clever and told him, I was a goldsmith and that my profession had not been included on the list they had called. The huge German was perplexed, as if he had paid no attention to my words or did not believe I was actually a goldsmith. As soon as I finished talking I took off my back the small tool bag I always carried and showed him its contents, as well as a monogram I had engraved on my own money wallet. This small proof of my professional skill was enough to make this brute a little more accessible and believe what I had told him. He finally decided I was to be taken from the files and I took advantage of the opportunity to add that I had three 'brothers' who also manufactured jewels and whom I would like to have with me. He nodded his agreement and my 'brothers' joined me. Before he could go on with his work I still found a little courage to tell him that my old father was in that crowd, although I had not been able to find him. The German then said we might be able to find my father next day. So ended that short but profitable dialogue.[53]

The SS officer who had selected Shlomo Szmajzner and his 'brothers' was the Austrian Gustav Wagner. Another Sobibór survivor, Moshe Bahir, described this cruel and much-feared member of the Sobibór SS personnel:

> He was a handsome man, tall and blond—a pure Aryan. In civilian life he was, no doubt a well-mannered man, at Sobibór he was a wild beast. His lust to kill knew no bounds. I saw such terrible scenes that they give me nightmares to this day. He would snatch babies from their mother's arms and tear them to pieces in his hands.

---

[53] Stanislaw Szmajzner, *Hell in Sobibor*, (Unpublished English Version in authors collection) pp.109-113.

57

> I saw him beat two men to death with a rifle, because they did not carry out his instructions properly, since they did not understand German. I remember that one night a group of youths aged fifteen or sixteen arrived in the camp. The head of this group was one Abraham (Fibs). After a long and arduous work day, this young man collapsed on his pallet and fell asleep. Suddenly Wagner came into our barrack and Abraham did not hear him call to stand up at once before him. Furious, he pulled Abraham naked off his bed and began to beat him all over his body. When Wagner grew weary of the blows, he took out his revolver and killed him on the spot. This atrocious spectacle was carried out before all of us, including Abraham's younger brother.[54]

Stanislaw Szmajzner received a description from his friend Abraham of his experience of conditions in *Lager III*. The exchange of correspondence was conducted in secret by Ivan Klatt, a *Trawnikimänner*, in exchange for gold. This information provided by Abraham, Stanislaw's friend from the Opole Ghetto, giving the Jewish perspective of *Lager III*, is unique:

> When the thousands of Jews pass through the gate you mentioned, they go down a long corridor and enter *Lager II*. There they are stripped of their last belongings, and made to stand there naked, until they are led into a large shack, where they are allegedly going to have a bath. Hundreds of people enter that shack at a time.
>
> When the shack is completely full, the door is locked and hermetically sealed. Then a large diesel motor is set to work, and its exhaust pipe is passed through a hole in the wall, so that the gases of combustion are blown inside, until everyone is asphyxiated.
>
> Before this operation, giant ditches are dug. After the mass extermination, we, the survivors of the same transport you came in, begin to pick up the bodies and throw them in the ditches. Not seldom, the ground has shaken under the weight of that human mass to be buried. Then, the monsters came and shot them, to make sure they were dead.

---

[54] Y. Arad, *Belzec, Sobibor, Treblinka*, Indiana University Press, Bloomington and Indianapolis 1987, p.191.

I am telling you this because, should you ever escape, you will be able to tell the world everything that happened here, because you must not expect to ever see me again. Whoever comes to *Lager III*, will never leave it. This place is the end for each and every Jew in the power of the Nazis.

I cannot describe all the scenes because you would never believe what happens in this horrible place. All of it is thoroughly inconceivable to the human mind. I wish you could see how the sadists like Bolender, Gomerski, and one called 'Red Cake' acted. While the slaughter was in progress, these monsters were delirious with happiness, as if they were at the opera. They seemed to take delight in looking at so many dead bodies naked and inert. I have written you this message for you to be aware of everything, since I no longer have any kind of fear. My end is coming and I already know what it will be like. It will be the same as the others. I have one foot in the grave, where I shall meet our brothers, who are gone forever.

I am not afraid of anything in writing to you because it does not make any difference to me whether they catch me or not, I am in the power of these scoundrels and I do not expect any good from them. You would be in trouble should they ever find out, I wrote you, but even so I decided to try. I have done this to warn you, because if you have any chance, try to escape. Unfortunately I am not that lucky. Since *Lager III* of Sobibór is the end of any Jew under the German yoke.

If you can, escape and avenge us.

Your friend Abraham[55]

One of the transports in June 1942, came from Vienna, Austria. A very detailed report from a member of the *Schutzpolizei*, an Austrian Lieutenant named Josef Fischmann, who was responsible for the transport, has survived the war:

> The Transport Guard consisted of Police Lt Fischmann in charge, 2 Senior and 13 policemen of the 1 Police and Reserve Company East. The Transport Guard commenced duties on the Aspang

---

[55] Stanislaw Szmajzner, *Hell in Sobibor*, (Unpublished English Version in authors collection) pp. 149-151.

station on 14.6.1942, at 11 o'clock having previously confirmed details with *SS-Hauptsturmführer* Brunner.

The Jews started to board the special train at 12:00 under the control and supervision of *SS-Hauptsturmführer* Brunner and *SS-Hauptscharführer* Girzik from the HQ office for Jewish Emigration. There were no incidents. The Transport Guards started their duties. A total of 1,000 Jews were transported. The official handover of the Jews according to transport lists took place at 16:00 hours. The transport had to be content with third class compartments, as there was a shortage of second class compartments.

The train, DA38, was dispatched from Vienna on June 14, 1942, at 19:08 and went via Lundenburg, Bruenn, Niesse, Oppeln, Tschentochau, Kielce, Radom, Lublin, Chelm to Sobibór and not, as expected to Izbica. The arrival in Sobibór was on June 17, 1942, at 8:15.

At the station of Lublin where we arrived on June 16, 1942, at 19:00 hours, *SS-Obersturmführer* Pohl[56] was waiting, and he ordered that fifty-one able Jews, between the ages of fifteen and fifty disembark and be brought to a labor camp. At that time he gave an order that the remaining 949 Jews were to be taken to Sobibór. The list of the people, three freight cars with food, and 100,000 zloty were handed over to the *SS-Obersturmführer* Pohl in Lublin.

At 23:00 we left Lublin for Sobibór, in the Jewish Camp of Trawniki, 30 kilometres before Lublin, we handed over the three freight cars with food and luggage to *SS-Scharführer* Mayerhofer.

The train arrived at 8:15 on June 17, at the labor camp, which was close to the Sobibór station. The 949 Jews were handed over to *Oberleutnant der Schutzpolizei* Stangl, who immediately had the wagons unloaded. By 09:15 hours they were empty. As soon as the Jews had been unloaded, the train left Sobibór as a *Sonderzug* at 10:00 hours, arriving at Lublin on 18 June at 02:30 hours.

No fares were charged for this journey. At 08:13 the train departed according to schedule as a fast train to Krakow, where it arrived at 17:30. Stayed overnight with the third company of Reserve

---

[56] Helmut Ortwin Pohl, an Austrian, was a member of Globocnik's staff in Lublin.

Police Battalion 74. Departure from Krakow on 19 June at 20:08 hours; arrival Vienna *Ostbahnhof* on 20 June at 06:30 hours.[57]

Eda Lichtman, who left Wielczka for Mielec, was then deported via Berdychow to Dubienka. From Dubienka, she was deported to Sobibór, by train, via Hrubieszow. She described her arrival in Sobibór, during June 1942:

> We have lost all sense of time. Have we already arrived in the Ukraine? The locomotive lets out an earsplitting shriek. The train comes to an abrupt stop. We remain halted for a while and then the car sets off again. The doors open. The light blinds us. I read the writing on the sign: '*SS Sonderkommando Sobibór.*'
>
> Facing us are officers and soldiers, on their shoulders or in their hands machine-guns ready to shoot. I make out a large St. Bernard dog. 'Hey you over there,' one of the officers shouts, pointing at me, 'What do you do for a living?' I'm a qualified kindergarten teacher.' The whole gang burst out laughing. 'Ok, you can do the washing for us.' They pull me and two other young girls—Bela Sobol and Sarka Kac from Dubienka out of line. They take us into the camp and put us in a small barrack. In it, in a great mess, are clothes and mouldy slices of bread. Who were the barrack's previous residents, and where are they now? Of the transport from Hrubieszow, 8,000 souls, three women remained in Sobibór. The only thing left of all the rest is heaps of clothes and shoes. Of those three, I am the only one to have survived.[58]

Another SS officer who also deserves recognition for his cruelty was *SS-Oberscharführer* Karl Frenzel, the commander of *Lager I*. He is remembered by Selma Engel, in a post-war interview:

> And also one day *Oberscharführer* Karl Frenzel came out. Frenzel was one of the worst SS in the camp and he came to Camp One. He went with his whip, he went in the barrack and everybody in the barrack was sick, had to go out and had to stay in the middle.

---

[57] Report by Lieutenant Fischmann, 20 June 1942. Copy Holocaust Historical Society UK.
[58] R. Saidel, *Mielec, Poland*, Gefen Publishing House, Jerusalem, Israel, 2012, p.74.

> I remember so vividly there was a boy I knew from Assen, from another town, from the Zionist organization, and he was standing there, and they were all standing for a long time in the middle of the camp and they all got shot right away.[59]

Sometime during June 1942, Theresa Stangl, the wife of Sobibór commandant Franz Stangl, was given permission by Odilo Globocnik to visit her husband. She travelled by train to *Krakau*, and then onto Chelm, with their two daughters, Brigitte and Renate. Theresa and the two girls stayed with *Baurat* Bruno Moser, in his house in Chelm, some 20 kilometres distance from Sobibór.

Stangl was able to secure some rooms for his family in a fish-hatchery in the village of Okuninka, some 10 kilometres north of Sobibór, which belonged to Count Chelmicki. There was also an officers country club built by the Germans at Perepsza Lake,[60] but this was unsuitable for small children, and was mentioned by Pan Gerung in conversation with Gitta Sereny:[61]

> You are probably confusing it with a big white house the Germans built as a kind of country club for their officers, on the other side of the lake. They used to go there for weekends, for the fishing—and other days too, in the evenings. An enormous amount of drinking went on there, and other things. Poles were not allowed in.[62]

It was at this fish-hatchery, mentioned above, where Theresa Stangl first learnt of what was happening in Sobibór:

> One of the members of the *SS-Sonderkommando* Sobibór Karl Ludwig visited the fish-hatchery to buy some fish. Ludwig became maudlin and told Theresa Stangl how fantastic numbers of Jews were being done away using gas at the Sobibór camp.

Theresa confronted her husband about this, when he returned to the fish-hatchery from Sobibór, which was only 4 kilometres from

---

[59] Selma Engel – Interview with USHMM on July 16, 1990.
[60] M. Bem, *Sobibor Extermination Camp 1942-1943*, Stichting Sobibor 2015, p. 116.
[61] Gitta Sereny, *Into That Darkness*, Pimlico. London 1974, p.132
[62] Ibid p. 132.

the death camp,[63] but Franz Stangl denied any involvement in the murder of the Jews, he said he was just in charge of construction.[64]

On July 19, 1942, Heinrich Himmler, *the Reichsführer-SS* visited Sobibór, as part of a visit to Lublin, where he had visited Odilo Globocnik. He also visited the Trawniki *SS-Ausbildungs-Lager*. This visit was documented, and is included in the documents section of this book. At the end of July 1942, the deportations to the Sobibór death camp temporarily ceased due to construction work on the Lublin-Chelm railway line. During the next two months only a few smaller transports from some nearby ghettos arrived at the camp.

During August 1942, Odilo Globocnik and Christian Wirth visited the Treblinka death camp commanded by Dr. Irmfried Eberl, where they found the camp in chaos, It was decided to move Franz Stangl to Sobibór and replace him with Franz Karl Reichleitner, a former Euthanasia colleague, who had worked with Stangl in Hartheim near Linz. Reichleitner arrived in Sobibór during September 1942. Christian Wirth's adjutant testified about Globocnik and Wirth's visit to Treblinka, on August 19, 1942:

> In Treblinka everything was in a state of collapse. The camp was overstocked. Outside the camp, a train with deportees was unable to be unloaded, as there was simply no more room. Many corpses of Jews were lying inside the camp. These corpses were already bloated. Particularly I can remember seeing many corpses in the vicinity of the fence. These people were shot from the guard towers.
>
> I heard then in Treblinka how Globocnik and Wirth summed up the following: Wirth would remain in Treblinka for the time being. Dr Eberl would be dismissed immediately. In his place Stangl would come to Treblinka, from Sobibór as Commander. Globocnik said in this conversation that if Dr Eberl was not his fellow

---

[63] It is actually 10 kilometres from Sobibor.
[64] Gitta Sereny, *Into That Darkness*, Pimlico. London 1974, p.132-133.

countryman he would arrest him and bring him before an SS and Police court.

Oberhauser also testified that it was at Treblinka, leaning against a door of a barrack in the square, that Globocnik also decided that Franz Reichleitner would be Stangl's replacement at Sobibór.[65]

Theresa Stangl recalled how their idyllic life in a forest in south-eastern Poland came to an end:

> We were rowing on the lake with the children that day, when Michel arrived on the shore. Michel called to us across the lake and said that a message had come through to say that Paul (Stangl) was to report to Globocnik. We rowed back to the shore and Michel said, 'They mean now, at once. You have to come with me right away.' We went back to the house, and I remember, I helped him get changed, and then he left.[66]

Franz Karl Reichleitner, a member of the Linz *Gestapo*, who also served with Stangl in the T4 Euthanasia Institution at Hartheim, came to Sobibór. Jewish inmate Stanislaw Szmajzner recalled his arrival:

> Not much later, Franz Stangl's substitute came. He was the new commandant of the extermination camp in Sobibór. We never learned his name. We—the Jews of Camp I, immediately nicknamed him '*Trottel*,' which means idiot, fool. We did that because that was the only word he used to call us by.
>
> '*Trottel*' an obese man, nearly as round as he was fat, was still very nimble and firm in the way he walked. Very red in the face, nearly as much so as 'Red Cake'. He loved to show off his authority by talking very little, even with the officers. He always shouted at us and he liked to give us continuous orders which had to be obeyed to the last dot. He was really a very tough fellow, his own subordinates respected him and promptly obeyed his orders.[67]

In the three *Aktion Reinhardt* death camps, Bełżec, Sobibór, and Treblinka, the initial gas chambers capacity were found to be

---

[65] Ibid. p.161.
[66] Ibid. p.137.
[67] Stanislaw Szmajzner, *Hell in Sobibor*, (Unpublished English Version in authors collection) pp.196.

wanting. After completing the construction of new gas chambers at Treblinka Erwin Herman Lambert and Lorenz Hackenholt, went to Sobibór to repeat the same activity. Erwin Lambert testified after the war:

> It was sometime in autumn 1942, but I don't know exactly when. At that time I was assigned by Wirth to enlarge the gassing structure, according to the model of Treblinka. I went to Sobibór together with Lorenz Hackenholt, who was at that time in Treblinka.
>
> First of all, I went with Hackenholt to a sawmill near Warsaw. There Hackenholt ordered a big consignment of wood for reconstruction in Sobibór. Finally both of us went to Sobibór. We reported there to the camp commander, Reichleitner. He gave us the exact directives for the construction of the gassing installation. Probably the old installation was not big enough, and reconstruction was necessary.
>
> Today, I cannot tell exactly who participated in the reconstruction work. However, I do remember that Jewish prisoners and so-called 'Askaries' (Ukrainian auxiliaries) took part in the work. During the time that building was in progress, no transports with Jews arrived.[68]

Franz Hödl, who was employed in *Lager III*, testified after the war, about the new gas chamber building:

> The airtight doors did not arrive until later. I collected them myself from Warsaw, but that was not until the rebuilding took place. Before then, there were wooden doors at the back, where the dead bodies came out. The fittings were not put in till later. I fetched them from Warsaw; they were real showerheads. Whether the pipes ran into the gas chambers from above or below, I do not know.
>
> In *Lager III*, a concrete building, 18 to 20 meters long with about 6 to 8 gas chambers had been erected. The gas chamber had either 4 or 6 chambers on either side of the central corridor, three on the left and three on the right. Inside these rooms it was dark.

---

[68] Y. Arad, *Belzec, Sobibor, Treblinka*, Indiana University Press, Bloomington and Indianapolis 1987, p.123.

There was a flat roof, in which to my knowledge there were no hatches. The external walls consisted of trap-doors that ran along the entire length, which would be raised after the gassing. This was also the means of ventilation inside the chambers.

In the engine room there were indeed two engines. There was a petrol engine, probably from a Russian tank and a diesel engine. The latter was never used, however. The people were pushed along through the corridor into the chambers. After the gassing, the outside doors could be raised, and the dead bodies removed.

I have drawn a rough sketch of my impressions of the *Lager* and have used this as a reference when giving my description, which I hand over as an appendix to this protocol.[69]

During the late autumn of 1942, according to Dov Freiberg in his memoirs the Germans erected a new building where the inmates lived in the centre of *Lager I*:

> A strange building was erected next to our barracks: at one end, close to us, there was a room that joined onto the long, rectangular, sloping building. This was a bowling alley, meant to provide entertainment for the Germans during the long winter evenings. It was beyond my understanding why this bowling alley was built in our camp, next to our barracks, and not in the German area. It was possible that in this way the Germans could keep a close eye on us during the long winter evenings to prevent the likelihood of rebellion or escape.
>
> One evening, a large group of Germans came to the entrance of the bowling alley. Somehow Graetschus hunted me down, and he ordered me to accompany him to the building. The Germans brought food and plenty of beer with them and already had been drinking before they entered the new structure.
>
> Graetschus explained to me that I was to stand at the end of the lane, where there was a platform marked with circles; I was to set up the wooden bowling pins and return the balls that reached me. I spent all that evening with the Germans, who talked and laughed and mostly drunk excessive amounts of beer. Now and then one of the Germans would give me something to eat and a beer. The drink was bitter and after one bottle my head swam.

---

[69] J. Schelvis, *Sobibor*, Berg-Oxford, New York, 2007, p104.

> When the Germans left I had to clean the place. I finally went back to the barracks, my pockets full of cigarette and cigar stubs, and within moments our barracks was filled with smoke.[70]

The commander of the Trawniki training camp, *SS-Sturmbannführer* Karl Streibel, testified about the cremating sites he saw during his visit to Sobibór at the end of 1942:

> Wirth led me through the Sobibór camp. I saw the gas chambers and the other facilities. I saw the ditches near the gas chambers. I could not see any corpses in the ditches, because they were covered with a layer of earth. But I saw the roaster made of railway lines where the corpses were burned. During my visit there were no extermination operation. There were also no corpses burned, but I could see the cremating sites. The roaster made from the railway lines was supported by a stone base.[71]

In December 1942, a daring escape took place on the night of December 26, 1942. This involved a Jewish woman named Pesia Liberman and two Jewish men, along with two Ukrainian guards, one named Viktor Kisilew and the other named Emil Zischer. Pesia Liberman stayed with the armed Ukrainians, whilst the Jewish men parted and went their separate ways. Whilst hiding in the village of Kozia Gorka, they were betrayed by a farmer. They were all killed in a shootout by three Polish Police Officers; Misnerowiec, Piescikowski, and Kwiatkowski.[72]

During December 1942, Paul Groth, one of the Sobibór NCOs was transferred back to the Bełżec death camp. Groth had fallen in love with a Jewess named Ruth. The day after he left, Ruth was no longer among the living. Erich Bauer takes up the story:

> I was blamed for being responsible for the death of the Jewish girls Ruth and Gisela, who lived in the so-called forresters house*[sic]*. As it is known, these two girls lived in the Forresters House and they were visited frequently by the SS-men. Orgies

---

[70] Dov Freiberg, *To Survive Sobibor*, Gefen Publishing House, Jerusalem, 2007, p.273.
[71] Y. Arad, *Belzec, Sobibor, Treblinka*, Indiana University Press, Bloomington and Indianapolis 1987, p.172.
[72] T. Blatt, *Sobibor—The Forgotten Revolt*, H.E.P, Issaquah, 1998, p.58.

were conducted there. They were attended by Bolender, Hubert Gomerski, Karl Ludwig, Franz Stangl, Gustav Wagner and Steubl.

I lived in the room above them and due to these celebrations could not fall asleep after coming back from a journey. One evening, Karl Ludwig banged on the girls' door. Evidently he wanted to enter. The girls opened the door in my presence. Ludwig ordered the girls to put on their dressing gowns, and both of us took them in direction of *Lager III*. I went half way only and then returned. Ludwig went with them alone. Next day Ludwig told me that by his order a Ukrainian had shot the two girls. [73]

On February 12, 1943, Heinrich Himmler paid his second visit to Sobibór. An armoured train with three wagons pulled into the camp and was received with a great deal of pomp and ceremony. Everything was prepared so that the extermination process, which Himmler had come to witness, would run as smoothly as possible. Wirth and his adjutant Josef Oberhauser, were also part of the group. They made their way directly to *Lager III*. [74] It is interesting to note that some survivors claim that Himmler and his entourage arrived in an aircraft, not a train.

SS-Oberscharführer Hubert Gomerski recalled Himmler's visit:

> I remember the visit of *Reichsführer* Heinrich Himmler in Sobibór. All the SS men, members of the police and the Ukrainian volunteers were lined up in a parade. I personally reported my platoon to Himmler for inspection. I know that on the day when Himmler was in Sobibór a certain number of Jews were gassed. I can tell for sure that Himmler visited Camp III (extermination area). I saw Himmler with the whole group going in the direction of Camp III. [75]

---

[73] Y. Arad, *Belzec, Sobibor, Treblinka*, Indiana University Press, Bloomington and Indianapolis 1987, pp. 116-117.
[74] J. Schelvis, *Sobibor*, Berg-Oxford, New York, 2007, p.94.
[75] Y. Arad, *Belzec, Sobibor, Treblinka*, Indiana University Press, Bloomington and Indianapolis 1987, p.166.

Moshe Szklarek (Bahir) recalled the visits of Heinrich Himmler to Sobibór at the Adolf Eichmann Trial in Jerusalem on June 5, 1961:

> It was in the month of July 1942. I remember this incident well. I remember that two hours before the arrival of a train, my friend Joseph Pines, and I were called to polish the officers' boots. The officers' quarters were near the platform. At approximately 11:00 or 11:30, two hours after I had been called, I saw a luxury train coming in to Sobibór.
>
> The victims who arrived in those days were brought in freight cars, and you could see all kinds of belongings hanging out of the cars. This one was a train with passenger carriages. A group of senior officers alighted from it, and it was headed by Himmler, who stood out with his spectacles and long coat. There were eight other officers, one of who was Eichmann, and together with them, three civilians......
>
> I saw him for the second time in 1943—roughly in the month of February, but then it was not a train that arrived—then the officers arrived by plane—we also knew that. I was then working in the German officers' casino. I worked there for eight months, starting the day after the first visit, for on the day after that first visit, the two Jewish girls who worked in the German casino were killed, and in their stead, I was chosen to work there, together with my friend Joseph Pines. From that day, I worked in the casino until March 1943, about one month after the second visit of Himmler and his colleagues.......
>
> Yes. On the day of that visit, when he had already returned from Camp 3. He visited only Camp 3, accompanied by Franz Reichleitner, who was camp commander at the time. My immediate superior in the camp Paul Bredow, heard from *Unterscharführer* Beckmann, who had returned from Camp 3, that the visitors were soon coming back from there. He was not even aware that the plane had already landed, as soon as he heard this, he sent me hurriedly to the camp with my friend Joseph Pines. When I arrived there, the gate was locked, and by the time the Ukrainian guard opened

the gate they had already come quite near, two or three meters away, and then I recognized them. [76]

SS-Oberscharführer Karl Frenzel was in charge of security during Himmler's visit:

> His visit was announced a few days in advance. The camp leadership spared no effort to demonstrate the proper functioning of the camp. The so-called *Aktiven* (trusted *SS* men) were put in position to ensure that all communications ran smoothly. I was assigned to patrol the outside of the camp with some of the *Unterführer* and Ukrainian guards to ensure Himmler's personal safety. While Himmler was observing the gassing procedure in *Lager III*, I secured the surrounding area (from *Lager IV*). [77]

Whilst Himmler was impressed with what he saw at Sobibór, he was disturbed to learn that the bodies of Jews were buried and not burned, so he ordered that the bodies should be exhumed and cremated, so that all traces of the mass murder committed here could be obliterated. He also thought the camp was idle, so he ordered that transports of Jews from France and Holland should be sent to Sobibór. The visit of Himmler brought about other changes. A German Jewess, named Johanna Koch[78], from Mainz, who had been deported from Mainz-Darmstadt on March 25, 1942, to the Piaski Transit Ghetto, and then onto Sobibór—cooked meals for the Germans. She was removed from this position, as Himmler feared that Jews employed serving food might poison the *SS*-Garrison. [79]

Four transports left France destined for the Sobibór death camp, between March 4, 1943, and March 25, 1943. On the March 25, 1943, transport was Josef Duniec, who was selected for work,

---

[76] The Adolf Eichmann Trial Transcripts, June 5, 1961. Session 65. Nizkor—online resource.
[77] J. Schelvis, *Sobibor*, Berg-Oxford, New York, 2007, p.94.
[78] Johanna Koch born July 18, 1892, in Mainz. www.bundesarchiv.de/Gedenkbuch—online resource.
[79] M. Bem, *Sobibor Extermination Camp 1942-1943*, Stichting Sobibor 2015, p. 117.

and who escaped in the revolt. He testified about the journey and his arrival:

> I remember that we left Drancy on 25 March 1943. We travelled for four days and arrived at Sobibór on 29/30 March 1943. We passed through Lublin and the same day came to Sobibór. Before we left Drancy, the Germans told us that we were going to Poland for work. They said we should take part in the war effort and not walk around the cities of France. We were just being tricked.
>
> The transports that left Drancy were quite big, 1,000 people in each, fifty people in a freight car, we were a group of friends from Drancy, and in spite of the fact that we did not know what awaited us there, we wanted to escape. We wanted to jump from the train, when the other people in the car were sleeping, otherwise they would try to prevent the escape, as they were afraid of collective punishment.
>
> We made a hole in the floor. We started to jump, without knowing in the last car were Gestapo with machine guns. When the Germans understood that people were escaping, they started to shoot. Some were killed. I do not know how many of those who jumped succeeded in escaping. We reached Sobibór.[80]

Josef Duniec described what happened next when his transport arrived in the Sobibór death camp:

> After we left the train, some SS men ordered that thirty people be selected for work. We did not know what was better, to be among the thirty people taken for work or among those who were going in the other direction. Where were they going? I saw that one of my friends from Drancy was among the thirty people taken to work. I joined this group. The Germans counted and found that we were thirty-one people. 'Let there be thirty-one,' he said. In this way I remained in the group.[81]

A total of nineteen transports left Westerbork Camp in Holland for Sobibór, commencing on March 2, 1943, and the final one

---

[80] Y. Arad, *Belzec, Sobibor, Treblinka*, Indiana University Press, Bloomington and Indianapolis 1987, p.146.
[81] Ibid. pp. 147-148.

departed on July 20, 1943. These transports carried 34,313 Jews in a mixture of passenger cars and freight wagons.

Selma Engel recalled in a post-war interview, the train journey from Westerbork, which departed on April 9, 1943, and her arrival at Sobibór, three days later:

> I can just recall the train ride was very scary, I remember we didn't have anything to drink—we were very thirsty. I think it was very hot. We had no idea where we went—I remember we came out at Sobibór. They opened the doors and then we heard screaming and the whips and we heard, 'Raus, Raus, Raus.'
>
> That we had to go out of the train with whips hitting us already, and everybody stumbled over each other. And I remember there was a trolley, you know it was a dump cart that goes over, we saw all the people who couldn't walk being thrown in them and little children went in that trolley. And it was very confusing, you know, we had to throw away our baggage, that little package, the backpack we had. We had to throw that in a place. I remember vividly also that one woman threw away her package and her baby went, and she said to a German, 'Oh my child! My child.' And he had a whip and he hit this woman and I saw blood coming from her face and he said, 'We will take care of this baby. You go!'
>
> So then we went farther and we stuck somehow together with these young girls and we passed all these Germans. All the SS were standing there on the side and we passed all these Germans and they say, 'You're Out, You're Out,' and they pull us out and we settled on the side. We didn't know what will happen to us—we stay [sic] on the side and I say to the girls, 'What will happen to us?' 'One shower,' she always said, 'One bath and it's all over.' I didn't know even what she was talking about—so we were standing there on the side—I think we were ten or twelve or twenty—I don't know exactly how many girls.
>
> That's the first transport that took young girls—Dutch young girls, we were standing on the side and we saw all the people passing by. I think the women went first and then the men went at last. But I don't remember exactly—I saw them walking already that side to the gas chamber, that they had to take their clothes off. And I remember also that we heard them speaking to the group of us standing there and said, 'You came to Sobibór and

everything will be okay.' And, 'Here is a little card, You can write home that you are here in Sobibór and you are—you go to a work camp.' And you have to take a shower because it is better for you, that you take a shower—so we will give you other clothes.' That I remember that they were talking to them, they say, 'Here is a card. You can write to Holland.' For us we were standing on the side and they brought us to Camp I.[82]

On July 5, 1943, Heinrich Himmler issued an order not to dismantle Sobibór. but to transform it into a concentration camp. This order was addressed to *SS-Obergruppenführer* Oswald Pohl who, as head of *WVHA*, was in charge of concentration camps, and to Odilo Globocnik, and to other *SSPF's* within the *Generalgouvernement* and the occupied Soviet Territories. The first paragraph stated, 'The transit camp Sobibór in the District of Lublin has to be transformed into a concentration camp. In the concentration camp a depot for booty ammunition has to be established.' Further the order stressed that the Higher *SS* and Police Leaders had to deliver to this camp all kinds of ammunition taken from the enemy, and it specified how it should be treated there.

The order that Sobibór was to become a concentration camp meant it would now come under the control of Oswald Pohl, instead of Odilo Globocnik. Both Pohl and Globocnik were not in favour of this, and on July 15, 1943, Oswald Pohl wrote to Heinrich Himmler:

Reichsführer

Following your order that the transit camp Sobibór in the District of Lublin should be transferred into a concentration camp, I had a talk on this subject with *SS-Gruppenführer* Globocnik. Both of us propose to give up the idea of the transformation into a concentration camp. Your desired aim, namely to install in Sobibór a depot for booty ammunition, can be achieved without the change. Everything else in the above-mentioned order can be achieved without this change. Please let me have your

---

[82] Selma Engel—Interview with USHMM on July 16, 1990.

endorsement, which is important for *Gruppenführer* Globocnik and myself.

On July 24, 1943, Pohl was informed that Himmler agreed to his proposal. [83]

Bunkers were built to store the captured ammunition and to improve the camp's security mines were laid, in the south and south west of the camp. Dov Freiberg described the activity undertaken by the Nazis following this decision:

> There was another wave of construction at Sobibór camp and again trains full of construction supplies arrived... now weapons and ammunition warehouses were being built, most of them underground. At this stage *Lager IV*, was set up, which the Germans called the *Nordlager*—North Camp—in the north-east corner of the existing camp, in the open area between the railway platform and the forest, and it continued into the forest, close to the *Lazarett*.

> High ranking officers landed in light planes and ran around the area with maps and plans, while our *SS* officers were dragged along behind them, the work was performed at a swift pace, before the first bunkers were completed, transports of ammunition had already arrived and were temporarily stored outside, next to the bunkers.[84]

Zelda Metz also recalled the camp expansion:

> In the summer of 1943, I was working on the construction of camp number IV. The *SS* were in a hurry to finish it, with its barracks and bunkers. To speed up the work, the *SS* formed a *Strafkommando* (penal commando). We were to eat while running. Forty to fifty of us died during the construction of the camp.[85]

Alexander Pechersky, also remembered the work in the *Nordlager*:

---

[83] Y. Arad, *Belzec, Sobibor, Treblinka*, Indiana University Press, Bloomington and Indianapolis 1987, pp.168-169.

[84] Dov Freiberg, *To Survive Sobibor*, Gefen Publishing House, Jerusalem, 2007, p.283.

[85] M. Novitch, *Sobibor, Martyrdom and Revolt*, Holocaust Library, New York 1980, p.131.

> Soldiers led us to the *Nordlager*, a new section of the camp. Nine barracks were already built there, and others were under construction. Our group was split in two: one part was sent to build, the other to cut wood. On our first day of work, fifteen people got twenty-five lashes each for incompetence.
>
> On September 25, we unloaded coal all day, and were given only twenty minutes for lunch. The cook was unable to feed us all in such a short time. Frenzel was furious and ordered the cook to sit down. Then he whipped him while whistling a march tune. The soup tasted as though it had been mixed with blood and although we were very hungry, many of us were unable to eat.[86]

Thomas 'Toivi' Blatt also witnessed the above event, and he recalled that:

> The cook, Hershel Cukiermann was flogged by Frenzel, because he had been unable to prepare that day's lunch for the prisoners within the allotted time. [87]

Whilst the date of the *Waldkommando's* (Forest Commando) revolt is confirmed as occurring on July 23, 1943, in a German Security Police report, other prisoner accounts recall this took part on July 20, 1943. Given the documented proof of the German report, I have concluded it took place on July 23, 1943.

The *Waldkommando's* role in the camp was to fell trees for expansion, collecting firewood and branches for camouflaging the barbed-wire fences, revolted, eight prisoners escaped and those recaptured were shot.

Kalman Werwyk recalled what happened that day:

> One spring day in 1943, about 30 men of the *Waldkommando* were taken out, under Ukrainian guards, to work. Later that day we saw the Ukrainians herding a much smaller body of Jews back to the camp. The Jews were bloodied, in bad shape. They were dragging many corpses with them.
>
> We were told that two of the Jews Kopf and Podchlebnik had asked for permission to go to a nearby well and bring back water

---

[86] Ibid. p.90.
[87] T. Blatt, *Sobibor—The Forgotten Revolt*, H.E.P, Issaquah, 1998, p.50.

for their fellow prisoners. This was around mid-day and the men were thirsty. When they got to the well they attacked the Ukrainian guard accompanying them, took his weapon and ammunition, tossed him into the well and took off.

When they didn't return with the water, the other Ukrainian guards became suspicious and herded the remaining Jews together, under heavy guard, until the matter would be clarified. These Jews understood what had occurred; they knew that they were finished, whatever would happen. When one or two escaped from a group, the whole group was killed. So these desperate Jews took off in all directions, the Ukrainian guards firing at them and pursuing them. Some of those Jews were said to have successfully escaped. However, those who were caught alive were brought back, tied up (hands and feet), sat down and ordered to look straight ahead, while they were savagely clubbed by the Ukrainians.

We were ordered to stand in a semi-circle and watch the 'spectacle.' We were also ordered to laugh loudly during the ordeal of our poor fellow Jews. These unfortunates, however, had the courage to shout out, while they were being tortured. One, a religious Jew, yelled, 'The end of Hitler is coming!' Another shouted 'Shma Yizroel!' Then the Ukrainians shot them all, one unfortunate had to be shot 3 times before he died. The Ukrainians were foaming at the mouth as they clubbed them. Sobibór was full of those Ukrainians, the henchmen of the SS. For 2 or 3 months after this incident we were tormented and abused even more than usual.[88]

During July and August 1943, an underground group was formed amongst the Jewish prisoners, under the leadership of Leon Felhendler, who prior to deportation to Sobibór had been chairman of the *Judenrat* in the Zolkiew ghetto. Transports started to arrive from the *Reichskommissariat Ostland* during September 1943, principally from Lida, Minsk, and Vilna.

The mass execution of seventy-two Dutch Jews is the subject of many conflicting dates, and theories. But it is thought it took place shortly after the *Waldkommando* revolt, whilst some survivors claim it was earlier, in April 1943.

---

[88] Kalman Werwyk, *To Sobibor and Back*—online version.

There is a school of thought that the escape was planned by Polish Jews, who blamed the Dutch Jews. Frenzel spared the painter Max van Dam, who was painting a portrait of him. One other Dutchman was saved that day, 47 year old Raphael Viool, from Rotterdam. The seventy-two Dutch Jews were taken *to Lager III*, and executed. The leader of the so-called 'Dutch revolt' was thought to be Jozeph Jacobs, who was born on July 11, 1902, in Amsterdam. But he was not deported until May 18, 1942, from Westerbork, to Sobibór, so that rules him out of being involved in a 'revolt' in April. Of course if the true date was sometime in August 1943, then this makes the account plausible.

However, the memoirs of Philip Bialowitz, '*A Promise in Sobibór*,' states that after his arrival on April 28, 1943, he was informed that, 'yesterday, about seventy Dutch Jewish prisoners were murdered in connection with an escape plot, that was apparently revealed by an informant. They were ordered forward at Roll Call and marched to Camp 3, where they were shot.'[89] This may point as to the clearest indication that the 'Dutch Revolt' in fact took place in April 1943. Max van Dam, the Dutch painter, was spared as he was still painting a portrait of Karl Frenzel. Another Dutch painter Li van Staden[90], and an unknown Dutch painter, were both spared as well.

Ursula Safran-Stern recalled how the Dutch Jews were executed and she commented that the executions took place during mid-April 1943. She arrived in Sobibór on April 9, 1943. So again this points to the April 1943, timeline:

> Once, after I had spent about a week at Sobibór, all the Dutch Jews were told to step forward at the roll-call. The men ended up in front, while we women had to line up behind them. Shortly after, Frenzel, standing by the gate to *Lager I*, ordered that the women could go back to their places in the line up.

---

[89] Philip Bialowtiz, *A Promise At Sobibor*, The University of Wisconsin Press, Madison, Wisconsin, 2010, p.73.
[90] This probably was Serline van Straten.

Frenzel walked over to the seventy-two men who were lined up, looking for the painter Max van Dam. Betrayed in the Alps on his way to Switzerland, he had arrived on a French transport as a criminal prisoner at the end of March 1943, and carrying his painters supplies and brushes, had put himself forward as a painter.

Frenzel did not want van Dam to be killed in *Lager III*, along with the other Dutch Jews because he had not finished his portrait, so he called him out. One other Dutchman was spared that day, 47 year old Raphael Viool from Rotterdam. The SS and their Ukrainians took the seventy other Dutchmen to the execution area in *Lager III*.[91]

Eda Lichtman testified about the same event, with some differences:

> Wagner appeared at the square and ordered all the seventy-two Dutchmen to march out. They were taken to *Lager III*. After a short while we could hear salvos of shots aimed at our comrades. We had to remain at the roll call during the entire time. The execution lasted half an hour. In the meantime Frenzel arrived and ordered the Dutch women to sing Dutch songs. The salvos of the shooting mixed with the tunes of the forced songs.[92]

Dov Freiberg provides yet another version with Wagner beating the Dutch Jew known as *Der Kapitän*, the alleged ringleader of the escape attempt:

> When Wagner realized it was no use beating *Der Kapitän*, he made one last attempt to break him and said, 'If you don't give up the names of your accomplices, we will cut off the heads of all your people in your block—and yours will be cut off last.' *Der Kapitän* did not waiver. Wagner ordered Block 6, to step forward, and we watched all of the men from Block 6, with *Der Kapitän* march towards death, accompanied by a group of armed Germans. Afterwards, we found out that Wagner had stood by his word, all of those men were beheaded in *Lager III*.[93]

---

[91] J. Schelvis, *Sobibor*, Berg-Oxford, New York, 2007, p.142.
[92] Y. Arad, *Belzec, Sobibor, Treblinka*, Indiana University Press, Bloomington and Indianapolis 1987, p.303.
[93] Dov Freiberg, *To Survive Sobibor*, Gefen Publishing House, Jerusalem, 2007, p.276.

On May 8, 1943, the Nazis closed the Bełżec death camp, and some time in May 1943 the Nazis transported to Sobibór the remaining worker-Jews who had helped dismantle the structures and remove all traces of the mass murder committed there. The dates quoted by a number of survivors and historians claim the transport took place in June 1943, whilst some claim it was in July 1943. But the clearing of the camp site at Bełżec was completed in April 1943, and it makes more sense to assume that the last worker-Jews were immediately sent from Bełżec to Sobibór. Moshe Bahir, a Sobibór survivor, testified after the war:

> One day in the month of May 1943, we were ordered to remain in our huts. We were not taken to work, and this aroused dark forebodings in us. In the afternoon the *Bahnhofkommando* (station / transport reception commando) was summoned to its usual work at the train station. When the men got to the train, a dreadful vision appeared before them. This train had brought the last of the Jews from the Bełżec death camp, who had been engaged in burning the bodies of those killed in the gas chambers.[94]

The system of *Kapos* was a well-known feature of German Concentration Camps right from their inception at Dachau, near Munich, in 1933. Dachau, under the brutal control of Theodor Eicke, used *Kapos* to police their fellow inmates, carry out orders and beat and sometimes murder the unfortunates if needs be.

The *Kapos* in Sobibór were privileged; they slept apart from the other prisoners, enjoyed better food and living conditions. Moshe Sturm was appointed the first Chief *Kapo* (*Oberkapo*) by Franz Stangl in June 1942. He was known in the camp as the 'Governor.' Karl Frenzel ordered the tailors to sew him a special outfit, it consisted of trousers with red stripes on the sides, a jacket with shiny buttons and three stars on the breast, red braces and a round hat with a red stripe around the crown. [95]

---

[94] Miriam Novitch, *Sobibor*, Holocaust Library, New York, 1980, p.159.
[95] M. Bem, *Sobibor Extermination Camp 1942-1943*, Stichting Sobibor 2015, pp. 196-197.

Moshe Sturm was allowed two assistants, Benjamin Katz, also known as 'Bunio', and Herbert Siegel who had also arrived in Sobibór in June 1942. Other notable *Kapos* were Szymon Pozycki, Walter Poppert, who commanded the *Waldkommando*, Chaskiel Menche, who supervised the tailors, and Stanislaw Szmajzner who was Head of the Maintenance work-brigade.

During the first half of September 1943, six *Kapos*, headed by *Oberkapo* Moshe Sturm, hatched a plan to escape from Sobibór. One of the other *Kapos*, Herbert Naftaniel, better known as *'Berliner,'* because he hailed from Berlin, informed the camp authorities of the planned escape. The six *Kapos* were arrested and executed in front of all the other prisoners. As a reward, *'Berliner'* was appointed *Oberkapo*, to replace Moshe Sturm.

However, *Berliner* did not enjoy this role for long. Several weeks before the main October revolt he was attacked by, Katz and the Austrian *Kapo* Siegfried Spitz, and he was beaten so badly he could not walk. Karl Frenzel ordered the Jews to finish him off, as *Berliner* had gone over his head when betraying Sturm and the other *Kapos* escape plan to Gustav Wagner. Poison was mixed with barley and *Berliner* ate his last meal, his body was burned in *Lager III*.

Another incident of note took place on September 13, 1943, which Stanislaw Szmajzner wrote in his book, *'Hell in Sobibor— The Tragedy of a Teenage Jew'*:

> One day we heard an explosion. As all news spread very fast in the camp, we soon learned what had happened. A grenade had just exploded in Getzinger's hand, and had instantly killed him. A Ukrainian guard had also died with him. The ignoble officer had met his well-deserved end through his curiosity and conceit. He had been checking one of the Russian artifacts stocked in the 'Bunkers' he was responsible for. He considered himself so competent about it that he certainly did not believe the possibility of

having any kind of accident. Of his body, only pieces were found. They were soon gathered and sent back to Germany.[96]

Hubert Gomerski, who was with Anton Getzinger at the time, explained what happened:

> We wanted to zero the aim of a machine-gun. We took two or three hand grenades, pounded a stake into the ground and wanted to put the grenades on top to hit them and blow them up. Toni hit it and was torn to shreds.

On September 18-19, 1943, a transport from Lida, in the *Reichskommissariat Ostland,* was deported to Sobibór. A German engineer, Otto Weisbecker, who was a *Bauführer* in the *Organization Todt,* testified at the Sobibór Trial:

> As a building engineer I came to Lida and worked there on the railways. In the ghetto, which was subordinated to the *Gebietskommissar,* were 1,400 Jews. At the building site that I headed, 1,300 Jews and their families, who were accommodated in a camp were engaged. Approximately in the middle of 1943, the Security Police arrived in Lida. All the Jews were then subordinated to the Security Police.
>
> One day, these Jews from the ghetto—men, women and children were loaded onto freight cars and under the direction of *Haupttruppführer* Bache from the *Organization Todt,* they were transferred to Sobibór. The next day I received an order from the head of my department, the architect Hans W. to transfer our Jews to Lublin for a working mission.
>
> The Jews were loaded on the train that day, sixty people to a freight car. I was the commander of the transport, and I had at my disposal a police sergeant and nineteen Polish policeman. In spite of the security measures, between twenty and twenty-five Jews escaped on the way.
>
> A sentry in Sobibór told me that the transport would be liquidated in the morning. Next morning I came into the camp and I was brought to the commander, who was in the breakfast barrack. On the wall of this barrack was a big plan of the camp. I could see

---

[96] Stanislaw Szmajzner, *Hell in Sobibor,* (Unpublished English Version in authors collection) p. 243.

on it that the 1,400 Jews that Bache had brought the day before, could not possibly be accommodated in the existing barracks. In reference to my question to the camp commander, where can he accommodate the Jews I had brought, he told me that of the 1,400 Jews of yesterday's transport, nobody remained.[97]

In one of the last transports from Minsk, on September 18, 1943, were Jewish soldiers serving in the Red Army. They arrived in Sobibór on September 22, 1943, from the labor camp in Sheroka Street. Among the prisoners was Alexander Pechersky, better known as Sasha. Due to his military experience, he became the camp's underground commander, with Leon Felhendler as his deputy.

Alexander Pechersky recalled his deportation from the labor camp in Minsk to Sobibór:

> On 18 September, all the Jews were ordered to assemble in the courtyard. It was four o'clock in the morning, still dark. We stood in a line to get the 300 grams of bread, we received for the journey. The courtyard was full of people, but no noise could be heard. Scared children kept close to their mothers.
>
> Commander Wat announced to us, 'Soon you will be taken to the station. You are going to Germany, there you will work. Hitler has made it possible to grant life to each Jew who will work honestly. You are going with your families.'
>
> The women and children were taken to the station in trucks, the men by foot. We were pushed—seventy people in a freight car. On the fifth day of travelling, we arrived in the evening at an isolated station. A white sign bore the name Sobibor. We were kept in the closed freight car overnight.
>
> On 23 September, in the morning, a locomotive pushed the train into the camp, tired and hungry we left the cars. *Oberscharführer* Gomerski shouted, 'Cabinet-makers, and carpenters without families forward!' Eighty men, most of them war prisoners reported. We were rushed into a fenced area inside a barrack. A Jew from the camp who returned from some work approached us. During

---

[97] Y. Arad, *Belzec, Sobibor, Treblinka*, Indiana University Press, Bloomington and Indianapolis 1987, pp.135-136.

the conversation I noticed grey smoke rising in the north-west direction and a sharp smell of burning hovering in the air. I asked, What is burning there?' They are burning the bodies of your friends who arrived with you,' the Jew answered. I was shocked.[98]

Shortly after his arrival in the camp, on September 26, 1943, a noteworthy event happened and Alexander Pechersky wrote about it:

> An ordinary day. About twenty-five men received twenty-five lashes for various infractions. I was almost one of them. This is how it happened: forty of our men were busy chopping wood. Hungry, emaciated, exhausted, they raised the heavy axes with great effort and dropped them on the chunky stumps. Frenzel kept hurrying them on, *'Schnell, Schnell.'*
>
> Quietly he walked over to one of the Dutch Jews... Frenzel let him have one with his whip, Frenzel noticed that I had stopped chopping. He called out to me, *'Komm.'* He pushed aside the Dutch Jew and said to me in broken Russian, 'Russian soldier, you don't like the way I punish this fool. I give you exactly five minutes to split this stump. If you miss by as much as one second, you get twenty-five lashes.'
>
> Frenzel gave the command, 'Begin' .... with all my strength and with genuine hatred, I hit it time and again, until I smashed it into pieces. Frenzel handed me a pack of cigarettes. 'Four and a half minutes,' I heard him say. But I literally could not take the gift from the scoundrel's hand. 'Thanks I don't smoke,' I said and resumed working. Frenzel went away quietly and returned in about twenty minutes holding half a roll and a slice of margarine in his hand.... 'Russian soldier take it,' he said. 'Thank you, the rations we are getting satisfy me fully.' Naturally, the German could not let the irony of my reply pass un-noticed. I saw Frenzel clench the whip in his hand, but he restrained himself, turned abruptly and left the yard.[99]

Pechersky's closest friends in the camp were Shlomo Leitman, Boris Tsibulsky, and Alexander Shubayev from Baku (nicknamed

---

[98] Ibid. pp.136-137.
[99] Y. Arad, *Belzec, Sobibor, Treblinka*, Indiana University Press, Bloomington and Indianapolis 1987, pp.306-307.

Kalimali). With them he discussed the different options and ways for organizing the escape. Pechersky's personality and prominent position among the prisoners drew the attention of Leon Felhendler, who was seeking an organizer and leader for a potential mass escape.

Once Felhendler overcame his doubts about Pechersky, he asked him to join his underground committee, and Felhendler said to him:

> Our aim is for as many people as possible to escape. Perhaps you are wondering why we have not done so yet. But trust me, we have been thinking about it for a long time. We just do not know how to organize it. You are an army officer, so you should be able to do it. If you tell us what to do, we will do exactly as you say.
>
> But you must promise us that there will be no escape attempts by individuals or smaller groups from this moment on. Our motto is: one for all and all for one. Because if at roll-call it turns out that some people have escaped, then the entire camp will almost certainly be liquidated, and we will all end up in *Lager III*. We cannot take that risk.[100]

Leon Felhendler and Alexander Pechersky met in the women's barracks and to disguise the true purpose of their meetings, a 'sham' girlfriend for Pechersky was proposed. This 'girlfriend' was the German Jewess Liselotte Karoline Rosenstiel, born on March 17, 1923, in Neustadt, Germany. She was always known as Luka, by her family, before her time in the camp, and in the camp itself. She escaped during the revolt, and was last seen with a group of escapees, heading toward Chelm. Her fate is unknown, but she probably lost her life in the forests.[101]

Pechersky discussed with Shlomo Leitman, the possibility of digging an escape tunnel, which was agreed to be undertaken. The attempt was to build a tunnel from the carpentry workshop, which was the closest barrack to the fences, it had to run beneath the fences and the minefields. The tunnel had to originate at the

---

[100] J. Schelvis, *Sobibor*, Berg-Oxford, New York, 2007, p.151.
[101] Information supplied by Aline Pennewaard—December 12, 2022.

stove in the carpentry workshop and exit behind the minefield, a distance of approximately 35 meters.

The digging of the tunnel was conducted by Boris Tsibulski, who was by profession in his civilian life a miner from the Donbas. Work commenced at the beginning of October 1943. The main work was done at night, but some work also took place during the daytime. The digging crew included four people; while two were digging, the other two disposed of the earth under the floor of the workshop and rested.

About fifteen prisoners, some of them Polish Jews, were involved in the digging work, and the digging progressed smoothly, but on October 8, and October 9, heavy rains fell on the camp and water penetrated the tunnel and flooded it completely. When Tsibulski entered the tunnel on the night of October 9, he found it utterly wrecked. The tunnel escape plan had to be abandoned. A new plan had to be developed.

Alexander Pechersky then came up with a simple plan for a mass escape, which involved killing members of the SS-Garrison in a short but sustained burst, and escaping with the onset of darkness. The revolt was planned to take place on October 13, 1943, but the unexpected arrival of SS troops from the labor camp at Osowa, resulted in a 24 hour delay.

From Alexander Pechersky's own diary account, the lead up to the day of the revolt, makes fascinating reading:

> **October 12:** It was a terrible day, eighteen of our friends, mainly from Sheroka were sick. Several SS men, under the direction of Frenzel, entered our barracks and asked the patients to follow them. Among them was a Dutch prisoner with his wife, and the unfortunate man could hardly walk. The woman was running after the group screaming, 'Murderers, I know where you are taking my husband. I can't live without him! Assassins! Murderers!' She died with the group.
>
> Shlomo and I ordered a meeting for 9:00 p.m. at the carpenters workshop. Baruch (Felhendler), Shlomo, Janek, the tailors Joseph and Jacob, Moniek and others were present. We posted a sentry at the entrance. Moniek went out to fetch Pozyczki and, when

both returned I asked Pozyczki again if he had thought over the consequences of his decision; if the plan failed, he would be the first to die. He said, 'I know it, but we must get rid of the SS officers and this should take one hour. If we could do it in less time, so much the better. For that purpose we need efficient and determined men, since one moment's hesitation would be fatal, and I know some capable people, who can do the job.'

At 3 p.m. Pozyczki was to lead three of his men to *Lager II*, under any pretext, that he would find himself. Their task would consist of liquidating the four officers present. Baruch (Felhendler) would lead the SS men to a place where the prisoners would be waiting and would prevent anyone from leaving *Lager II*, once the action had begun.

At exactly 4 o'clock, another team would cut the telephone wires from *Lager II*, to the guards quarters. The same team would hide those wires in such a way to make it impossible to reconnect the telephone on the same day. At the same time, we were to start killing SS officers; they would be invited one by one, into the workshops where two of our men would execute them. At 4:30 p.m. everything would be finished.

At the same time, Pozyczki and Geniek would assemble the prisoners for the usual evening roll-call. In front would be the Soviet prisoners who were to take over the arsenal and the rest of us would cover them. Once the arsenal was open, armed men would head the group and kill the guards at the gate. If they resisted we would fight with the arms taken from the officers.[102]

Eda Lichtman described the atmosphere in her barracks on the eve of the revolt:

When it became known to our small group that the next day, October 14, the uprising would finally happen, it caused excitement and nervousness among us. Esther Grinbaum, a very sentimental and intelligent young woman, wiped away her tears and said, 'It's not yet the time for an uprising. Tomorrow none of us will be alive. Everything will remain as it was—the barracks, the sun will

---

[102] Miriam Novitch, *Sobibor*, Holocaust Library, New York, 1980, pp. 94-95.

rise and set, the flowers will bloom and wilt, but we will be no more.'

Her closest friend Helka Lubartowska, a beautiful dark-eyed brunette, tried to encourage her, 'There is no other way. Nobody knows what the results will be, but one thing is for sure, we will not be led to the slaughter.'

The little Ruzka interrupted the conversation, 'What silly talk. What have we to lose—one day more of a life of suffering? Whatever will be, let it be. Esther Terner approached the group and said enthusiastically, 'Girls at least something is going to happen. I have a feeling that everything will go smoothly and will succeed. 'Sala a blond with blue eyes, who was always quiet, interfered, 'Stop chattering like old women. We have to prepare ourselves, and that's that,' It was wise advice. The talk stopped, but the whispers continued during the night. We made preparations for the escape. We could not fall asleep, and the night was a nightmare. Sala was singing quietly, sentimental songs, others were crying silently.[103]

Dov Freiberg recalled the morning of the revolt:

The morning of October 14: rising early, as usual. The weather cloudy, cold and gloomy, like before. The dispensing of ersatz coffee went on, as usual, but for some reason everything seemed to take longer and was more emphasised. I already knew, the rebellion would begin at 4 p.m.—half an hour before everyone returned from work.

At *Lager II*, in the possession-sorting barracks, our group was about twenty men. Our commander was *Scharführer [actually Oberscharführer*–C. Webb] Kurt Rudolf Beckmann,[104] a short thin German with a mousy face. He wore a large pistol on his belt and shouted incessantly, *'Schneller, Schneller'* (Faster, Faster). Time passed slowly. I counted every minute.[105]

---

[103] Y. Arad, *Belzec, Sobibor, Treblinka*, Indiana University Press, Bloomington and Indianapolis 1987, p. 321.
[104] His correct name was Rudolf Heinrich Beckmann.
[105] Dov Freiberg, *To Survive Sobibor*, Gefen Publishing House, Jerusalem, 2007, pp.291-292.

On October 14, 1943, with Reichleitner, Wagner, and Gomerski on leave, the SS-Garrison was considerably weakened, and now the die was cast. At about 4 p.m. deputy commandant Johann Niemann visited the tailors workshop to try on a new uniform. There he was killed by Shubayev and Yehuda Lerner.

Abraham Margulies, who was deported to Sobibór at the end of May 1942, from Zamość recalled:

> On October 14, I was sent along with Biskubicz, to do some work at the gate. I saw Niemann on his horse, leaving for the tailor's workshop. There he was to be killed with an axe.

Alexander 'Sasha' Pechersky recalled who were responsible for carrying out the killings:

> Each of us had a task: Shubayev, aged twenty-five, a Railway Engineer from Rostov, a good and simple buddy, would go to the tailor's workshop with Moniek. Tsibulsky, a thirty-five year old driver, a former truck driver from Donbas and accompanied by Michael and Bunio.[106]

Pechersky wrote about the killing of Johann Niemann in the tailor's shop:

> The operation in *Lager I*, started as planned at four o'clock. Exactly at that time the Deputy Commander of the camp, Niemann rode his mare into *Lager I*, and reined up in front of the bakery. He dismounted, left the horse to one of the prisoners, and entered the tailor's shop.
>
> There Josef, the head of the tailor's shop and a member of the underground committee, brought him his new uniform and began to take the fitting. At that moment, Shubayev approached him from behind and hit Niemann on the head with an axe. Niemann died on the spot. His body was dragged into the back room and stuffed under a bunk, and the bloodstains on the floor were wiped away and covered. The presence of Niemann's horse close to the tailor's shop for longer than the time needed for a uniform

---

[106] Miriam Novitch, *Sobibor*, Holocaust Library, New York, 1980, pp. 95.

measurement could arouse suspicion, so one of the underground members took it to the stables.[107]

Moshe Hochmann also recalled the death of Johann Niemann:

> I was working in the tailor's barracks. The Liberation Committee gave us the task of executing Niemann, while he was going to the workshop to try on new clothes. The plan worked and, when Niemann was putting on a suit, he was killed with an axe by a Russian prisoner. We wrapped his body in a blanket and hid it.[108]

At 4.15 p.m. *Oberscharführer* Siegfried Graetschus, the German officer in charge of the Ukrainian guards arrived at the shoemakers shop to pick up some new boots. During the fitting Arkady Wajspapier and Yehuda Lerner slipped out from the backroom and split the skull of the Nazi with an axe.

Arkady Wajspapier takes up the account of Graetschus's death:

> Lerner and I had hidden behind a curtain. Then Graetschus, Chief of the Guards, entered the workplace. He stood by the door and started putting on a coat, that had been made for him at the tailor's barracks.
>
> I came out from behind the curtain and walked past the officer, pretending I was leaving, but turned around and hit him on the head with the sharp edge of the axe. Graetschus cried out, but did not immediately fall down, tumbling forward instead, because I had evidently not him hard enough. Then Lerner came out of hiding and hit him on the head a second time with his axe. Graetschus at last fell down and gave up the ghost. I pulled his Walther pistol and extra ammunition from the holster and also took his personal papers from his inside pocket. I kept the pistol and covered him with a pile of clothing.[109]

The shoemakers barely had time to hide the body when the Ukrainian Ivan Klatt, entered the workshop calling his boss to the telephone. He too was attacked and killed. Chaskiel Menche, the

---

[107] Y. Arad, *Belzec, Sobibor, Treblinka*, Indiana University Press, Bloomington and Indianapolis 1987, p. 326.
[108] Miriam Novitch, *Sobibor*, Holocaust Library, New York, 1980, p. 123.
[109] J. Schelvis, *Sobibor*, Berg-Oxford, New York, 2007, p.163.

hat-makers foreman took his scissors to the lifeless body of Siegfried Graetschus, and he then described the killing of Ivan Klatt:

> Shortly after the Ukrainian came in. He bumped into the pile of clothing that was hiding Graetschus' body. Bending over he asked what it was. I approached him from behind and hit him on the head with my axe. Then Lerner hit him again with his axe. The guard fell to the floor. After we had confirmed that he was dead, we also took his pistol from the holster. Lerner kept it. Then Lerner and I left the barracks. I went over to Pechersky and told him what had happened.[110]

Selma Engel recalled Chaim Engel's killing *SS-Oberscharführer* Beckmann in the Forester's House:

> So I walked to Chaim and at four o'clock I arrive there. I remember I walked in there and one of the *Kapos*-Wieszubski[111] was his name, he killed already a few Germans and he was very nervous, and I said, 'Take a pill for it, something for your nerves to calm down,' and he took it. I remember it was bitter and he spat it out saying, 'I don't need it.' So I met Chaim—he was not involved in the uprising, but somehow he say to me, 'Come there, and from there we will go in the area for roll-call.' So he wanted to be sure that we are together when there is a roll-call, and there was a boy standing there and he was involved in the uprising and he had to kill one German. Together with the *Kapo* Wieszubski and he said—I was standing together with him and Chaim—he said, 'I am afraid to go.' Chaim said, 'You have to go.' And he said, 'I am afraid.' Chaim said, 'There is no way back.' What we knew already there was one young boy who had the chance to walk around the camp and we knew already there were ten dead. We know it's our death when we get caught—'that's the end.' The electricity was already cut off and the telephone was already cut off, so we knew there were no connections anymore. So Chaim had no choice, he run inside and took a knife, put it in his boots and he walked to this office where *SS-Oberscharführer* Beckmann was.
>
> And he had no choice. I remember that he was gone. I was inside to take the knife or something like that and I didn't see him going away to the barrack, and I went looking for him. I got so panicky,

---

[110] J. Schelvis, *Sobibor*, Berg-Oxford, New York, 2007, p.163.
[111] His real name was Hersz Pozycki, who perished in the revolt.

when I know already there was an uprising and there was something going on there, and I couldn't find Chaim. And then one of the boys said that, 'Chaim is in that barrack' and I went looking where Chaim was and I hear screaming, like someone killing a pig. This screaming was of course the *SS* man and they were killing him with knives. We couldn't use guns or anything because no one was allowed to hear—hear that we were killing Germans, because they were all over, the Ukrainians were standing there, and the Poles were all around.[112]

Thomas Steffl was also killed by Chaim Engel and Hersz Pozycki, in the Forester's House. Shortly after, *SS* men Fritz Konrad and Josef Vallaster met the same fate, at the Shoemakers workshop. Josef Wolf was killed in one of the sorting barracks. In the carpenters' workshop Friedrich Gaulstich lost his life at the hands of Szlomo Leitman. The background to the murder of Gaulstich was that returned with the prisoners from *Lager IV*, where they were chopping wood. He was headed for the carpenters workshop, followed by *SS*-man Gaulstich. Leitman, who was in the vicinity asked Gaulstich to enter the barrack. *Oberkapo* Spitz wanted to enter the carpenters workshop, in order to assist Gaulstich, but *Kapo* Pozycki took him by the arm, and told him, if he wanted to remain alive, not to go inside. Spitz, dumbfounded, heeded the warning, and meanwhile Leitman axed Gaulstich to death.[113]

Philip Bialowitz recalled the murder of Josef Wolf:

> Finally, just after 4 p.m., from my vantage point, I see *SS-Unterscharführer* Josef Wolf being approached by a teenage boy who like me, is one of the on-call messengers. According to plan the boy appears to tell Wolf that a very expensive coat has been found for him and that he is welcome to try it on for fit.
>
> Wolf nods in approval and walks away in the direction of the storeroom. From what Symcha has told me, I know this is one of the locations where ambush awaits. I am incredibly anxious to know if the conspirators in the storeroom have succeeded. After

---

[112] Selma Engel Interview with USHMM on July 16, 1990.
[113] Y. Arad, *Belzec, Sobibor, Treblinka*, Indiana University Press, Bloomington and Indianapolis 1987, pp. 327-328.

a few minutes I cannot stand to wait any longer. I need to know Wolf's fate. Have we really killed him. I go to the storeroom to see if I can find out what has happened. As I walk past, I glance inside as casually as possible. Wolf is on the ground, dead and covered in blood. Two of the Soviet POW's are dragging him behind the piles of clothes to hide him.[114]

Semion Rosenfeld, a Jewish Red Army Prisoner of War who arrived in Sobibór from Minsk on September 22, 1943, and who was a member of the underground, recalled:

> On the day of the uprising, Pechersky called me and gave me an assignment. I had to kill Frenzel when he came to the carpentry workshop at 4:00 or 4:30 to receive new cupboards. I prepared myself thoroughly for the task. I sharpened the axe and selected the proper place to carry out the mortal blow. But the scoundrel did not come. Until today I am sorry for that.[115]

In the afternoon, Stanislaw Szmajzner managed to steal some rifles from the Ukrainian barracks, which he recounted in his memoirs:

> Only thirty minutes were missing before the whistle to end the day's work was blown and the moment when I had to play my role had finally come. I started it right away. To perform my task and mislead the attention of the guards I went to my shop and picked up some tools and a thick tin pipe, one of those used in the chimneys of the stoves which heated the lodgings of the Ukrainian guards, and which I was responsible for maintaining. Next I went to the Ukrainians shack, under the pretext that I had to fix something there.
>
> I climbed onto the roof and started to do something with the chimney pretending I was fixing it. I stayed there for a few minutes, so as to make it very clear that there were no second intentions on my part. Soon afterwards I climbed down, this time

---

[114] Philip Bialowitz, *A Promise at Sobibor*, The University of Wisconsin Press, 2008, p.114.

[115] Y. Arad, *Belzec, Sobibor, Treblinka*, Indiana University Press, Bloomington and Indianapolis 1987, p.328.

to fix the stove, since I needed a reason to be inside the place should any guard come in and ask me what I was doing.

I soon faced two Jewish boys who worked there and made sure there was no one else inside. Luck still smiled on me. These two boys were responsible for cleaning the quarters and they also ran some other errands for the Ukrainians. They were even younger than my nephew.

Inside the shed, which was rather ample, there was a partition which was destined for the higher ranking guards in the abominable corporation. I started to observe the place, while the two youths stared at me, and they were very surprised when I headed for the place where the weapons were kept.

I threw a greedy glance at the machine guns right there, within reach of my hands. These weapons were only used by the sergeants and the higher ranking elements. I finally controlled my impulses, because I and possibly others, did not know how to use them and they would not fit inside the metal pipe I carried. Besides everything else, I did not know anything about that kind of armament.

I then turned my eyes to the rifles and soon noticed that they were accompanied by their own cartridge belts and a lot of ammunition. We had agreed before that I would only go out with the weapons when the work in the shops had finished and all were heading back to quarters.

I waited for some more minutes and then I heard the characteristic German song that the Jews were forced to sing, when they came back from their daily tasks. That was the moment for me to act. The initial plan had determined that three rifles should be taken away and placed inside the long thick pipe, I had taken with me to hide them. Thus I would be able to take them back to Camp I, without raising any suspicion. Something unexpected happened though. No rifle would fit inside the pipe, since the head of the bolt did not let it go inside and I did not know how to remove it.

For this reason, as soon as I heard the song, I wrapped the rifles in a blanket and asked the astonished boys to hand the bundle to me through the window, since I intended to go out and get it from the outside. However, they were terribly frightened and they refused to do what I had told them to. The moment was not one for arguments and I had no other choice but threaten to kill them by unsheathing my knife.

With the gleam of the blade before their very eyes, the poor creatures, who did not understand anything, decided to obey me. I went out of the shed with my empty pipe in my hand and the pockets full of cartridges. I went quickly round the house and stopped before the window where I got my bundle with the rifles.

I then walked towards my destination hardly able to carry all my awkward load, since the pipe was still in my hand. Luck was still on my side I had crossed the officers yard and I was already heading for the kitchen in Camp I, yet I had not yet met a single guard.

When I got there, there was a group waiting for me, made up of my three relatives, and the young Russian Jews who were going to use the weapons. At the same time, the large mass of workers were returning from work singing and getting nearer and nearer to the kitchen. My mission had been thoroughly successful, and we were in possession of the precious rifles and plenty of ammunition.[116]

One killing was not planned. *SS-Unterscharführer* Walter Ryba had wandered into the SS Garage, where he was stabbed to death by the locksmith Engel. This killing disturbed Perchesky greatly, as the body of Ryba could easily be discovered by the SS who were milling about in the post office building right opposite the garage. This prompted Pechersky to give the signal for the roll-call whistle to be blown. This was 4.45pm, some fifteen minutes earlier than usual. *Kapo* Pozyczki blew his whistle.

Yehuda, the barber, climbed the Forester's Tower and blew the bugle—the signal for the whole camp to stop work and gather for the daily roll call. Felhendler lined up the prisoners in *Lager II*, and slowly they began the march to *Lager I*. Dov Freiberg described the march:

> When we marched to *Lager I*, we were singing a German song in order not to provoke any suspicion. We arrived there after all the

---

[116] Stanislaw Szmajzner, *Hell in Sobibor*, (Unpublished English Version in authors collection) pp. 275-278.

other groups had already gathered. There was great excitement. Some of the Jews were armed with rifles and pistols. A Jewish boy climbed the Forester Tower and trumpeted for roll-call.[117]

A short time before the bugle was blown, a lorry with provisions and liquor driven by Erich Bauer returned to the camp from Chelm and drove in the direction of the Forester's House. Jakub Biskubicz and David (Surname unknown) were repairing the gate of *Lager I*. Bauer ordered them to help with the unloading of the lorry. Jakub Biskubicz testified:

> As we were unloading the first box from the truck, we saw inside the Foresters House a German whom we stabbed in the back. As we were taking the second box, a Ukrainian came running and called to Bauer, 'A German is dead.' Bauer did not immediately understand what he meant. But David, who had heard it, started to run in the direction of *Lager I*. Bauer shot at him twice and ran after him. I remained alone. Then I heard a cry, 'Hurrah' from *Lager I* and shooting.[118]

Thomas 'Toivi' Blatt recalled how Alexander Pechersky jumped up on a table and made a short speech in Russian. He told the prisoners that most of the Germans had been killed, and that there was no turning back. He ended with a call, 'Forward, Comrades! For Stalin! Death to the Fascists!'

Alexander Sasha Pechersky described the scene in *Lager I*:

> People came streaming from all sides. We had previously selected seventy men, nearly all of them Soviet Prisoners of War, whose task it was to attack the armoury. That was why they were in the forefront of the column. But all the others, who had only suspected that something was being arranged, but didn't know when or how, now found out at the last minute.
>
> They began to push and jostle forward, fearing that they might be left behind. In this disorderly fashion we reached the gate of Camp I. A squad commander, a German from Near-Volga, approached us, 'Hey, you son of bitches,' he shouted, 'didn't you

---

[117] Y. Arad, *Belzec, Sobibor, Treblinka*, Indiana University Press, Bloomington and Indianapolis 1987, p. 330-331.
[118] Ibid pp.330-331.

hear the whistle? So why are you pushing like a bunch of cattle? Get in line, three in a row!' As though in respond to a command several hatchets appeared from under coats and came down on his head.

At that moment, the column from Camp II, was advancing towards us. Several women shaken by the unexpected scene, began to scream. One prisoner was on the verge of fainting. Another began to run blindly, without any direction. It was clear that under these circumstances it would be impossible to line up the people in an orderly column.

'Comrades, forward,' I called out loud. 'Forward!' someone on my right picked up the slogans. 'For our Fatherland—forward.' The slogans reverberated like thunder in the death camp, and united Jews from Russia, Poland, Holland, France, Czechoslovakia and Germany. Six hundred pain-wracked, tormented people, surged forward with a wild 'Hurrah' to life and freedom.[119]

Thomas 'Toivi' Blatt described the same scene, including the murder of *Volksdeutscher* Schreiber at the *Lager I* exit:

The second, larger group, armed with an assortment of weapons, pushed its way forward towards the exit of *Lager I*, to reach the main gate. At that moment, a Guard Commander, the *Volksdeutscher* Schreiber, was riding his bicycle through the same exit. Not understanding what had happened, he yelled, 'Why are you pushing like cattle? Get in line!' When he understood it was too late. He was immediately surrounded, thrown from his bike, and knifed. His pistol was confiscated. Not far away I saw another guard in visible shock, continuously turning himself around, as if set in motion, his outstretched hand still holding his rifle.[120]

Eda Lichtman wrote:

Suddenly we heard shots. In the beginning only a few shots, and then it turned into heavy shooting, including machine-gun fire. We heard shouting, and I could see a group of prisoners running with axes, knives, scissors, cutting the fences and crossing them.

---

[119] Y. Arad, *Belzec, Sobibor, Treblinka*, Indiana University Press, Bloomington and Indianapolis 1987, pp. 329-330.

[120] T. Blatt, *From the Ashes of Sobibor*, Northwestern University Press Illinois, 1997, pp. 151-152.

> Mines started to explode. Riot and confusion prevailed, everything was thundering around.
>
> The doors of the workshop were opened, and everyone rushed through. We ran out of the workshop. All around were the bodies of the killed and wounded. Near the armoury were some of our boys with weapons. Some of them were exchanging fire with the Ukrainians; others were running towards the gate or through the fences. My coat was caught on the fence. I took off the coat, freed myself and ran further behind the fences into the minefield. A mine exploded nearby, and I could see a body being lifted into the air, and then falling down. I did not recognize who it was. Many were shot on the fences. Behind the mines was a ditch, luckily without water. With the help of two other women, I crossed the ditch and reached the forest.[121]

Alexander Pechersky described his breakout from Sobibór:

> The guards on the watchtower opened intensive machine-gun fire on the escaping prisoners. The guards who were at and between the barbed-wire fences joined them. Yanek the carpenter aimed and shot at the guards on the watchtower. The machine gun fell silent. The Locksmith Henrick used the captured sub-machine gun to silence the gunner from the second watchtower. But this machine gun continued to fire incessantly.
>
> The remaining SS men tried with automatic fire to cut off the way of the crowd of prisoners. The main body of the prisoners turned towards the fences of Camp I. Some ran directly over to the minefields. According to the plan, stones and planks had to be thrown on the mines to explode them, but in the confusion nobody did it. Many found their death there, but paved the way to freedom for the prisoners who followed them.
>
> A special group started to cut the fence close to the house where the Commander of the camp lived. When I passed by this house, I saw Frenzel crouching behind another house and shooting with a sub-machine gun. I shot at him twice with my pistol, but missed him. I did not stop. A large group of prisoners under the command of Leitman tried to cross the barbed-wire fences close to

---

[121] Ibid. pp. 151-152.

the main gate. The guards on the watchtower aimed his fire on Leitman's group. I was one of the last to leave the camp.[122]

Werner Dubois was in the armoury and, after the war, testified about the attack:

> On the afternoon of the day of the uprising, I was in the armoury with some of the Ukrainian guardsmen. The door was open. I saw a group of Jewish prisoners with axes approaching the armoury. I thought this was an ordinary work group. This group of five or six men passed by the armoury. They went around the armoury, crashed into the room and hit me with axes. My skull was fractured. Other axe blows injured my hands. Despite my wounds, I succeeded in extracting myself and escaping. After running about ten meters, I was shot in the chest and lost consciousness.[123]

Thomas 'Toivi' Blatt takes up the story:

> I could hear the bullets whistle. A friend fell in front of me, then others. The remaining Germans—Bauer, Frenzel, Rewald, Wendland, Floss, Richter and Wolf, and some Ukrainian guards with machine-guns, who had initially been in shock—now blocked the main gate. People were killed, and the front-line Jews, mostly unarmed, fell back for a few minutes. I stopped, my long knife of no use, and backed off about fifty feet, then headed to the right of the Germans' quarters, as a new wave of determined fighters pushed forward again toward the main gate in a suicidal thrust.
>
> A small group including Sasha, Szlomo, Sender and another man with an axe, ended up with me, between the fences in the peripheral guard's corridor. In the confusion we ran into the entrance of this corridor, avoiding two barbed-wire fences and the water ditch, which were now behind us. Ahead of us, only one more barbed-wire fence and about fifty feet of minefield.
>
> We stopped. Someone was trying to cut an opening in the fence with a shovel. Sasha armed with a pistol, stood by, waiting, as were Sender and myself, both with knives in hand. Only Szlomo Szmajzner, calmly shooting his rifle, was able to silence the guard

---

[122] Y. Arad, *Belzec, Sobibor, Treblinka*, Indiana University Press, Bloomington and Indianapolis 1987, p. 332.
[123] T. Blatt, *Sobibor—The Forgotten Revolt*, H.E.P, Issaquah, 1998, p.80.

in the tower. I still remember marvelling at his composure. Within minutes more Jews arrived.

Not waiting in line to go through the opening under the hail of fire, they climbed the fence. Though we had planned to touch the mines off with bricks and wood, we did not do it. We couldn't wait; we preferred sudden death to a moment more in that hell. While I was only halfway through the fence it crumbled and fell on top of me with the combined weight of so many. This possibly saved my life for, lying under the wires, trampled by the stampeding crowd, I saw mines exploding every second. I realized that had I been able to get through earlier, I would have been killed with them.

Corpses were everywhere. The noise of rifles, exploding mines, grenades and the chatter of machine-guns assaulted my ears. The Nazis shot from a distance while in our hands were only primitive knives and hatchets. Heavy casualties were inflicted by the Ukrainian guards on the towers. As I found out later, although some of them deserted, most were faithful to the Nazis.

The waves of escapees had passed over me. I was alone, lying among bodies on the perimeter. I tried to extricate myself but the trampling had embedded the barbed-wire in the thickness of my coat and it held me back. I had to think fast—was this the end? I didn't want to die. An idea suddenly flashed through me—and now it was relatively easy. I simply slid out from under my coat and left it tangled there.

I ran through the mine craters, jumped over a single wire marking the end of the mine fields and was outside the camp. Now to make it to the woods ahead of me. It was so close. I was behind the last of the fugitives. I fell several times, each time thinking I was hit. And each time I got up and ran further... 100 yards.... 50 yards..... 20 more yards... and the forest at last. Behind me—blood and ashes. In the greyness of the approaching evening, the machine guns shot their last victims from the towers.[124]

SS-Unterscharführer Franz Wolf, who arrived in Sobibór in March 1943, along with his brother Josef, Fritz Konrad, and Willi Wendland, recalled:

---

[124] Ibid, pp. 81-82.

> On the day of the revolt I spent the day in the forest with Willi Wendland overseeing a labor commando. Between 4:30 and 5 p.m. Wendland and I arrived back at the camp with the Jewish labor commando. Wendland took the Jews to *Lager I* and the horse and cart to *Lager II*, where the stables and the shed were. I still had to collect the Jewish women workers from the vegetable plots. So Wendland and I went our separate ways, and I went to the garden between *Lager I* and *Lager II*.
>
> When I was on my way back with the Jewish women, I suddenly heard shooting. I was between the *Forsthaus* and *Lager I* when I first heard the shots, I shouted to the Jews, 'Go over to your barracks and get inside.' I walked back to the writing room in the *Forsthaus*. There Beckmann and another permanent staff member had been shot.[125]
>
> I walked back out to make my way through the courtyard in *Lager II*, to the sorting barracks, to get to my brother. I saw no one on the way. The door that led from the courtyard to the sorting barracks was locked. After the shooting had died down, I went over to the posts in the *Vorlager*. There were several other bodies there and Werner Dubois, who was seriously wounded. I tried to find my brother but did not succeed. The next morning I was told that he had been found dead in the sorting barrack.[126]

Dov Freiberg also recounted how he escaped from the camp:

> I stood for a moment and looked around. I saw a lot of people near the gate, many of them falling. Frenzel had gathered his wits, taken position at a machine gun and fired non-stop into the masses that crowded the gate. When I saw a lot of people running for the barbed wire fences, I joined them.
>
> When I neared the fences I saw people climbing the barbed wire like a ladder. Some hung there and didn't move—they had been hit by bullets shot from the guard tower. By the time I got to the fenced area, the inner fence had already collapsed. I jumped toward the other side of the trench and climbed up quickly. The left guard tower, close to the gate, had been neutralized by our men. On the right side, a machine-gun still fired, and the wounded

---

[125] Beckmann and Steffl had been stabbed to death, not shot.
[126] J. Schelvis, *Sobibor*, Berg-Oxford, New York, 2007, p. 167.

were left hanging on the barbed wire. I passed through the third fence quickly, without noticing that my arm was cut by the barbed wire.[127]

Stanislaw Szmajzner recalled his breakout from the camp in his memoirs:

> At that time I had not crossed the fences yet and I had lost contact with Nojech, Moisze and Jankus. I tried to stop for a while to avoid being forced into the forward lines. I intended to stay on the back lines since no reaction was coming from the Boches. Only the nearest towers fired some shots against the fleeing multitude. It was then that I armed my rifle at one of the towers and fired four shots nearly at random. I later learned that one of these stray bullets had killed one of the guards.[128]

Jakub Biskubicz, who remained inside *Lager II*, later testified:

> All the prisoners escaped. I remained alone. I jumped over a 2 meter fence and reached the warehouse. It became dark, because in October, night fell early; therefore the bullet fired in my direction didn't hit me. Until midnight I lay on the earth. I could hear shouts and screams from all directions. At midnight, I heard shooting close to me and the voices of Germans saying, 'Nobody is here.' They left.
>
> I reached *Lager IV*. I saw the open door of a watchtower. Nobody was around. I climbed the ladder of the tower and jumped outside over the fences and mines. I fell on the railway and escaped to the forest.[129]

Kurt Thomas described at the Sobibór trial in Hagen on July 4, 1965, how he survived by hiding on a farm, following his escape from Sobibór:

> An understanding, freedom-loving, Polish farmer on whose farm I arrived, after a four day hike through the countryside, had mercy

---

[127] Dov Freiberg, *To Survive Sobibor*, Gefen Publishing House, Jerusalem, 2007, pp 295-296.
[128] Stanislaw Szmajzner, *Hell in Sobibor*, (Unpublished English Version in authors collection), p. 282.
[129] Y. Arad, *Belzec, Sobibor, Treblinka*, Indiana University Press, Bloomington and Indianapolis 1987, p. 335.

on me; he let me hide in the attic of his pig-sty, after I explained to him where I escaped, from November 1943 until the end of July 1944, when the Russian armies took the village, and I later joined the Czechoslovakian legion, with which I moved westward into my native country and town.

The existence above the pig-sty was another humiliating experience filled with terror. German soldiers often went through the yard of the farm, sometimes units were billeted on the farm of the hamlet and I was for days without food and in fear of being discovered by accident. The farmer could not bring me anything during these times.

In the attic in which I laid was even at the point of the gable so low, that here I could only kneel. I did not walk for nine months, never leaving my hideout. I ate only whenever it was possible for the farmer to bring me some food from his house. I had a bucket up there which I used as a toilet and which I handed my farmer once a week, if circumstances were favourable for being emptied.

I changed my laundry six times during those nine months, shaved that many times with a straight razor, with the help of a broken piece of mirror and a little bit of water from a small bottle and a piece of soap, all thrown up there by my farmer. I pushed the straw of the thatch roof apart by which I gained some light to shave. I was awfully cold in the winter, being covered only with one blanket, while in the summer the heat and the flies made it most uncomfortable.[130]

An at-a-glance table has been produced for readers to see who was killed, where and by whom. There is some conflict about who was killed where, and by whom, and this needs to be borne in mind, that in some cases the details are not known:

---

[130] YVA 033.717.

SS Officers and *Trawnikimänner* Killed in the Revolt on October 14, 1943

SS Officer	Killed Where	By Whom
Rudolf Beckmann	Forester's House	Chaim Engel and Hersz Pozycki
Max Bree	Sorting Barracks	Not Known
Friedrich Gaulstich	Carpenters Workshop	Szlomo Leitman
Siegfried Graetschus	Shoemakers Workshop	Arkady Wajspapier and Yehuda Lerner
Fritz Konrad	Shoemakers Workshop	Not Known
Johann Niemann	Tailors Workshop	Alexander Shubayev and Yehuda Lerner
Anton Nowak	Not Known	Not Known
Walter Ryba	SS Garage	Engel the locksmith
Thomas Steffl	Forester's House	Chaim Engel and Hersz Pozycki
Erwin Stengelin	Not Known	Not Known
Josef Vallaster	Shoemakers Workshop	Not Known
Josef Wolf	Sorting Barrack	Boris Cybulski
Trawnikimänner	Killed Where	By Whom
Ivan Klatt	Shoemakers Workshop	Chaskiel Menche, Arkady Wajspapier and Yehuda Lerner
Klaus Schreiber	By the Main Gate	By the escaping mob

On the evening of the revolt Christian Wirth and Gottlieb Hering arrived at Sobibór and those prisoners in *Lager I*, that had not tried to escape, were executed. The next morning saw the arrival of Jakob Sporrenberg, the *SSPF* Lublin, as well as Hermann Höfle and Georg Michalsen, senior members of the *Aktion Reinhardt Kommando*.

On October 15, 1943, the *SSPF* Lublin advised *SS-Brigadeführer* Wilhelm Gunther, his neighbouring *SSPF* in Luzk, that some 700 Jews had broken out of the Sobibór camp and would be escaping in Gunther's direction, and that counter measures should be taken. At that time Sobibór held about 700 Jews, and not all of them escaped, but approximately 300 managed to break out to the forest and taste freedom.

Erich Wulbrandt, a captain of the Security Police—Mounted SS and Police Regiment III, based in Chelm, was sent to Sobibór following the prisoner revolt on October 14, 1943. He testified about his role in the aftermath:

> When I returned to my quarters at Chelm, after several days of fighting the partisans in the Lublin district—I think in the autumn of 1943—I found the order to go to Sobibór already waiting for me. It was clear from the order that a revolt led by Jewish *Arbeitshäftlinge* had broken out at the Jewish camp at Sobibór. Apparently Jewish prisoners had taken over the armoury.
>
> I can no longer remember now whether the order was given verbally or in writing. It was also known that a number of prisoners had escaped. I cannot remember either whether the order contained any details of guards being killed. But it seemed obvious there would be danger to the guards, so *Schutzpolizei* Major Eggert, *Kommandeur der Reiterabteilung III*, took charge himself. It was suspected that the escaped Jews would plan an attack on the camp to liberate any prisoners still inside. To prevent this from happening and to protect the guards at the camp my squadron as well as that of Major Eggert were deployed, with Eggert in overall charge.
>
> As far as I can recall the squadron went to Sobibór by train. A train had been made available especially. We arrived at Sobibór close to daybreak. At Sobibór station, right by the camp entrance, two men of the *Waffen-SS* told us about the incident that had occurred earlier that day. Neither of them were officers. They claimed they had not been at the camp at the time of the incident, but as they were driving back in their truck, they had come across armed Jewish prisoners in the forest. They had managed to turn the truck around and flee to safety. I assume that both of these *SS*

men would have informed their superior authorities in Lublin about the revolt at the camp.

According to them, the German camp staff had been lured inside different workshops in the afternoon and murdered by Jewish prisoners using a variety of tools. It must have been a well-prepared revolt, because at the same time a large number of other prisoners had apparently stormed the armoury, taken the weapons and broken out of the camp.

By the time we arrived, the bodies had already been laid out in one of the offices. I saw them myself. I think there were about thirteen bodies in this room. They were quite badly mutilated, some with their skulls split open and deep knife wounds to their faces and the rest of their bodies.

How many prisoners got away I do not know. My estimate, considering the situation at the time, would be about fifty percent. I can no longer remember how many prisoners were still in the camp. When we arrived, they were inside their barracks. The watchtowers were manned by foreign *Hilfswilligen*. As the revolt had taken place several hours before we arrived at Sobibór, and the remaining guards had already restored order at the camp, there was not much for us to do.

We did not consider it necessary to protect the camp against attacks from the outside and, as the Jewish prisoners in their barracks were also quiet, the squadron stationed itself in the Vorlager buildings. That is to say, as they had just returned from a very tiring assignment fighting *the* partisans, they went to have a rest. I presume that a few men were assigned to guard us. The camp's own staff had already restored order at the camp by the time we arrived.

During the night and even before, in the evening, a few of the escaped Jews returned to the camp voluntarily. I actually saw four or five prisoners return. They reported to the camp watch by the entrance gate and were taken in by the *Hilfswilligen*, who were stationed there. I cannot recall them being ill-treated. The *Hilfswilligen* took them to the barracks where the other prisoners were. I have no idea what happened to them later. I could not say whether they were shot in the end.

After a quiet night we carried out a search of the surrounding forest in the morning, which was more of a formality, really. No prisoners were found. At some stage that morning I did see about 50 prisoners, who presumably had been shot by the *Hiwis* and brought into the camp from the surrounding area, and then placed on the rails.

That same day a commission of higher ranking *SS* officers arrived at the camp from Lublin. Major Eggert reported to them after they had entered the camp. The commission consisted of about ten people. They went to look at the bodies of the killed camp staff members, but did not linger at the camp for long. I never saw any of the escaped Jews again and never ran into any of them, while fighting the partisans either.[131]

Jakob Sporrenberg, who had taken over from Odilo Globocnik as *SS* and Police Leader in Lublin in September 1943, was interrogated in London on March 26, 1946, and he gave a description of his visits to Sobibór, before and after the revolt:

> When Sporrenberg arrived in Lublin he did not know of this camp's existence. Only on odd occasions some of Globocnik's men would talk of the camp 'S,' but Sporrenberg later heard through the *KdS* that it was an extermination camp. He also knew that the camp was situated in the Lublin district, about 120-150 kilometres from the town, i.e. the district in which Sporrenberg himself was *SSPF*.
>
> He wanted to inspect the camp and did in fact go there some time in October 1943. Sporrenberg maintains that the camp came directly under the command of Globocnik, and that the *SIPO* had nothing whatsoever to do with it. On arrival at Sobibor the Guard Commander, *Hauptsturmführer* Reichleitner, who also refused him access and informed him that he could only visit Sobibór in the company of the *RFSS* or Globocnik, preferably both. Sporrenberg had a quarrel with Reichleitner and told him that as *SSPF* Lublin, he was responsible for all camps in the district. But the Commandant would not permit him to get past the gate.

---

[131] J. Schelvis, *Sobibor*, Berg-Oxford, New York, 2007, pp. 175-176.

Sporrenberg returned to Lublin and, although he had told Reichleitner that he would complain, he did nothing about it, especially as Reichleitner had told him that the camp would be dissolved in three to four weeks and that he himself would then follow Globocnik to Trieste.

About three weeks later Sporrenberg received a report from Chelm that an uprising had taken place in the camp while it was being dissolved. This report reached Sporrenberg about 24 hours after the uprising had begun. He drove there at once and found that the police had taken over the guarding of the place. Sporrenberg had not given such an order himself.

He found out that the last remaining Jews there, about 150, had beaten to death all the German staff present—there were about 15—, and then made off together with their Russian guards. Reichleitner himself was unfortunately not present as he had already left for Trieste. Before leaving, the prisoners had also set the entire camp on fire.

By the time Sporrenberg arrived, the police had placed the bodies of the dead Germans in one room. He tried to have a look round the camp but nearly everything had been destroyed by the fire. He saw a heap of stone rubble which, he says were the former gas chambers, but as he also says that he had never been there before, had never seen a plan of the camp and that nobody ever told him about it, it seems peculiar that he should be so certain about it. He explains that this was the only stone building and all others were of wood, which gives rise to the assumption that it used to be the crematorium and not the gas chamber. Furthermore he does not know where the corpses were disposed of. There were railway lines which had originally led to the heap of stone rubble.

As stated above, the camp was in the process of being dissolved when the uprising began. One of the dead found there had been an *Oberscharführer*, which seems to confirm that the stone building had been dynamited only just before. Sporrenberg was told by the police that unsuccessful attempts had been made to recapture the escaped prisoners. When Sporrenberg returned to Lublin, he found a teleprint from Himmler, who had already been informed by the *SIPO* of the incident. In this teleprint Himmler blamed Sporrenberg, asked why the prisoners had not yet been recaptured, and ordered him to spare no effort to seize them without delay. Sporrenberg replied that he had nothing to do with the matter and that he had not even been allowed inside the camp. He told Himmler that it was impossible to recapture the escaped prisoners, as they had fled across the River Bug.

Next day Sporrenberg was told that Globocnik had arrived in Lublin from Berlin and that he had gone out to the camp without seeing Sporrenberg. He merely drove out and made arrangements for the rest of the camp to be completely obliterated so that no traces would be left.[132]

In the forest the escapees were hunted by SS, Police and Ukrainians, and most of them lost their lives. In addition to this an unknown number of Jews lost their lives to Polish underground groups, who took their money and then their lives. Those Jews who remained in the camp during the revolt—mainly the religious and foreign Jews, who did not know the language or the country—were killed on the spot. This also included the prisoners in *Lager III*, who because of their location knew nothing about the revolt.

Franciszek Parkola, the Polish Station Supervisor at Sobibór, recalled:

> After I had come into work that evening, the station master and other people told me that a shooting had taken place at the camp, and that the Jews had cut through the fence in two places, one was near the station and the other near the sawmill.
>
> I had heard the shooting and explosions while still at home, 3 kilometres away from the camp. When I was at the station the next morning I saw the damaged fence around the camp. I could see part of the camp square and dead people scattered about.
>
> That afternoon I saw Jewish prisoners carting injured Jews and dead Jewish women out of the forest and back to the camp in wheelbarrows. I saw two Jews being taken on a handcart, that is to say, their hands were tied to the handles with barbed wire, and they were being dragged along. People I spoke to also told me that the Jews who had escaped from the camp had spoken to some

---

[132] Jakob Sporrenberg Interrogation on March 26, 1946, in London—National Archives Kew WO 208/4673.

building workers and had literally said, '*Hitler kaput*,' and that the war had ended.[133]

Alexander Pechersky remembered what happened when they reached the forest:

> For some time we continued to hear shots from rifles and automatic weapons. This helped us orient ourselves. We knew that there, behind us, was the camp. Gradually the shooting became more distant until it died down altogether. It was already dark when shooting broke out again from the right, it sounded distant and faint. I proposed that we continue going all through the night, and that we should go in a single file, one behind the other. I would be in the front. Behind me, Tsibulsky, Arkady [Vaispapir] would close the line. No smoking, no talking, no falling behind, no running ahead. If a man in front lies down, all would do the same. If a rocket flared up, all would lie down at once. There must be no panic, no matter what happened.
>
> We were out of the woods, for about three kilometres we walked through an open field. Then our path was blocked by a canal about five to six meters wide. The canal was deep, and it was impossible to wade through it, so we walked along the shore of the canal. Suddenly I noticed a group of people about 50 meters away. We all lay down at once. Arkady was given the task of investigating who they were. At first he crawled on his belly, then he rose and ran up to the group. A few minutes later he returned, 'Sasha, they're ours,' he announced. 'They found wooden stumps lying by the shore and are crossing over to the other side. Kalimali (Shubayev) is with them'. We all crossed over the canal on these wooden stumps.
>
> Shubayev had no news about Luka, but he had seen Shlomo Leitman. He said Shlomo was wounded before he managed to get into the woods. He had continued to run for a distance of about three kilometres and then his strength gave out. He begged to be shot. What horrible, painful news that was! To break out of the camp and on the way to freedom to remain lying helpless.

---

[133] J. Schelvis, *Sobibor*, Berg-Oxford, New York, 2007, pp. 176-177.

By now our group numbered fifty-seven people, we covered another five kilometres and then heard the rumble of a passing train. Before us lay a broad open stretch of land, sparsely covered with short shrubs. We stopped it was getting close to dawn, time to give some thought to the question of where we should spend the day. It was clear that the Germans would be pursuing us through the day. The woods in these parts were not very thick and could be easily combed in all directions. I talked it over with Tsibulsky and Shubayev, and it was decided that the best thing to do would be to scatter around the bushes, precisely because it was an open space, not far from the railway line. Therefore it wouldn't occur to anyone to look for us there. But we would have no camouflage ourselves as well, lie motionless and not utter a sound.

Before we took to the bushes, I sent out a few people to comb through them carefully for some distance on all sides. Throughout the day airplanes circled overhead, some quite low over the bushes where we lay. We heard the voices of Poles who worked on the railway, our people lay glued to the ground, covered with branches, no one moved, until it grew dark, that's how the first day of our freedom passed. It was October 15, 1943.

Night fell, as we raised from our places we noticed two figures approaching us. They moved cautiously, we guessed at once they were our people. It turned out they had already been as far as the Bug and were now returning from there. 'Why didn't you cross?' we asked.

They reported that they had entered a hamlet not far from the river and were told that Germans had arrived at the shore during the night and that all crossings were heavily guarded. We walked in single file, in the same order as yesterday. Tsibulsky and I were in front. Shubayev and Arkady were the last in line.

After walking for about 5 kilometres we entered the woods and stopped. It made no sense to continue together in so large a group, we would be too conspicuous, also it would be impossible to provide food for so many people. Therefore, we divided ourselves into small groups, each going its own way. My group consisted of nine people, including Shubayev, Boris Tsibulsky, Arkady Vaispapir, Michael Itzkowitch, Semion Mazurkiewitch. We headed east, with the polar stars as our compass. The nights were starry. Our first aim was to cross the Bug. To do that we had to find the proper place and the proper time. In quiet deserted hamlets we obtained food and received vital information and directions.[134]

The escapees were close to the River Bug, and the long awaited freedom:

> We remained in the forest for the rest of the day. Then we started to make our way towards Stawki, which was one and a half kilometres from the Bug. Shubayev who had been sent on a reconnaissance with two of his comrades, knocked at one of the little houses to ask if they could come in. A young man answered positively in perfect Russian. Aside from him, there was a woman, a baby in a cradle and an old man. Shubayev asked if they knew where in the area might be a good place to cross the river, because they were Prisoners of War, who had escaped and wanted to return home, to Donbas and Rostov.
>
> After staying silent for a long while, the young man replied he did know of such a place. After Shubayev had come back for us and the woman had given us some bread to take along, the young farmer led us to a place not far from the river and left us there. That was in the night of 19 October. Two days later we met the first partisans near Brest, they were from the Worosjilkow group.[135]

Shlomo Alster described the events surrounding Pechersky's group of escapees departing:

> Sasha's people left us, and went away. We remained without a leader. What could we do? Without arms and without a man to lead us. Together with us were French, Dutch, Czechoslovakian Jews. They could not find their way without knowing the language and surroundings. Like us they also divided themselves into small groups. They went out to the road, which was full of SS men, and all of them were caught alive. Also the local people caught them one by one, and brought them to Sobibór, where they were liquidated. None of them survived.

---

[134] Y. Arad, *Belzec, Sobibor, Treblinka*, Indiana University Press, Bloomington and Indianapolis 1987, pp. 338-339.
[135] J. Schelvis, *Sobibor*, Berg-Oxford, New York, 2007, pp. 184-185.

We, the Polish Jews, remained a small group. What should we do? To stay in the forest was dangerous, because either the Germans or the local people would catch us. We had to get away from this place, and from Sobibór—as far as possible. But this was not so simple—where could we go?

I was hungry, my clothes were torn to pieces. I decided to go back to my native town, to Chelm, maybe there I could find some chance of survival. I couldn't see any other alternative.[136]

Azik Rotenberg recalled his escape from Sobibór:

On October 14, the revolt took place. I ran to the forest with my companions and met a naked fugitive. 'Come with me,' I said, and gave him my coat. We looked for partisans, but didn't find any. Then we were arrested by *Schupo's*, who didn't wish to kill us right away. They took us to Adampol, and a German called Zelinger, tied us up with chains in a stable. For weeks he treated us like dogs. However, we managed to break the chains and escaped to the forest of Parczew.

We met a group of Polish partisans, who didn't want to accept us. Later we found Jewish partisans, the Yehiel group, who were part of Chyl Grynspan's unit. They accepted us and we took part in several battles.[137]

Dov Freiberg recounts the difficulties faced in the forests near Sobibór following the revolt and escape from the camp:

We were murdered not only by Germans, but by Poles, Ukrainians and partisans, especially the men of the *Armia Krajowa*, gangs and farmers. More than once we considered suicide, after we saw that the whole world was against us. Every day of the ten months until the liberation is a story unto itself. Yet I would not have exchanged the whole terrible period in the forests for one day, even the best day in Sobibór. There were also a few good Poles and Ukrainians. These people helped us and risked their lives, because

---

[136] Y. Arad, *Belzec, Sobibor, Treblinka*, Indiana University Press, Bloomington and Indianapolis 1987, p. 340.
[137] Miriam Novitch, *Sobibor*, Holocaust Library, New York, 1980, p.105.

they had to fear every neighbour, every passerby, every child who might inform on them.[138]

On April 23, 1944, Thomas 'Toivi' Blatt, Szmul Wajcen and Fredek Kostmann were in hiding in the farm of a Pole Bojarski, who was a former classmate of Thomas Blatt in Izbica:

> We were lying quietly, resigned to our dreams when we heard faint footsteps about the barn. We recognized Bojarski's tread. Perhaps he was not as mean as we thought, he was bringing us food. We heard him stop before the entrance.
>
> Although it was my turn to pick up the food, Fredek was now close to the entrance. He stretched out on his belly and edged through the opening in the straw to the board, which would open any moment for our food. We heard the catch open and the board move.
>
> Suddenly a flash of light and the crack of a gunshot disturbed the stillness. I heard Fredek wriggling, screaming, 'Son of a bitch... Germans.' The rest became a mutter, and then an unrecognizable gurgle.
>
> The board was swung back in place. Silence. Only Fredek's hoarse gasping was heard. Szmul and I were sitting up against the wall. Fredek, in his convulsion, threw himself about, spraying us with his blood. After a moment of shock and confusion, we realized that he was dead, and knew it was our turn.[139]

That night both Thomas 'Toivi' Blatt and Szmul Wacjen were both shot by the Farmer Bojarski. They both survived and escaped from the farm, but Szmul lost his life later in the forest.

The British Intelligence Service staff at Bletchley Park, in the United Kingdom intercepted on October 15, 1943, a German police message from the *SS* Police Leader Lublin, to *SS-Brigadeführer* Wilhelm Guenther in Luzk, regarding the escape of 700 Jews from the camp at Sobibór,—which lies 5 kilometres from the Bug,

---

[138] Y. Arad, *Belzec, Sobibor, Treblinka*, Indiana University Press, Bloomington and Indianapolis 1987, pp. 347-348.
[139] T. Blatt, *From the Ashes of Sobibor*, Northwestern University Press Illinois, 1997, pp. 183-184.

between Chelm and Włodawa—who had fled over the River Bug border.[140]

On March 17, 1944, *SS-Untersturmführer* Adalbert Benda, who served in the Border Police unit in Chelm, wrote a report about the Jewish revolt in Sobibór, requesting medals for himself and a number of his comrades for their conduct in carrying out the manhunt. Benda himself was never brought to trial for his actions in the Lublin district of Poland, although he was indicted in Vienna, Austria and Wiesbaden in Germany. He passed away in Vienna during 1970.

Benda's report was written some five months after the revolt in Sobibór on October 14, 1943, makes the mistake of citing the wrong date, of October 15, 1943, on a number of occasions. But it describes the actions his unit took to secure the death camp, including the mass execution of Jewish prisoners:

Subject: Awards for Anti-Bandit Campaign

Ref: Kdr Order No 11, 11 March 1944. Art 105

In the afternoon of 15.10. 1943, some 300 prisoners of *Sonderlager* Sobibór attempted a breakout, having disarmed a number of guard units and killed one *SS-Führer*, as well as 10 *SS-Unterführer*. The attempt was partially successful.

An *Einsatzkommando* was sent from the *Grenzpolizeikommissariat* at Chelm, which included the following members:

SS-Untersturmführer Benda, Adalbert

SS-Hauptscharführer Pruckner, Ludwig

SS-Hauptscharführer Benzler, Hermann

SS-Oberscharführer Scholz, Erich

SS-Oberscharführer Theimer, Rudolf

SS-Oberscharführer Schlogel, Konrad

SS-Rottenführer Reinelt, Adolf

---

[140] National Archives Kew HW 16/38.

The *Wehrmacht* and *Schutzpolizei* were also summoned. In view of the nature of the *Sonderlager* and its inmates, it was decided that the *Wehrmacht* should take immediate responsibility for pursuing the fugitives, and the *Schutzpolizei* for securing the camp from the outside. The *Einsatzkommando* sent by the *Grenzpolizeikommissariat* at Chelm, carried out a thorough search of the camp interior in the night of 15.10. 1943, and in the early morning hours of 16.10.1943. In the process, the men repeatedly came under fire from the prisoners. During the actual search of the camp, the use of firearms was required as the prisoners resisted their capture. A large number of prisoners 159, ended up being shot, as per instructions. All members of the *Einsatzkommando* proved themselves worthy of the task throughout the entire operation.

Benda SS-Untersturmführer[141]

Erich Bauer recalled what happened to the SS men killed in the prisoner revolt regarding their burial at the Chelm Military Cemetery on October 18, 1943:

> I personally took seven caskets to Chelm: the other caskets arrived in Chelm by train. I picked them up from the station and took them to the town hall. In total between 21 and 23 people were killed, including a Ukrainian who, I believe, was in charge of all the tradesmen, his name was Klatt.
>
> The funeral took place at the military cemetery outside Chelm, where those who died at the Chelm *Lazarett* had also been buried. The cemetery was situated along the road to Bialystok.
>
> I refused to drive to the border patrol. I was supposed to warn them that the prisoners had broken out. I was afraid, because it was dark and they had taken all the weapons. Wirth shouted at me. He threatened me with a pistol or a whip. So I drove away from Sobibór, straight to a farm, where I hid behind one of the sheds. If I had not gone, he would have killed me. The next morning I drove to the border patrol."[142]

---

[141] J. Schelvis, *Sobibor*, Berg-Oxford, New York, 2007, pp. 179-180.
[142] Ibid. p. 179.

The fallen members of the SS-Garrison were buried with full military honours in the German Military Cemetery in Chelm, on October 18, 1943. Among the visitors, paying their respects were Gottlieb Hering, the former commandant of Bełżec death camp; Ernst Lerch, who was Adjutant for the SSPF in Lublin, Dietrich Allers, and Werner Blankenburg, who represented the T4 Organization from Berlin.

In a conference held by Hans Frank in *Krakau* on October 19, 1943, the Sobibór uprising was discussed along with the security issues of the Jewish Labor Camps, and inspections of all the labor camps were proposed.[143] Himmler however, wanted to move faster and ordered the liquidation of all the Jewish Labor Camps under the title of *Aktion Erntefest*.[144]

On October 20, 1943, three cargo wagons left the Treblinka death camp[145] bound for Sobibór, with a few dozen Jews, including *Oberkapo* Karl Blau and his wife Adele, to help dismantle the camp. They had been involved in dismantling the facilities in the Treblinka death camp following the revolt there on August 2, 1943. The work took about one month to complete, and when this was accomplished the Jewish workers were murdered in the most brutal fashion.

One of the SS-Garrison Erich Herbert Floss, on October 22, 1943, escorted a group of Ukrainian guards to the Trawniki *Ausbildungs-Lager* by train. Floss was killed by Wasil Hetmaniac in Zawadowka, near Chelm, using Floss's own weapon.

The British Intelligence Service at Bletchley Park intercepted another German Police message transmitted on October 27, 1943, regarding un-used ammunition sent to Munich from *Durchgangslager* Sobibór on October 25, 1943. This message

---

[143] Sobibor was not mentioned by name in the meeting minutes.
[144] Y. Arad, *Belzec, Sobibor, Treblinka*, Indiana University Press, Bloomington and Indianapolis 1987, p.365.
[145] Franciszek Zabecki Testinony—Judge Lukaszkiewice—Holocaust Historical Society.

originated from the *SS- und Polizei Russland Mitte*. The term *Durchgangslager* means 'Transit Camp.'[146]

Jan Piwonski, a railway employee, also recalled the last days of Sobibór:

> The Jews who had been put to work on demolishing the camp had to plant new trees after the ground had been levelled. I also know the Jews had to fill in and cover up the holes that had been caused by blowing up the concrete buildings inside the camp. I do not know what happened to the Jews who wound up in the camp, but no one ever saw them leave. I heard that all of them were killed.
>
> Later in the autumn, towards the end of October, or early in November 1943, the Germans who had been at the camp, left Sobibór. I know that the Germans dispatched clothing from the camp, because I saw it being loaded into wagons and transported out of the camp. I also know they sent crates full of something or other from the camp. The crates were one meter long and very heavy. I know the crates were very heavy because I weighed them myself. From the labels on the crates—I read them—I could make out they were sent to Berlin.
>
> The Ukrainians carried the crates into a luggage wagon and a German officer armed with a sub-machine gun, got into the same wagon. I learnt from the Ukrainians that the crates contained gold coins. The Vlaszows also said there might be expensive jewellery and precious stones inside.[147]

Early in the morning of November 23, 1943, Gustav Wagner announced the final liquidation. *Oberkapo* Karl Blau and his wife Adele committed suicide the night before, and the thirty remaining Jewish workers were forced to lie down on the cremation site, consisting of narrow-gauge rails, where they were shot in the back of the neck in groups of five.

Gustav Wagner and the Ukrainians Bodessa and Kaiser played a prominent role in the executions, which took about one hour.

---

[146] National Archives Kew HW 16/39.
[147] J. Schelvis, *Sobibor*, Berg-Oxford, New York, 2007, p. 191.

The bodies were cremated and, along with the cremation rails, were buried on the grounds of the former *Lager III*.

Robert Juhrs, who was sent from the Dorohucza Labor Camp to assist with the liquidation of the camp, was part of the security cordon that guarded the executions of the last Jewish workers:

> By the time I arrived at Sobibór, many of the buildings and the inner fence had already been torn down. I vaguely remember about thirty *Arbeitsjuden* still being at the camp, but perhaps there were a few more. These Jews had been put to work on demolishing and clearing away what had once been *Lager III*. I remember I had to supervise these Jews for one or two days as well.
>
> Mostly I was involved in putting back in order the buildings that were to be returned to the Polish Forestry Commission. I clearly remember that the last *Arbeitsjuden* were shot in early December 1943, in what had been *Lager III*, or in any case in a wooded area. I am certain that the Ukrainian train guard Alex Kaiser was very active on that day of the execution. He took part in all the beatings and shootings.
>
> At any rate, I can say that Wagner and Frenzel were also in the foreground on the day of the executions. What I mean is that they were actively engaged in the beatings and executing of the Jews. I saw them myself beating up the Jews and shooting them. But other camp staff at Sobibór, also actively participated in the executions: Bauer, Bodessa, Bolender, Hödl, Klier, Lambert and Unverhau.
>
> The fact is, though, that all of the camp staff were present at the executions. I formed part of the security cordon around the area of the execution. I saw with my own eyes, how the Jews were shot in the back of the neck with pistols, or machine pistols. I was about 10 meters away from where the executions took place and witnessed it all.
>
> As far as I can recall, there were no incidents—the Jews were submissive and offered no resistance when being taken to their execution. After this action I stayed at Sobibór for only a few more

days and assisted with demolishing the Jewish tailors workshop.[148]

With the final winding up of the camp, the vast majority of the *SS*-Garrison and a number of *Trawnikimänner* were posted to Northern Italy, to serve once again under Odilo Globocnik, who had been appointed the Higher-*SS* and Police Leader for the *Adriatisches Küstenland*.

The Germans dismantled the incriminating gas chamber installations and some other buildings, but a number of the former camp facilities were used by the *Baudienst*—Construction Service— until July 1944, when the Red Army forces defeated the Germans. Most of the barracks were not destroyed by the *SS*, but rather in the immediate post-war period. The railroad ramp for example was used until 1947, for gathering Ukrainians, who were destined for resettlement to the Ukraine or to the western parts of Poland. While these Ukrainians waited for their trains, sometimes this took one week, they demolished the remaining wooden barracks for their camp fires. The tall forester's watchtower was not destroyed, because this densely wooded area needed such a tower for observation in case of fire. The Forester's tower collapsed and was removed in 2003. The former commandant's house, was also not destroyed, since it originally belonged to the Forester's administration and was not strictly connected to the mass murder process. The unloading ramp was used until the 1960's but all railway traffic ceased in 1999, and since then the Sobibór railway station has stood idle.

The precise number of victims may never be known, however, with the discovery of the decoded message sent by Hermann Höfle, the deputy head of *Aktion Reinhardt* to *Obersturmbannführer* Heim in *Krakau*, showed the number of Jews sent to Sobibór up to the year end of 1942, amounted to 101,370. Official estimates of the number of victims range from 150,000 to 250,000.

---

[148] J. Schelvis, *Sobibor*, Berg-Oxford, New York, 2007, pp. 190-191.

Erich Bauer, known as the *'Gasmeister'* recalled after the war the following:

> I estimate that the number of Jews gassed at Sobibór was about 350,000. In the canteen I once overheard a conversation between Frenzel, Stangl and Wagner. They were discussing the number of victims in the extermination camps of Bełżec, Treblinka and Sobibór and expressed their regret that Sobibór came last in the competition.[149]

One of the most important finds in the modern field of Holocaust research was the discovery of a German police message which was decoded by the British Intelligence Service at Bletchley Park, discovered by Stephen Tyas, held by the National Archives in Kew.

The message was sent by Hermann Höfle, the Deputy Chief of *Aktion Reinhardt* in Lublin, to *SS-Obersturmbannführer* Franz Heim, Commander in Chief of the *BdS (Befehlshaber der Sicherheitspolizei)* office *in Krakau*. The message was a 14-day report and year end report up to December 31, 1942, covering the number of people sent to the *Aktion Reinhardt* death camps.

This was the second of two messages intercepted by the British Intelligence Service, the first one Höfle sent to Adolf Eichmann, the expert on Jewish affairs at the *RSHA* headquarters in Berlin, which was only partially intercepted. The second message sent to Heim was intercepted in full on January 11, 1943. The death camps were identified by their initial letters.

Camps	14-Day Report to 31-12-1942	Year End 1942
L – Lublin	12, 761	24,733
B – Bełżec	0	434,508
S – Sobibór	515	101,370
T–Treblinka	10,335	713,555
Totals	23,611	1274, 166

---

[149] Klee, Dressen, Riess, *Those were the Days*, Hamish Hamilton, London 1991 p.232.

In the original message the British Intelligence Service staff made a mistake and missed the last 5 digit off the Treblinka figure, it has to be 713,555 to fit the total figure. It must be stressed the message does not refer to the above as victims, but people sent to the camps—nevertheless this is a very important find.

What is interesting is that the figures for *Aktion Reinhardt* submitted by Höfle include the Lublin Concentration Camp (known as Majdanek in post-war times). Lublin came under the control of the *Wirtschafts-Verwaltungshauptamt (WVHA)* headed by Richard Gluecks in Berlin. Bełżec, Sobibór, and Treblinka were controlled by Globocnik, the *SSPF* for the Lublin District.[150]

There was a link, however, as the Old Airfield Camp was a storage depot for the clothing and footwear of the murdered Jews in the three *Aktion Reinhardt* Camps, as well as from the ghettos. The Old Airfield Camp was planned to become a sub-camp of the main Lublin Concentration Camp, but the liquidation of the labor camp, as part of the *Aktion Erntefest* mass murder frenzy in November 1943, meant this plan never came to fruition.[151]

In the immediate post war period several key SS Officers who had served at Sobibór were put on trial, such as Hubert Gomerski, who was arrested but acquitted during 1947, at a trial about euthanasia. When his participation in the crimes committed at Sobibór were proven, he was sentenced to life imprisonment on August 25, 1950. Former *SS-Unterscharführer* Johann Klier was arrested but, based on the testimony of Sobibór survivors that Klier was a person who felt compassion for the Jews and secretly tried to help them, he was released.

Josef 'Sepp' Hirtreiter, who served at Treblinka and briefly at Sobibór, was arrested in July 1946, and accused of having served at the T4 Institute at Hadamar. He was the first of the 'Treblinka Hangmen' to be brought to trial in Frankfurt-am-Main. On March 3, 1951, he was sentenced to life imprisonment. He was found

---

[150] Hw 16/32 National Archives Kew.
[151] T. Kranz, Extermination of the Jews at Majdanek Concentration Camp, Majdanek Museum, Lublin 2007, p.64.

guilty of killing young children, aged one or two, during the unloading of transports, seizing the infants by their feet, and smashing their heads against the boxcars. Because of ill-health, he was released from prison in 1977. He died on November 27, 1978.

One of the worst of the Sobibór murderers was *SS-Oberscharführer* Erich Bauer, the chief of the gas chambers, who was recognized on the streets of Berlin by survivors Samuel Lerer, and Estera Terner. On May 8, 1950, he was sentenced to death and then after the abolition of the death penalty in West Germany, to life imprisonment. He died in the Tegel Prison in Berlin on February 4, 1980.

On September 6, 1965, the West German court in Hagen initiated criminal proceedings against twelve former *SS*-men who served at the Sobibór death camp. This was in respect of participating in the mass murder of Jews. On December 20, 1966, the men on trial learnt their fate. Six of those charged were acquitted, only one Karl Frenzel, was sentenced to life in prison, whilst others were given sentences ranging from three to eight years in prison.

Only one member of the Sobibór *SS*-Garrison, former *SS-Unterscharführer* Werner Dubois, admitted guilt in his court testimony in Hagen:

> It is clear to me that in the extermination camp, murder was committed. What I have done was only to assist in the murder. If I were to be found guilty it would be justified, murder is murder. We are all guilty. The camp had a chain of command and if one link in the chain were to refuse to cooperate then the whole system would collapse.... We did not have the courage to disobey orders.

In their defence, the accused claimed that once assigned to serve in a death camp, there was no way out, citing the words of Christian Wirth, Inspector of the *SS-Sonderkommandos Aktion Reinhardt*, made to the *SS*-Garrison in Sobibór:

> If any of you don't like it here, you can leave. But under the earth not over it.[152]

Given the number of acquittals, it would appear the judges were swayed by this defence. It could be claimed that the world had grown weary about the Holocaust and the passage of time had somehow lessened the enormity of the crimes committed at Sobibór, but in reality the crimes committed there were so awful, this was no excuse for lenient sentences.

In 1970, Franz Stangl was brought to justice when he stood trial in Düsseldorf, West Germany, for the War Crimes committed at the Treblinka death camp. He was not tried for his time as the Commandant of the Sobibór death camp, for technical reasons.

Stanislaw Szmajzner testified at Stangl's trial on the last day of the hearings, during October 1970. Stanislaw even posed with Frau Stangl after the trial ended in Düsseldorf. He said he agreed to the press taking photographs, as he had nothing against Stangl's family, and he wanted to convey this to the media in Brazil.[153]

The table below shows the name of those charged with war crimes, what their current occupations were, the charges and the sentences handed out at the conclusion of the trial, in December 1966. It does not take into account any subsequent appeals.

---

[152] T. Blatt, *Sobibor—The Forgotten Revolt*, H.E.P, Issaquah, 1998, p. 97.
[153] Gitta Sereny, *Into That Darkness*, Pimlico. London 1974, p.130.

Name	Occupation	Charges	Sentence
Karl Frenzel	Carpenter	Accused of personally killing 42 Jews and participating in the murder of approximately 250,000 Jews	Found guilty of personally killing 6 Jews and in the participation in the mass murder of 150,000 Jews. Sentenced to life imprisonment.
Franz Wolf	Warehouse Clerk	Accused of personally killing one Jew, and participating in the mass murder of 115,000 Jews.	Found guilty of participation in the mass murder of 39,000 Jews. Sentenced to eight years in prison.
Alfred Ittner	Laborer	Accused of participating in the mass murder of approximately 57,000 Jews.	Found guilty of the participation in the murder of 68,000 Jews. Sentenced to four years in prison.
Werner Dubois	Railroad Employee	Accused of participating in the mass murder of approximately 43,000 Jews.	Found guilty of the participation in the murder of 15,000 Jews. Sentenced to three years in prison.
Erich Fuchs	Lorry Driver	Accused of participating in the mass murder of approximately 3,600 Jews.	Found guilty of the participation in the murder of 79,000 Jews. Sentenced to four years in prison.
Erich Lachmann	Mason	Accused of participating in the mass murder of approximately 150,000 Jews.	Acquitted
Heinz-Hans Schutt	Salesman	Accused of participating in the mass murder of approximately 86,000 Jews	Acquitted

Heinrich Unverhau	Male Nurse	Accused of participating in the mass murder of approximately 72,000 Jews	Acquitted
Robert Juhrs	Porter – Janitor	Accused of participating in the mass murder of approximately 30 Jews	Acquitted
Ernst Zierke	Saw Mill Worker	Accused of participating in the mass murder of approximately 30 Jews	Acquitted
Erwin Lambert	Ceramic Tile Salesman	Accused of participating in the mass murder of an unknown number of Jews.	Acquitted
Kurt Bolender	Hotel Porter	Accused of personally killing 360 Jews and participating in the murder of approximately 86,000 Jews.	Committed suicide in prison before sentencing

A few of the Ukrainian who served at Sobibór were brought to trial in the Soviet Union, they were:

W. Bielakow

M. Matwijenko

I. Nikifor

W. Podienko

F. Tichonowski

Emanuel Schultz

J. Zajcew

They were found guilty and executed for their crimes. In April 1963, in a court in Kiev, where Sasha Pechersky was the chief prosecution witness, ten former Ukrainian guards were found guilty and executed, while one of those tried was sentenced to fifteen years in prison. A third trial was held in Kiev in June 1965, where three former death camp guards from Sobibór and Bełżec were executed.

A number of Sobibór survivors testified at the Adolf Eichmann trial in Jerusalem during 1961. These included three survivors such as Moshe Bahir, Jakub Biskubicz and Dov Freiberg.

Ivan Demjanjuk was extradited from the United States of America and tried in Jerusalem in the mid-1980's for War Crimes. He was accused of being the so-called 'Ivan the Terrible,' who served at the Treblinka death camp. He was found guilty and sentenced to death, but was later freed following a successful appeal. At his trial a *Trawnikimänner* Identity Card showed an entry stating he was posted to Sobibór. He returned to the United States of America, but he was still pursued by the authorities.

Ivan Demjanjuk, a former Ukrainian guard who had served at Sobibór, was eventually brought to face trial in Bonn, Germany for alleged war crimes committed at the Sobibór death camp. In May 2011, he was convicted of 28,060 counts of being an accessory to murder and was sentenced to five years imprisonment. He passed away on March 17, 2012, in a nursing home in the southern Bavarian town of Bad Felinbach, after being released pending his appeal. According to German law, Demjanjuk went to his grave a free man, in the eyes of the law.

Chapter III
The *Arbeitsjuden* Remember

In this chapter we will recall the accounts of some of the Sobibór survivors on what they remember of the day to day living in the death camp. They will recall what work they performed, the friends they knew and those that were lost. They will recall the brutality they suffered and their day to day contact with their Nazi masters:

Moshe Szlarek, who worked as a *Putzer* in the *SS* canteen, recalled an incident involving Erich Bauer:

> Bauer told his comrades of an incident in which a naked woman in one of the gas chambers asked an SS-man who was about to close the door: 'What's that officer doing at the skylight window? How can we wash ourselves when he is peaking in?' Bauer and his cohorts erupted in laughter. The engine was started by *SS-Oberscharführer* Erich Bauer and a Ukrainian Emil Kostenko. Soon a horrible mass screaming could be heard over the rumble of the engine muffled by the thick walls of the chamber. At first it was very loud and terror-filled. After 20-30 minutes the people were gassed and dead.[154]

Philip Bialowitz was deported from Izbica to Sobibór by lorry on April 28, 1943. He worked as a member of the *Bahnhofkommando*, who dealt with new arrivals at the death camp:

> One day at Sobibór a transport arrived that had been underway for a long time; the people on it were starving and very weak, and many had already died in the wagons along the way. Shortly after, Frenzel led a group of men onto the platform to help with unloading. It was the most harrowing time of my life. I had been selected for the *Bahnhofkommando*.

---

[154] T. Blatt, *Sobibor—The Forgotten Revolt*, H.E.P, Issaquah, 1998, p. 36.

The wagon doors were opened to the most horrible sight. The people inside were terribly swollen, the children distended to almost the size of an adult; half of the wagon occupants were dead, the other half had gone insane. The order to unload was given. As we touched these people, their skin stuck to our hands and the bodies remained where they were.

But Frenzel urged us to carry on unloading, using his whip on us. In the second wagon a child was sitting on its mother's lap. The child was still embracing its mother. Both were dead. Frenzel said, 'What a wonderful picture.' The ones who were still alive were shot. Frenzel and some others whose names I do not know, shot them as they were being dragged from the wagons. The bodies were laid on the rail carts and taken to *Lager III*, along with people who were still alive, but too weak to walk.[155]

Moshe Szklarek recalled the arrival of a transport from Holland, when he was part of the *Bahnhofkommando*:

I remember one incident from the time I was in the *Bahnhofkommando*. A transport of Jews from Holland arrived at the camp in luxury wagons, with all their personal belongings. Our attitude towards them, compared to other transports was different, we were more patient.

After unloading the victims from the wagons, we started rounding them up to move them from *Lager II*. Franz Reichleitner was personally in charge. I saw with my own eyes how one Jew from this transport did not line up quickly enough, prompting *Oberscharführer* Frenzel to step in and start beating him.

Reichleitner immediately came across and the German stopped straight away. I saw how the Jew bent down, scooped up a handful of sand, and turning to face Reichleitner said to him, 'See how I pour this sand from my fist, down to the last grain, that is how you and your Reich will fall. Do not think that the world will not take revenge. It will revenge each and every drop of innocent blood you have shed.'

Then he turned back to face the other victims, while reciting 'Shema Israel' (The Jewish acknowledgement of God, also to be

---

[155] Y. Arad, *Belzec, Sobibor, Treblinka*, Indiana University Press, Bloomington and Indianapolis 1987, p.68.

said as one's last words). Before he had even finished, Franz Reichleitner pulled his revolver and shot him. The Jew died on the spot.[156]

Thomas 'Toivi' Blatt recalled his first meeting with members of the *Bahnhofkommando* on his first day of life inside Sobibór:

> I heard people singing, and I jumped down and went outside. The gate opened wide, and in marched a group of about of about twenty robust youths. They wore dark blue overalls and fancy caps, with the letter B embroidered within a yellow triangle. The leader held a whip and issued a sharp command in German: '*Abteilung ... Halt!*' A few steps forward and the group halted, with the next command everyone dispersed. If I hadn't heard them speak Yiddish after they broke ranks, I would have mistaken them for German soldiers. Though I had seen them with my own eyes, I still couldn't believe they were really Jews. I found out later that the B stood for *Bahnhofkommando*, train brigade.[157]

After the Jews were unloaded from the trains or by lorry the next step in the process was the removal of their personal belongings. Thomas 'Toivi' Blatt outlined the process:

> In the middle of the night I was awakened by a sharp whistle. My bunk neighbour explained that a transport had arrived, a Dutch one. The train usually came in around 3:00 A.M. While the transports of Jews from Eastern Europe usually arrived in Sobibór in overfilled cargo wagons or trucks, the Dutch transports sometimes came in standard passenger trains. The Jewish administration in Westerbork, Holland, their departure point, provided them with doctors and nurses for the sick, maids for the handicapped and babies. Food and medicine were in plentiful supply in attached freight wagons.
>
> *Kapo* Bunio tore into our barrack, and turning on the light, he shouted, Porters and barbers... get ready. Groups of prisoners jumped from their bunks, dressed quickly and went out to the square. Evidently a large transport was expected. Another *Kapo* dragged additional men from the bunks, myself included. A few

---

[156] J. Schelvis, *Sobibor*, Berg-Oxford, New York, 2007, p.67.
[157] T. Blatt, *From the Ashes of Sobibor* Northwestern University Press Illinois, 1997, p.94.

of us were designated 'porters' and a few others were called 'friseurs,' barbers.

The camp was well lit. Being led to the workplace, I could see some movement far off on the station platform. New arrivals were getting off the train. A narrow-gauge dumpcart passed by. Into it would be thrown, I was told, in addition to large pieces of baggage, the sick, the old, the crippled, and all those unable to walk on their own. The rest would follow the SS men to a long barrack.

The eight-member group I was with was led to this barrack and told to wait for the arriving Jews. It was a large windowless barrack; its entrance and exit gates were wide open. Two prisoners were placed by the entrance gate, four in the centre, and two by the exit. We were to tell the Jews passing through the barrack to leave their purses and small hand baggage there.

The first group of condemned drew near. First were the women. They were nicely dressed. I stood for a moment dumbfounded. It was early in the morning, and many small children slept in their arms. They had no idea they were going to their deaths. The sudden crack of the whip reminded me not to be a passive observer. The veteran prisoners repeated a sentence in Dutch over and over again, informing the passing people that they were to leave their belongings here. I mimicked them. At the exit gate stood an SS man, and woe to us if someone passed by still holding something after crossing the length of the barrack.

Thomas Blatt continued with his account:

Once in a while I would see bewilderment and suspicion on their faces. They had left their heavy luggage on the platform without worry, because all the luggage had tags, but here they were told to throw their very personal belongings into a huge heap. When someone refused to leave a purse or a handbag, the SS man would whip the victim until he or she complied. The column of about five hundred people passed through. We could hear more wagons arriving on the camp's side track. Now this place had to be emptied.

The barrack had several doors that led to attached smaller barracks. Several prisoners entered through these doors and together we quickly loaded the heaps of hand luggage into blankets and carried them to the adjoining rooms. Inside were tables where

> women stood sorting the booty. We threw down load after load. Soon the barrack was empty and the sand floor had been raked clean.
>
> Then the SS men led us to the gate of an enclosed courtyard and ordered us to wait. From inside the yard came a single German voice. I thought I heard the end of a speech. After a while the gate opened and we entered. The yard was now empty and quiet. Only heaps of neatly piled dresses, suits and underwear remained.
>
> We loaded the clothes onto blankets and carried them back through the gate. I understood that they were left by Jews who had just been ordered to undress. Moving along with others, I found myself in a large warehouse. We threw the clothes onto large, short tables. [158]

The clothes sorting commando employed hundreds of Jewish workers. Chaim Engel, who arrived in Sobibór on November 6, 1942, recalled how he was put to work immediately upon his arrival:

> So they took us—the 20 people—they took us in one side, and the others went to the camp, to the gas chambers—which we found out later. So we worked in there. We went in the afternoon and they took us with all the other people to separate the clothes. That started to be our work and I started to separate my pile of clothes—these were the clothes of the people who had just arrived with the transport that we came with. While I did that, I found the clothes of my brother, the pictures from my family, so I knew already—they had already told me what was going on, so I knew what had happened. He had gone to the gas chamber with my friend, and I am here separating his clothes. So you can imagine what went through my mind when that happened. [159]

Dov Freiberg arrived in Sobibór during May 1942, and he described his encounter with the dog Barry, who accompanied the SS on their rounds through the camp:

---

[158] T. Blatt, *From the Ashes of Sobibor,* Northwestern University Press Illinois, 1997, pp. 99-100.
[159] Interview with Chaim Engel by USHMM, July 16 1990.

Bolender, whose nickname was *Der Bader* (the bath-house attendant), while on his way to *Lager III*, or on the way back, would set the dog Barry on one of the workers. You could go out of you mind from the horrible sight of Barry attacking a man, tearing his clothes, biting his flesh, as the victim screamed horribly and was usually taken to the *Lazarett* afterwards.

One day, Paul Groth came to us with the dog. He sat opposite us and laughed, the dog lying at his side. Now and then he would set the dog upon someone, 'Man catch the dog,' he would order Barry. Paul Groth was amused. Sometimes he would set the dog on someone, then call him back when he was close enough to touch the victim; sometimes he just let the dog attack someone without intervening. The fear of the dog bite was so great, that fear alone could drive you insane.

Then suddenly I saw Barry coming straight at me. A weakness ran through my limbs. The dog jumped up on me with such force that I fell to the ground and he tried to bite me between my legs. I fought with him and pushed his head to the side, and his teeth sank into my thigh, until I felt them hit bone. I turned his head aside with all my strength and then he bit my backside. I do not know which was greater, my pain or my fear. Again I thought this was the end, but after the attack I continued working, my blood flowing into my pants. Later I changed my pants to a pair that I had taken from the ones I sorted.[160]

Kurt Thomas, born Kurt Ticho, was deported from Theresienstadt to Trawniki during April 1942, and was then sent to the Piaski Transit Ghetto. On November 6, 1942, he was deported from Piaski to Sobibór with approximately 3,000 Jews. He initially worked as a sorter:

After I had spent some time in the sorting barracks, I was transferred to a room where only smaller pieces of luggage were sorted. I found many valuables and a lot of notes. The Commandant's horses were stabled nearby and were looked after by Samuel Lerer, who was supervised by a Ukrainian called Dabizja. He

---

[160] Dov Freiberg, *To Survive Sobibor*, Gefen Publishing House, Jerusalem, 2007, pp. 204-205.

regularly came to visit my work place, taking anything he could lay his hands on.

When he came to see me one time, I gave him a few hundred Marks, for which he gave me a kilo of Polish sausage and a bottle of vodka. This became a routine. Every other day I gave him money, and he would give me the sausage and vodka. I used to pass the vodka on, because I did not drink myself, and just eat the sausage. That is what kept me going.[161]

Returning to the mass murder process, once the deportees had been stripped of all their possessions and clothes, the women were taken to have their hair cut off. Thomas 'Toivi' Blatt described what happened:

> Our job in this section done, *SS-Oberscharführer* Karl Frenzel randomly chose four prisoners, myself included, and led us to the hair-cutting barrack, less than twenty feet from the gas chambers. Inside were simple wooden chairs. Josef Wolf, a short, dark, middle-aged SS man stood in the centre of the room.
>
> I was given large shears and told to wait. The women began to come. I did not know what to do, 'Just snip quickly in bunches,' a comrade told me. 'It does not need to be close to the head.' I was terribly shy. I had never seen a nude woman before. Like all fifteen year olds I wanted to, but I felt embarrassed for the naked and humiliated women. I tried not directly at them, and they looked down and tried to cover themselves. Not all of the women reacted the same way. One woman resisted refusing to move. When the Nazi hit her with the whip, she attacked him with her fists and nails, but the German bullet was faster and killed her instantly. Now most were resigned and passive. A teenager wept at the loss of her lovely locks, asking not to have it cut too short.
>
> They were going to die in only a few minutes and there was nothing we could do. After the women left, we packed the hair into potato sacks, which were then brought to a nearby storeroom. After about three hours of work and over two thousand deaths, the SS men ordered us back to the barracks.

---

[161] J. Schelvis, *Sobibor*, Berg-Oxford, New York, 2007, p.84.

We were being counted. Everything was tallied—both the numbers of the murdered and those still living. As we moved on, the searchlights enveloping us were shut off one by one. It was a beautiful starry night. Nearing our barracks in *Lager I*, we heard rhythmic thuds coming from the direction of the gas chambers, like stones being thrown into a metal box. Later I learned what it was. Prisoners in the crematoria section were throwing the bodies onto the narrow-gauge dumpcarts that carried the corpses to the cremation site.[162]

In terms of the specialized *Arbeitsjuden*, Stanislaw Szmajzner who arrived in Sobibór on May 12, 1942, was a goldsmith and he was selected to work along with his brother Mosze, by Gustav Wagner. In his memoirs, Stanislaw Szmajzner remembered his work for the Germans:

> Next day, Wagner came in and told me: 'I have talked with Stangl and decided to have a ring made for each *SS-Scharführer*.' He then sat down and explained what he wanted the rings to be like. They must be made in silver with a gold badge. This badge would be in relief and consist of two letter Y's. The YY would be placed in such a way that one of them would be in a normal position, representing life. The other would be engraved right beneath it in an inverted position meaning death. It would then be a symbol of life and death, which incidentally suited the functions of their future owners. When Wagner finished his explanation, he urged me to work diligently and affirmed that the necessary metal would come to me soon. And then he left.
>
> For me to learn more about each of the SS Officers, I cut a small board into which I hammered as many nails as the number of rings I was to make. As the officers came in I would measure their fingers and hang the string with their names attached to it on each of the nails. The board hung on one of the walls and thanks to it I was able to not only make all the artifacts so as to please their owners, but also learn the names of nearly all of the torturers in Sobibór.

---

[162] T. Blatt, *From the Ashes of Sobibor* Northwestern University Press Illinois, 1997, pp. 101-102.

Stanislaw Szmajzner recalled how rings were made for the SS-Garrison:

> They began to come a few at a time and the number of nails with their names on gradually increased. Among the first gangs to appear I remember perfectly well, to this day, in an indelible way the following felons: Stangl, Gustav Wagner, Bolender and his bosom friend, nicknamed the 'Red Cake,' who will appear in the following lines in a sadly spectacular manner.
>
> Next to these prominent elements, there came the others whose perilousness and iniquity were no less remarkable, such as Karl Frenzel, Steubl, Bauer, Gomerski, Weiss, Poul, Vallaster and Michel. Besides these, I also remember other scoundrels whom I came to know later, such as Grinman, Graetschus, Richter, Beckmann, Groth, Getzinger, Bredow and another one who was called 'The Baker.'
>
> I received the silver and the gold sent by Wagner and started to make the sinister jewels. Once in a while a late-comer whose measure I had not taken yet, and whose name I had not copied would show up. The ones who most frequently visited our workshop were Stangl and Wagner. They went there to watch our work. Every time I would ask about the rest of my family and I always got the same answer—I should not worry because very soon we would be sent to the place where my parents were, it was only a matter of time.
>
> The days went by and the work on the rings went on without ceasing. The only ones who never came to watch us work were the Ukrainian guards. The same did not happen with the German officers, whose constant visits to our workshop made us interrupt our work quite frequently. They did not go there only to fetch the rings. It even seemed that these were not enough for them. They also wanted us to make them other jewels, since they had so much gold at their disposal, they did not know what to do with it. [163]

Stanislaw Szmajner recalled how Jankus his nephew was ordered by Kurt Bolender to come to him in *Lager II:*

---

[163] Stanislaw Szmajzner, *Hell in Sobibor*, (Unpublished English Version in authors collection) pp. 135-138.

In the afternoon, when I was already starting on the task, a *Scharführer* came to our workshops. His name was Bolender and brought very good company. It was a huge St. Bernard dog, which answered to the name of Barry. At first I thought it was tame. It did not bark at me, but stood quietly by its master. I was absolutely mistaken. I later learned it was a fierce watchdog.

Bolender was an officer with the *SS*. He was tall, stout and elegant looking. He was characterized by his manifest austerity and the constant use of a goatee, which gave him an imposing aspect. He was one of the leaders in *Lager III*, and one of the most important figures in Sobibór.

He approached me, threw a quick glance at the piece I had started to chase and then addressed me. It was soon evident that I was facing a very brutish man, because he ordered me in a very rude way to make a gold inlay in the handle of his whip. He also ordered me to fix a coin to the upper end of the handle. He had hardly finished talking when he threw on the table a handful of gold. It seemed to me that the Nazi did not know what he was doing, for the quantity of bullion he had brought was excessive. Before he left he ordered me to send my nephew, early next morning to *Lager II*, to fetch the coin, because he would be there then, although he worked in *Lager III*. I put away the material Bolender had brought and went on with my task for the rest of the afternoon and evening to be able to finish Wagner's monogram, as soon as possible. As the lights had been turned out, I worked by the light of an oil lamp.

During the day, another levy of prisoners had come to Sobibór, much larger than ours, as I later learned. However, as I supposed I was in a labor camp, I did not pay any attention to the fact, assuming that the Germans needed a larger number of men for the activities in the camp.

Soon after daybreak my ingenious nephew headed for the place Bolender had told him to go, without any suspicion. In order to get there he had to cross the yard where the rows of men who had come in the latest levy were waiting. By then the women had already left towards the mysterious gate and had disappeared behind it. He passed by the rows of Jews and went to the same gate through which he would reach the assigned place. He opened it and entered a long corridor which led to *Lager II*.

When he got to the end of the corridor he found himself inside a place which could very easily be taken for a giant corral, surrounded by boards so well juxtaposed that it would be impossible to see from the outside, what was going on inside it. The side of the corral nearest to the end of the corridor had a door which was guarded by a Ukrainian soldier. My nephew went up to him and said he was to meet Bolender, who had ordered him to be there at that hour. The brutal sentry did not pay any attention to him but opened the door and pushed him inside. Next he made the boy undress to the skin, without giving him the opportunity of explaining anything, heedless of his protests. Perhaps he acted like that because he thought the boy was part of the levy.

In the meanwhile I had finished Wagner's monogram and was starting to work on Bolender's whip. I was engrossed in my work and was already starting to worry about my nephew's delay, when the door was suddenly opened. It was the boy coming back, seized by indescribable panic. He was trembling and his face was ashen with terror. He was not able to say a word and he was obviously out of his mind. He sank into a deep depression, and did not make a simple gesture to justify his attitude. He was obviously deranged.

His nervous attack lasted for the rest of the day, and during the night, the others and I did all we could to make him tell us what had happened and what had shocked him in that way. All was in vain for he would not tell us anything. Only, at daybreak were we able to see him relax and come to himself again. He then started his unbelievable report. He told us that as soon as he had undressed inside what was known as *Lager II*, he had found himself face to face with a tragic scene, never before seen or imagined.

He saw a multitude of women, some of them naked and others in the process of undressing. Among the latter, the most reluctant to do so, had their clothes torn off their bodies by the brutal guards, while the others were forced to undress with whiplashes, rifle butts, and blows of every sort, not to mention the shots which were fired at them. At the same time, the loud noise made the place even more terrifying. There were shouts, weeping and laments mixed with begging for the Germans not to continue their nameless cruelty. The Nazis and their Ukrainian secretarians answered with shouts, curses, orders and blows.

He continued his petrifying description and told us he had witnessed right there something that would only be comparable with the times when Barbarian tribes roamed over Europe. Children of all ages were torn out of their mother's arms and held by the legs, they were twirled and violently thrown with their heads against the walls, falling dead to the floor. It was mass infanticide, impossible to conceive of in our modern age.

Amid the savage scene he had witnessed he had been able to see very clearly that one of the chiefs there was Bolender. This man apparently perfect for the task which he performed with the utmost pleasure, looked more like a jackal than a human being. His activity was feverish and he was resolute not only in emitting orders, but also in taking active part in the practice of vandalism.

To finish his report my nephew added that, by mere chance, he had been seen and recognized by the criminal who then called him. Bolender had next, amidst curses and rude words, taken out of his pocket a gold coin for twenty American dollars. He had next handed the coin to the boy and ordered a guard to lead him out of that place. Before he did that, though, he severely warned the boy not to go any place whenever a new levy came and to tell his companions to do the same. He also told him not to mention to anyone, under any circumstances, what he had seen there. [164]

Moshe Szklarek recalled the cruelty of Paul Groth, whom many prisoners, in their own accounts, remembered as being called Paul or Poul:

Groth was the leader of the Ukrainian columns, between the two rows of whom the camp prisoners were frequently ordered to pass. They were to be afflicted with leaden whips, rubber clubs and all kinds of flagellation instruments with which the servants of the Nazis, who stood on both sides of the row, were equipped.

Groth carried out this task with zeal and pleasure. He had a trusted assistant in this work, his dog Barry, a wild beast the size of a pony, well trained and obedient to the short, brutal orders of his master. When he heard Groth cry '*Jude*' the dog would attack his victim and bite him on the testicles. The bitten man was, of

---

[164] Stanislaw Szmajzner, *Hell in Sobibor*, (Unpublished English Version in authors collection) pp. 129-132.

course, no longer able to continue his work, and then Groth would take him aside and ask him in a sympathetic voice, 'Poor fellow, what happened to you? It certainly must be hard for you to keep working, isn't it? Come with me, I'll go with you to the clinic!'

And sure enough, Groth accompanied him, as he accompanied scores of workers every day to the *Lazarett*, to the giant grave behind the worn-out hut, where armed Ukrainian 'bandagers' greeted the sick and bitten men. In most cases, these men would place buckets on the heads of the victims, after they made them get into the pit, and would practice shooting, along with Groth, who was of course, always the most outstanding shot. Groth would return from the clinic satisfied and gay—and looking for more victims. His dog knew his masters temperament and helped in his murderous pleasures.

Sometimes Groth would have himself a joke, he would seize a Jew, give him a bottle of wine and sausage weighing at least a kilo and order him to devour it in a few minutes. When the lucky man succeeded in carrying out this order and staggered from drunkenness, Groth would order him to open his mouth and would urinate into his mouth.[165]

Stanislaw Szmajzner recalled the commandant Franz Stangl and Stangl's right-hand man Gustav Wagner in his post-war memoirs:

> Franz Stangl was at that time, extremely vain. He was always perfectly dressed, and his snobbery came to the point of being absurd. He regarded himself as being all powerful. And he actually was. His countenance reflected a lot of arrogance, in spite of some kind and tender traits. He doubtless looked snobbish. He was always well-groomed, his *Hauptmann's*—high ranking police officer—uniform was always shiny and well-pressed, and it fits beautifully his 1.74m of slender height.
>
> He usually wore a cap which showed that he still had all of his light-brown hair. He looked thirty years old and healthy. He always kept his white gloves swinging in one of his hands and his boots were like mirrors, clean and shiny. He had the air of a

---

[165] M. Gilbert, *The Holocaust—The Jewish Tragedy*, William Collins and Son, London 1986, p.326.

superior man, a peculiar characteristic of all Aryans, who revered their ancestry. He was always smiling, friendly, and happy, although at the cost of the unhappiness of others. He spoke slowly in a soft voice which betrayed his unshakeable calm. The words he pronounced sounded mild and affable, showing how well-bred and refined he was. His appearance was that of a University lecturer due to the mixture of attitudes that he deliberately presented.

The other one, Gustav Wagner, was a giant, nearly two meters tall. He had a huge body, must have weighed more than a hundred kilos and was as strong as an ox. His main peculiarity lay in the fact that he had extremely long arms, which went down to his knees, in an absurdly disproportionate way. He also had a severe deformity in one of his shoulders, which was much narrower than the other, and made him walk with a strange gait, always leaning towards the right. Besides, his way of swinging his body right and left gave him the appearance of an orangutan.

His face was like a skull made in granite, so rigid was it. His eyes were such a dark green that they could hypnotize anyone who looked fixedly at them. However, they were lusterless like those of a dead fish with no life or sparkle. [166]

Kalman Werwyk was deported from Chelm to Sobibór in November 1942, in the same transport as Shlomo Alster. He described the conditions in *Lager I*:

> At lunchtime they drove us into a big camp. There was one barrack there for Jewish women and two for Jewish men. Sobibór prisoners told me that 400 Jewish men and 200 Jewish women were kept there for work. They explained everything for me, one told me I was in a *'Vernichtungslager'*—an extermination camp. Although the Ukrainians had told me on the train, I had not believed them. But now I saw the place with my own eyes, I knew.
>
> The *Kapo's* yelled *'Eintreten!'* (line up), a *Kapo* stood by the kitchen with a whip in his hand and Jews lined up for food: a watery soup, a piece of bread, 10 deko (a deko is short for dekogram, and is a measure of weight) was given in the morning.

---

[166] Stanislaw Szmajzner, *Hell in Sobibor*, (Unpublished English Version in authors collection) pp. 120-121.

I slept in that area, called *Lager I*. We slept on bunks of rough wood made out of logs. There were four levels of bunks and 3-4 Jewish prisoners slept in each bunk. At night, people, some deranged and at the end of their sanity, were biting, scratching, tearing and clawing at each other. I heard many cry from hunger, others shrieked and moaned. The door was locked at night, so little pots were brought in as toilets. There was no light at all in the barracks—this was strictly forbidden—and hundreds of us were packed in there.[167]

Thomas 'Toivi' Blatt recalled the occasion he came close to the secret part of the camp, *Lager III*:

> *SS-Oberscharführer* Rudolf Beckmann, chief of the Administration Office, ordered two other prisoners and myself to go with him. He led us to a barren field between *Lager II* and *Lager III*. On a truck platform were two young girls about twenty-years of age, one of whom was completely nude and probably wounded. 'You,' he said, pointing at the other prisoners, 'carry the naked one. And you,' he pointed at me, 'go with the other one. Bring them to *Lager III*.' The girls were frightened but silent. I sensed their unspoken question, 'What was *Lager III*?' Beckmann followed briskly a few paces behind.
>
> As we walked, the girl whispered frantically in Polish, 'I've got money. Bribe the German. Help me do something!' She didn't know that the Germans would soon take her money as well as her life. 'Aren't you a Jew, how could you do this, doesn't your conscience bother you? Help us.' I didn't dare answer her. Beckmann was right behind me and it would be death for me as well. 'Am I going to die?' she asked. Should I answer yes? What good was the truth? I kept quiet.
>
> We came to the gate of the gas chamber compound. My heart pounded. I was terrified too. Would he order me in as well? 'Go back!' ordered Beckmann. I turned and ran like the wind. Minutes later I heard shots. The girls had been executed. I returned to my interrupted work, shaken. They were so young, good looking, in

---

[167] Kalman Werwyk, *To Sobibor and Back*, Private copy in author's possession.

the spring of their lives. And they were only two, out of hundreds of thousands like them.[168]

Stanislaw Szmajzner recalled an unexpected visit to his workshop by the *SS*-man Bolender accompanied by the *Kapo* in charge of *Lager III*, and his friend Abraham, who had written him the secret notes about conditions in *Lager III*:

> Some days later I had a great surprise. I was working in the machine shop when the criminal Bolender, the maniac Franz and my friend came in. They had come to look for nails. While these were being supplied, Bolender strolled over our quarters, and showed them to Franz. They looked as if they were close friends.
>
> There was a large number of Jews working at that time. As he walked slowly by, Franz started to deride us, calling us lazy. Franz and some others had things. He seemed to want to be taken for a *Scharführer*, because he said loud and clear, that our place should be *Lager III*, and not that paradise where we lived like princes.
>
> In his sickly enthusiasm, he added that he would like to see us in his camp and to show us how we would work under his command. When he passed by me, he made a point of pretending he did not know me, even after our eyes had crossed. Meanwhile, Bolender smiled in scorn, as if he approved of everything his faithful disciple said.
>
> A little later, Abraham gestured to me to make me understand I should not expect to see him again. He was unrecognizable. He looked extremely depressed and was dressed in rags. He showed he was in a state of severe moral collapse and he did not in the least resemble the strong happy boy of yesterday. He was not the same one I had known.
>
> Some minutes later they left, taking the nails with them, and headed towards their hell. From that day on I never had any other news from my dear friend Abraham.[169]

---

[168] T. Blatt, *From the Ashes of Sobibor* Northwestern University Press Illinois, 1997, pp. 103-104.
[169] Stanislaw Szmajzner, *Hell in Sobibor*, (Unpublished English Version in authors collection) pp. 190-191.

Leon Felhendler recalled how the corpses were disposed of:

> In the first period there was no crematorium. After gassing, the people were laid into the graves. Then out of the soil, blood and a bad odour of gas began to surface: terrible smells spread over the whole camp, penetrating everything. The water in Sobibór became rancid. This forced the Germans to build a crematorium. It was a large pit with a roaster above it. The bodies were thrown on the roaster. The fire was ignited from beneath, and petrol was poured on the corpses. The bones were crushed into ashes with hammers.[170]

Philip Bialowitz recalled the bartering went on between the *Arbeitsjuden* and the Ukrainian guards. The goldsmiths worked in the old Forester's House, which now served as the camp administration building in *Lager II*. This was located opposite to where the Jews undressed:

> I recall that *Arbeitsjuden* bartered with Ukrainian guards in the *Goldkammer* (Gold Room). Reichleitner the camp commandant got involved in the case and had three Jews and two Ukrainian guards shot. The Ukrainians were shot in *Lager IV* in front of all the men. We all had to witness the executions, as a warning against taking part in such bartering. The executions were led by an *Unterführer* (probably Graetschus) and carried out by Ukrainians.[171]

Kurt Thomas remembered his role as a Medical Orderly in Sobibór:

> As soon as I had been appointed *Sanitäter* (Medical Orderly), I set up a card system, recording the name, start date and temperature for each of the patients. I brought them water and food, and whatever else I could find or do for them. Most of the time, the permitted three days were insufficient for a full recovery. In order to stick to the legal term, I would replace the old cards with new ones on the fourth day, recording a new starting date, which was against the rules. It was my intention to give the patients—in spite of the danger I put myself in a better chance of being cured,

---

[170] Y. Arad, *Belzec, Sobibor, Treblinka*, Indiana University Press, Bloomington and Indianapolis 1987, p.172.
[171] J. Schelvis, *Sobibor*, Berg-Oxford, New York, 2007, p.84.

enabling them to return to their commandos, so they would not be sent to the *Lazarett*.

At every roll call I was required to report the number of patients. The number I gave would be added to that of those present and the number of deceased, so that the total matched the previous number. Frenzel accepted my figure, usually he was not concerned about the patients. For months I also sheltered two other men in barracks during the day. One was 20-year old Kiewe Herz, whose toes were frozen, he could not walk. The other was Jossel Siegel, about 15-years old, whose toes were also frozen. I kept them in the barracks illegally, as patients. They would attend roll calls only, so they were not counted among the patients.

I was allowed to get very basic medication, bandages and other supplies from a special storeroom. I got them from my friend Leon Halberstadt, who gave me whatever the doctors had advised me. There was a kind of spray, for instance, which I used for freezing wounds or bruises.

Once in a while, Frenzel would call for the patients and send them to *Lager III*, sometimes he would take them there himself. They would never be seen again. Wagner on the other hand, who hardly ever took roll calls, always wanted to verify their actual presence. In that case I had to reel off all the names on the cards, standing by the door to the barracks. He would count the voices of those who answered, to assure himself that no one was missing. My card index was therefore of great importance.

On October 11, 1943, the Monday before the revolt, Frenzel asked me again how many patients I had. I replied, 'Fourteen, *Herr Oberscharführer*.' This time he wanted to verify for himself. He recognized ten people who had been ill a few weeks earlier. He had them brought over and without any consultation with the Commandant sent them straight to *Lager III*. Then lashing out at me with his whip he said, 'Your turn next time.' Thanks to the revolt shortly after, it never got to that point.[172]

Itzhak Lichtman was deported on foot with other members of his family from Zolkiewka to Krasnystaw station, where they boarded

---

[172] Ibid, pp.86-87.

cattle cars bound for Sobibór on May 22, 1942. He takes up the story:

> Guards take us to the barracks of the shoemakers. In a corner we saw pieces of leather and on a table, remains of food. Who had been here before? Soon we would stop asking that question and understand we were in another Bełżec.
>
> An *SS* man gave us the measurements of the *Lagerkommandant* and ordered a pair of shoes immediately. We obeyed and the SS man seemed pleased. *'Ihr bleibt bis zum Schluss.'* (You will stay to the end). What end? The gas chambers?
>
> We were five shoemakers, Shaul Fleishhacker from Kalisz, Schlomo, nicknamed the 'Negro,' Berek Lichtman, a cousin of mine and I. In the second workshop, there were eight to ten Ukrainians, who mended the boots.
>
> The *SS* ordered two sets of boots and slippers for each of them, and shoes for their families. We wanted to live and avenge ourselves, and to see the end of Sobibór.[173]

Thomas 'Toivi' Blatt explained how the Germans destroyed the photographs and documents of the murdered Jews, and how he became known as the 'Fireman' by the *SS* and *Kapo's*:

> Not far from the sorting sheds was a big pit where teenagers Sznul Wajcen from Chodorow and Meir Ziss from Zolkiewka worked burning documents, photo albums, letters and so on. It was an ideal place to work. The ditch was deep and always surrounded by thick smoke. The Germans did not come close, and there was no supervision... I pitched in to help.
>
> Later a special oven was built in an enclosed building to prevent burning papers from being dispersed by the wind. The pit was levelled and we were now hidden in a building out of view. Szmul later was transferred and I was put in charge of the burning and given another helper, Blind Karolek, so nicknamed because he only had one good eye.
>
> To start a fire, I laid out some wood, identification papers, and torn books, and lit the pile. The oven ablaze again, was stuffed to

---

[173] Miriam Novitch, *Sobibo*r, Holocaust Library, New York, 1980, p.83.

> capacity. The flames hummed and crackled through the tall chimney. All books were supposed to be burned, but I always tried to save some to look at, if I could get away with it. I had always loved books, and I would risk my life to smuggle out a book to read in some barrack corner.[174]

Herschel Cuckierman and his family were deported from Nalencow during May 1942. He worked with his son Josef in the kitchen in *Lager I*, as a Cook, and he prepared the food for the workers in *Lager III*:

> I came up with the idea. Every day I used to send twenty or twenty-five buckets with food for the workers in *Lager III*. The Germans were not interested in what I cooked, so once I prepared a thick crumb pie and inside I put the following letter: 'Friends, write what is going on in your camp.' When I received the buckets back, I found in one of them a piece of paper with the answer: 'Here the last human march takes place from this place nobody returns. Here the people turn cold.' I informed some other people about the substance of this letter.[175]

Abraham Margulies was deported from Zamosc to Sobibór at the end of May 1942. He described his work in the kitchen for Jewish prisoners:

> There were three kitchens in the camp: one for the SS personnel under Wagner's supervision. He used to select very young girls whom he enjoyed beating up. A second kitchen was for the Ukrainian guards. Krupka, their chief, hated the Germans and often gave us news from the front. He promised to contact the partisans and we gave him some gold to take to them, but the attack on the camp never took place and Krupka disappeared.
>
> Hershel Cuckierman from Kurow, was in charge of the Jewish kitchen. After the cleaning of the carriages, I was assigned to help in the kitchen, but didn't stay long. I tried to smuggle some food to women who worked in the laundry, and Frenzel caught me and sent me back to the wagons. An old German Klier, supervised the

---

[174] T. Blatt, *From the Ashes of Sobibor* Northwestern University Press Illinois, 1997, pp. 121-122.
[175] Y. Arad, *Belzec, Sobibor, Treblinka*, Indiana University Press, Bloomington and Indianapolis 1987, p.79.

bakery and was quite humane. At night he used to bring bread into our camp.[176]

Eda Lichtman, who was deported to Sobibór on June 2, 1942, recalled her first day in Sobibór:

> We were ordered to clean thoroughly a villa where the Germans lived. After work we were taken to an area with some barracks, surrounded by a barbed-wire fence, where we were given a room with three wooden beds, one over the other. Close to our room lived the skilled workers.
>
> In the evening, two men brought two big boxes with dirty laundry, and a Ukrainian guard told us it should be ready within two days. The washing required many different kinds of work. The laundry was full of lice, so first of all it had to be disinfected. We had to raise the water from a deep well with heavy wooden buckets tied to a rope. The laundry had to be boiled, at a distant place. The wet laundry was transported in a baby carriage.[177]

Eda also recalled her first night in the death camp:

> I remember that first night. I heard screams, and opened the door, but received lashes of a whip across my face. *Oberwachmann* Lachmann, who was taking his dog for a walk, shouted, 'If I see you here again, I shall send you Barry (the dog).' Later I learned that these screams came from young girls who were raped before being gassed.
>
> From our barrack, I could hear people begging for water. From time to time, a prisoner was allowed to go to the well where the *Volksdeutsche*[178] Michel was waiting. With his bayonet, he pushed the wretched victim to the latrines. 'Gather your excrement with your bare hands!' he screamed. Then he led the prisoner to the guard Malinowski, who shot him.[179]

Regina Zielenski, formerly Feldman, was deported to Sobibór from the Staw-Nowosiulki Labor Camp on December 20, 1942,

---

[176] Miriam Novitch, *Sobibor*, Holocaust Library, New York, 1980, p.64.
[177] Y. Arad, *Belzec, Sobibor, Treblinka*, Indiana University Press, Bloomington and Indianapolis 1987, p.114.
[178] Michel was not *Volksdeutscher*, he was born near Berlin.
[179] Miriam Novitch, *Sobibor*, Holocaust Library, New York, 1980, p.55.

and she was selected to knit socks for the *SS*, but later she was put to work in the laundry:

> It was early in April 1943, when I had a middle-ear infection and was unable to do my work as a washer-woman. One day I found it hard to get started with my work and sat down for a bit in another room, just to have a little rest. I was discovered by an *SS*-man who took me to Gustav Wagner. Wagner decided I should get ten lashes. He led me to a woodpile and made me bend over it, pulled up my skirt and gave me the ten lashes himself, using a whip which was longer than a normal riding whip.
>
> It consisted of rubber-coated steel rods, with knots at the end. I sustained a permanent kidney injury, and later my right kidney had to be surgically removed. That was aside from the other injuries to my back and front caused by the rod ends coiling around my body as I received the lashes.[180]

Eda Lichtman described an incident with the Ukrainian guard Koszewadski, in the laundry:

> One day, the Ukrainian Koszewadski brought the white uniform of his chief *Oberwachmann* Lachmann, and ordered me to have it ready by 5 o'clock the next day. 'But it won't be ready!' I said. To answer a guard! The Ukrainian began to hit me, when the prisoner Itzhak caught his hand. 'Aren't you ashamed to hit a woman who is working so hard?' Koszewadski left the barrack, he never hit a woman again.[181]

There was a small farm *in Lager II*, where the Nazis kept their horses in a stable, and they also kept cattle, pigs and geese. Thomas 'Toivi' Blatt wrote in his memoirs:

> The Jews who worked in the stable and with other household animals were held responsible for the health of the animals. Max a stablemaster was severely beaten and sent to *Lager III*, where he was executed for lightly hitting a horse. Shaul Stark, in charge of the geese, was killed when one goose died.[182]

---

[180] J. Schelvis, *Sobibor*, Berg-Oxford, New York, 2007, p.91.
[181] Miriam Novitch, *Sobibor*, Holocaust Library, New York, 1980, p.61.
[182] T. Blatt, *Sobibor—The Forgotten Revolt*, H.E.P, Issaquah, 1998, p. 51.

Jakub Biskubicz testified at the Adolf Eichmann Trial in Jerusalem on June 5, 1961, about a narrow escape that he experienced in Sobibór:

> Not everyone had the opportunity, but by chance I was taken to bring a cart with a barrel of chloride. When I was passing by the two large stores in Camp II, I detached the cart and pushed it towards Camp III. I was supposed to leave it near the gate, but I couldn't hold the vehicle back. The gate opened and it pushed me inside. Since I knew I would not get out alive from there, I begun to run back at top speed and managed to reach my place of work without anyone noticing. I kept this a secret—I am stressing this—even from the inmates of the camp who worked with me.
>
> From a distance I saw the pit and the hollow and the small train that carried the dead bodies. I did not see the gas chambers from the inside: I only saw from the outside that there was a very prominent roof and that the floor opened and the bodies fell below. I did not see that the floor opened up—I merely saw that underneath the gas chambers, there was a hollow that already contained bodies.[183]

Dov Freiberg recounted his work in the forest with the *Waldkommando* near the *Lazarett*:

> Another parade, and all sorting workers joined the *Waldkommando* (Forest workers) this time. SS-men Gomerski and Getzinger along with some Ukrainians led us. We crossed the open area between *Lager II*, and the forest from the right side, near the camp fence and the railway tracks, passing the *Lazarett*—a small wooden building with a tiled roof. From the roof rose a cross—this must have been a church at a local cemetery. Close by rose a mound of earth next to a pit. This was the pit where our friends had been killed. A shudder passed through my body. Perhaps they had decided to execute us?
>
> But we continued marching into the forest. After about a hundred meters, we saw a barbed-wire fence on the left, and behind it, a hill of white sand about twenty meters high. Hills of sand are unusual in a forest and indeed the hill looked suspicious.

---

[183] www.Nizkor—online resource. Adolf Eichmann Transcripts.

We were ordered to barrel load logs that had been cut down by the *Waldkommando* onto our shoulders and bring them to the camp, where they were to be used for electricity poles and for the construction of the camp expansion. This loading work was crushing. The Germans and the Ukrainians whipped us mercilessly.

It was particularly difficult for me, because as I was short, my shoulders often did not reach the height of the log. As a result I had to work on the tips of my toes—both to help the others and so that the Germans would not notice that I was not helping in the loading. But sometimes the full weight of the heavy log pressed down on me, and every time this happened I was close to collapse.[184]

Philip Bialowitz explains the role of the *Waldkommando* in his memoirs:

One evening Symcha tells me how Wagner had selected him to join the *Waldkommando*. This group of prisoners had been sent to the woods with axes and saws to cut down trees and chop the wood that was probably necessary to fuel Camp 3's crematorium.

At one point the prisoners had to cut through nearly the entire trunk of a very tall tree. But just before they could finish, Wagner had ordered Symcha and several other prisoners to climb the trees and tie a rope near the top branches. This rope could be used to pull down the tree and thus save a small amount of time. But right after they placed the rope, Wagner had forced the remaining prisoners to pull the rope while the people were still in the tree.

The tree had toppled down with Symcha and several others perched on the branches. Every prisoner had hung on to the branches as best he could. Several had lost their lives in the tree. Others had broken bones, which itself is a death sentence, because now they will be killed for being unable to work. But Symcha has somehow escaped with only some scratches and bruises.[185]

---

[184] Dov Freiberg, *To Survive Sobibor*, Gefen Publishing House, Jerusalem, 2007, pp. 219-220.
[185] Philip Bialowtiz, *A Promise At Sobibor*, The University of Wisconsin Press, Madison, Wisconsin, 2010, p.86.

Thomas 'Toivi' Blatt recalled how the SS established an orchestra in the camp:

> A camp orchestra was formed with first rate musicians and the sentimental Polish Folk song, *Goralu, czy Ci nie zal?* (Highlander, Have you no regrets?) was often sung. It was probably introduced by the SS, who were transferred from the Bełżec death camp, where it had been the camp song since early summer of 1942. The orchestra performed after work, or whenever ordered. Jews were taught the SS military drill songs and were forced to sing in flawless unison, while marching to or returning from work.

This song indeed was the camp song at Bełżec, much loved by *SS-Oberscharführer* Reinhold Feix. It was also a favourite at the Treblinka death camp.

Dov Freiberg also recalled how the SS created an orchestra in Sobibór:

> The Germans selected musicians and established a small orchestra, which would play on Sundays. More than once we were forced to dance to its music. And sometimes, when transports arrived, the orchestra would be called to play, to the wonder of the people in the transport.
>
> A cabaret singer—from Holland or France—also arrived at the camp and she sang in many languages. Sometimes all the Germans would gather, the orchestra would play and the singer would sing. Her voice was pure and deep and she sang plaintive songs, and although I didn't understand their words, they made my tears catch in my throat. After a short while the singer was taken to the *Lazarett*, and we never heard her voice again.[186]

He also recalled the German marching songs that accompanied the military drillings:

> The Germans spent many hours training the new workers in parade exercises and German songs. On Sundays, in the afternoon, one could see the groups marching here and there under German,

---

[186] Dov Freiberg, *To Survive Sobibor*, Gefen Publishing House, Jerusalem, 2007, p.254.

Ukrainian and *Kapo* supervision, in the area between *Lager I* and *Lager II*.

Shouts and orders were given non stop: *Links, Links* (Left, left), *Marsch* (March). One group sang 'The Blue Dragoons,' other groups were made to run, and people fell and got up, crawled and jumped, and the orders followed each other closely. [187]

Continuing with the musical theme, Selma Engel recounted in a post-war interview, how the Germans made the prisoners dance in the evenings:

> I remember that we all assorted the clothes and then after four or five o'clock I had to assort even the clothes from the uncle, from the man with five children, who were also in the transport. At five o'clock we had to go on roll-call, and we were brought to *Lager I*, where we slept.
>
> And when we came to *Lager I*, we had to dance for the Germans. There were some Jews who had instruments, who were already longer in the camp. In between, the fire was burning—it was like this over the whole camp, it was very big, very big!
>
> And we had to dance, the Germans were standing there laughing and having fun... and it was an order, we had to dance. Chaim—my husband—asked me to dance and that was the first time I met Chaim.[188]

Estera Raab remembered the tragic murder of a seamstress and her baby by Gustav Wagner, in a post-war interview:

> She came into the camp with her husband, he was a good tailor, and she was an excellent seamstress and the Nazis didn't wear underwear from plain material, everything had to be made from silk, the shirts, the underwear, they brought a lot of silk from the parachutes, and she used to be able, if you told her out of this piece has to come three shirts and three items of underwear—it came out. I don't know how she did it.
>
> First of all was the baby, second of all, again to do something against the Nazis, you know maybe we'll be able; it was a

---

[187] Ibid. p.254.
[188] Interview with Selma Engel by USHMM on July 16, 1990.

> challenge at the same time, and so she kept it for two weeks. And once Wagner walked in unannounced, unexpected and he heard the baby, and he gave her a choice. He gave her a choice, just because they needed her, otherwise they wouldn't have.
>
> And what mother would give up her baby? And she just spat in his face right then and there and they shot them both. But they were such murderers, that they had to shoot the baby first, so the mother would die with more pain.[189]

Eda Lichtman recalled how Gustav Wagner and other members of the SS-Garrison raided the Sorting Barracks for gifts when they returned home on leave:

> Whenever other Germans came to visit. Wagner would order me to get some nice things together for him to pass on as gifts. They were all handed out these parcels containing Jewish property. One day Wagner came to me and said, 'My wife is tall and blonde. I am going on holiday and I need several things. Put a parcel together for me.' I put in some baby clothes for his daughter, and also a white fur cape, which must have belonged to a child of rich Jewish parents.
>
> We put parcels together for all the officers, always with dolls and clothing. Frenzel, Wagner and Niemann particularly wanted the dolls. We also sewed uniforms for the *Hitlerjugend* at the camp, which made the Urlaubers (officers on leave) very happy.[190]

In June 1943, an area surrounding the Sobibór death camp was mined to a distance of approximately seventeen yards from the outer fence, in order to fend off potential attacks by partisans. A single wire was suspended above the ground stating '*Achtung Minen.*' This was the direct result of a successful escape attempt by Josel Pelc, a carpenter from Tyszowice, and Yasha, a bricklayer from Chelm, who escaped in the middle of the night by cutting the barbed-wire fences. Thomas 'Toivi' Blatt takes up the story:

> The Germans consulted among themselves and *Scharführer* Frenzel announced the verdict: each tenth prisoner in the rows of the

---

[189] Interview with Ester Raab, by the USHMM, February 18, 1992.
[190] J. Schelvis, *Sobibor*, Berg-Oxford, New York, 2007, p.85.

> roll-call would be executed. He approached my group. I was seized with fear, he is in the row behind me. My God, only not me—a man is an egoist. The third from me became the victim. After the selection the doomed were taken to *Lager III*, and we went to work. Afterwards we heard shots, and later the clothes of those who had been killed were brought for sorting.[191]

A transport of some 5,000 prisoners arrived in Sobibór from the Lublin Concentration Camp, they were dressed in striped prisoners clothes. Many had died en-route, and many were in a very weakened state. Dov Freiberg was one of those who were ordered to remove the corpses that remained on the square. He wrote about what happened next:

> The SS man Frenzel selected twenty prisoners and told us we should work naked, because the corpses were dirty and full of lice. We had to take the dead to the trolley, a distance of about 200 meters. In spite of the fact that we were used to this kind of work, I cannot describe our feelings when we carried the dead on our naked bodies.
>
> The Germans urged us on with shouts and blows. While I was dragging a man's body, I stopped for a while, and not seeing a German nearby, I laid it on the ground. And then this body, which I thought was dead man, rose up, looked at me with great eyes and asked, 'Is it still far.' He said these words with great effort, and collapsed. At that moment I felt lashes on my head and back. The SS man Frenzel whipped me. I caught the living-dead by his feet and dragged him to the trolley.[192]

Herschel Cukierman, who worked in the prisoner's kitchen, and Volodia Koszewadski, the *Trawnikimänner* who supervised the kitchen, became friends. Koszewadski informed him that he had contacts with the partisans and needed money to spring an escape from Sobibór. Herschel Cukierman testified:

---

[191] Y. Arad, *Belzec, Sobibor, Treblinka*, Indiana University Press, Bloomington and Indianapolis 1987, p.266.

[192] Dov Freiberg, *To Survive Sobibor*, Gefen Publishing House, Jerusalem, 2007, pp. 245-246.

Koszewadski used to say that a day would come and he would open the gates of the camp for us. Whether his intention was that he would do it for money or for moral reasons, I did not know. I had full confidence in him. He told me that he was going to the friends in the forest and he needed money to get weapons. I spoke about this to Leon Felhendler.

Koszewadski told me about a talk he had had with a certain doctor in Chelm, who was in contact with the partisans. According to him an attack on the camp was impossible, because the camp was heavily guarded. In addition, he said such an attack would cause the death of the prisoners in the camp, because the Germans would kill them. Koszewadski and the doctor proposed to poison the Germans and the Ukrainians who collaborated with them. The poisoning had to be carried out by two Jewish boys who worked in the German kitchen. The poison was to take effect after six hours. The partisans would arrive that evening to liberate us. But this plan failed. An officer arrived from Lublin who ordered that no Jews were to work in the German kitchen. The prisoners who worked in the German and Ukrainian kitchens were transferred to another working place.[193]

Zelda Metz, who arrived in Sobibór on December 20, 1942, and Arkadij Wajspapir who arrived in Sobibór in September 1943, described the daily routine in Sobibór:

> In the early morning specially assigned prisoners, referred to as *Kapos* would wake us. Then there was breakfast, consisting of 150 grams of *Schwarzbrot* (dark rye bread) and a mug of hot water or coffee, after which we were put to work.
>
> If we worked in the *Nordlager*, we would go through a gate leading into the area where the SS men lived in their little cabins. We left them to the right of us as we went along the railway line and into the *Nordlager*. At lunchtime we were given some soup that we used to call *Plorre*, without bread. After finishing this dishwater, we would labour until dark.
>
> Then we were driven back to the *Lager I* area and given our evening meal: 100 grams of *Schwarzbrot* and a mug of hot water. After

---

[193] Y. Arad, *Belzec, Sobibor, Treblinka*, Indiana University Press, Bloomington and Indianapolis 1987, pp.300-301.

the evening meal, the *Kapo* would bring us to one of the smaller areas in *Lager I* for an inspection, after which we would go to sleep in the barracks. We slept on bare wooden bunks, there were no blankets....

I knew *SS*-officer Frenzel, who led our building commando. To call him barbaric would be an understatement. He was an outright sadist. Frenzel always held his leather whip at the ready, and would strike the prisoners over the head, across the face or any other part of the body, for no reason at all. Many prisoners were permanently crippled or even died as a result.

I remember one time when some prisoners were being flogged. One day early in October 1943, as they were marching us back into *Lager I* after our day's labour in the *Nordlager*, Frenzel, as usual forced us to sing songs as we went along. We sang, '*Immer höher und höher und höher, streben wir dem Flug unserer Vögel nach*' (higher and higher we go, after our birds in flight)—the birds referred to the Russian aeroplanes. As soon as Gomerski, who was standing by the gate to the first *Lager*, heard us singing this, he threw himself on us, screaming and cursing, and lashing out at the prisoners with his whip.[194]

Leon Felhendler wrote about a transport that arrived in Sobibór from *Lemberg*, in June 1943:

> There were fifty freight cars all together—twenty-five with living prisoners, and twenty-five with corpses. The living were nude. In the freight car with the killed, the corpses were mingled without any wounds, only swollen. The prisoners were forced to unload the freight cars and put the corpses on the trolley to the crematorium. The smell of the corpses made it impossible to enter the freight cars. The Germans whipped us to force us to enter them. From the state of disintegration of the bodies, these people had been dead for about two weeks.[195]

Thomas 'Toivi' Blatt recalled how the cremation rails were replaced, by stealing from the *Ostbahn:*

---

[194] J. Schelvis, *Sobibor*, Berg-Oxford, New York, 2007, pp. 87-88.
[195] Y. Arad, *Belzec, Sobibor, Treblinka*, Indiana University Press, Bloomington and Indianapolis 1987, p. 129.

In the middle of the night, *Oberscharführer Wagner* asked for volunteers. Because I was always on the alert for potential escape routes, I volunteered, despite Wagner's reputation as a volatile killer.... A group of twenty Jews assembled in pairs. *SS* Wagner led us to the main gate. From there under heavy Ukrainian guard, we marched outside the camp. The night was beautiful. In the moonlight, I could see the village train station and neighbouring cottages. It was so peaceful. If not for the silhouette of the tall *SS* man and the outstretched rifles of the guards, it might as well have been an evening stroll.

Wagner led us along the railroad for about five minutes, finally stopping next to a pile of neatly stacked reserve railroad rails. Beyond the alert chain of guards, the forest tempted me with its dark wall of trees. But it was impossible to get away.

Now we were ordered to pick up a rail. The gate opened again and we were back in another hellish world. We marched straight towards the direction of *Lager III*, and left the rails near the gate. This was simply the way the burned out grates of the pyres were replaced. I was wondering why, with all their might, the *SS* stole the rails at night. But I assume the clever *SS* Wagner had found that this eliminated the hassle of going through regular channels.[196]

Alexander Pechersky, who led the prisoner revolt, was taken to Sobibór on September 22, 1943, and he described the *Nordlager*:

> Soldiers led us to the *Nordlager*, a new section of the camp. Nine barracks were already built there and others were under construction. Our group was split in two: one part was sent to build, the other to cut wood. On our first day of work, fifteen people got twenty-five lashes each for incompetence.
>
> On September 25, we unloaded coal all day, and were given only twenty minutes for lunch. The cook[197] was unable to feed us all in such a short time. Frenzel was furious and ordered the cook to sit down. Then he whipped him while whistling a march tune. The

---

[196] T. Blatt, *From the Ashes of Sobibor* Northwestern University Press Illinois, 1997, pp. 113-114.
[197] The cook was Herschel Cuckierman.

soup tasted as though it had been mixed with blood, and although we were very hungry, many of us were unable to eat.[198]

Thomas 'Toivi' Blatt described the activity in *Lager IV*, the so-called *Nordlager*:

> A new extension of the camp was being built, called *Lager IV*, or North. Bunker—like storerooms were being constructed. Rumours were that this would be a sorting centre for Soviet ammunition. From conservations with prisoners working there, I found out that watchtowers on the newly enlarged perimeter were not yet completed and some stretches of forest were not yet fenced in. The Ukrainian guards there were cruel, but the area seemed not to be guarded heavily. Maybe this was the way to escape!
>
> I saw my chance. Prisoners from *Lager I* were building a road in the North Camp, and I volunteered to go there. In charge was *SS-Scharführer* Arthur Dachsel. At fifty-five, Dachsel was the oldest Nazi in Sobibór. He was also one of the least vicious, he seemed to protect 'his' prisoners from beatings by other guards, if only to keep us in good working condition. I cut down the small trees, cut the trunks into fifteen foot segments, and laid them aside to use as foundations for the new wooden road. I kept myself clean and walked straight, Dachsel took notice.
>
> When there were no more saplings in the immediate area, he put me in charge of a group of tree cutters deeper inside the forest. It was an easy job. I'd line up the men and march them off like an army platoon.... We were guarded only by Ukrainians, and I would have the men sing racy Ukrainian songs to keep the guards in a good mood and thereby prevent beatings. My strategy worked.[199]

Thomas 'Toivi' Blatt sought from *SS*-man Arthur Dachsel a transfer to the log road construction commando, and he was put in charge of this workgroup, and he explained the work:

> We dug long, narrow channels for larger logs, which would form the main support for the new wooden road. It was to run for about three hundred yards, through *Lager IV*. Where the road was to

---

[198] Miriam Novitch, *Sobibor*, Holocaust Library, New York, 1980, p.90.
[199] T. Blatt, *From the Ashes of Sobibor* Northwestern University Press Illinois, 1997, p.110.

make a left turn, I made an engineering mistake. Not understanding the instructions given by SS Dachsel, I built the turn flat instead of with a higher angle at the curve. The angry but still even-tempered German relieved me of my 'instructor job' and I was again a regular worker. Shortly thereafter the road was finished, and I returned to *Lager II*.[200]

Leon Felhendler's wife Estera gave a version of another planned escape during 1943, based on what her husband told her; It involved setting fire to the clothing stores, and that whilst the Germans and Ukrainians were busy putting out the fires, the prisoners would escape through the gates and flee to the forests:

> A young boy agreed to remain in the clothing store and set it on fire. This was to draw the attention of the Germans and be the sign for the mass escape. He was closed inside the store. As he bid farewell, he wished all the others luck and expressed his happiness for his sacrifice. But at the last moment, before the fire could be set, some Germans appeared, and being either drunk or suspecting something was wrong, they went round the storage barrack. And then Felhendler, seeing that this time the plan could not succeed, opened the store with the key he had, and pulled out the boy, who was in despair because the plan had failed.[201]

Some work was undertaken outside of the death camp by the inmates, and Stanislaw Szmajzner recalled a trip to the nearby former ghetto in Włodawa during early 1943:

> One day Wagner called me and ordered me to get my main tools ready. This time though, it was not going to be my goldsmith tools, but those I used to fix the metal parts of cars. He told me we were going on a trip. I gathered my tools... A few moments later there came a truck under heavy SS escort. We got in, twelve people altogether, for other Jews had also been called. We did not have the slightest idea as to the reasons of that strange trip.
>
> At the end of the trip we noticed we were approaching Włodawa, the truck drove to the sector where the old Włodawa ghetto had

---

[200] Ibid p. 112.
[201] Y. Arad, *Belzec, Sobibor, Treblinka*, Indiana University Press, Bloomington and Indianapolis 1987, p. 302.

been. The ghetto was already literally deserted. All its inhabitants had been evacuated and led away to be exterminated. The place was even gloomy with all the abandoned buildings. We could not see anyone nor hear anything.

Finally, the vehicle came to a halt. The Boches showed us two of the best houses there and told us to demolish them. They warned us, however, that all the material should be removed in the most perfect condition. Thus, both houses had to be taken apart very carefully. The roof, the doors, the windows, the boards, and the locks, as well as all the other components were to be carried intact to Sobibór, and re-assembled there. I was told to dismantle the zinc roof and to take off the locks and hinges. While I worked, my thoughts continuously turned to escape. In my mind, my ideas were in turmoil, but common sense prevailed.

We went back to the camp and we promptly started assembling the houses. One of them was destined to serve as lodgings for four officers. The other would be raised next to the small railroad station of the hamlet, which had given its name to the camp, outside its limits.

When the first one was completed, we had the opportunity of seeing what level the effrontery of the Boches would reach. They had a sign painted with the following words—'Birds Nest.' They should have written on the sign something referring to a snake pit, as that house would be called by us from then on.[202]

Thomas 'Toivi' Blatt also recalled how demolition work was also being undertaken in the nearby town of Włodawa, in his memoirs, titled *From The Ashes of Sobibór*:

The Germans were doing some demolition work in the nearby town of Włodawa. A small group of Jewish prisoners, with Ukrainian guards and *SS-Oberscharführer* Dubois in charge went there by train each day to work.

Before the morning roll call, I would hang around the group of prisoners designated to work in Włodawa. Maybe someone would get sick. Maybe they would take one more person. I waited for a chance. Within only a few days one prisoner was so brutally

---

[202] Stanislaw Szmajzner, *Hell in Sobibor*, (Unpublished English Version in authors collection) pp. 212-213.

beaten by Wagner that he wasn't able to work. I asked to take his place, and the Kapo agreed.

It was still dawn when we left the camp for the village train station. Soon a regularly scheduled train arrived. The Germans took one car, putting guards at each door and we made it to the town. We walked from the train station to the centre of town, a distance of about a mile. On the way, a group of Poles was walking towards us on the narrow sidewalk. One man didn't get out the way fast enough for our German guard. He beat the Pole until he was unconscious.

This day our work consisted of dismantling the ovens of a Jewish owned bakery. Sobibór needed fire-resistant bricks. Although Włodawa was already officially *Judenrein*, about 150 Jewish girls worked there under local supervision, sorting the spoils of the abandoned Jewish households. We could see them nearby and thought we might be able to help them. Risking torture and death—the likely result of unexpected searches often conducted by the SS guards—we smuggled money and other valuables to Włodawa. We hoped that the female slaves would find them and use them to save themselves by buying false papers or food. Eventually though, most of these girls were brought to Sobibór and gassed.

As we marched to and from work we were forced to sing. Poles stopped on the streets in confusion and looked at us. When had they last seen Jews, let alone young and healthy-looking Jews, singing happy songs? They didn't know what to make of it. When they found out we were from Sobibór, the whole street emptied in fear.

In a few weeks the brick transfer was finished. There had been no chance of escape. Not only did the Germans watch us closely, but the prisoners watched each other. We knew that if anyone escaped, everyone would be held responsible. And a mass escape in the middle of a town full of Nazi collaborators would be doomed to failure.[203]

---

[203] T. Blatt, *From the Ashes of Sobibor* Northwestern University Press Illinois, 1997, pp. 109-110.

Chapter IV
The Jewish Survivors, Escapees and Victims— Roll of Remembrance

This chapter is an attempt to record the names of Jewish survivors, escapees and victims who set foot in the living hell of the Sobibór death camp. This Roll of Remembrance also includes those Jews who were selected to live and work in Jewish forced labor camps within the Lublin district, such as Trawniki, and the Old Airfield Camp in Lublin.

What has been presented here is not simply a list of names; where known short biographies have been compiled, using as a foundation the excellent books by Jules Schelvis, Thomas 'Toivi' Blatt', Miriam Novitch and others. Also worthy of praise is the excellent Dutch website, *sobiborinterviews.nl*, as well as the Joodsmonument and the German website *Bundesarchiv Gedenkbuch*.

Whilst the list is extremely comprehensive, one simply cannot say whether there are other names to be added. This is not a precise science, and I apologize in advance if names have been missed off. Generally, the Germans did not maintain transport lists of Polish Jews, but comprehensive records were kept of the transports of Jews from Westerbork camp in the Netherlands to Sobibór, and transports from the Reich. There were nineteen transports from Holland, commencing on March 5, 1943, and the final one departed on July 23, 1943. These transports carried 34,313 Jews in a mixture of passenger cars and freight wagons.

The information has been compiled from a number of sources, and each entry has a quoted source, in order to authenticate the

Roll of Remembrance. It is respectfully presented, and hopefully their memory has been preserved in an accurate and fitting manner. All the names are shown in alphabetical order, surname first, and where known their forenames. One major improvement on my original book on Sobibór, published in 2017, is that the sources for each entry has been recorded, and thus a more accurate Roll of Remembrance can be constructed. However, it would be too large an undertaking to list all the victims names, so only a small percentage can be included. Readers can view the *Joodsmonument.nl* website for example for a full list of names.

This section of the Jewish Roll of Remembrance includes those that escaped from Sobibór and survived the Holocaust, and those that tasted freedom if only for an ephemeral time.

Survivors and Escapees A–Z

ALSTER, Schlomo. Born on December 1, 1908, in Chelm, Poland. He was deported from Chelm to Sobibór during November 1942, along with Kalman Wewryk. He worked in the death camp mainly as a carpenter, constructing barracks. He was also selected to work as part of the *Bahnhofkommando* on a few occasions. In his view Gomerski was the worst of all the *SS*-men in Sobibór. Alster escaped during the revolt on October 14, 1943. He settled in Israel, in Rehovot in 1946.[204]

BAHIR, Moshe (Born SZKLAREK). Born on July 19, 1927, in Plock, Poland. He was deported from Zamość on May 24, 1942, in one of the earliest transports. On his arrival he was among fifty men selected for work and was assigned to the *Bahnhofkommando* for the first three months. After that he worked in the provisions barracks and as a barber. Bahir escaped during the revolt on October 14, 1943. He later settled in Israel and he testified at the Adolf Eichmann Trial in Jerusalem during 1961.[205]

BARDACH, Antonius. Born on May 16, 1909, in Lwow, Poland. He arrived on the 53rd *RSHA* transport from France. He was deported from the Drancy internment camp to Sobibór on March 25, 1943. He escaped during the revolt on October 14, 1943. He was one of only two survivors from this transport, the other one was Josef Duniec. He settled in Belgium.[206]

BIALOWITZ, Philip. Born on November 25, 1929, in Izbica, Poland. As a thirteen-year old, he was one of 800 Jews deported from Izbica to Sobibór by lorry in January 1943. He was selected along with a few dozen others and worked in the sorting barracks, searching through the victims possessions for

---

[204] J. Schelvis, *Sobibor*, Berg-Oxford, New York, 2007, p.231.
[205] Ibid p. 231.
[206] Ibid. p.231.

hidden money and jewellery. He also served in the hair cutting barrack, where the women's hair was cut off before they went into the gas chambers. He also worked on the *Bahnhofkommando*. He escaped during the revolt on October 14, 1943. He later emigrated to the United States of America.[207]

BIALOWITZ, Symcha. Born on December 6, 1912, in Izbica, Poland. He arrived in Sobibór having been deported from Izbica in a lorry on April 28, 1943, three months after his brother Philip. Symcha was selected to work in the camp's pharmacy. He was also selected by Gustav Wagner to work in the *Waldkommando*. Symcha escaped with his brother Philip in the prisoner revolt on October 14, 1943. He settled in Israel.[208]

BISKUBICZ, Jakub. Born on March 17, 1926, in Hrubieszow, Poland. He was transported to Sobibór during May 1942, along with 3,000 others, including his parents and other family members. He was selected to work with his father, who was later shot and killed in the camp. He was a member of the *Bahnhofkommando* and the *Waldkommando* in the forest.

He escaped from *Lager IV*, the *Nordlager*, during the night of the prisoner revolt on October 14, 1943. After his escape he fought with the partisans and later in the Polish Army. He emigrated to Israel during 1949. He testified at the Adolf Eichmann Trial in Jerusalem during 1961. He died during March 2002, in Ramat Gan, Israel.[209]

BLATT, Thomas (Toivi). Born on April 15, 1927, in Izbica, Poland. He was transported from Izbica, to Sobibór in a lorry—via the camp in Trawniki—on April 23, 1943, with about 300 other Jews, including his father Leon, his mother Fajgele and his 10-year old brother Hersz. His parents and brother were sent to the gas chambers on arrival, and were murdered.

---

[207] Ibid pp, 231-232.
[208] Miriam Novitch, *Sobibor*, Holocaust Library, New York, 1980, pp.66-67.
[209] J. Schelvis, *Sobibor*, Berg-Oxford, New York, 2007, p.232.

Karl Frenzel selected Thomas to be a *Putzer*—polishing his boots, later he worked at repairing the fence, in the hair cutting barrack and as a fireman burning the documents and photographs of the murdered victims. Thomas Blatt escaped during the prisoner revolt on October 14, 1943. He emigrated to the United States of America, and has written two books: *Sobibór The Forgotten Revolt* (1996) and *From the Ashes of Sobibór: A Story of Survival* (1997). He passed away on October 31, 2015, at his home in Santa Barbara, California, United States of America.[210]

BORNSTEIN, Moshe. He escaped in the prisoner revolt on October 14, 1943. Nothing more is known.[211]

CUCKIERMAN, Hershel. Born on April 15, 1893, in Kurow, Poland. He arrived in Sobibór via Opole and Nalenczow, along with his wife and family, during May 1942. Although a gardener by profession, both he and his son Josef volunteered when the Germans asked for a cook to step forward. He worked in the kitchen in *Lager I*, right up until the revolt. He escaped during the revolt on October 14, 1943. He emigrated to the United States of America during the 1950's.[212]

CUCKIERMAN, Josef. Born on May 26, 1930, in Kurow, Poland. Josef arrived in Sobibór with his father Hershel during May 1942. He was 12 years-old and he became a cook's helper. He also worked in the SS canteen, and as a *Putzer*, polishing the boots of the SS. He escaped during the revolt, with his father, on October 14, 1943. Josef fought with the partisans and later settled in Stuttgart and then Karlsruhe, in Germany. Josef passed away on June 15, 1963.[213]

---

[210] T. Blatt, *From the Ashes of Sobibor*, Northwestern University Press, Evanston, Illinois, 1997.
[211] T. Blatt, *Sobibor—The Forgotten Revolt*, H.E.P, Issaquah, 1998, p.110.
[212] J. Schelvis, *Sobibor*, Berg-Oxford, New York, 2007, pp. 232-233.
[213] Ibid p.233.

DRESZER, Josef. He was from Zolkiewka, and was 13-years old on the day of the revolt. He was a *Putzer*, and at the start of the revolt he held the reins of Niemann's horse, whilst Niemann went into the tailor's workshop. Dreszer also played a role when Stanislaw Szmajzner stole some rifles from the Ukrainian barrack. He escaped from Sobibór, and reached the forest, but in all probability lost his life.[214]

DUNIEC, Josef. Born on December 21, 1912, in Kiev, but his parents settled in Rowno, Poland. Later he left for France to study chemistry at the University of Caen. He was on the 53rd *RSHA* transport from the Drancy internment camp near Paris, on March 25, 1943, via Lublin to Sobibór. On arrival at Sobibór he was selected to work along with thirty others, out of a transport of 1,000 people. He worked in the *Waldkommando* and in the sorting barracks. He escaped during the revolt on October 14, 1943, then lived in the forest and with peasants.

When the Second World War ended he became the chauffeur of a Polish minister of the first government of the Liberation in Chelm. He eventually made his way back to France, via Odessa.

Re-united with his wife, they decided to settle in Israel, where they had two more children. Although reluctant to talk about Sobibór, he agreed to testify at the Hagen Trial of former *SS*-men. One day before he was due to fly to West Germany, he died from a heart attack on December 1, 1965, in Haifa, Israel.

ENGEL, Chaim. Born on January 10, 1916, in Brudzew, Poland. His family moved to Lodz, where his father ran a textile factory and a store. Chaim served in the Polish Army at the time the Germans invaded Poland, and he was captured by the Germans. As a Prisoner of War he was sent to work near Leipzig. Released, he returned to Poland, and made his way to Lublin, where his family had been moved to. His father and stepmother were deported to Sobibór in June 1942. Chaim and his

---

[214] T. Blatt, *Sobibor—The Forgotten Revolt*, H.E.P, Issaquah, 1998, p.74 and 77.

brother worked and lived on a farm, and they decided to travel to Izbica.

They were deported to Sobibór from Izbica, and they arrived at the death camp on November 6, 1942. Chaim was selected to work sorting clothes of the victims, and whilst doing this found his brothers clothes.

Chaim worked as a member of the *Bahnhofkommando*, and in the hair cutting barrack. For a time he was also the *Kapo* of the Women's barrack. He formed a life-long relationship at the camp with Saartje (Selma) Wijnberg, a Dutch Jewess who arrived in Sobibór on April 9, 1943, from the Westerbork camp, in Holland.

On the day of the prisoner revolt, October 14, 1943, Selma provided Chaim with a pointed knife. Chaim used it to murder *SS-Oberscharführer* Rudolf Beckmann and Thomas Steffl in the Forester's House, with the able assistance of Hersz Pozycki.

Chaim and Selma escaped from the death camp and hid on a farm near Chelm, where they were liberated by the Red Army in June 1944. They travelled to the Netherlands, via Odessa and Marseille, along the way losing their little baby Emilchen, to food poisoning in 1945. They stayed in Holland until 1951, then they emigrated to the United States of America, via Israel in 1957. Chaim passed away on July 4, 2003, in New Haven.[215]

ENGEL, Saartje-Selma (formerly WIJNBERG). Born on May 15, 1922, in Groningen, Netherlands. She moved to Zwolle, where her parents ran a hotel on Voorstraat 26, Zwolle. Her father Samuel died in Apeldoorn on April 2, 1941. Her mother Alida died in Auschwitz Concentration Camp on October 12, 1942.

Saartje went into hiding, but was arrested by the *Gestapo*. She was imprisoned in Utrecht and then Amsterdam. She was then sent to the camp in Vught, and then onto Westerbork transit camp. Saartje arrived in Sobibór with 2,019 other Jews from Westerbork, on April 9, 1943. Selected for work, she worked

---

[215] Chaim Engel—Interview with USHMM on July 16, 1990.

mainly in the sorting barracks, but also in the *Waldkommando*.

On the day of the prisoner revolt, October 14, 1943, Selma provided Chaim with a pointed knife, that Chaim used to murder *SS-Oberscharführer* Rudolf Beckmann and Thomas Steffl in the Forester's House, with the able assistance of Hersz Pozycki.

Chaim and Selma escaped from the death camp and hid on a farm near Chelm, where they were liberated by the Red Army in June 1944. They travelled to the Netherlands, via Odessa and Marseille, losing their little baby Emilchen along the way in 1945, from food poisoning. They stayed in Holland until 1951, then they emigrated to the United States of America, via Israel in 1957. Selma passed away on December 4, 2018.[216]

FAJGENBAUM, Jakub. Escaped from Sobibór during the revolt on October 14, 1943. No other details are known.[217]

FELHENDLER, Lejba (Leon). Born on June 1, 1910, in Turobin, to an orthodox Jewish family. His parents were Symcha Felhendler, and Gitla, formerly Fersztendix. In 1911, the Felhendler's moved to Zolkiewka, where Symcha had designs on being the Chief Rabbi. This came to pass in January 1924.

On May 9, 1935, Lejba married Toba Wajnberg, and on October 20, 1935, they had a son, Chaim Szymon. Another child was born, but no details have been recorded. It is believed that prior to the Second World War, Lejba had been a trader, and he leased a mill and a sawmill.

In early 1940, Lejba became the head of the Jewish Council (*Judenrat*) established by the Germans in Zolkiewka. In April 1942, a branch of the Jewish Self-Help (*ZSS*) organization was formed, whose management also fell to him.

The Jewish history of Zolkiewka came to a close on October 16, 1942. On this day approximately 1,000 Jews, including

---

[216] Selma Engel—Interview with USHMM on July 16, 1990.
[217] T. Blatt, *Sobibor—The Forgotten Revolt*, H.E.P, Issaquah, 1998, p.110.

members of the *Judenrat* and their families, were driven on foot to the transit ghetto of Izbica. Whilst being subjected to another deportation '*Aktion*' and being loaded onto a train, the old Rabbi, his wife, and one of his daughters were shot on the railway ramp.

Felhendler and his immediate family remained in the Izbica ghetto for another two weeks in a previously prepared hiding place. This was discovered on November 2, 1942. Felhendler, his wife, children, brother and surviving sisters, along with their families, were transported first to Trawniki, and from there by train to Sobibór.

On his arrival at Sobibór Felhendler was saved by an unidentified cousin, who pointed him out as an exceptional carpenter. The remaining members of Felhendler's family were driven straight to the gas chambers.

Felhendler worked in the provisions barrack, and occasionally he worked as a member of the *Bahnhofkommando*. He started to become an influential figure in the underground in the camp, and he and Alexander Pechersky planned and led the revolt on October 14, 1943.

Felhendler found shelter after escaping from the camp, in the village of Maciejow Stary. In late July 1944, he found himself in Soviet-controlled Lublin, where he stayed at 4 Kowalska Steet. At this address he shared this apartment with other survivors from Sobibór.

Later he moved into a flat at 6/4 Zlota Street and in February 1945, he married Estera Muterperel, a twenty-year old woman from Krasnystaw. Lejba (Leon) Felhendler was shot and killed in his apartment, by Polish anti-Semites on April 2, 1945.[218]

FELENBAUM-WEISS, Hella. Born on November 25, 1924, in Lublin, Poland. She was taken along with her two brothers and others from the Labor Camp at Staw-Nowosiulki, by horse and

---

[218] A. Kopciowski, *Lejba (Leon) Felhendler: A Biographical Sketch*, Panstwowe Muzeum Majdanku Lublin 2018.

cart to Sobibór on December 20, 1942. Her two brothers escaped from the cart; one was killed immediately, the other ran, but he too did not survive.

She was selected to work knitting socks for the *SS* and Ukrainians and ironed shirts. She escaped from Sobibór during the revolt on October 14, 1943, and fought with the partisans and in the Russian Army. She received six decorations for fighting against the Germans, including the Red Star. In Czechoslovakia she met a Jew in General Swoboda's army, whom she married and settled with in Israel. She passed away in December 1988, in Gedera, Israel.[219]

FREIBERG, Dov. Born on May 15, 1927, in Warsaw. He left Warsaw for Turobin in the autumn of 1941. In May 1942, the Germans initiated a deportation *'Aktion'* and Dov walked with other Jews to the regional town of Krasnystaw. At Krasnystaw the Jews were loaded into boxcars and taken to the Sobibór death camp, arriving there on May 15, 1942.

Dov was selected to work sorting the clothes of the murdered victims under the supervision of *SS-Unterscharführer* Steubl. He was employed at cleaning the Ukrainian barracks along with another prisoner called Tsudik.

The *SS* man Paul Groth set the infamous St. Bernhard cross dog 'Barry' on Dov, and the animal bit him on the backside, he survived the attack, although he was in great pain.

Dov Freiberg escaped from Sobibór during the prisoner revolt on October 14, 1943. He settled in Israel in 1948. He testified at the Eichmann Trial held in Jerusalem during 1961.[220]

---

[219] Miriam Novitch, *Sobibor*, Holocaust Library, New York, 1980, pp.49-51.
[220] Dov Freiberg, *To Survive Sobibor*, Gefen Publishing House, Jerusalem, 2007.

FREIBERMAN, Szama. He was from Włodawa and was a member of the first successful escape attempt from Sobibór, along with Szmul Machles, and Matys. They were already naked and on their way to the gas chambers. They managed to hide in the bushes and slip under the barbed-wire to freedom. They returned to Włodawa during May 1942. His eventual fate is unknown.[221]

GOKKES, Catharina (Kathy). Born on September 1, 1923, in Den Haag, Holland. She lived at Beeklaan 192, Den Haag, in April 1942. She was an office clerk and was deported to Westerbork, via the camp in Vught, and Utrecht prison. She was deported from Westerbork to Sobibór on April 6, 1943, on the same transport as Ursula Stern).

During the revolt on October 14, 1943, Kathy was shot in the leg by Karl Frenzel, but she managed to escape into the forest, along with Ursula Stern and Eda Lichtman, and join a partisan group. There seems to be some confusion over her death. Ursula Stern testified at the Sobibór War Crimes Trial in Hagen that on June 22, 1944, Kathy Gokkes was killed by the Germans one day before they retreated from the area. Other reports claim she died of typhoid fever. Given the closeness of the two women, we believe that Kathy was killed in action.[222]

GOLDFARB, Moshe. Born on March 15, 1920, in Piaski, Poland. He was deported with his brother and Kurt Thomas on November 6, 1942, from the Piaski Transit Ghetto. In Sobibór he worked as a calligrapher, writing names and addresses on the suitcase labels of the *SS* staff who were going on leave.

He escaped from Sobibór during the revolt on October 14, 1943. He joined a partisan group along with Yehuda Lerner. He passed away on June 8, 1984, in Haifa, Israel.[223]

---

[221] T. Blatt, *Sobibor—The Forgotten Revolt*, H.E.P, Issaquah, 1998, p.58.
[222] Joods Monument and J. Schelvis, *Sobibor*, Berg-Oxford, New York, 2007, p. 166.
[223] J. Schelvis, *Sobibor*, Berg-Oxford, New York, 2007, p. 234.

HANNEL, Salomea. Salomea Hannel was deported to Sobibór from the village of Ustrzyki Dolne. She escaped during the revolt on October 14, 1943, and hid in the forest. She made her way to Krakau, and settled with the non-Jewish population.

HERSZMANN, Josef. Born during 1925, in Zolkiweka, Poland. Josef was transported from Chelm to Sobibór in one of the early transports in 1942. He was selected to work in the Sorting barracks, he was also a member of the *Bahnhofkommando* and the *Waldkommando*. He escaped from Sobibór during the revolt on October 14, 1943. He later settled in Israel.[224]

HOCHMANN, Moshe. At the end of spring 1942, Moshe Hochmann and his family were deported from Zolkiewka to Krasnystaw on foot. At Krasnystaw they were herded into cattle cars and transported to Sobibór. In the death camp he worked in the tailors workshop as a foreman. It was Moshe who requested that Johann Niemann visit the tailors workshop on the day of the revolt. After Niemann had been killed, Moshe wrapped his body in a blanket and hid it.

He escaped from Sobibór during the revolt on October 14, 1943, and hid in a farmer's barn in Papierzyn, until liberation by the Red Army during 1944.[225]

HONIGMAN, Zyndel. Born on April 10, 1910, in Kiev, USSR. He was a slave worker in Gorzkow near Izbica, Poland. He was taken to Sobibór by lorry in November 1942. Two days later he escaped by crawling underneath the barbed wire fence into *Lager II*, and finding his way out. He went to Izbica, but in April 1943, he was taken back to Sobibór via Trawniki.

Claiming to be a butcher, he was put to work in the kitchen, and he also was a member of the *Waldkommando*. He escaped from Sobibór for a second time following the revolt by the *Waldkommando* on July 23, 1943. He later settled in the United

---

[224] J. Schelvis, *Sobibor*, Berg-Oxford, New York, 2007, p. 234.
[225] Miriam Novitch, *Sobibor*, Holocaust Library, New York, 1980, pp. 122-123.

States of America. He testified at the Sobibór Trial in Hagen on December 13, 1965.[226]

ITZKOVICH, Michael. A member of Alexander Perchersky's group who escaped during the revolt of October 14, 1943, and joined the partisans.[227]

KATZ, Serka. She was deported from Dubienka, via Hrubesziow to Sobibór, along with Eda Lichtman and Bella Sobol, in the middle of June 1942. She worked as a cleaner in the SS quarters. She escaped from the camp on the day of the revolt on October 14, 1943, it is thought she perished in the forest.[228]

KOHN, Abram. Born on July 25, 1910, in Lodz, Poland. He was taken to Sobibór on a transport of several hundred Jews from Wisocka during May 1942, and was selected for work along with eighty other men, including his brother.

He worked in the Sorting Barracks, in the kitchen, and was a member of the *Waldkommando*. He escaped from Sobibór during the revolt on October 14, 1943. He settled in Australia, and turned down the opportunity to testify against Frenzel at his appeal trial in 1983. He passed away on January 19, 1986, in Melbourne, Australia.[229]

KOPF, Josef. Born in Bilgoraj, Poland. He was deported to Sobibór on one of the earliest transports. He worked in the *Waldkommando*, On July 23, 1943 he and Szlomo Podchlebnik, went to the village of Zlobek to fetch some water, with a *Trawnikimänner* guard. The German Security Police report stated the guard was an Armenian *Wachmann*. They escaped into the forest. Josef Kopf was murdered during August 1944, by Polish anti-Semites.[230]

---

[226] J. Schelvis, *Sobibor*, Berg-Oxford, New York, 2007, pp. 234-235.
[227] Miriam Novitch, *Sobibor*, Holocaust Library, New York, 1980, p. 98.
[228] Ibid p. 55.
[229] J. Schelvis, *Sobibor*, Berg-Oxford, New York, 2007, p. 235.
[230] T. Blatt, *Sobibor—The Forgotten Revolt*, H.E.P, Issaquah, 1998, p.64 and p.109.

KORENFELD, Chaim. Born on May 15, 1923, in Izbica, Poland. He arrived in Sobibór from Izbica on April 28, 1943, on the same transport as Thomas 'Toivi' Blatt. He escaped during the *Waldkommando* revolt on July 23, 1943. Chaim later claimed that his uncle Abraham Wang had covered for him, and that he escaped during the revolt on October 14, 1943. However, both Honigman and Wang both claimed that Korenfeld escaped from the *Waldkommando* with them. Having been in Italy, Chaim settled in Brazil during 1949.[231]

KOSTMANN, Fredek. He was from Krakow and at the age of 21, he escaped from Sobibór on the day of the revolt October 14, 1943, with his friend Szmul Wajcen. They met up with Thomas 'Toivi' Blatt in the forest, they formed a small group and headed for Thomas Blatt's home town of Izbica. They found shelter with a farmer named Bojarski, for five and a half months. However, on April 23, 1944, Bojarski and his accomplices shot all three hiding in the barn. Fredek Kostmann was killed outright, but Thomas Blatt and Szmul Wacjen were only wounded, and they managed to escape into the forest.[232]

LEITMAN, Szlomo. He was a cabinet-maker from Warsaw. He escaped to the Soviet Union after the German invasion and was incarcerated in the Sheroka Camp in Minsk, where he became friends with Sasha Perchersky. Szlomo arrived in Sobibór on the same transport as Boris Taborinskij on or near September 15, 1943. Szlomo was a key member of the Underground in Sobibór. He killed *SS-Unterscharführer* Friedrich Gaulstich in the Carpenters' workshop on October 14, 1943, during the prisoner revolt. He was wounded during the escape but he managed to reach the forest before his strength ran out.[233]

---

[231] J. Schelvis, *Sobibor*, Berg-Oxford, New York, 2007, p. 235.
[232] T. Blatt, *From the Ashes of Sobibor*, Northwestern University Press, Evanston, Illinois, 1997, pp. 183-184.
[233] Y. Arad, *Belzec, Sobibor, Treblinka*, Indiana University Press, Bloomington and Indianapolis, 1987, p. 338.

LEJST, Chaim. Born in Zolkiewka, his father was a farmer. He fled to Izbica and was deported from there to Sobibór. He arrived in Sobibór on April 23, 1943. He was selected by Gustav Wagner to grow vegetables and flowers. He acted as a liaison agent between *Lager I* and *Lager II*, as his job as a gardener enabled him to walk between the two camps. He escaped from Sobibór during the revolt on October 14, 1943. He later settled in Israel.[234]

LERER, Samuel. Born on October 1, 1922, in Zolkiweka, Poland. He was transported to Sobibór during May 1942, and he was selected to work in *Lager II*, looking after the horses and later on the chickens.
On October 14, 1943, he escaped from Sobibór during the prisoner revolt. In 1949, Samuel and Estera Raab, another Sobibór survivor, came across former *SS*-Garrison member Erich Bauer on a street in Berlin. This led to Bauer's arrest. Samuel lived in Berlin for a number of years before settling in the United States of America. He passed away on March 3, 2016.[235]

LERNER, Yehuda. Born on July 22, 1926, in Warsaw, Poland. His family were rounded up on the first day of the mass deportation '*Aktion*' on July 22, 1942, and they were deported to the Treblinka death camp. Yehuda was sent to work in Smolensk, building an airfield for the *Organisation Todt*.
He escaped in September 1942, but was recaptured and sent to the Minsk ghetto. He was moved from there to the Sheroka Labor Camp, and in September 1943, he was deported to Sobibór, via Chelm.
On the day of the revolt on October 14, 1943, he along with Arkady Wajspapier, killed *SS*-man Siegfried Graetschus and the Ukrainian *Volksdeutsche* guard Ivan Klatt in the Shoemakers shop.

---

[234] J. Schelvis, *Sobibor*, Berg-Oxford, New York, 2007, p. 235 and Miriam Novitch, *Sobibor*, Holocaust Library, New York, 1980; pp.114-115.
[235] J. Schelvis, *Sobibor*, Berg-Oxford, New York, 2007, p. 236.

After the revolt Yehuda joined a partisan group in the forest along with Moshe Goldfarb. From January 1945, until the summer of the same year he was Deputy Commander of the Police in Radom. He and his wife Manja settled in Bayreuth, Germany until 1949, when they moved to Israel. He worked for the police in Haifa from 1951.[236]

LIBERMAN, Pesia. She was one of three Jews—two men and one woman—who escaped from Sobibór on the night of December 25, 1942, along with two Ukrainian guards; Viktor Kisilew and Emil Zischer. In the forest the two Jewish men went their own way and Pesia stayed with the two Ukrainians, who were armed.

Five days later they were betrayed by a farmer whilst hiding in the village of Kozia Gorka. They were surrounded in a village hut, and all three were killed in a shoot-out with three Polish Police Officers, (Kwiatkowski, Misnerowiec, and Piescikowski).[237]

LICHT, Aron. He escaped during the *Waldkommando* revolt on July 23, 1943. No further information is known.[238]

LICHTMAN, Eda (formerly FISCHER). Born on January 1, 1915, in Jaroslau, Poland. When the war broke out she lived with her husband in Wieliczka, but they left for Mielec. She was deported from there to Berdychow for a few days and then onto Dubienka, where they were lodged initially in synagogues. They were then sent to Hrubieszow, where they boarded a train to Sobibór, in the middle of June 1942.

She was selected to work in the SS Laundry and the Ironing Room located in *Lager II*. She escaped from Sobibór in the revolt on October 14, 1943. She fled into the forest along with Ursula Stern, and Kathy Gokkes. She settled in Israel during

---

[236] Ibid, p.236.
[237] T. Blatt, *Sobibor—The Forgotten Revolt*, H.E.P, Issaquah, 1998, p.58.
[238] Ibid. p. 110.

1950, where she later married another Sobibór survivor Itzhak Lichtman.[239]

LICHTMAN, Itzhak. Born on December 10, 1908, in Zolkiewka, Poland. On May 22, 1942, Itzhak and his family were deported on foot from Zolkiewka to Krasnystaw railway station, where they were loaded onto cattle cars bound for the Sobibór death camp.

On arrival he was selected to work in the Shoemakers' workshop in *Lager I*, along with five others, including his cousin Berek Lichtman. He escaped during the prisoner revolt on October 14, 1943. In the forest he joined the Zukow partisans on December 15, 1943. He later settled in Israel with another survivor Eda, and they later married.[240]

LITWINOWSKI, Yefim. As a Soviet Prisoner of War he arrived in Sobibór on September 22, 1943. A member of Alexander Perchersky's group, he escaped during the revolt of October 14, 1943. He re-joined the Red Army.[241]

MACHLES, Szmul. He was from Włodawa and was a member of the first successful escape attempt from Sobibór along with Szama Freiberman, and Matys. They were already naked and on their way to the gas chambers. They managed to hide in the bushes and slip under the barbed-wire to freedom. They returned to Włodawa during May 1942. His fate is unknown.[242]

MARGULIES, Abraham. Born on January 25, 1921, in Zyradow, Poland. He was sent to Belzec during 1940, to work on the so-called 'Otto Line,' the defence ramparts along the Polish-Soviet demarcation line. Abraham was deported from Zamosc at the end of May 1942 to Sobibór.

He was selected to work in the *Bahnhofkommando*, cleaning the carriages under the supervision of Paul Groth. He also

---

[239] Miriam Novitch, *Sobibor*, Holocaust Library, New York, 1980, pp 52-55.
[240] J. Schelvis, *Sobibor*, Berg-Oxford, New York, 2007, p. 236.
[241] Sobiborinterviews.nl—online resource.
[242] T. Blatt, *Sobibor—The Forgotten Revolt*, H.E.P, Issaquah, 1998, p.58.

worked in the Sorting Barracks and in the kitchens. Abraham befriended Hella Weiss, and the two of them ended up together during and after the revolt on October 14, 1943. He later settled in Israel, where he became a printer.[243]

MATYS, (Forename unknown). He was from Włodawa and was a member of the first successful escape attempt from Sobibór along with Szama Freiberman, and Szmul Machles. They were already naked and on their way to the gas chambers. They managed to hide in the bushes and slip under the barbed-wire to freedom. They returned to Włodawa during May 1942. His fate is unknown.[244]

MAZURKIEWITCH, Semion. A member of Alexander Pechersky's group who escaped during the revolt on October 14, 1943, and who joined the partisans.[245]

MENCHE, Chaskiel. Born on January 7, 1910, in Kolo, Poland. In 1937, he married Hella Podchlebnik, the sister of Szlomo Podchlebnik, who escaped during the *Waldkommando* revolt on July 23, 1943.

In June 1942, he was transported to Sobibór along with 2,000 other Jews from Izbica. On arrival he was selected for work in the Sorting and Tailors barracks. He took part in the slaying of Ivan Klatt. He escaped during the revolt on October 14, 1943, and hid in the Parczew forest. He settled in Melbourne, Australia during 1949. He passed away in Melbourne, in 1984.[246]

MENDEL. He escaped during the revolt on October 14, 1943. He was wounded in the escape and, according to Moshe Goldfarb, he was a Tailor; although Thomas Blatt recalled a Baker in the camp called Mendel. Goldfarb remembered that Mendel asked

---

[243] J. Schelvis, *Sobibor*, Berg-Oxford, New York, 2007, p. 237.
[244] T. Blatt, *Sobibor—The Forgotten Revolt*, H.E.P, Issaquah, 1998, p.58.
[245] Y. Arad, *Belzec, Sobibor, Treblinka*, Indiana University Press, Bloomington and Indianapolis, 1987, p. 339.
[246] J. Schelvis, *Sobibor*, Berg-Oxford, New York, 2007, p. 237.

for them to kill him due to his injury. He perished in the forest.[247]

MERENSTEIN, Mosek. He escaped from Sobibór during the prisoner revolt on October 14, 1943. No further details known.[248]

METZ, Zelda (formerly KELBERMAN). Born on May 1, 1925, in Siedliszcze, Poland. She was deported with her family to an *Arbeitslager* in Staw-Nowosiulki. Zelda arrived in Sobibór on December 22, 1942, on a horse-drawn cart, along with her cousin Regina Feldman (Zielinski) and Estera Raab.

She was selected to work and she knitted socks and pullovers for the SS, and she also worked in the laundry and ironing barracks. In the summer of 1943, she was employed in the construction of *Lager IV*, the so-called *Nordlager* for captured ammunition.

She escaped during the revolt on October 14, 1943, and found shelter with peasants. She obtained false papers stating she was Aryan and she worked as a nanny for a family in *Lemberg* (now Lviv). Zelda settled in the United States of America during 1946. She passed away during 1980, in the United States of America.[249]

PECHERSKY, Alexander Aronowitz (Sasha). Born on February 22, 1909, in Kremenchuk, Ukraine, but his family moved to Rostov on the Don. He worked as an electrician at a locomotive repair factory. After graduating from university with a diploma in music and literature. He became an accountant and the manager of a small school for amateur musicians. He was married and had a daughter called Elochka.

He fought in the Red Army against the Germans and was captured during October 1941, in the city of Vyazma. After trying

---

[247] Y. Arad, *Belzec, Sobibor, Treblinka*, Indiana University Press, Bloomington and Indianapolis, 1987, p. 346.
[248] T. Blatt, *Sobibor—The Forgotten Revolt*, H.E.P, Issaquah, 1998, p. 110.
[249] J. Schelvis, *Sobibor*, Berg-Oxford, New York, 2007, p. 237.

to escape in May 1942, he was taken to Borisov, where a medical examination exposed him as being of Jewish extraction.

He was imprisoned from September 1942, in the Sheroka Labor Camp in Minsk, and when the Minsk ghetto and labor camp was liquidated, he was taken to Sobibór on September 22, 1943, along with 2,000 other Jewish Prisoners of War, and inhabitants from the Minsk ghetto. He was among eighty men selected by Hubert Gomerski for work in *Lager IV*, the so-called *Nordlager*, clearing the forest.

Along with Lejba (Leon) Felhendler, Pechersky planned the prisoner revolt. On October 14, 1943, the prisoners killed 12 *SS*-men and 2 *Trawnikimänner*, and escaped from the death camp.

Pechersky and a small band of Jewish former Soviet Prisoners of War, crossed the Bug River on the night of October 19-20, 1943, and joined the Voroshilov partisans fighting against the Germans. During this period, his comrades who had played a significant role in killing the *SS*-men in Sobibór, Boris Cybulski and Alexander Shubayev (Kali-Mali) lost their lives.

He re-joined the Red Army and in August 1944, he was severely wounded in the leg.as a result spent a short time in hospital, and received a medal for his bravery. Sasha returned to his homeland and resumed his civilian career as a music teacher. He was arrested and thrown in prison for a period, along with his brother, who died in prison due to a diabetic coma. Sasha passed away on January 19, 1990, in Rostov on the Don.[250]

PELC, Josel. In June 1943, Josel Pelc, a carpenter from Tyszowice and Yasha, a bricklayer from Chelm, successfully escaped in the middle of the night by cutting the barbed wire and evading the minefield and the guards.[251]

PLATNICKI, Naum. He was responsible for attacking the armoury during the revolt on October 14, 1943, and to command

---

[250] Miriam Novitch, *Sobibor*, Holocaust Library, New York, 1980, pp 89-99.
[251] T. Blatt, *Sobibor—The Forgotten Revolt*, H.E.P, Issaquah, 1998, p.60.

the group of prisoners columns marching towards the main gate after the evening roll call. No other details are known.[252]

PLOTNIKOW, Chaim. He was a member of Alexander Pechersky's group, a Jewish Soviet Prisoner of War. He escaped during the revolt on October 14, 1943. He escaped to the forest and departed with Pechersky's and others from the group which included Thomas Blatt.[253]

PODCHLEBNIK, Szlomo. Born on February 15, 1907, in Kolo, Poland. He arrived in Sobibór on April 28, 1943, from Izbica, on the same transport as Thomas 'Toivi' Blatt. At Sobibór, he found his brother-in-law Chaskiel Menche. Szlomo was selected for work digging wells outside the camp, and he was also a member of the *Waldkommando*.

Szlomo escaped from the *Waldkommando* on July 23, 1943, along with Josef Kopf after killing a *Trawniki Wachmann* in the village of Zlobek, where they had gone to fetch water. After the war he settled in the United States of America.[254]

POWROZNIK, Haim (POZNER, Herman). Born in Liubomil, Poland, during 1911. He went to a labor camp in Chelm, and from there he was deported to Sobibór during February or March 1943. On arrival at Sobibór he was selected by Gustav Wagner to work as a carpenter in *Lager II*. He escaped during the revolt in October 14, 1943, and lived in hiding in Chelm. After the war he settled in the United States of America.[255]

POZYCKI, Yankel. The father of two sons also in the Sobibór death camp, Hersz and Symon. He was a Shoemaker, and he escaped from Sobibór during the revolt on October 14, 1943. He survived the war.[256]

---

[252] Y. Arad, *Belzec, Sobibor, Treblinka*, Indiana University Press, Bloomington and Indianapolis, 1987, p. 324.
[253] T. Blatt, *Sobibor—The Forgotten Revolt*, H.E.P, Issaquah, 1998, p.102.
[254] J. Schelvis, *Sobibor*, Berg-Oxford, New York, 2007, p. 237.
[255] Miriam Novitch, *Sobibor*, Holocaust Library, New York, 1980, p. 125.
[256] T. Blatt, *Sobibor—The Forgotten Revolt*, H.E.P, Issaquah, 1998, p.101.

RAAB, Estera (formerly TERNER). Born on June 11, 1922, in Chelm, Poland. Estera arrived in Sobibór on a horse-drawn cart from the *Arbeitslager* Staw-Nowosiulki, on December 22, 1942. She arrived with Regina Feldman and Zelda Metz. Selected for work, she worked in the Knitting barrack for a few months, and later on she worked in the Sorting Barracks. She escaped from Sobibór during the revolt on October 14, 1943, though she sustained a head injury.

Along with Samuel Lerer, they recognized former *SS-Oberscharführer* Erich Bauer, walking on a street in Berlin, during 1949. She later settled in the United States of America. She passed away on April 13, 2015, in Vineland, New Jersey, United States of America.[257]

REISNER-BIALOWITZ, Lea. She was born in Zamość, to a well-to-do business family. In the autumn of 1942, she was deported from Zamość to Izbica, on foot. In the spring of 1943, she was deported from Izbica to Sobibór.

She was selected on arrival to work in the laundry. She escaped from Sobibór during the revolt on October 14, 1943. She reached the forest and found shelter in a stable. She travelled to a monastery in Radeczny, where she learned the Germans had left the country. She then returned to Zamosc, to find the family home occupied by Poles from Poznan. Later she met up with Symcha Bialowitz, and they married and settled in Israel.[258]

ROSENFELD, Semion. Born during 1922, in Baranowitz, (then in Poland). He arrived in Sobibór on September 22, 1943, from Minsk, in the same transport as Alexander Pechersky. He was put to work hauling bricks in *Lager IV*, the so-called *Nordlager*. He escaped from the camp during the revolt on October 14, 1943.

---

[257] J. Schelvis, *Sobibor*, Berg-Oxford, New York, 2007, p. 238.
[258] Miriam Novitch, *Sobibor*, Holocaust Library, New York, 1980, pp. 100-102.

He fought with the Red Army and ended his military career in Berlin, where he left a permanent mark on the *Reichstag* building, by scratching the words, *'Baranowitz-Sobibór-Berlin'* into one of the walls. He remained in the Soviet Union until the mid-1980's. He then settled in Israel.[259]

ROSENSTIEL, Liselotte, Karoline. Born on March 17, 1923, in Neustadt, Germany. She emigrated with her family to Holland. She lived at Van Ostadelaan 3, Naarden. She was deported from Westerbork to Sobibór on March 17, 1943.

In Sobibór, she was known as Luka, which indeed was the case whilst in Holland. She became the 'girlfriend' of Sasha Pechersky, prior to the revolt. She gave Sasha her father's shirt as a good luck charm. She escaped during the revolt on October 14, 1943. She was last seen among a group of escapees heading towards Chelm. She probably died in the forests.

ROTENBERG, Aizik. Born during 1925, in Włodawa, Poland. He arrived on foot at Sobibór, along with the rest of his family, on May 12, 1943. Both he and his brother were selected for work by Frenzel. He worked as a bricklayer building an arsenal, and he also worked as a member of the *Bahnhofkommando*.

Whilst his brother was killed during the revolt, Aizik managed to escape from Sobibór, on October 14, 1943, along with other prisoners. They were captured by members of the *Schutzpolizei* and were taken to Adampol, where a German called Zelinger tied them up with chains in a stable. They managed to free themselves and escaped to the forest of Parczew. They joined the Jewish Yehiel partisan group. He settled in Israel where he raised a family, and continued working as a bricklayer.[260]

SAFRAN, Ilona (Born Ursula STERN). Born on August 28, 1926, in Essen, Germany. When the Nazis came to power her father Albert Stern sold their lingerie business and sought refuge in

---

[259] J. Schelvis, *Sobibor*, Berg-Oxford, New York, 2007, p. 239.
[260] Ibid. p.239.

Epe, Holland. The family lived at Voorstraat 85 bis Utrecht. Her father joined the resistance, but was captured by the Nazis. Both Albert and his wife Anna, were deported to Auschwitz, where they both perished.

Ursula went into hiding with the Pompe family, but the hideout was discovered and Mrs Pompe was sent to Ravensbruck Concentration Camp in Germany. Ursula was sent to Utrecht Prison, then Amstelveen and then onto Vught Camp. Here she made friends with—amongst others—Kathy Gokkes, Selma Wijnberg and Minny Cats.

During April 1943, they were transferred to the Westerbork Transit Camp, from where they were deported on April 6, 1943. They arrived at the Sobibór death camp three days later on April 9, 1943. Selected for work, she worked mainly in the Sorting Barracks and the *Waldkommando*. She also worked in *Lager IV*, the so-called *Nordlager*, where she cleaned captured munitions.

She escaped from Sobibór during the revolt on October 14, 1943, along with Kathy Gokkes, and reached the forest, where they met Eda Lichtman. She fought with the partisans and witnessed the death in action of Kathy Gokkes. She made her way back to Holland after the war, and she settled in Israel. She passed away during 1985.[261]

SCHWARZ, Walter. The camp electrician who was in charge of the generator. He put the generator out of action, on the day of the revolt. According to Thomas 'Toivi' Blatt, he was one of their group who escaped from Sobibór during the revolt on October 14, 1943. He was a German Jew aged thirty-five years old. He chose to separate from Blatt's group, and in all probability perished in the forest.[262]

---

[261] Miriam Novitch, *Sobibor*, Holocaust Library, New York, 1980, pp 86-88.
[262] T. Blatt, *Sobibor—The Forgotten Revolt*, H.E.P, Issaquah, 1998, p. 78 and 101.

SENDER, (Forename unknown). A tall Jew from Lodz, who was with Thomas 'Toivi' Blatt when they escaped from Sobibór on October 14, 1943. It is likely he perished in the forest.[263]

SHUBAYEV, Alexander. He was originally from Baku, and was also known by the nickname 'Kalimali.' A Jewish Red Army Prisoner of War. He was heavily involved in the planning and the execution of the revolt, and was a close friend of Sasha Pechersky. He was responsible for killing Johann Niemann in the Tailors workshop, with a blow from the axe, on October 14, 1943. He broke out of Sobibór with Pechersky and his group of men. He later lost his life fighting with the partisans against the Germans.[264]

SIEGEL, Jossel. Recalled by Kurt Thomas, the medical orderly who sheltered Jossel in the barracks because his toes were frozen. Around 16 years of age he worked in the Sorting Barracks.[265] He is also remembered by Philip Bialowitz, who wrote, 'I recognize one of the people lying on the ground. He is my friend Jossel Siegel, a boy about my age from Siediszcze, who has worked with me in the Sorting shed. He is bleeding profusely.' It is likely he perished that day.[266]

SOBELMAN, Cvi. He escaped from Sobibór during the revolt on October 14, 1943. No further details are known.[267]

SOBOL, Bajle. She was deported from Dubienka, via Hrubiesow to Sobibór, along with Eda Lichtman and Serka Katz, during the middle of June 1942. She was selected to live and worked in the SS Laundry. She was remembered by Stanislaw

---

[263] T. Blatt, *From the Ashes of Sobibor*, Northwestern University Press, Evanston, Illinois, 1997, p.153.
[264] T. Blatt, *Sobibor—The Forgotten Revolt*, H.E.P, Issaquah, 1998, p. 75 and P.123.
[265] J. Schelvis, *Sobibor*, Berg-Oxford, New York, 2007, p. 87.
[266] Philip Bialowtiz, *A Promise At Sobibor*, The University of Wisconsin Press, Madison, 2010, p.118.
[267] T. Blatt, *Sobibor—The Forgotten Revolt*, H.E.P, Issaquah, 1998, p. 75 and P.110.

Szmajzner in his book *'Hell in Sobibór'*, 'Bajle had come with her husband and her little daughter, and that now, after what she had heard, she no longer nourished any hope of their still being alive.'[268]

She formed a relationship with Stanislaw Szmajzner, but that cooled. She escaped from Sobibór on the day of the revolt on October 14, 1943, but in all probability, she perished in the forest.[269]

STRATEN, Van, Rosette. Born on June 28, 1919, in Amsterdam, along with her twin sister Serline. She was a seamstress by occupation, and lived at Vechtstraat 5, 11 Amsterdam. She probably perished in the forest after escaping from Sobibór, after the revolt on October 14, 1943. Her date of death is listed as October 31, 1943.[270]

STRATEN, Van, Serline. Born on June 28, 1919, in Amsterdam, along with her twin sister Rosette. She, like her sister, was a seamstress by profession, and lived at Vechtstraat 5, 11 Amsterdam. She arrived in Westerbork Transit Camp on March 31, 1943, and was deported to Sobibór on April 6, 1943. According to a post-war statement by Ursula Stern, she confirmed that Deetje van Straten had a twin sister, who also used the painting room which Max van Dam used to paint pictures in Sobibór. According to Ursula Stern both sisters perished during their flight from Sobibór. Her date of death is listed as October 31, 1943. This could be the 'Li van Staden' mentioned by Jules Schelvis, as Max van Dam's painting assistant in his book.[271]

SZMAIS, Abraham. In early spring 1942, the Włodawa *Judenrat* were ordered to deliver 150 Jews to perform building work in

---

[268] S. Szmajzner, *Hell in Sobibor*, unpublished English version in authors possession, p.172.
[269] Miriam Novitch, *Sobibor*, Holocaust Library, New York, 1980, p.55.
[270] www.Joodsmonument.nl—online resource.
[271] www.Joodsmonument.nl—online resource. This could be the same Li van Staden, Max van Dam's assistant mentioned by Jules Schelvis, in his book *Sobibor*.

Sobibór. Two of those Jewish workers were Abraham Szmais, and Fajwel Cukierman's son-in-law (name not known). Both men were able to escape from Sobibór during April 1942. Their eventual fates are not known.[272]

SZMAJZNER, Mosze. He was deported from Opole Lubelski to Sobibór on May 12, 1942, along with other members of his family. He was selected by Gustav Wagner, to assist his Goldsmith brother Stanislaw. According to Stanislaw in his book *'Hell in Sobibór'* Mosze escaped with his Jewish sweetheart, and was free for one month. He was killed by Polish anti-Semites in the town of Lubartow.[273]

SZMAJZNER, Stanislaw. Born on March 13, 1927, in Pulawy, Poland. He was deported to Sobibór on May 12, 1942, from Opole Lubelski. He arrived in Sobibór with his father Josef, his mother Posel, and sister Rryrka, who were all gassed immediately.

Stanislaw was selected to work, along with his brother Mosze, and cousin Nojech (also a Szmajzner), by Gustav Wagner as a goldsmith, and he made rings and jewellery for members of the *SS*-Garrison. Wagner later appointed Stanislaw—better known as Szlomo—, as Chief of the Mechanics Shop. Szlomo joined the camp resistance and was responsible for stealing weapons from the Ukrainian living quarters, he visited their quarters in the *Vorlager*, under the pretext of repairing a stove. This brave action contributed to the success of the prisoner revolt, on October 14, 1943. His cousin Nojech and Jankus Rotter, his nephew, both died near the camp fences. In the forest he joined the partisans. He settled in Brazil after the war in 1947, and in 1968, published a book in his adopted Portuguese language titled, *'Hell in Sobibór. The Tragedy of a Teenage Jew'*.

---

[272] M. Bem, *Sobibor Extermination Camp 1942-1943*, Stichting Sobibor 2015, p.240.
[273] S. Szmajzner, *Hell in Sobibor*, unpublished English version in authors possession, p.286.

In May 1978, he identified Gustav Wagner at a Sao Paulo police station. Stanislaw committed suicide on March 3, 1989, in Goiania, Brazil.[274]

SZYMIEL, Leon. He escaped from Sobibór during the revolt on October 14, 1943. No further details known.[275]

TABORINSKIJ, Boris. Born during 1917, in Minsk. He was deported from the Sheroka Camp in Minsk, on or near September 15, 1943. He was on the same transport as Szlomo Leitman. He and Szlomo were selected for work as carpenters, although they were unskilled at this work. They worked on covering the roofs in *Lager IV*, the so-called *Nordlager*. He escaped from Sobibór during the revolt on October 14, 1943. He was in charge of a battle team that was ordered to cut the barbed wire fence near the Camp Commandant's house. He later joined the partisans and fought against the Germans.[276]

THOMAS, Kurt, Max (original name Kurt TICHO). Born on April 11, 1914, in Brno, Moravia, which is now part of the Czech Republic. Kurt was deported from Theresienstadt fortress Ghetto along with his father, mother and sister to the Piaski Transit Ghetto in Poland, on April 1, 1942.
In June 1942, his father Max, his mother Paula, (formerly Steiner), and his sister Marianne were deported from Piaski to Sobibór, where they all perished. Kurt followed them from Piaski to Sobibór on November 6, 1942, with around 3,000 other Jews. Kurt was selected to live, and initially worked in the Sorting Barracks, then was appointed as a medical orderly by Karl Frenzel, tending to the sick. Kurt escaped with Stanislaw Szmajzner during the revolt on October 14, 1943.
To honour his Dutch girlfriend Minny Hanny Cats, whom he got to know in Sobibór, he wrote an extensive account about

---

[274] Ibid.
[275] T. Blatt, *Sobibor—The Forgotten Revolt*, H.E.P, Issaquah, 1998, p.110.
[276] Y. Arad, *Belzec, Sobibor, Treblinka*, Indiana University Press, Bloomington and Indianapolis, 1987, p. 324.

his time in Sobibór on September 3, 1946, for the Dutch Red Cross. He settled in the United States of America, applying for citizenship during 1948. In the 1990's he wrote another account of his experiences in Sobibór. He passed away on June 8, 2009, in Columbus, Ohio, United States of America.[277]

TRAGER, Chaim. Born on March 5, 1906, in Chelm, Poland. He was transported from Chelm to Sobibór on May 22, 1942. On arrival he was selected to work as a bricklayer and helped construct a bakery. He claimed to have seen into *Lager III* whilst building a chimney on a roof top. He was also a member of the *Bahnhofkommando*.
Chaim escaped from Sobibór during the revolt on October 14, 1943. He later settled in Israel, and he died on August 1, 1969, in Tel Aviv, Israel.[278]

WAIZEN, Aleksej. Born on May 30, 1922, in Grigoriw, Russia. He arrived in Sobibór during the autumn of 1943, in a transport of Jews from Tarnopol, and was one of thirty men selected for work. He worked in the Sorting Barracks, sorting the murdered victims clothing. He escaped during the prisoner revolt on October 14, 1943. After the war in a court in Donetsk he declared that he was not Jewish, but he had not been able to convince the SS in Sobibór of this.[279]

WAJCEN, Szmul. He was employed in Sobibór burning the photographs, documents, prayer books and so forth, in an open pit, until the incinerator was built in mid-1943. He escaped during the revolt on October 14, 1943. During the escape he and Fredek Kostman met up with Thomas 'Toivi' Blatt in the forest. They were hidden by a farmer called Bojarski in a barn in Izbica. He survived an attack by Bojarski and his

---

[277] J. Schelvis, *Sobibor*, Berg-Oxford, New York, 2007, p. 240.
[278] Ibid. p.240.
[279] Ibid. p.240.

accomplices—they shot him, but did not kill him, on April 23, 1944. However, he was killed in the forest a short time later.[280]

WAJSPAPIR, Arkadij Moishejewicz. Born during 1921. Before the war he worked as an engineer in Donetsk. He served in the Red Army and was wounded and captured in Kiev. After his recovery he was sent to Minsk as a Prisoner of War. He was incarcerated in the Sheroka Street Labor Camp in Minsk.

On September 22, 1943, along with Sasha Pechersky, he arrived at the Sobibór death camp. He was selected for work, along with eighty others, on building barracks in *Lager IV*, the so-called *Nordlager*.

He played a leading role in the killing of the *SS*-men during the revolt on October 14, 1943. Along with Yehuda Lerner, he killed *SS-Unterscharführer* Siegfried Graetschus and the Ukrainian *Volksdeutsche* Ivan Klatt in the Shoemakers workshop After his escape from Sobibór as part of Sasha Pechersky's group, he crossed the River Bug and joined the partisans. After the war he returned to his profession as an engineer in Donetsk. He passed away on January 11, 2018, in Kiev.[281]

WAKS, Berl. He escaped from Sobibór during the revolt on October 14, 1943. No further details known.[282]

WANG, Abraham. Born on January 2, 1921, in Izbica, Poland. He was taken from Izbica to Sobibór by lorry, along with 280 other Jews on April, 23, 1943. He was selected to work in the Sorting Barracks, but he was also a member of the *Waldkommando*.

On July 23, 1943, whilst working in the *Waldkommando*, he was one of seven prisoners who managed to escape. After the war he settled in Israel. He passed away during 1978, in Rehovot, Israel.[283]

---

[280] T. Blatt, *From the Ashes of Sobibor*, Northwestern University Press, Evanston, Illinois, 1997, pp.186-187.
[281] J. Schelvis, *Sobibor*, Berg-Oxford, New York, 2007, p. 241.
[282] T. Blatt, *Sobibor—The Forgotten Revolt*, H.E.P, Issaquah, 1998, p.110.
[283] J. Schelvis, *Sobibor*, Berg-Oxford, New York, 2007, p. 241.

WEWRYK, Kalman. Born on June 25, 1906, in Chelm. He arrived at Sobibór on the same transport as Schlomo Alster. Selected to live he worked as a carpenter. He escaped during the revolt on October 14, 1943. He joined the partisans in the forest. After the Second World War ended, he married a survivor from Auschwitz Concentration Camp, and moved to France in 1956. During 1968, they settled in Canada. He wrote a book about his experiences during the war titled *'To Sobibór and Back. An Eyewitness Account.'*[284]

ZIELINSKI, Regina (formerly FELDMAN). Born on September 2, 1924, in Siedliszcze, Poland. She was taken on a horse-and-cart transport from the Staw-Nowosiulki Labor Camp, arriving at Sobibór on December 20, 1942.

Along with eleven other young women, she was selected to knit socks for the SS. Later she was put to work in the laundry and after that in the sewing room. She also worked in *Lager IV*, sorting and cleaning captured munitions.

She escaped during the prisoner revolt on October 14, 1943, and she eventually ended up in Frankfurt am Main, where she worked as a nanny with a German family. She married on December 24, 1945, in Wetzlar, and settled in Australia on August 3, 1949. She told her story to her son Andrew, who published her account in 2003, under the title, *'Conversations with Regina.'*[285]

ZISS, Meier. Born on November 15, 1927, in Lublin, Poland. He arrived in Sobibór during May or June 1942, and worked in the Sorting Barracks for six months, then he was employed as a barber. He also worked with Szmul Wajcen burning personal documents, photographs, prayer books in an open pit until an incinerator was installed in a barracks in *Lager II*. He escaped from Sobibór during the revolt on October 14, 1943. He later settled in Venezuela, from 1956, until 1961, then he settled in Israel.[286]

---

[284] Ibid p. 241.
[285] J. Schelvis, *Sobibor*, Berg-Oxford, New York, 2007, p. 242.
[286] Ibid.p.242.

Roll of Remembrance—
Poland and Other Countries A–Z

This Roll of Remembrance covers the victims who perished at Sobibór from Poland, Czechoslovakia, Soviet Union, and France.

This is a partial listing, in alphabetical order. This list has been compiled in the main from survivor testimony, either in written accounts, or during interviews with various Holocaust institutions.

BAJRACH, Abram. Born in Kalisz, Poland. Deported from a ghetto in the Lublin district, together with his brother Max. He was the youngest *Kapo* in the camp, aged seventeen years old, but he never beat anyone. This vexed the so-called 'Govenor', *Oberkapo* Moshe Sturm, and Abram was often cruelly beaten by the *SS*.

One night Abram returned to his barrack after an arduous working day, and fell asleep. He did not hear Gustav Wagner's order to stand up. Wagner furiously beat Abram and then shot him on the spot with his revolver, in front of all those in the barracks, including his younger brother Max. Abram was also known as Fibs.[287]

BAJRACH, Max. The younger brother of Abram. In the camp he worked in the stable. He was severely beaten and sent to *Lager III*, where he was executed for lightly hitting a horse, according to Thomas Blatt.[288]

BAUM, Lieb. Born during 1890, in Stropkov, Slovakia. He was a farmer by profession. He was deported from Stropkov on May 23, 1942. He was murdered at Sobibór.[289]

---

[287] T. Blatt, *Sobibor—The Forgotten Revolt*, H.E.P, Issaquah, 1998, p.51.
[288] Ibid. p.51.
[289] Yad Vashem Anonymous Project.

BLATT, Leon. A seventeen-year old from Izbica, no relation to Thomas Blatt, who escaped from the *Waldkommando* on July 20, 1943. He was caught hiding in the forest and brought back to Sobibór, where he was whipped to death on July 21, 1943, in *Lager II*, by a fellow prisoner known by the nickname of 'Radio.'[290]

BLAU, Adele (formerly Wallisch). Born on February 18, 1898, in Schaffa, Moravia. She was deported from Vienna to Kielce along with her husband Karl on February 19, 1941. They were deported to Treblinka during 1942, and have the unique distinction of being the only husband and wife couple allowed to live. She worked as a cook in the camp until she was taken along with her husband Karl, who was an *Oberkapo* appointed by Stangl, to the Sobibór death camp, following the prisoner revolt. When the dismantling of the camp was completed in November 1943, she committed suicide along with her husband.[291]

BLAU, Karl. Born on February 15, in Kollersdorf, Austria. He was deported from Vienna to Kielce along with his wife Adele, on February 19, 1941. They were deported to Treblinka during 1942. They have the unique distinction of being the only husband and wife couple allowed to live. Blau was described by Treblinka survivor Samuel Willenberg, 'as a man who was very fat, with the face of an imbecile and crooked legs, who had collaborated with the Gestapo in Kielce.'

He was appointed to the role of *Oberkapo* by Franz Stangl, They were both sent to the Sobibór death camp, following the prisoner revolt. When the dismantling of the camp was completed in November 1943, he committed suicide along with his wife.[292]

---

[290] T. Blatt, *Sobibor—The Forgotten Revolt*, H.E.P, Issaquah, 1998, p.64.
[291] Yad Vashem Central Database of Shoah Victims and Gitta Sereny, *Into That Darkness*, Pimlico. London 1974, p.209.
[292] Yad Vashem Central Database of Shoah Victims and Gitta Sereny, *Into That Darkness*, Pimlico. London 1974, p.209.

BOHM, Ernst. Born on December 12, 1893, in Krnov, formerly Jagerndorf, Sudetenland. He was a member of the *Judenrat* in Piaski. He was deported to Sobibór in 1942, where he perished.[293]

BRAND, Berek. According to Sobibór survivor Eda Lichtman who recalled what happened to him in Erich Bauer's private bar; 'One day, he broke a bottle; Berek Brand, a prisoner had to clean the floor with his tongue, the man's face was cut with glass.' He perished in the camp.[294]

BRAND, Hanka. Hanka was the sister of Eda Lichtman's husband. She was deported from Wieliczka together with her parents Susel and Leon Wiessberg in early 1943.[295]

BRESLER, Dr. Szulim. He was from Kolo. In Sobibór he was a dentist in *Lager I*. His son Josek was also in Sobibór. Dr Bresler gave medical attention to SS-man Werner Dubois after the attack on the armoury on the day of the prisoner revolt. He accompanied Dubois to the hospital in Chelm, but did not return. Most probably he was killed after delivering his patient.[296]

BRESLER, Jozek. Jozek was the son of Dr. Szulim Bresler from Kolo, as mentioned by Thomas Blatt. He knew Jozek before their time in Sobibór. This suggests he was one of the Jews resettled from Kolo, in the *Warthegau*, to Izbica.[297]

BRINKER, Motel. He was executed during the aftermath of the *Waldkommando* escape on July 20, 1943.[298]

CZEPIK, (Forename unknown). *Kapo* Czepik was in charge of the *Putzers* in Camp I. He was involved in the planning of the

---

[293] www.deathcamps.org—online resource.
[294] Miriam Novitch, *Sobibor*, Holocaust Library, New York, 1980, p.57.
[295] www.deathcamps.org—online resource.
[296] T. Blatt, *Sobibor—The Forgotten Revolt*, H.E.P, Issaquah, 1998, p. 86.
[297] Ibid, p. 59.
[298] Ibid p. 64.

revolt, he was a member of the camp's underground. He was active in the revolt itself on October 14, 1943. His fate is unknown, but probably he perished during the revolt.[299]

ELBERT, Hugo. Born on October 10, 1913, in Slovenska Lupca, Czechoslovakia. He was deported from Liptovsky on June 2, 1942, via Włodawa, to Sobibór.[300]

ENGEL, (Forename Unknown). A locksmith in the camp, who was responsible for killing *SS-Unterscharführer* Walter Ryba, in the *SS* garage during the prisoner revolt on October 14, 1943.[301]

FLAJSZHAKIER, Shaul. He was originally from Kalisz. Deported to Sobibór from the Lublin district. He was nicknamed 'Negro' because of his tanned complexion. He was a *Kapo* in the shoemakers workshop, but was beaten by the *SS* for not whipping prisoners.

He improvised a song on the orders of Gustav Wagner, which described life in the camp:

How happy is our life here

Fucked up

We are fed here

Fucked up

How happy we are in the green forest, where we live

Fucked up, fucked up

Fucked up, fucked up

Eda Lichtman recalled that the 'Negro', a cobbler, had lost his wife and two children. On the night before the revolt, he said to her, 'Let us swear that we shall fight and the young ones will

---

[299] Y. Arad, *Belzec, Sobibor, Treblinka*, Indiana University Press, Bloomington and Indianapolis, 1987, p. 313.
[300] Yad Vashem Central Database of Shoah Victims—online resource.
[301] Y. Arad, *Belzec, Sobibor, Treblinka*, Indiana University Press, Bloomington and Indianapolis, 1987, p. 328.

know freedom.' Then he knelt and kissed the ground while we were overcome with emotion.' Shaul lost his life during the prisoner revolt on October 14, 1943.[302]

FLEISCHER, Leibl. He was remembered by Eda Lichtman as a 13-year old boy with a stammer. He did not survive the revolt.[303]

Franz, *Kapo*. His surname is not known. He was a *Kapo* in *Lager III*. He was only 18-years old and came from the ghetto in Opole. Stanislaw Szmajzner recalled that he arrived in Sobibór, on the same transport as himself. His fate is unknown, but in all probability he perished in the camp.[304]

FRIEDBERG, Hans. Born on March 23, 1898, in Karlsruhe. He emigrated to France in 1936. He was deported from Drancy, the transit camp near Paris on March 25, 1943, to Sobibór. It is possible that this is the same person mentioned in other accounts by survivors as 'Alfred Friedberg', who convinced the Nazis he was once employed in a shoe factory in Frankfurt, and was thus selected to sort the mountains of shoes in *Lager II* left by the murdered Jews who perished in the gas chambers. Kurt Thomas recalled that he once lanced a boil for him, enabling him to return to work. In return Friedberg gave Kurt Thomas some gold coins. His fate is unknown.[305]

GENIEK, (Forename unknown). *Kapo* who was expected to blow the whistle for the prisoner roll-call on the day of the revolt, and march the prisoners to the main gate in rows of five,

---

[302] T. Blatt, *Sobibor—The Forgotten Revolt*, H.E.P, Issaquah, 1998, p.54 and Miriam Novitch, *Sobibor*, Holocaust Library, New York, 1980, p.58.

[303] Miriam Novitch, *Sobibor*, Holocaust Library, New York, 1980, p.60.

[304] S. Szmajzner, *Hell in Sobibor*, unpublished English version in authors possession, p.189.

[305] J. Schelvis, *Sobibor*, Berg-Oxford, New York, 2007, p. 160 and Yad Vashem Central Database of Shoah Victims.

escorted by *Trawnikimänner*. His fate is unknown, but probably he perished in the revolt.[306]

Gisela. An Austrian Jewess, who was thirty-five years old. She was known to *SS-Scharführer* Schutt. She was an actress or singer, who lived in the kitchen of the Forester's House in *Lager II*, with her niece Ruth. She was shot along with Ruth in *Lager III*.[307]

GOBERMAN, Moshe. Moshe and ten of his friends were killed by the Germans for planning a revolt. He was betrayed by an unknown prisoner, according to Moshe Bahir.[308]

GOLDSTEIN, Schlomo. Schlomo worked in the kitchen, according to Hershel Cukierman. He did not survive the revolt.[309]

GRINBAUM, Esther. Eda Lichtman recalled that Esther was a very sentimental and intelligent young woman, who feared on the night before the revolt, that they would all be killed. In all probability she perished during the revolt on October 14, 1943.[310]

GRINER, Chaim. Chaim came from Izbica. He was killed by Johann Niemann, following the revolt of the *Waldkommando* on July 20, 1943. Thomas Blatt recalled that Chaim, standing next to Motel Brinker, fell to the ground just before the execution. He was ordered to get up and was killed.[311]

Grisha. Grisha, whose full name is not known, was a Soviet Prisoner of War. On October 9, 1943, he was given twenty-five lashes for chopping wood in a sitting position. He decided, as

---

[306] Ibid. p.155 He is listed as Genjek, but in other accounts it is Geniek. I have opted for the latter.
[307] Y. Arad, *Belzec, Sobibor, Treblinka*, Indiana University Press, Bloomington and Indianapolis, 1987, p. 116.
[308] Miriam Novitch, *Sobibor*, Holocaust Library, New York, 1980, p.161
[309] www.deathcamps.org—online resource.
[310] Y. Arad, *Belzec, Sobibor, Treblinka*, Indiana University Press, Bloomington and Indianapolis, 1987, p. 321.
[311] T. Blatt, *Sobibor—The Forgotten Revolt*, H.E.P, Issaquah, 1998, p.64.

a result of this, to escape with others from Sobibór. Pechersky posted some of his men close to the fence by the latrine to forcibly stop the escape, which they did successfully. Grisha did not survive the revolt.[312]

HALBERSTADT, Leon. Remembered by Kurt Thomas, the medical orderly, who supplied him with medication and bandages from a special storeroom in the camp. His fate is unknown but in all probability he perished during the revolt.[313]

HERZ, Kiewe. Recalled by Kurt Thomas, the medical orderly, Kiewe was a 20-year old. His toes were frozen and he could not walk. Kurt Thomas kept in the barracks illegally. His fate is not known.

KAHN, Edgar. Edgar was born on October 12, 1907, in Merzig, Saarland. He fled from there in 1935, with all his family (parents, brothers, sisters, wife and baby girl). He was married to Thea Liselotte Salomon, who was still alive in 2006. A part of the family first gathered in Alencon (French Normandy) before some fled to the 'Free Zone.' Some survived the Holocaust, but most of them perished in Auschwitz-Birkenau.

Edgar Kahn was arrested in Lavelanet in the French Pyrenees, around February 20, 1943, triggered by the killing of two *Luftwaffe* officers in Paris on February 13, 1943. He was incarcerated in the Gurs Transit Camp.

On February 26, 1943,—the day when his daughter was born in Lavelanet, hidden in the attic of the local convent by sisters, who protected his wife and her daughters until the end of the war—he was taken to the Drancy Transit Camp near Paris, from where he was deported to Sobibór in Convoy Number 50, on March 4, 1943. He perished in Sobibór. This account was provided by the Grandson of Edgar Kahn.[314]

---

[312] Y. Arad, *Belzec, Sobibor, Treblinka*, Indiana University Press, Bloomington and Indianapolis, 1987, p. 321.
[313] J. Schelvis, *Sobibor*, Berg-Oxford, New York, 2007, p.87.
[314] www.deathcamps.org—online resource.

Karolek. Known in the camp as 'Blind Karolek' because he had only one good eye, he worked with Thomas Blatt in the incinerator building, burning photographs, documents, and letters of the murdered Jews. His fate is unknown, but he probably perished in the revolt.[315]

KATZ, Benjamin (aka Bunio). He was aged 26, and arrived in the camp during 1942, from Hrubieszow, along with Moshe Sturm. He was selected to be Sturm's assistant, along with Herbert Siegel. Bunio was part of the underground committee and played a leading role in the prisoner revolt on October 14, 1943. He was a *Kapo* who supervised a number of Jewish *Kommandos*, such as the *Bahnhofkommando*, the *Waldkommando* and the *Putzers*. He did not survive the revolt by the prisoners.[316]

KUPTSHIN, Sasha. A Soviet Prisoner of War who was one of the security team who safeguarded the meetings held by Sasha Pechersky in the women's barracks. His fate is unknown, but he probably perished during the revolt.[317]

LICHTMAN, Berek. According to Eda Lichtman, Berek was fifteen years old and was selected to work in the laundry, while the rest of his family perished. He later worked in the kitchen, and finally in the shoemakers barracks with his cousin Isaac. When *SS-Scharführer* Vallaster was killed during the revolt, Berek helped hide the body and clean the traces of blood. He fell during the revolt, while shooting at the guards.[318]

LUBARTOWSKA, Helka. A beautiful dark eyed brunette and a close friend of Esther Grinbaum. She was remembered by Eda

---

[315] T. Blatt, *From the Ashes of Sobibor*, Northwestern University Press, Evanston, Illinois, 1997, p. 121.
[316] M. Bem, *Sobibor Extermination Camp 1942-1943*, Stichting Sobibor 2015, p.196.
[317] Y. Arad, *Belzec, Sobibor, Treblinka*, Indiana University Press, Bloomington and Indianapolis, 1987, p. 310.
[318] Miriam Novitch, *Sobibor*, Holocaust Library, New York, 1980, p.60.

Lichtman, in her account of the conversations in the women's barracks the night before the day of the revolt. Helka said, 'There is no other way. Nobody knows what the results will be, but one thing is sure, we will not be led to slaughter.' Her fate is unknown, but in all probability she perished during the revolt.[319]

MARUM, Eva Brigitte. Born on July 17, 1919, in Karlsruhe, Germany. She was the youngest of three children. Her father Ludwig was arrested by the Nazis for anti-Nazi activity and he died in Kislau Concentration Camp on March 29, 1934.

In April 1934, Eva and her mother emigrated to France. Her sister obtained tickets to sail to the United States of America, but she could not sail as she was nine months pregnant. She gave birth in Marseille to a boy. Her son survived the Holocaust, because she gave him to a Jewish children's home in Limoges.

She was arrested by the Germans in January 1943, and taken to the transit camp at Drancy, near Paris. She was deported from Drancy on March 25, 1943. She perished in Sobibór on March 30, 1943.[320]

Moniek. His surname is unknown. He was promoted to a *Kapo*, when he became the conductor of the choir. He later became the *Kapo* of the *Putzers*. He was involved in the planning of the revolt by the camp's underground. He perished during the revolt on October 14, 1943.[321]

MORGENSZTERN, Rabbi Mendel. The last Rabbi in the Jewish community of Włodawa, he was a member of the Hassidic dynasty from Kock. He was deported in the summer of 1942, during the so-called '*Kinder Aktion*' when only children were

---

[319] Y. Arad, *Belzec, Sobibor, Treblinka*, Indiana University Press, Bloomington and Indianapolis, 1987, p. 321.
[320] USHMM—listed on the www.deathcamps.org—online resource.
[321] Y. Arad, *Belzec, Sobibor, Treblinka*, Indiana University Press, Bloomington and Indianapolis, 1987, p. 228.

sent to Sobibór. Rabbi Morgensztern voluntarily went on the transport because he wanted to accompany the children.[322]

Mundek. His surname is unknown. Mundek worked in the tailors workshop and his wife and children perished in Sobibór. Mundek was involved in the killing of Johann Niemann, as he held Niemann's new uniform, while Shubayev struck him with an axe.

Mundek the hat-maker broke down and stabbed Niemann's lifeless body with his scissors whilst calling out the names of his wife and children murdered in Sobibór. He was gagged and put in a closet. He did not survive the revolt.[323]

MUSSENFELD, Muniek. Muniek was a Polish Jew who worked in the camp bakery. According to Eda Lichtman, during the revolt he was killed on October 14, 1943, along with the other bakers.[324]

PINES, Joseph. Joseph was recalled by Moshe Bahir at the Adolf Eichmann Trial in 1961. He was his friend who had worked with him polishing the SS officers' boots and had also worked in the SS Casino with him. He perished in the revolt on October 14, 1943.[325]

POLISECKI, Mandel. Born in 1895, in Kamionka, Poland. He was the head of the *Judenrat* in Piaski. He was deported to Sobibór with his wife Rozalia and daughter Mania to Sobibór during July 1942, where he perished.[326]

POLISECKI, Mania. Born on November 8, 1919. She worked as a waitress in the *Volksküche* in the Piaski ghetto. She was deported along with her parents to Sobibór in July 1942, where she perished.[327]

---

[322] www.deathcamps.org—online resource.
[323] T. Blatt, *Sobibor—The Forgotten Revolt*, H.E.P, Issaquah, 1998, p.75.
[324] Yad Vashem Archives YVA 03/1291.
[325] www.Nizkor.org—Adolf Eichmann Transcripts—online resource.
[326] www.deathcamps.org—online resource.
[327] Ibid.

POLISECKI, Rozalia. She was Vice-President of the 'Help Committee for Refugees and Poor People' in the Piaski ghetto. Deported along with her husband and daughter to Sobibór in July 1942, where she perished.[328]

POZYCKI, Hersz. The son of Yankel, who was a shoemaker, and a younger brother to Szymon, the *Kapo* who was heavily involved in the planning and execution of the revolt by the prisoners. Hersz took part in the killing of *SS-Oberscharführer* Beckmann, holding him in a head-lock grip, whilst Chaim Engel stabbed Beckmann in the chest several times. Hersz grabbed the fallen Nazi's revolver. He did not survive the revolt.[329]

POZYCKI, Szymon. Described by Dov Freiberg as a man of twenty-something from Warsaw, although Thomas Blatt thought he was aged approximately thirty-five. He was a *Kapo* who supervised the *Waldkommando*. He played a leading role in the murder of *Oberkapo* Herbert Naftanial better known by the nickname of *'Berliner.'* He also played his part in the planning and execution of the prisoner revolt. He perished during the revolt on October 14, 1943.[330]

RABINOWITZ, Shimon. Shimon remembered by Eda Lichtman, as a Jew who cooked food for the sick in the camp in secret. He had found a little kerosene stove and cooked some rice. Once he was caught carrying food to a patient and was beaten up by Otto Weiss.[331] Another day Frenzel entered the barracks at the same time Shimon was cooking. The poor man hid the saucepan under his foot. I remember how much he suffered from the burns he got.' Shimon was killed during the prisoner revolt on October 14, 1943.[332]

---

[328] Ibid.
[329] T. Blatt, *Sobibor—The Forgotten Revolt*, H.E.P, Issaquah, 1998, p.76.
[330] T. Blatt, *Sobibor—The Forgotten Revolt*, H.E.P, Issaquah, 1998, p.62.
[331] The correct name was Bruno Weiss.
[332] Miriam Novitch, *Sobibor*, Holocaust Library, New York, 1980, pp. 60-61.

ROSENTHAL, Hedwig. Born on May 16, 1878, in Sinshelmer, in Worms, Germany. She emigrated to France. She was deported from Drancy, on March 23, 1943 to Sobibór, where she perished.[333]

ROTTER, Jankiel (Jankus). A nephew of Stanislaw Smajzner, he was deported with Stanislaw and other family members from Opole Lubelski in May 1942. On arrival he was selected by Gustav Wagner to work with Stanislaw as a jeweller. Later Gustav Wagner selected him to be his *Putzer*. Smajzner wrote in his book '*Hell in Sobibór*' that he learned in the forest, some time after his escape from Sobibór, that his nephew Jankus and his cousin Nojechhad died on the day of the revolt, against the barbed-wire fences trying to break out from the camp.[334]

Ruth. The 22-year old niece of Gisela from Austria, lived in the Forester's House. She became involved with *SS-Unterscharführer* Paul Groth, and many prisoners noticed that this had a positive effect on Groth, who was one of the most feared SS men. She was shot in *Lager III*, along with Gisela.[335]

SALZ, Sala. Sala was remembered by Eda Lichtman, as a blond with blue eyes, who calmed everyone in the women barracks on the eve of the revolt. She was probably killed during the revolt.[336]

SIEGEL, Herbert. He was a *Kapo*, who hailed from the Polish town of Rejowiec. He was also known in Sobibór as *Rajowiecer*. He was shot by Karl Frenzel in *Lager III*, along with *Oberkapo* Moshe Sturm, and other *Kapos* in the summer of 1943, for

---

[333] Yad Vashem Central Database of Shoah Victims.
[334] S. Szmajzner, *Hell in Sobibor*, unpublished English version in authors possession, p.285.
[335] Y. Arad, *Belzec, Sobibor, Treblinka*, Indiana University Press, Bloomington and Indianapolis, 1987, pp.116-117.
[336] Y. Arad, *Belzec, Sobibor, Treblinka*, Indiana University Press, Bloomington and Indianapolis, 1987, p. 321.

planning an escape that was aborted. They were betrayed to the Germans by *Kapo 'Berliner.'*[337]

SRULEK (Forename unknown). He was a baker in the camp. Before the killing of Johann Niemann, the deputy commandant as he dismounted his horse, asked Srulek to hold the reins until he returned. He did not survive the revolt.[338]

STARK, Shaul. According to Eda Lichtman, Shaul was from Zolkiewka, and he arrived on the same transport as Leon Felhendler in November 1942. He was in charge of the geese and he was whipped to death by Frenzel, Bredow, Wagner, and Weiss when a goose died. His last words were, 'Avenge me, comrades, avenge me.'[339]

STURM, Moshe. Moshe was deported from Hrubieszow to Sobibór. He was approximately 22-years old. He was appointed to the post of *Oberkapo* (Head *Kapo*), known as *'Governor'* and carried out his duties with zeal. Post war testimonies revealed that some of the prisoners called him 'Mad Moisze,' as no one knew what he would do next, since his mood would change unexpectedly. At times he was cruel and would beat people for no apparent reason, yet afterwards he would come back to beg for forgiveness, crying like a small boy.' Moshe was executed by the Germans in the summer of 1943, accused of planning an escape with some of his fellow *Kapos*. His position was taken by *Kapo 'Berliner'*, who had betrayed him to Karl Frenzel.[340]

SZMAJZNER, Josel. Father of Stanislaw Szmajzner, a deeply religious man who owned stores. Wholesaler of fruit, chiefly strawberries to Germany. He lived in Pulawy, and was transferred to the Opole Ghetto. He was deported from Opole on

---

[337] M. Bem, *Sobibor Extermination Camp 1942-1943*, Stichting Sobibor 2015, p.196.
[338] J. Schelvis, *Sobibor*, Berg-Oxford, New York, 2007, p.161.
[339] Miriam Novitch, *Sobibor*, Holocaust Library, New York, 1980, p.57.
[340] M. Bem, *Sobibor Extermination Camp 1942-1943*, Stichting Sobibor 2015, p.198.

May 11, 1942, on foot to Naleczow. From there he was brought to Sobibór where he arrived on May 12, 1942. He was murdered on arrival along with other members of his family.[341]

SZMAJZNER, Nojech. A cousin of Stanislaw Szmajzner, he was deported from Opole Lubelskie to Sobibór on May 12, 1942. He worked with Stanislaw as a jeweller, and was later on selected by Wagner as a *Platzmeister*, gathering all the pots and pans and other utensils brought by the Jews to the camp, and checking them for hidden valuables. According to Stanislaw he perished in the revolt on October 14, 1943, against the barbed wire along with his nephew Jankus.[342]

SZMAJZNER, Posel. Mother of Stanislaw Szmajzner. She divided her time between running the household and helping Josel in the family business. She lived in Pulawy, and then in the Opole Ghetto. She was deported from Opole on May 11, 1942, on foot to Naleczow. From there she was brought to Sobibór where she arrived on May 12, 1942. She was murdered on arrival along with other members of her family.[343]

SZMAJZNER, Ryrka. Older sister of Stanislaw Szmajzner. She married Josef who worked in the family business. She lived in Pulawy, and then in the Opole Ghetto. She was deported from Opole on May 11, 1942, to Naleczow on foot. From there she was brought to Sobibór where she arrived on May 12, 1942. She was murdered on arrival along with other members of her family.[344]

SZPIRO, Mira. Mira was deported from Siedliszcze to Sobibór. Eda Lichtman said that Mira was a beautiful young woman who was killed during the revolt on October 14, 1943.[345]

---

[341] S. Szmajzner, *Hell in Sobibor*, unpublished English version in authors possession, p.17.
[342] Ibid. p.285.
[343] Ibid. p.17.
[344] Ibid. p.17.
[345] Yad Vashem Archives—YVA 03/ 1291.

TUCHMAN, Zygmund. A seventeen-year old *Kapo*, who was transferred from *Lager II* to *Lager III*, because whilst delivering disinfectants to the secret part of the death camp, his group saw inside *Lager III*, and they were not allowed to return.[346]

WEISSBERG, Dr. Leon. Father-in-law of Eda Lichtman. He was a doctor by profession in Wieliczka, Poland. He was deported from there in early 1943, to Sobibór, along with his wife Susel. He arrived in Sobibór wearing his doctor's clothes. Eda saw him for the last time on his way to *Lager III*.[347]

WEISSBERG, Susel. Mother-in-law of Eda Lichtman. She was deported from Wieliczka, near *Krakau*, to Sobibór, along with her husband Leon. Eda saw her for the last time on her way to *Lager III*.[348]

WIESZUBSKI, *Kapo*. Remembered by Selma Engel. He took part in the revolt. His fate is unknown, but he probably perished during the prisoner revolt.[349]

---

[346] T. Blatt, *Sobibor—The Forgotten Revolt*, H.E.P, Issaquah, 1998, p.17.
[347] www.deathcamps.org—online resource.
[348] Ibid.
[349] Selma Engel Interview with USHMM on July 16, 1990.

Roll of Remembrance— Holland A–Z

Sobibór Museum—Wir wollen Sie nicht vergessen
(Chris Webb Private Archive)

The above list of German Jews—who emigrated to Holland but were deported from Westerbork to the Sobibór death camp—have not been forgotten. These, where possible, have been included in the following Roll of Remembrance, and their entry is duly noted with the memorial details.

This Roll of Remembrance covers the victims from Holland who perished at Sobibór, including both native-born Jews and German Jews who emigrated to Holland after the Nazis came to power in Germany. The main source of this information is the online resource *www.Joodsmonument.nl,* and the *www.deathcamps.org* online resource. The vast majority of the entries come from the *Joodsmomument,* and the source will not be individually stated. Where another source has been used then

211

this will be shown. We do not have the space to list all the entries from this database, and naturally apologize in advance for those names not selected. They are no less important, but the online resource can be consulted to see all the names of the deported Jews.

I have, in this edition, tried to capture more names, so have favoured more individual surnames, rather than multiple entries, and concentrated more on native-born Dutch Jews, instead of German Jews who settled in Holland after the Nazi's coming into power. Circa 150 native Dutch names have been recorded, and circa 80 German-born names, who settled in Holland, are included. Around 40 names from other countries, who ended up in Holland, and were deported to Sobibór, have also been included. This list is an extract and this must be taken into account. I apologize in advance if your relatives' names have not been included.

These pages are dedicated to my late friend Martin van Liempt, from Holland, who helped with a number of entries:

AALST-PRINS, Van, Emma. Born on September 17, 1874, in Den Haag. She lived at Valkenboslan 320, Den Haag. She was deported on the first transport, and was the first name listed on March 2, 1943. She died in Sobibór on March 5, 1943.

ADLER, Max. Born on January 1, 1864, in Schotmar a.d. Lippe, Germany. He emigrated to Holland, and he lived at Tintorettostraat 39 huis, Amsterdam. He was deported from Westerbork on May 4, 1943. He perished along with his wife Emmy on May 7, 1943.

ADLER-ENOCH, Emmy. Born on October 19, 1869, in Hannover, Germany. She emigrated to Holland and lived at Tintorettostraat 39 huis, Amsterdam She was deported from Westerbork on May 4, 1943. She perished along with her husband Max on May 7, 1943.

ADLER-HEYMANN, Sophie. Born on December 31, 1882, in Ahrweiler, Germany. Before the war she lived in Kassel. In 1938, she emigrated to Holland and lived at Uiterwaardenstraat 86 I, Amsterdam. She perished in Sobibór on May 21, 1943.[350]

ASSER, Mathilde. Mathilde was the daughter of Eva and was born in Amsterdam on July 25, 1901. She lived at Sarphatistraat 157 II, Amsterdam. She was a Seamstress by profession. She perished along with her mother in Sobibór on May 28, 1943.

ASSER, Israel. Israel was the son of Eva Asser and was born on July 23, 1906, in Amsterdam. He lived at Sarphatistraat 157 II, Amsterdam. He was a merchant by profession. He perished in Sobibór on May 7, 1943.

ASSER-VET, Eva. Born in Alkmaar, Holland, on June 28, 1870. She lived at Sarphatistraat 157 II, Amsterdam. She perished in Sobibór on May 28, 1943.

BACHRACH, Klara. Born on December 27, 1936, in Den Haag. She lived at Spaarnedwarsstraat 13, Den Haag. She was part of the Childrens Transport from Vugt. She perished in Sobibór on July 2, 1943.

BACHRACH-SCHWARZENBERGER, Lina. Born on December 4, 1872, in Heilbronn, Germany. She emigrated to Holland, and lived at Dintelstraat 84 I, Amsterdam. She was deported from Westerbork to Sobibór, where she perished on March 26, 1943.[351]

BIERMAN, Falk. Born on July 3, 1889, in Haarlem. He lived at Brinkgreverweg 248, Deventer. He was deported from the Westerbork Transit Camp on April 20, 1943. He died in Sobibór on April 23, 1943.

BIERMAN, Helene. Born on September 15, 1862, in Plettenberg, Germany. She emigrated to Holland, and lived at

---

[350] Listed on the memorial in the Sobibor Museum shown on the heading of this chapter.
[351] Listed on the memorial in the Sobibor Museum shown on the heading of this chapter.

Wakkerstraat 28, beletage, Amsterdam. She was deported from the Westerbork Transit Camp on June 29, 1943. She died in Sobibór on July 2, 1943.

BLOCH-WERTHEIMER, Melanie Erika. Born on July 31, 1871, in Regensburg, Germany. She emigrated to Holland and lived at Linnaeuspark 38 II, Amsterdam. She was held in Westerbork from March 6, 1943, until March 10, 1943, when she was deported to Sobibór. She perished there on March 13, 1943.

BLOK-ELIAS, Minna. Born on May 29, 1862, in Altona, Germany. She emigrated to Holland and lived at Uiterwaardenstraat 24 II, Amsterdam. She perished in Sobibór on July 2, 1943.

BORZYKOWSKI, David. Born on February 13, 1892, in Janow, Poland. He moved to Amsterdam after the First World War. The family home was located at Nieuwe Kerkstraat 103 III, Amsterdam. He was an upholsterer by profession. David and the rest of his family were deported to Westerbork on May 26, 1943. On June 1, 1943, he was deported 'East' to Sobibór, and he was murdered on his arrival on June 4, 1943.

BORZKOWSKI, Hermann. Born on October 30, 1927, in Amsterdam, the only son of David and Gitla. He lived at the family home that was located at Nieuwe Kerkstraat 103 III, Amsterdam. He was deported to Westerbork on May 26, 1943. On June 1, 1943, he was deported 'East' to Sobibór, and he was murdered on his arrival on June 4, 1943.

BORZKOWSKI-STROZ, Gitla. Born on April 18, 1895, in Czestochowa, Poland. She was married to David and mother to Herman. She lived at the family home that was located at Nieuwe Kerkstraat 103 III, Amsterdam. She was deported to Westerbork on May 26, 1943. On June 1, 1943, she was deported 'East' to Sobibór, and she was murdered on her arrival on June 4, 1943, along with her husband, and other members of her family.

BRUCK-FALKENBERG, Herta. Born August 2, 1899, in Zempelburg, West Prussia. She settled in Holland and lived at Eendrachtstraat 8 II, Amsterdam. She worked as a Clerk by profession. She perished in Sobibór on May 7, 1943.

BRUCK, Van; Family. A mother with a son and two daughters. They were deported from Holland, and the whole family was selected for work in the camp. The mother worked in the Tailors' workshop, her daughters segregated the clothes of the murdered people. The son transported the suitcases on the narrow-gauge railway into the camp. One day the son was brought to *Lager III*, and never returned. The whole family was killed in Sobibór.[352]

CATS, Minny, Hanny. Born on March 6, 1920, in Haarlem, Holland. She lived with her mother Elisabeth Speelman-Cats, who was born on December 11, 1890, at Schotersingel 7, Haarlem. Her mother was gassed on arrival, but Minny was selected to live. She became the girlfriend of Sobibór survivor Kurt Thomas. She lost her life during the revolt on October 14, 1943.

DALBERG, Julius, Jonas. Born on May 21, 1882, in Essentho, Germany. He was a member of the Jewish Community Council in Kassel until 1933, and redactor of the '*Jüdische Wochenzeitung für Kassel, Hessen und Waldeck*,' in which he published many articles about the Jewish history of Kassel and the surrounding areas. In September 1933, he was arrested and spent two weeks in the Breitenau Concentration Camp near Guxhagen.

After his release he emigrated together with his wife Bella to Amsterdam, Holland, where he ran a *Judacia* / Antique shop until 1940.They lived at Noorder Amstellaan 31 a III, Amsterdam. He perished in Sobibór on July 23, 1943.[353]

---

[352] Eda Lichtman YVA 031291.
[353] Listed on the memorial in the Sobibor Museum shown on the heading of this chapter.

DALBERG-NUSSBAUM, Bella. Born on January 28, 1883, in Hersfeld, Germany. Until 1933, she lived in Kassel, Germany, from where she emigrated with her husband Julius to Amsterdam. They lived at Noorder Amstellaan 31 a III, Amsterdam. She perished in Sobibór on July 23, 1943.[354]

DAM, Max, van. Born on March 19, 1910, in Winterswijk, Holland. He lived at Zomerdijkstraat 18 I, Amsterdam. He was the son of Aron van Dam and Johanna Leviticus. He was a painter by profession. He studied at the Royal Academy of Fine Arts in Antwerp, Belgium. He preferred to paint Socialist and Zionist themes. During 1938, he won the Prix de Rome, for his painting of '*Hagar and Ismael in the Desert.*'
During the Nazi occupation he was hidden by his friend, Professor Hemmelrjik, but in the course of trying to escape to Switzerland, he was arrested in the Swiss Alps. He was sent to the Drancy Transit Camp near Paris.
He was deported from Drancy on the fourth transport to Sobibór on March 25, 1943. Selected to work he was set up in a painters studio in *Lager I*. Max van Dam painted landscapes and portraits of the *SS*, including Karl Frenzel, and their animals. A painting of Fifi, a dog who belonged to Erich Bauer, was completed.
Karl Frenzel testified after the war that *Kapo* Benjamin Katz (aka Bunio) from the *Bahnhofskommando*, had told him that the Dutch Jews were planning an escape on April 20, 1943. Seventy-two Dutch Jews were executed in *Lager III*. In all probability the break-out was really a break-out planned by Polish Jews.
Max van Dam was amongst the handful of Dutch prisoners spared that day, as he was in the process of painting Frenzel's portrait. It was only a reprieve for Max, was murdered on September 20, 1943.

---

[354] Ibid.

DEEN, Helga. Born on May 6, 1925, in Stettin. She emigrated with her parents Kathe and Willy Deen in 1934, to Holland. They lived at Pelgrimsweg 45, Tilburg. She was incarcerated in Vught Transit Camp between April 1943, to June 1943. There she kept a diary about her beloved Tilburg. The diary and several letters survived the war and are now in the collection of the Regional Archives in Tilburg. She and other members of her family were deported from Westerbork, on July 13, 1943. She perished in Sobibór on July 16, 1943.

DEEN, Klaus Gottfried. Born on June 22, 1928, in Stettin. His family emigrated to Holland in 1934. The family lived at Pelgrimsweg 45, Tilburg. In the same year he attended the 'Openbare Lagere School Number 3' in Tilburg. He later went to the Rijks-HBS Koning Wilhelm II, also in Tilburg.
In October 1941, he was at the Joods Lyceum in Den Bosch. He was sent to Vugt Transit Camp and was accepted in the carpentry workshop as an apprentice. He was then sent to Westerbork between July 3-13, 1943. He was deported from Westerbork to Sobibór on July 13, 1943. He perished in Sobibór, three days later on July 16, 1943.

DEEN, Willy. Born on March 3, 1891, in Tilburg, Holland. After living in Stettin, Poland, he returned to Tilburg, with his family in 1934. They lived at Pelgrimsweg 45, Tilburg. A member of the Jewish Council in Tilburg. He was sent to Vught Transit Camp, where he was an administrator. He was sent, along with his family, to Westerbork, between July 3-13, 1943. He was deported from Westerbork to Sobibór on July 13, 1943. He perished on July 16, 1943.

DEEN-WOLF, Kathe. Born on May 20, 1894, in Nuremburg, Germany. She emigrated with her husband Willy and family to Holland in 1934. She lived at Pelgrimsweg 45, Tilburg. She and other members of her family were deported from Westerbork on July 13, 1943. She perished on July 16, 1943.

DRESDEN, Eva. Born on June 26, 1937, in Amsterdam. She lived at Van Woustraat 174 III, Amsterdam. She died along with her Mother Anna, in Sobibór on July 23, 1943. Her father Barend was murdered in Auschwitz on November 30, 1944.

DRESDEN-POLAK, Anna. Born on November 24, 1906, in Amsterdam. She was a daughter of Mejer Polak and Mietje Vischjager. She married Barend Dresden on June 25, 1936, in Amsterdam. She lived at Van Woustraat 174 III, Amsterdam. He was a tailor by profession. The couple had one daughter Eva, born in 1937. Anna Polak competed in the 1928, Olympic Games in Amsterdam. She won a gold medal in the women's gymnastic team event. She perished in Sobibór on July 23, 1943.

DRIEDUITE, Alexander. Born on October 27, 1919. He lived at Rapenburg 102 I, Amsterdam, and he worked as a Sales Representative. He was married to Mina Drieduite-Koopman, who died in Sobibór a week after him. He perished in Sobibór on July 2, 1943.

DRIEDUITE, Celine. Born on May 9, 1922. She was the daughter of David and Evelina Drieduite. She lived at Rapenburg 102 I, Amsterdam. She perished in Sobibór on July 2, 1943.

DRIEDUITE, David. Born on December 23, 1892. He lived at Rapenburg 102 I, Amsterdam and worked in Amsterdam as a bank clerk. He died in Sobibór on July 2, 1943, along with his wife Evelina, son Alexander and daughter Celine.

DRUCKER, Martin, Samuel. Born on May 11, 1889, in Berlin. He emigrated to Holland in December 1936. He lived at Blasiusstraat 58 I, Amsterdam. He was a Merchant by profession. He was held in Vught Transit Camp from March 25 until May 24, 1943. He was sent to Westerbork on May 24, 1943. A day later on May 25, 1943, he was sent on a transport to Sobibór. He perished in Sobibór, along with his wife Gitla, on May 28, 1943.

DRUCKER-EHRENFREUND, Gitla. Born in Przemysl, Poland on August 28, 1893. The wife of Martin Samuel Drucker, and they lived in Berlin. They emigrated to Holland in December 1936, and they lived at Blasiusstraat 58 I, Amsterdam. She was incarcerated in the Vught Transit Camp from March 25, 1943, until May 24, 1943. Following deportation to Westerbork on May 24, 1943, she was deported a day later on May 25, 1943. She was murdered in Sobibór on May 28, 1943.[355]

DRUCKER, Ruth. Born on March 4, 1913, in Bengel, Germany. She was the daughter of Abraham Drucker and Berta Bermann. She emigrated to Holland in 1933, and lived at Merwedeplein 14 II, Amsterdam. She was a domestic servant by profession. She was held in Westerbork between March 9, 1943, until March 17, 1943. She was deported from Westerbork on March 17, 1943, and she was murdered in Sobibór, three days later on March 20, 1943.

EHRENFREUND, Leo, Leib. Born on March 2, 1885, in Przemysl, Poland. He lived in Berlin before emigrating to Holland, with his wife Martha. They lived at Biesboschstrat 42 III, Amsterdam. He was a Tailor by profession. He perished in Sobibór on May 21, 1943.

EHRENFREUND, Martha (formerly Rosenstein). Born on November 24, 1883, in Neidenburg, Germany. She lived in Berlin with her husband Leo, before settling in Amsterdam. They lived at Biesboschstrat 42 III, Amsterdam. She perished in Sobibór on May 21, 1943.

ELIAS, Frieda. Born on January 6, 1877, in Hamburg, Germany. She emigrated to Holland, with her husband Moritz, and they lived at Sparrenweg 7 II, Amsterdam. She was deported from Westerbork on March 30, 1943. She perished in Sobibór on April 2, 1943.

---

[355] www.bundesarchiv.de/gedenkbuch—online resource.

ELIAS, Helen. Born on June 6, 1870, in Altona, Hamburg, Germany. She emigrated to Holland and lived in Amsterdam. She lived at Uiterwaardenstraat 24 II Amsterdam. She was deported from Westerbork on March 2, 1943, to Sobibór. She perished there three days later on March 5, 1943.

ELIAS, Moritz. Born on October 16, 1875, in Hamburg, Germany. With his wife Frieda they emigrated to Holland and settled in Amsterdam. They lived at Sparrenweg 7 II, Amsterdam. He was deported from Westerbork on March 30, 1943. He perished in Sobibór on April 2, 1943, along with his wife.

ELIAS-FRANK, Bertha (formerly Frank). Born on June 9, 1871, in Bad Kissingen, Germany. She emigrated to Holland on July 6, 1933. She lived in Jan van Eijckstraat 25 I, Amsterdam. She was held in Westerbork from December 3, 1942, until March 10, 1943. She was deported from Westerbork on March 10, 1943, and she perished in Sobibór on March 13, 1943.[356]

EMMERICH, Ile (Ilse). Born on December 10, 1926, in Frankfurt am Main, Germany. She emigrated to Holland and lived at Marnixstraat 398, I, Amsterdam. She died in Sobibór on July 9, 1943.

ERNST, Emil. Born on June 22, 1892, in Herbede, Germany. He lived at Tweede jan Steenstraat 104, III, Amsterdam. He was a laundry dispatcher by profession. He perished in Sobibór on May 28, 1943.[357]

FEIWEL, Jozef, Chaim, Benjamin. Born on October 31, 1889, in Tarnow, Poland. He lived and worked in Amsterdam, as a Merchant by profession. He lived at Zoomstraat 7 I, Amsterdam. He perished in Sobibór on July 23, 1943, along with his wife Fanny and son Norbert.

---

[356] Listed on the memorial in the Sobibor Museum shown on the heading of this chapter.
[357] Ibid.

FEIWEL, Norbert. Born on September 8, 1929, in Berlin. He was the son of Jozef and Fanny. He lived at Zoomstraat 7 I, Amsterdam. He was deported from Westerbork, he perished in Sobibór on July 23, 1943, along with his parents.

FEIWEL-NUSSBAUM, Fanny. Born on October 15, 1905, in Munich. Married to Jozef. She lived at the family home in Zoomstraat 7 I, Amsterdam. She was deported from Westerbork, she perished in Sobibór on July 23, 1943, along with her husband and son.

FRANK-ROSENBUSCH, Elsa. Born on December 29, 1889, in Dinslaken, Germany. She emigrated to Holland on January 2, 1939. She lived at Amstellaan 79 III, Amsterdam. She was deported from Westerbork on March 30, 1943, and she perished in Sobibór on April 2, 1943.

FRANK, Frederik. Born on September 3, 1886, in Gronningen, Holland. He lived in Bremen until he emigrated to Holland on January 23, 1933. He lived at Sint Antoniesbreestraat 52 I, Amsterdam. He was deported from Westerbork on April 6, 1943, and he perished in Sobibór on April 9, 1943.

FRANK, Hans. Born on May 26, 1894, in Quedlinburg, Germany. He emigrated to Holland and he lived at Cliostraat 20 I, Amsterdam. He was a Merchant by profession. He was deported from Westerbork on July 20, 1943, and he perished in Sobibór on July 23, 1943.

FRIEDMANN, Benno. Born on June 22, 1921, in Duisburg, Germany. The son of Jakob and Liebe. He emigrated to Holland and lived at Amstel 107 III, Amsterdam. He was a weaver by profession. He perished in Sobibór, on May 14, 1943.

FRIEDMANN, Jakob, Salomon. Born in Rzeszow, Poland on April 28, 1894. He settled in Germany, but emigrated to Holland, and he lived at Amstel 107 III, Amsterdam. He was a Merchant by profession. He perished in Sobibór, on May 21, 1943.

FRIEDMANN-SONNENBERG, Liebe, Rachela. Born on January 9, 1898, in Lancut, Poland Wife of Jakob, she lived in Germany, but emigrated to Holland. She lived at Amstel 107 III, Amsterdam. She died in Sobibór on May 21, 1943.

GERSON, Max. Born on October 28, 1869, in Kriescht, Germany. He emigrated to Holland and lived at Frans van Mierisstraat 78 bovenhuis, Amsterdam. He was the father of the well-known Kurt Gerson, also known as Kurt Gerron. Kurt was a famous actor and director of films. He acted with Marlene Dietrich in the film *Blue Angel* in 1930. In 1935, Kurt Gerron moved to Holland. In 1944, he was transported from Westerbork to Theresienstadt, just outside Prague. He directed a propaganda film for the Nazis, titled, 'The Führer Gives The Jews A City,' in 1944. Kurt was deported to Auschwitz, along with his wife Olga. They were both murdered in the gas chambers on October 28, 1944.

Max Gerson died in Sobibór on May 7, 1943, along with his wife Toni.

GERSON-RIESE, Toni. Born on July 25, 1874, in Berlin, Germany. She emigrated to Holland, and lived at Frans van Mierisstraat 78 bovenhuis, Amsterdam. She was the wife of Max Gerson, and the mother of Kurt. She died in Sobibór, along with her husband on May 7, 1943.

GEZANG-GOUDEKET, Florence. Born on September 17, 1908. She lived at Noordwijkschelann 9, Den Haag. She was the mother of Koenrad. She perished in Sobibór on April 9, 1943.

GEZANG-HUIB, Koenrad. Born on January 29, 1942, in Den Haag, Holland. His mother was Florence Gezang-Goudeket. In April 1942, he lived at Noordwijkschelann 9, Den Haag. In October 1942, an abandoned child was taken in by the creche opposite the Hollandsche Schouwburg (Dutch Theatre) in Amsterdam.

The little boy was given the name Remi van Dunwijk. When the creche was closed down, he was taken to Westerbork and from there he was deported to Sobibór. He perished there on May 21, 1943. After the war ended, his true identity became known, for his father survived the Holocaust.

GODFRIED-NUSSBAUM, Margarete Flora. Born on October 19, 1886, in Hannover, Germany. She was married to Samuel Godfried. She lived at Hoofdstraat 37, Hoogeveen. She died in Sobibór on May 21, 1943, along with her husband.

HABERMAN, Abraham. Born on April 17, 1929, in Chrzanow, Poland. He lived with his mother and sister in Ruyschstraat 43 III Amsterdam. He perished in Sobibór on May 28, 1943.

HABERMAN, Mina. Born on January 6, 1927, in Krakow, Poland. She lived with her mother and brother in Ruyschstraat 43 III Amsterdam. She perished in Sobibór on May 28, 1943.

HABERMAN-JUNGENWIRT, Chaja, Malka. Born on October 16, 1893, in Chrzanow, Poland. She lived in Amsterdam, with her son and daughter at Ruyschstraat 43. She perished in Sobibór on May 28, 1943.

HAHN, Augusta. Born on March 9, 1888, in Auerbach, Germany. She emigrated to Holland. She lived at Spoorlaan 5, Roermond. She was a Seamstress by profession. She was deported from Westerbork on May 25, 1943. She perished in Sobibór on May 28, 1943.

HAMBURGER-SCHLACHTER, Bertha. Born on October 29, 1873, in Braunsbach, Germany. She emigrated to Holland. She lived at Wooldstraat 26 a, Winterswijk. She was deported from Westerbork on July 20, 1943. She perished in Sobibór on July 23, 1943.

HAMBURGER, Jessie. Born on April 1, 1877, in London, England. She lived at Prinses Marielaan 24, Amersfoort. She perished in Sobibór on July 23, 1943.

HAMBURGER, Levie. Born on November 17, 1898, in Maarssevern, in the Dutch province of Utrecht. He was the head of the family, and was married to Bertha Hamburger-Korn. The family lived at Jonas Daniel Meijerplein 6 boven, Amsterdam. They had five children. Levie and his family were deported from Westerbork on June 1, 1943. He perished in Sobibór, along with all his family, on June 4, 1943.

HAMBURGER, Samuel. Born on February 26, 1869, in Colmberg, Germany. He emigrated to Holland. He lived at Wooldstraat 26 a, Winterswijk. He perished in Sobibór on May 14, 1943.

HAMBURGER-KORN, Bertha. Born on April 30, 1900, in Lichtenroth, Germany. She was the wife of Levie. The family lived at Jonas Daniel Meijerplein 6 boven, Amsterdam. Herself, her husband and five children were deported from Westerbork on June 1, 1943. Bertha, her husband and five children, all perished in Sobibór on June 4, 1943.

HAMME, Joel. Born on July 19, 1929, in Den Haag, Holland. In September 1941, he was enrolled in Grade 1 of the Municipal Commercial Secondary School in the Hague. In October 1941, Joel had to transfer to Grade 2a of the Joods Lyceum. In April 1942, he lived at Carel Reinierszkade 167, Den Haag. He was deported from Vught to Westerbork on the so-called 'Childrens Transport.' He perished in Sobibór on June 11, 1943.

HAMME, Marcus. Born on December 24, 1901, in Den Haag, Holland. He lived at Steenenstraat 10, Oud-Beijland. He worked in a Bank. He perished in Sobibór on July 16, 1943.

HAMMERSCHLAG, Sophie. Born on October 19, 1857, in Kassel. She emigrated to Holland and lived at Merwedplein 10 huis, Amsterdam. She was deported to Sobibór, where she perished on March 20, 1943.[358]

---

[358] Listed on the memorial in the Sobibor Museum shown on the heading of this chapter.

IKENBERG, Isaak. Born on May 8, 1875, in Nieheim, Germany. He emigrated to Holland and he lived at Krugerlaan 23, Gouda. He perished in Sobibór on May 7, 1943.

ISRAEL, Isaak. Born on August 18, 1882, in Wietzzno, Poland. He emigrated to Holland and he lived at Staalstraat 3 bis, Utrecht. He perished in Sobibór on July 9, 1943.

JACOBS, Jacob. Born on July 8, 1859, in Rotterdam. He lived at Rechter Rottekade 35, Rotterdam. He perished in Sobibór on April 23, 1943.

JACOBS, Jacob. Born on March 11, 1895, in Borne, Holland. He lived at Lantmanstraat 10, Borne. He was a Merchant by profession. He perished in Sobibór on June 11, 1943.

JACOBS, Jacob. Born on January 30, 1886, in Maasluis, Southern Holland. He lived at Klein Coolstraat 9 b, Rotterdam. He was an Inspector by profession. He perished in Sobibór on April 23, 1943.

JACOBS, Jacob. Born on May 9, 1886, in Amsterdam. He lived at H. Jacobszstraat 12 huis, Amsterdam. He perished in Sobibór on April 2, 1943.

JACOBS, Jozeph. Born on July 11, 1902, in Amsterdam. He lived in Nuhout van der Veenstraat 40, Castricum. He perished in Sobibór on May 21, 1943. He was, according to some survivors, the leader of the 'revolt' in Sobibór by the Dutch Jews. Some accounts claim the Dutch were executed in *Lager III* by beheading, whilst others claim they were shot.

JACOBS-LAZARUS, Julie. Born on September 21, 1897, in Trier, Germany. She was the wife of Jacob Jacobs, (born March 11, 1895) . They emigrated to Holland, and lived at Lantmanstraat 10, Borne. She perished in Sobibór, along with her husband, on June 11, 1943.

JACOBSON, Mariana. Born on December 25, 1881, in Amsterdam. She lived at Van Aerssenstraat 15 C, Scheviningen. She died in Sobibór on July 2, 1943.

JONGH, de, Lea. Born on February 16, 1919, in Amsterdam. She was the daughter of Izaak and Judic, who both perished in Auschwitz Concentration Camp on October 22, 1943. She lived at the Centraal Israelitisch Krankzinnigengesticht Het Apeldoornse Bos, Zutphensestraat 106, Apeldorn. She worked as a nurse in the Central Jewish Lunatic Asylum in Apeldorn Bos. She perished in Sobibór on July 16, 1943. (Her photograph and biography are included in *Appendix 4—The Transports from Holland*).[359]

JOURGRAU-FRIEDMANN, Lea. Born on October 5, 1904, in Tarnow, Poland. She settled in Holland from Palestine, probably in 1929. She lived at Eerste Boerhaavestraat 15 III, Amsterdam. She was in hiding from the Nazis but was arrested and sent to Westerbork. She was deported to Sobibór, where she perished on July 23, 1943.

KAPPER, Anna (Annie). Born on January 9, 1931, in Amsterdam. She lived at Oude Ijelstraat 44 huis, Amsterdam. She died in Sobibór on April 2, 1943. Her name tag was discovered by archaeologists in 2013.

KAR, Abraham, van de. Born on January 18, 1935, in Amsterdam. He lived at Vechtstraat 139 I, Amsterdam. He was deported from Vught to Westerbork on the so-called Children's Transport. He perished in Sobibór on June 11, 1943.

KAR, Anna, van de. Born on September 6, 1930, in Amsterdam. She lived at Louis Bothastraat 16 huis, Amsterdam. She was deported from Vught to Westerbork on the so-called Children's Transport. She perished in Sobibór on June 11, 1943.

---

[359] Benny Yacobi, in correspondence with the author and www.Joodsmonument.nl—online resource.

KAR, David, van de. Born on July 14, 1938, in Amsterdam. He lived at Louis Bothastraat 16 huis, Amsterdam. He was deported from Vught to Westerbork on the so-called Children's Transport. He perished in Sobibór on June 11, 1943.

KAR, van de, Betje (formerly Wurms). Born on February 23, 1883, in Amsterdam. She perished in Sobibór on May 28, 1943, along with her husband Jacob.[360]

KAR, van de, Jacob. Born on August 11, 1880, in Amsterdam. He perished in Sobibór on May 28, 1943, along with his wife Betje.[361]

KATZENSTEIN-ROSENBLATT, Sophie. Born on July 30, 1870, in Stadthengsfeld, Germany. She emigrated to Holland. She lived at Alexander Boersstraat 19 bovenhuis, Amsterdam. She perished in Sobibór on May 28, 1943.

KEEZER, Elsa, Virginie. Born on July 28, 1904, in Amsterdam. Before the Second World War she had a dancing school in Amsterdam. Her address was Jacob Obrechtstraat 65 huis, Amsterdam. During the occupation Elsa went into hiding. She refused to wear the Jewish Star and was arrested and sent to Westerbork on March 23, 1943, where she was placed in the Punishment Block. She was deported from Westerbork on March 30,1943, to Sobibór. She perished in Sobibór on April 2, 1943.[362]

KEIZER, Louis. Born on September 6, 1904, in Zwolle. He lived at Servaasbolwerk 3, Utrecht. He worked in Utrecht and was a Merchant by profession. He perished in Sobibór on April 9, 1943.

KEIZER-HAAS, Rebekka. Born on December 20, 1912, in Almelo. She lived at Servaasbolwerk 3, Utrecht. She was married to

---

[360] Earnest Cotton, USA—correspondence with the author.
[361] Ibid.
[362] My Family, the Holocaust and Me, Robert Rinder-BBC TV Program 2019 and www.JoodsMonument.nl—online resource.

Louis, and she perished in Sobibór on April 9, 1943, along with her husband.

KINDLER, Adolf. Born on July 3, 1899, in Rawa Ruska, Poland. He lived at Stationssingel 99 a, Rotterdam. His profession was a Merchant. He perished in Sobibór on May 7, 1943.

KINDLER, Gitta Bronia. Born on June 4, 1929, in Chemnitz, Germany. She lived at Stationssingel 99 a, Rotterdam. Her father was Adolf Kindler. She perished in Sobibór on May 7, 1943.

KINDLER, Herz. Born on October 19, 1938, in Rotterdam. He lived at Stationssingel 99 a, Rotterdam. He perished in Sobibór on May 7, 1943.

KINDLER-KORNFELD, Ides. Born on August 14, 1906, in Warsaw, Poland. She emigrated to Holland and lived at Stationssingel 99 a, Rotterdam. She perished in Sobibór on May 7, 1943.

KLEEREKOPER, Elisabeth. Born on October 14, 1928, in Amsterdam. She was the daughter of Gerrit and Kaate Kleerekoper. She lived at Rivierenlaan 94 I, Amsterdam. She perished in Sobibór on July 2, 1943.

KLEEREKOPER, Gerrit. Born on February 15, 1897, in Amsterdam. He lived and worked in Amsterdam as a Secondary School teacher. The family lived at Rivierenlaan 94 1 Amsterdam. Gerrit was the coach of the Dutch women's gymnastic team, which won the Gold Medal for the team event, at the 1928 Olympics in Amsterdam. He was deported to Sobibór with his wife Kaatje, and daughter Elisabeth. His son Leendert perished in Auschwitz Concentration Camp during July 1944.

KLEEREKOPER-OSSEDRIJVER, Kaatje. Born on August 29, 1895, in Amsterdam. She was married to Gerrit and they had two children Elisabeth and Leendert. They lived in the family home at Rivierenlaan 94 1 Amsterdam. She perished in Sobibór on July 2, 1943.

KLOOT, Abraham. Born on July 28, 1902, in Amsterdam. He was a hairdresser by profession. He was married to Helena. The family home was at Tweede Boerhaavestraat 40, II Amsterdam. He perished in Sobibór on July 2, 1943, along with his wife, and daughter.

KLOOT, Jacob. Born on September 20, 1916, in Amsterdam. He lived at Swammerdamstraat 51 II, Amsterdam. He was a publisher and the owner of Corunda on the Keizergracht. He helped people in hiding and arranged meeting venues for the Dutch underground workers by renting apartments. He operated under the alias El Pintor.

On May 30, 1943, he was arrested in Leiden, and incarcerated in the prison at Scheveningen, he was later transferred to Westerbork. He was deported from there to Sobibór where he perished on July 2, 1943.

KLOOT, Rebecca. Born on April 12, 1933, in Amsterdam. The daughter of Abraham and Helena. She lived at Tweede Boerhaavestraat 40 II, Amsterdam. She perished in Sobibór on July 2, 1943.

KLOOT-NORDHEIM, Helena. Born on August 1, 1903, in Amsterdam. She lived at Tweede Boerhaavestraat 40 II, Amsterdam. She was married to Abraham, and was a hairdresser by profession. Helena competed in the 1928 Olympic Games in Amsterdam. She and her team members won the Gold Medal in the team gymnastics event. She perished in Sobibór along with her husband, and daughter Rebecca on July 2, 1943.

KON, Mosiek, Markus. Born on January 14, 1878, in Plock, Poland. He emigrated to Holland, and he lived at Blasiusstraat 46 huis, Amsterdam. He was a Tailor by profession. He perished in Sobibór on July 23, 1943.

KON, Szymon. Born on January 15, 1927, in Plock, Poland. He emigrated to Holland and he lived at Blasiusstraat 46 huis, Amsterdam. He perished in Sobibór on July 23, 1943. Along with Szymon perished his father Mosiek and his mother Chana.

KON, Wolf, Majlech. Born on March 14, 1902, in Lodz, Poland. He lived at Amstelkade 64 huis, Amsterdam. He worked as a Merchant by profession. He perished in Sobibór along with his wife Veronika, and son Szymon on May 28, 1943. His son is not the Szymon listed directly above.

KON-DYDAKOV, Chana. Born on May 29, 1882, in Biezun, Poland. She was married to Mosiek Kon. She emigrated to Holland, and she lived at Blasiusstraat 46 huis, Amsterdam. She perished in Sobibór along with her family on July 23, 1943.

KOOPMAN, Levie. Born on October 31, 1874, in Amsterdam. He lived at Lepelstraat 74 I, Amsterdam. He married Deborah Vogel and they had eleven children, the family lived at Lepelstraat 74, 1 Amsterdam. He perished in Sobibór on May 21, 1943.

KOOPMAN-PORCELIJN, Clara. Born on June 13, 1885. She was married to Isaac Koopman, and they lived at Vrolikstraat 100, II Amsterdam. Isaac perished in Auschwitz Concentration Camp, on November 2, 1942. Clara perished in Sobibór on March 20, 1943.

KOOPMAN-VOGEL, Deborah. Born on April 12, 1873, in London, England. She was married to Levie. She lived at Lepelstraat 74 I, Amsterdam. She perished in Sobibór along with her husband on May 21, 1943.

KORNFELD, Josef. Born on March 28, 1885, in Nowy Sacs, Poland. He lived and worked in Amsterdam, as a Merchant by profession. He lived at Nieuwe Amstelstraat, 35 b, Amsterdam. He perished in Sobibór on April 2, 1943.

LAMPIE, Alida. Born on February 16, 1938, in Amsterdam. She lived at Vrolikstraat 62 III, Amsterdam. She perished in Sobibór on April 9, 1943, along with other members of her family.

LAMPIE, Maurits. Born on December 29, 1905, in Amsterdam. He lived with his family on Vrolikstraat 62 III, Amsterdam. He perished in Sobibór on April 9, 1943.

LAMPIE, Max. Born on November 20, 1931, in Amsterdam. He lived at Vrolikstraat 62 III, Amsterdam. He perished in Sobibór on April 9, 1943, along with other members of his family.

LAMPIE, Miep. Born on November 20, 1930, in Amsterdam. She lived at Vrolikstraat 62 III, Amsterdam. She perished in Sobibór, on April 9, 1943, along with other members of her family.

LAMPIE-POLAK, Mina. Born on January 17, 1908, in Amsterdam. Married to Maurits. She lived at Vrolikstraat 62 III, Amsterdam. She perished in Sobibór on April 9, 1943, along with Maurits and other family members.

LEEDA-van de Kar, Celina. Born on May 11, 1904, in Amsterdam. She lived at Lange Houtstraat 59 III, Amsterdam. She perished in Sobibór on March 20, 1943.

LEVI, Erich. Born on July 29, 1905, in Rotenburg an der Fulda, Germany. He emigrated to Holland. He lived at Zuider Amstellaan 254 I, Amsterdam. He was a Merchant by profession. He perished in Sobibór on April 9, 1943.[363]

LEVI, Rika. Born on April 8, 1904, in Burg Haslach, Germany. She emigrated to Holland and lived at Raphaelstraat 2, II, Amsterdam. She was married to Sally. She perished in Sobibór on June 11, 1943.

LEVI, Sally. Born on March 3, 1893, in Grebenhain, Germany. The family home was at Raphaelstraat 2, II Amsterdam. He was a merchant by profession. He perished in Sobibór on March 21, 1943.

---

[363] Listed on the memorial in the Sobibor Museum shown on the heading of this chapter. Although it should be noted his birthdate is listed as July 19, 1905.

LEVY-MOSES, Hedwig. Born on October 6, 1886, in Frielendorf, Germany. She emigrated to Holland. She lived at Uiterwaardenstraat 130 III, Amsterdam. She perished in Sobibór on July 23, 1943.

LEWANDOWSKI-Mecca, Karoline. Born on February 2, 1875, in Kassel. She emigrated to Holland. She lived at Dahliastraat 51 Enschede. She perished in Sobibor on May 14, 1943.[364]

LILLENTHAL, Fritz. Born on September 22, 1901, in Ehrenfeld, Germany. He emigrated to Holland, and he lived at Rozengracht 214 huis, Amsterdam. He was deported from Westerbork on July 13, 1943. He perished in Sobibór on July 16, 1943.

LOWENSTEIN, Else (formerly Goldberg). Born on August 11, 1893, in Herford, Germany. She emigrated to Holland. She lived in Merwedeplein 13 III, Amsterdam. She was deported from Westerbork on July 6, 1943. She perished in Sobibór on July 9, 1943.

LOWENSTEIN, Hannelore. Born on December 7, 1924, in Laufenselden, Germany. She emigrated to Holland, and lived at Rapenburgerstraat 171, Amsterdam. She died in Sobibór on November 30, 1943.

LOWENSTEIN, Inge. Born on October 15, 1923, in Hannover, Germany. She emigrated to Holland, and lived at Oranje Nassaulaan 60 huis, Amsterdam. She died in Sobibór on June 11, 1943.

LUSTBADER-PRESSER, Leja. Born on June 29, 1885, in Ciezkowicz, Poland. She emigrated with her daughter Helene from Vienna and they lived at Kribbeststraat 17 I Amsterdam. Her daughter Helene Lustbader perished in Auschwitz

---

[364] Listed on the memorial in the Sobibor Museum shown on the heading of this chapter.

Concentration Camp on September 30, 1942. Leja perished in Sobibór on April 9, 1943.

LUTOMIRSKI, Isidor. Born on June 18, 1892, in Amsterdam. He lived at Herengracht 64 huis, Amsterdam. He perished in Sobibór on April 9, 1943.

LUTOMIRSKI, Martha. Born on June 17, 1883, in Amsterdam. She lived at Herengracht 64 huis, Amsterdam. She perished in Sobibór on March 13, 1943.

MANUSKOWSKI, Wolf. Born on April 20, 1857, in Bialystok, Poland. He lived at the Israelitisch Oude Mannern—en Vrouwenhuis Newee Sjalom, Neuhuyskade 92-94, Den Haag. He perished in Sobibór on April 16, 1943.

MAR, De La GRAANBOOM, Esther. Born on June 16, 1867, in Brussels, Belgium. She lived at Monseigneur van de Weteringstraat 9, Utrecht. She perished in Sobibór on July 2, 1943.

MARX, Erich. Born on November 18, 1910, in Vechta, Germany. He emigrated to Holland, and he lived at Torenstraat 4, Weesp, and he was a Sales Representative by profession. His wife Henny Marx-van Pels, perished in Auschwitz Concentration Camp on September 17, 1943. Erich was deported from Westerbork to Sobibór on March 23, 1943. He perished in Sobibór on May 21, 1943.

MECHANICUS, Marianne. Born on March 30, 1924, in Amsterdam. She lived at Afrikanerplein 38 III, Amsterdam. She died in Sobibór on July 9, 1943.

MEYER, Berta. Born on April 21, 1927, in Kassel, Germany. She emigrated to Holland. She lived at Plantage Badlaan 19 huis, Amsterdam. She perished in Sobibór on May 28, 1943.[365]

---

[365] Listed on the memorial in the Sobibor Museum shown on the heading of this chapter.

MEYER, Levi. Born on July 4, 1890, in Grebenau, Germany. He emigrated to Holland. He lived at Plantage Badlaan 19 huis, Amsterdam. He perished in Sobibór on May 28, 1943.[366]

MEYER-STERN, Sophie. Born on December 28, 1892, in Allendorf, Germany. She emigrated to Holland. She lived at Plantage Badlaan 19 huis, Amsterdam. She perished in Sobibór on May 28, 1943.[367]

MORPURGO, David. Born on July 11, 1889, in Amsterdam. He lived at Jonas Daniel Meijerplein 18, II Amsterdam, and was a shipping agent by profession. He perished in Sobibór on July 23, 1943.

MORPURGO-MORPURGO, Sara. Born on February 8, 1909, in Amsterdam. She lived at Jonas Daniel Meijerplein 18 II, Amsterdam. She was married to David, and was a Seamstress by profession. She perished in Sobibór on June 11, 1943.

MULLER, David. Born on February 26, 1895, in Deventer. He lived at Walstraat 77, Deventer. He was a Shopowner by profession. He perished in Sobibór on July 2, 1943.

MULLER, Izaak. Born on May 29, 1935, in Deventer, son of David and Sophia. He lived at Walstraat 77, Deventer. He perished in Sobibór on July 2, 1943.

MULLER-LINDEMAN, Sophia. Born on October 4, 1897, in Almelo. She lived at Walstraat 77, Deventer. She married David Muller on July 2, 1919, in Almelo. She perished in Sobibór on July 2, 1943, along with her husband David and son Izaak.

NEUHAUS, David, Peter. Born on June 27, 1938, in Frankfurt am Main, Germany. He emigrated to Holland, and lived at Raphaelstraat 31, Amsterdam. He was deported from Westerbork on May 4, 1943. He died in Sobibór on May 7, 1943.

---

[366] Ibid.
[367] Ibid.

NEUHAUS-SELIGMAN, Helene. Born on September 14, 1909, in Ichenhausen, Germany. She emigrated to Holland and lived at Raphaelstraat 31, Amsterdam. She was deported from Westerbork on May 4, 1943. She died in Sobibór on May 7, 1943.

NEUHAUS, Justin, Jacob. Born on September 30, 1900, in Frankfurt am Main, Germany. He emigrated to Holland, and lived at Raphaelstraat 31, Amsterdam. He was a merchant by profession. He died in Sobibór on May 21, 1943.

NOL, Abraham. Born on November 2, 1919, in Uitgeest, Holland. He lived at Linnaueskade 14, Amsterdam. He worked as a Book-keeper by profession. He was arrested, along with his cousin Richard Nol, on May 18, 1942, during an aborted escape by fishing boat to England at Ijmuiden.

After spells in prison at Scheveningen, he was transferred to Westerbork. He was deported from there, along with Richard, to Sobibór. They both perished on May 21, 1943. His Red Cross notification of death is included in the Documents section of this book.[368]

NOL, Mozes, Richard. Born on November 8, 1920, in Amsterdam. He lived at Linnaeuskade 14 I, Amsterdam. He was a pupil at the First Montessori School in Amsterdam. He produced drawings from models. He tried to escape with his cousin Abraham in a boat to England, but they were arrested at Ijmuiden on May 18, 1942. He was taken to the convict prison at Scheveningen and from there to the Groot Seminarie, Haaren, the prison on Gansstraat in Utrecht. He was deported from Westerbork to Sobibór. He perished in Sobibór on May 21, 1943.[369]

---

[368] Joe Noel in correspondence with the author September 2003 and JoodsMonument—online resource.

[369] Joe Noel in correspondence with the author September 2003 and JoodsMonument—online resource.

NOORD, Elisabeth. Born on February 12, 1928, in Amsterdam. She lived with her family at Vrolikstraat 367 huis, Amsterdam. She died in Sobibór on May 28, 1943.

NOORD, Esther. Born on February 11, 1928, in Amsterdam. She lived with her family at Vrolikstraat 367 huis, Amsterdam. She died in Sobibór on May 28, 1943.

NORD, Joseph. Born on June 26, 1930, in Zwolle. He lived at Kerkstraat 5, Zwolle. He was deported from Westerbork to Sobibór on the so-called 'Children's Transport'. He perished in Sobibór on June 11, 1943.

NORD, Mozes. Born on April 22, 1937, in Zwolle. He lived at Kerkstraat 5, Zwolle. He was deported from Westerbork to Sobibór on the so-called 'Children's Transport'. He perished in Sobibór on June 11, 1943, along with his brother Joseph.

NORD, Rachel. Born on December 13, 1923, in Den Haag. She was the daughter of Mozes and Jeanetta Nord. She lived at Transvaalkade 113 huis, Amsterdam. She worked in October 1941, as a Seamstress with the lingerie—and ready made clothing company SIDVA (Simon de Vries Ateliers), in Amsterdam. She had commenced working there during 1939. She perished in Sobibór on April 30, 1943.

NORDEN, Alexander. Born on October 10, 1875, in Hamburg, Germany. In 1938, he was incarcerated in Fuhlsbüttel, Concentration Camp, and when he was released he emigrated to Holland, where he lived at Mecklenburglaan 23 a, Bussum. He perished in Sobibór on July 23, 1943, along with his wife Caroline.

NORDEN, Betsy. Born on December 27, 1926, in Den Haag. She was the grand-daughter of the Conductor Simon Jacob Henrique de La Fuente and the soprano Frederike Streletskie. She lived at Westeinde 201 a, Den Haag. She perished in Sobibór on April 30, 1943.

NORDEN, Hartog. Born in January 15, 1929, in Amsterdam. His mother was Beile Norden-Korn. He lived at Plantage Kerklaan 5 II, Amsterdam. He was deported from Vught to Westerbork on the so-called 'Children's Transport', and he perished in Sobibór on June 11, 1943.

NORDEN, Henni Sophia. Born on February 15, 1923, in Zwolle. She lived at the Centraal Israelitisch Weeshuis, Nieuwegracht, Utrecht. She worked in Veenendaal as a Domestic Servant for a Jewish family, who survived the war. She perished in Sobibór on May 28, 1943.

NUNEZ-VAS, Jacob. Born on September 20, 1906, in Amsterdam. He lived at Keizersgracht 524 h, Amsterdam. He was known as Jap and lived and worked in Amsterdam, with his wife. He worked as a journalist after completing secondary school education. He joined the Onafhankelijke Socialistische Partij (OSP). At first he worked for the Vaz Dias Press Agency. Later he joined the ANP, where he was fired for being Jewish. He then did translations and wrote a booklet on aviation.

The first meeting of the resistance group Parool editorial board was held in his room on the Keizergracht. He served on the editorial board and eventually became the Executive Editor and wrote leading articles. During a search, his hiding place was discovered. On October 25, 1942, he was arrested in Wageningen. From the convict prison at Scheveningen he was transferred to Westerbork. He was deported to Sobibór, where he perished on March 13, 1943.

NUNEZ-VAS, Philip. Born on November 18, 1934, in Amsterdam. He lived at Lepelstraat 64 III, Amsterdam. He perished in Sobibór on May 28, 1943.

NUNEZ-VAS, Samuel. Born on April 15, 1893, in Amsterdam. The family home was at Lepelstraat 64, III, Amsterdam. He was employed by a Municipal Utilities Company. He was deported to Sobibór where he perished on May 28, 1943, along with members of his family.

NUNEZ-VAZ-COHEN, Betje. Born on February 15, 1896, in Amsterdam. The family home was at Lepelstraat 64, III, Amsterdam. She was a Seamstress by profession. She was deported to Sobibór where she perished on May 28, 1943.

NUSSBAUM, Benjamin. Born on November 1, 1897, in Tarnobrzeg, Poland. He lived at Pletterijstraat 152, Den Haag, and he worked in Den Haag as a Shop-owner. He perished in Sobibór on May 28, 1943, along with members of his family.

NUSSBAUM, Hulda. Born on January 4, 1891, in Bad Hersfeld, Germany. She emigrated to Holland. She lived at Noorder Amstellaan 31 III, Amsterdam. She perished in Sobibór on July 9, 1943.[370]

OPPENHEIMER, Inge. Born on June 6, 1930, in Frankfurt am Main, Germany. The family emigrated to Holland on July 26, 1935. She lived at Michelangelostraat 61, Amsterdam. She died in Sobibór on May 28, 1943.

ORGELIST, Leentje. Born on November 3, 1894, in Amsterdam. She lived at Boterdiepstraat 11, huis, Amsterdam. She was deported from Westerbork on April 6, 1943, to Sobibór. She perished in Sobibór on April 9, 1943.

ORGELIST, Roosje. Born on August 3, 1883, in Amsterdam. She lived at Boterdiepstraat 11, huis, Amsterdam. She was deported from Westerbork on April 6, 1943, to Sobibór. She perished in Sobibór on April 9, 1943.

ORGELIST-de Leeuwe. Born on October 22, 1859, in Amsterdam. She lived at Boterdiepstraat 11, huis, Amsterdam. She was deported from Westerbork on April 6, 1943, to Sobibór. She perished in Sobibór on April 9, 1943.

---

[370] Listed on the memorial in the Sobibor Museum shown on the heading of this chapter.

OSSEDRIJVER, Dora. Born on December 9, 1934, in Eindhoven. She lived at Edelweisstraat 145, Eindhoven. She was deported from Westerbork on April 6, 1943. She perished in Sobibór on April 9, 1943.

OSSEDRIJVER, Jacques. Born on June 3, 1911, in Den Haag. The family home was located at Edelweissstraat 145, Eindhoven. He was a Warehouse clerk by profession. He was deported from Westerbork on April 6, 1943. He perished in Sobibór on April 9, 1943.

OSSEDRIJVER-WINKEL, Anna. Born on September 23, 1913, in Den Haag. Married to Jacques. The family home was located at Edelweissstraat 145, Eindhoven. She was deported from Westerbork on April 6, 1943. She perished in Sobibór on April 9, 1943.

OSTER, Raphael, Rafael. Born on February 10, 1856, in Alpen, Germany. He emigrated to Holland and he lived at Het Zand 10, Boxmeer. He was deported from Westerbork to Sobibór, where he perished on May 14, 1943.

OSTER-WINDMULLER, Rosalia, Rosalie. Born on February 24, 1866, in Beckum, Germany. She emigrated to Holland, and lived at Het Zand 10, Boxmeer. She was deported from Westerbork to Sobibór, where she perished on May 21, 1943.

PARIJS, David. Born on May 5, 1889, in Amsterdam. He lived at Nieuwe Hoogstraat 6 III, Amsterdam. He was a Rose Sharpener by profession. He perished in Sobibór on May 28, 1943.

PARIJS-VIEIJRA, Rosa. Born on August 23, 1885, in Amsterdam. She lived at Nieuwe Hoogstraat 6 III, Amsterdam. She perished in Sobibór on May 28, 1943.

PARIJS, Samuel. Born on February 21, 1913, in Amsterdam. He lived at Nieuwe Hoogstraat 6 III, Amsterdam. He was a Chemist by profession. He perished in Sobibór on June 4, 1943.

PENHA, de, la, David. Born on August 12, 1909, in Amsterdam. He lived at Graaf Florisstraat 5 I Amsterdam. He was a Paperhanger by profession. He perished in Sobibór, along with his wife Judith, and their young daughter Leah, on July 9, 1943.

PENHA, Elias. Born on January 24, 1912, in Amsterdam. The family home was located at Argonautenstraat 25 I, Amsterdam. He was a Paint supplies dealer by profession. He perished in Sobibór on March 13, 1943. His wife Mirjam Penha-Blits, who was selected for work in a Labor Camp outside Sobibór, survived the Holocaust. Elias on the other hand was gassed on arrival on March 13, 1943.

PENHA, de, la, Judith. Born on September 27,1903, in Amsterdam. She lived at Graaf Florisstraat 5 I, Amsterdam. A Tailor by profession. She perished in Sobibór on July 9, 1943, along with her husband David and daughter Leah.

PENHA, de, la, Leah. Born on May 11, 1937, in Amsterdam. She was the daughter of David and Judith. She lived at Graaf Florisstraat 5 I, Amsterdam. She perished in Sobibór on July 9, 1943, along with her parents. Her metal name tag was discovered by the archaeologists Yoram Haimi and Wojech Mazurek, at the site of the former death camp.

PLAUT-Mainzer, Bertha. Born on September 5, 1880, in Pfungstadt, Germany. She emigrated to Holland. She lived at Krammerstraat 6 I, Amsterdam. She perished in Sobibór on July 23, 1943.[371]

POLAK, Wolf. Born on January 9, 1904, in Amsterdam. He lived at Andreas Bonnstraat 19 I, Amsterdam. He was a Sales Representative by profession. He perished in Sobibór on May 21, 1943.

---

[371] Listed on the memorial in the Sobibor Museum shown on the heading of this chapter.

POPPERT, Erich, Karl. Born on April 20, 1912, in Dortmund, Germany. He emigrated to Holland, and he lived at Botenmakerstraat 68, Zaandam. He was deported from Westerbork to Sobibór where he perished on May 1, 1943.

POPPERT-SCHONBORN, Gertrud (formerly Schonborn) (aka Luka). Born on June 29, 1914, in Dortmund, Germany, the daughter of Anton and Selma (formerly Rosenbaum). She married Walter Michael Poppert, who was born on March 26, 1914, in Amsterdam, during 1938. They lived at Utrechtsedwarsstraat 113, I, Amsterdam.
She was deported from Westerbork Camp to Sobibór on May 18,1943. In *Lager II*, she tended the rabbits. Her date of death is unclear, the Joods Monument lists her date of death as November 30, 1943, whilst her *Stolpersteine* lists her death as October 14, 1943. Jules Schelvis claimed in his book that Gertrude was also known as Luka who became Sasha Pechersky's girlfriend. Thanks to modern research this claim has been found to be incorrect.

POPPERT, Walter, Michel. Born on March 26, 1914, in Dortmund, Germany. He emigrated to Holland, and on December 22, 1938, in Amsterdam he married Gertrud Schonborn. He was a clothing contracting dealer and lived at Utrechtsedwarsstraat 113, I, Amsterdam. He was deported from Westerbork on May 18, 1943, along with his wife.
At Sobibór he was selected for work and he was appointed to the post of *Kapo* in the *Waldkommando*. He perished in Sobibór on October 31, 1943.

PRAAG, van, Benjamin. Born on September 30, 1870, in Amsterdam. He lived at Lingenskamp 18, Laren. He perished in Sobibór on July 2, 1943.

PRAAG-HOLLANDER, Celina van. Born on December 25, 1887, in Amsterdam. She lived at Lingenskamp 18, Laren. She perished in Sobibór on July 2, 1943.

PREGER, Annie. Born on October 7, 1920, in Rotterdam. She lived at the Centraal Israelitisch Het Appeldoornse Bos, Zutphensestraat 106, Apeldoorn. She was the daughter of Levie Preger and Sara Swaan. She worked as a student nurse at the Appeldoornse Bos.

On September 19, 1942, she became engaged to Hans van Witsen, who also worked at the Appeldoornse Bos. The couple were transferred to Westerbork Transit Camp and they married there on January 28, 1943. They were deported from Westerbork on March 2, 1943, to Sobibór, where they both perished on March 5, 1943.

PRESSER, Kitty. Born on March 26, 1928, in Amsterdam. She lived at Tugelaweg 45 II, Amsterdam. She was deported from Vught to Westerbork on the so-called 'Childrens Transport.' She perished in Sobibór on June 11, 1943.

PRESSER, Simon. Born on December 29, 1930, in Amsterdam. He lived at Tugelaweg 45 II, Amsterdam. He was deported from Vught to Westerbork on the so-called 'Childrens Transport.' He perished in Sobibór on June 11, 1943.

PRINS, Eduard. Born on June 23, 1874, in Deventer. He lived at Regentesselaan 9, Bussum. He perished in Sobibór on July 9, 1943.

REITER, Frieda (formerly Keh). Born on August 21, 1878, in Bagienica, North-Central Poland. She emigrated to Holland along with her husband Moritz on August 5, 1939. They lived at Quellijnstraat 153 II, Amsterdam. She was deported from Westerbork on April 27, 1943. She perished in Sobibór on April 30, 1943.

REITER, Moritz, Moses. Born on July 17, 1869, in Popielniki, Ukraine. He emigrated to Holland along with his wife Frieda) on August 5, 1939. They lived at Quellijnstraat 153 II, Amsterdam. He was deported from Westerbork on April 27, 1943. He perished in Sobibór on April 30, 1943.

ROET, Rachel. Born on September 13, 1883, in Amsterdam. She lived at President Brandstraat 58 I, Amsterdam. She was deported from Westerbork on April 6, 1943. She perished in Sobibór on April 9, 1943.

ROOT, Juda. Born on November 4, 1882, in Amsterdam. She lived at Valkenburgerstraat 141 II, Amsterdam. She was a Cigar-maker by profession. She was deported from Westerbork on April 6, 1943. She perished in Sobibór on April 9, 1943.

ROSEN, Hella, Emmi. Born on August 12, 1935, in Berlin, Germany. She emigrated to Holland, and she lived at Prins Hendriklaan 6, Bussum. She was deported from Westerbork on June 8, 1943. She perished in Sobibór on June 11, 1943.

ROSEN-SUSSKIND, Margarete, Marianne. Born on May 10, 1904, in Stuttgart, Germany. She emigrated to Holland, and she lived at Prins Hendriklaan 6, Bussum. She was deported from Westerbork on June 8, 1943. She perished in Sobibór on June 11, 1943, along with her daughter Hella.

ROSENTHAL, Calman, Carl. Born on February 12, 1865, in Haaren, Germany. He emigrated to Holland and he lived at Beethovenstraat 67 bovenhuis, Amsterdam. He was deported from Westerbork on May 4, 1943. He perished in Sobibór on May 7, 1943.

ROSENSTIEL, Albert. Born on December 1925, in Neustadt, Germany. He emigrated to Holland, and lived at Van Ostadelaan 3, Naarden. He died in Sobibór, on March 20, 1943.

ROSENSTIEL, Wilhelm. Born on January 13, 1886, in Neustadt, Germany. He emigrated to Holland, and lived at Van Ostadelaan 3, Naarden. He died in Sobibór, on March 20, 1943.

ROSENSTIEL-OPPENHEIMER, Irma. Born on November 7, 1896, in Mergentheim, Germany. She emigrated to Holland, and lived at Van Ostadelaan 3, Naarden. She died in Sobibór, but the date is uncertain. It was recorded on the Joods

Monument as March 20, 1943. More modern research points to her surviving the initial selection, and being in the camp with her daughter Liselotte (Luka). Her fate is unknown.[372]

SALOMONSON, Rosalie, Johanna. Born on June 11, 1887, in Denekamp. Holland. She lived at Honthorststraat 42 huis, Amsterdam. She was a Domestic servant by profession. She perished in Sobibór on March 20, 1943.

SALOMONSON-PHILIPS, Esther. Born on March 25, 1895, in Winterswijk, Holland. She lived at B 132 Hardenberg. She perished in Sobibór on May 21, 1943.

SCHELVIS, Marie. Born on February 28, 1934, in Amsterdam. She lived at Hofmeyrstraat 12 II, Amsterdam. She was deported to Sobibór in June 1943, from Vught via Westerbork, on the so-called 'Children's Transport.' She perished in Sobibór on June 11, 1943.

SCHELVIS-BORZYKOWSKI, Rachel. Born on March 2, 1923, in Amsterdam. She lived in Nieuwe Kerkstraat 103 III, Amsterdam. She was a Seamstress by profession. She was married to Jules Schelvis during 1941. She was deported, along with Jules, from Westerbork on June 1, 1943. She was sent to the gas chambers on arrival, and she perished on June 4, 1943. Jules was selected to work in a labor camp outside Sobibór at Dorohucza. He survived the Holocaust and wrote a book on Sobibór.

SCHELVIS, Rebecca. Born on January 24, 1915, in Amsterdam. She was engaged to Raphael (Felix) Ensel, who was arrested in a raid during February 1941. The raid took place a couple of days before they were due to be married. He perished in Mauthausen Concentration Camp in Austria, on August 30, 1941. Following this she lived with her in-laws-to-be at Krugerplein 36 II, Amsterdam.

---

[372] Correspondence between Aline Pennewaard, December 12, 2022.

One day in September 1942, she came home to find the house empty, because the entire family had been taken away. She then moved in with her older brother Mozes and his wife. She was arrested in March 1943, but thanks to the efforts of her boss—she was a Seamstress—she was released the next day from the Hollandsche Schouwburg, which was a holding centre for deportees. Rebecca was arrested again on May 26, 1943, and she was deported to Sobibór, where she perished on May 28, 1943.

SCHLOSSER, Gompert. Born on July 30, 1931, in Den Ham, Holland. He lived at the family home which was located at B 127, Den Ham. He was deported to Sobibór, where he perished on March 20, 1943.

SCHLOSSER, Levi. Born on December 18, 1876, in Den Ham, Holland. He settled in Germany, but returned to Holland, where he lived at B 127, Den Ham. He was a Merchant by profession. He was deported from Westerbork on June 1, 1943, to Sobibór, where he perished on June 4, 1943.

SCHLOSSER, Miechel. Born on July 8, 1918, in Den Ham, Holland. He lived at B 127, Den Ham, he was a Brush Maker by profession. He was deported to Sobibór, where he perished on March 20, 1943.

SCHLOSSER, Simon. Born on December 22, 1885, in Den Ham, Holland. He lived at B 127, Den Ham, he was a Merchant by profession. He was deported to Sobibór, where he perished on March 20, 1943.

SCHLOSSER-van DAM, Judic. Born on September 1886, in Leek, in North Eastern Holland. She was married to Simon. She lived at the family home which was located at B 127, Den Ham. She was deported to Sobibór, where she perished on March 20, 1943.

SCHMIDT, SALOMON. Born on April 23, 1887, in Tarnow, Poland. He emigrated to Holland. He lived at Maria van

Rederstraat 21 bis Utrecht. He was deported from Westerbork on May 18, 1943, to Sobibór, where he perished on May 21, 1943.

SCHRIJVER, Abraham. Born on April 5, 1905, in Amsterdam. He lived at the family home which was located at Hoflandplein 14, Den Haag, Holland. He was a Fruit Merchant by profession. He was deported to Sobibór, where he perished on July 9, 1943.

SCHRIJVER, Betje. Born on June 18, 1929, in Amsterdam. She lived at the family home which was located at Hoflandplein 14, Den Haag, Holland. She was transferred from Vught to Westerbork, on the so-called 'Children's Transport.' She perished in Sobibór on June 11, 1943.

SCHRIJVER, Hermanus. Born on January 12, 1927, in Amsterdam. He lived at the family home which was located at Hoflandplein 14, Den Haag, Holland. He was deported to Sobibór, where he perished on July 9, 1943.

SCHRIJVER, Joseph, Nardus. Born on May 30, 1911, in Amsterdam. He lived at Neptunusstraat 41, Scheveningen. He was an Office Clerk by profession. He married Carla Okker in the Westerbork Transit Camp on April 24, 1943. He perished in Sobibór on April 30, 1943.

SCHRIJVER, Philip. Born on May 28, 1899, in Amsterdam. He lived at the family home which was located at Hoflandplein 14, Den Haag, Holland. He was a Merchant by profession. He was deported to Sobibór, where he perished on July 9, 1943.

SCHRIJVER, Salomon. Born on October 31, 1885, in Amsterdam. He lived at Lepelstraat 86 II, Amsterdam. He perished in Sobibór on March 26, 1943.

SCHRIJVER, Salomon. Born on May 25, 1917, in Amsterdam. He lived at Kleine Kattenburgerstraat 55 huis, Amsterdam. He perished in Sobibór on July 9, 1943.

SCHRIJVER-MENDELS, Flora. Born on October 15, 1919, in Amsterdam. In 1941, she lived at Nieuwe Uilenburgerstraat 34 II, Amsterdam. She perished in Sobibór on July 9, 1943.

SCHRIJVER-OKKER, Clara. Born on June 14, 1914, in Watergraafsmeer, Holland. In February 1941, she resided at Nicolaas Maesstraat 37 huis, Amsterdam. She was a Sales-lady by profession. She married Joseph Schrijver in the Westerbork Transit Camp on April 24, 1943. She perished in Sobibór on April 30, 1943.

SCHRIJVER-WOLFF, Mariana. Born on October 29, 1904, in Amsterdam. She lived at the family home which was located at Hoflandplein 14, Den Haag, Holland. She was deported to Sobibór, where she perished on June 11, 1943.

SCHULZ, Anna (formerly Haas). Born on August 16, 1890, in Bingen, Germany. She emigrated to Holland, and lived at Milletstraat 56 II, Amsterdam. She was deported from Westerbork on May 4, 1943, to Sobibór, where she perished on May 7, 1943.

SCHULZ, Emil. Born on February 9, 1879, in Frankenthal, Germany. He emigrated to Holland, and he lived at Milletstraat 56 II, Amsterdam. He was a Tobacco-dealer by profession. He was deported from Westerbork on May 4, 1943, to Sobibór, where he perished on May 7, 1943.

SCHWARZ, Herbert. Born on August 18, 1905, in Köln, Germany. He emigrated to Holland and he lived at Amstellaan 87 III, Amsterdam. He was a journalist by profession. He was deported from Westerbork on June 1, 1943, to Sobibór. He perished there on June 4, 1943.

SCHWARZ, Levi. Born on March 30, 1859, in Raesfeld, Germany. He emigrated to Holland. He lived at Havenstraat 51, Hilversum. He was deported to Sobibór, where he perished on May 28, 1943.

SCHWARZ-ROSENBAUM, Mathilde. Born on April 9, 1869, in Borken. She lived at Spoorstraat 42, Winterswijk. She perished in Sobibór on April 30, 1943.

SELIGMANN, Jacob Moritz. Born on July 25, 1884, in Hamburg, Germany. He emigrated to Holland, and he lived in Haringvlietstraat 15, III, Amsterdam. He was a Merchant by profession. He was deported from Westerbork on May 18, 1943. He perished in Sobibór on May 21, 1943.

SIMONS, Louis. Born on October 1, 1935, in Amsterdam. He lived in the family home located in Eerste Oosterparkstraat 165 huis, Amsterdam. He was deported to Sobibór, where he perished on June 11, 1943.

SIMONS, Salomon. Born on January 13, 1937, in Haarlem. He lived in the family home located in Eerste Oosterparkstraat 165 huis, Amsterdam. He was deported to Sobibór, where he perished on June 11, 1943.

SIMONS, Simon. Born on January 13, 1912, in Amsterdam. The family home was located in Eerste Oosterparkstraat 165 huis, Amsterdam. He was a Tailor by profession. He was deported to Sobibór, where he perished on July 23, 1943.

SIMONS-a COHEN, Rebecca. Born on May 18, 1910, in Amsterdam. The family home was located in Eerste Oosterparkstraat 165 huis, Amsterdam. She perished in Sobibór on June 11, 1943.

SLIER, Eliazar. Born on March 26, 1890, in Amsterdam. He lived at Vrolikstraat 128 III, Amsterdam. He worked as a typographer for the liberal newspaper *Algmeen Handelsblad* in Amsterdam. He was the father of Philip Slier, the subject of the book '*Hidden Letters.*' Eliazar perished in Sobibór on June 4, 1943.

SLIER, Elisabeth, Anna. Born on May 6, 1930, in Amsterdam. She lived at Scheldstraat 6 II, Amsterdam. She perished in Sobibór on April 9, 1943.

SLIER, Henri. Born on January 16, 1929, in Zandvoort. He lived at Scheldstraat 6 II, Amsterdam. He perished in Sobibór on April 9, 1943.

SLIER, Joseph. Born on April 9, 1885, in Amsterdam. He lived at Scheldstraat 6 II, Amsterdam. He was a Sales Representative by profession. He perished in Sobibór on April 9, 1943.

SLIER, Leentje. Born on September 18, 1926, in Rotterdam. She lived in Levendaal 8, Leiden, and she was a Domestic Servant by profession. She perished in Sobibór on April 23, 1943.

SLIER, Meijer. Born on December 27, 1888, in Amsterdam. He lived at Transvaalstraat 88 huis, Amsterdam. He was a Diamond worker by profession. He perished in Sobibór on July 16, 1943.

SLIER, Mozes. Born on November 16, 1893, in Amsterdam. He lived at Smaragdstraat 7 II, Amsterdam. He was employed by the Asscher Company in Amsterdam, as a Diamond Sawyer. On February 11, 1943, he was interned in the camp at Vught. On June 7, 1943, he was sent to Westerbork. A day later he was deported from Westerbork to Sobibór, where he perished on June 11, 1943.

SLIER, Philip. Born on December 4, 1923, in Amsterdam. He lived at the family home located on Vrolikstraat 128 III, Amsterdam. He worked in Amsterdam as a Typographer. He was incarcerated in the Molengoot Labor Camp, and the letters he wrote from there were published in a number of books including 'Hidden Letters,' which was published in 2007. Philip was deported from Westerbork on April 6, 1943, to Sobibór, where he perished on April 9, 1943.

SLIER, PLAS, Anna. Born on August 26, 1891, in Amsterdam. She lived at Oude Doelenstraat 12 II, Amsterdam, with her husband Jonas. She ran a stall selling fabrics and ornaments at the Nieuwmarkt in Amsterdam, with her husband Jonas. Anna perished in Sobibór on June 4, 1943. Jonas perished in Auschwitz Concentration Camp on November 5, 1942.

SLIER-SALOMONSON, Saline, Rozette. Born on March 14, 1890, in Denekamp. She lived at Vrolikstraat 128 III, Amsterdam, along with her husband and son Philip. She perished in Sobibór along with her husband Eliazar on June 4, 1943.

SLIER-VLEESCHHOUWER, Catharina. Born on June 28, 1898, in Amsterdam. She lived at Scheldestraat 6 II, Amsterdam. She was married Joseph and they had a son Philip, who perished in Auschwitz Concentration Camp on September 30, 1942. Catharina and Joseph were deported to Sobibór, where they both perished on April 9, 1943.

SLUIJZER, Levie. Born on November 3, 1916, in Amsterdam. He lived at Plantage Badlaan 11 II, Amsterdam. He married Serline Finsi in Westerbork on February 2, 1943. Levie, before he was deported to the 'East,' wrote as agreed to his brother Meijer, and hid the notes he had written in a spot underneath his wagon. His brother Meijer retrieved the notes when the train returned to Westerbork, about one week after its departure on April 6, 1943. The letter described the conditions of the journey through Germany, noting the destruction caused by the Allied bombing. Levie and his wife Serline were gassed at Sobibór on their arrival on April 9, 1943. The notes written by Levie survived the war and are held in the Westerbork archives. Meijer was murdered in Auschwitz Concentration Camp on April 30, 1943.

SLUIJZER-FINSI, Serline. Born on June 11, 1911, in Amsterdam. In February 1941, she lived at Joh. Vd. Waalsstraat 15 huis, Amsterdam. She worked as an Insurer at the Stock Exchange. She married Levie Sluijzer in the Westerbork Transit Camp on February 2, 1943. She was deported together with Levie and other family members from Westerbork on April 6, 1943. She perished in Sobibór on April 9, 1943.

SMEER, Elisabeth. Born on April 1, 1934, in Amsterdam. She lived at the family home which was located at Ruyschstraat 116 III, Amsterdam. She was transferred from Vught, to Westerbork, and was then deported to Sobibór, on the so-called 'Children's Transport'. She perished at Sobibór on June 11, 1943.

SMEER, Jacob. Born on December 17, 1904, in Amsterdam. He lived at Formosastraat 13 I, Amsterdam. He worked at the Hollandia-Kattenburg clothing factory in Amsterdam, where he patched coats. He lived at Formosastraat 13 I, Amsterdam.
In January 1943, Jacob was arrested and accused of having distributed *'Der Waarheid'* an illegal publication and for carrying out sabotage on the conveyor belt producing raincoats for the German Army. He perished in Sobibór on May 28, 1943.

SMEER, Jacob Philip. Born on December 26, 1938, in Amsterdam. He lived at the family home which was located at Ruyschstraat 116 III, Amsterdam. He was transferred from Vught to Westerbork. He was deported from Westerbork on the so-called 'Children's Transport'. He perished in Sobibór on June 11, 1943.

SMEER-ZWAAB, Dora. Born on August 13, 1910, in Antwerp, Belguim. She lived at the family home which was located at Ruyschstraat 116 III, Amsterdam. She worked as a Sticher by profession. She was married to Maurits Smeer, who perished in Auschwitz on August 10, 1942. She perished in Sobibór on June 11, 1943, along with her son Jacob Philip and her daughter Elisabeth.

SMIT, Engeline (formerly de-Vries). Born on November 27, 1908, in Amsterdam. In February 1941, she lived at Eendrachtstraat 15 I, Amsterdam. She married Leopold Smit, the Composer, during 1933. She was taken to Westerbork, and then deported from there to Sobibór, where she perished along with her husband on April 30, 1943.

SMIT, Leopold. Born on May 14, 1900, in Amsterdam. He lived at Eendrachtstraat 15 I, Amsterdam. He was a Composer and Music Teacher by profession. He was educated at the Conservatory in Amsterdam, where he studied modulation. He was considered one of the most talented students, and was one of the first to receive his *diploma cum laude.*

On June 28, 1925, his *'Silhouetten'* was performed by the *Concertgebouworkest* of Amsterdam. From 1929, until 1937, Leopold lived in Paris, where he came into contact with the *Group des Six*. During this period in 1933, he married Engeline de Vries), and he returned to Amsterdam during 1937.

During the Nazi occupation, he taught music and in February 1943, he completed his last work *'Sonata for Flute and Piano.'* He was deported to Sobibór, along with his wife, where they both perished on April 30, 1943.

SOMMER, Bruno. Born on May 29, 1929, in Kassel, Germany. He emigrated to Holland. He lived at Berenstraat 21 I, Amsterdam. He perished in Sobibór on March 13, 1943.[373]

SOMMER, Julius. Born on November 26, 1875, in Heinebach, Germany. He emigrated to Holland. He lived at Berenstraat 21 I, Amsterdam. He perished in Sobibór on March 13, 1943.

SOMMER-STRAUSS, Lina. Born on December 8, 1885, in Eiterfeld, Germany. She emigrated to Holland. She lived at Berenstraat 21 I, Amsterdam. She perished in Sobibór on March 13, 1943.[374]

SPITZ, Siegfried. Born on April 23, 1902, in Vienna, Austria. He settled in Holland, and he lived at Traansvalstraat 56, III, Amsterdam. He was deported from Westerbork to Sobibór on May 18, 1943. At Sobibór he was appointed to be one of the *Kapos.*

---

[373] Listed on the memorial in the Sobibor Museum shown on the heading of this chapter.
[374] Ibid.

Following the death of *Oberkapo 'Berliner'*, he was appointed to take his place as head of the *Kapos*. During the prisoner revolt on October 14, 1943, and the murder of *SS-Unterscharführer* Friedrich Gaulstich in the carpentry workshop, he was warned by *Kapo* Pozycki, at knife-point, not to get involved. He was murdered when the camp was finally liquidated on November 30, 1943.[375]

STERN, Maier. Born May 20, 1873, in Neustadt, Germany. He emigrated to Holland, where he lived at Geleenstraat 1 II, Amsterdam. He was deported from Westerbork on May 18, 1943. He perished in Sobibór on May 21, 1943.

STEINBERG, Salomon. Born on June 16, 1867, in Hagen, Germany. He resettled in Holland and lived at Maastrichterlaan 49, Beek. After one and a half years they had to leave the building because the new NSB Mayor urgently needed their house. They then moved to a small house in Grevenbicht. Following incarceration in Vught and Westerbork, he was then deported to Sobibór, where he perished on May 14, 1943.

STEINBERG-HERTZ, Selma. Born on October 29, 1868, in Goch, Germany. She resettled in Holland and lived at Maastrichterlaan 49, Beek, with her husband Salomon. After one and a half years they had to leave the building because the new NSB Mayor urgently needed their house. They then moved to a small house in Grevenbicht. Following incarceration in Vught and Westerbork, she was then deported to Sobibór, where he perished, along with her husband, on May 14, 1943.

STODEL, Albert, Leopold, Clement. Born on July 13, 1915, in Amsterdam. He lived at Geleenstraat 26 huis II, Amsterdam. He lived and worked in Amsterdam as a Textile worker. He married Lola Ronny Polak at the Westerbork Transit Camp on

---

[375] www.JoodsMonument.nl—online resource and Y. Arad, *Belzec, Sobibor, Treblinka* op it. pp. 327-328.

April 9, 1943. The couple were deported from Westerbork, to Sobibór, and they both perished in Sobibór on April 23, 1943.

STODEL-BORZYKOWSKI, Chaja. Born on August 6, 1921, in Amsterdam. In February 1941, she lived at Nieuwe Kerkstraat 103 III, Amsterdam. She was a Shop Assistant in Amsterdam. She married Abraham Stodel, on December 18, 1941. She was deported along with her husband to Sobibór on June 1, 1943. She was murdered on arrival in the gas chambers, but Abraham was selected to work outside Sobibór and was sent to the Jewish Labor Camp at Dorohucza, where he perished on November 30, 1943.

STODEL, Leo. Born on April 15, 1908, in Amsterdam. He lived at Israelitisch Weeshuis, Pletterijstraat 66, Den Haag. He worked as a farmhand by profession. He was married to Martha Katz. He perished in Sobibór on March 13, 1943.

STODEL, Levie. Born on April 12, 1877, in Amsterdam. He lived at Dongestraat 13 huis, Amsterdam. A potato vendor by profession, he owned a small shop selling vegetables in the Lazerussteeg, Amsterdam. He perished in Sobibór on April 9, 1943.

STODEL, Lola Ronny. Born on August 23, 1919, in Amsterdam. In February 1941, she lived at Ceintuurbaan 366 I, Amsterdam. She was a Sales Lady and Merchant by profession. She married Albert Stodel at the Westerbork Transit Camp on April 9, 1943. She was deported from Westerbork to Sobibór, along with her husband, and they both perished on April 23, 1943.

STODEL-KONIG, Martha. Born on September 18, 1912, in Vienna, Austria. She resettled to Holland, and she lived at Jekerstraat 92 I, Amsterdam. She was a Cutter by profession. She perished in Sobibór on May 21, 1943.

STODEL-KATZ, Martha. Born on January 19, 1913, in Regensburg, Germany. She resettled to Holland and lived at

Israelitisch Weeshuis, Pletterijstraat 66, Den Haag. She was a Seamstress by profession. She perished in Sobibór on March 13, 1943

STRAUS-KUPERSCHMID, Ester, Chaje. Born on March 11, 1910, in Bełżec, Poland. She lived at Van Limburg Stirumstraat 56, Den Haag. She perished in Sobibór on March 20, 1943.

STRAUSS, Abraham. Born on December 18, 1869, in Langenschwarz, Germany. He emigrated to Holland, and he lived on Merwedeplein 8 II, Amsterdam. He was deported from Westerbork on July 6, 1943, to Sobibór. He perished there on July 9, 1943.

TEITELBAUM, Israel Isi. Born on January 27, 1925, in Leipzig, Germany. He emigrated to Holland on February 15, 1939, and lived at Paviljoen Loosdrechtse Rade C 8 rood Loosdrecht. He was deported from Westerbork on April 27, 1943. He perished in Sobibór on April 30, 1943.

THEMANS, Bernard, Salomon. Born on April 5, 1909, in Oldenzaal. The family home was located at Nieuwegarcht 92, Utrecht. He lived and worked in Utrecht as a Religious Instructor. He perished in Sobibór on March 20, 1943, along with his wife Judik and their two children Leon and Sonja.

THEMANS, Judik (formerly Simons). Born on August 20, 1904, in Den Haag. The family home was located at Nieuwegrcht 92, Utrecht. She was a member of the Dutch Women's Gymnastics team that won a Gold Medal at the 1928 Olympics, that were held in Amsterdam. She perished in Sobibór on March 20, 1943, along with her husband and two children.

THEMANS, Leon. Born on February 28, 1940, in Utrecht. The family home was located at Nieuwegrcht 92, Utrecht. He perished in Sobibór on March 20, 1943.

THEMANS, Sonja. Born on March 9, 1938, in Utrecht. The family home was located at Nieuwegrcht 92, Utrecht. She perished in Sobibór on March 20, 1943.

TONNINGE, Mozes. Born on June 11, 1900, in Dordrecht. He lived at Sint Jorisweg 33, Dordrecht. He was a Tailor in Dordrecht. He perished in Sobibór on July 9, 1943.

TROOTSWIJK, Menno. Born on April 13, 1909, in Zwolle, Holland. He lived at Bilderdijkstraat 13, Zwolle. He worked in Zwolle as a Sales Supervisor. He was deported from Westerbork to Sobibór, along with his wife Annie Trootswijk-Hijmans on March 10, 1943. On arrival in Sobibór, she was selected for Labor in the Jewish Labor Camp at Trawniki, in the Lublin district, where she perished on January 7, 1944. Menno was selected to be gassed in Sobibór, and he perished on March 13, 1943.

TURTELAUB, Meier. Born on January 8, 1925, in Dortmund, Germany. He emigrated to Holland and he lived at Paviljoen Loosdrechtse Rade C 8 rood Loosdrecht. He was deported from Westerbork to Sobibór on May 18, 1943. He perished in Sobibór on May 21, 1943.

UNGER, Chaim. Born on October 12, 1908, in Rozdol, in Eastern Galicia. He emigrated to Holland, and he lived at Falckstraat 14 huis, Amsterdam. He worked in Amsterdam as a Merchant. He perished in Sobibór on July 23, 1943.

UNGER, Jakob, Wolf. Born on December 14, 1871, in Uhnow, Ukraine. He lived at Gravesandestraat 32 III, Amsterdam. He was married to Erna. He perished in Sobibór on April 30, 1943

UNGER-SCHUMIR, Erna. Born on April 14, 1884, in Kolomea, Ukraine. She lived at 's Gravesandestraat 32 III, Amsterdam. She was married to Jakob Unger. She perished in Sobibór on April 30, 1943.

VALK, Magdalena. Born on September 28, 1933, in Goch, Germany. She lived at Molenpad 71, Leeuwarden. She perished in Sobibór on May 21, 1943.

VALK-EMMERICH, Selma. Born on April 11, 1887, in Horstein, Germany. She emigrated to Holland and lived at Korte Kleverlaan 40, Bloemendaal. She was deported from Westerbork on April 13, 1943, and she perished in Sobibór on April 16, 1943.

VELDE, David Juda van der. Born on November 21, 1932, in Amsterdam. He lived at President Brandstraat 5 II, Amsterdam. He died in Sobibór on April 2, 1943. His partially burnt name tag was discovered by archaeologists in 2013.

Van KLEEF-Van DAMM, Saartje. Born on December 25, 1881, in Smilde. She lived at Rapenburgerstraat 35 huis, Amsterdam. She was deported along with her husband Salomon from Westerbork to Sobibór, on June 8, 1943, and she perished in Sobibór on June 11, 1943.

Van KLEEF, Salomon. Born on January 12, 1887, in Amsterdam. He lived at Rapenburgerstraat 35 huis, Amsterdam. He was a Shopkeeper by profession. He was deported along with his wife Saartje on June 8, 1943. He perished on June 11, 1943.

VERSTANDIG, Erna. Born on August 16, 1924, in Kassel, Germany. She lived at the Nederlands-Israelitisch Meisjesweehuis, Rapenburgerstraat 171, Amsterdam. She perished in Sobibór on July 16, 1943.[376]

VIOOL, Betje, Judik. Born on April 25, 1924, in Rotterdam. She lived at Nieuwe Binnenweg 65 a, Rotterdam. She was a Hairdresser by profession. She perished in Sobibór on October 31, 1943.

---

[376] Listed on the memorial in the Sobibor Museum shown on the heading of this chapter.

VIOOL, Raphael. Born on December 4, 1895, in Rotterdam. He lived at Nieuwe Binnenweg 65 a, Rotterdam. He was a Pastry cook by profession. He perished in Sobibór on October 31, 1943.

VISJAGER-PETERS, Rebecca. Born on December 28, 1918, in Amsterdam. She lived at Nieuwe Kerkstraat 30 huis, Amsterdam. She was a cardboard worker by profession. She died in Sobibór on June 4, 1943.

VISSER, Israel, Bernard. Born on April 16, 1918, in Amsterdam. He lived at Jodenbreestraat 3 I, Amsterdam. He was a Merchant by profession. He perished in Sobibór on May 28, 1943.

WAGNER, Ilse. Born on January 26, 1929, in Hamburg, Germany. She emigrated to Holland, and she lived at Grevelingenstraat 11 I, Amsterdam. She was friends with Anne Frank. She perished in Sobibór on April 2, 1943.

WAHRHAFTIG, Abraham. Born on June 4, 1931, in Berlin, Germany. He emigrated to Holland, and he lived at Van Limburg Stirumstraat 74, Den Haag. He perished in Sobibór on April 30, 1943.

WAHRHAFTIG, Adolf, Adi. Born on February 3, 1928, in Berlin, Germany. He emigrated to Holland, and lived at S.A. Rudelsheim Foundation Heideparkweg 51, Hilversum. He perished in Sobibór on July 23, 1943.

WEBER-BRASCH, Irma. Born on December 5, 1886, in Breslau. She emigrated to Holland and lived at Jan van Eijckstraat 22 II, Amsterdam. She was deported from Westerbork on March 23, 1943, to Sobibór. She perished in Sobibór on March 26, 1943.

WEIJL, Jules, Jacob. Born on January 4, 1915, in Amsterdam. He lived at Zomerdijkstraat 14 huis, Amsterdam. He attended the Amsterdamse Toneelschool between 1939-1941. He acted with the Joodsch Kleinkunst Ensemble at the Hollandsche

Schouwburg during 1941, and 1942. He perished in Sobibór on July 16, 1943.

WEISS, Rita. Born on April 29, 1925, in Berlin, Germany. She emigrated to Holland, and lived at Merelstraat 1, Utrecht. She was deported from Westerbork to Sobibór on March 2, 1943. She perished in Sobibór on March 5, 1943.

WINNIK, Elisabeth. Born on July 13, 1926, in Amsterdam. She lived at Nederlands Israelitsch Meisjesweehuis, Rapenburgerstraat 171, Amsterdam. She was deported from Westerbork Transit Camp on June 1, 1943. She died in Sobibór on June 4, 1943.

WINNIK, Keetje. Born on July 13, 1926, in Amsterdam. She lived at Nederlands Israelitsch Meisjesweehuis, Rapenburgerstraat 171, Amsterdam. She was deported from Westerbork Transit Camp on June 1, 1943. She died in Sobibór on June 4, 1943, along with her twin sister Elizabeth and other family members.

WOLF-NUSSBAUM, Maier. Born on February 10, 1874, in Fulda, Germany. He emigrated to Holland and lived at Krammerstraat 7 II, Amsterdam. He was deported from Westerbork on May 25, 1943, to Sobibór. He perished in Sobibór on May 28, 1943.

ZAK, David, Jacob. Born on February 23, 1935, in Amsterdam. He lived at Uiterwaardenstraat 71 III, Amsterdam. He was deported from Vught to Westerbork on the so-called 'Children's Transport'. He was deported from Weterbork on June 8, 1943, to Sobibór. He perished in Sobibór on June 11, 1943. A tag bearing the name 'Deddie', which presumably his nickname, also bearing his address in Amsterdam, and his date of birth was discovered by archaeologists on the former camp grounds in 2013.

ZANDER, Clara. Born on March 14, 1895, in Berlin. She emigrated to Holland, and she lived at Diezestraat 29, Amsterdam. She was deported from Westerbork on March 23, 1943. She perished in Sobibór on March 26, 1943.

ZEEMAN, Joseph. Born on July 6, 1914, in Duisburg, Germany. He emigrated to Holland and lived at Retiefstraat 16 I, Amsterdam. He was a Salesman by profession. He was deported from Westerbork on June 29, 1943, to Sobibór. He perished in Sobibór on July 2, 1943.

ZEEHANDELAAR, Abraham. Born on September 27, 1877, in Amsterdam. He lived at Nieuwe Achtergracht 55 huis, Amsterdam. He died in Sobibór on May 21, 1943.

ZEEHANDELAAR, Mozes, Gerrit. Born on October 20, 1915, in Zwolle. He lived at Jufferenwal 18, Zwolle. He was a Merchant by profession. There is some confusion about the date of his death. The Joods Monument lists his death on March 13, 1943. However Selma Wijnberg, during an interview, said Mozes was killed when the 70 Dutch prisoners were murdered en-mass during April 1943. As she came from Zwolle, and knew him, this is the most likely outcome.

ZIJTENFELD, Jacob. Born on July 14, 1900, in Lodz, Poland. He settled in Holland and he lived at Zwetstraat 87, Den Haag. He was a Merchant by profession. He perished in Sobibór on May 7, 1943.

ZIJTENFELD, Moniek. Born on January 23, 1928, in Pabiance, Poland. He settled in Holland and she lived at Zwetstraat 87, Den Haag. He perished in Sobibór on May 7, 1943.

ZIJTENFELD-HERSZKOWICZ, Rachela. Born on January 15, 1903, in Pabiance, Poland. She lived at Zwetstraat 87, Den Haag. She perished in Sobibór on May 7, 1943.

ZWARTVERWER-SPIER, Tilly. Born on December 31, 1920, in Amsterdam. She lived at Transvaalstraat 90 I, Amsterdam. She was an Office Clerk by profession. She was deported from the Westerbork Transit Camp on July 20, 1943. She was the last name on the last transport from Westerbork to Sobibór. She died in Sobibór on July 23, 1943.

Roll of Remembrance— Greater German Reich A–Z

List of German born Jews who were members of the Piaski Judenrat
(Courtesy of the Holocaust Historical Society UK)

Der Judenrat in Piaski.
Tgb.Nr. 49/42.

Piaski, den 27. April 1942

An den
Herrn Kreishauptmann Lublin-Land
L u b l i n .

Nachdem am 7.April 1942 auf behördliche Anweisung der Judenrat in Piaski neu konstituiert wurde, reichen wir nachstehend die Liste der 12 Mitglieder des Judenrates nebst Geburtsdaten dem Herrn Kreishauptmann ein und bitten ergebenst für die neuen Judenratsmitglieder von Nr.4 bis Nr.12/ drei Mitglieder des alten Judenrates sind verblieben/ entsprechende Ausweise auszustellen und für 6 der neu eingesetzten Judenräte, die in der untenstehenden Liste rot unterstrichen, die Erlaubnis zum Verlassen des Ghettos Piaski in Ausübung ihres Dienstes zu genehmigen:

1/ Polisecki Mandel, Obmann des Judenrates / Verbliebene
2/ Drajblat Moses, Stellvertreter des Obmanns / Judenratsmitgl.
3/ Aschmann Josef, Kassierer /
4/ Fried Moritz Israel,   geb. 9. 9. 1908 in Butzbach/Hessen/
5/ Schlüsser Ernst   "   "   16. 1. 1884 " Sürgenloch/Kr. Mainz/
6/ Kugelmann Siegfr."   "   17. 7. 1884 " Witzenhausen/b. Kassel/
7/ Sänger Fritz   "   "   12. 9. 1991 " Augsburg
8/ Railing Hugo   "   "   14. 5. 1886 " München
9/ Hirschmann Kurt   "   26.10. 1900 " Wien
10/ Böhm Ernst   "   12.12. 1893 " Jägerndorf
11/ Guttsmann Walter Isr.   "   8. 5. 1880 " Berlin
12/ Kempner Friedr.Wilh.Isr. "   29. 8. 1914 "   "

9 Lichtbilder und Lebensläufe der neuen Judenräte überreichen wir in der Anlage.

Der Obmann des Judenrates Piaski:

This Roll of Remembrance covers the victims who perished at Sobibór from the Greater German Reich, mainly sourced from the online resource *Bundesarchiv Gedenkbuch*. Where appropriate this has been checked with the Joodse Monument Database in the Netherlands. The online resource *www.deathcamps.og* has also been consulted.

Where there is doubt as to whether individuals were murdered in Sobibór or another camp, such as Auschwitz or Lublin, then these people have not been included. Jews that emigrated from Germany to another country—for example Holland—have been included in other lists.

ABELE, Berta (formerly Westerfeld). Born on February 14, 1880, in Frankfurt am Main. She was deported from Frankfurt am Main on June 11, 1942, to Sobibór where she perished.

ABELES, Renate (formerly Kahn). Born on December 9, 1882, in Frankfurt am Main. She was deported from Frankfurt am Main on June 11, 1942, to Sobibór where she perished.

ABRAHAM, Emanuel. Born on August 15, 1879, in Treysa. Deported from Kassel-Halle on June 1, 1942, to the Izbica Transit Ghetto in Poland. Sent from Izbica to Sobibór, where he perished on June 3, 1942.

ABRAHAM, Mathilde (formerly Mayer). Born on March 21, 1883, in Friedelsheim. She was deported from Frankfurt am Main on June 11, 1942, to Sobibór where she perished.

ABT, Bessy. Born on March 10, 1898, in Melsungen. She was deported from Kassel-Halle on June 1, 1942, to the Izbica Transit Ghetto. Sent from Izbica to Sobibór, where she perished on June 3, 1942.

ACKERMANN, Hedwig (formerly Lorig). Born on April 13, 1911, in Butzweiler. She was deported from Frankfurt am Main on June 11, 1942, to Sobibór where she perished.

ACKERMANN, Klara (formerly Schaffer). Born on September 12, 1892, in Dubiecko, Poland. She was deported from Frankfurt am Main on June 11, 1942, to Sobibór where she perished.

ACKERMANN, Lana. Born on August 6, 1941, in Aidhausen. She was deported from Wurzburg on April 25, 1942, to Krasnystaw in Poland. She perished in Sobibór.

ADLER, Adelheid (formerly Gollisch). Born on August 16, 1901, in Beuthen, Poland. She was deported from Frankfurt am Main on June 11, 1942, to Sobibór where she perished.

ADLER, Bertha (formerly Oppenheim). Born on January 17, 1888, in Abterode. She was deported from Kassel-Halle on June 1, 1942, to the Izbica Transit Ghetto. Sent on from Izbica to Sobibór, where she perished on June 3, 1942.

ADLER, Clothilde (formerly Nassauer). Born on May 26, 1882, in Wehen. She was deported from Frankfurt am Main on May 24, 1942, to the Izbica Transit Ghetto. Sent on from Izbica to Sobibór where she perished.

ADLER, Ida. Born on November 9, 1889, in Niedenstein. She was deported from Kassel-Halle on June 1, 1942, to the Izbica Transit Ghetto. Sent on from Izbica to Sobibór, where she perished on June 3, 1942.

AHRONSON, Klara (formerly Blumenthal). Born on April 4, 1888, in Oberlahnstein. She was deported from Frankfurt am Main on June 11, 1942, to Sobibór where she perished.

ALEXANDER, Luise. Born on December 13, 1890, in Kauernik, Poland. She was deported from Frankfurt am Main on June 11, 1942, to Sobibór where she perished.

ALTHEIMER, Kathinka. Born on January 30, 1883, in Bergen. She was deported from Frankfurt am Main on June 11, 1942, to Sobibór where she perished.

APPEL, Jenny (formerly Schwab). Born on March 4, 1888, in Berkach. She was deported from Kassel-Halle on June 1, 1942, to the Izbica Transit Ghetto. Sent on from Izbica to Sobibór, where she perished on June 3, 1942.

APPEL, Sofia. Born on September 10, 1880, in Scholkrippen. She was deported from Frankfurt am Main on June 11, 1942, to Sobibór where she perished.

APT, Benjamin. Born on July 9, 1882, in Niederaula. He was deported from Kassel-Halle on June 1, 1942, to the Izbica Transit Ghetto. Sent on from Izbica to Sobibór, where she perished on June 3, 1942.

APT, Berta (formerly Rosenberg). Born on January 5, 1884, in Mulbach. She was deported from Kassel-Halle on June 1, 1942, to the Izbica Transit Ghetto. Sent on from Izbica to Sobibór, where she perished on June 3, 1942.

ARM, Erna (formerly Munz). Born on March 2, 1912, in Glogow, Poland. She was deported from Frankfurt am Main on June 11, 1942, to Sobibór where she perished.

ARM, Rosel. Born on September 10, 1937, in Frankfurt am Main. She was deported from Frankfurt am Main on June 11, 1942, to Sobibór where she perished.

ARNHOLZ, Bertha (formerly Lewin). Born on January 12, 1883, in Labischin, Poland. She was deported from Kassel-Halle on June 1, 1942, to the Izbica Transit Ghetto. Sent on from Izbica to Sobibór, where she perished on June 3, 1942.

ARON, Sitta. Born on June 3, 1921, in Hamburg. She was deported from Frankfurt am Main on June 11, 1942, to Sobibór where she perished.

ARONSOHN, Fanny (formerly Rosenthal). Born on October 26, 1883, in Wetzlar. She was deported from Kassel-Halle on June 1, 1942, to the Izbica Transit Ghetto. Sent on from Izbica to Sobibór, where she perished on June 3, 1942.

ATZEL, Fanny (formerly Tannenberg). Born on January 1, 1887, in Schenklengsfeld. She was deported from Frankfurt am Main on June 11, 1942, to Sobibór where she perished.

BACARACH, Abraham. Born on September 2, 1878, in Nenterhausen. He was deported from Kassel-Halle on June 1, 1942, to the Izbica Transit Ghetto. Sent on from Izbica to Sobibór, where she perished on June 3, 1942.

BACHARACH, Betty (formerly Muller). Born on February 16, 1889, in Herleshausen. She was deported from Kassel-Halle on June 1, 1942, to the Izbica Transit Ghetto. Sent on from Izbica to Sobibór, where she perished on June 3, 1942.

BACHARACH, Frieda, Friederike. Born on April 24, 1880, in Fritzlar. She was deported from Kassel-Halle on June 1, 1942, to the Izbica Transit Ghetto. Sent on from Izbica to Sobibór, where she perished on June 3, 1942.

BACHARACH, Grete. Born on October 2, 1922, in Neukirchen. She was deported from Kassel-Halle on June 1, 1942, to the Izbica Transit Ghetto. Sent on from Izbica to Sobibór, where she perished on June 3, 1942.

BACHARACH, Klara (formerly Lazarus). Born on December 8, 1893, in Appenheim. She was deported from Kassel-Halle on June 1, 1942, to the Izbica Transit Ghetto. Sent on from Izbica to Sobibór, where she perished on June 3, 1942.

BACHARACH, Meta (formerly Spier). Born on March 31, 1895, in Hoof. She was deported from Kassel-Halle on June 1, 1942, to the Izbica Transit Ghetto. Sent on from Izbica to Sobibór, where she perished on June 3, 1942.

BACHARACH, Sophie. Born on August 12, 1874, in Fritzlar. She was deported from Kassel-Halle on June 1, 1942, to the Izbica Transit Ghetto. Sent on from Izbica to Sobibór, where she perished on June 3, 1942.

BACHENHEIMER, Hildegard. Born on November 4, 1921, in Wetter. She was deported from Kassel-Halle on June 1, 1942, to the Izbica Transit Ghetto. Sent on from Izbica to Sobibór, where she perished on June 3, 1942.

BACHENHEIMER, Paul. Born on December 26, 1930, in Wetter. He was deported from Kassel-Halle on June 1, 1942, to the Izbica Transit Ghetto. Sent on from Izbica to Sobibór, where he perished on June 3, 1942.

BACHMANN, Hilde (formerly Cohen). Born on November 18, 1897, in Preusisch. She was deported from Frankfurt am Main on June 11, 1942, to Sobibór where she perished.

BAER, Chana. Born on February 3, 1941, in Hannover. She was deported from Kassel-Halle on June 1, 1942, to the Izbica Transit Ghetto. Sent on from Izbica to Sobibór, where she perished on June 3, 1942.

BAER, Clementine. Born on March 24, 1924, in Frankfurt am Main. She was deported from Frankfurt am Main on June 11, 1942, to Sobibór where she perished.

BAER, Gunther. Born on March 11, 1918, in Worms. He was deported from Kassel-Halle on June 1, 1942, to the Izbica Transit Ghetto. Sent on from Izbica to Sobibór, where he perished on June 3, 1942.

BAER, Irma (formerly Ullmann). Born on October 13, 1894, in Westerburg. She was deported from Frankfurt am Main on June 11, 1942, to Sobibór where she perished.

BAER, Paula (formerly Bermann). Born on January 4, 1921, in Schwetzingen. She was deported from Kassel-Halle on June 1, 1942, to the Izbica Transit Ghetto. Sent on from Izbica to Sobibór, where she perished on June 3, 1942.

BAER, Sofie. Born on August 23, 1923, in Frankfurt am Main. She was deported from Frankfurt am Main on June 11, 1942, to Sobibór where she perished.

BAUCHWITZ, Kurt. Born on January 27, 1888, in Sangerhausen. He was imprisoned in the Sachsenhausen Concentration Camp. He was deported from Kassel-Halle on June 1, 1942, to the Izbica Transit Ghetto. Sent on from Izbica to Sobibór, where he perished on June 3, 1942.

BAUCHWITZ, Regina (formerly Meyer). Born on April 7, 1888, in Labenz. She was deported from Kassel-Halle on June 1, 1942, to the Izbica Transit Ghetto. Sent on from Izbica to Sobibór, where she perished on June 3, 1942.

BAUER, Rickchen (formerly Strauss). Born on April 15, 1886, in Rothenkirchen. She was deported from Frankfurt am Main on June 11, 1942, to Sobibór where she perished.

BAUM, Josef. Born on October 22, 1926, in Wiesbaden. He was deported from Frankfurt am Main on May 24, 1942, to the Izbica Transit Ghetto. He was sent from Izbica to Sobibór where he perished on September 10, 1942.

BAUM, Toni (formerly Bierig). Born on February 5, 1886, in Flehingen. She was deported from Frankfurt am Main on June 11, 1942, to Sobibór where she perished.

BECK, Rosa. Born on March 6, 1890, in Mainz. She was deported from Frankfurt am Main on June 11, 1942, to Sobibór where she perished.

BECKER, Gertrude (formerly Brodreich). Born on July 5, 1899, in Himbach. She was deported from Kassel-Halle on June 1, 1942, to the Izbica Transit Ghetto. Sent on from Izbica to Sobibór, where she perished on June 3, 1942.

BEER, de, Cacille. Born on March 29, 1891, in Mesenheim. She was deported from Frankfurt am Main on June 11, 1942, to Sobibór where she perished.

BENEDICK, Flora (formerly Scheuer). Born on September 20, 1897, in Gelnhausen. She was deported from Kassel-Halle on

June 1, 1942, to the Izbica Transit Ghetto. Sent on from Izbica to Sobibór, where she perished on June 3, 1942.

BENEDICK, Lothar. Born on August 13, 1923, in Gelnhausen. He was deported from Kassel-Halle on June 1, 1942, to the Izbica Transit Ghetto. Sent on from Izbica to Sobibór, where he perished on June 3, 1942.

BENEDICT, Amalie. Born on February 14, 1879, in Landau. She was deported from Frankfurt am Main on June 11, 1942, to Sobibór where she perished.

BERNEY, Rosalie (formerly Katz). Born on February 1, 1878, in Bobenhausen. She was deported from Frankfurt am Main on June 11, 1942. She perished in Sobibór on December 31, 1942.

BERNSTEIN, Eva. Born on June 15, 1935, in Frankfurt am Main. She was deported from Frankfurt am Main on June 11, 1942, to Sobibór where she perished.

BERNSTEIN, Eva, Mirjam. Born on April 2, 1938, in Berlin. She was deported from Kassel-Halle on June 1, 1942, to the Izbica Transit Ghetto. Sent on from Izbica to Sobibór, where she perished on June 3, 1942.

BERNSTEIN, Jutta (formerly Fleischmann). Born on January 28, 1911, in Sangerhausen. She was deported from Kassel-Halle on June 1, 1942, to the Izbica Transit Ghetto. Sent on from Izbica to Sobibór, where she perished on June 3, 1942.

BERNSTEIN, Lotte. Born on January 3, 1889, in Kolberg. She was deported from Frankfurt am Main on June 11, 1942, to Sobibór where she perished.

BEVERSTEIN, Adele. Born on June 5, 1894, in New York, United States of America. She was deported from Frankfurt am Main on June 11, 1942, to Sobibór where she perished.

BICKHARDT, Edith. Born on March 22, 1924, in Frankfurt am Main. She was deported from Frankfurt am Main on June 11, 1942, to Sobibór where she perished.

BINAMOWITSCH, Liba. Born on June 20, 1902, in Kielce, Poland. She was deported from Frankfurt am Main on June 11, 1942, to Sobibór where she perished.

BIOW, Alice. Born on April 20, 1893, in Frankfurt am Main. She was deported from Frankfurt am Main on June 11, 1942, to Sobibór where she perished.

BIOW, Hedwig. Born on October 14, 1894, in Frankfurt am Main. She was deported from Frankfurt am Main on June 11, 1942, to Sobibór where she perished.

BLEICH, Erna. Born on February 10, 1923, in Frankfurt am Main. She was deported from Frankfurt am Main on June 11, 1942, to Sobibór where she perished.

BLEICH, Ita (formerly Sturm). Born on April 3, 1897, in Biezdziedza, Poland. She was deported from Frankfurt am Main on June 11, 1942, to Sobibór where she perished.

BLEICH, Ruth. Born on July 31, 1934, in Frankfurt am Main. She was deported from Frankfurt am Main on June 11, 1942, to Sobibór where she perished.

BLOCH, Friederike (formerly Levi). Born on August 5, 1896, in Schluchtern. She was deported from Frankfurt am Main on June 11, 1942, to Sobibór where she perished.

BLOCH, Ilse. Born on May 20, 1894, in Sachenhausen. She was deported from Kassel-Halle on June 1, 1942, to the Izbica Transit Ghetto. Sent on from Izbica to Sobibór, where she perished on June 3, 1942.

BLOCH, Lina (formerly Kleinstrass). Born on December 7, 1881, in Steinheim. She was deported from Kassel-Halle on June 1, 1942, to the Izbica Transit Ghetto. Sent on from Izbica to Sobibór, where she perished on June 3, 1942.

BLOCH, Siegmund. Born on February 2, 1861, in Sachsenhausen. He was deported from Kassel-Halle on June 1, 1942, to the

Izbica Transit Ghetto. Sent on from Izbica to Sobibór, where he perished on June 3, 1942.

BLOCH, Siegmund. Born on June 2, 1878, in Schmieheim. He was deported from Kassel-Halle on June 1, 1942, to the Izbica Transit Ghetto. Sent on from Izbica to Sobibór, where he perished on June 3, 1942.

BLUHM, Lotte (formerly Weisfeldt). Born on July 20, 1889, in Zempelburg. She was deported from Kassel-Halle on June 1, 1942, to the Izbica Transit Ghetto. Sent on from Izbica to Sobibór, where she perished on June 3, 1942.

BLUM, Arthur. Born on January 2, 1886, in Gauersheim. He was imprisoned in Dachau Concentration Camp during 1938. He was deported from Kassel-Halle on June 1, 1942, to the Izbica Transit Ghetto. Sent on from Izbica to Sobibór, where he perished on June 3, 1942.

BLUM, Caroline (formerly Weinberger). Born on September 22, 1892, in Bremberg. She was deported from Frankfurt am Main on June 11, 1942, to Sobibór where she perished.

BLUM, Hanna. Born on September 24, 1930, in Saarbrucken. She was deported from Kassel-Halle on June 1, 1942, to the Izbica Transit Ghetto. Sent on from Izbica to Sobibór, where she perished on June 3, 1942.

BLUM, Ida (formerly Braumann). Born on May 6, 1887, in Unteralterheim. She was deported from Kassel-Halle on June 1, 1942, to the Izbica Transit Ghetto. Sent on from Izbica to Sobibór, where she perished on June 3, 1942.

BLUM, Leontine (formerly Lorch). Born on May 8, 1881, in Mainz. She was deported from Frankfurt am Main on June 11, 1942, to Sobibór where she perished.

BLUM, Martha. Born on February 5, 1898, in Helligenwald. She was deported from Kassel-Halle on June 1, 1942, to the Izbica

Transit Ghetto. Sent on from Izbica to Sobibór, where she perished on June 3, 1942.

BLUMBERG, Meta (formerly Lewald). Born on October 20, 1880, in Wurzburg. She was deported from Kassel-Halle on June 1, 1942, to the Izbica Transit Ghetto. Sent on from Izbica to Sobibór, where she perished on October 15, 1942.

BLUMENFELD, Georg. Born on March 22, 1910, in Berlin. He was deported from Berlin on June 13, 1942. He perished in Sobibór on September 11, 1942.

BLUMENTHAL, Adolf. Born on August 3, 1919, in Niederrodenbach. He was deported from Kassel-Halle on June 1, 1942, to the Izbica Transit Ghetto. Sent on from Izbica to Sobibór, where he perished on June 3, 1942.

BLUMENTHAL, Bernhard. Born on May 6, 1913, in Niederrodenbach. He was deported from Kassel-Halle on June 1, 1942, to the Izbica Transit Ghetto. Sent on from Izbica to Sobibór, where he perished on June 3, 1942.

BLUMENTHAL, Else. Born on August 24, 1886, in Nassau. She was deported from Frankfurt am Main on June 11, 1942, to Sobibór where she perished.

BLUMENTHAL, Hilde (formerly Schwarz). Born on March 2, 1912, in Ruckershausen. She was deported from Frankfurt am Main on June 11, 1942, to Sobibór where she perished.

BLUMENTHAL, Mathilde (formerly Kahn). Born on February 19, 1881, in Hergershausen. She was deported from Frankfurt am Main on June 11, 1942, to Sobibór where she perished.

BLUTSTEIN, Fanny. Born on July 4, 1911, in Dortmund. She was deported from Frankfurt am Main on June 11, 1942, to Sobibór where she perished.

BODENHEIMER, Martha (formerly Ermann). Born on March 25, 1903, in Trier. She was She was deported from Kassel-Halle on June 1, 1942, to the Izbica Transit Ghetto. Sent on from Izbica to Sobibór, where she perished on October 15, 1942.

BODENHEIMER, Siegfried. Born on January 14, 1895, in Brebach. Imprisoned in Dachau Concentration Camp. He was deported from Kassel-Halle on June 1, 1942, to the Izbica Transit Ghetto. Sent on from Izbica to Sobibór, where he perished on June 3, 1942.

BOHM, Ernst. Born on December 12, 1893, in Krnov, Czech Republic, formerly Jagerndorf, Sudetenland. He was a member of the *Judenrat* in Piaski. He was deported to Sobibór in November 1942, where he perished. [377]

BORGER, Rosa (formerly Melamed). Born on March 24, 1896, in Glogow, Poland. She was deported from Frankfurt am Main on June 11, 1942, to Sobibór where she perished.

BRACHOLD, Gisela (formerly Burstin). Born on October 22, 1880, in Janow, Poland. She was deported from Frankfurt am Main on June 11, 1942, to Sobibór where she perished.

BRASCH, Clotilde (formerly Frank). Born on February 24, 1880, in Forcheim. She was deported from Kassel-Halle on June 1, 1942, to the Izbica Transit Ghetto. Sent on from Izbica to Sobibór, where she perished on June 3, 1942.

BRAUNSBERG, Emile (formerly Stern). Born on June 1, 1892, in Betziesdorf. She was deported from Kassel-Halle on June 1, 1942, to the Izbica Transit Ghetto. Sent on from Izbica to Sobibór, where she perished on June 3, 1942.

BRAUNSBERG, Viktor. Born on March 29, 1887, in Breuna mit Rhoda. He was deported from Kassel-Halle on June 1, 1942, to the Izbica Transit Ghetto. Sent on from Izbica to Sobibór, where he perished on June 3, 1942.

---

[377] www.deathcamps.org—online resource.

BRIEFWECHSLER, Paula (formerly Blumenthal). Born on September 15, 1899, in Nordholen. She was deported from Frankfurt am Main on June 11, 1942, to Sobibór where she perished.

BRONNE, Emma (formerly Beisinger). Born on June 3, 1877, in Gondelsheim. She was deported from Frankfurt am Main on June 11, 1942, to Sobibór where she perished.

BRONNE, Gertrud. Born on June 18, 1911, in Rommersheim. She was deported from Frankfurt am Main on June 11, 1942, to Sobibór where she perished.

BRONNE, Ruth. Born on September 22, 1920, in Armsheim. She was deported from Frankfurt am Main on June 11, 1942, to Sobibór where she perished.

BRUCKMANN, Hulda. Born on December 20, 1882, in Xanten. She was deported from Frankfurt am Main on June 11, 1942, to Sobibór where she perished.

BUCHEIM, Johanna (formerly Simon). Born on May 1, 1902, in Ehringshausen. She was deported from Frankfurt am Main on June 11, 1942, to Sobibór where she perished.

BUCHEIM, Riga. Born on February 22, 1933, in Ehringshausen. She was deported from Frankfurt am Main on June 11, 1942, to Sobibór where she perished.

BUTWIES, Cornelie. Born on June 3, 1895, in Frankfurt am Main. She was deported from Frankfurt am Main on June 11, 1942, to Sobibór where she perished.

CAHN, Berta (formerly Jacobi). Born on February 4, 1891, in Sonnenberg. She was deported from Frankfurt am Main on June 11, 1942, to Sobibór where she perished.

CAHN, Erich. Born on August 2, 1877, in Aschersleben. He was imprisoned in Sachsenhausen Concentration Camp until November 23, 1938. He was deported from Kassel-Halle on June 1,

1942, to the Izbica Transit Ghetto. Sent on from Izbica to Sobibór, where he perished on June 3, 1942.

CAHN, Hedwig (formerly Ferse). Born on August 1, 1892, in Oberlistingen. She was deported from Kassel-Halle on June 1, 1942, to the Izbica Transit Ghetto. Sent on from Izbica to Sobibór, where she perished on June 3, 1942.

CAHN, Selma. Born on March 27, 1909, in Nastaltern. She was deported from Frankfurt am Main on June 11, 1942, to Sobibór where she perished.

CAHN, Toni. Born on May 19, 1898, in Eschwege. She was deported from Kassel-Halle on June 1, 1942, to the Izbica Transit Ghetto. Sent on from Izbica to Sobibór, where she perished on June 3, 1942.

COHN, Hannacha. Born on November 12, 1938, in Halle. She was deported from Kassel-Halle on June 1, 1942, to the Izbica Transit Ghetto. Sent on from Izbica to Sobibór, where she perished on June 3, 1942.

COHN, Recha (formerly Grunspan). Born on May 20, 1914, in Sonnberg. She was deported from Kassel-Halle on June 1, 1942, to the Izbica Transit Ghetto. Sent on from Izbica to Sobibór, where she perished on June 3, 1942.

COHN, Thekla (formerly Kaufmann). Born on November 20, 1879, in Coburg. She was deported from Kassel-Halle on June 1, 1942, to the Izbica Transit Ghetto. Sent on from Izbica to Sobibór, where she perished on June 3, 1942.

CZARLINSKI, Johanna. Born on November 13, 1905, in Erle. She was deported from Kassel-Halle on June 1, 1942, to the Izbica Transit Ghetto. Sent on from Izbica to Sobibór, where she perished on June 3, 1942.

DANNENBERG, Emmy (formerly Wolfes). Born on November 15, 1877, in Aurich. She was deported from Kassel-Halle on June

1, 1942, to the Izbica Transit Ghetto. Sent on from Izbica to Sobibór, where she perished on June 3, 1942.

DANNENBURG, Ruth. Born on March 3, 1910, in Kassel. She was deported from Kassel-Halle on June 1, 1942, to the Izbica Transit Ghetto. Sent on from Izbica to Sobibór, where she perished on June 3, 1942.

DANZIG, Mina. Born on August 6, 1879, in Selters. She was deported from Frankfurt am Main on June 11, 1942, to Sobibór where she perished.

DAVID, Hilda. Born on May 28, 1880, in Rohrenfurth. She was deported from Kassel-Halle on June 1, 1942, to the Izbica Transit Ghetto. Sent on from Izbica to Sobibór, where she perished on June 3, 1942.

DAVID, Klara (formerly Kahn). Born on January 20, 1879, in Freiburg. She was deported from Frankfurt am Main on June 11, 1942, to Sobibór where she perished.

DAVID, Magarethe (formerly Heymann). Born on July 16, 1902, in Wiesbaden. She was deported from Frankfurt am Main on June 11, 1942, to Sobibór where she perished.

DECKER, Getta (formerly Frank). Born on February 28, 1893, in Edelfingen. She was deported from Frankfurt am Main on June 11, 1942, to Sobibór where she perished.

DOENBERG, Henny (formerly Goldmann). Born on January 23, 1891, in Eschwege. She was deported from Frankfurt am Main on June 11, 1942, to Sobibór where she perished.

DOLLEFELD, Clara (formerly Wallach). Born on February 8, 1889, in Nesselroden. She was deported from Kassel-Halle on June 1, 1942, to the Izbica Transit Ghetto. Sent on from Izbica to Sobibór, where she perished on June 3, 1942.

DOLLEFELD, Mathilde. Born on November 27, 1872, in Bebra. She was deported from Kassel-Halle on June 1, 1942, to the

Izbica Transit Ghetto. Sent on from Izbica to Sobibór, where she perished on June 3, 1942.

DRUCKER, Aron. Born on May 11, 1876. He was deported on April 27, 1942, along with his wife Rosa, from Vienna to Włodawa, in Poland. He perished in Sobibór.[378]

DRUCKER, Rosa. Born on January 1, 1886. She was deported on April 27, 1942, along with her husband Aron, from Vienna to Włodawa, in Poland. She perished in Sobibór.[379]

ECKMANN, Emma (formerly Sulzbacher). Born on February 10, 1878, in Neustadt. She was deported from Kassel-Halle on June 1, 1942, to the Izbica Transit Ghetto. Sent on from Izbica to Sobibór, where she perished on June 3, 1942.

EHLBAUM, Hanni. Born on October 23, 1930, in Frankfurt am Main. She was deported from Frankfurt am Main on June 11, 1942, to Sobibór where she perished.

EHLBAUM, Perla (formerly Bernstein). Born on November 15, 1899, in Brzesko, Poland. She was deported from Frankfurt am Main on June 11, 1942, to Sobibór where she perished.

EHRLICH, Anita. Born on May 23, 1929, in Rosdorf. She was deported from Kassel-Halle on June 1, 1942, to the Izbica Transit Ghetto. Sent on from Izbica to Sobibór, where she perished on June 3, 1942.

EHRLICH, Ella (formerly Berlin). Born on September 24, 1891, in Grosen. She was deported from Frankfurt am Main on June 11, 1942, to Sobibór where she perished.

EHRLICH, Frieda. Born on January 19, 1893, in Rosdorf. She was deported from Kassel-Halle on June 1, 1942, to the Izbica Transit Ghetto. Sent on from Izbica to Sobibór, where she perished on June 3, 1942.

---

[378] www.deathcamps.org—online resource.
[379] www.deathcamps.org—online resource.

EHRLICH, Hermann. Born on July 2, 1891, in Rosdorf. He was deported from Kassel-Halle on June 1, 1942, to the Izbica Transit Ghetto. Sent on from Izbica to Sobibór, where he perished on June 3, 1942.

EHRLICH, Kathinka (formerly Simon). Born on October 1, 1888, in Niederweidbach. She was deported from Kassel-Halle on June 1, 1942, to the Izbica Transit Ghetto. Sent on from Izbica to Sobibór, where she perished on June 3, 1942.

EHRMANN, Henny (formerly Hahn). Born on February 22, 1893, in Bergen. She was deported from Kassel-Halle on June 1, 1942, to the Izbica Transit Ghetto. Sent on from Izbica to Sobibór, where she perished on June 3, 1942.

EHRMANN, Leopol. Born on October 14, 1881, in Bergen. He was deported from Kassel-Halle on June 1, 1942, to the Izbica Transit Ghetto. Sent on from Izbica to Sobibór, where he perished on June 3, 1942.

EHRMANN, Rosa. Born on December 13, 1891, in Frankfurt am Main. She was deported from Frankfurt am Main on June 11, 1942, to Sobibór where she perished.

EICHORN, Irma (formerly Pfifferling). Born on February 10, 1900, in Rhine. She was deported from Frankfurt am Main on June 11, 1942, to Sobibór where she perished.

EISENBERGER, Karoline (formerly Worms). Born on June 3, 1882, in Aschaffenburg. She was deported from Frankfurt am Main on June 11, 1942, to Sobibór where she perished.

EISENSTADT, Heinz. Born on February 10, 1938, in Hanau. He was deported from Kassel-Halle on June 1, 1942, to the Izbica Transit Ghetto. Sent on from Izbica to Sobibór, where he perished on June 3, 1942.

EISENSTADT, Henriette (formerly Lewkowitz). Born on November 23, 1890, in Buchsweiler. She was deported from

Kassel-Halle on June 1, 1942, to the Izbica Transit Ghetto. Sent on from Izbica to Sobibór, where she perished on June 3, 1942.

EISENSTADT, Herta. Born on February 4, 1913, in Strasbourg, France. She was deported from Kassel-Halle on June 1, 1942, to the Izbica Transit Ghetto. Sent on from Izbica to Sobibór, where she perished on June 3, 1942.

EISENSTADT, Marta. Born on October 6, 1915, in Strasbourg, France. She was deported from Kassel-Halle on June 1, 1942, to the Izbica Transit Ghetto. Sent on from Izbica to Sobibór, where she perished on June 3, 1942.

EISENSTADT, Rosa. Born on November 14, 1924, in Hanau. She was deported from Kassel-Halle on June 1, 1942, to the Izbica Transit Ghetto. Sent on from Izbica to Sobibór, where she perished on June 3, 1942.

EISENSTADT, Willi. Born on June 28, 1917, in Strasbourg, France. He was deported from Kassel-Halle on June 1, 1942, to the Izbica Transit Ghetto. Sent on from Izbica to Sobibór, where he perished on June 3, 1942.

ELIAS, Bella (formerly Weinstein). Born on June 19, 1881, in Eisenach. She was deported from Kassel-Halle on June 1, 1942, to the Izbica Transit Ghetto. Sent on from Izbica to Sobibór, where she perished on June 3, 1942.

ELIAS, Julie (formerly Pohly). Born on September 15, 1880, in Gottingen. She was deported from Kassel-Halle on June 1, 1942, to the Izbica Transit Ghetto. Sent on from Izbica to Sobibór, where she perished on June 3, 1942.

ELLINGER, Martha (formerly Birnzweig). Born on May 26, 1890, in Wiesbaden. She was deported from Frankfurt am Main on June 11, 1942, to Sobibór where she perished.

ELSOFFER, Selma (formerly Lichtenstein). Born on October 20, 1897, in Markobel. She was deported from Kassel-Halle on

June 1, 1942, to the Izbica Transit Ghetto. Sent on from Izbica to Sobibór, where she perished on June 3, 1942.

ELSHOFFER, Wilhelm. Born on November 7, 1887, in Battenfeld. He was deported from Kassel-Halle on June 1, 1942, to the Izbica Transit Ghetto. Sent on from Izbica to Sobibór, where he perished on June 3, 1942.

ELTBOGEN, Blanka. Born on October 10, 1891. She was deported on February 15, 1941, from Vienna to Opole Lubelski. She perished in Sobibór during May 1942.[380]

ELTBOGEN, Gertrud. Born on September 14, 1925. She was deported on February 15, 1941, from Vienna to Opole Lubelski. She perished in Sobibór during May 1942.[381]

ELTBOGEN, Katherina. Born on May 10, 1922. She was the daughter of Philipp and Blanka. She was deported on February 15, 1941, from Vienna to Opole Lubelski. She perished in Sobibór during May 1942.[382]

ELTBOGEN, Phillipp. Born on November 20, 1891. He was deported along with members of his family on February 15, 1941, from Vienna to Opole Lubelski. He perished in Sobibór during May 1942.[383]

ENGEL, Alexander. Born on February 23, 1892, in Berlin. He was deported on June 13, 1942, to Sobibór where he perished.

ENGELBERT, Wilhelmine (formerly Lipp). Born on March 26, 1888, in Bamberg. She was deported from Kassel-Halle on June 1, 1942, to the Izbica Transit Ghetto. Sent on from Izbica to Sobibór, where she perished on June 3, 1942.

---

[380] www.deathcamps.org—online resource.
[381] Ibid.
[382] Ibid.
[383] Ibid.

EPSTEIN, Sara (formerly Wechsler). Born on September 30, 1913, in Heilbronn. She was deported from Frankfurt am Main on June 11, 1942, to Sobibór where she perished.

ERBSEN, Lina. Born on July 19, 1919, in Frankfurt am Main. She was deported from Frankfurt am Main on June 11, 1942, to Sobibór where she perished.

ERL, Sophie (formerly Levy). Born on November 14, 1883, in Kurschawy, Russia. She was deported from Frankfurt am Main on June 11, 1942, to Sobibór where she perished.

ERMANN, Alfred. Born on July 11, 1891, in Rhaumen. He was imprisoned in Dachau Concentration Camp during 1938. He was deported from Koblenz, between April 30-May 3, 1942, to the Krasniczyn ghetto. He perished in Sobibór on December 31, 1942.

ERMANN, Hilde. Born on October 31, 1922, in Konigsfeld. She was deported from Koblenz, between April 30-May 3, 1942, to the Krasniczyn ghetto. She perished in Sobibór.

ERMANN, Julia (formerly Gottschalk). Born on May 25, 1897, in Konigsfeld. She was deported from Koblenz, between April 30-May 3, 1942, to the Krasniczyn ghetto. She perished in Sobibór.

ERMANN, Ruth. Born on November 9, 1927, in Ahrweiler. She was deported from Koblenz, between April 30-May 3, 1942, to the Krasniczyn ghetto. She perished in Sobibór on December 31, 1942.

ESCHWEGE, Felix. Born on October 19, 1927, in Fulda. He was deported from Kassel-Halle on June 1, 1942, to the Izbica Transit Ghetto. Sent on from Izbica to Sobibór, where he perished on June 3, 1942.

ESCHWEGE, Gabriel. Born on November 4, 1878, in Fulda. He was deported from Kassel-Halle on June 1, 1942, to the Izbica

Transit Ghetto. Sent on from Izbica to Sobibór, where he perished on June 3, 1942.

ESCHWEGE, Regina (formerly Michel). Born on November 4, 1885, in Frankfurt am Main. She was deported from Kassel-Halle on June 1, 1942, to the Izbica Transit Ghetto. Sent on from Izbica to Sobibór, where she perished on June 3, 1942.

ETTLING, Marie. Born on July 1, 1878, in Karlsruhe. She was deported from Frankfurt am Main on June 11, 1942, to Sobibór where she perished.

FALKENSTEIN, Frieda. Born on June 15, 1882, in Ermsleben. She was deported from Kassel-Halle on June 1, 1942, to the Izbica Transit Ghetto. Sent on from Izbica to Sobibór, where she perished on June 3, 1942.

FALKENSTEIN, Margarete. Born on April 14, 1920, in Rotenburg. She was deported from Kassel-Halle on June 1, 1942, to the Izbica Transit Ghetto. Sent on from Izbica to Sobibór, where she perished on June 3, 1942.

FARNTROG, Betty. Born on October 21, 1920, in Furth. She was deported from Frankfurt am Main on June 11, 1942, to Sobibór where she perished.

FEDERMANN, Sabina (formerly Jakubowicz). Born on June 14, 1892, in Zdunska Wola, Poland. She was deported from Frankfurt am Main on June 11, 1942, to Sobibór where she perished.[384]

FEILCHENFELD, Meta (formerly Kohler). Born on April 6, 1904, in Kassel. She was deported from Kassel-Halle on June 1, 1942, to the Izbica Transit Ghetto. Sent on from Izbica to Sobibór, where she perished on June 3, 1942.

---

[384] The Bundesarchiv Gedenkbuch shows Sabina has having been deported on May 24, 1942, to the Izbica Transit Ghetto. But this is disputed in the BBC TV Program *'My Family, the Holocaust and Me'* hosted by Robert Rinder. I took this up with the program producers and they confirmed their version was correct.

FEILCHENFELD, Ruth. Born on September 22, 1934, in Kassel. She was deported from Kassel-Halle on June 1, 1942, to the Izbica Transit Ghetto. Sent on from Izbica to Sobibór, where she perished on June 3, 1942.

FEINBERG, Sophie. Born on May 25, 1905, in Oberusel. She was deported from Frankfurt am Main on June 11, 1942, to Sobibór where she perished.

FELDMAN, Else. Born on February 25, 1884, in Vienna, Austria. Since 1912, she worked as a journalist. She was a founder member of *Vereinigung sozialkritischer Schriftsteller*. Her works were banned by the Nazis in 1938. On June 14, 1942, she was deported from Vienna, to Sobibór, where she perished.[385]

FIEBELMANN, Elsie. Born on May 21, 1879, in Haselunne. She was deported from Frankfurt am Main on June 11, 1942, to Sobibór where she perished

FISCHELBERG, Genia (formerly Spatz). Born on September 2, 1905, in Worms. She was deported from Frankfurt am Main on June 11, 1942, to Sobibór where she perished

FISCHELBERG, Mira. Born on January 16, 1930, in Frankfurt am Main. She was deported from Frankfurt am Main on June 11, 1942, to Sobibór where she perished

FLAMM, Efraim. Born on May 14, 1879, in Nenzeuheim. He was deported from Kassel-Halle on June 1, 1942, to the Izbica Transit Ghetto. Sent on from Izbica to Sobibór, where he perished on June 3, 1942.

FLAMM, Hermine (formerly Fleischer). Born on May 27, 1893, in Bayreuth. She was deported from Kassel-Halle on June 1, 1942, to the Izbica Transit Ghetto. Sent on from Izbica to Sobibór, where she perished on June 3, 1942.

---

[385] www.deathcamps.org—online resource.

FLEDEL, Ruth. Born on April 7, 1937, in Frankfurt am Main. She was deported from Frankfurt am Main on June 11, 1942, to Sobibór where she perished.

FLEDEL, Selma (formerly Lauh). Born on July 26, 1912, in Munich. She was deported from Frankfurt am Main on June 11, 1942, to Sobibór where she perished.

FLEISCHMANN, Otto. Born on December 11, 1879, in Prichsenstadt. He was deported from Kassel-Halle on June 1, 1942, to the Izbica Transit Ghetto. Sent on from Izbica to Sobibór, where he perished on June 3, 1942.

FLEISCHMANN, Rosa (formerly Friedmann). Born on January 26, 1878, in Kodlitz. She was deported from Kassel-Halle on June 1, 1942, to the Izbica Transit Ghetto. Sent on from Izbica to Sobibór, where she perished on June 3, 1942.

FLORSHEIMER, Gertrude. Born on January 24, 1904, in Gros-Geru. She was deported from Frankfurt am Main on June 11, 1942, to Sobibór where she perished.

FRANK, Dora. Born on August 6, 1899, in Wiesbaden. She was deported from Frankfurt am Main on May 24, 1942, to the Izbica Transit Ghetto. She perished in Sobibór.

FRANK, Ernst. Born on August 31, 1877, in Glan-Munchweiler. He was deported from Kassel-Halle on June 1, 1942, to the Izbica Transit Ghetto. Sent on from Izbica to Sobibór, where he perished on June 3, 1942.

FRANK, Eva. Born on February 20, 1933, in Fulda. She was deported from Frankfurt am Main on June 11, 1942, to Sobibór where she perished.

FRANK, Helena (formerly Zeilberger). Born on November 7, 1888, in Sulzdorf an der Lederhecke. She was deported from Wurzburg to Krasnystaw, Poland. She perished in Sobibór.

FRANK, Irene (formerly Schonfeld). Born on December 21, 1918, in Nordenstadt. She was deported from Frankfurt am Main on June 11, 1942, to Sobibór where she perished.

FRANK, Johanna (formerly Sender). Born on November 12, 1897, in Wiesbaden. She was deported from Frankfurt am Main on June 11, 1942, to Sobibór where she perished.

FRANK, Melitta (formerly Kern). Born on December 8, 1880, in Rodalben. She was deported from Kassel-Halle on June 1, 1942, to the Izbica Transit Ghetto. Sent on from Izbica to Sobibór, where she perished on June 3, 1942.

FRANK, Sara. Born on March 1, 1937, in Fulda. She was deported from Frankfurt am Main on June 11, 1942, to Sobibór where she perished.

FRANKENBERG, Brunhilde. Born on March 5, 1933, in Recklinghausen. She was deported from Frankfurt am Main on June 11, 1942, to Sobibór where she perished.

FRANKENBERG, Else (formerly Rose). Born on May 11, 1893, in Dornum. She was deported from Frankfurt am Main on June 11, 1942, to Sobibór where she perished.

FRANKL, Elli (formerly Schachtel). Born on August 12, 1896, in Charlottenbrunn. She was deported from Frankfurt am Main on June 11, 1942, to Sobibór where she perished.

FREUDENBERGER, Minna (formerly Stern). Born on June 16, 1877, in Lautenbach. She was deported from Frankfurt am Main on June 11, 1942, to Sobibór where she perished.

FREUDENTHAL, Berta (formerly Buchheim). Born on July 16, 1893, in Kirchain. She was deported from Kassel-Halle on June 1, 1942, to the Izbica Transit Ghetto. Sent on from Izbica to Sobibór, where she perished on June 3, 1942.

FRIED, Marrianne. Born on January 28, 1921, in Landau. She was deported from Frankfurt am Main on June 11, 1942, to Sobibór where she perished.

FRIED, Moritz. Born on September 9, 1908, in Butzbach. He was deported from Mainz-Darmstadt on March 25, 1942, to the Piaski Transit Ghetto in Poland. He was a member of the *Judenrat* in Piaski. He was deported to Sobibór in November 1942, where he perished.[386]

FRIED, Selma. Born on January 10, 1889, in Nordenstadt. She was deported from Frankfurt am Main on June 11, 1942, to Sobibór where she perished on December 31, 1942.

FRIEDLANDER, Minna (formerly Mayer). Born on February 24, 1877, in Biebrich. She was deported from Frankfurt am Main on June 11, 1942, to Sobibór where she perished.

FRIEDMAN, Beate. Born on August 13, 1924, in Wiesbaden. She was deported from Frankfurt am Main on June 11, 1942, to Sobibór where she perished on December 31, 1942.

FRIEDMAN, Betti (formerly Goldschmidt). Born on July 3, 1902, in Frankfurt am Main. She was deported from Frankfurt am Main on June 11, 1942, to Sobibór where she perished.

FRIEDMANN, Edith. Born on May 23, 1921, in Wiesbaden. She was deported from Frankfurt am Main on June 11, 1942, to Sobibór where she perished.

FRIEDMANN, Judith. Born on June 2, 1940, in Wiesbaden. She was deported from Frankfurt am Main on June 11, 1942, to Sobibór where she perished.

FRIEDMANN, Lina. Born on June 20, 1892, in Tscherkassy, Russia. She was deported from Frankfurt am Main on June 11, 1942, to Sobibór where she perished.

FRIEDMANN, Margarete (formerly Schwabach). Born on April 6, 1881, in Halle. She was deported from Kassel-Halle on

---

[386] www.deathcamps.org and www.bundesarchiv.de/gedenkbuch—online resources.

June 1, 1942, to the Izbica Transit Ghetto. Sent on from Izbica to Sobibór, where she perished on June 3, 1942.

FRIEDMANN, Margot. Born on June 24, 1928, in Frankfurt am Main. She was deported from Frankfurt am Main on June 11, 1942, to Sobibór where she perished.

FRIEDMANN, Susi. Born on June 14, 1926, in Wiesbaden. She was deported from Frankfurt am Main on June 11, 1942, to Sobibór where she perished.

FRIESEM, Ruth (formerly Liebmann). Born on December 3, 1921, in Geisen. She was deported from Frankfurt am Main on June 11, 1942, to Sobibór where she perished.

FRUCHTER, Gisela (formerly Braun). Born on December 12, 1883, in Szilsarkany, Hungary. She was deported from Kassel-Halle on June 1, 1942, to the Izbica Transit Ghetto. Sent on from Izbica to Sobibór, where she perished on June 3, 1942.

FRUCHTER, Mendel. Born on December 15, 1875, in Felsoviso, Hungary. He was deported from Kassel-Halle on June 1, 1942, to the Izbica Transit Ghetto. Sent on from Izbica to Sobibór, where he perished on June 3, 1942.

FURTH, Marie (formerly Amann). Born on December 21, 1881, in Prague, Czechoslovakia. She was deported from Kassel-Halle on June 1, 1942, to the Izbica Transit Ghetto. Sent on from Izbica to Sobibór, where she perished on June 3, 1942.

FULD, Bertha (formerly Joseph). Born on July 13, 1877, in Heppenheim. She was deported from Frankfurt am Main on June 11, 1942, to Sobibór where she perished.

FULD, Erna (formerly Junghaus). Born on December 4, 1909, in Frankfurt am Main. She was deported from Frankfurt am Main on June 11, 1942, to Sobibór where she perished.

GANS, Elfriede (formerly Meyer). Born on December 23, 1905, in Rotenburg. She was deported from Kassel-Halle on June 1,

1942, to the Izbica Transit Ghetto. Sent on from Izbica to Sobibór, where she perished on June 3, 1942.

GANS, Else. Born on July 10, 1884, in Darmstadt. She was deported from Frankfurt am Main on June 11, 1942, to Sobibór where she perished.

GANS, Judis. Born on February 18, 1940, in Kassel. She was deported from Kassel-Halle on June 1, 1942, to the Izbica Transit Ghetto. Sent on from Izbica to Sobibór, where she perished on June 3, 1942.

GANS, Rosa. Born on September 17, 1905, in Jesberg. She was deported from Frankfurt am Main on June 11, 1942, to Sobibór where she perished.

GANSS, Martha (formerly Altmann). Born on September 8, 1909, in Langenselbold. She was deported from Frankfurt am Main on June 11, 1942, to Sobibór where she perished.

GEISS, Franziska (formerly Levi). Born on May 20, 1902, in Mannheim. She was deported from Frankfurt am Main on June 11, 1942, to Sobibór where she perished.

GERNSHEIMER, Hans. Born on February 23, 1936, in Ruckingen. He was deported from Kassel-Halle on June 1, 1942, to the Izbica Transit Ghetto. Sent on from Izbica to Sobibór, where he perished on June 3, 1942.

GERNSHEIMER, Lothar. Born on December 19, 1937, in Ruckingen. He was deported from Kassel-Halle on June 1, 1942, to the Izbica Transit Ghetto. Sent on from Izbica to Sobibór, where he perished on June 3, 1942.

GERNSHEIMER, Ludwig. Born on September 2, 1897, in Ruckingen. He was deported from Kassel-Halle on June 1, 1942, to the Izbica Transit Ghetto. Sent on from Izbica to Sobibór, where he perished on June 3, 1942.

GERNSHEIMER, Therese (formerly Levi). Born on November 16, 1909, in Gladenbach. She was deported from Kassel-Halle on June 1, 1942, to the Izbica Transit Ghetto. Sent on from Izbica to Sobibór, where she perished on June 3, 1942.

GLOGOWSKI, Gertrud (formerly Lewinberg). Born on May 25, 1888, in Biziker. She was deported from Frankfurt am Main on June 11, 1942, to Sobibór where she perished.

GLUCKAUF, Friedericke (formerly Reiss). Born on March 3, 1877, in Egelsbach. She was deported from Frankfurt am Main on June 11, 1942, to Sobibór where she perished.

GORK, Betty (formerly Scheige). Born on October 27, 1895, in Schonlanke, Poland. She was deported from Frankfurt am Main on June 11, 1942, to Sobibór where she perished.

GOLDBERG, Frieda (formerly Lowenstein). Born on January 30, 1907, in Affoldern. She was deported from Kassel-Halle on June 1, 1942, to the Izbica Transit Ghetto. Sent on from Izbica to Sobibór, where she perished on June 3, 1942.

GOLDBERG, Lothar. Born on November 3, 1934, in Korbach. He was deported from Kassel-Halle on June 1, 1942, to the Izbica Transit Ghetto. Sent on from Izbica to Sobibór, where he perished on June 3, 1942.

GOLDMANN, Anna (formerly Seligmann). Born on November 30, 1889, in Gau-Algesheim. She was deported from Kassel-Halle on June 1, 1942, to the Izbica Transit Ghetto. Sent on from Izbica to Sobibór, where she perished on June 3, 1942.

GOLDMANN, Hugo. Born on March 24, 1885, in Gundersheim. He was imprisoned in Dachau Concentration Camp during November-December 1938. He was deported from Kassel-Halle on June 1, 1942, to the Izbica Transit Ghetto. Sent on from Izbica to Sobibór, where he perished on June 3, 1942.

GOLDMANN, Ruth. Born on July 23, 1924, in Neunkirchen. She was deported from Kassel-Halle on June 1, 1942, to the Izbica Transit Ghetto. Sent on from Izbica to Sobibór, where she perished on June 3, 1942.

GOLDMEIER, Karohne (formerly Muller). Born on January 10, 1880, in Marisfeld. She was deported from Kassel-Halle on June 1, 1942, to the Izbica Transit Ghetto. Sent on from Izbica to Sobibór, where she perished on June 3, 1942.

GOLDMEIER, Louis. Born on August 3, 1874, in Uttrichshausen. He was deported from Kassel-Halle on June 1, 1942, to the Izbica Transit Ghetto. Sent on from Izbica to Sobibór, where he perished on June 3, 1942.

GOLDMEIER, Meta (formerly Goldwein). Born on October 10, 1886, in Meimbressen. She was deported from Kassel-Halle on June 1, 1942, to the Izbica Transit Ghetto. Sent on from Izbica to Sobibór, where she perished on June 3, 1942.

GOLDMEIER, Nathan. Born on August 30, 1879, in Uttrichshausen. He was deported from Kassel-Halle on June 1, 1942, to the Izbica Transit Ghetto. Sent on from Izbica to Sobibór, where he perished on June 3, 1942.

GOLDSCHMIDT, Charlotte. Born on July 24, 1931, in Darmstadt. She was deported from Frankfurt am Main on June 11, 1942, to Sobibór where she perished.

GOLDSCHMIDT, Felix. Born on February 28, 1895, in Schluchtern. He was imprisoned in Dachau Concentration Camp from November 1938, until January 1939. He was deported from Kassel-Halle on June 1, 1942, to the Izbica Transit Ghetto. Sent on from Izbica to Sobibór, where he perished on June 3, 1942.

GOLDSCHMIDT, Freda (formerly Lowenstein). Born on July 21, 1894, in Lohra. She was deported from Kassel-Halle on June 1, 1942, to the Izbica Transit Ghetto. Sent on from Izbica to Sobibór, where she perished on June 3, 1942.

GOLDSCHMIDT, Freda (formerly Strauss). Born on November 23, 1902, in Ober-Seemen. She was deported from Frankfurt am Main on June 11, 1942, to Sobibór where she perished.

GOLDSCHMIDT, Gottfried. Born on December 4, 1902, in Ober-Seemen. He was deported from Kassel-Halle on June 1, 1942, to the Izbica Transit Ghetto. Sent on from Izbica to Sobibór, where he perished on June 3, 1942.

GOLDSCHMIDT, Henry. Born on January 6, 1913, in Falkenberg. He was deported from Kassel-Halle on June 1, 1942, to the Izbica Transit Ghetto. Sent on from Izbica to Sobibór, where he perished on June 3, 1942.

GOLDSCHMIDT, Helene (formerly Muller). Born on June 11, 1890, in Wernhausen. She was deported from Kassel-Halle on June 1, 1942, to the Izbica Transit Ghetto. Sent on from Izbica to Sobibór, where she perished on June 3, 1942.

GOLDSCHMIDT, Helene (formerly Borchert). Born on November 30, 1897, in Harmuthsachsen. She was deported from Kassel-Halle on June 1, 1942, to the Izbica Transit Ghetto. Sent on from Izbica to Sobibór, where she perished on June 3, 1942.

GOLDSCHMIDT, Hilda (formerly Stern). Born on August 9, 1882, in Hintersteinau. She was deported from Kassel-Halle on June 1, 1942, to the Izbica Transit Ghetto. Sent on from Izbica to Sobibór, where she perished on June 3, 1942.

GOLDSCHMIDT, Hilda (formerly Reiss). Born on July 22, 1886, in Florstadt. She was deported from Frankfurt am Main on June 11, 1942, to Sobibór where she perished.

GOLDSCHMIDT, Ilse. Born on August 28, 1933, in Frohnhausen. She was deported from Kassel-Halle on June 1, 1942, to the Izbica Transit Ghetto. Sent on from Izbica to Sobibór, where she perished on June 3, 1942.

GOLDSCHMIDT, Isidor. Born on March 27, 1907, in Langenselbold. He was deported from Kassel-Halle on June 1, 1942, to the Izbica Transit Ghetto. Sent on from Izbica to Sobibór, where he perished on June 3, 1942.

GOLDSCHMIDT, Jenny (formerly Hamburger). Born on September 1, 1889, in Langenselbold. She was deported from Kassel-Halle on June 1, 1942, to the Izbica Transit Ghetto. Sent on from Izbica to Sobibór, where she perished on June 3, 1942.

GOLDSCHMIDT, Johanna (formerly Lowenberg). Born on October 23, 1887, in Schenklengsfeld. She was deported from Kassel-Halle on June 1, 1942, to the Izbica Transit Ghetto. Sent on from Izbica to Sobibór, where she perished on June 3, 1942.

GOLDSCHMIDT, Johanna (formerly Rosenbach). Born on February 4, 1888, in Hoof. She was deported from Kassel-Halle on June 1, 1942, to the Izbica Transit Ghetto. Sent on from Izbica to Sobibór, where she perished on June 3, 1942.

GOLDSCHMIDT, Juda. Born on September 22, 1897, in Schluchtern. She was deported from Kassel-Halle on June 1, 1942, to the Izbica Transit Ghetto. Sent on from Izbica to Sobibór, where she perished on June 3, 1942.

GOLDSCHMIDT, Julius. Born on January 24, 1930, in Frohnhausen. He was deported from Kassel-Halle on June 1, 1942, to the Izbica Transit Ghetto. Sent on from Izbica to Sobibór, where he perished on June 3, 1942.

GOLDSCHMIDT, Karl. Born on July 14, 1884, in Hausen. He was deported from Kassel-Halle on June 1, 1942, to the Izbica Transit Ghetto. Sent on from Izbica to Sobibór, where he perished on June 3, 1942.

GOLDSCHMIDT, Lina (formerly Birk). Born on November 22, 1900, in Schluchtern. She was deported from Kassel-Halle on June 1, 1942, to the Izbica Transit Ghetto. Sent on from Izbica to Sobibór, where she perished on June 3, 1942.

GOLDSCHMIDT, Lothar. Born on June 9, 1910, in Langenselbold. He was deported from Kassel-Halle on June 1, 1942, to the Izbica Transit Ghetto. Sent on from Izbica to Sobibór, where he perished on June 3, 1942.

GOLDSCHMIDT, Markus. Born on April 18, 1880, in Flieden. He was deported from Kassel-Halle on June 1, 1942, to the Izbica Transit Ghetto. Sent on from Izbica to Sobibór, where he perished on June 3, 1942.

GOLDSCHMIDT, Minna. Born on January 28, 1885, in Raboldshausen. She was deported from Kassel-Halle on June 1, 1942, to the Izbica Transit Ghetto. Sent on from Izbica to Sobibór, where she perished on June 3, 1942.

GOLDSCHMIDT, Regina (formerly Wikowsky). Born on March 22, 1907, in Johannisburg. She was deported from Frankfurt am Main on June 11, 1942, to Sobibór where she perished.

GOLDSCHMIDT, Regina (formerly Nordhauser). Born on April 17, 1885, in Wustensachsen. She was deported from Kassel-Halle on June 1, 1942, to the Izbica Transit Ghetto. Sent on from Izbica to Sobibór, where she perished on June 3, 1942.

GOLDSCHMIDT, Selma (formerly Gutmann). Born on May 4, 1880, in Roth b. Nurnberg. She was deported from Kassel-Halle on June 1, 1942, to the Izbica Transit Ghetto. Sent on from Izbica to Sobibór, where she perished on June 3, 1942.

GOLDSCHMIDT, Sigmund. Born on July 27, 1909, in Langenselbold. He was deported from Kassel-Halle on June 1, 1942, to the Izbica Transit Ghetto. Sent on from Izbica to Sobibór, where he perished on June 3, 1942.

GOLDSCHMIDT, Simon. Born on October 5, 1876, in Heubach. He was deported from Kassel-Halle on June 1, 1942, to the Izbica Transit Ghetto. Sent on from Izbica to Sobibór, where he perished on June 3, 1942.

GOLDSCHMIDT, Simon. Born on February 17, 1884, in Hersfeld. He was deported from Kassel-Halle on June 1, 1942, to the Izbica Transit Ghetto. Sent on from Izbica to Sobibór, where he perished on June 3, 1942.

GOLDSTEIN, Betty. Born on November 29, 1901, in Nurnberg. She was deported from Munich on April 4, 1942, to the Piaski Transit Ghetto. She perished in Sobibór.[387]

GOLDSTEIN, Cacilie (formerly Keins). Born on July 6, 1878, in Königshütte. She was deported from Frankfurt am Main on June 11, 1942, to Sobibór where she perished.

GOLDSTEIN, Nora. Born on May 7, 1905, in Stolp. She was deported from Frankfurt am Main on June 11, 1942, to Sobibór where she perished.

GOLDSTERN, Eugenie. Born on March 1, 1884, in Odessa. She was an Ethnologist by profession. She was deported on June 14, 1942, from Vienna to Sobibór, where she perished.[388]

GOTTLIEB, Josef. Born on May 31, in Neuhof. He was deported from Kassel-Halle on June 1, 1942, to the Izbica Transit Ghetto. Sent on from Izbica to Sobibór, where he perished on June 3, 1942.

GOTTLIEB, Karoline. Born on December 10, 1875, in Neuhof. She was deported from Kassel-Halle on June 1, 1942, to the Izbica Transit Ghetto. Sent on from Izbica to Sobibór, where she perished on June 3, 1942.

GOTTLIEB, Lina. Born on July 19, 1881, in Neuhof. She was deported from Kassel-Halle on June 1, 1942, to the Izbica Transit Ghetto. Sent on from Izbica to Sobibór, where she perished on June 3, 1942.

GOTTSCHALK, Alice (formerly Ullmann). Born on October 12, 1903, in Westerburg. She was deported from Frankfurt am Main on June 11, 1942, to Sobibór where she perished.

---

[387] www.deathcamps.org—online resource.
[388] Ibid.

GOTTSCHALK, Jochanan. Born on March 26, 1940, in Aachen. He was deported from Frankfurt am Main on June 11, 1942, to Sobibór where he perished.

GROSS, Eva (formerly Grossmann). Born on November 25, 1896, in Gorodok, Ukraine. She was deported from Kassel-Halle on June 1, 1942, to the Izbica Transit Ghetto. Sent on from Izbica to Sobibór, where she perished on June 3, 1942.

GROSS, Josef. Born on December 30, 1889, in Brzesko, Poland. He was deported from Kassel-Halle on June 1, 1942, to the Izbica Transit Ghetto. Sent on from Izbica to Sobibór, where he perished on June 3, 1942.

GRUMBACHER, Emilie (formerly Grunbaum). Born on July 17, 1877, in Poppenlauer. She was deported from Frankfurt am Main on June 11, 1942, to Sobibór where she perished.

GRUNBLATT, Olga (formerly Pakula). Born on July 15, 1870, in Lodz, Poland. She was deported from Kassel-Halle on June 1, 1942, to the Izbica Transit Ghetto. Sent on from Izbica to Sobibór, where she perished on June 3, 1942.

GRUNEBAUM, Bella. Born on November 13, 1901, in Bergen. She was deported from Kassel-Halle on June 1, 1942, to the Izbica Transit Ghetto. Sent on from Izbica to Sobibór, where she perished on June 3, 1942.

GRUNEBAUM, Bella (formerly Strauss). Born on August 15, 1903, in Ober-Seemen. She was deported from Frankfurt am Main on June 11, 1942, to Sobibór where she perished.

GRUNEBAUM, Blanka. Born on January 16, 1919, in Schluchtern. She was deported from Frankfurt am Main on June 11, 1942, to Sobibór where she perished.

GRUNEWALD, Franziska. Born on March 3, 1877, in Frankfurt am Main. She was deported from Frankfurt am Main on June 11, 1942, to Sobibór where she perished.

GRUNEWALD, Ida (formerly Lazarus). Born on September 13, 1889, in Appenheim. She was deported from Frankfurt am Main on June 11, 1942, to Sobibór where she perished.

GRUNFELD, Margot. Born on April 17, 1927, in Vollmerz. She was deported from Kassel-Halle on June 1, 1942, to the Izbica Transit Ghetto. Sent on from Izbica to Sobibór, where she perished on June 3, 1942.

GRUNFELD, Rosa (formerly Hecht). Born on June 13, 1896, in Vollmerz. She was deported from Kassel-Halle on June 1, 1942, to the Izbica Transit Ghetto. Sent on from Izbica to Sobibór, where she perished on June 3, 1942.

GUNZENHAUSER, Betty. Born on September 30, 1889, in Tauberrettersheim. She was deported from Frankfurt am Main on June 11, 1942, to Sobibór where she perished.

GUTHMANN, Frieda (formerly Gerson). Born on December 17, 1887, in Kirchberg. She was deported from Frankfurt am Main on June 11, 1942, to Sobibór where she perished.

GUTTKIND, Annemarie. Born on October 30, 1906, in Berlin. She was deported from Kassel-Halle on June 1, 1942, to the Izbica Transit Ghetto. Sent on from Izbica to Sobibór, where she perished on June 3, 1942.

GUTMANN, Franziska. Born on January 6, 1891, in Hamburg. She was deported from Frankfurt am Main on June 11, 1942, to Sobibór where she perished.

GUTTSMANN, Walter Johann. Born on May 8, 1880, in Berlin. He was deported on March 28, 1942, from Berlin to the Piaski Transit Ghetto. He was a member of the *Judenrat* in Piaski. He was deported to Sobibór in November 1942, where he perished.[389]

---

[389] www.deathcamps.org and www.bundesarchiv.de/gedenkbuch —online resources.

GUTWIRTH, Fanny (formerly Bruder). Born on December 3, 1901, in Felsemorx, Hungary. She was deported from Frankfurt am Main on June 11, 1942, to Sobibór where she perished.

HAAS, Eugenie. Born on June 2, 1901, in Wiesbaden. She was deported from Frankfurt am Main on June 11, 1942, to Sobibór where she perished.

HAAS, Karoline. Born on July 14, 1880, in Neustadt. She was deported from Frankfurt am Main on June 11, 1942, to Sobibór where she perished.

HAAS, Recha (formerly Moller). Born on August 18, 1900, in Frankfurt am Main. She was deported from Frankfurt am Main on June 11, 1942, to Sobibór where she perished.

HAENDEL, Else (formerly Loser). Born on August 16, 1896, in Laufersweiler. She was deported from Frankfurt am Main on June 11, 1942, to Sobibór where she perished.

HAHN, Cacille. Born on April 6, 1877, in *Lissa* (Leszno), Poland. She was deported from Frankfurt am Main on June 11, 1942, to Sobibór where she perished.

HAHN, Cacille. Born on August 14, 1900, in Kassel. She was deported from Kassel-Halle on June 1, 1942, to the Izbica Transit Ghetto. Sent on from Izbica to Sobibór, where she perished on June 3, 1942.

HAHN, Franziska (formerly Levi). Born on October 25, 1876, in Eschwege. She was deported from Kassel-Halle on June 1, 1942, to the Izbica Transit Ghetto. Sent on from Izbica to Sobibór, where she perished on June 3, 1942.

HAHN, Frieda. Born on July 21, 1903, in Bergen. She was deported from Kassel-Halle on June 1, 1942, to the Izbica Transit Ghetto. Sent on from Izbica to Sobibór, where she perished on June 3, 1942.

HAHN, Johanna (formerly Strahlheim). Born on November 27, 1909, in Hofheim. She was deported from Frankfurt am Main on June 11, 1942, to Sobibór where she perished on September 26, 1942.

HAHN, Lenni. Born on March 24, 1905, in Bergen. She was deported from Kassel-Halle on June 1, 1942, to the Izbica Transit Ghetto. Sent on from Izbica to Sobibór, where she perished on June 3, 1942.

HAHN, Leonore. Born on June 26, 1902, in Kassel. She was deported from Kassel-Halle on June 1, 1942, to the Izbica Transit Ghetto. Sent on from Izbica to Sobibór, where she perished on June 3, 1942.

HAIN, Paula (formerly Marx). Born on July 23, 1895, in Langendiebach. She was deported from Kassel-Halle on June 1, 1942, to the Izbica Transit Ghetto. Sent on from Izbica to Sobibór, where she perished on June 3, 1942.

HAMBER, Amalie (formerly Mayer). Born on January 20, 1883, in Cologne. She was deported from Frankfurt am Main on June 11, 1942, to Sobibór where she perished.

HAMBERG, Betty (formerly Pulver). Born on September 11, 1897, in Westheim. She was deported from Kassel-Halle on June 1, 1942, to the Izbica Transit Ghetto. Sent on from Izbica to Sobibór, where she perished on June 3, 1942.

HAMBERG, Hermann. Born on September 12, 1890, in Breuna mit Rhoda. He was deported from Kassel-Halle on June 1, 1942, to the Izbica Transit Ghetto. Sent on from Izbica to Sobibór, where he perished on June 3, 1942.

HAMBERG, Moritz. Born on July 15, 1886, in Breuna mit Rhoda. He was deported from Kassel-Halle on June 1, 1942, to the Izbica Transit Ghetto. Sent on from Izbica to Sobibór, where he perished on June 3, 1942.

HAMBERG, Susanne. Born on August 11, 1929, in Breuna mit Rhoda. She was deported from Kassel-Halle on June 1, 1942, to the Izbica Transit Ghetto. Sent on from Izbica to Sobibór, where she perished on June 3, 1942.

HAMBURGER, Heinrich. Born on April 22, 1928, in Frankfurt am Main. He was deported from Kassel-Halle on June 1, 1942, to the Izbica Transit Ghetto. Sent on from Izbica to Sobibór, where he perished on June 3, 1942.

HAMMERSCHLAG, Mirjam (formerly Lillenfeld). Born on October 26, 1899, in Gudenberg. She was deported from Kassel-Halle on June 1, 1942, to the Izbica Transit Ghetto. Sent on from Izbica to Sobibór, where she perished on June 3, 1942.

HAMMERSCHMIDT, Cilla. Born on December 14, 1879, in Jastrow, Poland. She was deported from Frankfurt am Main on June 11, 1942, to Sobibór where she perished.

HAMMERSCHMIDT, Rosa. Born on August 29, 1886, in Roden. She was deported from Frankfurt am Main on June 11, 1942, to Sobibór where she perished.

Hana. A German Jewess from Berlin. She was chief of the Tailors workshop. During the revolt on October 14, 1943, she hid in the workshop together with other women and according to Eda Lichtman, she was killed along with the other women hiding there.[390]

HANAU, Leonie (formerly Mayer). Born on December 12, 1894, in Frankfurt am Main. She was deported from Kassel-Halle on June 1, 1942, to the Izbica Transit Ghetto. Sent on from Izbica to Sobibór, where she perished on June 3, 1942.

HANFF, Hans. Born on August 13, 1915, in Stettin, Poland. He was deported from Frankfurt am Main on May 24, 1942, to the Izbica Transit Ghetto in Poland. He was sent onto Sobibór, where he perished.

---

[390] Eda Lichtman Memoirs YVA 03/1291.

HANFF, Irmgard (formerly Openheimer). Born on November 24, 1914, in Berlin. She was deported from Frankfurt am Main on May 24, 1942, to the Izbica Transit Ghetto in Poland. She was sent onto Sobibór, where she perished.

HASE, Karl. Born on February 21, 1907, in Kassel. He was deported from Kassel-Halle on June 1, 1942, to the Izbica Transit Ghetto. Sent on from Izbica to Sobibór, where he perished on June 3, 1942.

HASE, Rolf. Born on March 10, 1937, in Kassel. He was deported from Kassel-Halle on June 1, 1942, to the Izbica Transit Ghetto. Sent on from Izbica to Sobibór, where he perished on June 3, 1942.

HASE, Selma (formerly Jakob). Born on March 15, 1901, in Osche. She was deported from Kassel-Halle on June 1, 1942, to the Izbica Transit Ghetto. Sent on from Izbica to Sobibór, where she perished on June 3, 1942.

HASENKOPF, Reisel (formerly Birnbach). Born on May 8, 1898, in Strzyzow, Poland. She was deported from Frankfurt am Main on June 11, 1942, to Sobibór where she perished.

HECHT, Else (formerly Bar). Born on December 24, 1895, in Crainfeld. She was deported from Kassel-Halle on June 1, 1942, to the Izbica Transit Ghetto. Sent on from Izbica to Sobibór, where she perished on June 3, 1942.

HECHT, Gitta (formerly Goldschmidt). Born on July 20, 1890, in Sterbfritz. She was deported from Kassel-Halle on June 1, 1942, to the Izbica Transit Ghetto. Sent on from Izbica to Sobibór, where she perished on June 3, 1942.

HECHT, Goldina. Born on September 28, 1878, in Nesselroden. She was deported from Kassel-Halle on June 1, 1942, to the Izbica Transit Ghetto. Sent on from Izbica to Sobibór, where she perished on June 3, 1942.

HECHT, Ida. Born on February 9, 1906, in Bruckenau. She was deported from Frankfurt am Main on June 11, 1942, to Sobibór where she perished.

HECHT, Jakob. Born on March 20, 1884, in Mottgers. He was deported from Kassel-Halle on June 1, 1942, to the Izbica Transit Ghetto. Sent on from Izbica to Sobibór, where he perished on June 3, 1942.

HECHT, Jettchen. Born on June 8, 1880, in Nesselroden. She was deported from Kassel-Halle on June 1, 1942, to the Izbica Transit Ghetto. Sent on from Izbica to Sobibór, where she perished on June 3, 1942.

HECHT, Jettchl (formerly Plaut). Born on December 21, 1897, in Rauschenberg. She was deported from Frankfurt am Main on June 11, 1942, to Sobibór where she perished.

HECHT, Lothar. Born on September 13, 1923, in Sterbfritz. He was deported from Kassel-Halle on June 1, 1942, to the Izbica Transit Ghetto. Sent on from Izbica to Sobibór, where he perished on June 3, 1942.

HECHT, Ludwig. Born on July 26, 1923, in Sterbfritz. He was deported from Kassel-Halle on June 1, 1942, to the Izbica Transit Ghetto. Sent on from Izbica to Sobibór, where he perished on June 3, 1942.

HECHT, Meier. Born on December 27, 1885, in Mottgers. He was deported from Kassel-Halle on June 1, 1942, to the Izbica Transit Ghetto. Sent on from Izbica to Sobibór, where he perished on June 3, 1942.

HECHT, Sophie. Born on February 9, 1926, in Sterbfritz. She was deported from Kassel-Halle on June 1, 1942, to the Izbica Transit Ghetto. Sent on from Izbica to Sobibór, where she perished on June 3, 1942.

HECHT, Steffi. Born on December 11, 1927, in Sterbfritz. She was deported from Kassel-Halle on June 1, 1942, to the Izbica

Transit Ghetto. Sent on from Izbica to Sobibór, where she perished on June 3, 1942.

HEILBERG, Meta (formerly Falkenstein). Born on December 30, 1907, in Meudt. She was deported from Frankfurt am Main on June 11, 1942, to Sobibór where she perished.

HEILBERG, Selma. Born on September 26, 1911, in Westerburg. She was deported from Frankfurt am Main on June 11, 1942, to Sobibór where she perished.

HEILBRONN, Julius. Born on November 19, 1897, in Falkenberg. He was imprisoned in Breitenau Concentration Camp. He was deported from Kassel-Halle on June 1, 1942, to the Izbica Transit Ghetto. Sent on from Izbica to Sobibór, where he perished on June 3, 1942.

HEILBRUNN, Frieda (formerly Eisemann). Born on August 2, 1887, in Laudenbach. She was deported from Frankfurt am Main on June 11, 1942, to Sobibór where she perished.

HEILBRUNN, Gertrud (formerly Strauss). Born on June 17, 1908, in Gelnhausen. She was deported from Frankfurt am Main on June 11, 1942, to Sobibór where she perished.

HEILBRUNN, Jettchen. Born on February 23, 1879, in Abterode. She was deported from Kassel-Halle on June 1, 1942, to the Izbica Transit Ghetto. Sent on from Izbica to Sobibór, where she perished on June 3, 1942.

HEILBRUNN, Maya. Born on March 26, 1935, in Frankfurt am Main. She was deported from Frankfurt am Main on June 11, 1942, to Sobibór where she perished.

HEILBRUNN, Meta. Born on October 15, 1883, in Oberaula. She was deported from Kassel-Halle on June 1, 1942, to the Izbica Transit Ghetto. Sent on from Izbica to Sobibór, where she perished on June 3, 1942.

HEIMENRATH, Hedwig. Born on September 16, 1881, in Gilserberg. She was deported from Frankfurt am Main on June 11, 1942, to Sobibór where she perished.

HELFT, Kuno. Born on October 18, 1873, in Bleicherode. He was deported from Kassel-Halle on June 1, 1942, to the Izbica Transit Ghetto. Sent on from Izbica to Sobibór, where he perished on June 3, 1942.

HELFT, Lucie (formerly Heinemann). Born on March 13, 1897, in Hannover. She was deported from Kassel-Halle on June 1, 1942, to the Izbica Transit Ghetto. Sent on from Izbica to Sobibór, where she perished on June 3, 1942.

HENE, Dora (formerly Nebel). Born on August 17, 1898, in Harburg. She was deported from Frankfurt am Main on June 11, 1942, to Sobibór where she perished.

HENLEIN, Martha (formerly Albert). Born on December 11, 1890, in Neustadt an der Haardt. She was deported from Frankfurt am Main on June 11, 1942, to Sobibór where she perished.

HERZ, Irma (formerly Fuld). Born on November 12, 1903, in Westerburg. She was deported from Frankfurt am Main on June 11, 1942, to Sobibór where she perished.

HERZBERG, Bronja (formerly Wajuryb). Born on August 27, 1900, in Konskie, Poland. She was resettled to Poland on October 28, 1938. She perished in Sobibór on July 16, 1943.

HERZBERG, Fabisch. Born on December 7, 1896, in Włocławek, Poland. He was resettled to Poland on October 28, 1938. He perished in Sobibór on July 16, 1943.

HES, Bernard. Born on July 16, 1879, in Hintersteinau. He was deported from Kassel-Halle on June 1, 1942, to the Izbica Transit Ghetto. Sent on from Izbica to Sobibór, where he perished on June 3, 1942.

HES, Fanny (formerly Idstein). Born on December 25, 1872, in Babenhausen. She was deported from Kassel-Halle on June 1, 1942, to the Izbica Transit Ghetto. Sent on from Izbica to Sobibór, where she perished on June 3, 1942.

HES, Nathan. Born on December 15, 1878, in Bergen. He was deported from Kassel-Halle on June 1, 1942, to the Izbica Transit Ghetto. Sent on from Izbica to Sobibór, where he perished on June 3, 1942.

HES, Paula. Born on April 16, 1895, in Bergen. She was deported from Kassel-Halle on June 1, 1942, to the Izbica Transit Ghetto. Sent on from Izbica to Sobibór, where she perished on June 3, 1942.

HES, Recha. Born on May 14, 1910, in Fulda. She was deported from Kassel-Halle on June 1, 1942, to the Izbica Transit Ghetto. Sent on from Izbica to Sobibór, where she perished on June 3, 1942.

HES, Rose (formerly Blumenfeld). Born on July 10, 1883, in Neustadt. She was deported from Frankfurt am Main on June 11, 1942, to Sobibór where she perished.

HESDORFER, Johanna (formerly Joseph). Born on January 14, 1887, in Altenbamberg. She was deported from Kassel-Halle on June 1, 1942, to the Izbica Transit Ghetto. Sent on from Izbica to Sobibór, where she perished on June 3, 1942.

HESS, Frieda. Born on June 5, 1912, in Fulda. She was deported from Kassel-Halle on June 1, 1942, to the Izbica Transit Ghetto. Sent on from Izbica to Sobibór, where she perished on June 3, 1942.

HESS, Lilly (formerly Suser). Born on June 11, 1887, in Wurzburg. She was deported from Frankfurt am Main on June 11, 1942, to Sobibór where she perished.

HESS, Martha (formerly Weil). Born on January 21, 1880, in Hechingen. She was deported from Frankfurt am Main on June 11, 1942, to Sobibór where she perished.

HESS, Selma (formerly Simons). Born on October 24, 1898, in Frankfurt am Main. She was deported from Frankfurt am Main on June 11, 1942, to Sobibór where she perished.

HESS, Thekla (formerly Buchheim). Born on October 19, 1893, in Dauborn. She was deported from Frankfurt am Main on June 11, 1942, to Sobibór where she perished.

HEYMANN, Anna (formerly Lerner). Born on July 30, 1896, in Berlin. She was deported from Kassel-Halle on June 1, 1942, to the Izbica Transit Ghetto. Sent on from Izbica to Sobibór, where she perished on June 3, 1942.

HEYUM, Johanna (formerly Israel). Born on October 29, in Kirchberg. She was deported from Frankfurt am Main on June 11, 1942, to Sobibór where she perished.

HIRSCH, Adele (formerly Simon). Born on June 28, 1905, in Ehringhausen. She was deported from Frankfurt am Main on June 11, 1942, to Sobibór where she perished.

HIRSCH, Alfred. Born on January 18, 1924, in Bergheim. He was deported from Koblenz-Köln-Düsseldorf on June 15, 1942, to Sobibór where he perished.

HIRSCH, Auguste. Born on December 17, 1880, in Langenselbold. She was deported from Kassel-Halle on June 1, 1942, to the Izbica Transit Ghetto. Sent on from Izbica to Sobibór, where she perished on June 3, 1942.

HIRSCH, Charleska (formerly Neuhaus). Born on March 1, 1880, in Bremerhaven. She was deported from Frankfurt am Main on June 11, 1942, to Sobibór where she perished.

HIRSCH, Else (formerly Stock). Born on June 13, 1903, in Schidlowitz. She was deported from Frankfurt am Main on June 11, 1942, to Sobibór where she perished.

HIRSCH, Emma (formerly Katz). Born on January 2, 1882, in Korbach. She was deported from Kassel-Halle on June 1, 1942, to the Izbica Transit Ghetto. Sent on from Izbica to Sobibór, where she perished on June 3, 1942.

HIRSCH, Emma (formerly Bach). Born on September 27, 1885, in Nieder-Moos. She was deported from Frankfurt am Main on June 11, 1942, to Sobibór where she perished.

HIRSCH, Frieda (formerly Lowenthal). Born on October 23, 1878, in Ueckmunde. She was deported from Kassel-Halle on June 1, 1942, to the Izbica Transit Ghetto. Sent on from Izbica to Sobibór, where she perished on June 3, 1942.

HIRSCH, Henriette (formerly Scharff). Born on August 23, 1897, in Freilaubersheim. She was deported from Frankfurt am Main on June 11, 1942, to Sobibór where she perished.

HIRSCH, Ilse. Born on October 16, 1911, in Bergheim. She was deported from Koblenz-Köln-Düsseldorf on June 15, 1942, to Sobibór where he perished.

HIRSCH, Mirjam. Born on July 24, 1937, in Haiger. She was deported from Frankfurt am Main on June 11, 1942, to Sobibór where she perished.

HIRSCH, Rosa (formerly Seufert). Born on March 13, 1903, in Dirmstein. She was deported from Frankfurt am Main on June 11, 1942, to Sobibór where she perished.

HIRSCHBERG, Alice. Born on October 27, 1920, in Fulda. She was deported from Kassel-Halle on June 1, 1942, to the Izbica Transit Ghetto. Sent on from Izbica to Sobibór, where she perished on June 3, 1942.

HIRSCHBERG, Rose. Born on December 1, 1886, near Feldheim in Graudenz, Poland. She was deported from Kassel-Halle on June 1, 1942, to the Izbica Transit Ghetto. Sent on from Izbica to Sobibór, where she perished on June 3, 1942.

HIRSCHBERG, Selma. Born on May 30, 1922, in Fulda. She was deported from Kassel-Halle on June 1, 1942, to the Izbica Transit Ghetto. Sent on from Izbica to Sobibór, where she perished on June 3, 1942.

HIRSCHBERGER, Betty. Born on April 17, 1908, in Oberlauringen. She was deported from Frankfurt am Main on June 11, 1942, to Sobibór where she perished.

HIRSCHBRANDT, Helga. Born on May 11, 1924, in Alzey. She was deported from Frankfurt am Main on May 24, 1942, to the Izbica Transit Ghetto in Poland. Sent on from Izbica to Sobibór where she perished.

HIRSCHBRANDT, Ida (formerly Strauss). Born on April 3, 1901, in Miehlen. She was deported from Frankfurt am Main on May 24, 1942, to the Izbica Transit Ghetto in Poland. Sent on from Izbica to Sobibór where she perished.

HIRSCHBRANDT, Otto. Born on March 31, 1889, in Erbes-Budesheim. He was deported from Frankfurt am Main on May 24, 1942, to the Izbica Transit Ghetto in Poland. Sent on from Izbica to Sobibór where he perished on December 31, 1942.

HIRSCHMANN, Kurt. Born on October 26, 1900, in Vienna. He was a member of the *Judenrat* in Piaski. He was deported to Sobibór in November 1942, where he perished.[391]

HIRSCHMANN, Salomon. Born on December 31, 1879, in Grosskrotzenburg. He was deported from Kassel-Halle on June 1, 1942, to the Izbica Transit Ghetto. Sent on from Izbica to Sobibór, where he perished on June 3, 1942.

HIRSCHMANN, Sara (formerly Rosenberg). Born on February 27, 1886, in Lichenroth. She was deported from Kassel-Halle on June 1, 1942, to the Izbica Transit Ghetto. Sent on from Izbica to Sobibór, where she perished on June 3, 1942.

---

[391] www.deathcamps.org—online resource.

HODDIS, Jakob van (DAVIDSOHN, Hans). Born on May 16, 1887, in Berlin. A German Jewish expressionist poet, who produced the poem 'Weltende,' which was published in 1911. Van Hoddis was an anagram of his surname Davidsohn. He suffered from mental health issues and was deported from the Berndorf-Sayn sanatorium on April 30, 1942, to the Krasniczyn Ghetto in Poland. From there he was deported to Sobibór where he perished, during 1942.[392]

HOFF, Martha (formerly Frankel). Born on October 5, 1890, in Mannheim. She was deported from Frankfurt am Main on May 24, 1942, to the Izbica Transit Ghetto in Poland. Sent on from Izbica to Sobibór where she perished.

HOFLICH, Gerda. Born on June 7, 1932, in Melsungen. She was deported from Kassel-Halle on June 1, 1942, to the Izbica Transit Ghetto. Sent on from Izbica to Sobibór, where she perished on June 3, 1942.

HOFLICH, Hilde (formerly Rothschild). Born on February 25, 1896, in Abterode. She was deported from Kassel-Halle on June 1, 1942, to the Izbica Transit Ghetto. Sent on from Izbica to Sobibór, where she perished on June 3, 1942.

HOFMANN, Selma (formerly Lowenberg). Born on August 5, 1908, in Reiskirchen. She was deported from Frankfurt am Main on June 11, 1942, to Sobibór where she perished.

HOHENBERG, Ella (formerly Levi). Born on May 13, 1882, in Kassel. She was deported from Kassel-Halle on June 1, 1942, to the Izbica Transit Ghetto. Sent on from Izbica to Sobibór, where she perished on June 3, 1942.

HOLLANDER, Elvira (formerly Troplowitz). Born on October 16, 1893, in Riesa. She was deported from Kassel-Halle on June

---

[392] https://en.wikipedia.org/wiki/Weltende_(Jakob_van_Hoddis)—online resource.

1, 1942, to the Izbica Transit Ghetto. Sent on from Izbica to Sobibór, where she perished on June 3, 1942.

HOLZMANN, Erna. Born on February 12, 1894, in Homburg von der Hohe. She was deported from Frankfurt am Main on June 11, 1942, to Sobibór where she perished.

HOLZMANN, Martha (formerly Ackermann). Born on October 29, 1896, in Wiesbaden. She was deported from Frankfurt am Main on June 11, 1942, to Sobibór where she perished.

HORMANN, Bella. Born on December 25, 1912, in Nowy Zmigrod, Poland. She was deported from Frankfurt am Main on June 11, 1942, to Sobibór where she perished.

HORN, Frieda (formerly Kerzner). Born on January 16, 1890, in Bohordczany, Poland. She was deported from Kassel-Halle on June 1, 1942, to the Izbica Transit Ghetto. Sent on from Izbica to Sobibór, where she perished on June 3, 1942.

HOXTER, Erika. Born on December 2, 1923, Schweinsberg. She was deported from Kassel-Halle on June 1, 1942, to the Izbica Transit Ghetto. Sent on from Izbica to Sobibór, where she perished on June 3, 1942.

HOXTER, Ilse. Born on October 2, 1926, in Marburg an der Lahn. She was deported from Kassel-Halle on June 1, 1942, to the Izbica Transit Ghetto. Sent on from Izbica to Sobibór, where she perished on June 3, 1942.

HOXTER, Rosa (formerly Nussbaum). Born on December 20, 1892, in Neukirchen. She was deported from Kassel-Halle on June 1, 1942, to the Izbica Transit Ghetto. Sent on from Izbica to Sobibór, where she perished on June 3, 1942.

IDSTEIN, Therese. Born on September 24, 1889, in Homburg von der Hohe. She was deported from Frankfurt am Main on June 11, 1942, to Sobibór where she perished.

IMMERGLUCK, Lotte (formerly Goldstein). Born on October 29, 1900, in Berlin. She perished in Sobibór on June 11, 1943.

ISAACSON, Anna (formerly Sondheim). Born on February 26, 1880, in Wiesenbronn. She resided in Essen. She was deported from Koblenz-Köln-Düsseldorf, on June 15, 1942, to Sobibór where she perished.

ISAAK, Beate. Born on April 9, 1938, in Niederkleen. She was deported from Frankfurt am Main on June 11, 1942, to Sobibór where she perished.

ISAAK, Betty. Born on July 20, 1907, in Hausen. She was deported from Kassel-Halle on June 1, 1942, to the Izbica Transit Ghetto. Sent on from Izbica to Sobibór, where she perished on June 3, 1942.

ISAAK, Billa. Born on March 1, 1884, in Oberkleen. She was deported from Frankfurt am Main on June 11, 1942, to Sobibór where she perished.

ISAAK, Edith. Born on October 11, 1936, in Niederkleen. She was deported from Frankfurt am Main on June 11, 1942, to Sobibór where she perished.

ISAAK, Elfriede. Born on May 2, 1929, in Oberaula. She was deported from Kassel-Halle on June 1, 1942, to the Izbica Transit Ghetto. Sent on from Izbica to Sobibór, where she perished on June 3, 1942.

ISAAK, Leopold. Born on October 29, 1882, in Langenselbold. He was deported from Kassel-Halle on June 1, 1942, to the Izbica Transit Ghetto. Sent on from Izbica to Sobibór, where he perished on June 3, 1942.

ISAAK, Lina (formerly Liebermann). Born on December 11, 1880, in Hausen. She was deported from Kassel-Halle on June 1, 1942, to the Izbica Transit Ghetto. Sent on from Izbica to Sobibór, where she perished on June 3, 1942.

ISAAK, Max. Born on April 5, 1879, in Oberkleen. He was deported from Kassel-Halle on June 1, 1942, to the Izbica Transit

Ghetto. Sent on from Izbica to Sobibór, where he perished on June 3, 1942.

ISAAK, Moritz. Born on November 17, 1884, in Oberkleen. He was deported from Kassel-Halle on June 1, 1942, to the Izbica Transit Ghetto. Sent on from Izbica to Sobibór, where he perished on June 3, 1942.

ISAAK, Rahel. Born on January 5, 1935, in Berlin. She was deported from Kassel-Halle on June 1, 1942, to the Izbica Transit Ghetto. Sent on from Izbica to Sobibór, where she perished on June 3, 1942.

ISAAK, Rosa. Born on October 24, 1880, in Oberkleen. She was deported from Frankfurt am Main on June 11, 1942, to Sobibór where she perished.

ISAAK, Selma (formerly Wallach). Born on May 10, 1888, in Oberaula. She was deported from Kassel-Halle on June 1, 1942, to the Izbica Transit Ghetto. Sent on from Izbica to Sobibór, where she perished on June 3, 1942.

ISAAK, Theodor. Born on June 19, 1914, in Oberaula. He was deported from Kassel-Halle on June 1, 1942, to the Izbica Transit Ghetto. Sent on from Izbica to Sobibór, where he perished on June 3, 1942.

ISENBERG, Berta. Born on November 26, 1888, in Buchenau. She was deported from Kassel-Halle on June 1, 1942, to the Izbica Transit Ghetto. Sent on from Izbica to Sobibór, where she perished on June 3, 1942.

ISENBERG, Emilie. Born on August 18, 1883, in Volksmarson. She was deported from Kassel-Halle on June 1, 1942, to the Izbica Transit Ghetto. Sent on from Izbica to Sobibór, where she perished on June 3, 1942.

ISENBERG, Selma. Born on July 29, 1890, in Marburg an der Lahn. She was deported from Kassel-Halle on June 1, 1942, to the Izbica Transit Ghetto. Sent on from Izbica to Sobibór, where she perished on June 3, 1942.

ISRAEL, Ada (formerly Robert). Born on September 16, 1897, in Graudenz, Poland. She was deported from Kassel-Halle on June 1, 1942, to the Izbica Transit Ghetto. Sent on from Izbica to Sobibór, where she perished on June 3, 1942.

ISRAEL, Amalie (formerly Falkenberg). Born on October 8, 1877, in Hammerstein. She was deported from Kassel-Halle on June 1, 1942, to the Izbica Transit Ghetto. Sent on from Izbica to Sobibór, where she perished on June 3, 1942.

ISRAEL, Bernhard. Born on June 30, 1886, in Dillich. He was deported from Kassel-Halle on June 1, 1942, to the Izbica Transit Ghetto. Sent on from Izbica to Sobibór, where he perished on June 3, 1942.

ISRAEL, Dina (formerly Falkenstein). Born on May 16, 1880, in Rotenburg an der Fulda. She was deported from Kassel-Halle on June 1, 1942, to the Izbica Transit Ghetto. Sent on from Izbica to Sobibór, where she perished on June 3, 1942.

ISRAEL, Hedwig (formerly Hallgarten). Born on October 5, 1895, in Winkel. She was deported from Frankfurt am Main on June 11, 1942, to Sobibór where she perished.

ISRAEL, Herta. Born on May 22, 1925, in Schierstein. She was deported from Frankfurt am Main on June 11, 1942, to Sobibór where she perished.

ISRAEL, Margot. Born on January 22, 1928, in Wiesbaden. She was deported from Frankfurt am Main on June 11, 1942, to Sobibór where she perished.

ISRAEL, Rosa (formerly Kaufmann). Born on May 9, 1880, in Gambach. She was deported from Frankfurt am Main on June 11, 1942, to Sobibór where she perished.

ISRAEL, Rosel. Born on March 7, 1922, in Schierstein. She was deported from Frankfurt am Main on June 11, 1942, to Sobibór where she perished.

ITZKOWITZ, Hilda (formerly Strauss). Born on July 26, 1892, in Strasbourg, France. She was deported from Kassel-Halle on June 1, 1942, to the Izbica Transit Ghetto. Sent on from Izbica to Sobibór, where she perished on June 3, 1942.

JACOB, Karl. Born on July 5, 1877, in Schmalkalden. He was imprisoned in Buchenwald Concentration Camp from November 10, 1938. He was deported from Kassel-Halle on June 1, 1942, to the Izbica Transit Ghetto. Sent on from Izbica to Sobibór, where he perished on June 3, 1942.

JACOB, Klarchen. Born on December 26, 1929, in Rhoden. She was deported from Kassel-Halle on June 1, 1942, to the Izbica Transit Ghetto. Sent on from Izbica to Sobibór, where she perished on June 3, 1942.

JACOB, Louis. Born on April 8, 1896, in Freienohl. He was imprisoned in Sachsenhausen Concentration Camp. He was deported from Kassel-Halle on June 1, 1942, to the Izbica Transit Ghetto. Sent on from Izbica to Sobibór, where he perished on June 3, 1942.

JACOB, Rolf. Born on July 12, 1928, in Rhoden. He was deported from Kassel-Halle on June 1, 1942, to the Izbica Transit Ghetto. Sent on from Izbica to Sobibór, where he perished on June 3, 1942.

JACOBS, Charlotte (formerly Rosenbaum). Born on March 15, 1887, in Grebenstein. She was deported from Kassel-Halle on June 1, 1942, to the Izbica Transit Ghetto. Sent on from Izbica to Sobibór, where she perished on June 3, 1942.

JACOBSOHN, Hedwig (formerly Cohn). Born on July 23, 1886, in Rugenwalde. She was deported from Frankfurt am Main on June 11, 1942, to Sobibór where she perished.

JAHL, Karla. Born on November 22, 1887, in Mulheim. She was deported from Frankfurt am Main on June 11, 1942, to Sobibór where she perished.

JAKOB, Hedwig (formerly Lowenthal). Born on September 16, 1883, in Meerholz. She was deported from Frankfurt am Main on June 11, 1942, to Sobibór where she perished.

JERET, Etta (formerly Kronfeld). Born on November 4, 1908, in Lancut, Poland. She was deported from Frankfurt am Main on June 11, 1942, to Sobibór where she perished.

JESSE, Rosalie (formerly Philipp). Born on July 29, 1887, in Ried. She was deported from Frankfurt am Main on June 11, 1942, to Sobibór where she perished.

JONAS, Kurt. Born on June 23, 1890, in Hagen. He resided in Köln. He perished in Sobibór.

JONASSOHN, Hans. Born on March 5, 1927, in Köln. He resided in Köln. He perished in Sobibór.

JORDAN, Hedwig (formerly Mendel). Born on October 6, 1891, in Ebersgons. She was deported from Frankfurt am Main on June 11, 1942, to Sobibór where she perished.

JORDAN, Hedwig (formerly Examus). Born on April 23, 1906, in Horn. She was deported from Frankfurt am Main on June 11, 1942, to Sobibór where she perished.

JOSEPH, Helene (formerly Buchheim). Born on June 24, 1889, in Wohra. She was deported from Frankfurt am Main on June 11, 1942, to Sobibór where she perished.

JOURDAN, Elisabeth. Born on April 6, 1894, in Mainz. She was deported from Frankfurt am Main on June 11, 1942, to Sobibór where she perished.

JUDA, Berta (formerly Simon). Born on June 23, 1896, in Kolschhausen. She was deported from Frankfurt am Main on June 11, 1942, to Sobibór where she perished.

JUDEL, Flora (formerly Susskind). Born on October 17, 1877, in Pinne. She was deported from Frankfurt am Main on June 11, 1942, to Sobibór where she perished.

JUNGHAUS, Rosa (formerly Lyon). Born on October 4, 1881, in Frankfurt am Main. She was deported from Frankfurt am Main on June 11, 1942, to Sobibór where she perished.

JUNGHEIM, Aron. Born on July 17, 1887, in Zwesten. He was deported from Kassel-Halle on June 1, 1942, to the Izbica Transit Ghetto. Sent on from Izbica to Sobibór, where he perished on June 3, 1942.

JUNGHEIM, Julchen (formerly Plaut). Born on April 6, 1894, in Wehrda. She was deported from Kassel-Halle on June 1, 1942, to the Izbica Transit Ghetto. Sent on from Izbica to Sobibór, where she perished on June 3, 1942.

KAEMPFER, Georg. Born on December 29, 1883, in Poznan, Poland. He was deported from Kassel-Halle on June 1, 1942, to the Izbica Transit Ghetto. Sent on from Izbica to Sobibór, where he perished on June 3, 1942.

KAEMPFER, Herta (formerly Bergheim). Born on February 14, 1893, in Schwersenz, Poland. She was deported from Kassel-Halle on June 1, 1942, to the Izbica Transit Ghetto. Sent on from Izbica to Sobibór, where she perished on June 3, 1942.

KAEMPFER, Irmgard. Born on January 22, 1922, in Saarbrucken. She was deported from Kassel-Halle on June 1, 1942, to the Izbica Transit Ghetto. Sent on from Izbica to Sobibór, where she perished on June 3, 1942.

KAEMPFER, Marion. Born on March 22, 1925, in Saarbrucken. She was deported from Kassel-Halle on June 1, 1942, to the Izbica Transit Ghetto. Sent on from Izbica to Sobibór, where she perished on June 3, 1942.

KAHN, Berta. Born on August 15, 1881, in Eschwege. She was deported from Kassel-Halle on June 1, 1942, to the Izbica Transit

Ghetto. Sent on from Izbica to Sobibór, where she perished on June 3, 1942.

KAHN, Betti (formerly Nusbaum). Born on April 29, 1900, in Masbach. She was deported from Frankfurt am Main on June 11, 1942, to Sobibór where she perished.

KAHN, Erna. Born on December 19, 1908, in Montabaur. She was deported from Frankfurt am Main on June 11, 1942, to Sobibór where she perished.

KAHN, Fanny (formerly Katz). Born on March 5, 1887, in Munzenberg. She was deported from Frankfurt am Main on June 11, 1942, to Sobibór where she perished.

KAHN, Frieda (formerly Strauss). Born on March 27, 1881, in Lauterbach. She was deported from Frankfurt am Main on June 11, 1942, to Sobibór where she perished.

KAHN, Frieda (formerly Kahn). Born on October 29, 1885, in Wiesbaden. She was deported from Frankfurt am Main on June 11, 1942, to Sobibór. She perished in Sobibór on December 31, 1942.

KAHN, Frieda. Born on January 28, 1887, in Eschwege. She was deported from Kassel-Halle on June 1, 1942, to the Izbica Transit Ghetto. Sent on from Izbica to Sobibór, where she perished on June 3, 1942.

KAHN, Frieda (formerly Strauss). Born on August 6, 1897, in Mittelsinn. She was deported from Frankfurt am Main on June 11, 1942, to Sobibór where she perished.

KAHN, Gertrud. Born on September 13, 1919, in Biskirchen. She was deported from Frankfurt am Main on June 11, 1942, to Sobibór where she perished.

KAHN, Henriette (formerly Weiss). Born on November 14, 1889, in Langenlonstein. She was deported from Frankfurt am Main on June 11, 1942, to Sobibór where she perished.

KAHN, Ida (formerly Simon). Born on June 3, 1885, in Gladenbach. She was deported from Frankfurt am Main on June 11, 1942, to Sobibór where she perished.

KAHN, Ilse. Born on September 27, 1920, in Florsheim. She was deported from Frankfurt am Main on June 11, 1942, to Sobibór where she perished.

KAHN, Irma. Born on November 4, 1911, in Langendiebach. She was deported from Kassel-Halle on June 1, 1942, to the Izbica Transit Ghetto. Sent on from Izbica to Sobibór, where she perished on June 3, 1942.

KAHN, Jakob. Born on December 30, 1882, in Kulsheim. He was deported from Kassel-Halle on June 1, 1942, to the Izbica Transit Ghetto. Sent on from Izbica to Sobibór, where he perished on June 3, 1942.

KAHN, Jenny (formerly Klein). Born on May 14, 1901, in Kirf. She was deported from Kassel-Halle on June 1, 1942, to the Izbica Transit Ghetto. Sent on from Izbica to Sobibór, where she perished on June 3, 1942.

KAHN, Johanna (formerly Levi). Born on August 27, 1872, in Langendiebach. She was deported from Kassel-Halle on June 1, 1942, to the Izbica Transit Ghetto. Sent on from Izbica to Sobibór, where she perished on June 3, 1942.

KAHN, Lore. Born on August 5, 1933, in Idstein. She was deported from Frankfurt am Main on June 11, 1942, to Sobibór where she perished.

KAHN, Melitta (formerly Dreyfus). Born on January 6, 1895, in Watzenborn. She was deported from Frankfurt am Main on June 11, 1942, to Sobibór where she perished.

KAHN, Selma. Born on November 19, 1890, in Esch. She was deported from Frankfurt am Main on June 11, 1942, to Sobibór where she perished.

KAHN, Toni. Born on February 8, 1927, in Gemunden. She was deported from Frankfurt am Main on June 11, 1942, to Sobibór where she perished.

KAHN, Werner. Born on March 14, 1935, in Kirf. He was deported from Kassel-Halle on June 1, 1942, to the Izbica Transit Ghetto. Sent on from Izbica to Sobibór, where he perished on June 3, 1942.

KAISER, Emilie (formerly Guggenheimer). Born on March 5, 1863, in Osterberg. She was deported from Kassel-Halle on June 1, 1942, to the Izbica Transit Ghetto. Sent on from Izbica to Sobibór, where she perished on June 3, 1942.

KAISER, Frieda (formerly Schonfrank). Born on January 16, 1901, in Thalmassing. She was deported from Frankfurt am Main on June 11, 1942, to Sobibór where she perished.

KAISER, Sara (formerly Heiser). Born on February 15, 1880, in Breitenbach. She was deported from Kassel-Halle on June 1, 1942, to the Izbica Transit Ghetto. Sent on from Izbica to Sobibór, where she perished on June 3, 1942.

KAMM, Emil. Born on August 25, 1877, in Pawonkau. He was deported from Kassel-Halle on June 1, 1942, to the Izbica Transit Ghetto. Sent on from Izbica to Sobibór, where he perished on June 3, 1942.

KAMM, Rosa (formerly Kamm). Born on June 12, 1884, in Radostowitz, Poland. She was deported from Kassel-Halle on June 1, 1942, to the Izbica Transit Ghetto. Sent on from Izbica to Sobibór, where she perished on June 3, 1942.

KAMM, Ruth. Born on May 3, 1926, in Weisenfels. She was deported from Kassel-Halle on June 1, 1942, to the Izbica Transit Ghetto. Sent on from Izbica to Sobibór, where she perished on June 3, 1942.

KANN, Ellen (formerly Kahn). Born on February 22, 1902, in Cologne. She was deported from Frankfurt am Main on June 11, 1942, to Sobibór where she perished.

KANTER, Kantel. Born on January 8, 1874, in Neustadt. She was deported from Kassel-Halle on June 1, 1942, to the Izbica Transit Ghetto. Sent on from Izbica to Sobibór, where she perished on June 3, 1942.

KANTER, Karoline (formerly Weinberg). Born on August 4, 1883, in Lichenroth. She was deported from Kassel-Halle on June 1, 1942, to the Izbica Transit Ghetto. Sent on from Izbica to Sobibór, where she perished on June 3, 1942.

KANTER, Ludwig. Born on December 30, 1906, in Neustadt. He was deported from Kassel-Halle on June 1, 1942, to the Izbica Transit Ghetto. Sent on from Izbica to Sobibór, where he perished on June 3, 1942.

KANTHAL, Baruch. Born on September 16, 1877, in Langenselbold. He was deported from Kassel-Halle on June 1, 1942, to the Izbica Transit Ghetto. Sent on from Izbica to Sobibór, where he perished on June 3, 1942.

KANTHAL, Bertha (formerly Summer). Born on May 7, 1888, in Grebenhain. She was deported from Kassel-Halle on June 1, 1942, to the Izbica Transit Ghetto. Sent on from Izbica to Sobibór, where she perished on June 3, 1942.

KAPLAN, Hans. Born on August 6, 1928, in Pirmasens. He was deported from Kassel-Halle on June 1, 1942, to the Izbica Transit Ghetto. Sent on from Izbica to Sobibór, where he perished on June 3, 1942.

KAPLAN, Helga. Born on January 28, 1932, in Pirmasens. She was deported from Kassel-Halle on June 1, 1942, to the Izbica Transit Ghetto. Sent on from Izbica to Sobibór, where she perished on June 3, 1942.

KARLE, Olga (formerly Grunstein). Born on February 2, 1901, in Frankfurt am Main. She was deported from Frankfurt am Main on June 11, 1942, to Sobibór where she perished.

KARLEBACH, Sophie. Born on December 10, 1909, in Wiesbaden. She was deported from Frankfurt am Main on June 11, 1942, to Sobibór where she perished.

KASCHMANN, Rosi. Born on September 18, 1900, in Kassel. She was deported from Kassel-Halle on June 1, 1942, to the Izbica Transit Ghetto. Sent on from Izbica to Sobibór, where she perished on June 3, 1942.

KATZ, Berta (formerly Katz). Born on May 15, 1885, in Guxhagen. She was deported from Kassel-Halle on June 1, 1942, to the Izbica Transit Ghetto. Sent on from Izbica to Sobibór, where she perished on June 3, 1942.

KATZ, Berta. Born on September 23, 1887, in Nesselroden. She was deported from Kassel-Halle on June 1, 1942, to the Izbica Transit Ghetto. Sent on from Izbica to Sobibór, where she perished on June 3, 1942.

KATZ, Edith. Born September 30, 1922, in Nieder Weidbach. She was deported from Frankfurt am Main on June 11, 1942, to Sobibór where she perished.

KATZ, Emilie (formerly Lowenstein). Born on July 1, 1875, in Netra. She was deported from Kassel-Halle on June 1, 1942, to the Izbica Transit Ghetto. Sent on from Izbica to Sobibór, where she perished on June 3, 1942.

KATZ, Frieda. Born on November 26, 1912, in Nentershausen. She was deported from Kassel-Halle on June 1, 1942, to the Izbica Transit Ghetto. Sent on from Izbica to Sobibór, where she perished on June 3, 1942.

KATZ, Gertrud. Born on July 10, 1891, in Frauenstein. She was deported from Frankfurt am Main on June 11, 1942, to Sobibór where she perished.

KATZ, Hedwig (formerly Plaut). Born on May 6, 1888, in Gottingen. She was deported from Kassel-Halle on June 1, 1942, to the Izbica Transit Ghetto. Sent on from Izbica to Sobibór, where she perished on June 3, 1942.

KATZ, Irma. Born on March 31, 1914, in Nentershausen. She was deported from Kassel-Halle on June 1, 1942, to the Izbica Transit Ghetto. Sent on from Izbica to Sobibór, where she perished on June 3, 1942.

KATZ, Johanna (formerly Rosenbaum). Born on May 15, 1876, in Hornsheim. She was deported from Frankfurt am Main on June 11, 1942, to Sobibór where she perished on June 13, 1942.

KATZ, Lina (formerly David). Born on July 9, 1904, in Unterethal. She was deported from Kassel-Halle on June 1, 1942. She perished in Sobibór on June 3, 1942.

KATZ, Martha. Born on July 29, 1908, in Netra. She was deported from Kassel-Halle on June 1, 1942. She perished in Sobibór on June 3, 1942.

KATZ, Recha (formerly Kahn). Born on July 3, 1886, in Nieder-Florstadt. She was deported from Kassel-Halle on June 1, 1942. She perished in Sobibór on June 3, 1942.

KATZ, Sally. Born on November 3, 1887, in Hochstadt. She was deported from Kassel-Halle on June 1, 1942. She perished in Sobibór on June 3, 1942.

KATZ, Salomon. Born on July 2, 1879, in Nentershausen. He was deported from Kassel-Halle on June 1, 1942. He perished in Sobibór on June 3, 1942.

KATZ, Selma (formerly Steinberger). Born on December 25, 1879, in Angenrod. She was deported from Kassel-Halle on June 1, 1942. She perished in Sobibór on June 3, 1942.

KATZ, Siegfried. Born on July 20, 1879, in Korbach. He was deported from Kassel-Halle on June 1, 1942. He perished in Sobibór on June 3, 1942.

KATZENHEIM, Alfred. Born on June 5, 1882, in Eisleben. He was deported from Kassel-Halle on June 1, 1942. He perished in Sobibór on June 3, 1942.

KATZENSTEIN, Abraham. Born on May 9, 1884, in Treysa. He was deported from Kassel-Halle on June 1, 1942. He perished in Sobibór on June 3, 1942.

KEMPNER, Friedrich-Wilhelm. Born on August 29, 1914, in Berlin. He was deported from Berlin to the Piaski Ghetto in Poland, on March 28, 1942. He was a member of the *Judenrat* in Piaski. He was deported to Sobibór in November 1942, where he perished.[393]

KOCH, Johanna. Born on July 18, 1892, in Mainz. She was deported from Mainz-Darmstadt on March 25, 1942, to Piaski, Poland. From there she was taken to Sobibór, where she was selected to work in the German kitchen preparing meals for the *SS*. When Himmler visited Sobibór in early 1943, she was removed from this position, as the Nazis feared she might administer poison to the German staff. Her subsequent fate is unknown, but it is probable that she did not survive.[394]

KUGELMANN, Siegfried. Born on July 17, 1884, in Witzenhausen, near Kassel. He was a member of the *Judenrat* in Piaski. He was deported to Sobibór in November 1942, where he perished.[395]

LOEWENSTEIN, Frieda (formerly Schwarzchild). Born on September 10, 1884, in Massenheim. She was deported from Frankfurt am Main on June 11, 1942, to Sobibór where she perished.

---

[393] www.deathcamps.org and www.bundesarchiv.de/gedenkbuch—online resources.

[394] M. Bem, *Sobibor Extermination Camp 1942-1943*, Stichting Sobibor 2015, p.117 and www.bundesarchiv.de/gedenkbuch—online resource.

[395] www.deathcamps.org—online resource. It should be noted that the Bundesarchiv Gedenkbuch says he was sent to the Lublin Concentration Camp, but all the other *Judenrat* members went to Sobibór.

LOEWENSTEIN, Friederike. Born on August 8, 1872, in Fronhausen. She was deported from Kassel-Halle on June 1, 1942. She perished in Sobibór on June 3, 1942.

LOEWENSTEIN, Gustav. Born on December 24, 1890, in Diemerode. He was deported from Kassel-Halle on June 1, 1942. He perished in Sobibór on June 3, 1942.

LOEWENSTEIN, Henriette. Born on June 30, 1879, in Krefeld. She was deported from Koblenz-Köln-Düsseldorf on June 15, 1942, to Sobibór where he perished.

LOWENSTEIN, Ilse. Born on October 10, 1923, in Idstein. She was deported from Frankfurt am Main on June 11, 1942, to Sobibór where she perished.

LOEWENSTEIN, Julie. Born on May 29, 1881, in Eisleben. She was deported from Kassel-Halle to Sobibór where she perished on June 3, 1942.

LOEWENSTEIN, Lilli, Lilly. Born on January 13, 1911, in Bydogoszcz, Poland. She was deported from Berlin on June 13, 1942. She perished in Sobibór.

LOEWENSTEIN, Mathilde, Mathilda (formerly Rosenthal). Born on November 26, 1887, in Hohebach. She was deported from Frankfurt am Main on June 11, 1942, to Sobibór where she perished.

LOEWENSTEIN, Minna (formerly Cohen). Born on September 7, 1875, in Bocholt. She was deported from Koblenz-Köln-Düsseldorf on June 15, 1942, to Sobibór where he perished.

LOEWENSTEIN, Mirjam. Born on April 25, 1889, in Ichenhausen. She resided in the Bendorf-Sayn sanatorium. She was deported from Koblenz-Köln-Düsseldorf on June 15, 1942, to Sobibór where she perished.

LOEWENSTEIN, Paula (formerly Gottschalk). Born on December 6, 1888, in Geilenkirchen. She was deported from

Frankfurt am Main on June 11, 1942, to Sobibór where she perished.

LOEWENSTEIN, Rudolf. Born on February 28, 1898, in Cheb, Czech Republic. He was deported from Berlin on June 13, 1942. He perished in Sobibór.

LOEWENSTEIN, Selma (formerly Vogel). Born on March 12, 1891, in Nieder-Salheim. She was deported from Kassel-Halle on June 1, 1942, to the Izbica Transit Ghetto. Sent on from Izbica to Sobibór, where she perished on June 3, 1942.

LOEWENSTEIN, Selma. Born on November 15, 1895, in Diemerode. She was deported from Kassel-Halle on June 1, 1942, to the Izbica Transit Ghetto. Sent on from Izbica to Sobibór, where she perished on June 3, 1942.

LOEWENSTEIN, Wilhelm. Born on December 28, 1882, in Hameln. He was deported from Koblenz-Köln-Düsseldorf on June 15, 1942, to Sobibór where he perished.

MARX, Bettina, Babette. Born on July 6, 1896, in Wiesbaden. She was deported from Frankfurt am Main on June 11, 1942, to Sobibór where she perished.

MARX, Elfriede. Born on October 2, 1898, in Kassel. She was deported from Kassel-Halle on June 1, 1942, to the Izbica Transit Ghetto. Sent on from Izbica to Sobibór, where she perished on June 3, 1942.

MARX, Ella (formerly Strauss). Born on December 4, 1881, in Golheim. She was deported from Frankfurt am Main on June 11, 1942, to Sobibór where she perished.

MARX, Emil. Born on June 12, 1887, in Seckmauern. He was deported from Frankfurt am Main on June 11, 1942, to Sobibór where he perished.

MARX, Emilie (formerly Ackerman). Born on December 23, 1878, in Weyer. She was deported from Frankfurt am Main on June 11, 1942, to Sobibór where she perished.

MARX, Emilie. Born on January 22, 1891, in Gemunden. She was deported from Kassel-Halle on June 1, 1942, to the Izbica Transit Ghetto. Sent on from Izbica to Sobibór, where she perished on June 3, 1942.

MARX, Sara (formerly Barmann). Born on May 2, 1855, in Haupersweiler. She was deported from Koblenz-Köln-Düsseldorf on June 15, 1942, to Sobibór where he perished.

MARX, Solly, Samuel. Born on September 25, 1877, in Biebrich. He was imprisoned in the Buchenwald Concentration Camp. He was deported from Frankfurt am Main on May 24, 1942, to the Izbica Transit Ghetto, Poland. He perished in Sobibór.

NAFTANIAL, Herbert. Born on January 30, 1900, in Thorn, Poland. He resided in Berlin and was deported from Berlin on March 28, 1942, to Piaski. From Piaski he was sent to Sobibór, where he was selected to work sorting the luggage of the murdered Jews.

In the summer of 1943, he betrayed 'Governor', *Oberkapo* Moshe Sturm, and another *Kapo* Herbert Siegel, who was known as *Rajowiecer*, because he came from the Polish town of Rejowiec, and another unknown *Kapo*. Herbert Naftanial was commonly known as 'Berliner,' because he lived in Berlin. Several weeks before the revolt, he was attacked by *Kapo's* Pozycki, Katz (Bunio) and the Austrian *Kapo* Siegfried Spitz. He was beaten so badly, he could not walk. Karl Frenzel ordered the Jews to finish him off, as 'Berliner' had gone over his head, when betraying the Head *Kapo* and the other *Kapos* escape plan to Gustav Wagner. Poison was mixed with barley and 'Berliner' ate his last meal. his body was burned in *Lager III*.[396]

---

[396] T. Blatt, *Sobibor—The Forgotten Revolt*, H.E.P, Issaquah, 1998, pp. 62-63 and www.bundesarchiv.de/gedenkbuch—online resource.

OSTER, Else. Born on April 21, 1899, in Berlin. She was deported from Koblenz-Köln-Düsseldorf on June 15, 1942, to Sobibór where she perished.

OSTER, Julie. Born on April 17, 1938, in Rheinbach. She was deported from Koblenz-Köln-Düsseldorf on June 15, 1942, to Sobibór where she perished.

RAILING, Hugo. Born on May 14, 1886, in Munich. He was arrested and imprisoned in Dachau Concentration Camp from November 10, 1938, until December 12, 1938. He was deported from Munich to the Piaski Transit Ghetto in Poland, on April 3, or 4, 1942. He became a member of the *Judenrat* in Piaski. He was deported to Sobibór during November 1942, where he perished.[397]

ROSEN, Jacob, Jakob. Born on October 17, 1879, in Bucharest, Rumania. He was deported from Koblenz-Köln-Düsseldorf on June 15, 1942, to Sobibór where he perished.

ROSEN, Kate, Kathe (formerly Neumann). Born on September 11, 1880, in Borent, Poland. She was deported from Berlin on June 13, 1942. She perished in Sobibór.

ROSENTHAL, Edith. Born on May 9, 1923, in Neustadt. She was deported from Frankfurt am Main on June 11, 1942, to Sobibór where she perished.

ROSENTHAL, Else. Born on August 11, 1906, in Culmsee, Poland. She was deported from Berlin on June 13, 1942. She perished in Sobibór.

ROSENTHAL, Ernst, Samuel. Born on September 1, 1900, in Konstanz. He was deported from Koblenz-Köln-Düsseldorf on June 15, 1942. He was initially deported to Izbica, and then onto Sobibór, where he perished.

---

[397] www.deathcamps.org and www.bundesarchiv.de/gedenkbuch —online resources.

ROSENTHAL, Friederike (formerly Lob). Born on September 26, 1872, in Tiefenbach. She was deported from Koblenz-Köln-Düsseldorf on June 15, 1942, to Sobibór where he perished.

ROSENTHAL, Georg. Born on October 16, 1907, in Berlin. He was deported from Berlin on June 13, 1942. He perished in Sobibór.

ROSENTHAL, Gerda. Born on January 17, 1930, in Wetzlar. She was deported from Frankfurt am Main on June 11, 1942, to Sobibór where she perished.

ROSENTHAL, Hans, Albert. Born on November 27, 1910, in Munich. He was deported from Koblenz-Köln-Düsseldorf on June 15, 1942, to Sobibór where he perished.

ROSENTHAL, Hertha. Born on December 5, 1891, in Halle. She was deported from Kassel-Halle on June 1, 1942, to the Izbica Transit Ghetto. Sent on from Izbica to Sobibór, where she perished on June 3, 1942.

ROSENTHAL, Ilse. Born on October 5, 1898, in Mayen. She was deported from Koblenz-Köln-Düsseldorf on June 15, 1942, to Sobibór where she perished.

ROSENTHAL, Karl. Born on March 2, 1880, in Lamstedt. He was deported from Kassel-Halle on June 1, 1942, to the Izbica Transit Ghetto, Poland. He perished in Sobibór on June 3, 1942.

ROSENTHAL, Kathe, Minna. Born on September 9, 1886, in Dessau. She was deported from Berlin on June 13, 1942. She perished in Sobibór.

ROSENTHAL, Mina (formerly Heilbronn). Born on June 14, 1883, in Dorndorf. She was deported from Frankfurt am Main on June 11, 1942, to Sobibór where she perished.

ROSENTHAL, Minna (formerly Wertheim). Born on March 19, 1892, in Neidenstein. She was deported from Kassel-Halle on June 1, 1942, to the Izbica Transit Ghetto. Sent on from Izbica to Sobibór, where she perished on June 3, 1942.

ROSENTHAL, Minna (formerly Gutheim). Born on September 17, 1896, in Ungedanken. She was deported from Frankfurt am Main on June 11, 1942, to Sobibór where she perished.

ROSENTHAL, Rosalie (formerly Hecht). Born on July 2, 1877, in Nesselroden. She was deported from Kassel-Halle on June 1, 1942, to the Izbica Transit Ghetto. Sent on from Izbica to Sobibór, where she perished on June 3, 1942.

ROSENTHAL, Selma (formerly Sondheimer). Born on September 27, 1889, in Uttrichshausen. She was deported from Kassel-Halle on June 1, 1942, to the Izbica Transit Ghetto. Sent on from Izbica to Sobibór, where she perished on June 3, 1942.

ROTH, Auguste (formerly Rosenblatt). Born on February 6, 1883, in Zimmersrode. She was deported from Kassel-Halle on June 1, 1942, to the Izbica Transit Ghetto. Sent on from Izbica to Sobibór, where she perished on June 3, 1942.

ROTH, Emil. Born on June 11, 1881, in Solopisk. He was deported from Berlin on June 13, 1942. He perished in Sobibór.

ROTH, Emilie (formerly Becker). Born on March 6, 1882, in Rockenhausen. She was deported from Berlin on June 13, 1942. She perished in Sobibór.

ROTH, Erna (formerly Grunpeter). Born on January 10, 1904, in Brzenskowitz. She was deported from Koblenz-Köln-Düsseldorf on June 15, 1942, to Sobibór where she perished.

ROTH, Hanna, Anna. Born on June 12, 1906, in Sawadka. She was deported from Berlin on June 13, 1942. She perished in Sobibór.

ROTH, Heinrich. Born on August 6, 1894, in Gleiwitz, Poland. He was deported from Koblenz-Köln-Düsseldorf on June 15, 1942, to Sobibór where he perished.

ROTH, Inge, Inga. Born on November 15, 1930, in Gleiwtz, Poland. She was deported from Koblenz-Köln-Düsseldorf on June 15, 1942, to Sobibór where she perished.

SANGER, Betty (formerly Bloch). Born on September 9, 1886, in Pillallen. She was deported from Koblenz-Köln-Düsseldorf on June 15, 1942, to Sobibór where she perished.

SANGER, Flora. Born on December 12, 1884, in Kischewo, Poland. She was deported from Berlin on June 13, 1942. She perished in Sobibór.

SANGER, Frieda. Born on December 14, 1884, in Czarnikau, Poland. She was deported from Berlin on June 13, 1942. She perished in Sobibór.

SANGER, Friedrich. Born on September 12, 1891, in Augsburg. He was imprisoned in Dachau Concentration Camp between November 10, 1938, and December 15, 1938. He was deported from Munich on April 3, or 4, 1942, to Piaski, in Poland. In Piaski he was a member of the *Judenrat*. He was deported to Sobibór during November 1942, where he perished.[398]

SCHLOSSER, Ernst. Born on January 16, in Sorgenloch. He was deported from Mainz-Darmstadt on March 25, 1942, to Piaski, Poland. In Piaski he was a member of the *Judenrat*. He was deported to Sobibór during November 1942, where he perished.[399]

SCHWARZ, Clementine (formerly Hanau). Born on September 5, 1880, in Kerprichhemmersdorf. She was deported from Kassel-Halle on June 1, 1942, to the Izbica Transit Ghetto. Sent on from Izbica to Sobibór, where she perished on June 3, 1942.

SCHWARZ, Elizabeth (formerly Backhaus). Born on December 23, 1878, in Wittenberg. She was deported from Kassel-Halle on June 1, 1942, to the Izbica Transit Ghetto. Sent on from Izbica to Sobibór, where she perished on June 3, 1942.

---

[398] www.deathcamps.org and www.bundesarchiv.de/gedenkbuch—online resources.
[399] Ibid.

SCHWARZ, Fanny (formerly Kowler). Born on January 5, 1880, in Nikolajew, Ukraine. She was deported from Frankfurt am Main on June 11, 1942, to Sobibór where she perished.

SCHWARZ, Harry. Born on June 8, 1928, in Castellaun. He was deported from Koblenz-Köln-Düsseldorf on June 15, 1942, to Sobibór where he perished.

SCHWARZ, Helene (formerly Birnzweig). Born on April 1, 1893, in Wiesbaden. She was deported from Frankfurt am Main on June 11, 1942, to Sobibór where she perished.

SCHWARZ, Irmgard (formerly Lillenfeld). Born on August 28, 1915, in Ruckingen. She was deported from Kassel-Halle on June 1, 1942, to the Izbica Transit Ghetto. Sent on from Izbica to Sobibór, where she perished on June 3, 1942.

SCHWARZ, Leo. Born on February 23, 1897, in Marienthal. He was deported from Koblenz-Köln-Düsseldorf on June 15, 1942, to Sobibór where he perished.

SCHWARZ, Leopold, Leo. Born on March 7, 1916, in Embken. He was deported from Koblenz-Köln-Düsseldorf on June 15, 1942, to Sobibór where he perished.

SCHWARZ, Lili (formerly Forst). Born on October 6, 1904, in Castellaun. She was deported from Koblenz-Köln-Düsseldorf on June 15, 1942, to Sobibór where she perished.

SCHWARZ, Lina. Born on May 2, 1885, in Pirmasens. She was deported from Kassel-Halle on June 1, 1942, to the Izbica Transit Ghetto. Sent on from Izbica to Sobibór, where she perished on June 3, 1942.

SCHWARZ, Lina (formerly Kahn). Born on June 23, 1886, in Ruckershausen. She was deported from Frankfurt am Main on June 11, 1942, to Sobibór where she perished.

SCHWARZ, Moritz. Born on October 3, 1879, in Schmelz. He was imprisoned in Dachau Concentration Camp between November 15, 1938, and December 2, 1938. He was deported from

Kassel-Halle on June 1, 1942, to the Izbica Transit Ghetto, Poland. He perished in Sobibór on June 3, 1942.

SIMONS, Hans. Born on May 27, 1923, in Köln. He was deported from Koblenz-Köln-Düsseldorf on June 15, 1942, to Sobibór where he perished.

SIMONS, Ilse (formerly Albesheim). Born on March 4, 1913, in Soest. She was deported from Koblenz-Köln-Düsseldorf on June 15, 1942, to Sobibór where she perished.

STRAUSS, Adelheid (formerly Braunschwiger). Born on October 2, 1880, in Burghaun. She was deported from Kassel-Halle on June 1, 1942, to the Izbica Transit Ghetto. Sent on from Izbica to Sobibór, where she perished on June 3, 1942.

STRAUSS, Anna (formerly Rosenberger). Born on July 26, 1884, in Eschenau. She was deported from Kassel-Halle on June 1, 1942, to the Izbica Transit Ghetto. Sent on from Izbica to Sobibór, where she perished on June 3, 1942.

STRAUSS, Anneliese. Born on February 15, 1936, in Herschbach. She was deported from Frankfurt am Main on June 11, 1942, to Sobibór where she perished.

STRAUSS, Berta. Born on September 19, 1896, in Weinheim. She was deported from Frankfurt am Main on June 11, 1942, to Sobibór where she perished.

STRAUSS, Bertha (formerly Strauss). Born on February 21, 1879, in Steinach. She was deported from Frankfurt am Main on June 11, 1942, to Sobibór where she perished.

STRAUSS, Berthold. Born on October 7, 1923, in Langenselbold. He was deported from Kassel-Halle on June 1, 1942, to the Izbica Transit Ghetto, Poland. He perished in Sobibór on June 3, 1942.

STRAUSS, Berthold. Born on June 11, 1927, in Fulda. He was deported from Kassel-Halle on June 1, 1942, to the Izbica Transit Ghetto, Poland. He perished in Sobibór on June 3, 1942.

STRAUSS, Else. Born on January 30, 1897, in Ostrich. She was deported from Frankfurt am Main on June 11, 1942, to Sobibór where she perished.

STRAUSS, Else. Born on June 12, 1920, in Niederrodenbach. She was deported from Kassel-Halle on June 1, 1942, to the Izbica Transit Ghetto. Sent on from Izbica to Sobibór, where she perished on June 3, 1942.

STRAUSS, Emma (formerly Nussbaum). Born on December 11, 1882, in Weimarschmieden. She was deported from Kassel-Halle on June 1, 1942, to the Izbica Transit Ghetto. Sent on from Izbica to Sobibór, where she perished on June 3, 1942.

STRAUSS, Fanny. Born on April 7, 1877, in Geisenheim. She was deported from Frankfurt am Main on June 11, 1942, to Sobibór where she perished.

STRAUSS, Grete. Born on January 30, 1905, in Geisenheim. She was deported from Frankfurt am Main on June 11, 1942, to Sobibór where she perished.

STRAUSS, Gretel. Born on April 11, 1923, in Rod am Berg. She was deported from Frankfurt am Main on June 11, 1942, to Sobibór where she perished.

STRAUSS, Hannchen (formerly Lorge). Born on November 17, 1893, in Harmuthsachsen. She was deported from Kassel-Halle on June 1, 1942, to the Izbica Transit Ghetto. Sent on from Izbica to Sobibór, where she perished on June 3, 1942.

STRAUSS, Hanni. Born on January 31, 1920, in Berlin. She was deported from Berlin on June 13, 1942. She perished in Sobibór.

STRAUSS, Hanni. Born on October 2, 1907, in Meerholz. She was deported from Kassel-Halle on June 1, 1942, to the Izbica Transit Ghetto. Sent on from Izbica to Sobibór, where she perished on June 3, 1942.

STRAUSS, Hulda (formerly Eichberg). Born on July 23, 1875, in Bochum. She was deported from Koblenz-Köln-Düsseldorf on June 15, 1942, to Sobibór where she perished.

STRAUSS, Irma. Born on February 14, 1895, in Wollstein. She was deported from Frankfurt am Main on June 11, 1942, to Sobibór where she perished.

STRAUSS, Isaak. Born on June 2, 1890, in Niederrodenbach. He was deported from Kassel-Halle on June 1, 1942, to the Izbica Transit Ghetto, Poland. He perished in Sobibór on June 3, 1942.

STRAUSS, Karl. Born on April 22, 1876, in Grebenau. He was deported from Kassel-Halle on June 1, 1942, to the Izbica Transit Ghetto, Poland. He perished in Sobibór on June 3, 1942.

STRAUSS, Liebmann. Born on December 9, 1883, in Schluchtern. He was deported from Kassel-Halle on June 1, 1942, to the Izbica Transit Ghetto, Poland. He perished in Sobibór on June 3, 1942.

STRAUSS, Lucie. Born on March 28, 1886, in Pirmasens. She was deported from Frankfurt am Main on June 11, 1942, to Sobibór where she perished.

STRAUSS, Margarete. Born on April 28, 1899, in Barchfeld. She was deported from Frankfurt am Main on June 11, 1942, to Sobibór where she perished.

STRAUSS, Marie (formerly Eisenger). Born on October 28, 1877, in Mannheim. She was deported from Frankfurt am Main on June 11, 1942, to Sobibór where she perished.

STRAUSS, Marie (formerly Glass). Born on January 30, 1889, in Katowice, Poland. She was deported from Koblenz-Köln-Düsseldorf on June 15, 1942, to Sobibór where she perished.

STRAUSS, Martha (formerly Meyer). Born on January 7, 1887, in Beerfelden. She was deported from Kassel-Halle on June 1, 1942, to the Izbica Transit Ghetto. Sent on from Izbica to Sobibór, where she perished on June 3, 1942.

STRAUSS, Meier. Born on January 28, 1890, in Sterbfritz. He was deported from Koblenz-Köln-Düsseldorf on June 15, 1942, to Sobibór where he perished.

STRAUSS, Minna (formerly Plant). Born on December 4, 1878, in Frielendorf. She was deported from Kassel-Halle on June 1, 1942, to the Izbica Transit Ghetto. Sent on from Izbica to Sobibór, where she perished on June 3, 1942.

STRAUSS, Rosa (formerly Jacob). Born on December 22, 1881, in Homburg. She was deported from Frankfurt am Main on June 11, 1942, to Sobibór where she perished.

STRAUSS, Rosa (formerly Katz-Stiefel). Born on August 30, 1899, in Ziegenhain. She was deported from Kassel-Halle on June 1, 1942, to the Izbica Transit Ghetto. Sent on from Izbica to Sobibór, where she perished on June 3, 1942.

STRAUSS, Rosa. Born on January 5, 1901, in Heerholz. She was deported from Kassel-Halle on June 1, 1942, to the Izbica Transit Ghetto. Sent on from Izbica to Sobibór, where she perished on June 3, 1942.

STRAUSS, Sally. Born on December 5, 1899, in Grumbach. He was imprisoned in the Dachau Concentration Camp between November 15, 1938, and December 19, 1938. He was deported from Kassel-Halle on June 1, 1942, to the Izbica Transit Ghetto, Poland. He perished in Sobibór on June 3, 1942.

STRAUSS, Selma (formerly Strauss). Born on November 18, 1897, in Herschbach. She was deported from Frankfurt am Main on June 11, 1942, to Sobibór where she perished.

STRAUSS, Siegfried. Born on August 2, 1923, in Niederrodenbach. He was deported from Kassel-Halle on June 1, 1942, to the Izbica Transit Ghetto, Poland. He perished in Sobibór on June 3, 1942.

WEISS, Bertha (formerly Levy). Born on October 6, 1881, in Mainbernheim. She was deported from Berlin on June 13, 1942. She perished in Sobibór.

WEISS, Charlotte (formerly Hirsch). Born on March 27, 1891, in Halle. She was deported from Kassel-Halle on June 1, 1942, to the Izbica Transit Ghetto. Sent on from Izbica to Sobibór, where she perished on June 3, 1942.

WEISS, Erich. Born on March 21, 1886, in Dabrowka, Poland. He was deported from Koblenz-Köln-Düsseldorf on June 15, 1942, to Sobibór where he perished.

WEISS, Frieda (formerly Friedman). Born on April 12, 1892, in Rawa Ruska, Ukraine. She was deported from Berlin on June 13, 1942. She perished in Sobibór.

WEISS, Grete (formerly Hendler). Born on March 4, 1886, in Beuthen, Poland. She was deported from Koblenz-Köln-Düsseldorf on June 15, 1942, to Sobibór where she perished.

WEISS, Mina (formerly Sonnenberg). Born on February 18, 1888, in Kelsterbach. She was deported from Frankfurt am Main on June 11, 1942, to Sobibór where she perished.

WEISS, Theodor. Born on June 4, 1876, in Halle. He was imprisoned in Sachsenhausen Concentration Camp. He was deported from Kassel-Halle on June 1, 1942, to the Izbica Transit Ghetto, Poland. He perished in Sobibór on June 3, 1942.

ZUCKER, Chana (formerly Sockel). Born on September 5, 1877, in Lomza, Poland. She was deported from Berlin on June 13, 1942. She perished in Sobibór.

ZUCKER, Sara. Born on July 22, 1917, in Berlin. She was deported from Berlin on June 13, 1942. She perished in Sobibór.

Selected to work at Sobibór for Outside Labor Camps A–Z

This Roll of Remembrance covers the Jews selected in Sobibór to work in Labor Camps such as Dorohucza, the Old Airfield Camp in Lublin, Lublin Concentration Camp and Trawniki, and other camps. I have listed some of those who perished in various Labor Camps, as well as listing the survivors.

This is a partial listing—in alphabetical order.

ADEJES, Albert. He was transported from Drancy, France, on Convoy Number 50 on March 4, 1943, via Chelm to Sobibór. He was selected at Sobibór to work in Lublin. He was also incarcerated in Auschwitz Concentration Camp. He survived the Holocaust.[400]

COHEN, Alex. Alex Cohen, along with his wife Saartje, and Abraham, his four year old son lived at Rijnstraat 26, Groningen. They were deported from Westerbork on March 17, 1943, to Sobibór. They arrived in Sobibór on March 20, 1943, in the dead of night. Cohen volunteered as a metal worker and was put back on the same train. His wife and child were sent to *Lager III*, and murdered in the gas chambers.

Alex was sent to the Lublin Concentration Camp, where he worked in the kitchen. After three months in Lublin, he was sent to the Skarzysko-Kamienna Labor Camp digging pits for corpses. He was evacuated to a Labor Camp near Czestochowa. As the Red Army advanced he was sent first to Buchenwald Concentration Camp, and then to Theresienstadt in Czechoslovakia, where he was liberated by the Soviet forces.[401]

---

[400] J. Schelvis, *Sobibor*, Berg-Oxford, New York, 2007, p. 217.
[401] www.Sobiborinterviews.nl—online resource.

CZAPNIK, Zina. She was deported from Minsk along with her husband to Sobibór during September 1943, and her cousin Raja Mileczina. She and her cousin were selected at Sobibór for work at the Trawniki Labor Camp.

She survived the *Aktion Erntefest* massacre on November 3, 1943, although her husband was killed in Trawniki during this '*Aktion*.' She stayed at Trawniki until the spring of 1944, then she was sent to the Lublin Concentration Camp. She was then sent to Auschwitz Concentration Camp, and as the Red Army advanced, she was sent to the Bergen-Belsen Concentration Camp, and then onto Oschersleben. Finally Zina was sent to Theresienstadt, the fortress ghetto, where she was liberated by the Red Army.[402]

ELIAZER, Judith. On March 10, 1943, Judith, a 28-year old hairdresser from Rotterdam was deported from Westerbork Transit Camp to Sobibór. At Sobibór she was immediately selected for work at the Lublin Concentration Camp, where she was put to work building barracks and mending roads.

After six months in Lublin, Judith was taken to Milejow, to work in a marmalade factory, and from there she was sent to the Trawniki Labor Camp in November 1943, to sort the clothes of those workers murdered as part of *Aktion Erntefest*. In the summer of 1944, she returned to the Lublin Concentration Camp, but as the Red Army advanced she was forced to march to Auschwitz Concentration Camp. From Auschwitz she was sent to Bergen-Belsen Concentration Camp in Germany. Judith was liberated by Allied Forces at the Salzwedel Labor Camp.[403]

ENSEL, Bertha. On March 10, 1943, Bertha Ensel an 18-year old seamstress from Amsterdam was deported from Westerbork Transit Camp to Sobibór. At Sobibór she was immediately

---

[402] J. Schelvis, *Sobibor*, Berg-Oxford, New York p.128 and 220.
[403] www.sobiborinterviews.nl—online resource.

selected for work at the Lublin Concentration Camp, where she was put to work building barracks and mending roads.

After six months in Lublin, Bertha was taken to Milejow, to work in a marmalade factory, and from there she was sent to the Trawniki Labor Camp in November 1943, to sort the clothes of those workers murdered as part of *Aktion Erntefest*. In the summer of 1944, she returned to the Lublin Concentration Camp, but as the Red Army advanced she was forced to march to Auschwitz Concentration Camp. From Auschwitz she was sent to Buchenwald Concentration Camp in Germany. Bertha returned to Holland via Lippstadt, where she had worked in an ammunition factory.[404]

GOMPERTZ, Klaartje (Clara). Born on April 14, 1905, in Den Haag. She lived at Turfmarkt 34 a, Den Haag. She was deported along with other family members from Westerbork Transit Camp on March 10, 1943. Clara and other Dutch women were selected at Sobibór to work in Lublin. Their destination was the *Alter Flugplatz* (Old Airfield), where she sorted the clothes of the murdered victims, of Sobibór and Treblinka.

During October 1943, she volunteered to work in a marmalade factory in Milejow. She perished in the Trawniki Labor Camp on August 31, 1944.[405]

HUISMAN, Sophia. On the night of February 26, 1943, all patients and staff of the Jewish hospital in Rotterdam were rounded up by the *Sicherheitsdienst (SD)* and the Dutch WA forces and taken to Westerbork Transit Camp. Among them was 17-year old Sophia Huisman, a trainee nurse. She was deported from Westerbork to Sobibór on March 10, 1943.

On arrival at Sobibór, Sophia and a number of other Dutch women were put back on the same train and sent to the Lublin Concentration Camp, and then she was sent to the *Alter*

---

[404] Ibid.
[405] www.joodsmonument.nl—online resource.

Flugplatz (Old Airfield) Camp where she sorted the clothes of the murdered victims, of Sobibór and Treblinka.

In October 1943, she volunteered to work in a marmalade factory in Milejow. After the *Aktion Erntefest* massacre in November 1943, she was transferred to the Trawniki Labor Camp, until June 1944, where she returned to the Lublin Concentration Camp.

With the advancing Red Army, Sophia was sent to the Auschwitz Concentration Camp. As the Soviet forces advanced she was sent to a munitions factory in Raguhn. She was moved for the last time to the Theresienstadt fortress ghetto near Prague. She was liberated there by the Red Army in May 1945.[406]

LOWENSTEIN, Kurt. Born on June 10, 1904, in Barmen-Elberfeld, Germany. He emigrated to Holland. He lived at Jan Pietersz Coenstraat 13, Tilburg. He was deported from Westerbork Transit Camp on July 20, 1943, along with his wife Rosa Lowenstein-Eis. He was selected for forced labor in Dorohucza, whilst his wife was gassed immediately. He perished in Dorohucza on November 30, 1943.[407]

MENDELS, Heijman Sallij. Born on November 28, 1908, in Amsterdam. He lived at Hammemstraat 246, Den Haag. He was a Pastry Cook by profession He was deported from the Westerbork Transit Camp on May 11. 1943, to Sobibór. He was selected for forced labor in Dorohucza. He died there on November 30, 1943.

MILECZINA, Raja. She was deported from Minsk to Sobibór during September 1943, along with her cousin Zina Czapnik. At Sobibór she was selected to work at the Trawniki Forced Labor Camp. She managed to hide from the Germans during *Aktion Erntefest* in November 1943, and Raja survived the war.[408]

---

[406] www.sobiborinterviews.nl—online resource.
[407] www.joodsmonument.nl—online resource.
[408] J. Schelvis, *Sobibor*, Berg-Oxford, New York, 2007, p. 220.

MONTEZINOS, Salomon Levie. Born on May 6, 1924, in Den Haag, Holland. He lived at Centraal Israelitich Wees-en Droorganshuis Roodenburgerstraat I a Leiden. He was deported from the Westerbork Transit Camp on April 27, 1943. He arrived in Sobibór on April 30, 1943, where he was selected to work in Dorohucza Forced Labor Camp. He perished in Dorohucza camp on November 30, 1943.[409]

PENHA-BLITS, Mirjam. She lived with her husband Elias, also known as Eddy, and they lived at Argonautenstraat 25 I, Amsterdam. On February 25, 1943, in Amsterdam, 26-year old Mirjam Penha-Blits and her husband Eddy were arrested by the *Sicherheitsdienst (SD)*. First they were taken to the SD headquarters in the Euterpeststraat. They were then taken to Westerbork Transit Camp and from there they were deported to Sobibór on March 10, 1943.

On arrival she was selected for forced labor outside of Sobibór. She was taken to a barrack where she handed over all of her personal possessions and returned to the train she had arrived in. Elias was murdered in the gas chambers immediately.

Other Dutch women also selected were Judith Eliazer, Bertha Ensel, Sophie Huisman, Cato Polak, sisters Suze and Surry Polak and Sientje and Jetje Veterman, they were transported to the Lublin Concentration Camp.

After several days they were moved the short distance to the *Alter Flugplatz* (Old Airfield) Camp in Lubin. There the Dutch women were employed in the hangers sorting the clothes which belonged to the victims that had been murdered in the *Aktion Reinhardt* death camps of Sobibór and Treblinka.

In October 1943, Mirjam and the other Dutch women volunteered to work in a marmalade factory in Milejow and they worked there until they were moved to the Trawniki Forced Labor Camp, just after the *Aktion Erntefest* massacre, where

---

[409] www.joodsmonument.nl—online resource.

they were employed sorting the clothes of those murdered workers.

In May 1944, the Trawniki Labor camp was evacuated and Mirjam was once again sent to the Lublin Concentration Camp, where she worked in the *SS* Laundry. With the Red Army advancing, Mirjam and the other Dutch women were forced to walk to Auschwitz Concentration Camp. After a short stay there she was moved to Bergen-Belsen Concentration Camp in Germany. As the Third Reich diminished she was sent to Fallersleben and then onto another camp at Salzwedel, where she was liberated.[410]

PEPERWORTEL, Nathan. Born on January 29, 1898. He lived at Waterlooplein 89 I, Amsterdam. He was a driver in Amsterdam, by profession. He was deported from Westerbork Transit Camp to Sobibór on April 20, 1943. At Sobibór he was selected to work in the Dorohucza Forced Labor Camp, where he became a *Kapo*. His wife Saartje was murdered in Sobibór on May 7, 1943. Nathan was murdered in Dorohucza on November 30, 1943.[411]

PHILIPS, Meijer. Born on August 15, 1922, in Amsterdam. He lived with his family at Dondersstraat 11, Hilversum. He arrived in Sobibór on July 9, 1943. On arrival he was selected to work in Dorohucza Forced Labor Camp. He was murdered in Dorohucza on November 30, 1943.[412]

POLAK, Cato. On the night of February 26, 1943, all patients and staff of the Jewish hospital in Rotterdam were rounded up by the *Sicherheitsdienst (SD)* and the Dutch *WA* forces and taken to Westerbork Transit Camp. Among them was 22-year old Cato Polak, a nurse from the Hague. She continued her profession in Westerbork. She was deported from Westerbork to

---

[410] www.sobiborinterviews.nl—online resource.
[411] www.joodsmonument.nl—online resource.
[412] Ibid.

Sobibór on March 10, 1943, when she was put on a passenger train to Sobibór.

On arrival at Sobibór Cato, and a number of other Dutch women were put back on the same train and sent to the Lublin Concentration Camp. Then she was sent to the *Alter Flugplatz* (Old Airfield) Camp where she sorted the clothes of the murdered victims, of Sobibór and Treblinka.

In October 1943, Cato and the other Dutch women volunteered to work in a marmalade factory in Milejow and they worked there until they were moved to the Trawniki Forced Labor Camp, just after the *Aktion Erntefest* massacre, where they were employed sorting the clothes of those murdered workers. She was then transferred to the Trawniki Forced Labor Camp, until June 1944, when she returned to the Lublin Concentration Camp.

With the advancing Red Army, Cato was sent to the Auschwitz Concentration Camp. As the Soviet forces advanced she was sent to a munitions factory in Raguhn. She was moved for the last time to the Theresienstadt fortress ghetto near Prague. She was liberated there by the Red Army in May 1945.[413]

POLAK, Surry. On March 10, 1943, sisters Surry and Suze Polak were deported from Westerbork Transit Camp to Sobibór. They were both selected to work, Surry and a number of other Dutch women, including her sister Suze were put back on the same train and sent to the Lublin Concentration Camp. Their next destination was the *Alter Flugplatz* (Old Airfield) where she sorted the clothes of the murdered victims of *Aktion Reinhardt* camps Sobibór and Treblinka.

In October 1943, Surry and the other Dutch women volunteered to work in a marmalade factory in Milejow and they worked there until they were moved to the Trawniki Forced Labor Camp, just after the *Aktion Erntefest* massacre, where they were employed sorting the clothes of those murdered

---

[413] www.sobiborinterviews.nl—online resource.

workers. She was incarcerated in the Trawniki Forced Labor Camp, until June 1944, when she returned to the Lublin Concentration Camp. With the Red Army advancing she was sent to Auschwitz Concentration Camp.

As the Soviet forces advanced she was sent to a munitions factory in Raguhn. She was moved for the last time to the Theresienstadt fortress ghetto near Prague. She was liberated there by the Red Army in May 1945. Surry contracted spotted typhus after the liberation and both she and Suze returned to Holland after Surry had recovered.[414]

POLAK, Suze. On March 10, 1943, sisters Surry and Suze Polak were deported from Westerbork Transit Camp to Sobibór. They were both selected to work, Suze and a number of other Dutch women, including her sister Surry, were put back on the same train and sent to the Lublin Concentration Camp. Their next destination was the *Alter Flugplatz* (Old Airfield) where she sorted the clothes of the murdered victims of *Aktion Reinhardt* camps Sobibór and Treblinka, and helped construct barracks.

In October 1943, Suze and the other Dutch women volunteered to work in a marmalade factory in Milejow and they worked there until they were moved to the Trawniki Forced Labor Camp, just after the *Aktion Erntefest* massacre, where they were employed sorting the clothes of those murdered workers. She was incarcerated in the Trawniki Forced Labor Camp, until June 1944, when she returned to the Lublin Concentration Camp. With the Red Army advancing she was sent to Auschwitz Concentration Camp.

As the Soviet forces advanced she was sent to a munitions factory in Raguhn. She was moved for the last time to the Theresienstadt fortress ghetto near Prague. She was liberated there by the Red Army in May 1945. Surry contracted spotted typhus

---

[414] www.sobiborinterviews.nl—online resource.

after the liberation and both she and Suze returned to Holland after Surry had recovered.[415]

SCHELVIS, Jules. Born on January 7, 1921, in Amsterdam. Jules lived at Nieuwe Kerkstaat 103 III, Amsterdam. Jules worked as a typographer and was arrested with his wife Rachel, who was 20-years old, on May 26, 1943, and sent to Westerbork Transit Camp, with other members of Rachel's family.

They were all transported from Westerbork on June 1, 1943, and they arrived in Sobibór on June 4, 1943. The whole family including Rachel, were murdered in the gas chambers apart from Jules. He was selected for work and entered the train that had brought them, destined for the Dorohucza Forced Labor Camp, where he worked cutting peat in very harsh conditions. Jules Schelvis and other prisoners volunteered for work in a print-shop at the *Alter Flugplatz* (Old Airfield) Camp in Lublin. However, there was no print-shop, just heavy labor. After a short time on June 28, 1943, he was transferred to the Radom ghetto, along with other Dutch Jews, this time to work in a genuine print-shop. When the Radom ghetto was finally liquidated on November 8, 1943, he was moved to the nearby Szkölna Camp.

With the advance of the Soviet forces, Jules Schelvis was forced to walk to Tomaszow Mazowiecki, where they were locked in a rayon factory. Schelvis was then sent to the Auschwitz Concentration Camp, where he was again selected on the ramp for forced labor in another camp.

He was sent to work in a Labor Camp in Vaihingen, near Stuttgart. He was liberated from there by the Allies on April 8, 1945. Jules Schelvis has been extensively quoted throughout this book. He passed away on April 3, 2016. [416]

SCHELVIS, Salomon. Born on July 26, 1916, in Amsterdam. He lived at Vrolikstraat 195 I, Amsterdam and was a Rag Sorter by

---

[415] Ibid.
[416] J. Schelvis, *Sobibor*, Berg-Oxford, New York, 2007.

profession. He was deported to Sobibór, where he was selected to work in the Dorohucza Forced Labor Camp. He perished in Dorohucza on November 30, 1943.[417]

STODEL, Abraham. Born on July 2, 1920, in Amsterdam. He lived at Muiderstraat 19 huis, Amsterdam. He was a Leather-worker by profession. He was deported along with his wife Chaja Stodel-Borzykowski on June 1, 1943, from Westerbork Transit Camp. She was murdered in the gas chambers on June 4, 1943, but Abraham was selected to work in the Dorohucza Forced Labor Camp. He perished in Dorohucza on November 30, 1943.[418]

STRAUSS, Siegfried. Born on March 8, 1905, in Ober-Seemen, Germany. He emigrated to Holland. He was deported from the Westerbork Transit Camp to Sobibór. On arrival at Sobibór he was selected to work at the Dorohucza Forced Labor Camp. He perished in Dorohucza on November 30, 1943.[419]

TROOTSWIJK-HIJMANS, Annie. Born on September 29, 1917, in Amsterdam. During the occupation she lived at Bilderdijkstraat 13, Zwolle. She was deported from Westerbork Transit Camp on March 10, 1943, along with her husband Menno, who was murdered in the gas chambers immediately after arriving. Annie was selected for work in Lublin, at the *Alter Flugplatz* (Old Airfield) Camp, sorting the clothes of the murdered victims from the *Aktion Reinhardt* Camps of Sobibór and Treblinka.

In October 1943, Annie and other Dutch women volunteered to work in a marmalade factory in Milejow and they worked there until they were moved to the Trawniki Forced Labor Camp, around November 12, 1943, just after the *Aktion Erntefest* massacre. In Trawniki they were employed sorting the

---

[417] www.joodsmonument.nl—online resource.
[418] Ibid.
[419] www.bundesarchiv.de/gedenkbuch—online resource.

clothes of those murdered workers. Annie died in Trawniki from Tuberculosis in November 1944.[420]

VERDUIN, Lena. Born on October 6, 1927, in Amsterdam. She lived at Korte Konigsstraat 24 I, Amsterdam. On March 7, 1943, Lena was taken to Westerbork Transit Camp. Three days later on March 10, 1943, she was deported to Sobibór. On arrival she was selected to work, and with a number of other Dutch women, including her sister Sophia, was put back on the same train that they arrived in. They were sent to the Lublin Concentration Camp. The next destination was the *Alter Flugplatz* (Old Airfield) Camp in Lublin, where she sorted the clothes of the murdered victims of the Aktion Reinhardt Camps of Sobibór and Treblinka.

In September 1943, Lena and her sister Sophia were sent to the Blizyn Labor Camp, where they knitted clothes for the Germans. Lena died of Tuberculosis on November 30, 1943, in Blizyn.

VERDUIN, Sophia. Born on April 30, 1926, in Amsterdam. She lived at Korte Konigsstraat 24 I, Amsterdam. On March 7, 1943, Lena was taken to Westerbork Transit Camp. Three days later on March 10, 1943, she was deported to Sobibór. On arrival she was selected to work, and with a number of other Dutch women, including her sister Lena were put back on the same train that they arrived in. They were sent to the Lublin Concentration Camp. The next destination was the *Alter Flugplatz* (Old Airfield) Camp in Lublin, where she sorted the clothes of the murdered victims of the Aktion Reinhardt Camps of Sobibór and Treblinka.

In September 1943, Sophia and her sister Lena were sent to the Blizyn Labor Camp, where they knitted clothes for the Germans. Lena died in Blizyn of Tuberculosis on November 30, 1943. In the spring of 1944, Sophia was taken to Radom and the Szkölna Labor Camp, where she worked on the land.

---

[420] J. Schelvis, *Sobibor*, Berg-Oxford, New York, 2007, p.130.

As the Red Army advanced she was taken to Auschwitz Concentration Camp and on new years eve was sent to Bergen-Belsen Concentration Camp in Germany, where she was liberated by British Forces on April 15, 1945.[421]

VETERMAN, Jetje. In November 1942, Jetje Veterman, who was aged 19-years old, and her sister Sientje were arrested and sent to Westerbork Transit Camp. On March 10, 1943, the two sisters were deported from Westerbork to Sobibór. They were selected to work, Jetje her sister, and other women were put back on the same train they arrived in and were sent to the Lublin Concentration Camp.

The next destination was the *Alter Flugplatz* (Old Airfield) Camp in Lublin. Here they sorted the clothes of the murdered victims from the *Aktion Reinhardt* camps of Sobibór and Treblinka. Jetje contracted typhoid fever here, but recovered and returned to work.

In October 1943, she volunteered to work in a marmalade factory in Milejow. After the *Aktion Erntefest* massacre in November 1943, she was transferred to the Trawniki Labor Camp, where she made clothes for the Germans, until June 1944. Then she returned to the Lublin Concentration Camp, where she worked in the vegetable gardens.

With the advancing Red Army she was transferred to the Auschwitz Concentration Camp. In September 1944, she was put on a transport to Bergen-Belsen Concentration Camp in Germany, without her sister. She was liberated from there by British Forces and she returned to Holland.[422]

VETERMAN, Sientje. In November 1942, Sientje Veterman, and her sister Jientje were arrested and sent to Westerbork Transit Camp. On March 10, 1943, the two sisters were deported from Westerbork to Sobibór. They were selected to work, Sientje and her sister and other women were put back on the same

---

[421] www.sobiborinterviews.nl—online resource.
[422] www.sobiborinterviews.nl—online resource.

train they arrived in and were sent to the Lublin Concentration Camp.

The next destination was the *Alter Flugplatz* (Old Airfield) Camp in Lublin. Here they sorted the clothes of the murdered victims from the *Aktion Reinhardt* camps of Sobibór and Treblinka.

In October 1943, she volunteered to work in a marmalade factory in Milejow. After the *Aktion Erntefest* massacre in November 1943, she was transferred to the Trawniki Labor Camp, where she made clothes for the Germans, until June 1944. Then she returned to the Lublin Concentration Camp, where she worked in the vegetable gardens.

With the advancing Red Army she was transferred to the Auschwitz Concentration Camp. In September 1944, she was put on a transport to Buchenwald Concentration Camp in Germany. Then she was sent to Lippstadt and saw the end of the war in Kaunitz. She returned to Holland and was reunited with her sister Jetje.[423]

VISSER, Kurt Alfred. Born on February 14, 1910, in Nuremburg, Germany. He lived at Konningstraat 41 huis, Amsterdam. He was deported from Westerbork Transit Camp to Sobibór on June 1, 1943. On arrival he was selected to work in the Dorohucza Labor Camp. He perished in Dorohucza on November 30, 1943.[424]

WINS, Jozef. Born on September 25, 1915. He was a typographer who was arrested on March 12, 1943, in Amsterdam. He was sent to the Westerbork Transit Camp, and was deported to Sobibór on May 11, 1943. Three days later he arrived in Sobibór, where he was selected for work in the Dorohucza Labor Camp. Jozef and other typographers were taken to the *Alter Flugplatz* (Old Airfield) Camp in Lublin.

---

[423] Ibid.
[424] www.joodsmonument.nl—online resource.

On June 28, 1943, they were taken to the Radom ghetto to work in a print-shop. When the ghetto was liquidated on November 8, 1943, he was sent to the nearby Szkölna Camp, and after a while he was forced to march to a factory in Tomaszow Mazowiecki. Then Wins found himself in a camp in Kochendorf, near Heilbronn. Jozef was then forced to march to Dachau Concentration Camp, near Munich, where he was liberated by the Allies on April 29, 1945.[425]

---

[425] www.sobiborinterviews.nl—online resource.

Chapter V
The Perpetrators

**Former Nazis who served at Sobibór—
Heinrich Matthes and Kurt Franz, second from right and far right
during the Treblinka Trial in Düsseldorf during 1965
(Image courtesy of the Süddeutsche Zeitung)**

The following chapter is based on information disclosed at the trials of those men who served at the *Aktion Reinhardt* camps, or from survivor accounts and accounts by their fellow officers.

Almost all of them came from the lower middle class—their fathers were factory workers, craftsmen, salesmen or shop workers. Most of the men who served in the death camps had finished extended elementary school, some had been to lower high-school, and a few had attended a secondary school. Some had attended commercial schools or had received vocational training.

351

Those who were former Euthanasia Program employees were mostly former nurses, craftsmen, farm workers, or salesmen.

Almost all of the accused were members of either the *NSDAP* (The Nazi Party), the police, the *SS* (*Schutzstaffel*) or the *SA* (*Sturmabteilung*). Some had joined these organizations before Hitler came to power, others joined the Party later. Their average age at the time they served in the death camps, was between thirty and forty.

The personnel who ran the camps and supervised the extermination activities were absolutely ordinary people. They were not assigned to these roles because of any exceptional qualities or characteristics. The anti-Semitism that festered within them was no doubt part of their milieu and was an accepted phenomenon among large segments of German society. Many of them were married, and most had no criminal record. They had either volunteered to serve in the *SS* or had been drafted into its ranks. It was not unusual that a man wore an *SS* uniform but received his salary from his real employer; the German police, or *Aktion T4*- the Nazi euthanasia program

These men always carried out the murder of hundreds of thousands of men, women and children loyally and without question. What is more, they constantly displayed initiative in trying to improve the extermination process. An integral aspect of their duties was that they were also to exhibit cruelty towards their victims, and many of them contributed their own ideas and innovations for various forms of torture, which served to entertain them all. Under the Nazi regime, these perfectly ordinary people were turned into something extraordinarily inhuman.

Sources and pertinent materials on the daily lives of these men in Sobibór, on their personal feelings about the tasks that they carried out, and their relationship to their innocent victims is almost non-existent. Men more than anxious to cover up their past, were not about to sit down and record their memoirs. Even at their trials, at which some of them were forced to attest to their deeds, very little was brought out about their personal feelings and experiences. The primary sources on the behaviour of these perpetrators and their actual relationship to their victims are the testimonies of those who survived the camps, as well as some material and evidence which was submitted during their trials. The prisoners used to give nicknames to the various *SS* men, and these names were indicative of their reputations and activities in the camp. These nicknames were also a type of code to be used as a warning when a particular *SS* man appeared in a certain area of the camp.

Taking the above restrictions on information into account, it is nevertheless possible to compile a reasonably comprehensive staff list of Sobibór perpetrators. The staff list is compiled from known evidence and information, from various sources however scant, about the perpetrators. The *SS*-garrison only comprised of about twenty to thirty men stationed in the camp at any given time. This list contains the names of mainly *SS* men who were assigned duties at Sobibór during the time of its existence.

Members of the *SS* held key positions in the camp and many of the staff belonged to a police detachment of unknown origin, a few were civilians. *SS* men were sometimes transferred between the three *Aktion Reinhardt* camps, and may have served in Sobibór only briefly. It cannot be ascertained if this list contains all of the staff that served at the camp, as not all of the names of the camp staff or their specific functions could be gleaned from eyewitness reports. Most of the *SS* camp personnel first worked in the euthanasia program (*Aktion T4*) although not all of their functions were known, where this is known it has been included.

After the three *Aktion Reinhardt* camps were demolished, most of the personnel were posted to Northern Italy, assisting with the suppression of partisan activities, rounding-up Jews, confiscating Jewish property and valuables. As the war drew to a close the Nazi command realised that the staff and commanders could incriminate their superiors, and consequently they were sent to dangerous areas where some of them such as Christian

Wirth and Franz Reichleitner, were killed by partisans. As Franz Stangl said afterwards:

> 'We were an embarrassment to the brass. They wanted to find ways to incinerate us.'

What follows are biographies of the members of the key *Aktion Reinhardt* High Command and members of the *SS*-Garrison who served at the Sobibór Death Camp. I am grateful for the recent book by Sara Berger, *'Experten der Vernichtung: das T4 Reinhardt-Netzwerk in den Lagern Bełżec, Sobibór und Treblinka,'* for providing new information. I am also deeply indebted to the research skills of my colleague Georg Biemann, who through sheer persistence, skill, and determination, ended a very long search for me in respect of finding out the real life details of Rudolf Beckmann, who did not come from Osnabruck, as first thought. He also carried out detailed research into the lives of the Wolf brothers from Krumau, their friend Thomas Steffl, and Franz Paul Stangl. I simply cannot thank him enough.

I am also extremely grateful for the research and publication of the book by Ernst Klee, *'Euthanasie im Dritten Reich'*, which provided invaluable biographies on the T4 personnel who worked in the various Euthanasia institutes, before being posted 'east' to work in Bełżec, Sobibór and Treblinka death camps, as part of *Aktion Reinhardt*.

Aktion Reinhardt—Leading Personalities

GLOBOCNIK, Odilo
SS and Police Leader Lublin
Head of Aktion Reinhardt

Odilo Globocnik was born on April 21, 1904, at Via Guilia 34, in Trieste. Globocnik's father was Franz Globocnik, who was born on February 8, 1870, in Trzic. He was a cavalry officer in the Austro-Hungarian Army, and on his discharge he found employment with the postal service in Trieste. Globocnik's mother was Anna Globocnik, formerly Petschinka, who was born on July 24, 1870, in Werschetz.

Odilo Globocnik was imprisoned for over a year on account of political of offences though, he re-emerged as a key liaison figure between Hitler and the Austrian National Socialists. He was appointed provincial Nazi Chief of Carinthia in 1936, and was further promoted to the post of *Gauleiter* of Vienna on May 24, 1938. He was dismissed from this position for illegal speculation in the foreign exchange on January 30, 1939, and was replaced by Josef Burckel.

Globocnik was pardoned by Himmler, and he was appointed to the post of *SS* and Police Leader for the Lublin district on November 9, 1939. He was chosen by Himmler as the central figure in *Aktion Reinhardt*, the mass murder program of Polish Jewry, no doubt because of his scandalous past record and well-known virulent anti-Semitism.

Globocnik built up a special company of *SS* men, not subordinate to any higher authority, and responsible only to Himmler. Globocnik established three death camps in Poland—Bełżec, Sobibór, and Treblinka, as part of *Aktion Reinhardt*. He also had a hand in the creation of Lublin (Majdanek) Concentration Camp. He also built up an economic empire, including the Jewish Labor Camps at Budzyn, Krasnik, Poniatowa, and Trawniki, as well as a number of camps in Lublin itself, such as Lipowa and the Old

Airfield, and various enterprises throughout the Lublin district. Globocnik had offices in Lublin and Warsaw; as confirmed by Franz Stangl, in his 1970's interviews with Gitta Sereny. The Lublin *SS und Polizei* headquarters office was located on *Ostland Strasse 8*, while the Warsaw office was located in the *Befehlsstelle* at 103 Zelazna Street. This location housed the *Einsatz Reinhardt* staff from Lublin during the *Grossaktion*.

Globocnik was also responsible for clearing Polish peasant farmers from the Zamość Lands and replacing them with ethnic Germans. Globocnik and some of his cohorts amassed rich rewards, from the slaughter of approximately 1.6 million Jews whose property and valuables were seized by the SS, and his various business interests. As his situation reports showed, Globocnik carried out Himmler's orders with brutal efficiency, by November 1943, *Aktion Reinhardt* had been completed and the three death camps under his control had been liquidated.

On September 13, 1943, Himmler wrote to Globocnik appointing him to the post of Higher *SS* and Police Leader for the Adriatic Coastal Zone, based in Trieste, and replacing him in Lublin with Jakob Sporrenberg. Himmler instructed Globocnik to produce a final accounting statement regarding the assets and economic achievements of *Aktion Reinhardt* by December 31, 1943. Globocnik provided a portfolio and, on January 5, 1944, produced a detailed appendix. This appendix demonstrated that 178 million Reichmark had been added to the Reich's finance coffers, as a result of *Aktion Reinhardt*.

Odilo Globocnik married Lore Peterschinegg in October 1944, she was head of the Carinthian BDM *(Bund Deutscher Mädel)*. They had one son, Peter, born in January 1946.

At the end of the Second World War, Globocnik succeeded in evading arrest by returning to his native country, in the mountains south of Klagenfurt. He was eventually tracked down and arrested by a British army patrol at Wiessensee. He committed suicide by swallowing a cyanide capsule at Paternion, Austria, on May 31, 1945.

HÖFLE, Hermann Julius
Deputy Head of Aktion Reinhardt

Born on June 19, 1911, in Salzburg, Austria. Hermann Höfle was a trained mechanic and drove a taxi in Salzburg, and then went on to own his own taxi company. He married Berta Duehr on October 29, 1933. The couple lived at Elisabethstrasse 10a in Salzburg, and later they moved to Hubert Sattlergasse 13. Höfle and his wife had four children, though two of his children, who were twins, died, and at their graveside he lamented; 'This is punishment for the children of Warsaw.' His personnel file lists the birthdates of his children, but not their names.

He joined the Nazi Party and the SS on August 1, 1933. He led *SS-Sturmbann 1/76* after serving a brief prison sentence. He served for three months in Znaim, in the Sudetenland and attended the *Führerschule* in Dachau. After the invasion of Poland, he served in a *Selbstschutz* unit in Nowy Sączs (Neu Sandez). During 1940, he was the Leader of the Labor Camps employed on building the border fortifications known as the *'Bug-Graben'*, near Bełżec in the Lublin district.

On July 17, 1941, *RFSS* Heinrich Himmler appointed Odilo Globocnik as his Plenipotentiary for the Construction of *SS* and Police bases in the newly occupied Eastern Territories, and Höfle was sent from Lublin to Mogilev to supervise construction work there. Höfle was then recalled by Globocnik to Lublin and was responsible for overseeing the construction of the death camp at Bełżec. He was appointed by Globocnik to act as the Deputy Head of *Aktion Reinhardt*, which was the name given in 1942, to the mass murder program of Polish Jewry, following the death of Reinhard Heydrich in Prague.

Höfle was highly regarded by Globocnik and he played a leading role in the mass deportation *'Aktion'* in Warsaw, during July-September 1942,—which sent hundreds of thousands of Jews to their deaths in the Treblinka death camp—and the clearance of the Białystok Ghetto during the summer of 1943.

Whilst in Lublin, Höfle lived and worked in the *Julius Schreck Kaserne*, the headquarters of *Aktion Reinhardt* at *Litauer Strasse 11*. his associate Georg Michalsen, who worked for Höfle in the mass deportations from Warsaw and Białystok, provided a description of this building:

> The staff building was a three-storey house. On the ground floor—immediately by the entrance—there was a transport squad. On the first floor—on one side—there was the administration, accounts and archive (documents) offices. Here the chief-of-staff also had a room and an ante-room. On the second floor there was located the personnel department was located. Here Hermann Höfle also had his living quarters in one room.

Höfle also played a key administrative role in the destruction of the remaining Jewish workers, according to the post-war testimony of Jakob Sporrenberg—the SS and Police Leader for Lublin,—who had replaced Odilo Globocnik. This mass murder frenzy, ordered by Himmler, was known as 'Aktion Erntefest'— Harvest Festival—and this resulted in the mass murder of over 40,000 Jewish workers on November 3-4, 1943, in a number of labor camps in Lublin itself, and also at the camps in Poniatowa and Trawniki, by means of shooting in specially prepared ditches.

Höfle left Lublin and briefly served as the Commander of a Guard Unit at Sachsenhausen Concentration Camp. This was followed by spells of duty in Belgium and the Netherlands. He was re-united with Globocnik, who was now in Trieste, probably in late 1944. Höfle was amongst a group of SS men who were captured by the British Army. He was photographed beside the body of Globocnik—who had swallowed poison at Paternion, Austria on May 31, 1945.

Höfle learned in 1948, that the Polish Communist government wanted to extradite him to Poland to stand trial for war crimes he had allegedly committed there. With help he fled first to Italy and then returned to his native Austria. Making his way to Bavaria, he worked for the American Counter Intelligence Corps (CIC) as a low level agent. Höfle was again arrested in 1961 and he committed suicide on August 21, 1962, in a Vienna prison cell during pre-trial detention.

LERCH, Ernst
Chief of Globocnik's Personal Office

Ernst Lerch was born in Klagenfurt, Austria on November 19, 1914. According to his initial British interrogation report, he was educated in Klagenfurt and briefly studied at the *Hochschule fur Welthandel* in Vienna. From 1931, to 1934, he worked as a waiter in various hotels in Switzerland, France and Hungary to learn the hotel trade. From 1934, until Austria was annexed by the Reich, he was employed in the café of his father in Klagenfurt. It was during this time at the café—before the *Anschluss*—that he met Odilo Globocnik, Ernst Kaltenbrunner and Kurt Kutschera and other leading Austrians who served the Nazis after the *Anschluss* in March 1938. In 1939 Kurt Kutschera changed his surname to Claasen, and later, along with Lerch, worked with Globocnik in Lublin.

Lerch had become a member of the illegal Nazi Party and the *SD* from 1936, the annexation brought him promotion to the rank of an *SD-Hauptsturmführer*, and he became an *SD-Leiter*, a post he resigned from in July 1938. He was called up to serve in the German Army and served in the Polish campaign as a signals corporal, in 1940, he was released from the army and employed with the *Fremdenverkehrsverband Kärnten* in connection with the resettlement of German hotel proprietors from South Tyrol. According to Lerch, in his interrogation with the British in September 1941, he joined the *Waffen-SS* and was appointed *Rasse- und Seidlungsführer* based in Krakow in the *Generalgouvernement*. However, Lerch joined Globocnik (the *SSPF* Lublin), on December 20, 1941, became chief of Globocnik's personal office, and *Stabsführer der Allgemeinen-SS*.

Lerch played a leading role in *Aktion Reinhardt;* responsible for Jewish affairs, he was also responsible for the radio link between the *Aktion Reinhardt* Headquarters in Lublin and Berlin. During his interrogation by the British forces after his capture Lerch conveniently lied about his time in Lublin during the incriminating years between 1942, and 1943, stating he was in Klagenfurt and *Krakau*. At the former trial of the former *Gestapo* Chief in Lublin, Hermann Worthoff, it was stated that Lerch had overseen the liquidation of thousands of Jews from the Majdan Tatarski Ghetto in Lublin at the nearby Krepiec Forest. Lerch also attended the funerals at the Chelm Military Cemetery, when the SS men who were killed in the prisoner revolt were buried on October 18, 1943.

When *Aktion Reinhardt* was finished, Lerch was transferred to Italy in September 1943, together with some of Globocnik's staff. In Trieste he continued to serve as chief of Globocnik's personal staff in Adriatic Coastal Area. He was also involved in anti-partisan operations, and for a few weeks Lerch was provisional police commander in Fiume. After the German surrender in Italy he made his way back to Carinthia, his homeland, where he was captured along with Odilo Gobocnik, Hermann Höfle, Georg Michaelsen and Karl Helletsberger, near the Wiessensee Lake. He was interrogated by the British forces in Wolfsberg, from where he escaped and went into hiding between 1947, and 1950. Lerch was eventually brought to trial on May 15,1972, but the trial was suspended and adjourned *sine die*. Ernst Lerch died in 1997, in Klagenfurt, having never been brought to justice.

MICHALSEN, Georg
Einsatz Reinhardt Member

Georg Michalsen was born as Georg Michalczyk, on September 13, 1906, in Wendrin, Upper Silesia. The son of a school-teacher, he attended school in Opole between the years 1912 to 1920. He then served an apprenticeship in a law firm in Opole. Afterwards, he worked in agricultural co-operatives and in the construction industry.

Michalczyk joined the *'Wehrwolf'*, a regional organization, in 1924, and on November 1, 1928, he became a member of the Nazi Party. He served in a number of roles in Opole, such as treasurer. He also belonged to the *SA*-Reserve. On January 10, 1932, Michalczyk transferred from the *SA* to the *SS*. His *SS* number was 29337.

Following the German attack on Poland in September 1939, Michalczyk belonged to an *SS* unit which occupied Częstochowa. In Poland Michalczyk commanded a 70 strong squad of *SS* men, who trained *Volksdeutsche Selbstschutz* units in Petrikau, Opoczno and Rawa. This para-military organization was established as an auxiliary police force.

During 1940, Michalczyk married, and in the same year he changed his Polish sounding name to Michalsen. Following service in the *SS* and Police Leader's office in Radom, he was transferred to serve in the same capacity in Lublin, which was under the control of *SSPF* Odilo Globocnik.

Globocnik had been appointed by *RFSS* Heinrich Himmler after the German invasion of the Soviet Union to construct *SS* and Police strongpoints in the East- and Michalsen was appointed to head this activity in Riga. Michalsen returned to Lublin and became part of the *Aktion Reinhardt Kommando*, under Hermann Höfle. Michalsen assisted Höfle in the resettlement of the Jews of the Warsaw Ghetto, commencing in July 1942. Michalsen, along with Hermann Höfle, met with Adam Czerniaków and other members of the Warsaw *Judenrat* on July 22, 1942, to order the start of deportations in Warsaw to the Treblinka death camp.

After July 27, 1942, Michalsen, the Deputy Head of the resettlement commando, was deployed at the *Umschlagplatz*, the place where the cattle cars left for Treblinka. During the mass deportation *'Aktion'* in Warsaw, the resettlement squad, under Michalsen's command, was deployed to the nearby towns of Otwock, Wolomin and Miedzyrzec-Podlaski, during August 1942.

Michalsen was then involved in deportations within the Lublin district in Piaski and Włodawa. Michalsen returned to the

Warsaw Ghetto in the spring of 1943, during the Jewish uprising, to organize the transfer of major factories, such as Többens and Schultz, to the Poniatowa and Trawniki Labor Camp sites.

Between February 1943, and August 16, and 23, 1943, Michalsen was involved in the dissolution of the ghetto in Białystok, where over 17,000 Jews were deported to the Treblinka death camp.

In the autumn of 1943, Himmler appointed Globocnik to the post of Higher SS and Police Leader for the Adriatic Coastal Zone, based in Trieste, where Michalsen soon joined him. He became head of the *HSSPF*'s personnel department and was later involved in anti-partisan combat in Istria.

Michalsen was captured by British Forces in Paternion, in Carinthia, Austria, along with Globocnik, Höfle, Lerch, and others on May 31, 1945. Both Michalsen and Lerch were interviewed by the British Army on June 5, 1945, but both of them failed to disclose that they had participated in the mass murder of Jews when serving under Globocnik.

Michalsen was released from captivity during 1948, and he settled in Hamburg, where he worked as an accountant. He was arrested on January 24, 1961, but released. He was arrested again in 1961 and stood trial. On July 25, 1974, Georg Michalsen was sentenced to twelve years imprisonment by the Regional Court of Hamburg. He died on May 21, 1993.

GÖTH, Amon
Einsatz Reinhardt Member

Amon Leopold Göth was born on December 11. 1908 in Vienna. He was married twice, being divorced in 1934, and again in 1944. He had two children. He studied agriculture in Vienna until 1928, then from 1928, until 1939, he was employed by the company of *'Verlag für Militär und Fachliteratur'* in Vienna.

In 1932, Göth joined the *NSDAP*, his party membership number 510764, he joined the SS in 1940, his SS number was 43673. On

5 March 1940 he was drafted into the *Wehrmacht*, with the rank of *Unterfeldwebel*.

He was promoted in succession to *SS-Obersturmführer* in 1940, and *Untersturmführer* in 1941, with the letter F denoting professional officer in war time. The final rank Göth obtained was *SS-Hauptsturmführer*, in 1944, and he was a holder of the Cross of Merit with swords besides. After serving at Cieszyn and the *Volksdeutsche Mittlestelle* in Kattowice, Göth was transferred to Odilo Globocnick's staff in Lublin in June 1942, for participation in *'Judenumseidlung'* (Jewish Deportations), as part of *Aktion Reinhardt*. He commanded the deportation *'Aktion'* in the Zamość ghetto. In February 1943, he left Lublin after a conflict with SS Major Hermann Höfle, Globocnik's Chief of Staff for *Aktion Reinhardt*. He was transferred to *Krakau* with the rank of *SS-Unterscharführer*, as the Commandant of Plaszow Labor camp.

Göth served in *Krakau* from 11 February 1943, until 13 September 1944, and it was clear that Göth had arrived in *Krakau* with a brief to destroy the remaining Jews of *Krakau*. In order to wipe out the Jews of *Krakau* the Germans chose a most symbolic site for a camp—the new Jewish cemetery on the outskirts of the city, in the suburb of Plaszow. There huts were constructed, in desecration of the freshly-dug graves, and a sign was hung up 'Arbeitslager' (Labor Camp). Amon Göth played a leading role in the destruction of a number of Jewish ghettos; including the Zamość and Rzeszow Ghettos in 1942, where the Jews were deported to the death camp at Bełżec; the *Krakau* ghetto on 14 March 13-14, 1943, where he personally shot about 50 children. He also supervised the liquidation of the Tarnów Ghetto in early September 1943, when 10,000 Jews were deported to Plaszow, and 4,000 were killed. During the liquidation of the Tarnów Ghetto, he shot a girl who asked him for a transfer to a different working group to be together with her fiancé.

Göth also prepared, under the leadership of Willi Haase, plans for the liquidation of ghettos in Bochnia, Rzeszow and Przemysl. On September 13, 1944, Göth was arrested by the *SS- und*

Polizeigericht VI (Police Court) in *Krakau* for large-scale fraud. Göth was also interrogated by the *Sicherheitspolizei* (Security Police) for giving information to the engineer Grunberg about the liquidation of the *Krakau* Ghetto. Grunberg, a German, was sympathetic to the Jews and closely associated with Stern, Pemper and Oskar Schindler. He had passed the information on to Schindler, who in turn warned the ghetto leaders. Göth was released from prison in January 1945, due to his diabetes and was moved to a sanatorium in Bad Tolz. There he was arrested by the Americans. The Americans agreed to the request to extradite Göth to Poland following a request by the Polish authorities and Göth was tried before the Polish Supreme Court on charges of committing mass murder during the liquidations of the ghettos in Krakow and Tarnów and the camps at Plaszow and Szebnie. He was sentenced to death in Krakow on September 5, 1946, and hung in the former camp at Plaszow on September 13, 1946, defiantly saluting Hitler.

THOMALLA, Richard
Construction Supervisor—Otto Line
Chief of Construction for *Aktion Reinhardt* at Sobibór and Treblinka Camps

Born on October 23, 1903 in *Sabine-bei-Annahof* (today, Sowin in Polish Silesia), in the Falkenberg District of Upper Silesia. A builder by profession, he was bi-lingual in German and Polish, and joined the *SS* on July 1, 1932, and the Nazi Party a month later. On October 5, 1935, Thomalla married Margarete Bruckner. He saw military service in Falkenberg and Oppeln, and service in the *SS* in Wohlau and Breslau (Wrocław)—in the present-day southeastern part of Polish Lower Silesia. His *SS* Number was 41206.

On September 6, 1940, Thomalla was transferred from Breslau to the *Generalgouvernement* where he was a member of the *SS-Hilfspolizei* (auxiliary police) in the cities of Czestochowa and Radom. On August 22, 1940, he was transferred by Friedrich-

Wilhelm Krüger, the *HSSPF Ost,* based in Krakau, to serve under Odilo Globocnik, *SSPF* Lublin. From August to October 1940 was a Section Leader of the *SS*-Border Defence Construction Service in Bełżec, on the demarcation line between the *Generalgouvernement* and Soviet-occupied Galicia (Western Ukraine). He lived in the Bełżec village at Zamojska Street 15.[426] His first task was the establishment of a construction depot of the *Waffen-SS* and Police in Zamość, about 40 kilometres north of Bełżec.

After the invasion of Russia, Thomalla was also in charge of constructing *SS* strongpoints in the Ukraine, with branch offices in Zwiahel, and Kiev. He was recalled by Globocnik to Lublin at the beginning of 1942, whether he was involved at all in the construction activities at Bełżec is open to question. What is not open to any doubt is, that after returning to the Lublin district he was the construction chief at the next two death camps. He oversaw construction of the *Aktion Reinhardt* camps at Sobibór and Treblinka, in early 1942. At both camps, he was the senior *SS*-officer at each site until the camps became operational.

In 1943, he headed *Waffen-SS* construction offices in Riga, the capital of Nazi-occupied Latvia, and at Mogilev in White Russia. Later during 1943-44, Thomalla also played a role in the 'pacification' operations of the *SS* and police in Zamość district.

He was last seen in Zamość in June 1944, a few weeks before the entry of the Red Army into the town the following month. He was arrested by the Russians near Jicin, on the Czechoslovakian side of the Czech-Polish border. He was held in a special prison nearby for members of the *SS* and Nazi Party officials at *Karthaus-Waliditz*. On May 12, 1945, Thomalla was 'ordered out of his cell, with all his belongings'. This was a typical order by the Soviet *NKVD* immediately before the prisoner was executed.

---

[426] Information supplied by Tomasz Hanejko on May 26, 2021.

WIRTH, Christian
First Commandant of Bełżec Death Camp &
Inspector of SS Sonderkommando *Aktion Reinhardt*

Born on November 24, 1885 in Oberbalzheim, a small village in the Upper Swabian part of Württemberg in south-west Germany. After completing elementary education at the age of 14, he was employed as an apprentice carpenter with the Bühler brothers' timber firm in Oberbalzheim. From 1905-1907 he served his two year draft with Grenadier Regiment 123 in Ulm, and after a short break, re-enlisted for another two years as an army instructor.

After honourable discharge from the army in 1910, Wirth joined the Württemberg State Police as a uniformed constable in Heilbronn. In the same year he married Maria Bantel with whom he had two sons; the first was Eugen, who was born on May 22, 1911; his second son, Kurt, was born on September 22, 1922. Two other children died shortly after birth.

In 1913, Wirth transferred to the *Kriminalpolizei (Kripo)*, the plain clothes detective squads, at their headquarters on *Büchsenstrasse*, near the city centre in Stuttgart. In October 1914, two months after the outbreak of World War I, he volunteered to serve in the army of *Kaiser* Wilhelm II and saw action on the Western Front in Flanders and northern France in the ranks of Reserve Infantry Regiprograment 246. He received a field promotion to acting officer (*Offiziersstellvertreter*) and was awarded several medals and decorations for bravery, including the Iron Cross I and II Class, and the Gold Württemberg Military Service Medal. At the end of 1917, Wirth was transferred back to Stuttgart as an officer in the Military Police, guarding a supply depot for Reserve Infantry Regiment 119. During this duty he won high praise for defending the depot against the *Spartakists*, the forerunners of the German Communist Party, who attempted to raid the depot for weapons and ammunition.

Wirth re-joined the *Kripo* in 1919, and by 1923, was the head of Precinct II (*Dienststelle II*) on *Büchsenstrasse* in Stuttgart. He earned a reputation for solving difficult crimes that had defeated other officers, often by using brutal methods of interrogation. His 'dedication and zealous methods' finally led to questions being asked about him in the Württemberg Regional Parliament (*Landtag*).

In 1937, Wirth was the head or deputy head of all police and Party organizations, not only in Stuttgart, but the whole of Württemberg. This resulted in his recruitment by Reinhard Heydrich's Security Service (*Sicherheitsdienst–SD*) as a '*V-Mann*' (*Vertrauensmann*), a confidential agent spying and informing on his Party and police comrades. His SS Number was 345464.

By 1939, Wirth had reached the rank of *Kriminalinspektor*, in charge of *Kommissariat 5*, a special detective squad for investigating serious crimes, including murder. Wirth then carried out special police duties in Vienna, Austria and in Olmütz, Czechoslovakia. In the spring of 1939, a special remark was inserted into his personal file: 'At the disposal of the *Führer* ('z.V. *Führer*'). He had been earmarked for future 'special tasks'.

In the autumn of 1939, Wirth began the first 'special task', as founder member of the euthanasia planning team in Hitler's private Chancellery. His well-known reputation for 'meticulous administration and organization' was put to use in setting up the bureaucracy. In mid-January 1940 he was among a group of high-ranking Nazi officials who witnessed the first test-gassing of psychiatric patients in the abandoned prison in Brandenburg-an-der-Havel. Among this group were *Reichsleiter* Philipp Bouhler, head of Hitler's private Chancellery; Dr. Karl Brandt, Hitler's escorting physician; Dr. Leonardo Conti, Secretary of State for Health; and *SS-Standartenführer* Viktor Brack, chief of Head Office II in Hitler's private Chancellery. Brack was soon to be in charge of the daily running of the euthanasia operation under the code designation 'T4', named after its headquarters in a villa at *Tiergartenstrasse 4* in Berlin-Charlottenburg.

At the beginning of February 1940, Wirth arrived at the first 'T4' euthanasia institute established in Grafeneck castle in the Swabian mountains, 60 kilometres south of Stuttgart, in charge of administration and security. In May 1940, Wirth was appointed 'roving inspector' of the euthanasia institutions; to tighten-up discipline among the staff—which had deteriorated alarmingly—, improve security, and streamline the killing process, and ensuing paperwork. He spent much of his time in the Euthanasia Institution in Hartheim castle, near Linz in Upper Austria. It was here that he encountered the police officer Franz Stangl, the future commandant of the *Aktion Reinhardt* death camps at Sobibór and Treblinka. At Hartheim castle, Stangl was in charge of administration and security, and his first meeting with Wirth made a profound impression on him:

> Wirth was a gross and florid man. My heart sank when I met him. He stayed at Hartheim for several days that time and often came back. Whenever he was there he addressed us daily at lunch. And here it was again this awful verbal crudity: when he spoke about the necessity for this euthanasia operation, he was not speaking in humane or scientific terms ... he laughed. He spoke of 'doing away with useless mouths', and that sentimental slobber about such people made him puke.'[427]

Stangl also testified during a pre-trial interrogation that Christian Wirth was involved in liquidating mentally ill patients at a hospital in Chelm, during 1941.

Just before Christmas 1941, Wirth arrived in Bełżec where the first *Aktion Reinhardt* death camp was under construction, and in the New Year returned to the 'T4' Euthanasia Institution at Bernburg to select the first group of 15 men to staff the camp.

Between mid-January and the beginning of March 1942, he experimented with different methods of gassing, including, in the early days, using the exhaust fumes from a Post Office parcel delivery van converted into a mobile gas chamber. He also tried pumping the exhaust fumes from army trucks into three primitive gas chambers, before trying *Zyklon B*, a pesticide issued to all German military units in the field, and bottled carbon monoxide

---

[427] Sereny, *Into That Darkness*......, op.cit., p.54.

(CO) gas. This was the method used in the 'T4' euthanasia institutes.

He finally decided that CO gas produced from engines was the most efficient and had a Russian tank engine brought from a depot of captured Russian vehicles in *Lemberg* (today Lvov in the Ukraine). This method for gassing was then applied in the other two *Aktion Reinhardt* death camps Sobibór and Treblinka.

In time, Wirth also perfected the 'conveyor-belt' method of mass murder, in which the Jews themselves carried out most of the tasks in the extermination process, working permanently at specific points to ensure its smooth continuity. This method, too, was also adopted at Sobibór and Treblinka. Wirth ran the Bełżec death camp with a rod of iron, feared not only by Jews, but also by his own staff; Germans and Ukrainians alike.

After ensuring that Bełżec was operating efficiently, on August 1, 1942, *SS-Brigadeführer* Globocnik appointed Wirth to the post of Inspector of the three SS-*Sonderkommando's* operating at Bełżec, Sobibór and Treblinka—'*Abteilung Reinhard—Inspekteur der SS-Sonderkommando Aktion Reinhardt*'—with his office at first in the '*Julius Schreck* Barracks', the headquarters of *Aktion Reinhardt* in Lublin. At the end of the year, Wirth's Inspectorate was moved to a building on the Old Airfield just outside Lublin and close to the Lublin concentration camp (Majdanek).

Dov Freiberg, a survivor from Sobibór, recalled in his memoirs about Christian Wirth in Sobibór:

> 'Wirth riding a horse dressed in a white uniform with a cape over his shoulders.'

From mid-August 1942, Wirth played a leading role in the re-organization of Treblinka, including the construction of the new gas chambers, and thereafter visited the camp frequently. Wirth was also present when *RFSS*-Heinrich Himmler visited Sobibór death camp on February 12, 1943.

On September 20, 1943, Globocnik, Wirth, Stangl, and several Ukrainian guards from the *Aktion Reinhardt* death camps, were transferred to Trieste in northern Italy—where Globocnik had been appointed the Higher *SS* and Police Leader for the Adriatic Coastal Region. Wirth was given command of three special units formed from former *Aktion Reinhardt* personnel, including many of the Ukrainian guards, most of whom had arrived in Trieste by the end of the year.

Based in the buildings of an old rice husking factory in the San Sabba suburb of Trieste, their task was rounding-up and deporting the remaining Italian Jews to *Auschwitz-Birkenau,* and confiscating their property. Under the code designation '*Einsatz R*' (Operation 'R') these tasks were merely an extension of *Aktion Reinhardt*, albeit on a far smaller scale.

Wirth, however, turned the San Sabba factory into an interrogation centre and mini-death camp for Jews and captured Italian and Yugoslav partisans. Executions were carried out by shooting, hanging or beating to death with a mallet. For a time, a gas-van was also used. Erwin Lambert, who had constructed the gas chambers at the 'T4' euthanasia institutions and supervised construction of the new and bigger gas chambers at Treblinka and Sobibór, converted a basement heating furnace into a crematorium to dispose of the bodies of the victims. The charred and burnt human bones and ashes were dumped into the Adriatic from a boat or a jetty in the harbour.

Christian Wirth returned to Lublin and, on behalf of Globocnik, played a leading role in the mass murder of the Jewish workers employed in a number of labor camps; those within the Lublin district; in Lublin itself; and at Poniatowa and Trawniki. The mass murder of 18,000 Jews alone at Lublin, 15,000 at Poniatowa and 10,000 at Trawniki was the last mass killing of the Jews within the *Generalgouvernement*. Wirth's involvement in these mass killings were revealed during post-war interrogations with Jakob Sporrenberg, *SSPF* Lublin, who had taken over this post from Globocnik.

By the spring of 1944, Globocnik was aware that the tide of the war was turning against Germany and became concerned about the mass murders in Poland and Italy, for which he was ultimately responsible. He therefore forbade Wirth to carry out any more killing of prisoners in San Sabba. Wirth's special units were switched instead to anti-partisan duty on the Istrian peninsula, where they committed atrocities against the Yugoslav and Italian population under the guise of 'pacification operations'.

Christian Wirth was ambushed and killed by Yugoslav partisans of the First Battalion of the *'Istrska'* (Istrian) Division on May 26, 1944, near Kozina, just outside Trieste. He was on his way by car to inspect one of his *SS*-units in Fiume (today, Rijeka in Croatia) on the other side of the peninsula.

Wirth was buried with full military honours in the German Military Cemetery in the small village of Opicina, up on the Karst above Trieste. During the late 1950's-early 1960's, the remains of all German war dead in Italy were exhumed from their widely-scattered graves and reinterred in a new and large German Military Cemetery at Costermano, on the south-eastern shore of Lake Garda, near Verona in northern Italy. For many years, the presence of Wirth's grave at Costermano has been a matter of bitter dispute, although his *SS*-rank has been erased from his gravestone and his name removed from the Roll of Honour in the Propylaeum.

Sobibór Death Camp— Commandants

STANGL, Franz Paul
First Commandant of Sobibór and Second Commandant of Treblinka

April 1942–August 1942

Born on March 26, 1908, in Altmünster, a market town on the western shore of the Traunsee, near Gmunden in Upper Austria. His parents were Albert Stangl, who was born on April 21, 1853, in Pinsdorf, Austria, and his mother was Theresia, who was born on January 15, 1872, in Talheim, Austria.

Although his father was already advanced in years and his mother was still a young woman, they had only one other child, a daughter. In 1916, when Franz was eight years old, his father Albert died of malnutrition. A year later, his mother remarried a widower and Franz gained a step-brother and a step-sister.

After leaving school aged 15, Stangl became an apprentice in the weaving trade and three years later qualified as a master weaver, the youngest in Austria. Five years later in 1931, he realized that his job held no future prospects and he applied to join the Federal Austrian Police.

After acceptance and a year's training at the police school in Linz and a probationary period, he served in the Traffic Division and then with the Riot Squad. He recalled his tough training with some bitterness and that his colleagues were 'a sadistic lot, who were indoctrinated with the feeling that everyone was against them, that all men were rotten.'

During 1935, he was transferred to the Political Division of the Criminal Investigation Department (CID) in Wels, the biggest city in Upper Austria, not far from Linz. Franz Stangl married Theresa Eidenbock in October 1935, in Wels. They had three girls between the years 1936, and 1944. Brigitte, the eldest, was born in 1936, Renate in 1937, and the youngest, Isolde, was born in 1944.

In 1936, Stangl joined the Nazi Party, which had been banned in Austria since the assassination of Chancellor Dolfuss by the Nazis in 1934. After the Nazi annexation of Austria in March 1938, the so-called *Anschluss*, Stangl's department was absorbed into the *Gestapo*, and the Wels department was transferred to Linz. Stangl was promoted to the rank of *Kriminal-Oberassistent*, under the supervision of Georg Prohaska, a Bavarian police officer. The two officers took an immediate dislike to one another. Stangl also held the equivalent rank of *Polizei-Oberleutnant* in the uniformed police—the *Schutzpolizei (Schupo)*—and like Christian Wirth, he was also a member of Reinhard Heydrich's Security Service (*Sicherheitsdienst–SD*). Stangl's SS Number was 296569. His Nazi Party Number was 6370447.

On November 3, 1940, Stangl was recruited into the T4 Organization and was posted to the *Schloss Hartheim* Euthanasia institute near Linz, as Deputy Head of Administration and in charge of security. Later he carried out the same role at the Bernburg Euthanasia institute, where Dr Irmfried Eberl, who was later the commandant of the Treblinka death camp, was the Medical Director.

In the early spring of 1942, *SS-Obersturmführer* Franz Stangl was ordered to report to *SS-Brigadeführer* Odilo Globocnik in Lublin, who appointed him as the first Commandant of the latest death camp at Sobibór, on the River Bug in eastern Poland. The camp began its mass murder operations a few weeks later in May 1942, although a few transports are known to have arrived at the end of April, whose occupants were used in trial gassings to test the gas chambers.

In Sobibór, Stangl made use of his skill as a weaver to sew himself the famous white linen uniform, which later gave him the nickname 'White Death.' Sobibór was surrounded by swamps and in the heat of summer the area was plagued by all kinds of insects, especially mosquitoes. Stangl claimed that because of this, he preferred to wear this uniform.

Sometime between mid-August 1942, and the end of that month, Franz Stangl was transferred from Sobibór to Treblinka, to take over command of the death camp from Dr Eberl, who had created chaos in the camp. In Treblinka, Stangl had very little contact with the victims he sent to their deaths, or the Jewish prisoners employed in the camp. He was seen only on rare occasions, in summer wearing his distinctive white tunic. Through Stangl's flair for organization and his dedication in running the death camp, he earned an official commendation as the 'best Camp Commandant in Poland.' He was promoted to the rank of *SS-Hauptsturmführer,* according to the promotion list dated March 20, 1943.

Just prior to the revolt in Treblinka, on August 2, 1943, Stangl was attacked by partisans on July 30, 1943, in his car, on an official journey between the Sobibór death camp and Chelm,—according to a *KdO* Lublin report dated July 31, 1943.

Soon after the Treblinka revolt on August 2, 1943, Stangl was expected to be summoned to face a court martial because of the Jewish prisoners' actions. Instead he was posted to Trieste in Northern Italy, where he spent a short time at San Sabba. He did not face a court martial because no *SS* had been killed during the revolt and he was therefore not obliged to submit a report to Berlin.

In Italy, Stangl was appointed as the Commander of special *SS* and Police units in Fiume (today, Rijeka in Croatia), and Udine, with the task of rounding-up Jews, confiscating their property and shipping them to San Sabba. Later he was engaged in construction projects, defending the Po Valley against the Allied advance from the south.

At the end of the Second World War, Stangl fled over the border to Austria, where he was interned by US Forces, because of his membership of the *SS*. From the late summer of 1947, he was imprisoned in Linz, accused of having participated in the gassing of mentally-ill patients at *Schloss Hartheim.*

In May 1948, he escaped and made his way to Rome, where he received help from the Austrian Bishop Alois Hudal, who arranged for a Red Cross passport and money for Stangl to flee to Syria. In Damascus Stangl found employment in a textile factory, his wife and family joined him soon afterwards. He was later employed by the Imperial Knitting Company.

In 1951, he emigrated with his family to Sao Paulo, Brazil, where he worked in the Volkswagen factory. He started as a mechanic, but gained promotion and was in charge of preventative maintenance.

It was not until the mid-1960's that the Nazi hunter Simon Wiesenthal (in Vienna), learned of Stangl's whereabouts. For a total of $7,000—one cent for every Jew killed—an informer agreed to divulge Stangl's address. He was arrested by the Brazilian authorities and in 1967, was extradited to West Germany.

Stangl was sentenced to life imprisonment in 1970, by a court in Düsseldorf. He passed away a year later, due to a heart attack, in Düsseldorf prison on June 28, 1971.

REICHLEITNER, Franz Karl
Second Commandant of Sobibór

Born on December 2, 1906, in Ried, Austria. He was a member of the Linz Gestapo, with the rank of *Krimminalsekretär.* After service in the T4 Euthanasia Institute at *Schloss Hartheim* in Austria, he was appointed to the post of the second Commandant at Sobibór, replacing Franz Stangl, who had been transferred to the Treblinka death camp in August 1942. Reichleitner was also a member of the *SS*-Security Service (*Sicherheitsdienst–SD*). His *SS* Number was 357065, and his *SS* rank on becoming the Commandant of Sobibór was *SS-Obersturmführer.*

Moshe Bahir, one of the Sobibór inmates who escaped during the revolt on October 14, 1943, wrote about Reichleitner:

Reichleitner, a man in his late forties, with an Austrian accent, was dressed always with great elegance and wore gloves. He did not have direct contact with the Jews and the transports. He knew that he could rely on his subordinates, who were very frightened of him. He ran the camp with German precision. During his time the *Aktionen* went smoothly, and all the transports that arrived on a certain day were liquidated. He never left them for the following day.[428]

He ruled the death camp more strictly than Stangl, but was seldom seen in the camp. The prisoners nicknamed him *'Trottel'* (Idiot), as that was his favourite expression. Stanislaw Szmajzner described him as obese.

Reichleitner was promoted to the rank of *SS-Hauptsturmführer* as indicated on the promotion list dated March 20, 1943, along with other key members of *Aktion Reinhardt*. Reichleitner was on leave when the Sobibór revolt took place on October 14, 1943. When he returned to Sobibór he was responsible for dismantling the gas chambers and the other camp facilities. He was transferred to Italy, and he was shot and killed in action by partisans on January 3, 1944, in Fiume.

HERING, Gottlieb Jakub
Second Commandant Bełżec

August 1942–May 1943

Temporary Commandant Sobibór

Born on June 2, 1887, in Warmbronn, near Leonberg, Württemberg. On leaving school he worked as an agricultural labourer on estates in the Leonberg area. In 1915, he was conscripted into a Machine Gun Company of Grenadier Regiment 123. He fought on

---

[428] Y. Arad, *Belzec, Sobibor, Treblinka*, Indiana University Press, Bloomington and Indianapolis 1987, p.188.

the Western Front in northern France, where he was awarded the Iron Cross First Class, among other medals. Discharged from the Army in 1918, he joined the police at the end of December 1918, and served in the *Kripo* office at Goppingen, Württemberg. He later worked for the Stuttgart CID, where he became acquainted with Christian Wirth.

From December 1939, until December 1940, he served in a team of *Kripo* officers in *Gotenhafen* (Gdynia) dealing with the resettlement of ethnic Germans on the Baltic coast. In 1941, Hering was drafted into 'T4' and served in Bernburg, then later at Hadamar, and Pirna-Sonnenstein, before arriving in Bełżec death camp in July 1942. One month later, in August 1942, he was appointed commandant of Bełżec, when Wirth became the Inspector of *Sonderkommando Aktion Reinhardt*.

After the liquidation of Bełżec in May 1943, he became the commandant of the Jewish Labor Camp at Poniatowa until its liquidation on November 4, 1943, as part of *Aktion Erntefest* (Harvest Festival). Hering was temporary commandant of the Sobibór death camp, during the dismantling and closure of the death camp, during November 1943. He attended the funerals of the SS personnel, murdered during the revolt in Sobibór, in the Chelm Military Cemetery in October 1943. In 1944, he was ordered to Italy, where he again replaced Christian Wirth as chief of *Kommando R1* in Trieste, after Wirth was killed by partisans. On October 9, 1945, he died in unknown circumstances in the patient's waiting room of the Katherinen Hospital in Stetten-in-Remstal, Württemberg, while under investigation by the French military authorities.

SOBIBÓR DEATH CAMP

Garrison
Listed in Alphabetical Order

BARBL, Heinrich. Born on March 3, 1900, in Sarleinsbach, Austria. He worked at the T4 Euthanasia Institution at Hartheim and Grafeneck, before being sent to the Bełżec death camp in Poland where he helped install the gas pipes. He referred to himself as the *Hausklempner* (plumber) he worked with Erich Fuchs on the installation of gas pipes in the gas chambers in Sobibór.

BAUCH, Ernst. Born on April 30, 1911, in Grinsdorf. He served in the T4 Euthanasia Institutions at Grafeneck and Hadamar. He arrived in Sobibór during April 1942. He worked in *Lager I*. Bauch committed suicide on December 4, 1942, in Berlin. Karl Frenzel attended his funeral in Berlin.

BAUER, Hermann, Erich. Born on March 26, 1900, in Berlin. A former Tram Conductor, he also worked as a driver for the T4 organization at its headquarters in Berlin. Bauer was sent to Sobibór during April 1942, and he was in charge of the gas chambers in *Lager III*. He described himself as the *'Gasmeister'* of Sobibór during his trial. His SS number was 22113. He was also the camp's lorry driver, responsible for transporting the coffins of the SS-men killed in the revolt to the Chelm German Military Cemetery. When Sobibór was closed down Bauer was posted to Italy, where he served in Trieste and Fiume.
In 1946, he worked in Berlin, clearing the ruins. Whilst doing this, during 1949, he was spotted on the street by former Sobibór inmates Samuel Lerer and Estera Raab, who reported him to the Police.

On May 8, 1950, at his trial in Berlin-Moabit he was sentenced to death for war crimes committed in Sobibór. This was commuted to life imprisonment in November 1971, after the abolition of the death penalty. He passed away in the Berlin-Tegel prison on February 4, 1980.

BECHER, Werner. Born on April 26, 1912, in Annaberg, Aue. He worked at the T4 Euthanasia Institution at Pirna-Sonnenstein as a chauffeur. He served in Sobibór from August 1942, until November 1942. He supervised the sorting barracks in *Lager II*. He also worked in *Lager III*. He passed away in East Germany on November 29, 1977.

BECKMANN, Rudolf Heinrich. Born on November 21, 1904, in Buer, *Kreis* Gelsenkirchen, Westfalen. His father was Johann Beckmann, who was a miner by profession, who passed away during 1917. His mother was Antoinette Beckmann, formerly Eltrop. Rudolf Beckmann was one of six children, three brothers and two sisters.

In the mid-1920's, he earned his living as an office worker in Buer. Later on he became a farmer, and was presumably employed as a farmer in Ottmarsbocholt until April 1940.

He put his farming skills to good use at the T4 Euthanasia Institutions of Grafeneck and Hadamar. He was transferred to the Sobibór death camp in April 1942, where he was in charge of sorting the Jewish victims possessions in *Lager II*, he was also in charge of the farm. He also supervised the camps administration, based in the Forester's House. Thomas 'Toivi' Blatt' described that Beckmann, who whipped him once, was of slim build.[429]

It was in the Forester's House that Rudolf Beckmann was killed during the prisoner revolt on October 14, 1943. He was stabbed to death by Chaim Engel and Hersz Pozyczki, and he was buried at the Chelm German Military Cemetery in grave number 402, on October 18,1943. On his *Grabmeldung* issued by WGO

---

[429] Telephone conversation with the author.

No 3 Lublin, his rank was listed as *SS-Unterscharführer*, although it is generally accepted that his proper rank was that of an *SS-Oberscharführer*.

BEULICH, Max. Born on March 9, 1905, in Sornzig in Sachsen. He was a male nurse at the T4 Euthanasia Institute at Pirna-Sonnenstein. He served in Sobibór, but no other details known.

BLAUROCK, Emil. Born on January 25, 1897, in Kleinbauschlitz. He was a male nurse at the T4 Euthanasia Institute at Pirna-Sonnenstein. He served in Sobibór. He was detained by the US Army in Bad Aiblingen, Bavaria. He was discharged from internment on April 19, 1946. He passed away during 1980, in Leipzig.

BOLENDER, Heinz, Kurt. Born on May 21, 1912, in Duisburg. He joined the *SS* in 1932, his number was 47553. He served at the T4 Euthanasia Institutions at Brandenburg, Hartheim, and Pirna-Sonnenstein. Bolender arrived in Sobibór on April 22, 1942, along with a group that included Stangl, Frenzel, and Gomerski. In Sobibór he served in *Lager III*, supervising the mass graves.

In July 1942, he was arrested for perjury during his divorce case between him and his wife Margarete Bolender, and was punished by an *SS*-Court in *Krakau* on December 19, 1942. He was sent to the *SS*-Penal Camp at Matzkau, near Danzig (now Gdansk, in Poland.)

Bolender was transferred to the *DAW (Deutsche Ausrüstungswerke)* in Lublin, and he was sent back to Sobibór to assist with the dismantling of the camp following the prisoner revolt in October 1943. Bolender was posted to Italy after Sobibór was closed down, he served in Trieste and Fiume.

Kurt Bolender was arrested in May 1961, and he attended the trial of the former *SS*-Garrison members in Hagen during 1965-1966. He committed suicide before he was due to be sentenced on October 10, 1966.

BORNER, Gerhard. Born on October 28, 1905, in Dresden. He joined the SS. His number was 3832. He served at the T4 Euthanasia Institute at Pirna-Sonnenstein, as Chief of the Economics office. He was photographed in Sobibór, at the Stangl party in the Commandant's villa. After Sobibór he was posted to Italy. Nothing further is known.

BREDOW, Paul. Born on October 31, 1903, in Guttland, Danzig District. He was a male nurse who served at the T4 Euthanasia Institutions at Grafeneck, Hadamar, and Hartheim. He was posted to Sobibór along with Stangl and others during April 1942. At Sobibór, Bredow was in charge of the *Lazarett*, where he displayed untold cruelty in shooting Jewish deportees and prisoners. He remained in Sobibór until the spring of 1943, when he was posted to the Treblinka death camp, where he was in charge of Sorting Barracks 'A,' the clothing barracks.
After the closure of Treblinka, he was posted to Trieste in Italy. After the end of the Second World War he worked, together with another former Sobibór SS-Garrison member Karl Frenzel, as a carpenter until November 1945. He was killed in an accident in Gottingen, on July 10, 1963.

BREE, Max. Born on November 28, 1906, in Lubben im Spreewald. Following service in the T4 Organization, where he served in the T4 Euthanasia Institutions at Grafeneck and Hadamar, he was posted to Bełżec from June/July 1942 until September 1942, when he was transferred to the Treblinka death camp. In the spring of 1943, he was again transferred to the Sobibór death camp. He met his death at Sobibór, during the prisoner revolt on October 14, 1943.

DACHSEL, Arthur. Born on March 11, 1898, in Bohlen in Sachsen. In civilian life, he had a number of professions; he was a blacksmith, locksmith, cigar handler, police officer, and a carer. Arthur Dachsel worked at the T4 Euthanasia Institution at Pirna-Sonnenstein, where he incinerated bodies. He served at the Bełżec death camp in Poland and in July 1942, he was transferred to the Sobibór death camp, where he supervised the *Waldkommando*. He was promoted to the rank of *Oberwachtmeister* in March 1943. After Sobibór was closed he served in Trieste and Fiume in Italy. He was remembered by Thomas 'Toivi' Blatt as one of the least brutal SS men. He passed away on November 10, 1958.

DIETZE, Erich. Born on January 2, 1915, in Chemnitz. He worked at the T4 Euthanasia Institution at Pirna-Sonnenstein as an administrator. He was posted to Sobibór. He also served in Trieste, Italy. No further details known.

DUBOIS, Werner. Born on February 26, 1913, in Wuppertal-Langenfeld. He was brought up by his grandmother. After school he worked as a joiner, brushmaker, printer and on a farm. He joined the *SS* in January 1937, and he worked as a driver for the *Gruppenkommando Oranienburg*, and he also served as a driver and a guard at the Sachsenhausen Concentration Camp. His Nazi Party Membership number was 5229440.

In August 1939, he was transferred to the T4 organization where he drove the buses and worked as a burner in a number of T4 Institutions in Bernburg, Brandenburg, Grafeneck, and Hadamar. Following a brief spell in Russia working for the *Organisation Todt*, he, was transferred to the Bełżec death camp in March /April 1942, where he admitted shooting Jewish prisoners. In the summer of 1943, he was transferred to the Sobibór death camp after Bełżec was closed.

At Sobibór he was in charge of the *Waldkommando*. He was attacked in the armoury on the day of the prisoner revolt on October 14, 1943, and suffered serious wounds. Dubois was acquitted at the Bełżec trial in August 1963. However, he was sentenced to three years imprisonment at the Sobibór trial in Hagen in 1966. Dubois passed away on October 22, 1971, in Munster.

EBERL, Dr. Irmfried, Georg, Rolf. Born on September 8, 1910, in Bregenz, Austria. He had two older brothers, Harald and Ekhard. His mother's name was Josefine and his father's name was Josef Franz, an engineer by profession.

Eberl attended four years of elementary school, moving onto *Bregenz Gymnasium* (Secondary School). He took his A-Level[430] examination on June 15, 1928, as a seventeen-year old youth, the youngest one in his class. At first he wanted to study law, but later he decided in favour of medicine.

He started his medical studies during 1928/29, and two years later, he joined the Nazi Party on December 8, 1931, and his Party Number was 687095. He became the National Socialist representative of the student's chamber. He was also a member of the *Motorsturm I* and *SA-Sturm 14*.

Eberl achieved his Doctorate in February 1935, at 24 years of age, as a Medical Doctor. From February 20, 1935, to May 27, 1935, he was employed in the 2nd Medical Section of the *Krankenanstalt Rudolfstiftung*, and from May 28, 1935, to March 8, 1936, at the *Lungenheilanstalt Grimmenstein*.

After a period of unemployment in Austria, Eberl went to Germany (he earned the status of a political refugee: No 13943), There, for a month in April 1936, he was employed at the *Deutsches Hygiene Institut* in Dresden, and then from May 1, 1936, he was *Chief of Amt fur Volkswohlfahrt* in Dessau near Magdeburg. He subsequently served at the *Hauptgesundheitsamt* in Berlin. From February 1940, Eberl served at the *Gemeinnützige Stiftung fur Anstaltspflege*, which was the code name for the T4 Euthanasia program.

Eberl was appointed to the post of Director at the Brandenburg T4 Euthanasia Institution and during 1942, he went to the Bernburg T4 Euthanasia Institute, also as a Director. He later also served at the T4 Euthanasia Institute at Grafeneck.

After a brief spell on the Eastern Front working for the *Organization Todt* in the Minsk area, he was sent to the Sobibór

---

[430] Potentially the '*Abitur*' examination, leading to higher education.

death camp for training, in anticipation of being appointed to be the Commandant at the Treblinka death camp.

He was duly appointed as the first Commandant of Treblinka, but he was over-ambitious in his desire to exceed all other camps in their destruction of the Jews. A month after becoming operational, Eberl had overseen a chaotic breakdown in operations at Treblinka, and he was relieved of his command by Odilo Globocnik, sometime towards late August 1942.

Eberl's wife Ruth, formerly Rehm, knew at least on August 24, 1942, that her husband's time at Treblinka had come to an end. Her letter, dated the same day, starts with the words, *'Damit Du zum Schluss Deiner Tätigkeit in Treblinka.'* (Well, to the end of your activity in Treblinka.)

According to a post-war statement by Fritz Bleich, (who worked for T4), given to the International Military Tribunal in Nuremberg, Eberl also went to Auschwitz Concentration Camp to perform medical experiments on inmates, along with Dr. Georg Renno, and Dr. Horst Schumann in October 1943, for a period of six months.

Eberl then served in the *Wehrmacht* and his second marriage left him a widower. On the western front he found himself in taken into custody by American forces in Luxemburg, at the beginning of April 1945. He was sent to a Prisoner of War camp in Dietersheim, near Bingen, where he worked in the T.B. department. In July he was released, and when the war ended, he settled in Blaubeuren.

He was again imprisoned during 1947, and he committed suicide by hanging himself on February 16, 1948, during his pre-trial detention in the custodial prison in Ulm. At that time he was not yet accused for his activities in Treblinka, but for his service in the Euthanasia mass murder program.

FLOSS, Erich Herbert. Born on August 25, 1912, in Reinholdsheim. He attended extended elementary school. After school he was trained in textile dyeing, but he could not secure a position in this line of work, and consequently worked in several other jobs.

From April 1, 1935, he served in the 2 *Totenkopf-Sturmbann Elbe*, and saw service in the Buchenwald Concentration Camp. he also served at the T4 Institutions at Bernburg, Grafeneck and Hadamar. His SS Number was 281582,

Erich Herbert Floss was to make a name for himself as the *Aktion Reinhardt* cremation expert; which he put to good effect at Bełżec, Sobibór and Treblinka death camps during 1943. Floss was nicknamed by the Jews at Treblinka, as *Tadellos* (perfect)—that was his favourite expression. Floss served mainly at Sobibór death camp, he was one of the SS men who took the victims' last possessions before they entered the 'Tube,' leading from *Lager II* to the gas chambers.

One week after the revolt at Sobibór on October 14, 1943, Floss escorted a group of Ukrainian guards to the Trawniki training camp, in Zawadowka, near Chelm, when he was killed by his own machine-gun by *Trawnikimänner* Wasil Hetmaniec.

FORKER, Alfred. Born on July 31, 1904, in Seeligstadt. He served as a male nurse at the T4 Euthanasia Institute at Pirna-Sonnenstein. Forker served in the Treblinka death camp as a guard in the Sorting Yard and in the *Totenlager*. Described by his colleague Otto Horn in a post-war testimony, as being small, with a tapering peaky face and dark blond hair.'

He also served at Sobibór, and when Sobibór was closed down he was posted to Italy. No further details are known.

FRANZ, Kurt Hubert. Born on January 17, 1914, in Düsseldorf. He attended elementary school from 1920, until 1928, in his home town. From 1929, he trained as a cook, firstly at the '*Hirschquelle*' restaurant, then in '*Hotel Wittelsbacher Hof*,' in Düsseldorf without taking his final examination.

Franz then served as a soldier between the years 1935, to 1937, and in October 1937, he joined the *Waffen-SS* as part of the *SS-Totenkopfstandarte Thüringen*. As a member of the 6th battalion he served as part of the guard unit at the Buchenwald

Concentration Camp. At the end of 1939, Franz was summoned to the *Führer's* Chancellery in Berlin and detailed for service as a kitchen chief in the T4 Institutions at Grafeneck, Hartheim, Sonnenstein and Brandenburg. His *SS* Number was 316909.

During March 1942, he was ordered to the *Generalgouvernement*, and he reported to Odilo Globocnik *SSPF* in Lublin, and was then posted to the Bełżec death camp. In Bełżec Kurt Franz was responsible for supervising the Ukrainian guards and military training. He was promoted to the rank of *SS-Oberscharführer* on April 20, 1942.

In August 1942, he was ordered to the Treblinka death camp as Deputy Camp Commandant and took over control of the Ukrainian guard unit. On March 20, 1943, he was promoted to the rank of SS-*Untersturmführer*, according to the promotion list produced by Odilo Globocnik. After the revolt on August 2, 1943, he was appointed to the post of the last Commandant of the camp. He was responsible for the liquidation of the death camp, from August 27, 1943, until November 1943.

Franz was one of the most brutal and murderous members of the camp staff when it came to the day to day running of the camp. To the prisoners Franz was the cruellest and most feared among the SS personnel. His physical appearance was extremely deceiving, he was handsome and had a round, almost baby-face, and was nicknamed '*Lalka*' (Doll) by the prisoners. He was accompanied on his rounds of the camp by Barry, a Saint Bernard cross, who attacked and maimed prisoners on Franz's command. Franz is mentioned frequently in survivor accounts—all paint the same evil picture.

When Treblinka closed down he briefly went to the Sobibór death camp, and then to Trieste and Goriza in Italy, where he was head of the *Landesschutz* school.

In May 1945, he was arrested by the Americans, but escaped back to Germany, where he was re-arrested by the Americans, but later released. He then lived undisturbed in Düsseldorf until his arrest in 1959. He was tried as a War Criminal in the Treblinka Trial in Düsseldorf and sentenced to life imprisonment by the German *Landesgericht* on September 3, 1965. Kurt Franz died in an old people's home in Wuppertal on July 4, 1998.

FRENZEL, Karl, August Wilhelm. Born on August 20, 1911, in Zehdenick on the Havel, the son of a *Reichsbahn* employee. Both his brothers lost their lives in the First World War. Frenzel took on a four year apprenticeship as a carpenter, but work in this field was difficult to find. He managed to find agricultural work, then became a driver for a butcher. He joined the Nazi Party and became an *SA* man from August 1930. Due to his fervent belief in National Socialism, he received a dagger of honour from Hitler in person, which Frenzel described as 'his greatest experience.'

At the end of 1939, he was employed by T4. Frenzel first went to the Grafeneck Euthanasia Institute, where he worked as a guard. He then went to the T4 Euthanasia Institute at Bernburg, and then onto Hadamar, where he became involved in the gassing and cremation of mentally-ill and disabled people. After returning to Bernburg to help dismantle the gassing facilities, in mid-April 1942, Frenzel was summoned to Berlin and, together with other T4 comrades, he was ordered to report to Odilo Globocnik, *SS und Polizeiführer* in Lublin. Frenzel was given the rank of *SS-Oberscharführer* and was posted to Sobibór, he arrived there on April 28, 1942.

After a short while Frenzel was placed in charge of *Lager I* and the *Bahnhofkommando*. He was the *SS*-Officer, along with Gustav Wagner, who selected the workers who were to live, while the rest were consigned to the gas chambers. *SS-Scharführer* Erich Bauer, who served with Frenzel in Sobibór, recalled; 'He (Frenzel) was one of the most brutal members of the permanent staff in the camp. His whip was very loose.'

Frenzel was one of the main targets of the prisoners during the revolt on October 14, 1943, but he escaped because he was in the shower. Because Franz Reichleitner, the Commandant, was absent, and his deputy Johann Niemann was killed by the prisoners, Frenzel took command of the camp in the immediate aftermath of the revolt.

Once the Sobibór death camp had closed down he was sent to join Globocnik in Trieste. He was assigned to *Sondertruppe R*, as a *Polizeihauptwachtmeister* in Trieste and Fiume, hunting Jews and fighting partisans. In the spring of 1944, he was involved in a motoring accident and spent a long time in a hospital in Udine.

After being captured by the American Forces he was taken to a Prisoner of War Camp in the Munich area. He was released in November 1945, and made his way back to his home in Lowenburg. He arrived home the very day his wife Sofia died. He found employment as acting Stage Manager for a film studio in Gottingen.

Karl Frenzel was arrested for war crimes committed at Sobibór on March 22, 1962, and following a trial in Hagen, he was sentenced on December 20, 1966, to life imprisonment. Frenzel passed away in a retirement home in Garbsen-Hannover on September 2, 1996.

FUCHS, Erich. Born on April 9, 1902, in Berlin. After his education in an elementary school he trained to become a skilled motor mechanic and automotive foreman. Before the Second World War he was a driver in Berlin. He joined the Nazi Party in the early 1930's, and became a member of the *SA* and later the *SS*. His address in Berlin was SW 29 *Gneisenaustr*.

He was drafted to T4 where he worked as Dr Eberl's driver in the T4 Institutions at Brandenburg and Bernburg, and was, as he expressed himself, 'an interested spectator' at the gassing of 50 mental patients.

In the winter of 1941, Fuchs was selected at Bernburg by Christian Wirth and posted to Bełżec death camp. At Bełżec he installed the 'showers' the disguised gassing facilities; drove the converted parcel van that was turned into a *gas-wagen*; and worked as a truck driver in the motor pool, transporting material to the death camp site. In April 1942, he collected a Russian water-cooled petrol engine from *Lemberg*, which was to produce the lethal gas for exterminating the Jews at Sobibór death camp. He installed the engine with Erich Bauer and ensured that it worked with a trial gassing of Jews.

Erich Fuchs was then posted to Treblinka to assist with the installation of an engine in the gas chamber, which he testified; 'Subsequently I went to Treblinka. In this extermination camp I installed a generator which supplied electric light for the barracks. The work in Treblinka took me about three to four busy months. During my stay there transports of Jews who were gassed were coming in daily.'

In December 1942, Fuchs managed to arrange his release from T4 and from early 1943, he worked for the German oil company *Ostland-Öl-Vertriebsgesellschaft* in Riga. In February 1945, he became a soldier and member of the *Waffen-SS*, where he served in a tank transport unit. In March 1945, he was wounded during a bombing raid. Fuchs was taken prisoner by the Russians, and then subsequently he was held as a Prisoner of War by the Americans in Western Germany. He was employed by the British Army as a driver/ mechanic in Bergen Belsen, until his release in 1946.

Fuchs worked till 1962, at a number of jobs; as an assistant worker, locksmith, and truck inspector at the *TUV* in Koblenz. He was arrested and held in custody from April 8, 1963. The *Schwurgericht am Landgericht* Hagen sentenced him to four years imprisonment on December 20,1966, for being an accessory to the murder of at least 79,000 people. He died in Koblenz on July 25, 1980.

GAULSTICH, Freidrich. Freidrich Gaulstich was born in Oels. He was recruited by T4, and he worked at their headquarters in Berlin. He arrived in Sobibór during August 1943. He was killed by a blow from an axe wielded by Szlomo Leitman, in the Carpenters workshop, during the prisoner revolt on October 14, 1943.

GENTZ, Adolf. Born c.1912. He served in Treblinka death camp from August 1942, until October 1943, where he helped supervise the ramp. After the prisoner revolt in Treblinka, he was posted to Sobibór to assist with the liquidation of the camp. He was later posted to Udine, Italy. No further details are known.

GETZINGER, Anton. Born on November 24, 1910, in Oeblarn, Austria. He was described by his *Ortsgruppenleiter* as a 'fanatical National Socialist, and a fighter for the ideas of our *Führer*, Adolf Hitler.' Getzinger served at the T4 Euthanasia Institute at Hartheim, near Linz, Austria.

Getzinger arrived in Sobibór during April 1942, and he worked in *Lager III*. A few weeks before the revolt he was killed by a grenade in *Lager IV*—the so-called *Nordlager*—where captured Soviet munitions were stored, on September 13, 1943.

Hubert Gomerski, who was with Anton Getzinger at the time, explained what happened:

> We wanted to zero the aim of a machine-gun. We took two or three hand grenades, pounded a stake into the ground and wanted to put the grenades on top to hit them and blow them up. Toni hit it and was torn to shreds.

To cover up this embarrassing incident, an official Nazi Party report dated December 9, 1944, stated that Anton Gerzinger was killed in action fighting against bandits, while serving in a *Sonderkommando* in Serbia.

GOMERSKI, Hubert. Born on November 11, 1911, in Schweinheim. He worked at the T4 Euthanasia Institutions at Grafeneck, Brandenburg, Hadamar and Hartheim. He arrived in Sobibór at the end of April 1942. Initially he was put in charge of a group of Ukrainian guards, but then worked alongside Kurt Bolender and Sepp Vallaster in *Lager III*.

Gomerski could be found on the ramp whenever a transport arrived, looking for the sick and disabled. He was known as the 'doctor,' because of his past experience in handling the sick, and his speciality was braining the half-dead with a steel water-can as they were taken off the trains.

He also carried out executions in the *Lazarett*, of the sick and disabled, and worker-Jews sent there. He often took to balancing a bottle on the head of an *Arbeitshäftling*, getting him to stand against a wall, and then shooting him with his carbine.

His accomplishments at Sobibór earned him a promotion to the rank of *SS-Unterscharführer* at Christmas 1942. He supervised the *Waldkommando* and the *Nordlager* with the utmost brutality. He was on leave when the revolt took place on October 14, 1943.

At the end of 1943, he was posted to Fiume in Italy. The *Schwurgericht* in Frankfurt-am-Main sentenced Gomerski to life imprisonment on August 25, 1950, for murdering an undisclosed number of people. He asked for a re-trial, which started on December 12, 1972, but this was ended prematurely on ill-health grounds. Hubert Gomerski passed away on December 28, 1999, in Frankfurt-am-Main.

GRAETSCHUS, Siegfried. Born on June 9, 1916, in Tilsit, East Prussia. After extended elementary education, he became a farmer and was a member of the *NSDAP* from 1936. He served at the Sachsenhausen Concentration Camp, as confirmed by the War Crimes Group in 1947.

Graetschus was recruited into the T4 Organization and served in the T4 Euthanasia Institutions of Grafeneck, Brandenburg, and Bernburg.

Graetschus was posted to the Bełżec death camp and was involved in the early gassing experiments, including the conversion of a Post Office parcel van into a gas-van. Siegfried Graetschus was transferred to Treblinka death camp in May 1942, where he served until August 1942, when he was dismissed at the same time as Dr. Eberl. He was sent to the Sobibór death camp, where he commanded the Ukrainian guards, replacing Erich Lachmann as their chief. Graetschus was killed during the prisoner revolt on October 14, 1943, by Yehuda Lerner, in the Shoemakers workshop.

GROMER, Siegfried. Born on April 7, 1903, in Austria. He worked in the T4 Euthanasia Institute at Hartheim, near Linz. Gromer was posted to Sobibór in August 1942, as a cook. Gromer carried out a number of duties in Sobibór, such as overseeing the gassing and transporting of the bodies to the mass graves, where they were buried. He also supervised the *Waldkommando*.

Erich Bauer, in post-war testimonies, recalled Gromer as, 'a drunk who frequently resorted to violence.' Commandant Reichleitner removed Gromer from Sobibór in June 1943, because of his drinking problems. In a number of survivor testimonies Gromer was known by the nickname 'Red Cake.' No further details known.

GROTH, Paul Johannes. Born on January 21, 1918, in Zopprt, near Danzig. He served at the T4 Euthanasia Institute at Hartheim near Linz, Austria. Groth was posted to the Bełżec death camp in January 1942. Christian Wirth transferred Groth to Sobibór in April 1942, where he supervised the sorting activities in *Lager II*.

He was regarded by the prisoners as one of the worst sadists. However, Groth fell in love with a Jewish girl called Ruth, who was shot in *Lager III*. Groth was transferred back to the Bełżec in December 1942. Groth was in charge of the transport that brought the last Jewish work-brigade from Bełżec to Sobibór in May 1943. In 1951, his wife declared that Groth had died in order to claim her widow's pension.

HACKEL, Emil. Born on November 9, 1910, in Windisch-Kamnitz, in the Sudetenland. He served in the T4 Euthanasia Institute at Pirna-Sonnenstein, as a 'burner.' He was transferred to Sobibór, but no other details known.

HACKENHOLT, Lorenz Maria. Born on June 25, 1914, in the coal mining area of Gelsenkirchen, North Rhine-Westphalia, in the northern part of the Ruhr. After attending the local elementary school until the age of 14, he became an apprentice bricklayer and, on passing the trade examinations, worked on various building sites.

In 1934, he joined the 2 *Totenkopfstandarte* (Death's Head Regiment) 'Brandenburg' stationed at Oranienburg, north of Berlin. In March 1938, he was transferred to the nearby Sachsenhausen Concentration Camp, where he was employed in the motor pool and as a driver for the camp *Kommandantur* and personnel. His SS Number was 84133.

In November 1939, he was one of a group of 10 SS-NCOs summoned to the *Führer's* Chancellery on *Vosstrasse* in Berlin. During a meeting with *SS-Standartenführer* Viktor Brack, the head of Main Office II of the *Führer's* Chancellery, they were informed of the euthanasia program and their roles within its ranks—mainly as bus-drivers conveying the patients and as corpse incinerators. This duty was to be performed in civilian clothes. After the SS-NCOs were sworn to secrecy, civilian clothes were brought for them and Hackenholt drove them in a bus to Grafeneck castle in the Swabian mountains, south of Stuttgart. From the beginning of 1940, when Grafeneck became operational, until the summer of 1941, when the gassings were temporarily halted on Hitler's orders, Lorenz Hackenholt served in all six 'T4' Euthanasia Institutions, both as a bus driver and as a so-called 'disinfector/ burner,' unloading the corpses from the gas chambers and incinerating them.

After the temporary halt in the 'T4' gassings, Hackenholt, together with a small group of SS-NCO's from 'T4' was transferred in the autumn of 1941, to serve under *SS-Brigadeführer* Odilo Globocnik, the SS- and Police Leader of the Lublin District in the *Generalgouvernement*. Hackenholt was assigned to Bełżec, a remote village in the far south-eastern corner of the

Lublin District, on the main road and railroad between Lublin and *Lemberg* (Lvov).

Here, on the outskirts of the village, the first *Aktion Reinhardt* death camp was under construction. When the camp became operational on March 17, 1942, Hackenholt became the supervising mechanic, who started the Russian tank engine which then pumped its lethal exhaust fumes into three primitive gas chambers in a wooden shed. He rapidly became the gassing expert of *Aktion Reinhardt*, and a few months later designed and supervised the construction of a new and bigger gassing building with six chambers. It was named the 'Hackenholt Foundation' (*'Stiftung Hackenholt'*) in his honour.

In August 1942, Hackenholt was ordered to Treblinka by Christian Wirth—by then the Inspector of the three *Aktion Reinhardt SS-Sonderkommandos* operating at Bełżec, Sobibór, and Treblinka—to replace the original three gas chambers with a new and bigger building containing ten gas chambers. He was assisted in this task by Erwin Lambert, the 'T4' construction expert. On completion of this task both men were sent by Wirth to Sobibór death camp to construct new and bigger gassing facilities there.

Hackenholt then returned to Bełżec, where in the late autumn of 1942, he became involved in the exhumation and cremation of the hundreds of thousands of corpses buried in the mass graves. In the spring of 1943, Hackenholt returned to Treblinka on orders from Wirth to assist with the exhumation and cremation operations as one of the excavator drivers. Following the liquidation of Bełżec during May 1943, Hackenholt was transferred to the Old Airfield camp just outside Lublin, which was the main sorting, cleaning and storage depot for the vast amounts of belongings and valuables seized from the Jews murdered in the *Aktion Reinhardt* death camps.

Valuable furs were disinfected with *Zyklon B* in four specially constructed chambers; after Hackenholt arrived at the airfield, he used the chambers for killing prisoners who were unfit for work, instead of sending them to the gas chambers in the nearby Lublin Concentration Camp (Majdanek).

In the autumn of 1943, Hackenholt was transferred to Trieste in northern Italy, where he served in the *R-I Sonderkommando* of *Einsatz R* at San Sabba. In 1944, he was awarded the Iron Cross II Class for his dedicated service to *Aktion Reinhardt*. Shortly after Easter 1945, he was arrested and interned in San Sabba, awaiting execution for selling arms to the partisans. However, Dieter Allers, the head of *Aktion T4* and *Einsatz R*, who had replaced Christian Wirth after his assassination, realized that the war was all but over and released Hackenholt, who promptly disappeared. Hackenholt was next seen driving a bus for a Trieste motor company.

After that, he disappeared until during the retreat of the *Einsatz R* troops into Austria, the convoy passed him on the road to Kirchbach. He was driving a horse-drawn milk float. In the summer of 1945, his wife Ilse received news of him in Berlin from Rudolf Kamm, a former *SS*-comrade from the Bełżec death camp. Kamm wanted to collect Hackenholt's civilian clothing. In 1946, two former *SS*-comrades from Sobibór death camp, Erich Bauer and Wenzel Rehwald, claim to have met him near Ingolstadt in Bavaria, where he was living under an assumed name and employed in a motor accessories shop.

A year later, Hackenholt's brother, Theo, believed he passed him driving a delivery van near their hometown of Gelsenkirchen in the Ruhr. After that nothing more was heard of Lorenz Hackenholt. However, after a fruitless four-year hunt by the West German police, and intensive and repeated interrogations of his wife Ilse and other family members, it seemed likely that Hackenholt could have been living under a false name in the area of Memmingen, in the Allgäu region of southern Germany. His wife, Ilse, lived in the same area. The Allgäu region was close to the border with Austria, a country that had no extradition treaty with West Germany. Lorenz

Hackenholt, wanted for participation in the mass murder of at least 1.5 million people, has never been found.

HILLER, Richard. Born during 1899, in Braunsdorf bei Freiberg. At Treblinka death camp he worked in the administration office in the Lower Camp from September 1942, until October 1943. According to the post-war testimony of Erich Bauer, he served in Sobibór when the camp was being dismantled. He later served in Fiume, Italy. His eventual fate is unknown.

HIRTREITER, Josef 'Sepp'. Born on February 1, 1909, in Bruchsal, which is 20 kilometres northeast of Karlsruhe. After attending extended elementary school, he trained as a locksmith, but failed the final examination. Later he worked as an unskilled building worker and bricklayer. On August 1, 1932, he became a member of the Nazi Party and the *SA*.

In October 1940, he was posted to the T4 Euthanasia Institute at Hadamar, where he worked in the kitchen and the office. In the summer of 1942, he was drafted into the *Wehrmacht* for a brief time, before returning to Hadamar, and then onto Berlin. Christian Wirth transferred Hirtreiter first to Lublin, then he was posted to the Treblinka death camp. In Treblinka, he was greatly feared by the prisoners, and was known by his nickname 'Sepp.'

Josef Hirtreiter was stationed at Treblinka from August 20, 1942, until October 1943, when he was transferred to Sobibór to assist with the dismantling of the camp. When that was complete he was posted to Italy, where he joined an anti-partisan police unit.

After the end of the Second World War, he was arrested in July 1946, and accused of having served at the Euthanasia Institute at Hadamar. He was the first of the 'Treblinka Hangmen' to be brought to trial in Frankfurt-am-Main. On March 3, 1951, he was sentenced to life imprisonment.

Among the crimes he was found guilty of were those of killing many young children, aged one or two, during the unloading of transports, seizing the infants by their feet and smashing their heads against the boxcars.

Because of ill-health, Josef Hirtreiter was released from prison during 1977. He spent the last six months of his life in an old people's home in Frankfurt-am-Main. He passed away on November 27, 1978.

HÖDL, Franz. Born on August 1, 1905, in Aschbach, Austria. Franz Hödl served at the T4 Euthanasia Institutes at Grafeneck and Hartheim, near Linz, Austria. There, from April 1939, to January 1942, he drove the buses which transported patients. Thereafter he was drafted into an *Organization Todt* unit in Russia, where he was employed transporting wounded soldiers. He was a member of the SS, and his SS Number was 302133.

After a period of training at the Trawniki *SS-Ausbildungslager*, he was posted to Sobibór in October 1942, where he operated the gassing engine in *Lager III*. He also served as a chauffeur to Commandant Reichleitner. After the prisoner revolt on October 14, 1943, he helped with the dismantling of the facilities. When Sobibór was closed down, Hödl was posted to Italy, and he witnessed the death of Franz Reichleitner, who was ambushed in his car, and killed by partisans in Fiume on January 3, 1944.

ITTNER, Jakob, Alfred. Born on January 13, 1907, in Kulmbach. He joined the Nazi Party as early as 1926, and the SA in 1936, with the rank of *Scharführer*. After working for the T4 organization in Berlin as a book-keeper, he was in the first group of arrivals in Sobibór on April 28, 1942, and remained there until the end of July 1942.

He spent the first five weeks in administrative duties as an *SS-Oberscharführer*. The Jews had to hand over their money and other valuables as they filed past his counter naked, on their way from *Lager II* to the gas chambers. After that he became a guard in *Lager III*, where he supervised prisoners as they extracted gold teeth from the bodies of those gassed, and carted the bodies over to the mass graves.

At the end of June 1942, he managed to get himself transferred back to the T4 Headquarters in Berlin. In the 1965-1966, Hagen Trial he was sentenced to four years in prison for his part in the murder of an undisclosed number—though at least 68,000-Jews.

JUHRS, Robert Emil. Born on October 17, 1911, in Frankfurt-am-Main. By profession he was a painter, but he also worked as a labourer, caretaker, and usher at the Frankfurt Opera House, and as an office clerk. Until late 1941 he served at the T4 Institute at Hadamar, where he was employed as a male nurse, painter and clerk.

He was posted to the Bełżec death camp in June 1942, where he served at the ramp and at the *Lazarett* shooting the sick and disabled. In late February or early March 1943, he was posted to the Jewish labor camp at Dorohucza, where peat was dug and he remained there until early November 1943.

Juhrs escorted the *Arbeitshäftlinge* from Dorohucza to Trawniki, where all of them were shot during *Aktion Erntefest* (Harvest Festival). Following the revolt in Sobibór in October 1943, Juhrs was sent to Sobibór to help with the dismantling of the camp and he formed a guard cordon of the last prisoners to be killed at Sobibór, once they had finished with the clean-up of the death camp.

Juhrs was ordered to Italy in December 1943. He was acquitted at the pre-Trial Bełżec hearings at the *Landgericht* Munich in 1963. He was also acquitted at the Sobibór Trial in Hagen on December 20, 1966, on charges arising from his involvement in the demolition of the camp.

KAMM, Rudolf. Born on January 19, 1905, in Sedenz, a village near Teplitz Schonau in the Sudetenland. He was a glazier by profession. He served at the T4 Institute at Pirna-Sonnenstein as a 'burner.'

He was posted to the death camp at Bełżec in 1942, and records from the nearby hospital at Tomaszow Lubelski show that he was hospitalized on June 17, 1942, until the June 25, 1942, and again on the December 30, 1942, until January 31, 1943, with typhus.*

He was transferred to Sobibór in 1943, where he supervised the sorting barracks. He was posted to Italy. Franz Suchomel testified that he saw him for the last time after the end of the war, 'in a *Gasthaus* between Mauthern and Hermagor, Carinthia (Austria), the last lodgings of our former unit' (*R-1* in Trieste).

*Note; A number of the *SS* garrison were also hospitalized at Tomaszow Lubelski, including Gottfried Schwarz and Heinrich Unverhau, as well as Rudolf Kamm, and a number of *Trawnikimänner* such as Peter Aleksejev, Maks Bauman, Wasyl Hulyj, Petro Litus, Franz Pamin, Alexander Prus, Arnold Rosenko, Alexander Szwab, Jakub Wysota, Ignatz Zuk and many others.

KLIER, Johann. Born on July 15, 1901, in Stadtsteinach. After completing school he qualified as Master Baker. From 1934, until 1940, he worked at the Heddernheimer Copper Works factory and in the same year he was posted to the T4 Euthanasia Institute at Hadamar, where he worked as a builder and looking after the heating system. He also served at the T4 Euthanasia Institute at Hartheim.

He was posted to Sobibór early in August 1942. He was in charge of the bakery, first outside and later inside *Lager I*. He also supervised the sorting and storage of the shoes of the murdered victims in *Lager II*.

Klier was on leave when the prisoner revolt took place on October 14, 1943, and when Sobibór was closed, he was posted to Italy. Klier was regarded by the prisoners as relatively humane, and they testified to that effect at his trial in Frankfurt-am-Main. On August 25, 1950, he was found not guilty of war crimes. Klier passed away on February 18, 1955, in Frankfurt-am-Main.

KLOS, Walter. Born in 1906. Was from Dresden, according to post-war testimony by Werner Dubois. He served as a T4 driver at the T4 Euthanasia Institutions at Bernburg and Pirna-Sonnenstein. He served at the Bełżec from June 1942, and Sobibór death camps. He was transferred to the Lublin Concentration Camp, where he died in unknown circumstances.

KONRAD, Fritz. Born on September 21, 1914, in Gudellen. He served in the T4 Euthanasia Institutes at Pirna-Sonnenstein and Grafeneck, as a male nurse. He was posted to Sobibór in March 1943, along with Franz and Josef Wolf; the brothers from Krummau, and Willi Wendland. He worked both as a Supervisor in the Sorting Barracks in *Lager II*, and in *Lager III*. Sobibór survivor Zelda Metz testified that he was killed in the Shoemakers' workshop during the revolt on October 14, 1943.

LACHMANN, Erich, Gustav, Willie. Born on November 6, 1909, in Liegnitz. A member of the Police, he trained Ukrainian volunteers at the Trawniki *SS-Ausbildungslager* from September 1941, and he testified he was only at Sobibór a few months from August 1943, as an *Oberwachtmeister* and Chief of the Ukrainian guards. However, it has been confirmed that in fact he was in Sobibór a year earlier. Erich Bauer recalled that Lachmann was a thieving alcoholic. Jewish survivors Abraham Marguiles and Eda Lichtman witnessed him raping young Jewish girls. Commandant Reichleitner sent Lachmann back to Trawniki because of his incompetence, from where he deserted with his Polish girlfriend. He was arrested after roaming the streets of Warsaw for six weeks. He was sentenced by an *SS* Court in Lublin to six years in prison. In the Sobibór Hagen Trial of 1965-66, he was acquitted. He passed away on January 23, 1972, in Wegscheid.

LAMBERT, Erwin, Hermann. Born on December 7, 1909, in Schildow, Kreis Niederbarnin, near Berlin. He was a member of the Nazi Party since 1933, and a Mason by profession. In January 1940, he was recruited into the T4 organization, and his first assignment was the renovation of the T4 headquarters at *Tiergartenstrasse 4*, in Berlin. Examples of further work he carried out for T4 was the installation of gas chambers at the Euthanasia Institutes at Hartheim, Pirna-Sonnenstein, Bernburg, and Hadamar.

In the spring of 1942, he was ordered to Lublin, and then onto Treblinka death camp. He arrived there with August Hengst and, under the command of Richard Thomalla, was responsible for the construction work on the first gas chambers and other buildings.

In August 1942, Lambert was responsible for the demolition of a Glass Factory chimney in Malkinia, and he was photographed in the process by Kurt Franz. The bricks were salvaged and used in the construction of the larger gas chamber at Treblinka. Lambert was known as the 'Flying Architect of T4,' because he also undertook construction work at T4 establishments, such as the *Haus Schoberstein* villa at Attersee, which was used by death camp personnel for recreation and relaxing. Erwin Lambert was also involved with Lorenz Hackenholt in the construction of larger gassing facilities at Sobibór. He was also involved in other building projects at Dorohucza and Poniatowa, Jewish Labor Camps.

After *Aktion Reinhardt* ended he was posted to Trieste, Italy. After the Second World War ended, Lambert was arrested on March 28, 1962. He was tried at the Treblinka Trial which was held in Düsseldorf during 1964/65. He was found guilty and sentenced to four years in prison. He passed away on October 15, 1976, in Stuttgart.

LUDWIG, Karl, Emil. Born on February 7, 1901, in Zehdenick. He joined the Nazi Party during 1933. A driver by profession, he was the chauffeur of Reichsleiter Martin Bormann, and also for the T4 Organization, in Berlin. He served at the T4 Euthanasia Institutes at Grafeneck, and Hadamar.

He was posted to Sobibór during April 1942, and he served there in *Lager III*, the extermination area, until January 1943.

In that month he was transferred to Treblinka death camp, where he served in the *Totenlager*—the extermination area.

Former Treblinka inmate and survivor Joe Siedlicki recalled, in an interview with Gitta Sereny, that Karl Ludwig was viewed as, 'A good, good man. The number of times he brought me things, the number of times he helped me, the number of people he probably saved, I can hardly tell you.'

After the Treblinka death camp closed down, he served in Fiume in Italy. Ludwig passed away on August 3, 1963, in Gransee.

MATTHES, Heinrich, Arthur. Born on January 11, 1902, in Wermsdorf, *Kreis* Leipzig. He attended extended elementary school and became a tailor. In 1924, he served an apprenticeship as a male nurse and educator, and took his examinations at the mental home at Pirna-Sonnentein, near Dresden.

At the Psychological Clinic in Arnsdorf, also near Dresden, he was employed as a male nurse and educator. In 1930, he worked as an educator and welfare worker to an institute in Braunsdorf, near Freiburg/ Sachsen, returning in October 1933, to Arnsdorf.

Matthes became a member of the *SA* during 1934. In 1939, he was drafted into the *Wehrmacht,* where he served as a soldier in Poland and France until September 1941. His final rank in the *Wehrmacht* was an *Obergefreiter.*

Released from the *Wehrmacht,* Matthes was ordered to the *Kanzlei des Führer (KdF)* where he was posted to the T4 Organization. There he spent a short time in the photographic section, in the Berlin headquarters. He also served in the T4 Euthanasia Institute at Pirna-Sonnenstein. In the winter of 1941/42, he served as a member of the *Organization Todt,* in Russia. He served as a male nurse in the Minsk and Smolensk areas. In February or March 1942, he returned from the Eastern Front and worked once more in the T4 photographic section.

In August 1942, he was ordered to Lublin, where he was drafted into the *SS,* and given the rank of *SS-Scharführer,* and posted to the Treblinka death camp. He arrived there on August 20, 1942, and was appointed by Christian Wirth to be in charge of the *Totenlager*, which included the gas chambers and the burial pits.

From Treblinka he was posted to Sobibór during September 1943, where he stayed until the camp was liquidated, afterwards he was stationed in Berlin. In early 1944, he was posted from Berlin to Trieste in Italy, now with the rank of *Polizei-Oberwachtmeister*. In Trieste he fought against the partisans, took part in military construction work and served as a guard until the end of the war.

In 1945, he was captured by US forces, but was released the same year. Returning to Germany he worked in Nuremberg as an ambulance man, also helping removing rubble. He resumed his medical career, by working as a male nurse again at a number of mental homes in Ansbach, Andernach, and finally in Bayreuth.

In the Treblinka Trial held during 1964/65 in Düsseldorf, Matthes was sentenced to life in prison for war crimes committed at Treblinka. Arthur Matthes passed away on December 16, 1978.

MATZIG, Willy. Born on August 6, 1910, in Berg, Oberlausitz. After leaving school his first profession was a Glass-cutter. In October 1933, he became a member of the *Allgemeine SS*, with the rank of an *SS-Unterscharführer*.

In July 1939, he was posted to an infantry unit in Freistadt, Silesia. Then in early January 1940, he was posted to an *SS* infantry unit in Linz, Austria. Matzig fell ill with a septic bone marrow, as a result he was suspended on medical grounds and ordered to report to Berlin.

In Berlin, Matzig was recruited as a member of the T4 Organization from February or March 1940, and he served as a guard at the T4 Euthanasia Institute at Brandenburg for one year. In 1941, he was posted to the T4 Euthanasia Institute at Bernburg, where he again served as a guard and an administration assistant until August 1942.

In August 1942, he was posted to the Treblinka death camp, where he performed book-keeping and administrative duties. Along with *SS-Sturmscharführer* Otto Stadie, he was one of Commandant Franz Stangl's two senior administration assistants, housed in the *Kommandantur*.

Matzig was also part of the squad which received prisoners on the ramp when transports arrived. After the Jews disembarked, Stadie or Matzig would have a brief conversation with them. They were told something to the effect that, 'they were a resettlement transport, they would be given a bath and they would receive new clothes. They were also instructed to maintain quiet and discipline. They would continue their journey the following day.'

Following the closure of Treblinka, Matzig served in Sobibór for a short while, as the camp was dismantled. He was then posted to Trieste in Italy, until the end of the Second World War. His fate is unknown.

MAUERSBERGER, Werner. Born on May 15, 1916, in Meldenau. He worked at the T4 Euthanasia Institutes at Grafeneck, Hadamar, and Pirna-Sonnenstein, where he drove the buses. He was posted to Sobibór. No other details are known.

MENTZ, Willi. Born on April 30, 1904, in Schonhagen, *Kreis* Bromberg. After completing school he found employment as an unskilled worker in a sawmill, and then passed his master milkman's examination. In 1940, he took care of cows and pigs at the T4 Euthanasia Institute at Grafeneck. From 1941, to the early summer of 1942, he worked in the gardens at the T4 Euthanasia Institute at Hadamar.

During June or July 1942, he was posted to the Treblinka death camp, where he was assigned at first to *Lager II*, then to *Lager I*, as Chief of the *Landwirtschaft Kommando* (Agricultural Commando). Willi Mentz was also assigned to supervise the *Lazarett*, a small booth with its long velvet covered bench, where the sick, disabled and elderly victims undressed and were ordered to stand by a large fire-filled ditch, where they were killed by a shot in the back of the head. Mentz was regarded as one of the camp's most brutal killers, much feared by the Jewish prisoners.

After Treblinka was closed, he served for a short time at Sobibór, and from there he was posted to Italy, fighting partisans and persecuting Jews. At the war's end he was in Udine. After the Second World War ended he worked again as a Master Milkman. In the Treblinka Trial held in Düsseldorf during 1964/65, he was sentenced to life imprisonment.

MICHEL, Hermann. Born on February 20, 1909, in Heegermuhle near Berlin. He served at the T4 Euthanasia Institutes at Brandenburg, and Bernburg. He also served at T4 Euthanasia Institute at Hartheim, where he met and became friends with Franz Stangl. He was posted to Sobibór from April 1942, and he used to welcome the new arrivals in *Lager II* with a short speech in order to win their confidence, by pretending that they had arrived at a Labor Camp, and must be disinfected and bathed for reasons of hygiene. For this deception, he earned the nickname the 'Preacher.'

Michel was later posted to the Treblinka death camp in November 1942. At the end of the Second World War he was arrested and detained by American Forces at Bad Aiblingen, Bavaria. He was released on April 19, 1946. He cashed a certificate of credit for $191.60 on January 15, 1948, and simply disappeared. It was believed he fled to Egypt. He passed away on August 8, 1984.

MULLER, Adolf. Born during 1902, in Berlin. He served in T4, as an usher, and he arrived in Sobibór in late June 1943. He served predominantly in *Lager II*, in the Sorting Barracks, and was also in charge of the *Waldkommando*. During the prisoner revolt on October 14, 1943, he kept a group of prisoners, working in the *Waldkommando*, under armed guard. When Sobibór was closed he was posted to the Adriatic Coast in Italy. He passed away on March 10, 1949, in Berlin.

MUNZBERGER, Gustav. Born on August 17, 1903, in Weiskirchlitz, Teplitz-Schonau District in the Sudetenland. He attended extended elementary school, then a public school in Turn, Schonau District, for two years. After school he worked until 1923, as a carpenter for his father's firm, then afterwards for a few months in the Weiskirchlitz Paper Factory.

He served eighteen months military draft in a Railroad Regiment (*Eisenbahn Regiment*) in the industrial town of Pardubice, 95 kilometres east of Prague. From the autumn of 1925, he returned to work in the paper factory in Weiskirchlitz and in 1931, took over the management of his father's firm for the next nine years.

In August 1940, he was sent by the T4 Organization to the T4 Euthanasia Institute at Pirna-Sonnenstein, where he served as a carpenter and assistant cook. Together with about fifteen other men he was posted to Lublin in August 1942. From Lublin he was sent to the Trawniki *SS-Ausbildungslager* for basic military training. His *SS* Number was 321758.

In late September 1942, he was assigned to the Treblinka death camp, with the rank of *SS-Rottenführer* and employed in the *Totenlager* as an assistant to Heinrich Matthes, at the gas chambers. He was responsible for chasing the Jews into the gas chambers, and he also supervised the Corpse Transport Brigade (*Leichentransportkommando*).

On June 21, 1943, Munzberger was promoted to the rank of *SS-Unterscharführer*. At the time of the prisoner revolt on August 2, 1943, he was at home on leave. After the liquidation of Treblinka, he served at the Sobibór death camp for a short time, according to Erich Bauer, in a post-war testimony.

During November 1943, Munzberger was posted to *Einsatz R* in Trieste, northern Italy. He was arrested on July 13, 1963, and at the First Treblinka Trial in Düsseldorf during 1964-65 he was sentenced to twelve years imprisonment. In July 1971, he was released from prison after serving only seven years,' due to good behaviour.' He passed away on March 23, 1977, in Garmisch-Partenkirchen.

NIEMANN, Johann. Born on August 4, 1913, in Wollern *Ostfriesland*. He served at a number of concentration camps, such as Oranienburg, Esterwegen, and Sachsenhausen, between the years 1934-1941. He was a member of T4 and was employed as a 'burner' at the T4 Euthanasia Bernburg Institute, as well as at Grafeneck, and Brandenburg. His *SS* Number was 270600.

Niemann was posted to service in the east at the Bełżec death camp, where according to Kurt Franz, he was in charge of the *Totenlager*,—which included the gas chambers and mass graves—before being posted to Sobibór in January 1943. Niemann was promoted to the rank of *SS-Untersturmführer* following Himmler's visit to the death camp on February 12, 1943. He was acting camp commandant when the prisoner revolt took place on October 14, 1943, and he was killed in the Tailors' workshop by a blow from an axe wielded by Alexander (Kalimali) Shubayev.

NOWAK, Anton Julius. Born on May 22, 1907, in Janow. He was a member of the *SS*, and his *SS* Number was 27196. He supervised the 'Haircutters' barrack near the gas chambers. Sometimes he supervised the *Waldkommando*. Survivor Estera Raab often saw him going into *Lager III*, and said he stank of dead bodies. Anton Nowak was killed during the revolt on October 14, 1943.

NOWAK, Walter. Born during 1921. He served at the T4 Euthanasia Institute at Pirna-Sonnenstein as a male nurse. He was posted to Sobibór and served in *Lager III*, as confirmed by fellow *SS*-man Paul Rost. After Sobibór was closed down, he was posted to Trieste, Italy. He was there when the war came to an end. During a post-war Euthanasia Trial in Dresden in 1947, his service in Sobibór was not included in the indictment.

The fact that he served in Sobibór came to light in a letter dated March 6, 1946, from the local police in Pirna. It noted that during the interrogation of his wife, she had admitted that her husband had served in the *SS-Sonderkommando* at Sobibór. A search of her house had revealed a hoard of valuable items, 'from a camp in Poland, where many Jews had been burned.'

Paul Rost also confirmed that he had come across Walter Nowak after the war, in an American *Entlassungslager*. After his release during 1947, he was pursued by the authorities but without success.

POST, Philip. Born on January 30, 1911, in Bad Vilben, Hessen. He joined the Nazi Party during 1933,—in civilian life he worked as a baker and on the railways. He was recruited into the T4 organization, and served at the T4 Euthanasia Institute at Hadamar.

He served in the Treblinka death camp from August 1942, until September 1943. He was then transferred in the same month to Sobibór, where he worked in the bakery until the camp was closed. He then served in Trieste, Italy, until the war ended. Reported to have passed away on November 9, 1964.

PÖTZINGER, Karl. Born on October 28, 1908, in Marktredwitz, in Oberfranken. He joined the Nazi Party in 1932, and the SA in the same year. In civilian life he was a brewer. He was recruited into the T4 Organization and he served at the T4 Euthanasia Institute at Brandenburg, and also at the T4 institute at Bernburg, where he incinerated the corpses of the murdered victims.

He was posted to Treblinka death camp, where he worked in the *Totenlager*, in charge of the mass graves and then the cremations. When Treblinka was closed he served briefly in Sobibór. He was then posted to Italy. Karl Pötzinger was killed on December 22, 1944, by shrapnel in an air-raid in Udine. He was buried at the German Military Cemetery in Costermano, near Verona, Italy.

REWALD, Wenzel (Fritz). Born during 1910, possibly in Moldau. A bricklayer by profession. He joined the SS, his *SS* Number was 321745. He was a member of the T4 Organization. He served at the Bernburg, Hadamar, Hartheim, and Pirna-Sonnenstein T4 Euthanasia Institutes.

He was posted to Sobibór in April 1942. He supervised the women's undressing barrack and the construction of new barracks. During the revolt on October 14, 1943, he held prisoners under guard at gunpoint. After Sobibór was closed down, he was posted to Trieste, in Italy. His post-war fate is unknown.

RICHTER, Kurt. Born during 1914, in Karlsbad, Bohemia. He was a butcher in civilian life. He was recruited into the T4 Organization. He served at the T4 Euthanasia Institute at Pirna-Sonnenstein and the T4 Euthanasia Institute at Hartheim.

He was posted to the Treblinka death camp as a cook, and was then transferred to Sobibór in October 1942, where he worked in the *SS* kitchen, and the *SS*-casino. He also used to take sick from the ramp to the *Lazarett,* and he also supervised the work in the women's haircutting barrack. He took part in the execution of the workers in the *Waldkommando* on July 23, 1943, After Sobibór closed down he was posted to Italy, and he was killed in a fight with partisans on August 13, 1944, near Trieste. Erich Bauer testified after the war, that he transported Richter's body to the local cemetery.

ROST, Paul. Born on June 12, 1904, in Deutschenbora, near Meissen. After attending extended elementary school he trained to become a butcher. In 1925, he became a member of the police in Dresden, and in 1937, he became a member of the Nazi Party.

On May 21, 1940, he was posted to the T4 Euthanasia Institute at Pirna-Sonnenstein, where he commanded the police squad and transportation *Kommando.* He also served at the T4 Euthanasia Institute at Hartheim.

Paul Rost was posted to Sobibór in April 1942, he was initially the Deputy Commandant, but he was succeeded by Floss and then Niemann. He supervised the sorting of the Jewish victims property in *Lager II*. He also had to spy secretly on the other SS staff.

Rost was transferred to Treblinka during May 1943. When Treblinka was closed down Rost was transferred to Trieste, in Italy in December 1943. He was promoted to the rank of Police Lieutenant on November 9, 1944, and awarded the *Kriegsverdienstkreuz* (Class II).

After the Second World War ended, he was a Prisoner of War in an American Forces camp, but was released and he returned to his family in Dresden. He was subsequently imprisoned by the Soviet Military authorities until the summer of 1946, then once again released. He lived and worked, untroubled, in Dresden, until he passed away on March 21, 1984.

RUM, Franz, Albert. Born on June 8, 1890, in Berlin. In civilian life he was a waiter in a nightclub. He joined the Nazi Party in 1933, and he became a member of the T4 Organization in 1939, where he worked in the photographic section of the T4 headquarters in Berlin.

He was then posted to the Treblinka death camp in December 1942, where he supervised the Body-Transport *Kommando*, in the *Totenlager*. He also chased the Jews into the gas chamber with a whip in his hand. He also supervised Sorting Barrack B in the Lower Camp.

He took part in the final liquidation of the Treblinka death camp, and he was part of the transport, along with Kurt Franz, in a truck that went to Sobibór, during November 1943.

Franz Rum was then posted to Trieste, in Italy. After the war, he returned to Germany. He was tried at the Treblinka Trial held during 1964-65, in Düsseldorf. He passed away during 1970.

RYBA, Walter. Born on July 18, 1900, in Heydebreck, Kozle. He was killed in the *SS*-Garage during the prisoner revolt on October 14, 1943. This was not planned, more of a spontaneous act of revenge. According to the Berlin Document Centre, his name was Walter Hochberg.

SCHAFER, Herbert. Born in Liegnitz. After service in T4, Schafer was transferred to the Trawniki *SS-Ausbildungslager*, near Lublin. He served in Sobibór between April and June 1942, and was responsible for the *Trawnikimänner*.

SCHARFE, Herbert. Born on February 13, 1913, in Konigstein, Sachsen. He served at the T4 Euthanasia Institute at Pirna-Sonnenstein, in the Economics office. He was posted to the Treblinka death camp, where he was in charge of the *Tarnungs-Kommando* (Camouflage Commando). He also served in Sobibór. Nothing further is known.

SCHIFFNER, Karl. Born on July 4, 1901, in Weiskirchlitz, under the name of Kresadlo. He attended extended elementary school and later studied at the public school in Weiskirchlitz. He served a three year apprenticeship as a carpenter at a Trade School. He then served in the Czech army during the years 1921-23.

Schiffner married in 1928, and became a member of the *Sudetendeutsche Partei*. He joined the *SA* once Czechoslovakia was occupied. He changed from the *SA* to the *SS*, 'because the black uniforms looked better.' His *SS* Number was 321225.

He received the *Ehrenwinkel* (Chrevon of Honor) because of his membership in the *Sudetendeutsche Partei*. He changed his name from Kresadlo to Schiffner in 1941.

Until 1942, he served at the T4 Euthanasia Institute at Pirna-Sonnenstein. Then he was posted to the Treblinka death camp, where he was in charge of the camp joinery and construction team.

During June and July 1943, Schiffner, and a group of twelve Ukrainian *Trawnikimänner* under his command, went to Bełżec, to construct a farmhouse on the former camp site. This was to be occupied by a Ukrainian family in order to keep a close watch on the site.

He also served at Sobibór, from there he was posted to Trieste, to serve in a police unit which fought against the partisans, until the end of the Second World War. After the war Schiffner made his way to Karnten, Austria, where he was captured by British Forces, and interned in a Prisoner of War Camp at Usbach. He was released in October 1945, and he made his way to Salzburg, and then disappeared. No further details are known.

SCHMIDT, Fritz. Born on November 29, 1906, in Eibaum, Gorlitz district in eastern Saxony. A motor mechanic by trade, in 1940, he was employed in the T4 euthanasia Institute at Pirna-Sonnenstein, as a guard and driver. In 1941, he was transferred to Bernburg Euthanasia Institute. He served in Bełżec from June /July 1942, until September 1942, when he was transferred to the Treblinka death camp, to supervise the maintenance and running of the gassing engines in the Upper Camp. He was also in charge of the *SS* garage, and also supervised the metal-workshop. He was then transferred to Sobibór death camp during September 1943, and he stayed there until the camp was liquidated in November 1943. His *SS* Number was 276737. After that he served with *Einsatz R* in Trieste, northern Italy. He was captured by the Americans at the end of the war, but was released and he returned to Germany. He was arrested by the Soviet military authorities, and placed on trial. On December 14, 1949, he was sentenced to nine years imprisonment. He escaped and fled to West Germany, where he died on February 4, 1982, aged 76.

SCHULZE, Erich. Born on September 3, 1902, in Adlershof, Berlin. After serving in T4 Euthanasia Institutes at Grafeneck, Hadamar, and Pirna-Sonnenstein, he was posted to the Treblinka death camp, where he served from September 1942, until the spring of 1943. He was then transferred to Sobibór, where he supervised the *Waldkommando*, and the *Strafkommando* (Penal Colony), until the camp was liquidated. He was then posted to Trieste, Italy. His fate is unknown.

SCHUTT, Hans-Heinz. Born on April 6, 1908, in Dummersdorf. As early as 1938, he became a *Sturmbannverwaltungsführer* with the SS, and subsequently a *Verwaltungsführer* in the T4 Euthanasia Institutes at Grafeneck and Hadamar. His SS Number was 169099.

From April 28, 1942, until mid-August 1942, he served at Sobibór, where he was responsible for paying the SS-Garrison, and manning the counter in *Lager II*, taking the last money and valuables from the naked Jews as they made their way to the gas chambers.

Schutt also worked at the ramp and in *Lager III*, where he was responsible for the cleanliness of the barracks that housed the workers.

Schutt was tried at the Sobibór Trial in Hagen during 1965-66, and on December 20, 1966, he was acquitted of all charges.

SCHWARTZ, First name unknown. This member of the SS-Garrison was recalled by Jewish survivor Dov Freiberg, as an SS-*Untersturmführer* in rank, who wore a black uniform rather than the normal green coloured one. This German was unlike most other members of guard personnel, he did not shout nor beat anyone, and treated the prisoners decently. After a few weeks he left Sobibór, after visiting the Jewish prisoners in their barracks, shaking their hands and wishing them well.

SCHWARZ, Gottfried. Born on May 3, 1913, in Furth. He served at Brandenburg, Grafeneck and Bernburg T4 Institutes as a 'burner.' Schwarz was deputy commandant of Bełżec and he assisted in the construction of the death camp. According to Erich Fuchs, Schwarz also served at Sobibór taking part in trial gassings. His SS Number was 37768.

Schwarz was regarded by Rudolf Reder as being one of the most cruel SS guards. When Bełżec was liquidated he was appointed the commandant of the Dorohucza Labor Camp, in either late February or early March 1943. Schwarz was ordered to Trieste, and he was killed by Italian communist partisans in

San Pietro, near Civdale on June 19, 1944. He was buried at the German Military Cemetery at Costermano, Italy.

SIEFERT, Rudolf. Born on July 29, 1913, in Leipzig. He served as a male nurse at the T4 Euthanasia Institute at Pirna-Sonnenstein. He was posted to Sobibór. He passed away on December 31, 1953.

STEFFL, Thomas. Born on September 17, 1909, in Roiden, a small village circa 9 kilometres from Krummau, Sudetenland. He was the son of a wealthy homeowner Thomas Steffl Senior and his wife Theresia Steffl, formerly Schicho. After finishing school Thomas Steffl junior moved to Weichseln, located on the northern outskirts of Krummau. He became a painter and decorators assistant.

On November 19, 1932, he married Aloisia Wagner, who worked in a spinning factory. The couple lived in the house of Aloisia's, father, a master carpenter in Weichseln. In the same year Aloisia's brother Franz left the region and moved to Berlin, where he joined the Nazi Party in 1933. Franz Wagner had been trained as a photographer in the photo studio of Josef Wolf in Krummau. Because he had already joined, in his homeland, the pro-fascist DNSAP (German National Socialist Workers Party) in 1931, the T4 Organization showed an interest in him.

In the nursing institution of *Schloss Hartheim*, near Linz, in Austria, Franz Wagner was appointed, as the first photographer to take pictures of mentally ill people, before they were gassed—until April 1940.

In the late summer of 1940, Thomas Steffl was released from service in the German *Wehrmacht*. A short time later a life-changing, pivotal, event occurred. His brother-in-law Franz Wagner travelled from Berlin to Krummau to act as a witness in the marriage of his second sister Katharina. Franz Wagner probably recruited Thomas Steffl, his brother-in-law, for service in T4 in Berlin, because only one day later, on Sunday November 17, 1940, Steffl requested his transfer to Berlin.

On joining the T4 Organization Thomas Steffl worked as a painter and decorator in the photographic department in Wilhelmstrasse. But he did not stay there long, as between 1940, and 1941, he was employed in the Euthanasia mass murder Institution at *Schloss Hartheim*.

In February 1943, Thomas Steffl, now the father of three children, was transferred to the Sobibór death camp in Poland. A month later the Wolf brothers from Krummau also arrived at Sobibór. With the rank of *SS-Unterscharführer*, Steffl supervised the sorting of gold and valuables, which had been taken from the Jews who had been murdered in the gas chambers.

During the uprising on October 14, 1943, Thomas Steffl was killed by the Jewish prisoners Chaim Engel and Hersz Pozycki. According to the post-war testimony of Erich Bauer, the Sobibór '*Gasmeister*', Steffl was found lying in the entrance to the former post office house, in the *Vorlager*, after the uprising, having been shot in the stomach. Other accounts say that he was stabbed. Thomas Steffl was buried in German Military Cemetery in Chelm, on October 18, 1943.

STENGELIN, Erwin. Born on August 10, 1911, in Tuttlingen. He served at the T4 Euthanasia Institute at Hadamar. He was then posted to the Treblinka death camp, where he was assigned to the Lower Camp. He was transferred to Sobibór in September 1943. He was killed during the prisoner revolt on October 14, 1943.

STEUBL, Karl. Born on May 25, 1910, in Linz, Austria. He was recruited into the T4 Organization, and served as a male nurse at the T4 Euthanasia Institute at Hartheim. He was posted to Sobibór during April 1942. He supervised the Sorting Barracks in *Lager II*, and was described by Dov Freiberg,' as a tall, thin Austrian.'

Karl Steubl witnessed the murder of the Jews from Treblinka, who were assisting with the dismantling of the structures. He committed suicide after the Second World War ended on September 21, 1945, in Linz.

SUCHOMEL, Franz. Born on December 3, 1907, in Krummau, Sudetenland, now the Czech Republic. In civilian life he was a tailor. He served from 1940, until 1942, in the T4 program at the headquarters in Berlin and at the T4 Euthanasia Institute at Hadamar.

He was ordered, together with Sepp Hirtreiter, Philipp Post, Alfred Loffler, Hermann Sydow, Arthur Matthes and two other men from Frankfurt-am-Main, to the Treblinka death camp. They arrived in Treblinka on August 20, 1942.

Initially, he was employed at the unloading ramp, then as a supervisor in the women's undressing barrack, leading the victims to the 'Tube'. Later he was in charge of the *Goldjuden*, and the tailor workshop. When Odilo Globocnik and Adolf Eichmann visited Treblinka, Suchomel had to report to them about the work of the *Goldjuden*.

In late October 1943, he was posted to Sobibór to assist with the dismantling of the facilities in the death camp. After the closure of Sobibór he was posted to Trieste, Italy. At the end of the Second World War, he was captured by American Forces, and incarcerated in a Prisoner of War Camp.

In August 1945, he was released and he went to Germany. From 1949, he lived in Alotting, Bavaria. He was arrested there on July 11, 1963. At the Treblinka Trial in Düsseldorf during 1964-65, he was sentenced to six years in prison, but was released during 1969.

SYDOW, Hermann. Born in 1899, or 1900. He was a docker in Hamburg prior to the Second World War. In Treblinka. In Treblinka he was in charge of the *Tarnungs-Kommando* (Camouflage Commando). Richard Glazar, a prisoner recalled that Sydow was, 'A short little guy, but very tough, with an unbelievable appetite for alcohol.'

After the revolt Sydow was posted to Sobibór, to help with the dismantling of the facilities. After that was completed he was posted to Italy. No further details are known

THOMAS, Martin. He served at the T4 Euthanasia Institutes at Hadamar and Pirna-Sonnenstein as a driver. He was posted to Sobibór. No further details are known.

UNVERHAU, Heinrich. Born on May 26, 1911, in Vienenburg, Goslar. In April 1925, he became a plumber's apprentice, but as a result of an accident at work, he lost the sight in his right eye, and he was forced to end his apprenticeship. He became a musician and from 1934, he worked as a nurse.

In January 1940, he was ordered to join T4 and he was employed at Gafeneck and Hadamar Institutes, as a nurse. In the winter of 1941/42, he was drafted to the Eastern Front for service in the *Organisation Todt,* looking after the wounded in Raume Wjasma.

In June 1942, he was posted to the Bełżec death camp and whilst there in November 1942, he was hospitalized at Tomaszow Lubelski with spotted typhus and this disease caused him to lose his right eye completely. At the death camp he was responsible for sorting the possessions in the railway sheds located just outside the death camp, opposite Bełżec railway station.

In the summer of 1943, he was posted to the Sobibór death camp, where he supervised the cleaning up of the undressing area in *Lager II,* and in one of the sorting barracks. Unverhau was ordered back to the former death camp site at Bełżec to help with the planting of trees to erase the traces of the crimes committed there. He returned to Sobibór in November 1943, just in time to help with similar re-planting there.

Unverhau was cleared at the Bełżec pre-Trial hearings in 1963, and was also acquitted at the Sobibór Trial in Hagen in 1966. Unverhau passed away on July 25, 1983, in Bad Harzburg.

VALLASTER, Josef. Born on February 5, 1910, in Silbertal, Austria. He served in the T4 Institute of Hartheim. He was posted to Bełżec, where he served from January 1942, until April 1942.

He was then posted to Sobibór in the same month—April 1942. He worked in *Lager III*, supervising the gassing and burial—later burning—of the victims. He often drove the narrow-gauge railway engine that pulled the trucks, filled with the elderly and disabled, from the ramp to *Lager III*. One of the most brutal SS-NCO's in Sobibór, he was killed in the prisoner revolt on October 14, 1943, in the Shoemakers' workshop.

WAGNER, Gustav, Franz. Born on July 18, 1911, in Vienna, Austria. His parents were Franz Wagner and Marie Wagner, formerly Kutscherer, and they lived at Wulzendorfstrasse 14, in Wien 21. Gustav Wagner joined the Nazi Party during 1931, and the SS in 1939. His SS Number was 276962.

He joined the T4 Organization and served in the T4 Euthanasia Institute at Hartheim. He was posted to Sobibór in April 1942. His robust posture earned him the nickname *Welfel* (Wolf), and among the Jewish inmates he was regarded as one of the most brutal and dangerous of the SS-men, alongside Karl Frenzel and Hubert Gomerski. Along with Frenzel, Wagner would select workers on the Ramp, either for Sobibór itself, or outside Labor Camps, such as Dorohucza, Trawniki, and others.

Heinrich Himmler promoted Gustav Wagner to the rank of *SS-Oberscharführer*, following his visit to Sobibór on February 12, 1943. Gustav Wagner was on leave when the prisoners staged the revolt on October 14, 1943. His absence was one of the major factors in the eventual success of the prisoners uprising.

Wagner played a leading role in the execution of the Jewish workers sent from Treblinka, to assist with the dismantling of the facilities at Sobibór. After the end of the Second World War, he fled to Brazil, having adopted the name of Gunther Mendel.

During May 1978, he was traced by Simon Wiesenthal, the renowned Nazi-Hunter. Wagner's identity was confirmed at a Sao Paulo police station, by former Sobibór prisoner Stanislaw Szmajzner, who had also settled in Brazil.

Confronted with the evidence against him, he had to admit to being Gustav Wagner from Sobibór. Wagner was duly arrested, but requests for his extradition to the German Federal Republic and Israel were rejected. On October 15, 1980, Gustav Wagner committed suicide in Itabaia, Brazil. Stanislaw Szmajzner, however, stated that he (Szmajzner) had not been an entirely passive bystander at his death.

WALTER, Arthur. Born on October 22, 1907, in Reichstein. A *Reserveleutnant der Schutzpolizei*. He was a member of the *SA*, and joined the Nazi Party in 1930, and the *SS* in 1931. He served in the T4 Euthanasia Institutes at Pirna-Sonnenstein and Hartheim. He also served at Sobibór from September 1942. When the camp closed down, he was posted to Udine.

WEISS, Bruno. Born between 1905, and 1910, he lived in Berlin. In civilian life he was a male nurse and was recruited by the T4 Organization. In April 1942, he was posted to Sobibór, and in the early phase of the camp's operations he was the chief of *Lager I*, but Karl Frenzel took over this function. Weiss then served *in Lager III*—the extermination area—, at the Ramp, and in *Lager II*.

He was notorious for mocking the Jewish prisoners through songs such as, 'Gott. Du erhöre unsere Lieder, mach dem Juden die Klapp zu, dann haben die Menschen Ruh.' (Dear God, hear our song, shut up the Jews, so people will have some peace and quiet).

Weiss was released by T4 because he had tuberculosis. He left Sobibór in the spring of 1943, and he passed away in 1944.

WENDLAND, Wilhelm. Born during 1907, in Berlin. In civilian life he was a cook. He was recruited by the T4 Organization, and he served in the T4 Euthanasia Institute in Bernburg, as a cook, and as a 'burner' of bodies. He arrived in Sobibór in March 1943, along with Franz Wolf, Josef Wolf, and Fritz Konrad. According to Erich Bauer in his post-war interrogations, Wilhelm Wendland lost an arm in an accident.

Wendland supervised the Sorting barracks and the *Waldkommando*, on the day five prisoners escaped on July 23, 1943. During the prisoner revolt on October 14, 1943, he held prisoners at gunpoint.

He was posted to Trieste and Fiume, where he was killed in action in December 1944.

WOLF, Franz. Born on April 9, 1907, in Krummau, Sudetenland. He was a photographer, like his father Josef Wolf senior, and he took over the family business when his father passed away. He served in the Czech and German army. He was recruited by the T4 Organization and he served in the T4 headquarters in Berlin, in the photographic department, and also at the T4 Euthanasia Institute at Hadamar, and a psychiatric clinic in Heidelberg, where he took 'scientific' photographs of the mentally ill patients.

He was sent to Lublin, Poland, with a small group of men, and from there he was posted to Sobibór in early March 1943, along with his brother Josef, Fritz Konrad, and Willi Wendland.

Franz Wolf usually supervised the Sorting Barracks, where he mocked the women who worked there, with the saying, *Dalli, dailli, meine Damen: Arbeit macht das Leben süss'* (Come along now girls, work makes life worth living.). Franz Wolf also served in the barrack near the gas chambers where the women and girls had their hair cut off, and he sometimes supervised the *Waldkommando*.

He survived the prisoner revolt on October 14, 1943, and when Sobibór closed, he was posted to Trieste and Fiume, in Italy. At the Sobibór Trial in Hagen on December 20, 1966, he was sentenced to serve eight years in prison, on account of his participation in the murder of an undisclosed number of people, thought to be at least 39,000 people.

WOLF, Josef. Born on April 26, 1900, in Krummau, Sudetenland. He was the second son of the photographer Josef Wolf senior, and his wife Magdalena Wolf, formerly Mugrauer. Josef Wolf junior learned the profession of a photographer in his father's company, and was involved in the management of the company after his father's death in February 1938.

After the German assault on Poland, Josef Wolf served in the German *Wehrmacht* and was released from service during mid-1941. Wolf belonged to a group of people from Krummau, who knew each other very well, as friends, or family relatives. This is why a number of them, including Thomas Steffl and Franz Suchomel ended up working for the T4 Organization—responsible for the Euthanasia mass-murder of mentally-ill and disabled people.

This Krummau circle is important to the history of Josef and Franz Wolf. Thomas Steffl was the first one to be recruited into T4, on November 17, 1940, probably recommended by his brother-in-law Franz Wagner. Then Wagner recommended his friend Franz Habada, whom he shared an apartment with in Berlin since 1939. Steffl and Habada both came from villages near Krummau. Habada was a photographer, who had learned his trade at the photographic studio of Josef Seidel, where co-incidently Josef Wolf senior had also learned his trade during the years 1881-1884.

Franz Wagner had learnt the photographer's craft at the Atelier Wolf in Krummau. He rose through the ranks to become head of the T4 Photographic Department, whilst Franz Habada served as his deputy.

Wagner recommended the late Josef Wolf's son Franz, who was born in 1907, as well as the tailor Franz Suchomel, who later served at Treblinka and Sobibór death camps in Poland, also from Krummau, to join the T4 Organization. The last member of this group to join T4 in Berlin was Josef Wolf, now a father of three children.

Both of the Wolf brothers were employed from October 29, 1941, in the photographic department of T4, developing film negatives and producing enlargements of pictures which had been taken from victims. Both of the Wolf brothers were then employed as photographers in various Euthanasia killing institutions

In March 1943, both of the Wolf brothers arrived at the Sobibór extermination camp in Poland. Josef Wolf was employed in the clothes sorting barracks, driving the *Arbeitsjuden* to work at speed. Josef also supervised the *Waldkommando*, which worked in the forest outside the camp perimeters. For what Josef Wolf did in Sobibór the Nazi regime paid him a net salary of 300 *Reichsmark* per month.

During the Jewish prisoner revolt in Sobibór on October 14, 1943, Josef Wolf and Thomas Steffl were killed, amongst other SS and *Trawnikimänner*. Wolf was killed in the Sorting Barracks No. 25, with a blow from an axe wielded by Jewish Soviet Prisoner of War Boris Cybulski, who later died fighting the Germans in the forest. Josef Wolf was buried in the German Military Cemetery in Chelm.

ZANKER, Hans. Born on September 8, 1905, in Sachsen. In civilian life he was a butcher by profession. He served in the T4 Euthanasia Institutes of Pirna-Sonnenstein as a cook, and he also served at the T4 Euthanasia Institute at Hartheim. He served at the death camps in Poland including, Bełżec, Sobibór and Treblinka. He arrived in Bełżec during September 1942, and stayed until the camp closed, when he was transferred to the Jewish Labor Camp in Poniatowa. He was then transferred to Italy, where he was based in Trieste. No further details are known.

ZASPEL, Fritz. Born on October 31, 1907, in Waldheim. He was recruited by the T4 Organization and he served in the T4 Euthanasia Institute at Pirna-Sonnenstein, as a male nurse. He served in Sobibór. He passed away during 1988.

ZIERKE, Ernst Theodor Franz. Born on May 6, 1905, in Krampe, the son of a railroad worker. After he graduated from elementary school he worked as a forester, and in 1921, he was apprenticed to be a blacksmith. After passing the blacksmith apprenticeship exams he was employed in agriculture from 1925.

In 1934, he changed careers and became a nurse at a clinic at Neuruppin near Brandenburg and was summoned to the T4 Headquarters in Berlin in December 1939, and he served at the T4 Institutes at Grafeneck and Hadamar.

In the winter of 1941/42, he was drafted into the *Organisation Todt* for the care of the wounded in Russia. He returned to Germany and worked at a T4 institute at Eichberg, near Rudesheim. He was posted to the Bełżec death camp in June 1942, where he served until March 1943. At Bełżec he served on the ramp. His *SS* Number was 272096.

In March 1943, he was transferred along with Robert Juhrs to the Jewish Labor camp at Dorohucza, which dug peat, until November 1943. Zierke was amongst the SS who escorted the Jewish *Arbeitshäftlinge* from Dorohucza to the nearby Jewish Labor camp at Trawniki, where all of them were shot, as part of *Aktion Erntefest* (Harvest Festival).

Zierke was sent to Sobibór death camp, to help with the closure of the camp, and he formed part of the cordon that watched over the final liquidation of the Jewish workers from Treblinka. He was then posted to Italy. Zierke was released prior to the Bełżec Trial in Munich in 1964. He was subsequently tried in Hagen for war crimes committed at Sobibór, but was released from custody on health grounds. Zierke died on May 23,1972.

SUPPORT STAFF

BUCKSTEEG, Josef. He was born on March 18, 1888. As remembered by Georg Holzel, a *Reichsbahn* official, Bucksteeg was the station master at Sobibór. He came from the Kleve area, and was interrogated after the end of the Second World War.[431]

MOSER, Bruno (*Baurat*). Very little is known about Bruno Moser, who was in charge of providing construction material for the building of the Sobibór death camp. He was based in Chelm (*Cholm*), working for the *Kreishauptmann* Dr. Werner Ansel. Later he moved from Chelm to work for the *Technische Hauptamt* in *Krakau*. No further details about his fate are known.

Hans-Heinz Schutt testified on November 22, 1962, that he knew *Baurat* Bruno Moser and recalled that:

> I knew the *Baurat* Moser. At that time he had his office in *Cholm*, in the German administration building of the district Cholm. It is true that he established the Sobibór camp of that time. I visited him several times at the time and received instructions from him on where to pick up the necessary materials. The camp manager at the time, Stangl, had informed me that Moser was responsible for procuring the items mentioned. In my opinion, Moser, was a South German. However, I can't say where he came from. He was about 50-55 years old then.

---

[431] Georg Holzel Interrogation—Holocaust Historical Society UK.

Chapter VI
Post War Testimonies by *SS*-Men

Sobibór Trial (Used with permission from Ullstein Bild)

This chapter has been possible due to the excellent co-operation with the NIOD-Institute for War, Holocaust and Genocide studies in Amsterdam, Holland, who have generously made available their extensive archive. I would like to place on record my heartfelt thanks to Rene Pottkamp for all his help and advice, and the NIOD have given me permission to include these post-war testimonies.

Indeed this is the heart of the book, and the testimonies shed much light on Sobibór and the *SS*, who ran the death camp on a day to day basis. It is fair to say that the many testimonies cover the same ground, the same people. But that is the nature of this grisly, small, compressed world of life and death, in a small village in south-eastern Poland. Many of these are appearing in English for quite probably the first time ever, and they are the *raison d'etre* for this second edition. I am eternally grateful for the immense translation of these documents from German to English by Ena, who—as a young mother raising her little son Otto—, has undertaken the translation work with skill and dedication. I cannot thank her enough, and I should also mention her father-in-law John Lewis, for introducing Ena to me.

Former SS Men Testimonies

Erich Bauer

September 13, 1960
Berlin

I work as a driver and I did this job in Berlin before and during the war. In 1940, I was called up to be the driver for patient transfer for the armed forces in Berlin. I was mainly deployed for patient transfer and got to know drivers from German departments, who were assigned to move irretrievable patients to different institutions. It is the so-called '*Gemeinnützige Stiftung fur Anstaltspflege*' (Charitable Foundation for Institutional Care), which was based in *Berlin W30, Tiergartenstrasse 4*. Head of that department was the now known Professor Heyde, or rather the doctors working for him were always out and about to select the apparently irretrievable patients from all the mental homes in the whole of Germany, and what I found out later, to shift to concentration camps or rather mental homes. I have myself driven *Oberstabsarzt* Straub during my time there. As far as I know Straub was from Saxony and was *Wehrmachtsangehöriger*, who somehow got the position in the *Sonderkommando*.

In addition to Professor Heyde, Professor Nitsche, who lived in Berlin-Frohnau, who was apparently already condemned by the Russians, Haus[432] who was the head of personnel in the department and another person called Becker[433], who served as a fellow passenger. Becker continuously accompanied the transport of gas bottles, which were used for the extermination of the above sick people.

I need to mention that I myself was taken over to the department of Professor Heyde in the beginning of 1941, after I got acquainted with a driver of his department. We called the department T4, and from there in around April 1942, I was moved to the department of the *Höhere SS- und Polizeiführer* in Lublin.[434] Head of this department in Lublin was the *SS-Oberführer* Globocnik,[435] his adjutant *Obersturmbannführer* Höfle, who was in charge of the *Vernichtungslager* in the area Lublin.

Whilst I certainly know that Globocnik came from Salzburg, I think that I can remember that Höfle came from Berlin.[436] After a few days I got moved up from Lublin to Cholm, there I was in the *SS-Reiterstandarte* for about two days, until I came to the *Vernichtungslager* (extermination camp) Sobibór, which was under construction.

During my deployment there until about September 1943, I was only used as a driver to transport food and construction materials. I wore an *SS* uniform with the rank of a *SS-Oberscharführer*. I have never been a member of the General-*SS*.

The camp Sobibór consisted of about 30 barracks, and was subdivided into 'Lager I, II, III'. *Lager III* was the extermination camp, where the gas chamber and crematorium were. Sobibór was built by *SS-Führer* Thomalla. Later head of the camp were in the order of *SS-Obersturmführer* Franz Stangl and *SS-Hauptsturmführer* Franz Reichleitner, deputy head of camp was

---

[432] Friedrich Haus, Personalchef T4—Ernst Klee Namensliste, p.561.
[433] August Becker, Gasspezialist T4—Ernst Klee Namensliste, p.546.
[434] This statement is incorrect, it was the SSPF Lublin.
[435] Globocnik's rank at this time was *SS-Brigadeführer*, and the spelling used by Bauer in his testimony was Lobodscheck.
[436] Höfle's rank at the time was *SS-Hauptsturmführer*, and Globocnik was born in Trieste, lived in Klagenfurt and Vienna. Höfle was born in Salzburg.

SS-Untersturmführer Niemann, who was to my knowledge back then from Belzec, and subsequently after an uprising by prisoners lost his life.[437]

25-30 *SS* people were continually part of guarding the camp, alongside about 200-250 Russian volunteers, who were educated by members of the police from *Schlesien* in a camp in Trawniki. I have to mention that the actual guarding of the camp was carried out by the volunteers and the *SS* people were mainly acting as heads of the *'Arbeitskommando'* (Work command). So the head of the volunteers was *SS-Scharführer* Gomerski,[438] that means the volunteers continued to come under the police, and were only assigned to guard the camps.

In the *Stammlager I* and *II*, were continuously about 150 prisoners accommodated, who belonged to the *'Arbeitskommando,'* whereas *Lager III*, only served the extermination of the incoming Jew transports. I estimate the number of murdered people in Sobibór to about 30,000-40,000[439]. I can't specify numbers about this because the incoming train transports were directly brought to *Lager III*, and were murdered in the gas chambers after a few hours.

The unloading of the transports as well as the extermination in the gas chambers and the burning of the dead bodies in the crematorium were exclusively performed by prisoners. Only the unloading was supervised by former *SS-Scharführer* Karl Frenzel. As far as I know Frenzel came from the area around Neuruppin. I don't know anything about his whereabouts.

I would like to mention that the extermination in the gas chambers did not take place, as mistakenly assumed in my procedure, by poisonous gas, but by emissions of combustion engines.

---

[437] Thomalla held the rank of *SS-Hauptsturmführer*, Franz Stangl held the rank of *SS-Obersturmführer* as did Franz Reichleitner. Nieman held the rank of *SS-Oberscharführer* between August 1941, and August 1942.
[438] Listed as Komerski, by Bauer.
[439] This figure is far too low, and official estimates range from 150,000 to 250,000.

To the people listed here by name, who are guilty of any crime, I would like to give truthful declarations as far as this is still possible today.

SS-Unterscharführer **Becker or Becher** was in Sobibór for about 3-4 months. He had a work command in the Sorting Department, and represented me as a driver whilst I was on holiday. Becker / Becher came from Saxony, the area of Pirna.

SS-Unterscharführer **Beckmann**, he was the supervisor of the Economy Department in *Lager II*, in Sobibór. Beckmann was a qualified farmer and came from the area of Oldenburg, and he was about 30 years old back then.[440]

Dr. Blaurock, during my employment in Sobibór, I didn't get to know this name. I also haven't learnt that there was a chemist working.

SS-Unterscharführer **Kurt Bolender** was an active 'SS-Mann' and came from the mental home Hartheim, near Linz, where the already Stangl and Reichleitner were also working. Bolender was in *Lager III* in Sobibór. It is absolutely possible that he was leading the crematorium.

SS-Oberscharführer **Paul Bredow** also came from a mental home and led various work commands. I am not aware he shot Jews. Bredow is native-born from Berlin.[441]

The one listed under the name **Bree**, would be the security guard of the volunteers, who's name from my knowledge would be Rehl, and who lost his life in the revolt.

SS-Scharführer **Sepp Vallaster**, was allegedly from the mental home Hadamar, and was the head of *Lager III*. As such, he was mainly in charge of the burning. Vallaster lost his life in the Tailor Shop during the revolt.

---

[440] Beckmann was born in Buer, Gelsenkirchen, on November 21, 1904.
[441] Bredow was in fact born in Guttland, a district of Danzig.

The alleged listed **SS-Oberscharführer Franz** should be the same as the former commander from Treblinka, Kurt Franz, because I know that Franz was promoted at that time.[442]

SS-Oberscharführer **Herbert Floss**, was as far as I know, mostly in Belzec, and only came to Sobibór after the revolt. He constantly was with *Untersturmführer* Niemann.[443]

I don't know an *Unterscharführer* called **Friedrich Gaulstich**.

SS-Scharführer **Toni Getzinger** was also from the mental home in the area of Linz, like Stangl, and was leading *Lager III*, together with Vallaster. He was supervising the gas chambers. I would like to mention that Getzinger did the task that mistakenly was on me. He died in August or September 1943, when he wanted to try out discovered Russian hand grenades.

It is possible that a *SS-Scharführer* **Hans Greimer** came to Sobibór after the revolt. I can't say that for sure.[444]

SS-Scharführer **Paul Groth** was the successor of Beckmann, as the head of the *Lager* in Sobibór, and was also from a mental home. I think I can remember that he was from the Berlin district Treptow. He was a butcher and because of illness transferred. I don't know his whereabouts.

I don't know a *SS-Oberscharführer* Herbert Helm.

SS-Oberscharführer **Hermann Michel** was leading the removal of valuables and the undressing before the extermination together with Beckmann. He was also active as a paramedic and like his father before, he was a male nurse in the mental home Buch near Berlin. He was moved before the liquidation of the camp.

I don't know a person called **Hoffmann** from Sobibór.

SS-Oberscharführer **Paul Ittner** was leading the personnel department in the camp guard and was also from a mental home.

---

[442] Kurt Franz was promoted to the rank of *SS-Untersturmführer* in the spring of 1943.

[443] Johann Niemann was promoted to the rank of *Untersturmführer* in the spring of 1943.

[444] This might be Ferdinand Gromer.

Scharführer **Kamm**, first name unknown, was probably also a former male nurse in a mental home, and came to Sobibór shortly before the liquidation of the camp.[445]

Alex Kaiser was '*Oberwachmann*' in Sobibór and belonged to the Russian volunteers.

SS-Oberscharführer **Graetschus** was presumably called Hans by first name, and became the head of volunteers in 1943.[446]

SS-Scharführer **Konrad** came to Sobibór presumably after the revolt.[447]

Erich Lachmann a *Polizei-Oberwachtmeister* became known to me as a relative from the training unit mentioned before in Trawniki. He deserted in 1942, with valuables taken off the Jews. He came from *Schlesien*.

I got to know **Karl Ludwig, a** *SS-Scharführer* and driver of Professor Heyde. He is probably staying in the Soviet Zone.

SS-Oberscharführer **Hermann Michel** and Michel Hermann named under number 15, should be identical. As far as I know his surname was Hermann.[448]

SS-Unterscharführer **Karl Muller** came, like me from T4. At times he was leading the *Sortierungsabteilung* in Sobibór and came from Berlin-Kreuzberg. He passed away in Berlin after the war.

SS-Unterscharführer **Nowak**, first name presumably Kurt, used to belong to the police in Sonnenstein near Pirna, and died in the revolt.[449]

SS-Scharführer **Karl Pötzinger**, was in Sobibór only for a short time and used to be a male nurse in mental homes in Berlin.

---

[445] Rudolf Kamm, was his full name. He also served at Bełzec.
[446] Graetschus first name was Siegfried.
[447] Fritz Konrad was posted to Sobibór in March 1943. He was killed during the prisoner revolt on October 14, 1943.
[448] The correct name is Hermann Michel. The rank should read *SS-Oberscharführer*.
[449] The correct name is Anton Julius Nowak. The rank should read *SS-Unterscharführer*.

He died during a home visit. It was said that he drowned while being drunk at the Schlossbrücke in Berlin-Mitte.[450]

SS-Unterscharführer Wenzel Rehwald worked as a bricklayer and was supervising construction works in the camp. He practically constructed the Sobibór camp and had nothing to do with anything else. He was a *Sudetendeutscher*.

SS-Unterscharführer Kurt Richter worked as a butcher, came from the mental home Sonnenstein, and was head of the kitchen in Sobibór. He was shot by partisans.

I don't know **SS-Unterscharführer Walter Ribe**[451].

I know **SS-Unterscharführer Karl Schiffner** by name, he was probably in Bełżec, and could only have come to Sobibór for a short period of time after the revolt. He was, like most of all, a male nurse in a mental home before.

I don't know **SS-Oberscharführer Schmidt**.

I don't know **Emil Schumacher**.

I don't know **SS-Oberscharführer Schulz**.

I know **Hans Schutt** from my time in T4, he lived in Berlin-Niederschonweide and he appeared as *Untersturmführer* and Revisor in Sobibór.

SS-Untersturmführer Friedl Schwarz only came to Sobibór for a short time and must have otherwise been employed in other camps.

SS-Scharführer Karl Steubl was my passenger and came from a mental home near Linz. He was born there and committed suicide after the war.

I can't remember **Steffl**, but I think I have heard of that Nazi.[452]

I don't know **Unverhau**, closer, he presumably came to Sobibór after the revolt.[453]

---

[450] Karl Potzinger was killed on December 22, 1944, in an air raid in Italy.
[451] Possibly Walter Ryba.
[452] In Bauer's statement the name is shown as Staffl.
[453] Unverhau was posted to Sobibór.

SS-Oberscharführer **Gustav Wagner** was in charge of the '*Spies*' and is as far as I know, imprisoned in Vienna.

SS-Scharführer **Bruno Weiss** was the head of the *Arbeitskommando* and came from Berlin-Adlershof. He left because he suffered from tuberculosis and died later.

I know **Kurt Werner**.

SS-Scharführer **Wolf** was in the Sorting department in Sobibór. They were brothers, who's first names I don't know for sure and the younger one died in the revolt. They came from the Sudetenland.[454]

I know about *SS-Sturmbannführer* **Christian Wirth**, that he was a former criminal superintendent in Stuttgart, came to T4 after and was leading the facilities in the extermination camps in Poland. He got shot during an operation with our unit in Italy, apparently by partisans, but probably got shot by his own people, and was buried at the cemetery in Trieste.

Polizei-Oberwachtmeister **Arthur Dachsel** was the only one of our group who wore a police uniform. He came from the surroundings of Sonnenstein and didn't have a specific role in Sobibór. Back then he already was an old man and was hardly used.

I can't give any more details.

January 11, 1962
Berlin

Mentz: I know the name Mentz. However, I can't remember seeing Mentz in Sobibór. It is possible that he came to Sobibór after the camp was already taken down. If that had been in November 1943, there would have been no more gassing taking place in Sobibór.

---

[454] Josef Wolf, who was killed in the revolt, was 7 years older than his brother Franz Wolf who survived.

433

On demand: It is true that the demolition of the camp in Sobibór was executed by worker Jews. I don't know where those worker Jews stayed after that. The assumption is close that the worker Jews were shot in Sobibór, after the demolition of the camp. I can't confirm that assumption. I assume that the last Jews from Sobibór were taken to Auschwitz, after they finished the demolition of the camp.

Munzberger: I know him. He was—if any—only a short time in Sobibór. I can't give exact details about his activities or his behaviour in Sobibór.

Oberhauser: Was to my knowledge a short time in Sobibór. He was one of the very active. I think I can remember that he abused the female Jews with the words, 'Hey, you old whore!' In any case, I think the statement is inaccurate that Oberhauser was in Sobibór in the role of a demolition master. There were no duties for a demolition master in Sobibór.

Paetesser: Was actually called Bodessa. He was a Ukrainian unskilled worker in Sobibór.

Roil: Was to my knowledge an unskilled worker in Sobibór. I cannot identify him more closely.

Paul Rost: Police Chief from Saxony. He was in Sobibór for a short time as a supervisor. I can't give any other relevant information about him.

Rum: Came to Sobibór after the gassings had stopped. After the dissolution of the extermination camp in Treblinka, Sobibór was meant to be rebuilt as a working camp. For this purpose members of the permanent staff in Treblinka were moved to Sobibór in about November 1943. Sobibór, however, was also dissolved, so that we were all assigned to Italy. Therefore it might be true that Rum didn't participate in any extermination action in Sobibór.

Schafer: Was the predecessor of Lachmann in Sobibór for a few months. He performed the usual functions in the camp.

Schluch: I know the name. I can't say for sure if Schluch was in Sobibór. I would like to ask for a photo for further identification.

Schulz: Was a Ukrainian unskilled worker in Sobibór. I can't say anymore to identify him.

Schutt: He was merely employed for administrative work-procurement of food, administration of jewellery taken from Jewish prisoners, mail traffic, in Sobibór. I don't think Schutt was participating in any extermination actions in Sobibór.

Stich: I know the name. I think Stich was in Sobibór too. Ms Allers should know him.

Unverhau: Was in Sobibór. I would like a photo so that I can give a thorough statement about his activity and behaviour. Only based on his name I can't give specific information about him.

Wendland: The person recorded as Vetland, was called Wendland (possibly Hermann) to my knowledge. Wendland belonged to the permanent staff in Sobibór. He was originally from Berlin and lost an arm in an accident. Wendland performed the usual functions in the camp.[455]

I have already given details about the members of the permanent staff in Sobibór. I can't make any other relevant statements at this moment. The above interrogation transcript was read aloud and clearly. I confirm the correctness with my signature.

November 20, 1962
Dortmund

Erich Bauer, born 26.3.1900, is presented into the interrogation room in Berlin-Tegel, he is familiar with the subject of the interrogation and admonished the truth, he says the following:

Apparently out of false camaraderie I've been silent so far, to not burden my former comrades. I would like to say everything

---

[455] The correct name is Willhelm Wendland.

and tell the whole truth, because I don't accept that Gomerski and I get blamed for it all.

Fuchs: Until now someone has been spared who built the extermination camp Sobibór. It is the former *SS-Scharführer* Erich Fuchs born 1901, or 1902, who lived in *Berlin SW, 29 Gneisenaustr.* Fuchs was the technical manager of the T4 department. He has built all of the extermination camps of the *Aktion Reinhardt*, Treblinka, Sobibór and Bełżec.

In his private life he was an engine fitter. I got to know Fuchs in the *Kämpferzeit* as *Freidenker* and later as a former member from the T4 department. He was seconded from *T4* to Bełżec to build the extermination camp there. Later he set up the extermination camps Sobibór and Treblinka. Fuchs has told me about these activities himself. I worked together with him in Sobibór. We set up the engine together. Fuchs was associated with the Jeckel family, who owned a petrol station in Berlin, *Gneisenaustr./ corner Behrwald-Schleimacherstr.*

I suppose you can determine Fuchs through Jeckel. After setting up the extermination camps, Fuchs was seconded to the organization 'Samt und Seide' in Berlin, Tiergartenstrasse 3. This office was responsible for carrying out secret confiscation actions.

Bolender: At first Bolender dug the pits by hand in *Lager III*. Later the pits with buried corpses were excavated by a backhoe and the dead bodies were burned to tens of thousands. This work was Bolender's responsibility. It is a shame what happened back then.

Bolender and his men set up a log cabin during this 'work' in *Lager III*. They baked hash browns there and lived in the lap of luxury. Bolender was the lead in *Lager III* and was responsible for the business. *Er hatte ein Maul bis zum Alexanderplatz.* In Sobibór there was an 'insane' work Jew and Bolender made him fight other work Jews until they were half-dead for his entertainment. Bolender had a dog, who he set, because he was a member of the translation commando, on Jews, if they didn't walk fast enough.

Dubois: He trained the Ukrainian unskilled workers and deployed them to guard the camp.

Frenzel: I have already given detailed information about him. He was one of the most brutal members of the permanent staff. His whip was 'pretty loose.' For the rest I may refer to my earlier statements.

Ittner: If Ittner testified that he was in Sobibór in the beginning of the camp, he can confirm my statements about Fuchs. As far as he was deployed in *Lager III*, he must have been involved with the transports of the Jews to the gas chambers, burying the dead bodies and digging pits. I can't remember having seen Ittner in *Lager III*. However, I would like to mention again in this context that the digging of the pits stopped during the gassing process. The camp staff in *Lager III*, was involved in the proper destruction during the gassing process.

Juhrs: I can confirm that there were working Jews from Sobibór and Bełżec in Sobibór in the autumn of 1943. I can't remember working Jews from Treblinka. In the autumn of 1943, all the working Jews in *Lager III*, in Sobibór were shot. Because Frenzel was in charge of the working Jews, I assume he directed the execution or at least knew about it. I don't know who else was involved in the execution. I also don't know whether Juhrs was involved.

Lachmann: He supervised the Ukrainian unskilled workers, deployed them to guard the camp and participated in the destruction process in this way.

Lambert: In autumn 1942, new fittings and doors were installed in the gas chambers in Sobibór.

Schutt: As I have already testified, no former member of the camp staff can exclude himself from having participated in the gassing operation. We were a 'sworn group' in a foreign country, surrounded by Ukrainian unskilled workers, who you couldn't rely on. In these circumstances we depended on each other. In this context I would like to reveal a secret. We were so sworn, that Frenzel, Stangl, and Wagner made a ring out of a 5 *Deutsche Mark* coin for every member of the permanent staff with the *SS* Rune. These rings were used as identification marks for all camp staff, to make it clear who the 'sworn group' was. There was a division of labor in the camp. Everyone has at one point performed every function in Sobibór (station command, undressing, gassing process). This also applies to Schutt. I myself have seen him in various parts of the camp. On these occasions he belonged to the station command and supervised the undressing. Besides, he was corrupt, he had taken advantage of his position of power and celebrated orgies with female Jews and enriched himself with the Jewish wealth.

Unverhau: I can't remember him

Wolf: The Wolf brothers are known to me from Sobibór. Josef Wolf was the younger brother.[456] He got killed during the revolt. Franz Wolf was very saddened by the death of his brother. I comforted him then and therefore can't understand why he now calls me a 'rowdy.' The Wolf brothers were employed in the sorting department. I can't say anything negative about them.

The Jews had to undress in *Lager II* and were directly guided to *Lager III* to be gassed. After the Jews were taken away, the Wolf brothers and their *Kommando* turned up in *Lager III* to carry the clothes to the sorting barracks to clear the Lager for further undressing.[457] The floor was raked so that the Jews who followed wouldn't notice that undressing had already taken place there. It was the Wolf brothers' job together with their *Kommando* to sort the clothes into individual pieces (coats, jackets, trousers etc) and so look for valuables.

The sorting department had to work towards extreme acceleration because the duration of the extermination process depended on the duration of the undressing. The pieces of clothing therefore had to be removed in *Lager II* as quickly as possible, so

---

[456] Josef Wolf was actually the eldest of the two brothers, he was born on April 26, 1900, and Franz Wolf was born on April 9, 1907.

[457] This might be *Lager II*, as workers in *Lager III* were kept isolated from the rest and no worker was allowed to cross over the threshold, as Bauer confirmed in later testimony.

that the following Jews could be undressed and gassed more quickly. The supervising of the undressing, the removal of the clothes from *Lager II*, and the sorting were all part of the actual termination process, which began with the unloading of the transports and ended with the burying of the corpses.

I estimate the number of gassed Jews in Sobibór to be 350,000 people. I once overheard a conversation in the canteen in Sobibór between Frenzel, Stangl and Wagner. They were talking about the number of victims in the extermination camps Bełżec, Treblinka and Sobibór and they expressed their regrets for competitive reasons, that Sobibór ranked last.

I have given my consent for my interrogations to be dictated on tape. My interrogation was dictated loudly and clearly in my presence and then listened to. I confirm the correctness of the playback.

December 10, 1962
Berlin

From April 1942, until the termination of the camp Sobibór in October or November 1943, I belonged to the permanent staff. In that time I had 3 weeks holiday during New Years 1942/43, and in the summer 1943, again 2 weeks holiday. I was also in the hospital in Włodawa after my first holiday for 4-5 weeks.

I was mainly occupied as a lorry driver and drove a HGV-Ford, to get groceries, building material etc. I was occupied with these transports and the maintenance of the truck for more than two thirds of my total activity. I was assigned to the camp itself. I didn't have any other specific job in the camp. In *Lager III*, the actual extermination camp, I was involved in the construction and took part in the first 3-4 exterminations, together with Erich Fuchs.

The whole camp Sobibór consisted of three individual camps. In *Lager I*, which Frenzel (Karl Frenzel) was in charge of, the reception camp, there were workshops, cobbler shops, tailor, locksmith, carpentry, saddlery, the kitchen and later on the bakery. Furthermore there were the sleeping barracks for the 'working Jews.' In this camp were also the working tools. All three camps were fenced off from each other. In front of *Lager I*, was a pre-camp, where the German staff and the Ukrainian unskilled workers slept in buildings. The entire camp area was again fenced and mined.

The *Lager II* was the economy camp and it contained the office with the valuables department, a horse stable and the magazine. 5-6 men slept in the administration building and myself in a special chamber. In the administration building was also the first bakery. The administration building and the Forest House are identical: the whole of *Lager II*, belonged to the former Forest House.

The *Lager III*, was the actual extermination camp. On this site were the gas chambers, living barracks for the Jews, who were responsible for the operation of the gas chambers, as well as the crushing of the stubs and other work in connection with the extermination.

The permanent staff of the whole Sobibór camp contained of 20-30 German members of the *SS* and *SA*. Furthermore also about 200 men of the Ukrainian unskilled workers were active. Additionally there were usually about 150 working Jews in *Lager I*, and about 40-50 Jews in *Lager III*, who were dealing with the extermination work. The Jews of *Lager III*, were totally isolated from everyone and never got together with the others again.

In May 1942, a narrow-gauge railway train was set up. The bottom of the wagons came from dump trucks, on which a wooden box was placed. The train had a track of about 80 cm. The train had a connection to the unloading ramp, about 20 meters from the station, but was already inside the camp and led into *Lager III*, and from there down into the excavated pits. In addition a track led from the gas chambers to the pits.

I was first deployed in the winter of 1941/42, on a large scale operation on the Eastern Front, namely for the transport to the front in large buses and for the return transport of wounded people. I drove an ambulance. Back then the people from the euthanasia institute in Linz were already there. Leader was a certain Dr. Ulrich. It was around Christmas 1941, or perhaps a bit later I was back in Berlin and after around 10 weeks I was assigned by Dieter Allers to Poland, to the *SS- und Polizeiführer*[458]. Allers was one of the key people under the head of department T4, Professor Heyde. As far as I know, he had at least the fleet of vehicles under him and also assigned me to work. At the time I didn't know more about the purpose of my assignment. I only found out the actual purpose in Sobibór. Maybe the others already, who had previously been to smaller institutions knew more.

We met at the department T4 in *Tiergartenstrasse* in the beginning of April 1942. There were definitely Stangl, Wagner, Steubl, Rehwald), Gomerski, Beckmann, maybe already Frenzel, Vallaster, in total 12-15 men. We drove to Lublin from Berlin-Charlottenburg, where we reported to the *SS-und Polizeiführer*, and stayed for about 8 days. There we got dressed by the SS as SS men and came to Cholm to the cavalry squadron, and at the end of April-beginning of May 1942, we came to Sobibór by a small train. There we set up the camp, which had partially been set up, put up the barbed wire fences, set up the *Lager III*, and dug two pits of at least 30m x 30m floor space and at least 5m depth with Ukrainian unskilled workers and a few Jews from Włodawa.

The actual gas chambers have already been erected by the SS (a wooden barrack with cement flooring and two rooms of at least 6m x 6m floor space and maybe for 50 men). The engine (a French tank engine, Renault make) had already been lying there, as well as the connection pipes.

Erich Fuchs and I then made the connection to the two gas chambers for the line of engine exhaust gasses. Moreover the living barracks in *Lager III*, were built. The actual lines of gas were already laid by Erich Fuchs and Heinrich Barbl. Barbl did the

---

[458] Bauer in his testimony stated this was the Higher SS and Police Leader, but the correct rank was SS and Police Leader, which was Odilo Globocnik.

same in other camps also and was stationed in Bełżec. As far as I know, in the spring of 1943 (maybe February / March), the previous wooden barracks were built as solid concrete buildings with probably 6 or 8 gas chambers. I haven't seen the chambers myself but only brought the doors and fittings.[459]

The so-called 'Tube' which will be discussed later, led from *Lager II*, to *Lager III*, and consisted of a path about 300 m long, which was surrounded on the right and left by a wall of barbed wire, which was covered with fir branches. The purpose of this was to make it impossible to see the railway about 200m away.

The extermination transports of certain Jews started about the end of May/ beginning of June 1942. It started with only small transports of Polish Jews. I can't give precise information about the frequency of the transports, since I was mostly used as a driver and then always away for a day, and after long drives also 2-14 days. But I assume there were about 2 transports a week in the beginning. Those transports may have contained on average 150-200 people in the beginning.

Then, around August there was a long break because the burial pits burst open as a result of the heat. They were dug up with an excavator and burned. The transports started again in the winter. Again it was about 2 transports a week. It also happened there were 2 transports in a day. All in all, it can be said that the sequence of transports was very irregular, because the railway line, which the narrow-gauge railway to Sobibór had to cross, was repeatedly overloaded with transports bound for the front.

There were bigger transports arriving with the same frequency in 1943, sometimes also from Holland. These transports may have included about 350-450 people each, but I would like to emphasise that I can't say anything precise in this regard. The trains

---

[459] The new gas chambers were constructed in the autumn of 1942. Bauer stating that he never saw the insides of the new gas chambers, was a downright untruth. He was seen on the roof by the women victims looking through the observation windows, who he said complained of his presence.

consisted of up to 10 cattle cars, some of which were real passenger cars.[460]

The wagons were unloaded in the forecourt of *Lager I*, which probably still belonged to *Lager I*, and was also located within the general camp fence, but not within the special fence of *Lager I*. When a train arrived, it was shunted in groups of 3-4 wagons to the forecourt of *Lager I*.[461]

Frenzel or Wagner were supervising the offloading. The shunting work was carried out by Polish railwaymen. Sometimes Stangl was there too. As far as I know, Bolender was not present when the wagons were unloaded, but only when the items being transported from the warehouse were loaded. Later a proper ramp was built at the forecourt.

When some wagons arrived, the doors were opened and the people who could walk had to get out. A station *Kommando* of about 12 working Jews and about 3-4 *Hiwis* (Ukrainian unskilled workers) were active during the unloading.[462]

After the able-bodied people had left the wagons—if this didn't happen quickly enough, the working Jews would use force to help, they climbed into the wagons, took out the luggage that had been left behind and threw out the sick and frail people (unable to walk). Children were only very rarely on the transport and usually stayed with their mothers. It was practically impossible for the children to separate from their mothers because otherwise they would have known what was ahead of them. At most, only older sick children or left behind small children stayed behind in the wagons.

The Jews who could walk were directly led to *Lager II*. In the meantime the Jews unable to walk were thrown out of the wagons by the 'working Jews,' occasionally with such brutality that even

---

[460] This figure is far too low, transports from Holland ranged from 964 to 3,017 deportees. There were 19 transports which carried 34,313 people with an average quota of circa 1800.
[461] The ramp was 120m long, and could accommodate eleven wagons and one locomotive.
[462] Both these numbers seem too low.

the Germans present sometimes intervened. The loading ramp was about 8-10 m wide and on the other side of the ramp stood the wagons of the narrow-gauge train. People who were unable to walk were loaded into these wagons and driven down to the pits in *Lager III*. As I had to gather from the bullets that I heard come out from *Lager III*, that they were shot there. I have never seen it myself, but I knew from the others, that the shootings were carried out by the *'Hiwis'* who had already gone to *Lager III*, and were equipped with Russian rapid-fire rifles (12 rounds per magazine). In the beginning the narrow-gauge trucks were pulled by horses. About one month after commissioning, a diesel locomotive arrived.

In front of *Lager II*, the men had to step to the left and line up behind a wooden wall. The women were then led into the camp to the right under a covered corner of *Lager II*. The two legs of this corner were covered with boards. The SS man Hermann Michel then spoke to them in white scrubs and explained to them that they have to undress and give away their valuables; they would be bathed and disinfected and would be able to take their soap with them, and would then be assigned to work.

Besides Michel there were usually Rudolf Beckmann, Karl Richter, Paul Groth and others present as well as 4-5 *Hiwis*. Sometimes, if Stangl or Wagner found me, as I lived there, I was there too. After the undressing the Jews had to go to the entrance of 'The Tube,' at a booth. In there sat a Jew, who we called 'Little Max,' to hand over their valuables.

They were then led through 'The Tube,' with one of the regular German crew leading the way to the gas chambers and 3-4 *Hiwis* driving the Jews through and following them. The foreman stopped in front of the entrance. Someone from the regular crew in *Lager III*, would take over the Jews, they walked up the ramp into the building, where they were walking from the corridor into the gassing chambers. The doors (air raid shelter doors) were closed by members of the *Lager III*, crew. Either Vallaster, or Getzinger or Hödl, and the *Hiwis* (sometimes Bodessa, first name

Iwan, they called him 'Iwan the Terrible'), then started the engine in the engine room. As far as I know Barbl did not do it, he was a fitter, who had fitted the gas chambers together with Fuchs and did this also in other camps.

Then the gassing was carried out. On the other side of the gassing building were also doors. It was like this in the first gassing barracks and later at the massive gassing building. The 'worker Jews' of *Lager III* and the *Hiwis* were already waiting at those doors. After gassing, about 20-30 minutes, the engine was stopped. After the doors were opened, we waited until the exhaust gasses were removed. Then the dead bodies were loaded onto the narrow-gauge railway trucks and driven to the pits. In the pits the corpses were burned on grates, made from railway tracks.

Fuchs and I participated in the gassings of the first 3-4 transports. Later I wasn't there anymore. Those present at the gassings, usually 2 Germans for supervision, while the actual work was carried out by the Jews and the *Hiwis*. After Fuchs and I stopped doing it, Vallaster and a man who was the head chef at the very beginning took over (I didn't mention him in my list of names and I still can't remember his name). From about June or July 1942, Getzinger and Hödl did it. Bredow was there too. In the summer, I can't give a more precise date, but it was before the uprising in the camp, the exterminations were stopped.[463]

Shortly before the exterminations in Sobibór ceased, I think when exterminations by engine gasses were no longer taking place, 'working Jews' who worked at the extermination camp Bełżec are said to have come to Sobibór. I don't know anything more about this, just that the chef from the camp in Bełżec and his wife and some other Jews employed in the administration

---

[463] Transports from the *Reichskommissariat Ostland* were gassed in Sobibór during September 1943.

were brought to Sobibór, of which the wife and his wife poisoned themselves.[464]

At that time the so-called *Lager IV,* was set up by 'working Jews.' This was outside the original camp area in a forest behind *Lager III.* There were several pits about 1.5m deep were dug for the storage of ammunition and a 'stick dam' was laid. Apparently after the absence of further transports and other indications, the 'working Jews' expected that they would also be exterminated shortly.

Then there was the uprising. Only about 40-60 working Jews were left after the uprising and a part of them were taken away to Auschwitz, as it was initially, but later they said to Trawniki. The remaining 30 people came to *Lager III,* and were shot there and burnt with petrol. I know that, because I heard the shooting and Wagner asked me for a canister which he received. At these shootings Reichleitner, Wagner and Karl Steubl at least had the supervision over the *Hiwis* and over the whole action too. It is possible that Bredow was there too. I don't know if they shot themselves, as I wasn't there myself. Steubl borrowed my pistol. On behalf of Wagner, Hans Klier picked up the petrol canister for the cremation of the corpses from me.

I want to include the following: After a group of about 50-100 Jews undressed in the corner of *Lager II,* and had laid the clothes on the floor and then been led through the 'Tube,' the discarded pieces of clothing, with the exception of shoes, were taken through a gate by one of the work crews under the command of the brothers Wolf and moved to another part of *Lager II.* This area was behind the wooden fence, in front of which the Jews had to take off their clothes in the corner. A gate led through the wooden fence, which was opened for that purpose.

The clothes were initially left lying around in the sorting barracks and were continuously sorted there after the end of the

---

[464] This actually was post-revolt, and the worker Jews came from the Treblinka Death Camp. The couple mentioned are Karl and Adele Blau, who committed suicide in November 1943.

respective extermination operation and examined for valuables. The shoes were brought to a special shoe barracks in between *Lager II* and *Lager I,* by a work crew who reported to Hans Klier. After the clothing had been removed and before another group was led to the corner of the camp, this was cleaned under the supervision of Beckmann and Groth, so that the groups who followed would not become suspicious. When the destruction of a transport was finished, this place and the 'Tube' were raked. I would also like to note that in the early days, when there was less to do in *Lager III,* Bolender was also involved for a short time in the supervision of and after the undressing in *Lager II,* and sometimes in the unloading from the wagons.

I can say with certainty that every member of the permanent crew has gradually participated in every extermination-related activity carried out over time, however, the actual gassing process after the Jews entered the gas chambers is an exception to this. This activity was the responsibility of the *Lager III* crew I have already mentioned. So nobody can exclude themselves. Apart from Vallaster, the man I no longer know by name belonged to the crew of *Lager III* that I mentioned—but now I remember that his name was Ferdl Gromer, Getzinger, Hödl and Bredow, also Graetschus, as well as lorry driver Becher from the institution in Pirna, at times also Erich Lachmann, Karl Ludwig, Muller and Karl Pötzinger. The only thing I can't say about the people who came to Sobibór from Bełżec after it was dissolved in the summer 1943, was that they participated in any way in the gassings in Sobibór. At that time the gassings had stopped, as far as I can remember.[465]

I don't know anything about a larger children's transport being brought to Sobibór at some point, in particular I don't know anything about a children's transport from Włodawa. Incidentally, the ghetto in Włodawa was not liquidated in the summer 1942, but only in the summer 1943.

---

[465] It has already been stated this claim is factually incorrect

Mistreatment of Jews occurred when a Jew had violated camp regulations in some way. He was then punished by other Jewish inmates with 20 or 30 lashes by order of the German warden. I am still aware of the cause and effect of a case that I was mistakenly accused of, Little Max, who sat in the valuables booth and did spy services for us, hit the horse's foot with his iron-shod boot, while harnessing a horse, when it didn't work right away. I have seen that myself. Later the horse became lame. I have told this to Beckmann. As Klier later told me, Beckmann then whipped 'Little Max' himself.

In addition, a short burly Jew in particular—a *Kapo* who was called a General and was in charge of the station *Kommando* distinguished himself by abusing other Jews.

First the camp commander was *Obersturmführer* Stangl, he was perhaps replaced by *Obersturmführer* Reichleitner at the end of 1942.[466] The first deputy camp commander was *Untersturmführer* Gustav Wagner and from about mid 1943, *Untersturmführer* Niemann.

When we came to the Sobibór camp in May 1942, the construction of the camp was already well advanced. The commander with the highest rank during construction was the *Hauptscharführer* Thomalla. There was also a *Unterscharführer*, who gave the most details during the construction work, but I don't know his name, maybe it was Moser. In addition, some of the guards from Trawniki were there.

With the two girls—allegedly film actresses from the theatre, it was as follows: Maybe in late autumn both were accommodated in the former kitchen in the Forester's lodge. With them there was noise and singing almost every night and there were parties. I slept diagonally across from them and upstairs slept Karl Ludwig, Richter and another guy. We often got upset about the noise and knocked when the noise was too strong. One evening there was a loud noise again. There was a knock on the back door of the

---

[466] Stangl left for Treblinka in mid-August 1942 and was replaced by Reichleitner.

kitchen. I woke up and went to the hallway. Karl Ludwig was in the kitchen and when I asked why the girls had to leave, he yelled. He took them and went towards *Lager III*, in the darkness. I accompanied him a bit, but soon turned back because it was already quite cold and I was only lightly dressed. Ludwig went on alone with the girls. The next morning the girls were no longer there. When I asked him about it, Ludwig told me that he had a security guard shoot them. He didn't tell me the name of the security guard.[467]

December 11, 1962
Berlin-Tiergarten

Moser—This man is completely unknown to me. I only found out the name during the interrogations after the war. But I don't know which person it means. Possibly it is a sub-sharp watch, which I spoke about yesterday on page 11 in my interrogation. [468]

October 6, 1965
Hagen

I was drafted to the army in July 1940, (transport squadron), I got to know the T4 people during ambulance transports. I knew Allers, he used to be my boss. I didn't know what to expect from T4, so I applied there and I was hired. For two weeks I was employed in the porter's lodge, then I drove a car and was the driver of Professor Nitschke, Blankenburg and Haus.

In the winter 1941/1942, I was deployed in the east, after that I came back to T4 in Berlin and was then transferred to Poland. We just arrived in Lublin on the 20th April 1942, a few days later we came to Cholm, where we stayed 8-10 days. I came to Sobibór at

---

[467] The two Jewish girls were named Ruth and Gisela.
[468] This was *Baurat* Bruno Moser, who worked for the *Kreishauptmann* in Chelm.

the end of April or beginning of May. I was *Oberscharführer*. I can't say for sure because it's been so long. Besides me who came to Sobibór there was Stangl, Steubl, Wagner, Frenzel, Ittner. I don't know if Bolender was there from the beginning, as far as I can remember Schutt came later. The command was 10-12 men strong and led by Stangl, who wore a '*SD Winkel*' on his uniform. I was hired by Stangl in Sobibór after verbal instruction and didn't have to sign anything. I don't know if I had to sign anything before I joined T4, Oels, Allers, Haus and Kaufmann had instructed me about secrecy.

The post office was about 20-25 meters away from the station. Next to the camp—on the left of the map—was a sawmill. Another command had already been there before us. It could have been led by Thomalla.

At first there were no transports, fences were put up and the camp was set up further, Bolender, Gomerski, I and as far as I know, Klier helped from the start. Later the digging started, Bolender and Vallaster did that. When we arrived *Lager III*, wasn't completely fenced in, it certainly wasn't fenced across to the right. I don't know if it was fenced in towards the forest.

The gas chamber was already there, a wooden building stood on a cement base, about the same size as this conference room here, but significantly lower, as low as a normal apartment. There were 2 to 3 rooms, in front of it was a corridor that you entered from the outside via a footbridge. There were probably wooden doors that were later changed when the gas chamber was completely rebuilt. The air raid shelter doors came later, I got them myself from Warsaw, but that was only when the building was newly built. Before there were wooden doors at the back where corpses came out, folding doors. Those were big doors. I don't know whether Wirth complained about the doors. In an extension was the engine room, with the engine, from where the exhaust pipes went into the chambers. The fittings were installed later, I got them from Warsaw, they were real shower heads. I don't know whether the pipes entered the gas chamber at the top or bottom. A French Renault engine was already there in the engine room, as were the connections. I don't know whether the engine has been working (gassing) with before. Fuchs was already there when we got there. He was in charge of the engine and trained me. He showed me how to use it. A few of the *Askaris* were still there, one later stayed there all the time.

When I came to Sobibór I was first involved with the fence and the construction of the 'Tube,' then I was sent to the engine, where I met Fuchs. I don't know whether someone came and tested the gas in the gas chamber with a measuring device.

About 2-3 weeks after we arrived, the first transports came. I can't exactly pinpoint myself. They came by train, only at the end before the uprising did smaller transports not come by train, but from Cholm, for example. From there, German police brought them with horse-drawn carriages.[469] The transports were an average of 100-200, mostly freight trains, sometimes also second class passenger cars.[470]

3-4 wagons entered the camp. On the approach that others state 8-10 wagons, I can't say. Later the track was probably extended and a ramp was built to alight, it wasn't like that at first. Later the ramp was filled in, around the summer of 1942. The first transports did not have a ramp. Later the ramp was so high that it was about a normal step below the height of the wagon floor.

I know the walk from the ramp to the camp by sight. I was ordered to the engine at about the 3rd to 4th transport. The Jews were separated according to gender led to *Lager II*, first the women had to undress and were led through the 'Tube' into *Lager III*, into the gas chambers, where they were gassed and taken to the pits, then it was the men's turn. When the transports came the *Askaris* started the engine, it was running until the Jews got into the gas chamber. I brought the transport from *Lager II*, to the

---

[469] This statement does not ring true, smaller transports from the vicinity of Sobibór came either by cart or in the case of Izbica, by lorry in the spring of 1943.

[470] The transport numbers depended on the size of the ghettos being cleared, but the figure Bauer quotes is not accurate at all.

back through the 'Tube' and opened the door. The *Askaris* and the 'working Jews' in *Lager III*, then pushed the Jews into the chambers and closed the doors, when the chambers were full. The chambers were firmly attached to the engine, it was like that, when a wooden peg was pulled out, the exhaust fumes went into the open, when the peg was put into the pipe, the exhaust fumes went into the chamber. The gassing lasted about half an hour, I assume that about 50-60 people went in per gas chamber, but I don't know exactly.[471] The corpses were unloaded by Jewish workers under the supervision of German wardens. The chief supervisor was Vallaster from the start, he died in the uprising, he was a very good friend of mine.

In *Lager III*, there were carts on rails. The tipper wagons were arranged and a square wooden frame made like luggage carts at the train station. The corpses were driven in those to the pits. There were Jews at the pits, who dragged the corpses into the pits. I don't know how big the pits were. On the reproach that he used to say 30x30x5m I don't remember. It was sandy soil, which was first dug out by hand, later a digger came. The digger came just as Getzinger came to the camp.

I was only at the engine for a short time, basically almost not at all. I had to drive a lot. I wasn't there at all during the first transports, since Fuchs was still there. On the reproach that he said earlier that he gassed together with Fuchs during the first transports. Yes, it is supposed to have been gassed (but I don't know personally) before our arrival. I didn't see any corpses. The cremation of the corpses only started later.

When I wasn't in the camp, Vallaster tended the gas chamber, as did Ferdl Gomer. Barbl was a plumber, he was already there when we arrived and connected the pipes. I knew Fuchs from T4. I didn't know him from the earlier fights. I only got to know him through T4, at the service station on Eliendorf-Strasse. In 1934, it

---

[471] The capacity of the original 3 chambers gassing facility was 600 people, and the improved facilities had a capacity to nearly 1,300 people. A view could be formed that Bauer underestimated numbers throughout his testimony.

could have been 1933, in the *SA*. I was never an old fighter. I didn't know Fuchs as a free thinker. I had nothing to do with a search of his house. If Fuchs said otherwise, he lied. I was only in *Sturm 24*, later in another *Sturm*. I occasionally did repairs in the free-thinker garage. I know Suchomel from later.

On objection to Fuchs who only claims to have brought the Russian engine from *Lemberg* one afternoon and is said to have been brought back by Wirth the next morning to rectify a fault in the starter, because Bauer might have been drunk. No we did sleep together in Sobibór, several times. In the evenings we even made fried potatoes with a blow torch. Fuchs explained, that's not true. Bauer said we left the blowtorch on to keep us warm.

We initially had two Renault lorries from Lublin in the camp, then two Ford V8 lorries, one of them was attacked by partisans in the forest, Gomerski was there. After that we only had one truck, which was driven at first by Ludwig. Then it was used for a while by Schutt to get provisions; later we got a *VW-Kübelwagen*, a Mercedes stood in the garage. Schutt wasn't there for long, I guess one and a half to two months.

After me there was Vallaster, Gromer, then Hödl, and then Getzinger, the last one already in 1942. Later the machine house was enlarged and a new engine—diesel engine was installed. Fuchs wasn't there, he was in Treblinka.

A Jewish work command of 10-12 men were busy with the unloading; Wagner and Frenzel and the camp manager were in charge. Lachmann was in charge of the *Askaris*. Bolender, Ittner, Schutt didn't belong to the main unloading team. Later Niemann came from Bełżec. I collected his luggage by car from Bełżec. He was *Stellvertretender Lagerkommandant* (deputy Commandant) and was at the unloading.

When Niemann came, Reichleitner was probably already the *Lagerkommandant*, who came went Stangl went to Treblinka in the summer, maybe August or September 1942. In any case, I went to Treblinka with Reichleitner in the summer when it was still warm. It was said that the corpses were bloated by the heat and the ground rose. I don't know whether that was still in the days of Stangl.

Wagner was the 'right-hand man' for the *Lagerkommandant*, both of Stangl and Reichleitner. Graetschus only came later and then died. Frenzel commanded *Lager I*, and the supervision of the working commands. They all lived in *Lager I*, and that's where they also worked for example the craftsmen. *Lager II*, was for itself. The Jews who worked there also had their own accommodation, and as far as I know, from the very beginning. In the beginning the food from *Lager I*, was carried over there, but later they fitted their own kitchen. Frenzel was in charge of organizing the different commands. There was no *Appell*. In the morning there was the counting. One got so and so many to fetch wood, the others to sort. Frenzel divided that up.

There were *Kapo's* (prisoners who had a function in the camp), they supported the Germans and wore red stripes, they looked like Generals. The 'working Jews' wore civilian clothes and the people from the station command had a blue combination and a ship's hat. The *Kapo's* had whips to hit.

Question: Was there beatings and was it necessary?

(Witness smiles). Only the *Kapo's* whipped and every now and then the supervisors. Whips belonged to the uniform, even I as a truck driver had a whip. I made this sketch at the beginning of my imprisonment. If someone had done something, for example stolen, bartered with *Askaris* etc, the whip was used, not to spur on. The penalty was 25 strokes. Who ordered that? Probably Stangl, I wasn't there.

Once a case happened with a horse and 'Little Max.' He was probably a better calculus; the general was probably the 'fat one' in *Lager I*. I was in the Forester's lodge. I saw the stables from the window and saw the horse kicking Max. He kicked the horse with his boot again. Beckmann was actually in charge of the stables. In the evening they talked about the horse having a swollen foot. I said 'Little Max' will know. Now I found out I should have ordered

25 strokes for Max. I don't know anything about this, that was Beckmann. It's not supposed to be true that Max was killed, he is said to have lived until the end. Afterwards he took away valuables in *Lager II*, behind house number 2. In my opinion, the supervisors were not responsible for imposing penalties.[472]

When the ramp was extended, there were two *Askaris* who drove the people. The *Bahnhofkommando* (Jews) threw old people out. I saw it myself. I saw myself that Frenzel intervened. On the reproach that Frenzel doesn't say so himself, but I saw it myself that he scolded. Everything had to happen quickly.

The Jews only realized what was going on at the end, at first they were in the best of faith. The last transports from Cholm, they probably knew about it, partly also from foreign broadcasts on the radio. Some of the Jews had a lot of luggage, including bedding.

There was no great shouting on the ramp; the train station Sobibór was very close. Personally, I can only say that 1-2 women with children arrived (means babies).[473] I once saw that Stangl personally selected 2 boys for the work command. I assume the youngest was 'Little Max.' A woman had a school-age daughter in the camp.

Cuckierman was the chef. I don't know whether he had a son.[474] I don't know anything about a children's transport from Włodawa. I only heard about it in the court proceedings against Nitschke in Hannover.

Frenzel was a bit tough; everything just had to work.

Question: Did Frenzel yell at people, insult, scream?

I was almost never in the camp at all. When we lined up it said: Quick, quick, count begin.

---

[472] There were plenty of examples where SS –Officers flogged prisoners for infractions of the camp rules.

[473] This statement is clearly hard to believe is true.

[474] Bauer stated the name as Zuckermann. This was Hershel Cuckierman, and his son Josef worked with in the Jewish kitchen.

Number 12 in the pre-camp was the garage. I sometimes heard Frenzel scream and yell. I couldn't see anything. I got wedges from Wagner myself, he also beat Jews. Frenzel wasn't like that, they both worked together. I was there very little, because I was mostly on the road in the truck. How is anyone supposed to prove to me that I had hit. I hit someone only once, one from the *Bahnhofkommando*. Whilst unloading he smashed a 25 litre juice bottle and a bag of sugar. I gave him 2 slaps from the car and didn't report him. Once Wagner threw a drunk man into a well.

Some of the *Unterführers* have excelled in getting ahead. If you were mild and human, you were despised. Wolf, Lachmann, and Dubois were not involved in fights, as far as I know. Schutt was there the least time. Unverhau didn't hit. Lambert was only with us a little. Juhrs was only there a short time, all I know about Ittner is that he was in the office. I was amazed when I heard that he was also supposed to have been in *Lager III*. Fuchs soon left again. In my opinion Klier came to Sobibór with us, he was a peaceful man, in the bakery and later in the shoe sorting command. At first I collected bread and food from Trawniki, then we received an allocation of flour from Cholm and partly from Włodawa; there was bread baked by a baker in Cholm, if it wasn't enough, Klier would bake bread from flour in the camp. Klier was a sick man, with one leg and a speech impediment.

Beckmann was probably a graduated farmer, he was in charge of the stables and the sorting rooms in *Lager II*. Of the two Wolf brothers, the younger one probably died. I don't know his first name, they looked alike.[475] Wolf sitting here is in my opinion the older one. He worked in the barracks. The people from barracks 22-27 had nothing to do with the undressing. They only took away the clothes and suitcases.

In the corner behind the building in *Lager II*, was a wooden fence that was covered. That's where the undressing took place and that's where the clothes were laid out and hung up on hooks

---

[475] This has been covered already Josef Wolf, the elder brother was killed in the uprising.

in the wall boards. When the Jews went through the 'Tube' about 10 men quickly dragged the things into barracks 25-27. Later barracks 23 and 24 were added. Then the luggage was handed into barrack 22, and after the Jews had moved on they were taken to barracks 23 and 24.

Frenzel did not belong in the group of mild camp guards. Bolender was in *Lager III*. He had a barracks-like tone and was also an active soldier. He yelled. Once he allowed boxing. I saw that. The Jews challenged themselves, they boxed until they knocked themselves out with their bare fists.

I also saw Jews chasing another Jew, who wasn't quite right mentally, up a tree, then they quickly cut down the tree. The Jews themselves sent him out, the command included one of the *SS*-men and five or six *Askaris* who were able to prevent it. One of us was Ferdl Gromer when I saw it. Two security guards were once killed in a forest command. On hold 2 or I, two maybe it was just one. But that wasn't the command with the fallen trees.[476]

Bolender had a very loud organ (*Authors Note: Probably means voice*), he was initially used to build fences, later he was in charge of digging pits. He was in charge of the Jewish work command from barrack 1, in *Lager III*, about 40 men. Fuchs, I, Vallaster and Gertzinger were in charge of the gas chambers, not Bolender. The unloading from the gas chambers was done by the same people who drove the Jews in. It was not these Jews who carried away the corpses on the carts, but those from Bolender's command. Bolender was not alone in supervising the pits. I don't know that Ittner was there. Bolender supervises down the hole (pit), the *Askaris* stood on top, during the day there were 10-12 *Askaris* in *Lager III*. At night on the machine gun stand, on the tower in *Lager III*, the Askaris guard.

Initially there were kerosene lamps in *Lager III*, the floodlights were installed later. Around June or July 1942, I fetched a portable light device, which was set up near the gas chambers, next to the

---

[476] This was probably the *Waldkommando* revolt on July 23, 1943, when a *Trawnikimänner* was killed.

engine room, around building 4 in *Lager III*, of the sketch. In August 1942, Getzinger and Hödl and another expert from *Lager I*, who was possibly called Preuss, set up the lighting device opposite the Forester's lodge.

The floodlights and later also the housing for the Jews in *Lager III*, were connected to a small unit in *Lager III*, I can't remember the gas chambers too. In *my* opinion, one could not see anything even with the lighting in the gas chamber room, since everything was a vapour from the urination etc. When asked whether there really was a searchlight, which all accused deny. But there was a searchlight behind barrack 1 in *Lager III*, and it shone on the door. It was an ordinary car headlight that was fixed. There was a lantern in the corner of the barracks. The barracks were fully illuminated from the outside. There had been kerosene lamps on the corners in front of the headlights.

At the gate to *Lager III*, there were double guards. The remaining Ukrainians guarded the Jews. They had Russian guns, only the chief guards had whips. Very ill people were driven to the rear in carts and shot in the pits. They were Ukrainians who had special orders to do so. They had automatic weapons and a 12-round magazine. They were not commanded by a German[477], it was a well-rehearsed command who shot the people, who were being transported on the narrow-gauge railway train.

The narrow-gauge railway was not there at the beginning, it was built about 1-2 months after our arrival. From the gas chamber to the pit there was already a piece that was later extended to the ramp. Transports were shot at the pit, which was called the 'Lazarett.' The carts were initially pushed, later came a diesel locomotive.

Before the carts were used, the sick and infirm were taken to the '*Lazarett*' by horse carriages. It is also possible that in the beginning the carts were not pushed but pushed by horses. In my

---

[477] This is probably false, every Kommando was controlled by an *SS* Officer. The Ukrainian shooters were under the command of Bredow, whilst he was at Sobibór.

opinion the locomotive was already there before the digger. Sometimes one, but mostly 2-3 carts full of sick people, who were unable to walk, were taken to *Lager III*. The track went straight into the pit. I don't know that there was a bridge-like footbridge above the pit, over which the rails of the narrow-gauge railway ran. The firing squad had been assigned by Stangl. Vallaster mostly drove the locomotive. Frenzel had work to do at the front of the ramp. It needed to be cleaned and cleared out, so I don't think he was in command of the firing squad. I said earlier that I thought it was possible that the crew of *Lager III*, could have carried out the shootings in *Lager III*.

There were three dogs in the camp. A little young one, a Saint Bernhard named Barry and a Russian bastard who was a little smaller than a German Shepherd. I don't remember the dog Zeppi. Barry was part of the security guard. Frenzel and Michel had him. He slept in the anteroom of Frenzel's barracks.

Bolender once loaded things at the ramp. I stood by. Bolender is said to have rushed the dogs. That was not true. The dogs playfully bit the blankets and pieces of clothing worn by the Jews. They were difficult dogs. This incident happened when no transports came. Before the uprising, Barry left for Treblinka. Stangl took the dog with him. I don't know whether the incident with Bolender happened when there were no more transports coming or when there were finally no more transports shortly before the uprising.

Bolender was gone for a while. For several months. I don't know what happened. I heard he's in a prison camp; it was said that something had happened to a woman. I don't know exactly what happened. It was said he was in a camp near Hamburg. On the objection that Bolender states that he was on vacation from mid-September to mid-October 1942, and he was arrested in Lublin on October 16, 1942, the last may be correct, whether he was on vacation in September I don't know. When Bolender came back, he was torn and emaciated and completely run down. He looked like a bogeyman. That must have been before the uprising.

In Italy I was still with Bolender. I was already in Italy for Christmas 1943, and had been on vacation before that.

After the uprising all the Jews were shot. I remember that. After October 20th, 1943, Jews came from Treblinka or from Bełżec.[478] I don't remember exactly. I don't know whether Hering was *Kommandant* after the uprising. After the uprising I stayed in the camp at first because I had to drive a lot—take away valuables. The Jews then came to tear down the camp and the barracks. I assumed they came from Bełżec. I can't remember whether Bolender was in the camp after the uprising.

The dogs weren't chased, they had difficult dispositions. **When questioned by the AG Berlin-Tiergarten.** Yes, it was true that it was said, 'do you want to run.' The dogs reacted and bit into the blankets they were carrying.

Even before the uprising, the transports stopped. Sobibór was supposed to become a labor camp.

On objection that Bolender denies the incident with the dogs:

Bolender was there. He said to the Jews, 'Do you want to run?' The Jews ran. The mutts ran after them, Bolender was happy. I never dashed the dogs. I was only present once in this incident with Bolender. In my opinion, no Jew was hurt.

Whether other people have dashed the dogs, Frenzel for example. I don't know I wasn't in the camp often. On reserve of B1. 44R/45 of the criminal file against Bauer, I stated that Frenzel and Paul Groth were there when the dogs were chased. Lachmann's predecessor, Schafer had brought the dog with him. In the picture folder 'dogs,' photo 2 is in my opinion Barry, the bastard is not in the pictures. A guide dog or shepherd dog was not in the camp. Stangl later brought Barry to Treblinka, perhaps after visiting with the Opel car, shortly after his transfer to Treblinka. After the uprising or after Treblinka was dissolved, Barry was back.

---

[478] It was Treblinka. Belzec was closed in May 1943.

Case: Gisela and Ruth

The two Jewish girls slept in the Jewish kitchen of the Foresters Lodge/ I don't know if they were related, they spoke German and I think they came from Prague. They made tea and did the cleaning work in the house and in Schutt's room. They were not used in work commands. They were about 24. I don't think it was an aunt and niece. There were no Polish Jews in the house.

In the evenings there were parties in the girls room, orgies, they drank, they had a good time and sang, the girls played guitar, one of the crew had a piano. One of the girls could sing wonderfully. I didn't see anything about kissing or sexual things. However, much has been rumoured. All sorts of things are said to have happened. I once saw that there was one sitting on the edge of Schutt's bed when Schutt laid in bed. He lived opposite the girls' room in the Forester's House. Steubl and Stangl were also present at the celebrations. I was only there once, it didn't suit me. If you got caught doing it, it would have been bad. That was already in 1942. A kind of competition broke out around the girls. Ludwig was a swift man and was always with them. Some of the SS-men didn't join in, neither did Bolender. It was more the people from Lager II, who celebrated with the girls. Frenzel drank tea there.

Ludwig arranged for the girls to be killed by *Askaris*. I came from a trip. Ludwig and Richter and others slept upstairs in the Forester's Lodge. The two girls had had a row before. There had been several people there, playing and singing. At night Ludwig knocked on my door, telling me to come. He had the girls and wanted to bring them to *Lager III*.

What's that to do with me, went half-way to *Lager III*, and then turned back. Ludwig then gave the girls to the post in *Lager III*. In my opinion he did it out of jealousy of the competition. The next morning Ludwig told me that the Ukrainian Bodessa had shot the two girls. I didn't ask Schutt about these girls, not even in relation to individual Jewish women. I also didn't tell Schutt he could see the nice ass of the Jewish girls in the pit. I have never spoken to Schutt about it. But there probably a rivalry between

Schutt and Ludwig. When asked about Schutt's statement Bd 4BL 191 f, I don't know about the third Jewish girl, I never took Schutt up to *Lager III*, either, never. Schutt was never in *Lager III*, at all. According to Ludwig, the girls were shot. After Ruth and Gisela, no girls came back into the Forester's House.

Question: Why didn't you state in your proceedings that Ludwig took the girls away to be killed?

Does not answer

It is possible that a Jewish girl once came out of my room, but only when I was not in the room. I was often gone, it couldn't have been at night.

When he was reproached, he said with regard to Frenzel at the AG Berlin-Tiergarten, that Frenzel's whip was loose and he whipped at roll call. Yes that's the way I said it earlier. But the penalties imposed by Stangl. That must be a misunderstanding Frenzel whipped well.

I slept in House 2 together with Fuchs.

I'm not aware of any individual shootings. Nor whether individual Jews in *Lager III*, were shot. I don't know anything about the fact that a Jewish *Kapo*, who is said to have gone too close to *Lager III*, or people injured by dogs or pig master, Schohl or Stark has been shot in *Lager III*.

The hearing was interrupted from October 6th, 1965, 3pm until October 7th, 9 a.m. The protocol was completed on October 16th, 1965.

November 30, 1965

The telephone was not placed in the camp until later, at first there was no telephone, so you had to go to the post office to make a call. Later a telephone connection was established from the Forester's House, from the office to the post office outside the camp.

The telephone was on the desk in the office. The telephone had been destroyed beforehand during the uprising.

During the uprising I came back from a trip to Cholm. I was earlier than usual that day and got to the camp before 5 p.m. I pulled up in front of the post office. When I heard shots, I ran to the car and got my gun. Then I ran back, Beckmann was dead in the office.

After the uprising, the remaining Jews were imprisoned in the camp. Wirth came late in the evening. I do not know whether higher SS officers came. Wirth sent me to Włodawa to notify the border police. I do not know how many Jews remained in the camp. The next day they came (maybe it wasn't until the others had returned from vacation) in *Lager III*. I assume that, I wasn't there, just heard it, it was general talk.

I don't know whether new working Jews came. The *Askaris* did the cleaning up. I don't believe that new working Jews came. At last the *Askaris* were alone.

I transferred 7 coffins to Chelm; the other coffins came to Chelm in a wagon. I drove them from the train station to the Town Hall. A total of 21 or 23 people had been killed, including a Ukrainian. I think he was in charge of the craftsmen; his name was probably Klatt. The burials took place outside of Chelm, at the military cemetery, where those who had died in the Chelm hospital were also buried. The cemetery was on the road to Bialystok. Dead were Niemann, Klatt, Beckmann, Wolf (I found him myself), Graetschus, and the clerk from the writing room, a compatriot of Wolf's. Dubois was injured.

I know the name Sporrenberg. I don't know if he came to Sobibór. Blankenburg and Allers also wanted to come out, but they only got as far as Chelm. I have never heard of a list of names of SS people who should be killed or spared. I don't know if anyone has accused Frenzel.

There was talk of other SS-men giving 25 strokes across the bottom, as punishment for the Jews. I didn't see that. There is even said to have been a billy goat. I haven't seen it either. Wagner hit a lot more than me. The 'Tube' was so narrow, that it was impossible to beat in it. On the reproach that in this main hearing about the order of corporal punishment he had made postponing statements: As far as I know the *Kapo's* whipped.

Dubois: He came later and was present in Włodawa when the houses were being demolished and in the forest. He also had, I think a squad of Ukrainians. He also had the armoury.

On objection to the statement of 20 December 1962: Yes Dubois assigned the Ukrainians to guard towers. He didn't have all the Ukrainians but one squad. If his platoon was on watch, he probably assigned them. I don't know where he was deployed when the transports arrived.

Lachmann: On objection to his statement of January 10, 1962, Whether Lachmann had all the functions of the camp crew:

Yes, he had to divide the Ukrainians. I also often saw Lachmann checking the Ukrainians. In general, the student assistants knew where to go when the transports arrived; that was recorded. Only a small remainder was to be allocated separately. I also saw Lachmann looking after his luggage. Lachmann's predecessor was Schafer from Breslau. Although Rost was a chief of police, he had nothing to do with Schafer and Lachmann. Rost came late, he had probably been in Pirna-Sonnenstein before. This euthanasia facility was then probably dissolved. At that time, a large labor camp was to be built at ours, around the time he came.

A.B. RA. Doctor Freibertshauser

Rost was wearing a police uniform, not an *SS* uniform. He came from Berlin T4. He had nothing to do with Trawniki. When asked whether Lachmann was not involved in anything, he stalked everywhere. I don't know exactly why Lachmann drank. I don't know who gave orders to the Ukrainians on the ramp. There were no orders to be given, they were only supposed to guard. Lachmann had to make sure that the guards were there at all. The Ukrainians had often gone away from the towers and into the forest. Lachmann had nothing to do with the individual stages of a transports passage through the camp.

A.B. StA

Lachmann didn't take part in anything, the burning etc. Not even when his colleagues finished work.

A.B. RA. Doctor Freibertshauser

If Lachmann wasn't there and a transport arrived, everything ran smoothly. Lachmann was on the road a lot and was often wanted.

A.B. StA

Even when others were on vacation, it all went smoothly

A.B. Lgr Doctor Hohler

There was no successor for Lachmann from Trawniki. I don't know whether the Ukrainians were then under Wagner or Reichleitner. There were Ukrainian train drivers, they were ethnic Germans who spoke German well.

When asked if someone had a name similar to Lachmann?

I don't know, but I don't think so

A.B Vorsitzender (chairman)

I don't know whether Lachmann only spoke German. I don't know how he spoke to his Polish bride, nor how he communicated with the Ukrainians. Lachmann was there long after Reichleitner was there. In my opinion Lachmann was there until 1943. I saw him later in Trawniki. Lachmann still walked around the camp in his work wear. When it was still summer and we were driving vegetables from Trawniki, he was still in Trawniki. I can't remember exactly.

On New Year's Eve 1942, I was on vacation, probably 2 or 3 weeks. Was Lachmann still in the camp at that time? I assume so.

Graetschus was later with the Ukrainians. Schafer was ill and went on vacation as soon as the Sobibór camp began. Barry arrived with Schafer. Lachmann wore a police uniform. I didn't see that he was wearing a Ukrainian uniform. He had a glengarry and no peaked cap.

A.B. StA

Lachmann's girlfriend lived in the last house on the right with farmers. I don't know if the house was ever whitewashed. I do not believe it.

I don't know who wore glasses in Sobibór, maybe Unverhau. Bolender and Frenzel didn't wear glasses. I don't remember whether Fritz Konrad wore glasses. I don't know Gley.

A.B. Lgr Doctor Hohler

I haven't seen Bolender with a beard. I wore a beard occasionally until my surgery.

A.B. StA

I don't know if Bolender was wearing blue trousers. We had a good hairdresser in the camp.

Ittner: Ittner was often in the sorting department while undressing and sorting. That was when Schutt replaced him. I didn't even know that he was in *Lager III*, until the beginning of this trial. Beckmann was usually there when undressing. I can't remember exactly now. I assume that because Ittner was involved in the sorting, he was occasionally involved in the undressing. But I don't remember exactly. It's been too long.

A.B. Lgr Doctor Hohler

I was involved with the engine in *Lager III*. Bolender and Weis worked on the pits. I and Vallaster were in charge of the corpse squad that had to pull the corpses out of the gas chamber. I didn't see Ittner there. The gold teeth were broken off when the corpses were laid on the wagon to be driven to the pits. Getzinger was already there. I didn't see Ittner there either.

A.B. RA Bongart

Question: Is it possible that Ittner was involved in sorting and undressing while he was in the office?

Ittner stood there. I don't know who was in charge. I don't know when that was.

A.B. SyA

Schutt: He also stood at the train station. He also kept valuables in the room that used to be the kitchen. After Michel's speeches, the Jews handed in their valuables. Two or three *'Goldjuden'* stood at the window and took the things. Schutt did not belong to the station command; he stood there and watched. I don't know if he had a whip. I don't believe it, since he was busy in the writing room. He also stood by for the undressing, out of curiosity, as did I. When I was in the camp, I too watched them undress.

When asked whether he had received mail from the accused or relatives of the accused, or whether he was indirectly connected to the accused in this case?

No, I only receive mail from my wife

When reproached, he had said earlier that Stangl and Wagner had prevented the Jews from throwing the sick onto the wagons, now he says that for Frenzel.

The three Stangl, Wagner and Frenzel always stood together. Stangl and Wagner also prevented Jews in the work command from being treated too harshly. I don't know which transports it was, especially not if it was the western transport.

When asked whether the Jews didn't want to get out of the wagons?

I have such a faint memory of them going out too slowly and having helpers force them out. I don't know exactly. There was no shooting. I don't remember if they were whipped. There was always only two or three Germans on the ramp—Frenzel, Wagner, and Stangl—they mostly stood at the big wing door.

It's true that people didn't want to undress out of shame. Beckmann or Michel encouraged them. Not friendly, but yelled at them. Then people started to cry. Well there was no shooting there. I didn't see the use of whips there when undressing.

Whether 70 Dutchmen were shot?

I don't know anything about that. I've never heard of that. There was a painter. In the Casino was a picture that he had painted. It was an elderly gentleman. He also painted my dog Fiffi, who came with Niemann. When the Dutch transports came I was no longer in *Lager III*.[479]

I don't know anything about a *Lumpen* command, everything was bundled together.

I don't know anything about a suicide attempt by a Jew by cutting open his wrists. I don't know anything about punitive commands. I've never heard of it.

---

[479] The painter was Max van Dam, a Dutchman who was sent to Sobibór from Drancy in France. Max van Dam was murdered in Sobibór on September 20, 1943.

A.B. Lgr Doctor Hohler

Is it true that the corpses were examined for valuables in the body cavities? It should be hidden in praservatis valuables in the body.

I had nothing to do with it. I heard it from telling. Good things are said to have been found. The things were first carried to the front, later the gold things were melted down by a few *Goldjuden* in *Lager III*.

Allers and Blankenburg attended the funerals of the victims of the uprising in Chelm. Before the uprising they had been to Sobibór several times. I knew Allers from before, he was probably an *Obersturmführer*. He was respectively in Sobibór for inspections. I don't know exactly whether Wirth came along. How often was he there? I saw him once, that wasn't at the beginning of the time in Sobibór, because I wasn't at the gas chamber anymore. I don't know who accompanied him at the time.

A.B Vorsitzender (chairman)

Allers and Haus sent us to Lublin. Allers ran the house. I went there alone from T4 and I had no written marching orders. Allers told me to go to Lublin and that I would get a truck to drive there. I wouldn't have gone there, if I knew what was going on in Sobibór. If I had refused, then my u.k. position would have been abolished and I would have rejoined the *Wehrmacht*. Allers wore civilian clothes in Berlin. In Sobibór he wore *SA* uniform. The picture in the photo folder is probably from Trieste.

A.B. StA

Whether Jews were hanged—as punishment for another Jew fleeing?

I do not know anything about that.

Torture with an electrifying machine?

Next to the machine at the well, which was dug deeper, there was a bucket pulled up by an electro-magnet, which the *Askaris* did. A Jew was busy in the well below. He was electrified with the electro-magnet. This is not torture. The Jew also survived because it was low power.

A.B. RA Rothardt

I assume that Schutt managed the objects because he was the administrative person, so that he probably had the keys to the valuables room. With regard to Schutt's activities at the train station. I think it's possible that Schutt wanted to get instructions from the commander who was standing there.

A.B. RA Doctor Zinkann

I know Olchewski. I drove to Włodawa with him. I didn't drive to Berlin with him in the car. Fuchs drove a small Opel van that was in Sobibór. I have never been to Sadowna. I've been to Treblinka. I don't know exactly whether I met Fuchs there, but I think so. After the war I didn't see Frau Jackel again.

A.B. RA Doctor Klinkhardt

Wolf was employed in Barracks 22 to 24. Barracks 25 to 27 were open, the bolts of clothes were stacked there. Wolf's brother also worked there. I also found him in Barrack 25. Whether individual workers from *Lager I* and *Lager II*, occasionally came to work in *Lager III*, I don't know anything about that. I don't know whether working Jews from *Lager III*, were later taken to work in *Lager IV*.

Contacts between Jews from *Lager I* or *II*, and those in *Lager III*, were not allowed. *Lager III*, was completely closed. Barracks 23 and 24, were demolished between Bełżec and Zamosc and rebuilt in Sobibór. They were German *Wehrmacht* (Army) barracks. I don't know whether floorboards were installed.

I don't know the nickname 'idiot.' I assume there were 2 *kapos* in the camp, they were specially dressed. I don't remember when the mines were laid around the camp.

A.B. RA Reintzsch

The mines were laid in 1942. A former air-force member sang a song in Sobibór on Christmas Eve. It was from the squad that laid the mines. I can't remember an escape at that time.[480]

Transports also came in the evening. As long as I was in *Lager III*, no gassings took place at night. The lights were on until 10 p.m. possibly 11 p.m. There was no electricity at all at the ramp, only in the barracks, not even in the inmate barracks, electricity may have been put in there later. I don't know anything about a transport from Majdanek. Once on a Sunday a very small transport came in convict clothes. Back then there was a pile of stones because a garage was being built. They threw stones.

A.B Vorsitzender (chairman)

I don't know when the talk about the gassing of the hundred thousand Jews took place, nor whether it was before or after the Himmler visit. I don't know anything about a celebration on the occasion of the one millionth gassing. I assume the witness Blatt (whose testimony was put before him) means one of the farewell celebrations for a comrade who had been transferred.

October 9, 1974

I experienced something like that in Sobibór. That was when the uprising was back then. I had refused to go to the border guard at the time. I was supposed to alert the people, because the prisoners had left. I was afraid because it was dark and they had taken all

---

[480] There was an escape on December 26, when Pesia Liberman, two Jewish men and 2 *Trawnikimänner* escaped. Pesia and the 2 *Trawnikimänner* were killed in a shoot-out with 3 Polish policemen.

the weapons. Wirth yelled at me. He didn't threaten me with a pistol or a whip. Then I drove out to the farmers in Sobibór and I hid behind a barn there. If I hadn't driven he would have shot me dead. It wasn't until the next morning that I drove to the border guard. He would have killed me and he never hesitated for long.

Wirth was not in the camp when the Uprising took place. Immediately after the Uprising, he came back. They all came straight from Cholm and Lublin. The riot was around 5 or 5.30 p.m. I have not seen Wirth give orders to SS-people in Sobibór, that were not carried out. I wasn't there during the day. I saw that he started to rage and played crazy in the evening, when I came back. He didn't like me.

In the period from April 1942, to October 1943, I personally did not see Wirth raging with others. I don't know how it was with Bolender. I was rarely with the others. Nor did I hear whether Wagner whipped an SS member in the Sobibór camp. I also don't know whether Wagner threatened an SS man with concentration camps or beatings if they didn't carry out an order.

I know that Bolender boxed with an inmate in *Lager III*. It was in the pit where the shooting range was built. I don't know how that turned out. Otherwise I didn't see another SS man boxing with an inmate. I can't remember having heard of that either. The only athlete we had with us was Wagner.

Now follows the literal recording of the following part of the testimony of the witness Bauer.

Question: Have you ever experienced an SS member boxing with a Jewish prisoner?

Answer of the witness Bauer: Yes Bolender in *Lager III*, in the range where the shooting range was set up. I don't know what came out of it. I didn't watch this until the end.

Question: Have you ever experienced or heard that another SS member boxed with a Jewish prisoner?

Answer of the witness Bauer: No

Question: Was an SS man known as a boxer in the camp?

Answer of the witness Bauer: Only Wagner was an athlete. He still had a silver medal from the javelin at the Olympics, if he wasn't lying.

Question: Did you know Gomerski as a boxer?

Answer of the witness Bauer: No. Nor have I seen or heard that he once boxed with a Jewish inmate. Bolender also had the prisoners box among themselves. They did that without an order.

Question: Was it once you watched boxing or was it different incidents?

Answer of the witness Bauer: I've seen that more often.

Question of Lawyer Schweizer: Do you know anything about boxing in other parts of the camp, such as Lager II?

Answer of the witness Bauer: I don't know anything about that. Where are they have supposed to boxed? Everything was occupied. Then they must have boxed in the yard in *Lager II*. After all, they were all boys, the same size as the witness teacher. In *Lager III*, it was all big guys who boxed.

Question of the Chairman. Do you know if prisoners were brought to Sobibór from other camps?

Answer of the witness Bauer: Yes from the Bełżec camp when that was dissolved. I was not in the camp, when the transport arrived from Sobibór. Later, however, I saw a couple in the kitchen who had previously worked in the kitchen in Bełżec, and were therefore known to me. I don't know how many prisoners from Bełżec were brought to us. Nor have I heard anything about the fact this was subject to special treatment.

Question of the Judge Wachter: Do you know if any of the inmates from Bełżec camp who were taken to Sobibór were killed or were they all integrated into the Sobibór camp workforce?

Answer of the witness Bauer: No, I didn't hear anything about inmates being killed.

Question: How many prisoners were brought to Sobibór?

Answer of the witness Bauer: There weren't many. About one or one and a half wagons

Question: How do you know that?

Answer of the witness Bauer: I later saw the wagons parked at the ramp. There they were loaded with shoes and blankets. I was told that these were the wagons that were used to bring the prisoners from Bełżec.

Question: How many prisoners from Bełżec did you see in the Sobibór camp?

Answer of the witness Bauer: Several

Objection of the Lawyer Schweizer: Other witnesses have stated that the prisoners from Bełżec were unloaded under special security precautions and immediately taken to Lager III, and exterminated there.

Answer of the witness Bauer: Then I have to cheat or they cheat. We needed the people for work.

Objection of the Lawyer Schweizer: Did only one transport come from Bełżec or several?

Answer of the witness Bauer: No. As far as I know only one transport came. Those were the last workers from Bełżec. Some of the *Askaris* were there too.

Objection of the Lawyer Schweizer: Frenzel testified that although he was not there himself, he had heard that the prisoners from Bełżec had been shot.

Answer of the witness Bauer: This is news to me, I haven't heard of it. If Frenzel said that, I'm surprised that he shouldn't have been there. He was always in the camp. If he had been in *Lager I* or *II*, he would have had to have heard of the cracking over there. Because the gas chambers were no longer working when the people from Bełżec came, it should all happen quickly. They had already been torn down.

Question: Do you know if Frenzel was in the camp when the transports arrived?

Answer of the witness Bauer: No. I just assumed it after what was said here

Question of the Judge Wachter: Can you say approximately when this transport arrived at the Sobibór camp?

Answer of the witness Bauer: No. It was dark pretty early. Long before that no more transports had arrived. The offensive had already started and the *Wehrmacht* transports all went via Cholm. Such transports swarmed there. I do not know whether other transports of prisoners came to Sobibór after that.

Question of the Lawyer Lorenzen: Do you know if transports of Russian prisoners came afterwards?

Answer of the witness Bauer: We had two Russians in the camp. These were the leaders of the uprising. They've been in the camp for a long time. They were two strong guys. One was a butcher. They worked in *Lager II*, feeding pigs and cleaning horses. I don't know when they came.

Objection of the Lawyer Lorenzen: A witness from Russia, who is still alive, told us that he came to Sobibór in a larger transport about three weeks before the uprising and that the prisoners from this transport also took part in the uprising.

Answer of the witness Bauer: I definitely don't think so. The two had been in the camp for quite a while. You still slaughtered pigs.

Question of the Lawyer Lorenzen: How were the gas chambers eliminated?

Answer of the witness Bauer: They were blown up and broke everything. I had nothing to do with it, because I had my vans. The *Askaris* must have done that, they also loaded the things later. We only had a few Jews there. The Bełżec transport came after the uprising. The gas chambers was demolished before the uprising. At the time of the Uprising they were already working in *Lager IV*, in the ammunition bunkers.

Objection of the Prosecutor Eckert: Is it possible that the transport you just mentioned also came from Treblinka?

Answer of the witness Bauer: I didn't hear anything about a transport coming from Treblinka to Sobibór.

Question of the Lawyer Pfeiffer: Have you been to Treblinka yourself?

Answer of the witness Bauer: Yes. But I didn't know any labor inmates from Treblinka. I only got leather there.

Question of the Lawyer Schweizer to the accused: The gas chambers were still there when you went on vacation before the Uprising. Even when you came back?

The accused Gomerski declared to the question: When I went on vacation the gas chambers were still there, just as it was when I came back. The elimination began when I was assigned to Italy.

Question of the Lawyer Schweizer to the witness Bauer: Mr Bauer, what do you have to say to this?

Answer of the witness Bauer: I wasn't that much into it then. In any case, even before the Uprising people had stopped working in the gas chambers. We didn't have that many people anymore. I've noticed it from the petrol. There was no more petrol for the engine back there.

Question of the Lawyer Schweizer: How long has it been since they brought any petrol back there?

Answer of the witness Bauer: I cannot say that. Sometimes I wasn't there, then they did it themselves, for example Vallaster

Question of the Chairman: Can you remember when a transport came from the Majdanek camp, which is said to have been in Lager I?

Answer of the witness Bauer: No. I can't remember such a transport. In my trial, Miss Raab testified that five thousand inmates came from Majdanek, right at the beginning of the camp. They sat in *Lager I,* because our motor broke down. I am said to have stood at the well and made sure no one fetched water and shot everyone who came to the well. However, I know nothing about it.

Question of the Lawyer Lorenzen: Did you see whether on this transport the incapacitated or the dead were carried to the carts by labor prisoners who had undressed?

Answer of the witness Bauer: I didn't see any of that. At that time there were no lorries, we still had horse-drawn carriages. This transport came right at the beginning, after the SA arrived.

One cannot speak of the transport that arrived in concentration camp clothes. That was a misery. They were taken to the back and shot. They had to go, they would have infected the whole camp. They had dysentery. The Security Guards took them straight to the back. The SS left immediately for fear of contamination. I also fled. They threw bricks, it was such a mess. One of the SS-men was injured. The Askaris then did it all by themselves. Lachmann or Beckmann were still there. The camp commandant was not present. He was never there on Sundays. I didn't see if one of the SS was there.

Now follows the literal recording of the following part of the testimony of the witness Bauer.

I am not aware of a Jewish inmate Shul Stark. I also don't know anything about the fact, that he was called to account after pigs had died.

There were also dogs at the camp. A St. Bernard called Barry, a big Russian shepherd and a German shepherd who didn't understand German. Everyone ran around with the St. Bernard. Most of the time he was with the one standing on the ramp pretending to be a doctor. Bolender sometimes had the dog too. The dog was still in the camp during the Uprising.

Before the Uprising, the dog from Stangl was taken to Treblinka. He was later brought back. Afterwards he was taken to Linz by Wagner. The prisoners were not rushed with the dog. That wasn't a bloodhound, he was just playing. The dog was so big, if he jumped at you, you would fall. He jumped at me once too. Bolender once urged the inmates to load the wagons, which means he just told them to hurry. The prisoners were afraid of the dog and screamed. As they ran, the blankets in which they were storing things waved. Barry then jumped in and snapped at it. He just wanted to play. I don't remember the inmates being chased by the dogs or any one setting the dogs on the inmates. I don't know anything about that.

The witness Bauer was now held up to the first paragraph by public prosecutor Eckert from his first judicial interrogation

Witness Bauer explained: That's not true. Maybe I was misunderstood.

Question of Prosecutor Eckert: Did Gomerski, Michel, Frenzel or a man with the first name Paul set the dogs on the inmates?

Witness Bauer explained: No. no one could rush them
The representative of the public prosecutor's office objected to this form of verbatim recording of part of witness Bauer's testimony on the question of the dogs, since it was not complete.
The defense attorneys of the accused agreed with this objection.
The representative of the public prosecutors office requested that the dog complex be recorded verbatim in its entirety, since the accused is directly affected by it.
The defense attorneys agreed with this motion
The Jury retired to deliberate
After the consultation: The statements made by the witness Bauer are also to be recorded verbatim insofar as they refer to the presence of dogs in the camp. The verbatim transcript of the following part of the testimony of the witness Bauer follows:

Question of the Chairman: Were there dogs in the camp?

Answer of the witness Bauer: Yes, three. Barry a St.Bernard, also a shepherd dog with long hair and a black German shepherd dog, who didn't understand German. The Jews and the Polish women at the train station were afraid of Barry. He looked like a calf, if he jumped you, you fell over. He jumped at me once.

Question: Who did the dog belong to?

Answer of the witness Bauer: He went with everyone

Question: With whom did Barry mainly go?

Answer of the witness Bauer: With the Doctor, he was wearing a white scrub. He wasn't really a doctor, he just pretended to be one. His name was Michel. Bolender also walked the dog. Actually it belonged to the policemen. Beckmann brought it with him from Treblinka with Stangl. That was before the uprising. After the uprising he returned to Sobibór and went to Linz with Wagner in a wagon.

Question: Did you see if the dog Barry was once set on prisoners?

Answer of the witness Bauer: I only remember one incident at the ramp. But you can't say 'rush' to that. Bolender supervised the loading of a wagon. The Jews carried the things from the barracks to the wagon with blankets. Running back Bolender asked them to go faster. The blankets flapped and Barry ran after them, yanking on the blankets.

Question of the Judge Wachter: Did you ever go with Barry yourself?

Answer of the witness Bauer: No

Question: Did Gomerski go with Barry?

Answer of the witness Bauer: Yes. I've seen Gomerski walking with him in the camp

Objection of the Prosecutor Eckert: Were dogs sometimes set on the prisoners?

Answer of the witness Bauer: I don't know anything about that

Public Prosecutor Eckert's reproach from the interrogation of the witness Bauer on November 1, 1949, from 'That much until rushed!'

Answer of the witness Bauer: That must have been misunderstood at the time. I am not aware of dogs being set on inmates.

Objection of the Prosecutor Eckert: Which of the two statements is now correct. Today or then? Did you only provide the information at the time, because you yourself were accused of rushing dogs?

Answer of the witness Bauer: I've always said that nobody could rush Barry, that was a dog that was just playing. Bolender's expression was always, 'Do you want to run?' Then the Jews ran off, followed by Barry who ripped at the blankets.

Question of the Judge Wachter: Have others used similar expressions?

Answer of the witness Bauer: Not others. Only Bolender has loaded

Question of the Lawyer Lorenzen: Have you only seen such incidents on the ramp once or more than once?

Answer of the witness Bauer: There were multiple incidents. Since the garage was by the ramp, I could watch the loading. But I have only seen Bolender doing it, others hardly ever bothered with Barry, because he was so full of lice. I remember that a sergeant from the *Askaris* and *Askaris* were there.

On submission of sheet 187 of the Hague Protocols III paragraph, the witness Bauer explained:

Today I have no recollection of Frenzel and Paul Groth standing by when these incidents took place at the ramp.

Question of the Judge Wachter: Did you ever hear anything in the camp about a prisoner being injured by dogs?

Answer of the witness Bauer: I haven't heard anything about that

Now the expert Professor Dr. Dr Schumacher received the right to ask general questions. As soon as he tried to answer the first question, the witness Bauer began to cry. The hearing was therefore adjourned.

After re-entering the main hearing, the expert stated that he would no longer be available tomorrow, because he had to provide an expert opinion in the Einstadter criminal case in Frankfurt. In addition he had to take part in the main hearing in the Guhlen criminal case.

The witness Bauer was only able to be questioned to a limited extent. He said he had been in the courthouse since 8:30 a.m. At the first question about Gomerski's personality, he burst into tears. As expected, the questions to be asked would represent a particularly emotional burden for the witness and at the same time touch on central problems in the Gomerski trial. He therefore considered the continuation of the questioning of the witness Bauer to be dubious today.

Kurt Bolender

December 21, 1961
Düsseldorf

Present
Court Clerk Dr Schermer
Detective Master Neuert as an interrogator

The accused Kurt Bolender appears in an interrogation room of the Düsseldorf-Derendorf detention centre and, familiarized with the

subject of the interrogation and admonished to the truth, says the following on the matter:

First of all, I refer to my interrogation of May 29, 1961, and June 5, 1961. In addition I would like to add the following:

During my stay in Sobibór I always worked in *Lager III*. There, I oversaw the deployment of a Jewish Labor squad, tasked with cutting down trees in the nearby wooded area, laying barbed-wire and digging a pit intended for the burial of the Jews.

After the first pit was dug, the squad had begun digging a second pit when I was remanded in custody for inciting perjury. In this context, I would also like to point out that before I was imprisoned, I spent about four weeks on vacation at home. In addition, three weeks before my vacation, I was in the military hospital in Cholm for three weeks.

On objection:

It is true that Jews were gassed in *Lager III*, during my stay in Sobibór. There were about six transports with a total of about 2,000 to 3,000 Jews. Even during the actual extermination process, I did not interrupt the work with my work squad. On further objection, I declare that during the gassing in *Lager III*, I divided up working Jews in such a way that some had to empty the gas chambers and transport the dead Jews to the pits.

I don't know anything about the so-called military hospital in *Lager III*. I am of the opinion the narrow-gauge railway train only led from the gas chambers to the pit. I think I know exactly that no living or dead Jews were transported to Lager III, on the narrow-gauge railway train who had not been gassed in the chambers beforehand.

It is true that the members of the camp crew each carried a whip. I too was in possession of such a whip, which I carried with me. However, I did not use the whip. I also did not see other members of the permanent staff hitting people with their whips. If witnesses claim otherwise, I can only deny it.

In addition to the function I have described, I was also responsible for supervising the 3rd platoon of the Ukrainian guards. The Ukrainian platoon commander of the 3rd platoon who reported to me was a certain Mr. Maurer. The 3rd platoon had to take over the external security of the camp at night. However, there was a change between the individual platoons.

It was my job to control the posts of the 3rd platoon. During the day the 3rd platoon was used for all camp tasks. This included guard duties, unloading the Jews, undressing and probably transports to the gas chambers. Although it sounds unbelievable, I maintain that I did not do the classification of the 3rd platoon. Rather I stayed exclusively in *Lager III*. There was no fixed division of the individual platoons.

Werner Dubois

September 7, 1962

In June or July 1943, in any case it was the summer of 1943, I was sent to Sobibór. Before that, I delivered the Ukrainian guards from the Bełżec camp to the Trawniki training camp and then reported to Wirth in Lublin. He then told me that I would continue to be deployed in Sobibór. As far as I can remember, *SS-Hauptsturmführer* Reichleitner was head of the Sobibór camp. I believe that the camp commander from Bełżec, *SS-Hauptsturmführer* or Police Captain Hering, was also in Sobibór. I think that Hering was also active in the camp's administration. Reichleitner first reassigned me as a driver. I made trips to Lublin and had to fetch groceries and other consumer goods. I practiced this activity as a driver for about four months. In the meantime I was also the leader of a Jewish work squad for three weeks. This squad had to clear tree stumps. The actual guarding was carried out by Ukrainian volunteers. I was in charge. There were no irregularities during this mission. I have not killed or abused any Jew.

However, I remember the following incident.

During the time of this squad a Ukrainian security guard was killed[481] by two Jews while fetching water 400 or 500 m from the actual work site. The two Jews managed to escape. I had sent a security guard after it seemed to me that the water fetchers had been gone too long. He came back and reported to me that the other guard had been killed and the Jews had fled. I then gave the order that all Jews had to lie down on the ground to avoid further incidents.

I sent another security guard to the camp who informed the camp manager Reichleitner. Reichleitner appeared at the site, shortly thereafter, and had the entire squad drafted into the camp. The squad did not move out again in the next few days. I was replaced as squad leader. Reichleitner reproached me for sending a security guard with two Jews to fetch water. I do not believe that this squad was subsequently destroyed. As far as I can remember, the squad went back to work after a few days. I then worked as a driver again.

About 14 days before the uprising in the Sobibór camp, I was deployed as a weapons officer. This means I was deployed as a deputy for *SS-Oberscharführer* Hubert Gomerski, who was on vacation at the time. On the day of the uprising between 2:00 and 4:00 p.m. I was with a Ukrainian guard in the armoury on the ground floor. The door was open, I saw a group of Jewish inmates carrying axes approaching the armoury. I assumed it was a work squad. This group of five or six first walked past the armoury. They walked around the armoury and then entered the room. They beat me with axes. My skull was split open by an axe blow. My hands carry more axe blows.

Nevertheless, I was able to free myself and flee outside. After about 10m a shot in the lung hit me and I lost consciousness. Some Ukrainian security guards treated me with vodka, which brought me back to my senses. Now I learned out that an uprising

---

[481] According to a Security Police Lublin report the Trawniki guard killed was of Armenian descent.

had broken out and that I was the only SS man who had survived the uprising.[482]

I was then immediately taken to the hospital in Chelm. Here I was told that about 15 SS men died in the uprising. In this context I would like to mention that the head wound was so severe that my memory is still impaired to this day. Therefore, if I no longer remember some events from that time and various names, I would like to trace it back to that. In any case I know that the following SS people died in the uprising: Johann Niemann, Siegfried Graetschus and a certain Wolf, who I remember was a policeman.

I have already mentioned that Reichleitner was the head of the camp at the time of my stay in Sobibór. I can also remember the following names: Hubert Gomerski, Erich Bauer, Gustav Wagner, Hans Klier, and the three names who died. Several names were now read out to me by the interrogating officers. They are said to be members of the permanent SS staff at the Sobibór extermination camp. I would now like to provide relevant information on this.

Bauer, Erich: When I was seconded from Oranienburg to Berlin, Bauer was already working as a driver at the T4 office. I only met him again during my time in Sobibór. Like me, he was a driver there. I know nothing about his activities in *Lager III*.

Becker, Joachim: I can't remember him

Beckmann, Rudolf: I remember that he was in the Grafeneck and Hadamar euthanasia institutions. He was employed there in agriculture. I don't know whether he was in Sobibór.[483]

Bauch: The name sounds familiar to me, but I don't know where I met him

Berg, Ernst: I don't remember him

Dr. Blaurock: During my time there were no SS members with a PhD in Sobibór. I can't remember the person Blaurock.

---

[482] That is incorrect a number of SS men survived the uprising.
[483] Incorrectly listed as Kurt Beckmann.

Bolender, Kurt: I met him during my assignment in Trieste. I think I used to share a room with him. He was wounded there shortly before collapsing and getting lumbago. I took him to the hospital in Leibach and have never heard of him since. I didn't meet him in the euthanasia centres or in the extermination camps.

Bredow, Paul: I only remember that I was with Bredow in the Trieste area. I mean that he experienced the collapse in May 1945, and came into British captivity. On the day the English marched in, when we were disarmed by the English vanguard, we were called in by Dieter Allers and said goodbye. I believe that Bredow was still present. I didn't see him in the euthanasia centres or in the extermination camps.

Dachsel, Arthur: He was in Bełżec with me. There he was in *Lager II*, and collected and sorted the Jewish clothing. I don't know where he ended up after the Bełżec camp was dissolved. I didn't see him in Sobibór. I can't say whether he was in Sobibór before his time in Bełżec. In any case, I didn't see him again after the dissolution of the Bełżec camp

Fiffeck: I have in mind that I met Fiffeck in Hadamar. I mean that he came from Frankfurt am Main. As far as I can remember, I didn't come into contact with him in Bełżec or Sobibór.

Floss, Herbert: I was in Hadamar together with him. As already mentioned, he also worked there as a disinfectant. After that I heard nothing more from him.

Frenzel, Karl: I met him in 1939, at the T4 office in Berlin. I don't know where he was later. I haven't seen him again. I mean that Frenzel comes from the Brandenburg or the area.

Gaulstich, Friederich: I don't know this name

Girtzig, Hans: I met him in 1939, at the T4 office. I know that he was then in Grafeneck euthanasia facility and that he was later in the Bełżec camp. Whether he was in Sobibór, I can't say. I also met him again later in Trieste.

Groth, Paul: I don't know this name

Ittner, Paul: I don't know this name

Klatt: I can't remember him. I think his first name was Heinrich. I think he was a nurse in Hadamar. I cannot say whether he was in Sobibór.[484]

Konrad, Fritz: I can't remember him. I never heard the name.

Lachmann, Erich: I can't remember him

Ludwig, Karl: As I mentioned, I was with him at the Todt Organization. Later I met him again in the Trieste area. Karl Ludwig was present at the already mentioned farewell by Allers on the day of the English occupation. He must therefore have survived the end of the war. I know nothing about his stay in euthanasia institutions and extermination camps. I didn't meet him there either.

Michel, Hermann: The name is probably familiar to me. But I can't say where I met him.

Niemann, Johann: I got to know him for the first time in the T4 office in Berlin. Later I met him again in Sobibór. At that time he was an SS-Untersturmführer. It is possible that he was head of *Lager II*, or *III*. As I mentioned, he died in the uprising.

Pötzinger, Karl: I somehow got to know him during my deployment in euthanasia. Then I was with him in the Trieste area. I know he died there. I cannot say anything about his functions in the extermination camps. I didn't meet him in Bełżec and Sobibór.

Reichleitner, Franz, Karl: During my time in Sobibór, he was the camp manager. During this period he was responsible for the actions that happened in Sobibór. I can't say where he is. It is possible that I heard that he died in the Trieste area.[485]

Rehwald, Wenzel: He was in Hadamar together with me. He was a nurse there. I don't know where he ended up later.

Richter, Kurt: I can't remember the person

Rost, Paul: I met him in Bełżec. He wore the uniform of a police chief. I wasn't sure about his job. Sometimes it gave the

---

[484] Ivan Klatt was a Ukrainian Trawnikimänner who was killed in the prisoner uprising on October 14, 1943.
[485] Listed incorrectly as Hans.

impression that he was assigned to monitor us. Later he worked at customs in the Trieste area. I think he came from Saxony.

Ryba, Walter: I don't know him

Schiffner, Karl: I can remember him. He was active in euthanasia facilities. I can no longer say whether I met him in Brandenburg or Hadamar. I mean he was from Berlin. I didn't see him in the extermination camps.

Schmidt, Fritz: I can remember a person by the name of Schmidt, who was deployed either in a extermination camp or in euthanasia. I no longer know the exact details of the person and their activities.

Schulz: I can't remember him.

Schumacher, Emil: I don't know him.

Schwarz, Gottfried: I met Schwarz in 1939, at the T4 office in Berlin. I mean that he was also in Grafeneck and Brandenburg. When I arrived in Bełżec, he was already there. About three to four months before the Bełżec camp was closed, he left Bełżec and I heard that he ran an outside camp near Lublin. Anyway, he wasn't in Sobibór. I didn't see him there. I only met him again in Trieste. There he died.

Stefel, Thomas: I don't know him.[486]

Steubl, Karl: I don't know him either.

Stangl, Franz: I only heard that he ran an extermination camp and later also went to Trieste. However, I never came into contact with him personally.

Unverhau, Heinrich: I got to know him during my work in the euthanasia facility. Later I met him again in Bełżec. In Bełżec he was either sorting clothes or sorting shoes. I didn't meet him in Sobibór.

Vallaster, Josef: I think I've heard the name Vallaster in connection with a euthanasia facility. However, I did not see him in Bełżec or Sobibór .

Wagner, Gustav: I can remember clearly that during my time in Sobibór he was active as 'Stabsscharführer' and announced the

---

[486] Incorrectly listed as Adolf.

orders of the day. I don't know where he went after his stay in Sobibór. I did not see him in the Trieste area.

Weiss, Bruno: I don't know him.

Werner, Kurt: I can't remember him.

Wolf, Hans: I can remember that he worked as a photographer in Hadamar. There he had to photograph the mentally ill people selected for killing, before they were killed. I don't know where he went later. I only met him again in Trieste. I don't know whether he survived the end of the war. I met his brother, whose first name I do not remember, in Sobibór. As I mentioned he died in the uprising. They were both Austrians. I can't say exactly where they came from.[487]

During my stay in Sobibór, the camp was still full with Jews. It is possible that transports were still arriving there at the time. I was sometimes on the road for days, so I didn't notice everything that was happening in the camp. In any case, I have no recollection that I saw incoming transports or even took part in them. I never entered the actual extermination camp the so-called *Lager III*. I was not allowed to.

A map of the Sobibór extermination camp was presented to me. I recognize the camp as far as it relates to *Lager I* and *Lager II*, and also the front camp. However, I never entered the complex of camps III, or IV. I lived in building number 11 (the former post building).

The vehicles were housed in the garage (number 4) so I didn't have to go into distant parts of the camp complex. I am aware that Jews were gassed and burned in the Sobibór extermination camp from the existence of the Sobibór camp when I was still in Bełżec. However, I do not know who led and directed the extermination action in Sobibór. I was not spoken to about this and I did not ask about it.

On September 6, 1961, based on a search warrant issued by AG Schwelm a search was carried out in my apartment by the interrogating officers. Although this search was ordered by a judge, I

---

[487] The Wolf brothers, were both from Krummau in the Sudetenland.

voluntarily permitted it. Three pictures were secured. The first shows me in the *Waffen-SS* weapon uniform. It was at the time when I was in Oranienburg. In the second picture you can see me with my son. I'm about 28 years old, it was at the time I was on vacation in Berlin. I think I came from Hadamar on vacation. The third picture is from the post war period and shows me in work clothes during American captivity in 1946. I voluntarily provided these three pictures. Please return the same pictures to me, if you no longer need them.

I cannot give any further information on the matter, should we still need to clarify further points, I am available at any time for questioning. I have a permanent residence here in Schwelm and intend to stay here as well.

November 29, 1962

In June or July 1943, operations in the Bełżec extermination camp were discontinued. One day I received an order to transport parts from Bełżec to Lublin with a truck. The day after next I was seconded from Wirth to Sobibór. I reported to the camp manager there (Reichleitner or Hering). The *Stabsscharführer* Wagner or Steubl, in Sobibór gave me quarters and familiarized me with my tasks. I lived in the barracks marked number 11 in the front camp.

In Sobibór I worked as a driver and got food together with Steubl from Cholm and Trawniki. The rest of the time I supervised Jewish work squads. A sugar beet factory was to be built to the west of the camp. I led Jewish work squads to this forest work and supervised the execution of the work. The squad included 15 to 20 Jews and seven to eight Ukrainians who were responsible for guarding the Jews.

I also did forest work south of the camp with a Jewish work squad. One day it happened that two Jews had fled and killed a Ukrainian guard as they fled. I then ordered the Jews to lie flat on the ground and then I had the camp director informed. Reichleitner appeared at the scene of the crime and ordered the work squad to return to the camp immediately. The next day I was working as a driver again. I can't say what happened to the Jews. The incident I described was resented by the camp management, I was no longer assigned to supervise work squads.

During my assignment in Sobibór, I witnessed the handling of two Jew transports. Each transport consisted of about 40 to 50 wagons (freight cars). About 40 to 50 Jews were accommodated in each wagon. When one of these two transports arrived, I listened to the station command. The unloading of the transport proceeded as follows:

The northern siding south of the front camp had a width of about ten wagons. Therefore, initially ten wagons drove to the northern siding. Members of the Jewish station command opened the doors and asked the Jews to leave the wagons and line up.

When the Jews were taken to *Lager II*, they were told not to worry because it was a resettlement camp. I accompanied the Jews from the front camp to *Lager II*, and saw some of them being undressed there. The Jews had to undress on a sandy floor in *Lager II*, and take off their clothes there. Then they were led through the so-called 'hose' into the gas chambers in *Lager III*. I did not observe the transport of the Jews from *Lager II*, to the gas chambers in *Lager III*, because immediately after the arrival of the Jews in *Lager II*, I returned to the sidings in the front camp where the rest of the transport had to be dispatched. The further discharges were repeated in the manner described. I also accompanied these Jews from the front camp to *Lager II*.

Since the transport consisted of around 2,000 Jews, the unloading and undressing had to be carried out more quickly in order to be able to carry out exterminations as soon as possible. No incidents occurred during my stay at the siding. The Jews got out without resistance and went to the camp. To my knowledge the Jews were not beaten with whips.

Sick and infirm Jews were carried out of the wagons by members of the Jewish train station detail. They were taken over by a special squad in the front camp, loaded onto lorries and shot in

Lager III. The wagon squad belonged to the staff of *Lager II*. I do not know whether the shootings were carried out by members of the wagon squad or by the staff of *Lager III*. I never saw the shootings myself. The instruction in the camp was to shoot as little as possible. It is therefore possible that some of the sick and infirm Jews were also gassed. I no longer have a clear idea of the destruction of further transports of Jews.

Question: I have never entered *Lager III*, during the gassing operation. During my work as 'U v D' I had to check the camp posts at night. During this round of inspections I also entered *Lager III*. However, there was no activity there at the time. I did not look into the gas chambers. I can therefore not provide any relevant information about the condition of *Lager III*.

On Objection: The Ukrainian guards reported to Wagner and Feix. They drilled with the Ukrainians and divided them into individual services. Perhaps I once took over supervision of the Ukrainians on a deputy basis.

A few days before the camp uprising, I took over as Gomerski's representative in the armoury. There my fate overtook me. Several Jews armed with axes and knives broke into the armoury to take the weapons. I was hit on the hand and head by several axe blows and sustained a bullet in the lung. Because of these injuries, I am still receiving medical treatment today. I suffer from constant headaches. In this context, I would like to mention that during the Italian mission, two pieces of shrapnel penetrated the back of my head.

I am willing to comment on people whose names are held up to me:

Frenzel: He was very cheeky in Sobibór. I think I saw him operating the lorry-train.

Schutt: He was an accountant in Sobibór. Whether he also performed other functions there, I cannot say.

Unverhau: Was transferred from Bełżec to Sobibór a few days before me. He had to supervise the undressing in *Lager II*, and was probably assigned like me in other respects.

Wolf Brothers: The Wolf brothers were also assigned to the undressing in *Lager II*. Otherwise I cannot give any relevant information about them. I ask you to take into account that the events happened 20 years ago and that my memory has faded due to the injuries suffered. After the war I have only seen Gomerski and Hirtreiter.

I am aware that there was murder in the extermination camps. What I did was an accessory to murder. If I were to be convicted, I would think that's correct. Murder is murder. In my opinion, the assessment of guilt should not be based on the respective camp functions. Wherever we have been deployed, we are all equally guilty. The camp functioned in a chain of functions, if just one link in this chain is lost, the entire operation comes to a standstill.

The actual 'work' in the extermination process was carried out by the working Jews. However, they acted under duress and lived in constant fear of death. All members of the German camp staff were in charge of the camp and are responsible for the extermination of the Jews. However, it had to be taken into account that we did not act on our own initiative, but within the framework of the 'end solution to the Jewish question,' decided by the Reich leadership. None of us had the courage to defy the orders.

The outcome of such a refusal to obey orders is anyone's guess. I mean that I only had the following choice, either work in a Jewish camp or, if I disobeyed orders, be imprisoned in a concentration camp.

My above interrogation was dictated loud and clear in my presence. I confirm the correctness with my signature.

Karl Frenzel

March 6, 1962

About the person:

I was born on August 20, 1911, the son of the points warden Otto Frenzel in Zehdenick, district of Templin. I had three other siblings, of whom I was born the second oldest child. I spent my childhood in Gruneberg, North Baden. In the years 1917, to 1926, I attended elementary school n Oranienburg. I always achieved my class goal and was released from the eighth grade.

From 1927, to 1930, I learned the trade of a carpenter in Zehdenick. Since unemployment prevailed after the end of my apprenticeship, I was forced to work in a butcher's shop in Oranienburg. Because of the bad economic situation, I became a member of the *NSDAP,* and the *SA* in 1930, because I promised myself an improvement in living conditions from the National Socialist system. At the time, I was convinced of the correctness of the National Socialist goals. However, I could not foresee the later consequences. In this context, I would also like to emphasise that I did not take part in '*Kristallnacht*' and did not take anyone to a concentration camp.

In the years 1933, to 1935, I worked in the Gruneberger metalware factory. I then worked as an administrator in a country year centre in Lowenberg/ Mark. From August 27, 1939, to December 1939, I belonged to the construction battalion 211. Around the turn of the year 1939/1940, I was conscripted into the so-called 'charitable foundation for institutional care.' I had to report to the T4 office (Berlin, Tiergartenstr. 4). There we were conscripted and sworn in by Allers and Blankenburg for a secret 'Reich' matter.

We were told it was supposed to be a hospital transfer. I was first deployed in Grafeneck, where I worked in the laundry for about 3 months and later as a security guard. Here I realized what was going on in Grafeneck. It was about the extermination of the mentally ill, who were given a mercy death in the context of so-called euthanasia. I would like to expressly emphasize that I had nothing to do with the actual euthanasia. As already pointed out, I was mostly employed as a security guard in Grafeneck.

In the years that followed, I was employed in the Hadamar and Bernburg sanatoriums. In Hadamar, I first worked as a porter and later dealt with cremations. I have been given the printout order for this. While I was working in Bernburg, the sanatorium there was already in the process of being closed. I just did some cleanup work there.

Around the spring of 1942, I received the order to report to the SS and Police leader in Lublin.[488] We were supposed to be seconded to the police. In reality, however, we were dressed in SS uniforms. The respective SS rank was determined according to the last SA rank. So I got the uniform of an *SS-Oberscharführer*. A few days later I was seconded to the Sobibór extermination camp, via Cholm.

I was deployed in Sobibór from April 1942, until the camp uprising. I was then transferred to Italy, where I belonged to a police battalion commanded by Wirth. My battalion comrades and I had the task of registering Jewish property. The apartments of the Jews were sealed and handed over to the disposal of the 'Wehrmacht.' There were no exterminations of the Jews in Italy. At least I didn't know anything about it. Above all, I don't know that there is said to have been an incinerator in San Sabba. Instead gang activity soon set in, so that we were deployed in Italy, exclusively to fight partisans.

I suffered a fall from a motorcycle and was in hospital in Udine until September 1944. Then the retreat began and I was taken to an American internment camp near Munich, from which I was released on May 15, 1945. After temporary voluntary work in the internment camp, I returned to Langsdorf, Giesen district, in August 1945, where I worked as a carpenter until November 1945. I

---

[488] Incorrectly stated as the Higher SS and Police Leader.

have lived in Gottingen since November 25, 1945. I'm currently working as a vice stage master at the local film studio.

In 1934, I got married to Sophie Aumann. The marriage produced five children who are currently 26, 25, 24, 23, and 20 years old. Four of my children live in Gottingen, another son of mine lives in Hannover. My wife died in 1945. I've been a widower since then. I am currently engaged to Mrs Gruber, who is also widowed and lives with me at Rote Strasse 10. We each have our own apartment there.

To the business

When I reported for duty in the Sobibór extermination camp in April 1942, the so-called active members were already there. By these active people I understand the following people in particular Niemann, Floss, Gomerski, Bolender, Graetschus, Dubois etc. I will comment on the individual names in more detail later.[489]

An SS leader was in charge, whose name I can no longer remember. If the name Thomalla is mentioned to me in this context, it may be true that he was the first camp manager. At that time the camp was still under construction. Since I am a craftsman, I was involved in construction work when the camp was set up. Because of the space in the camp, the interrogating officers presented me with a site plan and visualized the layout of the camp again. I can therefore remember that when I took up my duties in Sobibór, the front camp, and *Lager I*, and *II*, were partially in place, while *Lager III*, had not yet been set up.

Questioned:

When I took up my duties in Sobibór, there were not only the so-called 'active' but also numerous working Jews who were supposed to set up the camp. The first transports of Jews destined for extermination only arrived a few weeks later. At first, I was

---

[489] In April 1942, Bolender, Floss, Gomerski, Graetschus were in post at Sobibór, Niemann and Dubois arrived much later.

exclusively occupied with working with a Jewish work squad to set up the camp. The barracks had to be built, the camp fenced in, barbed wire laid etc. I often worked with the work squad outside the camp to demolish houses in the village of Sobibór and rebuild them in the Sobibór camp.

At first there was talk in the camp that it should be a re-training camp. Later, however, Wirth appeared in the camp and explained to us that Sobibór was supposed to be a Jewish extermination camp. *Lager III*, with three gas chambers was built accordingly. I cannot say anything about the size of the gas chambers because I was never deployed in *Lager III*.[490]

As already pointed out, the first transports of Jews destined for extermination arrived in Sobibór by train a few weeks after I took up my duties. The Jews were received by the so-called '*Bahnhofskommando.*' The station command consisted of the former camp manager Reichleitner, or the deputy Niemann, working Jews, Ukrainian volunteers and some members of the permanent staff. For the most part, the Jews willingly left the wagons of the railway trains. Only rarely were there difficulties with unloading, then it was just 'helped out.' Guards were armed with carabiners and *Kapo's* with whips. They went into the wagons and made sure that the wagons were unloaded as quickly as possible. Violence may have been used in the process. However, I cannot say who hit the Jews, while unloading the Jewish transports.

On Objection

It is true that members of the permanent staff were also equipped with whips. I also had a whip in the camp. I cannot say whether I have ever used my whip. The transport of Jews was carried out as follows: after being unloaded by the so-called '*Bahnhofskommando,*' the Jews were led to *Lager II*, in rows of four or five. There they had to hand in their things and undress. In *Lager II*, the Jews were told that they should be bathed, disinfected and then

---

[490] Stated as *Lager II*, in his testimony.

assigned to work. In fact, however, the Jews were led through the so-called 'hose,' into the gas chambers of *Lager III*, where they were gassed and thrown into pits after their death and later burned.

When asked about my work in the Sobibór camp, I was able to explain that I was a member of the station command on a number of occasions. In my presence, there were no difficulties unloading the transport. The *Kapo's* probably helped with the unloading with whips. There is also the possibility that I used my whip myself on such an occasion.

Furthermore, I once accompanied a group destined for gassing through the so-called 'hose' to the intermediate barracks (see number 28 on the site plan). Later it was decided that the Jews did not have to defecate in *Lager II*, but only in intermediate barracks number 28.

Apart from the routine extermination process in the gas chambers of *Lager III*, Jewish children as well as frail or sick Jews were transported directly from the front camp to the so-called military hospital of *Lager III*, on a narrow-gauge railway. However, the expression 'hospital' is out of place in this context, because the so-called hospital in *Lager III*, was not used to heal the Jews, but to destroy them.

The gassing in the Sobibór camp had started under Reichleitner.[491] Reichleitner commissioned me to take over the transport of the narrow-gauge railway. I have only carried out this assignment a few times. I then asked Reichleitner to relieve me of this activity because I was personally shocked by what was happening there.

Bolender and Gomerski worked in *Lager III*. I cannot remember the other names of the members of the permanent staff who worked in *Lager III*, at the moment. The Jews were received in *Lager III*, by the members of the permanent staff working there

---

[491] This is incorrect—the gassings in Sobibór started under Franz Stangl, who was the commandant before Reichleitner.

and gassed there and some were shot. I myself had no insight into *Lager III*, during the gassing.

Questioned:

It is difficult for me to estimate the number of Jews gassed in Sobibór. However, I seem to remember that about two trains with Jews arrived in Sobibór every week. I cannot say how many people were in the trains, but I would assume that there were tens of thousands of Jews who were gassed in Sobibór.

I cannot say who operated the gassing engine in Sobibór. However, I believe that it could have been Anton Getzinger, who died while handling a hand grenade. However, I think I can say with certainty that Bauer did not operate the gassing engine. Bauer was only allowed to be a driver in the camp.[492]

On Objection:

Although it may seem unbelievable, I would like to emphasise that I was mainly occupied with Jewish working squads. It is true that the camp was completed after a few months. But then I worked in *Lager I*,—workshops, watchmaker, tailor, bakery etc— and was busy setting up *Lager IV*.

On another Objection:

It may have happened that working Jews were killed. I myself neither ordered the killing with working Jews nor carried it out myself. I even think I can say that I was popular with the Jews. The testimonies of the witness Ilana Safran dated April 3, 1960, were held up to me. It is true that I supervised a Jewish forest squad. However, I deny having beaten the working Jews for no reason. I also deny having participated in the killing of a work squad in retaliation for the flight of two Jews.

As far as the camp uprising is mentioned in the testimony, I would like to make the following statement: working Jews—it was

---

[492] Bauer's own testimony would seem to refute this claim.

actually a female worker Jew—had told me about the planned uprising. However, since I did not consider the message to be serious, I refrained from informing the camp administration. So it happened that the Jews were able to escape, when it is claimed that I shot flying Jews with a rifle, I counter that the armoury was occupied by Jews. However, we had no weapons in our accommodation, so that for this reason alone the testimony of the witness Ilana Safran cannot be correct.

After the camp uprising, there were no more gassings in the Sobibór camp. There were still about 150 Jews in the camp, who had not managed to escape. When a few days later an *Obergruppenführer* (successor of Globocnik) inspected the camp, he ordered that the Jews should be shot. I asked the *Obergruppenführer* to refrain from the shooting because the Jews were still needed for work. However, the *Obergruppenführer* insisted on the shooting and gave the shooting order to an *Untersturmführer* who was with him. He then had the shooting carried out by the Ukrainian guards. The shootings took place in *Lager III*. I also deny shooting a Jew who attempted suicide.

April 18, 1961

Dortmund

The site plan of the Sobibór extermination camp was shown to me again. I estimate the width of the northern siding from barbed wire to barbed wire to be about 150m and therefore I think I can say with certainty that it was not necessary to maneuver when unloading the transports. It is true that some transports carried up to 18 wagons. Among them, however, were luggage and personnel carriers that were unhooked in front of the entrance to the northern siding, so that the entire train could be parked on the northern siding.

The Jews were unloaded across the entire width of the northern siding and taken directly to *Lager II*. There the Jews had to hand in their luggage and their valuables and get undressed. I once attended such a 'clearance' myself and accompanied a group after the Jews through the so-called 'hose' to the border of *Lager III*.

The so-called 'hose' was surrounded by barbed wire about 3 to 4m wide and covered with twigs, so that the Jews could see the area neither to the right nor to the left. The group I accompanied consisted of about 100 naked Jews who were escorted by Ukrainian guards. The group was preceded by a few *Unterführers* while I walked behind the group. The Jews were taken to the gas chambers in *Lager III*. I stopped at the border of *Lager III*, and didn't look at the gassing.

On Objection:

I know *Lager III*. I was in *Lager III*, also when there were no gassings. I saw the pits there. I remember a pit about 25 to 30m long. The width may have been 6 meters. I estimate the depth to be about 3 to 4 m. Several hundred corpses lay in the pits. On the occasion of my stay in *Lager III*, I cast a glance at the gas chambers in passing. The chambers were painted white and gave the impression of shower rooms.

On another Objection:

I remember that in the fall of 1942, or spring of 1943, Himmler was on an inspection visit in the Sobibór camp. The visit had been announced a few days in advance, so the camp management endeavoured to carry out the camp functions properly. The individual workplaces were filled with the so-called active to ensure the reimbursement of proper reports. I was given the task of taking over the external security of the camp, with a few Ukrainian guards in order to guarantee Himmler's personal protection.

While Himmler looked at the gassing operation in *Lager III*, I secured the area (from *Lager IV*). I remember that all the *Unterführer* were called together in the canteen and that Himmler gave a speech. Although I was present at the speech, I cannot remember the details. However, Himmler praised Sobibór and arranged for the promotion of some *Unterführer*. I haven't been promoted.

On the site plan, I designate the canteen as building number 3 of the front camp. I lived in building number 9 or 10 in *Lager I*. I designate the individual buildings of *Lager I*, as follows:

No 1: Tailoring
No 2: Shoemaker
No 3: Carpentry
No 4: Bakery
No 5: Tailoring for the guards
No 6: Kitchen
No 7: Accommodation for female working Jews
No's 8 and 9: Accommodation barracks for male working Jews

The pigsty is shown as building number 6 in *Lager II*. Since I am a trained carpenter, I was responsible in particular for the carpentry. I have already described my other area of work in my earlier interrogations.

On Objection:

It is possible that I—apart from the case I have already described—ordered the flogging of other Jews. However, I cannot remember this exactly. I still remember the case I have already described, because I was present at the flogging myself. In addition, I concede the possibility that I have given the order to the Jewish *Kapo* to punish other working Jews, with about 10 lashes. In such cases, I did not attend the execution, so I cannot remember exactly the flogging.

On another Objection:

I often heard shots in Sobibór. Shots were nothing special in the camp. One has to imagine the situation in such a way that Ukrainian guards cordoned off the entire camp and fired whenever someone approached the camp border too closely from the outside or inside. I cannot say whether these were just warning shots.

I am also not in a position to accuse individual members of the permanent staff of having shot Jewish people. If I were to say that Wagner, Muller or others had shot this or that Jew, I had to lie. However, it is true that in Sobibór were not only gassed but also shot. The following incidents occurred to me:

In the camp it was said that working Jews in *Lager III*, should have dug a canal in order to break out. The project is said to have been discovered. I was told that about 50 Jews were then shot in *Lager III*.

I can remember that working Jews in the gold chamber had bartered with Ukrainian guards. The camp manager Reichleitner took over the clarification of the case and caused three Jews and two Ukrainian guards to be shot. The Ukrainians were shot in *Lager IV*, in front of the assembled team. We all had to witness the shooting at the time, to be warned against repeating barter deals. The shooting was led by an *Unterführer* (probably Graetschus), and carried out by Ukrainians.

Question: Did you shoot Jews yourself in Sobibór or get them shot?

Answer: I've been thinking about all the events in Sobibór for the whole day and I'll take a chance on a confrontation with the witnesses who claim that I'm supposed to have shot Jews.

I think I can say with certainty that the Lorenbahn was completed in the summer of 1942. I can remember the point in time because the narrow-gauge railway was already in operation several months before the suicide committed by Bauch—December 4, 1942.

My above interrogation transcript was dictated loudly and clearly in my presence and then read out. I confirm the correctness.

Franz Hödl

March 29, 1966

Linz

I was in Sobibór from about October 1942, to about March 1943. Before I came to Sobibór I was in Trawniki near Lublin. There was a military training camp there. As far as I calculated it afterwards, I had to have been there for 2 to 3 months. Before Trawniki I was in Alkoven near Linz (Hartheim) as a driver with a post bus. Before this time I was again from January 8th until March 30th, 1942, in Russia, in winter service. I was assigned there by the *Reichspost*. Before the incorporation of Austria I was a bus driver with *Oberkraft* Wels. From there I was taken on by the *Reichspost* again as a bus driver and from here I was transferred to Alkoven for this job, again as a bus driver.

I had been in the Austrian *NSDAP* since 1937, and I was in the *SS* here until 1938, specifically with the General *SS*. At that time we were selected for work in Alkoven by the '*Gauleitung*' (manager of the *NSDAP*). I don't know what aspects that was based on. Three of us were chosen. At first we didn't know what job we were supposed to do.

We were instructed in Alkoven by the police officer Wirth about the fact that the mentally ill were being killed in a secret 'Reich' matter. That was the law, we didn't have to worry about it. Things would be processed and checked by responsible doctors. We were asked to maintain secrecy here and threatened with the death penalty in the event of a violation and were finally sworn to this obligation. In my opinion Wirth was a major squadron leader in the police force. As far as I can remember, he was wearing an *SS* uniform but with a police badge and an *SD* on the sleeve.

I had to drive one of the existing buses, which were then used to fetch sick people from the various institutions in Austria. The whole thing ran under the company 'Public Fund for Institutional

Care' and the transport facility was called *Staffel Hegener*. But I also know the term '*Gekrat.*'

The following names are still known to me, from the time in Hartheim: Barbl, Bolender, Wirth, Reichleitner, Stangl, Wagner, Steubl, Reisenberger, Gomerski. Of the names of the 12 accused in the ongoing jury trial in Germany that have now been given to me. I know the names of Frenzel, Lambert, perhaps Unverhau, as well as the two Wolf brothers and perhaps Zierke. In addition to the already mentioned Bolender. Of these, only Lambert, who was a furnace mason, was in Alkoven. I mean, he was there in the beginning, maybe a month, may be longer. I can no longer say exactly. As far as I know he only built the furnace for burning the corpses there. Then he left and later built a chimney for this incinerator in the courtyard of the castle. That could have been early 1940. The rest of the accused I know only from Sobibór.

On Objection:

As far as I can remember, Bolender and Gomerski were in Alkoven at the same time. As far as I can remember, they were both active SS men. Bolender '*Rottenführer*' and Gomerski *Unterscharführer*. I think they both came to Alkoven at the same time. As far as I can remember, both were still in Alkoven when we left for the winter service in early 1942. Anyway, I didn't know that both or one of them had gotten away from Alkoven before. As, drivers we didn't get into the inner workings at all. Therefore, I cannot say what Bolender and Gomerski had to do in the institution, it is possible that they were burners or disinfectors.

As far as I remember, Wirth was the boss in Hartheim, as well as the doctors Dr Lonauer[493] and Dr Renno. Stangl was also somehow active in administration. I mean, Wirth was no longer in Hartheim when I returned from winter deployment in March 1942. Reichleitner was the boss there at the time. But Stangl was still there.

---

[493] Written as Dr Lohnmauer in his testimony.

One day, after the winter deployment, I received marching orders from Alkoven to Berlin, *Tiergartenstrasse 4*. I have a memory gap about the time that followed until my stay in Trawniki. I don't know whether I came from Berlin to Lublin alone or with others, and I don't remember who sent me there either.

In Lublin I had to report back to Christian Wirth, who was with the *SSPF* Globocnik at the time.[494] That must have been in July 1942. Up until then I had always been in civilian clothes, except during the disaster operation in Russia, where we wore OT uniforms.[495]

On Objection:

In Trawniki we only wore a drill suit, no specific uniform. We received some basic military training there. We were a group of about 8 people. I can no longer say who by name was listening.

Answer to Question:

I think I can remember that a policeman trained us in Trawniki.

It's possible, but I don't remember, that there were Ukrainian units in Trawniki. I also don't know the names of training police ranks from Trawniki. I tried to get away from there with Reichleitner in Trawniki. I knew Reichleitner from Alkoven and was on first name terms with him. I had this terrible burden of what was happening in Alkoven behind me, and I feared that something similar would be done in the future, or that somehow they wanted to get rid of us. There was already talk in Alkoven, that if we had already done our work there well and when the war was over then we were allowed to go on a sea voyage with the *KdF* ship 'Wilhelm Gustloff.' We think we know that on this journey we should disappear. It probably wouldn't have made it onto the ship.

I want to mention here that Wirth was a man who constantly made threats: he wanted to shoot someone and things like that.

---

[494] Incorrectly stated as *HSSPF* Globocnik.
[495] Organization Todt.

That's what happened to me, for example, when he threatened to shoot me when I once refused to clean the shitty and pissed-off bus. That was in Alkoven.

In this overall situation in Trawniki, I spoke to Reichleitner about whether I could leave or whether he could help me. Reichleitner explained to me that he couldn't do it himself, I have to stay where I am. I mean Reichleitner was already in Sobibór when we were having this conversation.

Answer to a Question:

I don't know that we were taught and sworn in again in Berlin. I think the Alkoven oath would still have applied there. As far as I can remember, I was only instructed again and sworn to secrecy under the threat of punishment, namely by Wirth, when I came from Trawniki to Sobibór. Whenever someone came, we were instructed again about this duty of confidentiality.

On Objection:

It is true that in Trawniki there was vague talk of the extermination of the Jews in certain camps. Later in Sobibór, the names of Bełżec and Treblinka camps also became known to me. At that time I came alone from Trawniki to Sobibór, received an SS uniform there and was assigned to be a driver for Reichleitner. At that time, Reichleitner was camp leader for the entire camp.

On Objection:

I don't know who Reichleitner's predecessor was as camp leader of Sobibór. In particular, I haven't heard anything that it was Stangl. In this context, I also do not know the name Wirth. I don't know the name Thomalla in this respect and otherwise, Wirth was still ahead of Reichleitner. Wirth was in Lublin at the time. He has been to Sobibór a few times. He made inspections in the camp.

My idea of the camp is as follows:

When you came in through the gate, there was a guard house on the left, then wooden houses on the left for the guards and a little further on the left a larger barrack for the kitchen. There is also a dining room. To the left behind this building was *Lager I*, which was specially fenced off. A Jewish work detachment was housed there, including tailors, locksmiths, carpenters, cobblers, and women for cleaning the accommodation and for laundry and leafing.

From the gate on the right hand side there was a larger house that if I remember correctly was called the 'Swallow's Nest.' Behind it was an armoury as far as I can remember, in a small house a little further to the right then a larger barrack for the Ukrainians. Further to the right of the gate was a larger gate for the introduction of a railway siding. This track led a bit into the camp there, so that if I remember correctly about five or six wagons could be pushed in. To the left of this was a ramp and to the left of this again began a lorry train that led through the camp to *Lager III*. There was the gas chamber with an attached room for a motor. Its exhaust gases were fed into the chambers to gas the Jews there.

There were even two engines in the engine room. It was a petrol engine, probably from a Russian tank and a diesel engine. But the last one wasn't used. The gas chamber contained either four or six chambers located on either side of a central aisle (three on the left and three on the right, or two on the left and two on the right). People were herded into the chambers from this central aisle.

After the gassing, the flap doors could be opened from the outside, from which the corpses could be taken out. In *Lager III*, there was also a watchtower. In addition, a small part of this camp was again fenced off. The work detail for *Lager III*, lived there in a barrack.

There was also a smaller barrack as a workshop, another small barrack as a kitchen and a clothes shed as a changing room for the work detail. In addition there was a large water tub in this part of *Lager III*, where the Jewish workers could wash themselves. As far as I know, there was no well in this camp. As far as I know there was a shaft well in *Lager III*, near the engine compartment near the gas chamber.

On Objection:

I thought the petrol engine in the gas chamber was an air-cooled four stroke V-engine. But I don't know exactly anymore.

In this *Lager III*, there was also a large grate outside, on which the corpses of the gassed were burned in an open fire.

Between *Lager I*, already described, and the residential camp for the German and Ukrainian wardens on the one hand and *Lager III*, on the other, there was a larger house in a garden more towards *Lager I*, and the German residential camp than an administrative building, there was a large tree, which I can remember as the only one in this area. *Lager I*, ended with a plank wall. Behind this wall of boards up to the barbed wire fence that boarded *Lager III*, was the area of *Lager II*.

There was at least one barrack where people had to hand in their belongings and another barrack where people's clothes were collected. I didn't see it, but I think its possible that the people there also had to undress before they started the journey through the 'hose' into the gas chamber. Around the camp was a 'hose' passage surrounded by a barbed wire fence, through which the guards had to patrol. I have now made a short hand sketch of my idea of the camp and I am including this sketch, which I will take into account in a description, as an appendix to this report. I can't find my way around all the details on the drawing of the camp from the files that have now been presented to me. In broad terms, however, I consider this plan to be correct.

Question: Who did you meet in Sobibór, from those you already knew from the euthanasia—apart from Reichleitner?

Gomerski, Wagner, Steubl, Getzinger, Weiss, to the question of Bolender, yes, then spontaneously no, again hesitant. I can't say for sure. Maybe yes, maybe also no.

Question: You know Bolender from Hartheim?

Yes

Do you know Bolender in Sobibór?

I almost wanted to say no. I later saw him again in Italy. I know that for sure. Didn't he go to Bełżec or to Treblinka?

Do you know if Bolender was in Sobibór at all?

I can't summon that. When Bolender says he wasn't there, I had to believe it. That's how weak I stand on my feet. If, as is now being accused, I said during the police interrogation in Linz on April 18, 1963, that Kurt Bolender was also a stoker in Alkoven and a trainer and commander of the guards in Sobibór, then that must be correct. At the time, I tried my best to make my statement.

If I said at this point that Bolender was commander of the guards, that could give a wrong picture, because a certain 'Jonny' whose other name I don't know—at least I cannot think of it at the moment—an *Untersturmführer*, had the entire Ukrainians among themselves. The man, a slender man, was killed in the riot and I heard it was in the tailor's workshop. Its possible that his name—as I'm being told now—was Niemann.

The question of whether I saw Bolender again in Sobibór in the summer of 1943, is in my opinion, settled by the fact that I left Sobibór in March 1943, specifically for the disaster operation in Germany to Hosel in the Rhineland and to Luneburg, that was in April 1943. After this assignment I was on home leave.

I would like to say today that the home leave took place in October. I'm sure I wasn't in Sobibór when the uprising took place there and when Getzinger died there. I think I had already found out about his death in Luneburg (after discussing the extent to which the witness could have received such a message in Luneburg and after objecting that he had stated on April 18, 1963, that he had found out about Getzinger's fatal accident in Sobibór in November 1943). It is true that I heard on the way from Luneburg via Berlin at the T4 in Berlin that 'something terrible' had happened in Sobibór, but without hearing any further details.

When I came to Sobibór in November 1943, I was told in detail about Getzinger's fatal accident. I would like to restrict that I could have been back in Sobibór at the end of October 1943, because we were already in Italy on November 18, 1943.

I went there with Reichleitner, Gomerski. I think Bolender, Benno Weiss, Frenzel was there too. Wagner, Steubl, one of the Wolf's (the other one died in the revolt), there could have been a few more. Others stayed behind, including Ukrainians, some Ukrainians also came to Italy with us, a certain Spilny[496], I also remember Libodenko.

Our transport went first to Lublin, others joined our tour group, e.g. Hackenholt. As far as I know he wasn't in Sobibór before, but in another camp. Hackenholt may also have been in Lublin with *Hauptsturmführer* Wirth. Wirth was later *Sturmbannführer*.

On Objection:

Of course after my return to Sobibór, apart from details about Getzinger's death, I also heard details about the uprising. I also have to admit that I heard after the uprising Jews who remained in the camp were killed here. However, when I came back to Sobibór, that is after the uprising, there were still Jewish workers in the camp. They must have come in later. These Jews were not liquidated when we left, but stayed in the camp.

---

[496] This was Heinrich Szilpny, a *Volksdeutscher*.

On Objection:

I cannot say anything about which of the guards who were still in the camp after the uprising were involved in the liquidation of the remaining Jews immediately after the flight. I don't even know whether these remaining Jews were killed by members of the camp crew, or by people outside of the camp.

On Objection:

I don't know how I'm being blamed now whether Bolender and Gomerski brought new Jews to work in Sobibór after the uprising took place. I would like to think that I must have come to Sobibór later, when these later transports of working Jews got there.

On Objection:

I do not know whether Bolender was involved in criminal proceedings outside the camp at the time and whether he left the camp as a result.

On another Objection:

I remember that when I came to the camp there was a young St Bernard dog there. I couldn't say that this dog belonged to a specific camp member, but rather that the dog walked around like that. I vaguely remember that this dog disappeared from the camp a little later, but I don't know where it went in particular. I do not know whether Stangl picked this dog up from the camp. Anyway, I don't know whether Stangl was commander of the camp before Reichleitner and where he ended up.

On Objection:

Apart from the St. Bernard dog, I don't remember any other dogs in the camp.

On Objection:

Gomerski was one of the active *SS*. He also had to supervise the guard and drill with the Ukrainians.

Question: What did he do when transports arrived?

In my time, not many transports came, maybe two or three. Then he was there like everyone else.[497]

Question: What about yourself?

I stood at the back of *Lager III*. I had nothing to do with the engine there. I stand by that even if I am told that witnesses are said to have charged me with working on the engine, the Ukrainian Szilpny was also active there. In my time I didn't know that Bauer had anything to do with the engine. I know Bauer. He was one of the little guys who drove the utility vehicle in my day, an Opel Blitz truck. Wagner was the *Spies* (skewer). He supervised the entire camp, and in particular divided up the work. That was the work for the Jews and also for the Ukrainians. Wagner wasn't an active *SS* man, so he didn't command the Ukrainians either. Jonny Niemann took care of the guard division of the Ukrainians.

Question: What did Frenzel do in the camp?

He was not an active *SS* man. He shouted 'to each other,' in the camp. He had such a shrill, loud voice that also sounded unpleasant. He was more in *Lager I* and *II*, where most of the work was done. You could say, he 'had a big mouth.'

Answer to a question:

Almost every guard carried a whip. I did not hear or see Frenzel screaming or whipping the Jews with his whip

---

[497] There was a steady stream of transports, so this statement is completely untrue.

On Objection:

I can't say anything about whether the Jews were mistreated outside of the extermination camp. Nor do I know anything about special measures taken against Jews outside of the general extermination for any special reason, for example if someone should have fled. In particular, I know nothing about the escape of 2 Jews around Christmas 1942, and a possible subsequent 'decimation' of the Jews from *Lager I*.

On Objection:

I don't know anything about the camp being mined around the outside. I don't think that happened when I was in Sobibór either.

On another Objection:

Although I heard that Himmler is said to have visited the camp, I was certainly not in the camp at the time, although I am told that Himmler's visit can be documented for mid-February, and I myself until March claim to have been in the camp in 1943. I also heard nothing about the fact that a number of girls were gassed 'for demonstration' during the Himmler visit. I do know, however, that the routes for Himmler's visit to the camp have been cleared. But I must have been absent somewhere during the visit.

The interrogation was interrupted at 4:45 p.m. The witness stated that he fully understood today's dictation and approved the content. The witness was summoned again for March 30, 1966, at 8 a.m. in room 208 of the regional court in Linz.

Alfred Ittner

November 28, 1963
Kulmbach

My name is Jakob Alfred Ittner. I was born in Kulmbach on January 13, 1907, and now live in Seidendorf near Kulmbach, Neue Siedlung 37a.

Soon after, although I cannot give the exact time, the organization was renamed the 'Public Institutional Care Foundation.' It took over the house at *Tiergartenstrasse 4*, where I had previously worked. I worked there until about April 1942.

We were a group of maybe 20 people who, as far as I remember, were under the command of Stangl. Hermann Michel belonged to the group, who later became a *'Spies'* (skewer) in Sobibór. I believe that the following people also belonged to the group at that time: probably Schutt, also Bauer, probably Bolender, Frenzel, Gomerski, Bredow, Wagner, Ernst Bauch. There were more, but today I can't remember any more. We were all given *Waffen-SS* (weapon) uniforms in Lublin.

We then drove from Lublin to Sobibór via Cholm, where, as I remember, we stayed in the soldiers hostel. Stangl has taken over the camp. It was basically done. It is possible, however, that perimeter fences still had to be erected. But I had nothing to do with that because I initially took over the administrative business.

Difficulties soon arose with camp manager Stangl. In the meantime the first transports of Jews had come to Sobibór. In addition to their valuables, considerable sums of money were taken from the Jews. Stangl wanted me to use this money to make additional purchases. I rejected that. Rather, I have separated this income administratively. Since no agreement was reached, Stangl replaced me without further ado. Schutt took my place. He had previously worked as my representative. He was particularly good at purchasing. He knew how to find something everywhere. He was also the one who slandered me to Stangl. In any case, Stangl deployed differently than Berlin had planned. I went to Sobibór convinced that I had nothing to do with the actual extermination of the Jews, and only had to do administrative business. Due to Stangl's decision, I was suddenly assigned to *Lager III*, the actual killing department of the Sobibór camp.

According to my current estimate, the first transports arrived two weeks after we arrived in Sobibór. In any case, before I was replaced as administrative leader, there were several transports of Jews. The money that was taken from the Jews played a role in my redemption, as I have just described. But I was administrative leader in Sobibór for only three or four weeks at the most. Accordingly, as I have already remarked, the Jewish transports to Sobibór must have started after about 2 weeks, at the latest.

When I was still an administrative manager, I also looked at the handling of the first transports. I went out of the forester's lodge and watched how the transaction went. As far as I can remember, the Jews mainly came in passenger cars. These wagons were pushed into the camp on the siding and then the camp gate was closed. Then the wagons were opened and the Jews were asked to get off.

The able-bodied Jews were asked to go to the *Lager II*, area. Occasionally there was congestion. Then they shouted, 'Keep going, keep going.' The whip was also used. I didn't do that myself, because I didn't have a whip. It has just been pointed out to me that, according to the other accused, all German camp members had such a whip. But that is not true. I certainly did not have a whip.

In *Lager II*, the 'spear' of our camp Hermann Michel, spoke to the Jews. I remember that he was wearing a white coat and looked like a doctor. He said that the Jews would now have to bathe and be disinfected. They would then be settled and put to work.

Apparently, the Jews had no idea of their fate here either, because I heard approval and shouts of bravo. The Jews were then asked to undress and then hand in their valuables and the money they had brought with them in a window of the forester's lodge. I myself took the valuables and money with a Ukrainian. We did not issue receipts. We didn't keep a list either. We just collected everything. I only held these positions while I was administrative manager. As far as I can remember, there were 2 or 3 transports that I handled in this way.

The Jews were then sent unclothed through the 'hose' to the gas chambers. I cannot remember whether SS leaders preceded them and whether the respective group was accompanied by Ukrainians. I think that's likely though. I have never done this service myself.

In *Lager III*, there were two or three gas chambers. I estimate the size to be about the same as today's interrogation room. I would say today that such a chamber was three to four meters big. It was furnished like a shower room. I can't say today whether the correct shower nozzles were attached. In any case, there was a pipe system in these rooms that could give the impression of a shower facility. In fact, the gas was conducted through these pipes. It is the exhaust fumes from a large engine that was placed in a special room at the end of the gas chamber building.

I only saw the gas chambers empty, but I did not watch a gassing. Such a gassing lasted about 20 minutes, I estimate. After the gassing, the Jews were pulled out of the gas chambers, that was done by a Jewish work detail. As far as I can remember, this command was under the direction of Ferdl Gromer. The gold teeth were broken out of the corpses, then they were taken to the corpse pit on a lorry-train.

While I was working in *Lager III*, most of the bodies went into the first pit. Some had already been placed in the second pit shortly before I left. I remember exactly that we were still digging on this second pit when the first corpses were already being placed at the finished end.

At this point the interrogation was broken off due to the late hour. It is to be continued tomorrow at 9 o'clock. The protocol has so far been dictated aloud. It is correct, however, the final approval should only come after the conclusion of the interrogation.

Signed: Alfred Ittner

The interrogation that was interrupted yesterday was continued today.

November 29, 1963

After inspecting this sketch of the situation and thoroughly discussing the localities and my experiences at Sobibór, the case with the Jewish woman also comes to mind. It was as follows:

I was already working in *Lager III*. When I came to the front camp during this time, Stangl called me over. He had a Jewish woman with him. He said to me, 'This woman wants to speak to her husband. Take her to her husband in *Lager III*.' He gave me the woman. As she turned to go, Stangl said, 'Take her there.' With this word he makes a movement with his right index finger, which I could only understand as an order to shoot. I then accompanied this woman to the gate of *Lager III*.

But I didn't want to shoot her myself, so I handed her over to the Ukrainian guard at the entrance to *Lager III*. I told him what Stangl had said, 'The woman wants to see her husband. Bring her there.' I don't know whether I also made a hand gesture or passed on Stangl's order, by making a brief remark behind the woman's back. In any case, the Ukrainian knew that the woman was not supposed to talk to one of the male working Jews in *Lager III*, but that she was to be shot.

Shortly afterwards I heard the shot, which I was convinced was aimed at the Jewess. However, I cannot say whether the Ukrainian shot, Bolender, or someone else. Anyway I went back to Stangl. I reported to him that his order had been carried out. It is correct, as I have just been told, that Stangl asked me, 'Was it you?' I replied that I handed her over to the Ukrainian at the camp gate of *Lager III*, and that he probably heard the shot himself. Its true that he then called me a coward.

I can't tell the name of the Ukrainian. My stay in the Sobibór camp was relatively short. I believe today that I got away around the end of June 1942, maybe even a little earlier, after staying in the camp for about 2 months. I had applied for it when I was on a short leave home and only had to do a few days of duty before I was ordered back. In any case, the success was that I was called back and from then on was employed in the administration of the T4, until I became a soldier in 1944.

When I left Sobibór, I estimated that around 20,000 Jewish prisoners had been killed in this camp. I can only estimate this number roughly. I use my idea of the full burial pit and the mountain of dead in the second pit, as a point of reference. The number can of course deviate considerably, the figure of 20,000 is only an estimate. The camp was a large and closed organization with the purpose of killing as many Jews as possible quickly. That went smoothly because at all points German camp members acted as overseers to ensure that there were no difficulties. Everyone helped where they were assigned to ensure that the whole organization worked.

Johann Klier and Hubert Gomerski

August 21, 1950
Johann Klier

He explained further. On July 15, 1901, I was born the son of a weaver. We had five children, my mother married twice. I am married and have no children, my parents are no longer alive.

I attended elementary school for seven years, according to the type of school at that time. In 1914, I was apprenticed to a baker. I learnt a baker's job in Frankfurt am Main, at my own request.

After completing my apprenticeship, I went to the Austrian Fine bakery. I was unemployed for a while, but then got a job again. Unemployed in 1929, I got work nine months later, until 1931, when I became unemployed again. In 1931, I passed the master's examination.

After the seizure of power in 1933, I joined the Party, because it was said that there was work. In 1934, I was employed at the Heddernheim copper works, where I remained employed until October 1940. On October 1, 1940, I received a letter from the Party's *Gau* leadership. Before that I was mustered out by the *Wehrmacht* and G.V. home had been written. On the *Gau*, I was told that I had to, since it was not K.V. work for the Fatherland, somehow I was conscripted at the employment office. From 1938, I was an *Oberscharführer* in a medical squad, from 1938, to 1940, block leader. In 1933, I joined the *SA*.

After enlisting in October, I was ordered to Hadamar. I was not told what it was about. I was initially employed on auxiliary construction work. In January 1941, I took over the steam heating for the kitchen and living rooms. In 1942, I left there. I had nothing to do with the whole thing. The heating had nothing to do with the combustion. It was intended only for the living rooms, the kitchen.

I was sworn to secrecy and had to sign a pledge. I was told that if I resisted and refused to do my job, I could be sentenced to death. I said to myself what should I refuse when I am a stoker. The threat of the death penalty referred to confidentially, I don't remember exactly how the commitment came about.

I was in Hadamar until June 1942. There I met Major Wirth, with whom I had nothing to do. At the beginning of 1942, work in Hadamar was stopped. I continued to work, after the institution was set up as a hospital.

In June I was ordered to report to the 'Charitable Foundation' office in Berlin, where I drove alone. I was told that a task in the East would await me, without giving me any further details. Two days later we went to Lublin. We had previously been reminded again in Berlin of the duty of confidentially and that we were under the laws of war.

Several of us drove to Lublin, where we were received by Major Wirth, who told us, we were going to a camp. We were only given more details about the camp on the last day. We were made aware that if we refused to carry out the ordered work, we would be put against the wall. Knowing what a radical and ruthless person Wirth is, I never for a moment was in the dark about what was about to happen to me. It was only said that it was a Jewish camp and a labor camp. We were only told in the camp (Sobibór) how to behave towards the Jews. We were two. My comrade whose name I have forgotten, died in the uprising in the camp.

I came to Sobibór at the beginning of August 1942, after we had been dressed in field grey in Lublin. I had no rank. Wirth told me I could possibly apply according to my rank in the *SA*—I wore a star without a *lietze* (*Unterscharführer*). The Sobibór camp was still partially set up. It was divided into *Lager I, II and III, Lager IV* was built in the summer of 1943, as was *Lager* V, which was intended to house the guards (Ukrainians). The guards consisted of about 80 to 90 men, 15, to 20, of them members of the *SS*, and the rest Ukrainians. I myself was housed in *Lager I,* which was divided into the German camp and the Jewish camp.

The Ukrainians also lived in *Lager I*. I worked as a baker. The bakery was in the administration building in *Lager II*, but was later transferred to *Lager I*. I was in a wooden house with two men. The one whose name I no longer remember, had come with me. The other's first name was Sepp, who was employed as an administrator in *Lager III*. The one with the first name Sepp was named Vallaster. Major Wirth was responsible for the whole camp. In the Sobibór camp, a police captain Reichleitner, was employed as the camp leader. The German camp consisted of three or four houses. *Lager I*, was led by Karl Frenzel, *Lager II*, by Paul Rost. Frenzel wore a star on the epaulets. Sepp Valaster was in charge of *Lager III*.

I didn't talk to Vallaster, because I didn't like him. Our room was portioned. In the back slept Vallaster and the third roommate. I slept at the front and didn't bother with the other two. I have withdrawn everywhere. I didn't want to have anything to do with anyone because I found the whole thing disgusting.

Lager I and *II*, were surrounded by barbed wire. *Lager III*, was fenced off for itself. The entire complex was surrounded by barbed wire. This was not electrically charged. It was partially drawn twice. The watchtowers were on the outer wire fence. There were more than four watchtowers. *Lager III*—the so-called extermination camp—was not surrounded by special towers. During the day it was possible to go from *Lager I* to *Lager II*, which was about 100 to 150 meters away. The distance to *Lager III*, was about 250 to 300 meters. *Lager II*, could not see into *Lager III*, which was surrounded by trees. Around *Lager III*, there was a double, sometimes triple fence, which was shielded by bushes.

The accused Gomerski:

Lager III, could not be seen from outside. Only from a further distance could one see a wooden watchtower.

The accused Klier explained further:

The distance between *Lager I*, and *Lager III*, was about 350 meters to 400 meters. *Lager II*, was between the two camps. The people who were needed as workers in the camp were selected when undressing. The extermination of the Jews, was the sole purpose of this camp.

Three days after my arrival Major Wirth came. He said if we refused, we would be killed without mercy; he would wipe us away. He made this statement in front of the general public. He said we should not do anything stupid, and refuse, because he would find no mercy.

The transports arrived in freight trains. Once I saw about 120 people coming on foot, another time people came in trucks. I saw two trucks parked in the camp. There were some women who were brought to the camp a few days before Himmler's visit.

As a rule, people came in goods wagons. The train pulled onto a siding near the camp. *SS* men were present when they were unloaded. Ukrainians were also active. I didn't see people being unloaded. My workplace was about 150 meters away and there was a building in between.

The trains came in the morning, when I was in the Bakery. I wasn't interested in these events, because I didn't want to know anything about the matter.

I've never watched the unloading. The people were then taken to *Lager II*. The carts pulled by a diesel locomotive, were used for work transport. The inmates who were unable to walk were also transported in this way. The lorry-train led from *Lager I*, to *Lager III*, to which the inmates who were unable to walk were taken immediately upon arrival. I myself have not seen any people being transported on the lorry-train, since the lorry-train ran behind a wooden fence.

Those who arrived had to undress in a place fenced off with boards, separated by sex. The children were mostly with the women. The men came first to undress. I only saw the women take off their shoes. They undressed in a barrack. The luggage of the newly arrived prisoners was laid down on the way from the train ramp to the undressing area. The valuables had to be handed in at a table in front of a barracks after undressing. This barrack was inside the undressing area.

The exit from *Lager II*, to *Lager III*, was directly at the undressing area, no more than three meters away.

The accused Gomerski:

The distance between the undressing place for men and the undressing barrack for women was about 250 meters. It was only in the early days that a permanent staff of about 300 men were selected from the inmates who had arrived. Later, with few exceptions, no more people were selected. There were 6 to 7 members of the *SS* in the camp, and a total of 15 to 20 Germans.

The accused Klier:

The people who were killed in the camp came mainly from Poland and the Eastern countries. Some also came from Holland. The distances between the individual transports varied. In exceptional cases two or three transports arrived one after the other on one day.

I once stated that I estimated the number killed would be around 25,000. It is technically impossible that 60,000 people should have been exterminated.

Later I came to the shed where the prisoners shoes were sorted. There were several tens of thousands of shoes in it. As far as I know, no more transports came from August onwards. I estimate the number of pairs of shoes at around 40 to 45,000. Some of the prisoners carried several pairs of shoes with them.

I had nothing to do with undressing and transporting the disabled. I stood by while undressing, until I could pick up the shoes with my team, which consisted of about five to six people. We stood outside the wooden fence. The shoes were taken to the shoe shed and sorted there. I didn't accompany anyone to the gate.

I only walked a few steps back and forth on the undressing place. I have said nothing in a previous interrogation that I went to the gate. I only had to receive the shoes. I don't know what the other three or four men had to do. One or two men were appointed for the clothes. I wasn't part of every transport, but was represented by someone else. The shoes were collected after the prisoners left the gate towards *Lager III*.

As people undressed, checkpoints stood inside the room. They were Germans and Ukrainians armed with carbines. I carried a pistol and a whip in the camp. When I went to the undressing, I didn't wear a whip.

The prisoners, suspecting their misfortune, hesitated to undress. They didn't cry. People were told to undress, have their clothes disinfected and go to the bathhouse I don't know how many times I've been there. In the barracks between *Lager II*, and *III*, the women's hair was cut off.

I didn't get into *Lager III*. Vallaster from the Germans and another named Toni Getzinger, who died in the uprising in the camp,[498] went to *Lager III*. I don't know who else was employed in Lager III. We got 14 days of vacation every three months. I went on vacation three times. We didn't get any special food, only an allowance of 15 *Reichsmark*.

Gomerski:

I only got my military pay, no foreign allowance

Klier:

I worked every day with the work detail of four to five, later about ten men. I don't think people knew exactly what was going on in *Lager III*. In *Lager III*, there was also a Jewish squad who slept there. I don't know how often this command was gassed. Replaced that is, killed and replaced by other people, it was from time to time.

All I knew was that people were being gassed by exhaust fumes from an internal combustion engine. I assume that about 300 people were gassed each time, the bodies were cremated as far as I know. There was a foul odour in the camp. The fire in which the corpses were probably burned has often been seen. The flame must have been four to five meters high.

I tried to get out of the camp, but I couldn't. I turned to the camp commander Reichleitner and asked for a different command. I declared I couldn't stand the foul smell. Reichleitner replied that I would have to endure it. I've tried many times to get away. Wirth came and once said, you are here and must stay here, even if you die. I could not report for service at the front, because

---

[498] Toni Getzinger died in an accident before the uprising on September 13, 1943.

I was also decommissioned, during a second examination in early 1943.

A few days before Himmler's visit, the camp was put in order and two trucks with two young women arrived. It was said that they were to be gassed when Himmler visited. The next day Himmler came to inspect the camp. Major Wirth led him through the camp. We had to go to our place of work. I didn't see the women and girls, and I don't know where they undressed either.

Himmler then made a speech and said, for example, that the camp was set up quite well, and that it was fairly orderly. The task would be difficult, but hopefully done soon. But we still have to hold on. Finally, he said, 'SS men hold on. The order is there. If you give up, you have to take the consequences.' We thought the consequences would be that we would get killed.

I was told about a man in another camp who had been shot. From time to time other Germans came from the office and said one thing or another, it was said that the one who had been shot had refused to continue to participate.

I was perfectly healthy then. Only once I was ill for a few days and suffered from nausea. I was on vacation when the revolt broke out in October. After my return I heard that on Wednesday some Germans had been lured into the shoemakers workshop and other rooms and killed. Germans also died in *Lager II*. It was said to be around 4:30p.m. The inmates from *Lager II*, ran into *Lager I*, and broke over the fence. Some Jews who were in the armoury blocked it and shot at the guards, while others were said to have climbed over the fence. I don't think many were shot in the breakout, as the guards only carried five or six rounds of ammunition and could not get into the armoury.

When I came back from vacation, the search for the escapees was no longer carried out, no reprisals were taken. The camp has been dissolved. It was supposed to be a labor camp, and *Lager IV* was already being built accordingly. But this plan was abandoned. After my return there were no more Jews in *Lager I*. I was in the camp until the end of October. The fences were torn down and the material taken away. The barracks were partly burned. *Lager III*, no longer existed, with the exception of a barrack in which the prisoners slept. Everything else has apparently been blown up.

At the end of October I came to Italy with the police, where I fought through the war to the end without being wounded. I was taken prisoner on May 5th, and was released on June 15th, 1945. I was interned from December 1945, to February 1948. In Dachau I was interrogated by a Polish man, who told me I would have to expect extradition (it was in May). In September I heard that Poland was not interested in my extradition. In October I was sent to the German camp and from there in December to Darmstadt, where I was released in February 1948. I worked for the Jost company until I was arrested on October 8th.

Whereupon the accused Gomerski was questioned and stated:

The statements made by co-accused Klier are generally correct. I came to Sobibór in April, which was still being built at the time. After the camp was fenced off, the first inmates came to help set it up. *Lager III*, was fenced off and no one was allowed to enter at that time. The people in *Lager III* were given special duties and were not allowed to speak to us.

The burning started much later. Clouds of smoke were seen and an unpleasant odour was noticed. When we went to the shooting range, we heard the sound of engines. The *SS* man Herbert Floss was specifically assigned to train the guards. I was also entrusted with guard training. Graetschus, Niemann, Rost and I from the *SS* were in the camp. We originally came to the camp to train the 130 to 140 Ukrainians.

At first I was involved in construction work such as fencing, camouflage and laying mines, later I started training the Ukrainians, who were divided into three platoons. A unit of Ukrainians was permanently in *Lager III*.

When a transport came, all the prisoners had to go to the barracks. Only the individual commands such as the

Bahnhofkommando and supervisor were outside. The posts were set up along the path that the prisoners had to walk from the train station to *Lager III*. Graetschus and I had to check the posts. I saw how the Jews were unloaded. When a transport arrived, the command 'disembark' sounded. Those who did not obey the request were whipped. The luggage was left on the railway embankment, where those unable to walk initially, remained seated. They were then loaded onto the lorries and driven to *Lager III*. Then the luggage was driven away. It was relatively quiet. Except for the loud commands. The station command which consisted of prisoners, often whipped. The Ukrainians brought the luggage to the designated barracks. Those free from each command stood around the train. Those unable to walk were placed in carts, in which there were no seats. There were about 20-25 people.

I didn't drive the lorry-train, nor did I shoot into the lorry-train. I could have injured myself if a ball had rebounded on the iron wall of the wagon. I didn't stand on the lorry-train wearing a white apron. I have never worn a white apron. If there had been a shot, the whole transport would have been in an uproar. We had to make sure everything went smoothly. The lorry-train was generally not accompanied by a guard, but at most one guard went with it.

Only one person in the camp was wearing a white apron, namely the one who told the people when they were undressing that they had to bathe etc. I only came to the undressing area to check on the guards. After undressing, the prisoners were led through the corridor to *Lager III*, with someone walking away in front. The people were not prodded by whips.

In addition to training the Ukrainians, I was responsible for checking the posts. I drove into town once or twice a week to go shopping, and was often on the road once for four weeks. I was twice on a coal transport to Katowice, which took two to three weeks.

529

The defendant was countered with earlier statements that differed from his statement today. He explained: I was too nervous at the first statement.

I only came to the area of *Lager III*, on the way to the shooting range. There is no way I've ever been to *Lager III*. I only saw the hair cutting once. In the barracks in front of *Lager III*, the women's hair was cut off.

When Himmler visited I had commanded a unit which reported to *Oberscharführer* Graetschus. I was only there for the speech. I was not in the barrack where the women were taken.

An estimated 30,000 were gassed in the camp. The individual transports arrived at the camp at different intervals. They have been registered before. The number of prisoners was not previously known. The names of the prisoners were not registered before the people were gassed.

I went on vacation shortly before the camp was closed. When I came back it was all over. I don't know where the written documents ended up.

I then came to Italy, where I was an *Oberscharführer* at last. I had been promoted to *Unterscharführer* in the camp at Christmas. After the end of the war I was sent to a camp in Kufstein and from there to internment. I was then in custody until July 2, 1947. After that I was employed as a driver.

I have the following to say about the indictment: I don't know which transport came from Majdanek. Once a transport came with nothing but seriously ill people who wore striped clothing. There were already dead people in the goods wagon when the transport arrived. The people dragged themselves, leaning on one another, to the undressing place. I didn't kill anyone with a can, as the witness claims. The witness could not have seen such a thing. The people were very weak. I didn't kill anyone in the square. It is not true that I killed people trying to get up, because the people were all infected with contagious diseases, so we stayed away from them. It can't be true that I once got this from the armoury, with the remark that I only need 40 rounds of ammunition.

I don't know anything about the fact that I once shot an inmate named Stark. A prisoner had stolen fat at the time. I went to his *Kapo* and told him what had happened. The inmate then received 25 lashes. I don't know what happened to Bredow. I did not shoot any *Kapo's* suspected of escaping. I didn't shoot anyone. It is unknown to me that someone fled. I was never present at a shooting. I have not whipped anyone.

Klier:

I haven't gotten rawer lately. But when people forced me to do it, and where I knew I was being watched, I had to hit them every once in a while to show that I wasn't in league with the inmates. It often happened that I gave bread to prisoners. I also allowed people to smoke near me, but had to stop smoking when a supervisor approached. When I hit, I only pretended to hit hard. In reality it wasn't that bad. No one can say when I hit someone they were in pain.

In general, the detainees were not treated harshly. But they were usually beaten by their own *Kapo's*. *Kapo's* often came and told things about other prisoners. It often happened that I gave a prisoner something that the camp manager knew a few hours later. I treated the people I dealt with in a way that I could stand up to myself. I seldom had a whip.

Reichleitner hadn't been particularly gentle with the prisoners. I didn't see him shoot, kick or hit anyone. I've always avoided Wagner. I heard he hit someone. I haven't seen anything. Frenzel was a screamer. He hit too. But he also had human features again and let some things pass. I can't say anything about Graetschus because he only dealt with the Ukrainians. Niemann was a very good man.

Gomerski:

When I came to Sobibór, I was again instructed about confidentiality. I was told by Major Wirth, that I could be killed if I disobeyed orders. On Christmas 1942, I burned myself by a flare. I couldn't stand it there anymore. We had wives and children at home ourselves. But we didn't dare, one after the other, because there were informers everywhere. Floss was shot. Another time a man from Berlin went on vacation and never came back.[499]

A third one also had something and one heard from vacationers that he was shot while trying to escape.

A day before my vacation in January, Wirth came and saw my burned hand. Niemann said to me that if I didn't come back from vacation, Wirth wanted to report me for self-mutilation. During my vacation I was being treated by a doctor in Frankfurt am Main. I begged to be allowed to go back because I knew that otherwise I would have to believe in it. The station commando were responsible for unloading the arriving prisoners. The sentry chain was there to guard the camp.

Klier:

In my command were two men who were recalcitrant. I made them aware that they should be considerate of their other comrades, otherwise they would all end up in *Lager III*. All the people in my command the revolt in the camp. When I got back from vacation, people were already gone. I would have liked to write down their names because I told myself that this could not go well.

Gomerski:

I had to check the sentries.

---

[499] This was probably Ernst Bauch, he committed suicide in Berlin, on December 4, 1942.

The sitting was adjourned for three quarters of an hour.

Erich Lachmann

June 21, 1961
Wegscheid

I was born in Legnica in 1909, and attended elementary school in Legnica for eight years. During my school days I did not reach the target of the class in 2 cases and had to repeat these classes.

After I left school, I learned the bricklayer's trade in Legnica. I learned my trade at the Hertrampf and Schroter company in Legnica. I had to study for three years. Meanwhile, the year 1927, had arrived. From 1927, until the beginning of the war in 1939, I worked as a bricklayer for various companies in the Legnica area. I have often changed my companies, because that is so common with bricklayers. This is due to the fact that one or the other company starts working earlier in the spring than the other. If possible, go to a company who starts work at the earliest.

On September 1, 1939, I was drafted into service and drafted into the police, as an auxiliary police officer. I came to the auxiliary police in the city of Legnica. I received provisional training in Legnica, but during the training period, I was already partially doing road service. I was on duty in Legnica until January / February 1940.

In January / February 1940, I was transferred to Charnow (Poland) with the police company that I belonged to, it was the third company of Police Battalion 82. In Charnow we received mainly military training. We did not do any service other than the training service in Charnow. In the spring or summer of 1941, I went through an *'Unterführer's'* course near *Kattowitz*. I didn't pass the course. I have to say that I failed the course, because I had no interest in the police force.

In the meantime our company had been moved to Orlau (Upper Silesia). I had to report back to the company after the *'Unterführer's'* course in Orlau. In Orlau we only did training service. We didn't have any assignments. After a short stay in hospital, I was transferred back to Legnica in 1941. My company had meanwhile been sent to Russia.

After I served in Legnica and Bunzlau for about half a year, I was transferred to Lublin in the fall of 1942. I think it was August or September 1942. I was informed of the transfer in Bunzlau by a police sergeant. I have to correct myself, in Bunzlau, I wasn't told that I was coming to Lublin. This announcement was made later in Breslau. From Bunzlau we were marched to Breslau, about 12 to 15 men. In Breslau, we received new clothes. We got a green police uniform instead of the blue uniform we had been wearing until then. In Breslau we were told that we were coming to Lublin. We went to Lublin about two to three days after we were dressed. We were guided by a chief constable. I can't remember the name of this constable. But I know that he later died back home.

We went to Lublin by train. The journey took about a day. In Lublin I was taken to the Wolinien barracks, and assigned to an active police regiment there. I can't remember the exact number of the regiment. I think it was 23/24. I believe this regiment was subordinate to the SS and Police Leader in Lublin.

Objection:

A document stating that you were nominated for the award of the War Merit Cross, 2nd Class with Swords shows that you must have been in Lublin as early as July 1, 1942. You could not have been in Lublin for just a short time on July 1, 1942, because after only a short period in Lublin you would not have been proposed for a medal award, unless you had distinguished yourself in some special way. During your interrogation you say that you only came to Lublin in the autumn, you mean August or September 1942. So your information cannot be correct.

Question: Why are you making these false statements? Can't you remember exactly or are you deliberately giving this false information?

Answer:

I have deliberately not given false information. It's possible that I've been to Lublin before, but I really can't remember.

Question: Why were you nominated to be awarded the War Merit Cross? To what extent have you 'best proven yourself' in various official positions and assignments, as is written in the award proposal?

Answer

I never knew that I had been nominated for the War Merit Cross. I can't give any specific information about a 'preservation' on my part. I'm not aware that I've 'proved the best.'

I stayed at the Wolinien Kaserne for three weeks at the most. I came to Trawniki from the Wolinien Kaserne in Lublin with about ten or twelve other auxiliary police officers. This must have been in the summer of 1942. I can't remember the exact time. In Trawniki, the SS trained Ukrainians for auxiliary service. I myself only acted as a *'Fourier,'* that is I drove to Lublin every day with a driver and fetched provisions. It may also be that I didn't drive every day. It happened that I stayed in Trawniki. I didn't do anything on those days. I had nothing to do with the education of the Ukrainians themselves. In the summer of 1943, I was transferred alone, from Trawniki to Sobibór.

Objection: To Mr Lachmann, in a brief informational conversation during today's interrogation, you explained that you knew Karl-Heinz Schutt, as the head of administration in Sobibór. According to our knowledge, however, Schutt had already been transferred in Sobibór in the spring of 1943. So in the summer of 1943, he was no longer in Sobibór. If you know Schutt from Sobibór, you must have been in Sobibór before the summer of 1943. Can you improve your previous information? If so, why did you state that you were only transferred to Sobibór in the summer of 1943?

Answer:

I can only say that Schutt was still in Sobibór when I was transferred back to Trawniki.

Objection: So you must have been in Sobibór before the summer of 1943?

Answer:

I cannot remember. I mean that I was in Sobibór for about eight weeks. However, it is also possible that I was there for a short time longer. I actually can't remember exactly. I also have to mention that before I came to Sobibór, I knew exactly what was going on in Sobibór. I knew that Sobibór was an extermination camp where Jews were killed. I knew this from the fact that transport trains with Jews who were brought to Sobibór passed through Trawniki. I have often seen such trains in Trawniki. It was common knowledge in Trawniki that the transports going to Sobibór were destined for extermination. It was mostly freight trains, but I can't say whether they were always full, you couldn't tell.

At this point I would always like to mention that I have never been a Party Member or member of the SS. I was not politically active.

To the Case

When I was transferred from Trawniki to Sobibór, I didn't have to sign a declaration of commitment, as I had to answer the question.

From Trawniki I took the train to Sobibór. In Sobibór I had to report to police lieutenant Stangl, who was the camp commander at the time.[500] Stangl behaved very decently towards me and familiarized me with my task. He explained to me that I had to take over the supervision of the Ukrainian volunteers. Stangl also did not oblige me to remain silent towards outsiders. Apart from the fact that I already knew what happened in the camp when Jews arrived.

Stangl did not tell me what the function of the Sobibór camp was. I have to mention at this point that I didn't like going to Sobibór. But I couldn't defend myself. I had to carry out the task assigned to me. There was no way for me to get ahead of this task.

In the camp, I was allocated a room in a permanent house right at the entrance to the living quarters. The Ukrainian volunteers lived about 50 meters away in the camp. The railway line to the camp went through the entrance where I lived. It was much more a siding on which the trains with the Jews drove directly into the camp. In addition to me, two other SS members lived in the room in which I lived. One was Anton Getzinger, the second one was *SS-Unterscharführer*, whose first name was Paul. I can't remember the last name of this Paul at the moment. If I remember it, I'll mention it.

When I arrived in Sobibór there were about 100 or 150 Jews in the camp, who were familiar with all sorts of jobs. Some of these Jews also worked in *Lager III*, which was actually the extermination camp. The Jews who worked in the death camp were busy

---

[500] The fact that he reported to Stangl, means that Lachmann had to arrive in Sobibór prior to August 1942, when Stangl left for Treblinka. Indeed Eda Lichtman encountered Lachmann on her first night in Sobibór in the middle of June 1942. Clearly Lachmann was in Sobibór, much earlier than he claimed.

digging up a large pit for the corpses. As long as I was in Sobibór, I always saw the same Jews at work. I didn't see any other Jews working.

I didn't have much work with the Ukrainian volunteers. The volunteers had the task of guarding the camp. A sentry post was set up at intervals of 60 to 70 meters. These sentries guarded the camp the camp from the outside. In addition, there were still guards in the actual extermination camp who ensured the internal security of the camp. My job was just to check the posts. There was never any friction between the Ukrainians and me. It must have happened that some Ukrainians fled. But then I wasn't blamed because it was practically impossible to watch these guards in such a way that nobody could escape. By checking the guards I ended up in *Lager III*, the actual extermination camp. For this reason I am also familiar with the facility in *Lager III*.

The house where the gassings took place was 12 meters long and 5 meters wide. In the house, it was a solid stone house, which consisted only of a ground floor, there were three chambers that were accessible from the outside. The chambers were locked to the outside with thick wooden doors. In these doors there were small holes the size of today's 5 mark coin. These holes were covered with glass.

A small chamber was attached on side of the house. In this chamber stood a large engine. The gassing of the Jews was carried out with the exhaust gasses from the engine. The exhaust gasses were fed into the gas chambers through a system of pipes. The pipes ran under the ceilings of the individual chambers and were provided with small holes. The small holes were in the tubes down and to the sides.

In response to questions, I have to say that one could assume that the gas chambers were shower rooms. I didn't see any inscriptions of the kind ‚bath for Jews,' or anything like that, so I can't remember. When asked, I have to say that I mean that there was room for around 50 to 60 people in each chamber.

The mass graves I saw in *Lager III*, were about 60 to 70 meters from the gas chambers. I myself saw a mass grave that was still open. The corpses lay in several layers, naked, one on top of the other. However, even with the most superficial estimate, I cannot state how many bodies lay in this mass grave. The corpses were sprinkled with chlorinated lime. It smelled horribly. This mass grave was about 60 x 60 meters in size. In any case, there must have been several thousand Jews who lay in this pit.

When asked, I also have to say that later in *Lager III*, I also saw an excavator, with this excavator new pits were dredged. Otherwise there were no special features in Lager III. However, there were still accommodations for the Jews, in which the Jews slept at night. These accommodations were in a barrack.

The Jews who worked in *Lager III*, did not come out of this part of the Sobibór camp. I cannot give any information *about* the extermination of these Jews, the entire *Lager III*, separated from the actual camp Sobibór. Barbed wire was drawn around *Lager III*, which was located directly in a dense forest area. One could not look into *Lager III*, from the outside, that is, into the actual Sobibór camp. I checked the guards in *Lager III*, that is the Ukrainians, two or three times a day. I never saw Jews being gassed during these controls.

It should be mentioned that the mass graves were always dug near a lorry-train that led from the siding to *Lager III*. The lorry-train led directly to the gassing chamber. When gassings were carried out, I must answer the question, the corpses were taken to the mass graves in carts. I have to say though that I've never seen it. I can only imagine it like this. I've also heard stories about it. I also heard that gold seals and the like were broken out of the corpses. These gold seals, as well as other valuables, were collected and later delivered to higher authorities.

During the time I was in Sobibór, only one transport with Jews arrived. They were two wagons that had been attached to another train. These two wagons were detached from the actual train at Sobibór station and pushed into the Sobibór camp, by a locomotive. If I am asked, I have to say that there were about 60 to 80 Jews in these two wagons. I cannot say where these Jews came from.

The Jews had to get out of the wagons in the camp, after the gates had been closed again. The Jews carried small luggage that they took with them to the camp. About twenty Ukrainians volunteers and a few SS men were present when the wagons were unloaded. Today I can no longer say which of the SS men were there. The Jews had to go from the wagons to a kind of barn and undress there. I then only saw how the Jews walked towards the gas chambers, through a narrow corridor that was overgrown with bushes on both sides, and bordered with wire mesh. I did not see the Jews being driven. An SS man went in front, and on the sides and behind them were Ukrainians and other SS men.

The whole action was relatively quiet. I didn't hear any screams. I didn't hear any lamentations either. I had the impression that the Jews suspected no evil. I cannot say where the valuables of the Jews were handed in. I didn't see them having to hand in their valuables. On that day I was also in *Lager III*, for a check.

I then saw that the Jews were already in the mass grave. I was in *Lager III*, about three to four hours after the action. The doors to the gas chambers were open at this time. At the time when the Jews were being taken to the gas chambers, I also heard the gassing engine running. The engine was operated by SS Oberscharführer Bauer. I mean Bauer's first name was Erich. If I am told that Bauer's first name is Rudolf, then I can't remember it. I did not take part in the whole action. I wasn't there when the Jews were unloaded, I only watched the action from a distance.

No other transports arrived during the time I was in Sobibór, although I was in Sobibór for at least eight weeks. I don't know anything about cremation of corpses. I didn't see any grates or anything like that on which corpses could be burned.

Information on various members of the camp crew in Sobibór:

Bauer, Rudolf: Bauer is known to me by his first name Erich. Bauer was an *SS-Oberscharführer* and carried out the gassings in *Lager III*. Before he carried out these gassings, he was a driver in the camp. During the gassings, Bauer replaced *SS-Scharführer* Anton Getzinger, who then became a driver for Bauer. Apart from the gassings, I can say nothing about Bauer.

Bolender, Kurt: I know the name Bolender, but I can't think of anyone by that name right now.

Beckmann, Kurt: I don't know Beckmann.[501]

Bock: I don't know a *Scharführer* called Bock

Berg, Ernst: I don't know a *Unterscharführer* called Ernst Berg

Bredow, Paul: I know Bredow. Bredow was an *SS-Unterscharführer*. As far as I know he came from Berlin. Bredow managed the clothing taken from the Jews. I'm not aware of any mistreatment on the part of Bredow. I don't know if he killed any Jews either.[502]

Becker, Joachim: I don't know Becker

Dr Blaurock: I don't know Dr. Blaurock. I also don't know if there was ever a chemist in Sobibór.

Bauch: I don't know a *SS-Unterscharfüh[r]er* called Bauch

Dachsel, Arthur: I don't know of a police sergeant with the name Dachsel

Frenzel, Karl: I know *SS-Oberscharführer* Frenzel. I cannot say where Frenzel came from. Frenzel also managed the items of clothing taken from the Jews. I can't say anything special about Frenzel for the procedure.

Floss, Herbert: I don't know Floss. I don't know what function he had in the Sobibór camp. I can't specify specifics.

---

[501] His name was Rudolf Beckmann.
[502] Bredow was born in Guttland, Danzig District.

Franz, Kurt: I don't know Franz. If I am told that Franz was an *SS-Untersturmführer*, then he was not in Sobibór during my time.

A person with the first name Fritz: I don't know anyone with the first name Fritz

Gomerski, Hubert: I don't know Gomerski

Graetschus, Siegfried: I don't know Graetschus

Goetzinger, Eduard: I know the name, but I can't think of anyone by that name.

Getzinger, Anton: I know SS-Untersturmführer Getzinger. I lived in a room with Getzinger. Getzinger carried out the gassings before Bauer. He was Austrian.

Groth, Paul: *SS-Unterscharführer* Groth is known to me. Groth sorted the clothes taken from the Jews. I can't say where Groth came from, it's possible that he came from Hamburg or Hannover based on his dialect.

Greimer: Greimer is not known to me.

Gley, Heinrich: Gley is not known to me.

Helm, Herbert: Helm is not known to me.

Hetzinger, Adolf: Hetzinger is not known to me.

Hermann, Franz: Hermann is not known to me.

Hermann, Michel: Hermann is not known to me.

Hirtreiter, Josef: Hirtreiter is not known to me.

Hoffmann: Hoffmann is not known to me.

Heinsch, Konrad: Heinsch is not known to me.

Ittner, Paul: Ittner is not known to me.

Klier, Johann: Klier is not known to me.

Konrad, Fritz: Konrad is not known to me.

Kaiser, Alex: Kaiser is not known to me.

Klatt: Klatt is not known to me.

Kamm: Is not known to me.

Ludwig, Heinrich: Ludwig is not known to me.

Michel, Hermann: *SS-Oberscharführer* Michel is known to me. Michel led the Jews to the death camp. I do not know where Michel came from. I can't say anything special about him.

Muller, Adolf: Muller is not known to me.
Niemann, Johann: Niemann is not known to me.
Nowak, Anton: Nowak is not known to me.
Neumann: Neumann is not known to me.
Neubauer: Neubauer is not known to me.
Olf: Olf is not known to me.
Pötzinger, Karl: Potzinger is not known to me.
Rost: Rost is not known to me.
Richter, Kurt: Richter is not known to me.
Rose: Rose is not known to me.
Reichleitner: I know Police Captain Reichleitner. Reichleitner was camp commandant in Sobibór. I do not know where Reichleitner came from. Reichleitner sent me back from Sobibór to Trawniki. I can't say anything special about him.
Ryba, Walter: Ryba is not known to me.
Rewald, Wenzel or Fritz): Rewald is not known to me.
Schutt, Hans-Heinz: *SS-Oberscharführer* Schutt is known to me, as the administrative leader in Sobibór. Schutt travelled a lot and was generally a good natured person. I don't think he did anything to harm the Jews in any way. I mean that he came from Berlin. As far as I know, when I was transferred from Sobibór to Trawniki, Schutt was still in the camp.
Schumacher, Emil: Schumacher is not known to me.
Schwarz, Gottfried: Schwarz is not known to me.
Schiffner, Karl: Schiffner is not known to me.
Schulze: Schulze is not known to me.
Schmidt, Fritz: Schmidt is not known to me.
Steffel, Adolf: I know Steffel, at least when I was in Sobibór, we didn't have Adolf Steffel. I do know an Adolf Steffel, but from Police Battalion 82. Steffel came from Legnica. Steffel was my age.
Steubl, Karl: Steubl is not known to me.
Stangl, Franz: Stangl is not known to me.
Thomalla, Richard: Thomalla is not known to me.
Unverhau, Heinrich: Unverhau is not known to me.

Weiss, Bruno or Otto: Weiss is not known to me.[503]

Wagner, Gustav: *SS-Oberscharführer* Wagner is known to me. Wagner divides up work in the camp. I can't say anything special about him. I mean that he was Austrian.

Wolf, Hans: Wolf is not known to me.

Werner, Kurt: Werner is not known to me.

Vallaster, Josef-Sepp: I don't know Vallaster.

Zierke, Ernst: Zierke is not known to me.

Apart from the people I have mentioned so far, I also know Herbert Schafer from the camp crew in Sobibór. Schafer was an auxiliary policeman before me in Sobibór. I practically replaced Schafer in his work in Sobibór. When I relieved Schafer, he already told me that he was relieved from Sobibór. As far as I know Schafer was transferred back home to Liegnitz. I also think I know that Schafer came from Liegnitz. Where Schafer is today, I cannot say.

I was just read a witness statement, according to which I am said to have beaten Jews and raped Jewish girls. This statement is a lie. I never hit a Jew who came to the camp on a transport. It must have happened that I hit Jews who were already there when I arrived in Sobibór. Then I only ever hit with my hand, although like all the other members of the camp crew, I had a whip. I received this whip in Sobibór.

Whenever I hit a Jew, it was always just a Jew who had behaved in a way that was unruly. It happened that I found out that a Jew had secretly slipped cigarettes from our kitchen boy, who was also a Jew. When I confronted this Jew about the cigarettes, he lied to me, and said he didn't get any cigarettes. I hit him because of that lie. Other cases were similar. So I think for example that Jews stole food. For this I beat them, which means I beat them, because they lied to me, when I asked them if they had stolen food. Mostly it was about cigarettes though.

---

[503] His correct name was Bruno.

Objection: Mr. Lachmann you should be aware that Jews who were caught stealing in the camp were ruthlessly murdered. There are enough known cases from Sobibór that Jews were shot or gassed for petty theft.

Question: What did you want to achieve with your questions to the Jews. Did you want to persuade the Jews to admit a theft in order to then subject them to 'punishment' by shooting or gassing, or in any case by killing the Jew. If not why did you ask the Jews, even though you knew exactly about the theft?

Answer

I was not aware that the Jews were subject to the types of punishments just mentioned. I definitely didn't want to get the Jews killed because of theft. They got their punishment from me, because I hit them. But I also have to mention that it wasn't often that I hit Jews. I would like to emphasize again that I never hit a Jew on incoming transports. Incidentally, it is the case that during my time there only once came two wagons with Jews. On this transport I was not present when the Jews were unloaded. I just watched from afar.

If the witness continues to say that I am said to have raped Jewish girls, this is not correct either. I have never hung out with a Jewess. I request that I be confronted with this witness.

When it is said in another interrogation that I deserted with stolen valuables from the Jews, that is not correct either. After a stay of about weeks or a little more, I came back to Trawniki. In Trawniki I left the troops without permission. After being on the road with a Polish women for about eight days, I was arrested in Warsaw. I met the Polish woman when I was in Trawniki, before I started working in Sobibór. The Polish woman's name is Helena Gepla. The Polish woman lived in Warsaw. I can't say if the Polish woman is still alive today.

The Polish woman was currently about 24 to 25 years old. After being arrested in Warsaw, I was taken to Lublin. The arrest took place in the summer of 1943. I remained in custody in Lublin for four or five months, and was then sent to the Dachau Concentration Camp. In March 1945, I was released from Dachau, although I had received a prison sentence of six years. After my release I was sent to a penal company at the military training ground near Prague. This is where we were trained.

But I was no longer deployed because the war was over. In Brandenburg I was captured by the Russians and was held prisoner by the Russians for five years. After my imprisonment, I came to Lower Bavaria in May 1950. Since that time I have lived in Untergriesbach. Today I work again in Untergriesbach, as a bricklayer.

If I am asked, I have to say that I never thought that I would be held accountable for the events in Sobibór. In itself, my conscience is clear. I didn't kill any Jews. The activity I carried out in Sobibór has nothing directly to do with the extermination of the Jews.

As I already mentioned, I only commanded and controlled the Ukrainian auxiliaries. I also assigned the Ukrainian volunteers, although I must mention that I did not assign the people when a transport of Jews arrived. The SS did that. By the way, only one transport arrived during my time.

I would also like to mention that I could not evade the job that was given to me. If I tried that, I would certainly have been locked up, or something else would've happened to me.

All the persons named in the process, accused as well as witnesses, had to be able to state that I always behaved decently towards the Jews. Except for the slight blows, I described myself. I have not been guilty of any abuse.

I can't give any more details at the moment.

Erwin Lambert

October 2, 1962

As I mentioned at the beginning, I was in Sobibór extermination camp for about 14 days to three weeks. It may have been in the fall of 1942. However, I can't commit to the exact time. At that time, I received an order from Wirth to enlarge the gas chamber in Sobibór. I was supposed to build the system based on the model of Treblinka.

At that time I went to Sobibór with Lorenz Hackenholt. Hackenholt was staying in Treblinka at the time. First, I drove with Hackenholt to a sawmill near Warsaw. There, Hackenholt ordered a large shipment of wood for the renovation work in Sobibór.

Then we both drove to Sobibór. There we reported to camp manager Reichleitner. He then gave the corresponding instructions for the construction of the gassing annexes. Before I arrived, the camp was already in operation, and there was already a gassing facility. The conversion probably had to be done because the old system wasn't big enough or wasn't solid enough. Today I can no longer say who was involved in the conversion work back then. In any case, Jewish prisoners and the so-called '*Askaris*' (Ukrainian volunteers) helped out.

During the period of reconstruction, no transports of Jews arrived. The extermination action rested during this time. When asked about this, I reply that I did not know the individual functions of the permanent staff in the Sobibór camp. I also cannot say who was working in *Lager III*, at the time.

A map of the Sobibór death camp was shown to me in front of the interrogating officer. I still remember the locations in Sobibór, as they are marked on the site plan. However, I would like to mention that during my stay I was only in the front camp and in *Lager III*. In the so-called template I lived and slept in the accommodation for the members of the permanent staff. During the day, I worked on the gas chamber in *Lager III*.

After the construction work was finished I went back to Treblinka. Later I was in Sobibór again, namely during my stay in the Dorohucza labor camp. I drove Friedel Schwarz to Sobibór on a motorbike. I then only stayed the night in Sobibór and drove back to Dorohucza the next day. Even during this stay, I did not gain any closer insight into the activities of the Sobibór extermination camp. I would therefore like to emphasise once again that I had nothing to do with the actions to exterminate the Jews in Sobibór.

Paul Rost

May 4, 1946

As mentioned earlier, I was then ordered to Lublin at the end of 1941, beginning of 1942. Around 20 men from Sonnenstein went with us. The purpose of the command was only communicated to us on the spot and became clear there and then. The command was subordinate to the SS Police Chief in Lublin. We came to a police major Wirth from Stuttgart, who was in charge of camps for the extermination of Jews in Sobibór, Bełżec, and Treblinka.

In the first few months, I only did internal work in the personnel department. In March 1942, I was sent to the Sobibór camp. There I supervised the Jewish inmates in *Lager II*, who had to sort out the valuables of the gassed Jews, I had nothing to do with *Lager III*, where the Jews were exterminated.

Altogether we had about 350 permanent working Jews. During the approximately 3 months in which I was on duty there, about 15 transports of Jews, each transport around 1,000 people—men, women and children—may have arrived and been gassed. Most were from Poland: one as far as I remember, from Holland, and the rest probably from the Reich.

I was in Sobibór in the capacity of foreman of the Security Police. To protect my belongings, I wore the uniform of the General

SS, not the *Waffen-SS*, i.e. without a victory gourd and with the narrow epaulets of the General-*SS*. My emphatic efforts to get away from the command were unsuccessful. Most of us wanted to leave and we didn't succeed.

I can assure you with certainty that I did not enrich myself from the Jewish camp inmates, neither before their gassing, nor after.

In the command to Lublin belonged from Sonnenstein, Schemmel, and Tauscher, the drivers Richter, Klos, Becher, Thomas, and from the nursing staff, Max Beulich, Rudolf Seifert, Kurt Blaurock, Erich Dietze, head nurse Gley, Gustav Munzberger from the Sudetenland, Walter Nowak, Ernst Seidler, Fritz Rehwald, also from the Sudetenland, Herbert Scharfe, probably from Konigstein, a certain Walther from Bielathal, Kurt Vey from Chemnitz, Hans Zanker from Freiberg, and Kurt Seidel from Chemnitz, possibly also Fritz Zaspel from Pirna.

Of these, there were in Sobibór camp, Vey, Walther, and Rewald—these 3 with me in *Lager II*, Richter as a cook and Becher, who was the driver and also supervised *Lager II*. Nowak was active in *Lager III*—alternately also in *Lager II*—and also did service there directly with the gassing of the Jews. However, I have not observed this myself. I only take it from the fact that he was commander in *Lager III*.

At the beginning of June 1942, I left Poland, as a result of other assignments while the gassing of the Jews was still going on. Since then I have had nothing to do with either the extermination of the mentally ill or the extermination of the Jews. I also explain that the rest of the command from Sonnenstein did not work in the Sobibór camp, but in other camps, and that I therefore do not know what posts they held.

The driver Werner Mauersberger was not assigned to Poland. He may have been to Sobibór once or twice on a business trip from Berlin, he brought allocations for the staff.

I am now a construction worker at Abbruch—Matscke in Dresden—Omsewitz, at Lehmberg 56. I have no intention of leaving Dresden, because I have my family and my own apartment here. As I have just been instructed, I will report a possible change of address for the matter at hand, as soon as possible.

Read out, approved and signed.

Hans-Heinz Schutt

November 22, 1962

In my interrogation on June 7, 1961, I already expressed that I was a member of the General *SS* during the so-called Third Reich. From 1938, until the outbreak of the war, I was a full-time member of the *SS-Sturmbann II/6* as *Sturmverwaltungsführer*. I can still remember '*Kristallnacht*' clearly because this event coincided with my wedding anniversary. At that time, I was assigned to work, and I had to go to a police station in the immediate vicinity of Alexanderplatz and patrol the area every hour with an active police officer. I was not directly involved in the actions against the Jews and their homes. I only provided auxiliary police service to maintain order on the streets.

At the time, I had nothing to do with the preparations for the campaign. This matter came as a surprise to me. I was presented with a *fait accompli* that night. Since I wasn't able to influence the action at the time, I came to terms with the secrets. I was surprised at the extent of the destruction. I didn't want to say that I wasn't an anti-Semite at the time, after all we *SS* members were trained in this regard at the time.

However, I did not at all agree with the solution to the Jewish question, especially with the destruction of the Jewish homes. Today, however, I see things differently and it is clear to me that great suffering and injustice was inflicted on the Jews.

The interrogating officers told me that I should again be interrogated about events and people in the Sobibór extermination camp, because certain points arose during the course of the investigation that still require clarification.

I have just been given the details of Erich Bauer from his interrogation on October 10, 1961. Accordingly, I am said to have had an intimate relationship with a Jewess named Edith or Gisela. I am also said to have supplied valuables to Dieter Allers at the time.

Here, I would like to reply that it is true that I treated the two Jewish women kindly, and well at the time. So it also happened that I invited one or the other of the Jewish women or both to my room and listened to music with them. In my first interrogation, I already expressed that it was not me, but Herbert Floss who administered valuables taken from the Jews. I have nothing to do with the removal of these valuables and jewellery. It is not true that I supplied Dieter Allers with such items.

I was also informed of Dieter Allers statements, according to which he claims to have seen me in the Sobibór camp. I would like to say that he is most certainly mistaken. I have never seen Allers in Sobibór. I haven't seen a funeral Allers attended in Sobibór. I only found out about the funeral after the uprising from hearsay.[504]

Furthermore, the statements of Karl Frenzel were held up to me, in which he expresses that I not only performed administrative tasks in Sobibór, but was also used for other camp activities. I would like to reply that at the time I was basically working as a '*Fourier*' in Sobibór, but it happened that I lined up at the siding for incoming transports. However, I expressed this during my first interrogation. Frenzel may have given the impression that I also held other positions.

When asked why I lined up at the siding for incoming transports, even though I had no business there, I might reply that it was out of curiosity. I wanted to convince myself of the inhuman performance of the '*Endlösung*' (Final Solution) and describe my impressions in Berlin, so that I could be relieved. Under no circumstances did I actively work on the siding. I was much more disgusted by the rude manner in which the Ukrainian volunteers,

---

[504] The funeral Allers attended took place in Chelm.

in particular acted. At that time, the arriving Jews were often hit and pushed by the Ukrainian volunteers. They acted heartlessly. When asked about this, I would like to reply that the members of the German camp command did not actively participate in the emptying of the wagons. They stood by to supervise. I can particularly remember Frenzel and Wagner as supervisors for incoming transports.

When Frenzel stated in his interrogation that I had had an affair with a Jewess and had been transferred for this reason, I would like to reply that he may have given the impression that in reality it was different. In previous interrogations I have already mentioned that I was friendly towards the Jewish women who lived in the Foresters House.

I also had closer contact with these women than the other members of the camp. However, intimate relationships never came about. The Jewish women were probably eliminated out of envy or hatred. In any case, I was not dismissed or transferred because of my relationships with these Jewish women. In fact, because of my efforts at the 'Public Foundation' in Berlin, I received exemption from the *Waffen-SS*.

I was then informed of Alfred Ittner's statements from his interrogation on July 18, 1962, according to which I should have ousted Ittner from his administrative position in Sobibór. I would like to reply that I have very bad memories of Alfred Ittner in connection with the Sobibór camp. I did recognize him in a photograph that was provided, but I can't remember when I came into contact with him.

In Sobibór, I was in charge of the administration from the start. In the first three to four weeks, I was outside the camp almost continuously and went shopping. It is possible that Ittner maintained internal operations during this time. I don't have a precise idea about this, however, I don't know anything about Ittner's work in *Lager III*.

I have just made corresponding statements regarding his statements regarding my relationship to the Jewish women. It must have been the case that Ittner only heard vague rumours about this.

When asked about this, I reply that I know that the frail and sick Jews and children were transported directly to *Lager III*, after their arrival. I would like to qualify that in my time the children were taken to *Lager I*. The frail and sick Jews were fooled into believing that they were being taken to a hospital. In fact, however, they were taken to *Lager III*, and killed there. I have already made statements about this in my first interrogation. However, if I am asked today about the exact course of events, I would like to say that I can no longer remember the details of the events at that time.

Although I know that the frail and sick Jews were taken to *Lager III*, for extermination, I cannot determine how they were transported there. There was a lorry-train that led from the siding to the sorting barracks. It is possible that this railway was later expanded and then led to *Lager III*. I also have in mind that the sick and infirm were transported directly to *Lager III*. It must have been that they were taken to *Lager III*, with this lorry-train, but I didn't notice it.

Nor can I say how the extermination of the frail and sick in *Lager III*, was carried out. They could have been gassed or shot there. I can't say anything specific about that, though, because I've never seen it. These exterminations in *Lager III*, were also not described to me in conversation. I would like to emphasise again that I did not have close contact with the other members of the German camp staff in Sobibór because I did not live and eat with them. Now and then I must have met them in the dining room. But that happened very rarely. Even in my free time, I hardly came into contact with them. As I have already mentioned several times, I always stayed in what was then the Foresters lodge.

After an urgent objection, I reply that I have never been present at an execution in Sobibór or have any knowledge of an execution at all. It was shot a lot. However, I cannot say exactly where the shots were fired. It was well known that Ukrainian auxiliaries were very fond of shooting and often shot in the air for no reason.

When questioned further, I reply that in my time there was no morgue in the part of the so-called *Lager IV*, and no shootings were carried out there either. In my time this part of the camp was densely wooded.

More names were read out to me today by the interrogation officers. I was told that these people should also have been in Sobibór. Although I know the names of various people, I didn't get to know them in Sobibór, but had previously been with them either in Berlin, Grafeneck, or Hadamar. I can therefore not provide any useful additional information that could be of importance for the present proceedings.

I know the *Baurat* Moser. At that time he had his office in Cholm, in the German administration building of the district of Cholm. It is true that he established the Sobibór camp of that time. I visited him several times, at the time and received instructions from him on where to pick up the necessary materials. The camp manager at the time, Stangl, had informed me that Moser was responsible for procuring the items mentioned. In my opinion, Moser was a South German. However, I can't say where he came from. He was about 50-55 years old then.

When asked again about the origin and place of residence of Paul Groth, I can only say that he came from northern Germany. However, I cannot say where he lived at the time. A photo album was just presented to me by the interrogating officers. I have clearly recognized and identified the following people:

Wirth, Stangl, Bauer, Gomerski, Dubois, Bolender, Bredow, Ludwig, Frenzel, Oberhauser, Franz, Rose, Hackenholt, Girtzig, Floss, Niemann, Ittner, Groth. I cannot give any further information on the matter.

Franz Wolf

June 14, 1962

After I arrived in Sobibór, I reported to Reichleitner, the camp manager at the time. Up to this point I knew nothing about the extermination of the Jews. Reichleitner enlightened me about the purpose of the camp. He explained to me roughly that Jews were being exterminated here in the camp. A certain number of working Jews were selected from the arriving transport of Jews, who would then be assigned to work.

When asked by Reichleitner about my professional skills, I said that I had also worked in the forestry industry. For this reason, in the years that followed, I was temporarily put under the command of the Jewish lumberjacks. When transports of Jews arrived, I was assigned to sorting clothes in *Lager II*. There, a group of Jewish women was subordinate to me. It was about 150 Jewish women, that I had to supervise at work. Rudi Beckmann was in charge of *Lager II*. For a time Franz Hodl and Heinrich Unverhau were in charge of *Lager II*.

Regarding my work, I would like to say that when transports arrived, I was only employed in the transit barracks, where the Jews' luggage and suitcases were stacked. These are the barracks indicated in the sketch with the numbers 22, 23, and 24. I did not enter barracks 25, 26, and 27, in which the clothes were sorted, when the transports arrived. Work in these barracks was suspended during the extermination actions, because the Jewish workers who worked there, were locked up in their living barracks in *Lager I*.

I would like to explain the following about the course of events and the activities of the Jewish work squad, the Ukrainian volunteers and the members of the permanent staff:

There were definitely three Jewish work squads in the Sobibór camp that were used to empty the wagons. It was the so-called *'Bahnhofskommando'* (station squad), consisting of about 20 Jews, who had to see to it that the Jews got out of the wagons. Then there was another squad of Jewish workers who were deployed in barracks 22, 23, and 24, already mentioned. There may have been three or four Jews who cleared away the luggage with me. Another detachment of Jews, about 10-12 men, was used in *Lager II*, for the incoming transports, as a so-called undressing detachment. This squad had to ensure that the clothes that had been laid down, disappeared from the storage area as quickly as possible and were taken to the sorting barracks.

Another Jewish squad will then have to carry out the gassing and the removal of the corpses in the actual extermination camp. But this is just an assumption on my part. Improbable as it sounds, I would like to say that I never set foot in *Lager III*, during my time there. There were only the members of the permanent staff who had their permanent jobs.

The Ukrainian volunteers, there must have been about 100, took care of external security. They also used warnings when unloading the wagons and helped with this with rifle butts. They also led the Jews into the so-called 'hose' and transported the frail and old Jews to the so-called hospital in *Lager III*, with the lorry-train. I also heard that they shot these Jews there.

The permanent staff in the Sobibór extermination camp were in charge of all these processes. In principle, there were no fixed functions for members of the permanent staff on incoming transports. Everyone was deployed where it was needed. However, there were also exceptions. So I know for sure that Frenzel mostly supervised the Jewish station command and that Gustl Wagner mostly gave the speeches to the arriving Jews in *Lager II*. Frenzel and Wagner were also the ones who would choose working Jews from the arriving transports.

I, too, was an exception: as already mentioned, I was constantly deployed in the sorting and packing barracks. That was because I always successfully 'printed' myself before the other tasks. My stay and work in the Sobibór camp disgusted me. For this reason, I have always tried to be deployed where I could cause the least harm to the Jews. It will be common knowledge that there were two kinds of people among the permanent staff, at one time the 'shouters' and 'bullies' on the other hand quiet and withdrawn. Among the former are Bauer, Gomerski and Frenzel. I would like to count Beckmann, Wendland, Steubl, Unverhau and myself among the latter.

I have always tried to make the stay as good as possible for the Jews. In this context I would like to mention that I tolerated the Jewish working women subordinate to me receiving additional food, cigarettes, and chocolate by taking these things from the luggage of the arriving Jews and hiding them in the barracks, and then consuming them. Because of this generosity, which I take for granted, I was once warned by Frenzel. He checked me once and the sorting barracks and found a lot of these adhesives that had been put aside. He yelled at me, implying that I would 'fly,' if I kept giving in like that. But that didn't bother me and I acted as if I had never seen anything. Any living witnesses had to be able to confirm this. I was also beaten up once by camp manager Reichleitner, because I had once taken a cigarette break for a Jewish fieldwork squad and had extended it too long. I also ignored this and always treated the Jews on the external work details humanely.

In this context, it is also worth mentioning how I felt at the time about the so-called punishments of the Jewish workers. There was an order that all names had to be removed from the clothing of the gassed Jews. We had to make sure that this order was followed exactly by the Jewish workers. If a worker accidentally didn't remove a name, we should flog her with lashes. If my subordinate Jewish workers made a mistake like this, I took the 'sinner' in question out of the barracks and just pretended to hit her. In fact, I slung the whip on the top of my boot and whispered to her, 'Now scream!' If those who were reprimanded in this way are still alive, they can confirm it.

All members of the permanent staff were equipped with a whip and a pistol. I also know that some of the permanent staff used the whips. However, I was never an eyewitness to these floggings. I found out about it in conversation with comrades. Only once did I witness Gustl Wagner hitting a Jew with his fists because he had stolen food.

When the Jews were unloaded at the siding, terrible and sad scenes played out. So I saw that frail, sick and elderly Jews were thrown into the lorries of the lorry-train and then transported to *Lager III*. This robust treatment was carried out were carried out by the members of the Jewish station squad. However, these machinations were approved by the supervisors. As already mentioned, Frenzel was the one who led the discharges several times.

During the transports where I was deployed, there were no shootings on the sidings. I did not see at all that Jews were shot by the members of the camp occupation. That wasn't in the old days either, because the exterminations were carried out in the actual extermination camp, part III of the camp. As I have already stated, I only heard about shootings in *Lager III*, from comrades. However, I cannot give any specific information about the reasons for and by whom the shootings were carried out.

The transports of Jews arrived at irregular intervals. Sometimes two to three transports arrived in a week, then 8 to 14 days went by again without a transport. I have no idea about the total number of Jews killed in Sobibór. During my time, however, the number went into the thousands.

I would like to mention that I am not guilty of any crime and have never killed or mistreated a Jew. What happened in the Sobibór camp is unfortunate, but there was nothing I could do about it.

November 14, 1962
Heidelberg

Before the Sudetenland was incorporated I belonged to the Sudeten German Party. Almost all Germans in the Sudetenland belonged to this party at the time. After the German troops marched in, it was said that the members of the Sudeten German Party were to be transferred to the *NSDAP*. I didn't become a member of the *NSDAP* at the time. I never bothered to. On August 28, 1938, I was drafted into the *Wehrmacht*. After this, I never heard anything about the fact that I was automatically accepted into the *NSDAP*. I never belonged to a subsidiary organization of the *NSDAP*.

The so-called *'Kristallnacht'* during which Jewish homes were stormed and Jews mistreated, did not take place in Krummau. I only heard about this action much later. I myself did not actively take part in such attacks. I opposed anti-Semitism, rather I had business connections with many Jews. I was always hostile to the persecution of the Jews. I only got involved in the later extermination of the Jews by force.

I was told by the interrogating officers that I should testify again today in detail about what happened in the Sobibór Jewish extermination camp at that time, because a few points still need to be clarified.

When asked about this, I reply that I am not aware of the execution of the last Jews in Sobibór and the Jews who had come to Sobibór from the camp in Treblinka. Despite urgent reproaches, I have to say that I did not take part in this execution. As I already expressed in my interrogation on June 14, 1962, I was only there for a few days after the uprising in Sobibór, and then spent a 14-day home leave.

After my return, I was only in Sobibór for a few days and then drove to Italy, via Lublin, with an advance detachment. About four or five people from Sobibór belonged to this detachment. I can remember that Wendland and possibly also Zierke belonged to this group. In Lublin we met another five or six people who had previously served in other extermination camps. We then drove from Lublin to Italy with this group of 10 to 12 people.

The other Sobibór people came to Trieste later. I mean that we were in Trieste for about 10 days when they arrived. I know for certain that there were still over a hundred Jews in the Sobibór camp, when I left this camp. I have not heard anything more specific about the fate of these Jews. I guess I learned through conversation that they had been liquidated. At the time, I was not able to find out where this liquidation took place and by whom it was carried out. I believe that at that time someone said, 'The last Jews have all been killed.'

I only know of one execution that took place in Sobibór in the summer of 1943. On the day in question a group of about 25 Jewish workers had left for an external squad. This squad was guarded by four SS men and several Ukrainian volunteers. I still remember that Willi Wendland and my brother Josef Wolf were part of the guard. On the return march, some Jews fled. My brother described the incident to me, as follows:

The Jews suddenly scattered and ran into the forest. He ran after those who were fleeing while the other guards shot at the Jews. Some of the Jews stayed on the forest path and some were caught again. They were taken back to the camp.

[From the NIOD Archives, there are a number of pages missing from the Franz Wolf interrogations, so sadly this is an incomplete record, for which I apologize. The following is what we have]:

Becker, Jochen: He wasn't in Sobibór when I was there.

Bolender, Kurt: I think he was in Sobibór for a while during my time. However, I can't pinpoint myself exactly. I recognized him from a photograph that was shown to me, and I believe that I saw him in Sobibór at the time.

Bree, Max: I know him. I can't say whether he was in Sobibór though. I can hardly believe it. Rather, I would like to assume that we were together in Hadamar.

Dachsel, Arthur: Was not in Sobibór during my time. I guess I only met him in Italy.

Dahlke: Was a Ukrainian volunteer in Sobibór.[505]

---

[505] Dalke's full name: Heinrich Dalke.

Dubois, Werner: Was in Sobibór in the armoury there. He was an active *SS* man and belonged to the Frenzel, Wagner, and Bauer group. What I mean by that is that he paid his respects to the old tribe and hardly got involved with us newcomers and latecomers. However, he didn't count among the bullyheads, already mentioned, but was a little quieter.

Ferdl: I can remember that an *SS* man with the first name Ferdl was in Sobibór and was the camp manager in *Lager III*. When I arrived, he was already transferred, or only there for a short time. Ferdl was still often mentioned in connection with *Lager III*. I don't know his family name.[506]

Frenzel, Karl: Belonged to the tribe of the Sobibór camp. During my time he was the head of *Lager I* and *II*. He supervised all working Jews and regulated their deployment. In Sobibór he could decide whether the Jews would prosper or die. As already mentioned, he selected the workers on incoming transports of Jews and determined their assignment. He was also able to pronounce punishments and exercised harsh and strict camp justice.

It can be said, that he was even cruel. On minor occasions he had the' Jewish sinners' beaten with whips by the *Kapo's*. I never witnessed this torture. But I heard about this several times from my comrade at the time, Thomas Steffl, who was in the writing room. Frenzel was a screamer and always behaved very wildly. I had bad contact with him because I seemed too humane and forgiving to him. I have already testified that Frenzel reprimanded me for being so lenient. I cannot say that Frenzel shot a Jew.

Hackenholt, Lorenz: Was not in Sobibór during my time.

Hödl, Franz: Was Austrian and temporarily headed *Lager III*, in Sobibór. He was also in *Lager II*, from time to time. He was a quiet person and did not belong to the 'wild group.'

Hoffman: A member of the permanent staff named Hoffman was not in Sobibór during my time.

Kamm, Rudi: Was a Sudeten German and probably came from Tetschen/ Sudetenland, or Teplitz-Schonau. It Italy I had

---

[506] The correct name was Ferdinand Gromer.

closer contact with him. In conversation he told me that he was my landsman. But I don't think he was in Sobibór. In any case he wasn't there when I was there.[507]

Kaiser, Alex: Was a Ukrainian train guard in Sobibór.

The interrogation was interrupted at this point because it was late and will be continued on June 15, 1962, at 8:00 a.m.

Ludwig, Karl: I have a firm idea about him, that he was in Italy with me and that he left in a vehicle together with Frenzel and Bauer. That was when Austria collapsed. I cannot say whether Ludwig was in Sobibór during my time.

Maurer: Mauer was in Sobibór during my time. I can remember that he married a Ukrainian woman in Sobibór.[508]

Michel, Hermann: Definitely wasn't in Sobibór during my time

Rost, Paul: Was in Sobibór at the beginning of my time, i.e. from March 1943, and was in *Lager II*. He then left, I don't know where he is. Later he was in Trieste.

Schulze, Erich: Was in Sobibór during my time. He mostly led road construction commands. He drank a lot, as far as I can remember. He spent a lot of time with Frenzel and Gomerski. He was also with Wagner a lot. I recognized him perfectly in the photo number 78, that was shown to me.

Steffl, Thomas: Was with me in Sobibór. I was in close contact with him. He was in Sobibór in the writing room, and he also came from Krummau. I know for certain that he died in the uprising on October 14, 1943. I saw his dead body the next day and was present at the funeral.

Suchomel, Franz: Came to Sobibór shortly after the uprising and was there for a few days. I mean that he then went to Italy with the *Vorkommando*. He also comes from Krummau.

---

[507] Rudolf Kamm hailed from Sedenz near Teplitz-Schonau. And he was in Sobibór briefly at the same time as Franz Wolf.
[508] Mauer was a *Volksdeutscher* member of the Trawnikimänner.

Unverhau, Heinrich: I knew him from Hadamar. In Sobibór he was temporarily the head of *Lager II*. It is possible that he was only in charge of this camp on a temporary basis.

Wagner, Gustl: Was the spear and the right hand of the camp manager in Sobibór. He shared responsibility for what happened in Sobibór and for the most part made all the arrangements. I have already said about him that once in my presence he hit a Jew with his fists. He was a tough and brutal man. He belonged to the already mentioned group of bullies. I recognized him perfectly in photo number 20.

Wendland, Willie: I already mentioned about him, that he came to Sobibór with me, and stayed there until the end. Then he was in Italy. I remember that he came from Berlin, or at least lived there. However, he did not speak with a distinct Berlin dialect. In Sobibór, he was mainly employed in the sorting barracks. He also led external work details. He was a quiet person and, to my knowledge, never harmed a Jew.

Wolf, Josef: It is about my brother, who died on October 14, 1943, during the uprising in Sobibór. He was born in Krummau on April 18, 1900, and was also a photographer. At the beginning of the war he was initially drafted into the Wehrmacht and then came to the T4 in the autumn of 1941.

He didn't get there through arrangements from my side. Like me, he was also employed as a photographer at the T4. As already mentioned, he came to Sobibór with me. Most of the time he was employed in sorting barracks number 25, 26, and 27. He was found dead in one of these barracks after the uprising.

My brother Josef was married. His wife now lives in Okriftel-Main, near Hochst, Hattersheimerstrasse 32. Her first name is Anna. Her birth name is Schwarz. It is possible that she has my brother's death certificate. In any case, I don't have any documents or certificates about my brother's death.

Zierke, Ernst: I can definitely remember that he was in Sobibór. I think he belonged to the group of five or six that I went to Sobibór with. I assume that he was also assigned to sort clothes in Sobibór. I have identified him perfectly from the submitted photographs.

Questioned

On the day of the uprising, I was with Willi Wendland in the woods during the day, with an external work detail. Between 4:30 and 5:00 p.m. Wendland and I returned to the camp with the Jewish work detail. Wendland delivered the Jews to *Lager I*, and drove the horse-drawn carriage to *Lager II*, where the horse stables and carriage shed were located. On that day I still had the job of picking up the Jewish women workers from the garden after work. That's why I left Wendland and went into the garden, which was between *Lager I*, and *Lager II*.

When I came back from there with the Jewish women, I suddenly heard shooting. I was between the so-called Foresters Lodge and *Lager I*. When the shooting began, I called out to the Jewish women, 'Run over to the Bunker!' I ran back to the office in the Foresters Lodge. In the meantime, Beckmann and another member of the permanent staff had been shot there.[509]

I ran back and wanted to go through the courtyard of *Lager II*, to the sorting barracks to get to my brother. I haven't seen anyone on the way there. The door that separated the courtyard from the sorting barracks was also locked. After the shooting had subsided, I ran to the guard of the front camp. There were already several dead and Werner Dubois, who was badly injured.

I then kept trying to find my brother, but I couldn't. Only the next morning I was told that he had been found dead in the sorting barracks. Now I took care of my dead brother first. I washed him and prepared him for burial. Understandably, I was nervous. For this reason, I no longer concerned myself with further events in the Sobibór camp. Because of the death of my brother, I was also left alone, and I was not used for any duties until the funeral.

As far as I know, the following people survived the uprising:

---

[509] Beckmann and his comrade had been stabbed to death not shot.

Karl Frenzel, Erich Bauer, Karl Richter, Adolf Muller, Hubert Gomerski, and Willi Wendland.

As far as I know, the rest of the survivors were on vacation at the time. As I have already stated, I definitely saw the bodies of Thomas Steffl, Rudi Beckmann, Jonny Niemann and my brother. More than ten people died. However, I can no longer remember the rest.

I attended the funeral in Cholm. The death of my brother affected me very deeply. That's why I was given a 14-day holiday the day after the burial. I know that some Jews managed to escape. Some of those who fled came back to the camp voluntarily. I cannot say what happened to these Jews.

When I came back from vacation, there were still about 100 Jews in the camp. But there could have been more. Two days after returning from vacation I went to Trieste with the advance detachment. This *Vorkommando* consisted of about 10 people. It was led by Lorenz Hackenholt. I can't say what else happened in the Sobibór camp. In particular I don't know whether the Jews who came back were shot.

I would like to make the following statement about the mission in Italy:

I arrived in Trieste with the advance detachment. Then we moved into a villa for three or four days, which was already occupied by people from T4. I found out that we had to record Jewish property in northern Italy. After that I went to Fiume with some people. Initially, Otto Stadie led the unit in Fiume. Later Franz Reichleitner and after his death, Franz Stangl came there.

I was busy in the clerks office and had to make lists of registered Jewish property. I stayed in Fiume until January 1945. Then I was transferred to the unit in Trieste. Here, too, I was again active in the office and drew up lists of confiscated Jewish property. I had nothing to do with partisan operations. I also know exactly that Jews were arrested in northern Italy. They were forwarded to Trieste at the time I was in Fiume. There they were sent to a prison camp, only to be transferred to concentration camps in Germany.

I personally did not take part in the arrests or transports of Jews. I know for certain that around 50 Jews were arrested in the Fiume area. When I was back in Trieste in January 1945, I was told that a Jewish extermination facility had been set up in the rice factory and was also working.

I only saw this facility from the outside and did not enter it. Regarding the deployment in Italy, I can say that the main thing was that we were supposed to register Jewish property and arrest any Jews we found. Subsequent partisan operations were only marginal. As already mentioned, I did not take part in any partisan operations, when I was deployed to Italy, but was only assigned to the clerk's office to record Jewish property.

The interrogating officers gave me a map of the former Sobibór extermination camp for Jews. The buildings and facilities shown correspond to the actual conditions at the time. Photographs from the corresponding period were also presented to me. I could not identify any other people.

In conclusion I would like to say that terrible things happened in Sobibór extermination camp at that time. But I don't feel guilty in any way, because I was forced to be there and didn't cause anyone any harm.

Franz Stangl

April 29, 1969
Duisburg—Hamborn

In Berlin I was only told at the time that I was coming to Lublin to join the SS and Police Leader. I was further told that I had to supervise the people who were going to Lublin with me. I remember knowing several of these people, particularly from Hartheim.

In Lublin, Globocnik told me that a store was to be expanded to store ammunition and equipment for the *Waffen-SS*. He introduced me to these tasks in a conversational manner.

In Sobibór I noticed that there was a brick building in the partially wooded area that was not yet fenced off. This building was not marked in the plan sketch. In connection with this building, the suspicion arose after a few days that it could be the site of gas chambers. Among the people who had come from the institutions were those who were 'burners.' We called burners in Hartheim—Wirth always used this expression—the people who had to do with the incineration of the gassed sick. I would like to assume with certainty that the burners had to bring corpses out of the gas chambers into an anteroom and from there into the incineration room.

Wirth got there about 3-4 weeks after I arrived in Sobibór. He complained about practically everything that had happened, and used rude language. He went to the brick building with some of the camp staff. I was also there. On this occasion, Wirth said that the engine went to a certain place in the brick house. As soon as the people were called together, Wirth clearly stated that the aim of this camp was to kill Jews.

An engine was then brought in and set up immediately afterwards. I would like to think that at that time the gas chambers were not yet usable. As far as I can remember, there were no doors in it, nor any pipes.

On enquiries:

I remember that a first test gassing took place. Wirth was in the camp on this occasion. Wirth was already at the gas chambers, and I was called. Oberhauser was standing in front of this brick building. I still remember that he pointed his finger at his head and said, 'Christian is crazy.'

Wirth raged and scolded again. It was on the back side of the building, where the exit doors were. Wirth complained that the doors were too narrow. The people to be gassed had been driven through the exit doors into a gas chamber. If they had been herded in on the entrance side, it might have been possible to see it from outside the camp.

As far as I can remember, the ramp on this side of the building wasn't finished either. I myself did not see the people being driven in. I went to Wirth immediately after the doors were closed. As far as I can remember, some of the working Jews who had been assigned to me from the start were gassed. I estimate the 20, 25, or 30 Jews, and only men, were gassed on this occasion. I no longer saw the corpses being taken out of the gas chamber. I left before. Wirth's way that when he pissed someone off, by swearing at them, he didn't pay any more attention to them afterwards.

I believe the bodies were buried near the brick building. There was no prepared pit. I would like to say with certainty that the bodies were not naked, but were buried with their clothes on. At the time I heard that the people had resisted being locked in the gas chambers. That's also why Wirth was angry.

Only after this first gassing did burial pits begun to be dug. As far as I can remember, the first large burial pit was dug by hand. Then it was done with an excavator. I can't say where the excavator came from. As far as I can remember, the excavator driver wore a uniform. I would like to think that he wore the same uniform as the other *Unterführer*, i.e. *SS* uniform without runes.

On objection:

The public prosecutor's interrogation of the witness Fuchs on the record of April 8, 1963

    a) I can't remember Fuchs, even after I was told details about him.
    b) Bauer was the one who worked as a mechanic in Sobibór. He was in charge of the engine in the gas chamber building.

c) I have no recollection that Wirth brought a chemist with him to the test gassing. The name Dr. Blaurock says nothing to me. Also the name Dr. Kallmeyer tells me nothing.
d) I would like to venture that in the first gassing that I can remember only male Jews were killed. If Jewish women were brought into the camp on this occasion only for the purpose of gassing, I should have seen that. I mean, even if I hadn't been there, I would at least have experienced that.
e) As far as I can remember, there was a period of at least 14 days between the time the engine was delivered and the time of the test gassing.
f) I have the recollection that a corresponding number of new working Jews came to Sobibór to replace the gassed men, as well as an additional number for the pit command.

The testimony of the witness Schutt on the court record dated September 16, 1968.

a) I can still remember Schutt.
b) Schutt was an administrative officer.
c) Before I went to the East, I heard in Hartheim that Christian Wirth was in the East, specifically in Cholm, and oversaw the killing of the mentally ill there. I heard that before I had to report to Berlin.
d) I have no recollection that in Berlin we were told anything about the resettlement of Jews from Europe to the East. I was only personally told that I had to report to the *SS* and Police Leader in Lublin.
e) I did not tell the *Unterführer* in Sobibór what the real purpose of the camp was. It was Wirth who told me and the *Unterführer* after 3-4 weeks that the Jews were being killed in Sobibór.

f) I was Schutt's superior insofar as I was in charge of the camp staff.
g) I have no recollection that initially Ittner was administrative manager and that Schutt only took over this position after about 4 weeks.
h) When transports were dispatched in Sobibór, I was in the camp, outside of my office, but not always. I had nothing to do with clearing the transports, I was a site manager. I had no orders from Wirth to take care of the clearance and the orderly process.

According to the allegation of the accused to the Judicial record of June 26, 1967, to II:

I received no instructions from Wirth to stop torture of the Jews by the *Unterführer*'s. Wirth only told me in Treblinka that I should make sure that people didn't go too far.

If in this context, I am held up to my own admission to the Judicial record of June 27, 1967, I declare that:

If I said then that I went around the camp and made sure that the *Unterführer*'s weren't committing any excesses and that I had prevented un-necessary beatings on people, I would like to say today that I did it of my own accord in Sobibór, but not because of an order from Wirth.

The testimony of the witness Ittner on the Judicial record of August 29, 1968

a) I first met Ittner on the trip from Berlin to Lublin. If he already found out something in Berlin that the operation in the East was about the planned extermination of the Jews, then he must have better connections at the T4 office.
b) All I know is that Schutt was an administrative officer and that Ittner supported him. I don't remember replacing Ittner and putting Schutt in his place.

If the findings of the Hagen jury court in the criminal case against Dubois and others, page 244, are held up to me in this context, I declare:

I don't know anything about the fact that I replaced Ittner as head of administration because he refused to use money from the exploitation of the transports to buy additional food for the camp crew. I also don't know anything about the fact that because of this refusal, I assigned Ittner to Lager III, where he then had to supervise the digging of the pits for the corpses by working Jews. I would welcome a comparison with Ittner and Schutt to clarify where this idea came from. Ittner's statements, on which the judgement is based, are wrong. It doesn't exist that I gave Ittner orders or transferred him.

The testimony of the witness Cuckierman on the Consular record of May 9, 1968:

I can't say anything about the fact that, as commander, I should have attached importance to the quick handling of transports. In Sobibór I never gave any instructions to the *Unterführer*'s about the clearance. To that extent I had neither an order from Globocnik nor from Wirth. It is not me who is said to have told the witness to take a stick and beat the kitchen workers when they weren't working hard.

In Sobibór I heard that Bolender tortured the Jewish prisoners by forcing them to climb trees. Then they had to whistle or sing there and then jump down. Bolender was the leader of *Lager III*, i.e. the part of the camp where the gassing of the Jews took place and where the corpse pits were located. I confronted Bolender and told him that as long as I was in the camp, it wouldn't happen again. I forbade him such torture. Then, the next time I was together with the other *Unterführer*, I announced that I didn't want to tolerate such torture. I was put above the team in Sobibór by Globocnik, I was the gang leader, so I felt obliged to stop the torture. I then heard nothing more about such tortures committed by Bolender.

I later came across Bolender for the following reason. I got a procedure at the SS and Police Court in Krakau. I was accused of advising Bolender to induce someone to commit perjury. As far as I know, Bolender was punished. I think he came to the penal company. Nothing was done against me.

I note that, as far as I can remember, there was an order from the Reichsführer-SS, according to which a unit leader had to advise his *Unterführer* if they turned to him about off-duty matters.

Bolender came back from vacation very depressed. When questioned, he told me his wife wanted a divorce. I then talked to him about the matter and, after a phone call in Lublin, was able to get him to go home again.

When we presented him with the wording of Bolender's third letter to the then accused Gertrud Klahn from the judgement of the long court in Heidelberg of November 13, 1942, I declare:

When we were talking to *Unterführer*, I once said, 'If you say yes, you will stay, if you say no, you will go home.' That was the saying in Austria at the time, according to which the illegal National Socialists acted when they were arrested. Bolender must have related this saying to his divorce process and to Gertrud Klahn. I was also questioned about this sentence at the SS and Police Court in Krakau.

If Bolender refers to me as Franz Stangl according to the wording of the letter put before, I declare:

It has nothing to do with a friendly connection between Bolender and me. It was probably the same as here in the house, where I am called Franzl. I wasn't on first name terms with Bolender, not even off-duty.

During the discussion with Bolender about his wife's intention to divorce, it was said that he had had an affair with Gertrud Klahn, and that his wife knew that. I also remember the following now:

It has already been said that Bolender brought dental gold with him from Hartheim, which he had acquired while working as a 'burner' in Hartheim. His wife turned him over with this knowledge. She has promised him a complaint if he doesn't give up his relationship with Getrud Klahn.

I no longer remember whether I learned all this from Bolender himself, or on the occasion of the hearing before the SS and Police Court in Krakau. After my return from Krakau, I informed Wirth about it.

I don't remember that a labor prisoner once escaped from Sobibór. I only found out about it when I was already in prison in Brazil. I was confronted with a prisoner who explained that he had come to the Sobibór camp at the age of 15, and later escaped. This inmate knew me, but I couldn't remember him.

I have no recollection of a labor inmate who was shot outside the camp by a guard after escaping. I am not aware of the fact that another prisoner was hanged in the camp after a prisoner who also belonged to my work detail was shot outside the camp. I have no idea that another 8 members of the same work detail are said to have been shot after a prisoner escaped.

If the certified copy of the Judicial minutes of December 3, 1963, about the interrogation of the then accused Bolender, is presented to me, I declare:

I can't remember anything like that happening at all. I know for a fact that I wasn't involved in anything like that. I don't have the slightest recollection of the fact that once in Sobibór, a Jewish woman came from outside the camp and, unaware of the actual circumstances, asked to speak to her husband.

If the testimony of the then accused Ittner to the Judicial record of November 28, 1963, is held up to me, I declare:

Ittner said something that doesn't exist. If I am further accused of having been convicted of Ittner, for what happened in Hagen, I declare:

I request a comparison with Ittner to clarify this matter. It is quite impossible that I gave such an order to shoot this Jewess. I can't remember anything like that ever happening, that a Jewess came to the camp and asked to speak to her husband. It could be possible that something like this happened at the beginning, because at first there was a big sign at the outer gate of the camp with the inscription 'Resettlement Camp.' This inscription was then changed to '*SS-Sonderkommando.*' This happened by order of Lublin.

I don't remember that once a transport arrived in Sobibór, on which occasion a member of this transport handed over a letter asking for good treatment. The name Biala Podlaski is known to me. It is the name of a city in Poland. It is likely that Jews came to Sobibór from this place, I don't remember.

Subject to the testimony of the witness Lerer on the Consular record of May 10, 1968:

I would ask you to first present the camp's plan, which was mentioned in the testimony of the witness.

After reading plan B1.63, of the judgement in Dubois and Others, have seen, I declare:

I claim that Barracks 25, 26, and 27, were only built by my successor Reichleitner. The incident described by the witness can therefore only have taken place under my successor. From Treblinka I went to Sobibór again and saw that one of these barracks were there. These three barracks were probably marked in the plan sketch, I can remember that.

Incidentally, I would like to point out that in my time no clothes were loaded into goods wagons and taken away. The clothes of the dead Jews were piled up in the so-called 'Heustadel.' It was a barn that stood next to the farm building, which used to be the Foresters Lodge.

If I am further accused of the fact that the transport in question from Biala Podlaska arrived in Sobibór on June 10, 1942, according to the findings of the Hagen court, i.e. at a time when Reichleitner was not yet commandant in Sobibór, I declare:

At that time, i.e. on June 10, 1942, I was still commander of Sobibór. But I know that I didn't build barracks 25, 26, and 27.

If the further findings of the jury court in Hagen are held up to me, and it is pointed out to me in particular that these findings are based on the testimonies of a whole series of witnesses and have also been confirmed by Bolender roughly according to the findings made, I declare:

I don't know that all this happened in Sobibór.

In Sobibór I had nothing to do with registering the valuables of the murdered Jews or with delivering the accumulated textiles. That was a matter for the administration, i.e. Schutt and his successor Floss. As already mentioned, the textiles were collected in the 'Heustadel,' the valuables in the administration.

To a Question:

The valuables have been safely delivered, probably to Lublin. I had nothing to do with it. I didn't deliver any valuables to Lublin from Sobibór.

On Objection:

The testimony of the witness Rzepa on the Judicial record of February 21, 1968.

It is possible that I took valuables with me to Lublin from Sobibór and then delivered them. We didn't have our own car in Sobibór. It is possible that a ride presented itself and that I then took the valuables with me.

On Objection:

I have not been assigned to do anything about the valuables. If I'm not meant to do something, then I don't care about it. If I took any valuables with me, it was only as a courtesy.

I don't remember there were two or three Jews in Sobibór who were goldsmiths. They did goldsmithing for the camp staff. They made rings and badges in gold or silver that were fastened to riding crops. The badges were monograms. It may be that monograms for purses and briefcases were also made. I would like to think that gold coins from the killed Jews were used for these works. I don't know whether any pieces of jewellery were worked or re-worked.

When the statements of the witness Szmajzner are held up to me, I declare:

a) I remember the man. He was 15, years old at the time, that's the one I was confronted with in Brasilia.
b) One can say that at the time, the golden monograms in Sobibór were fashionable among the German camp staff.
c) A ring was also made for me at that time. It was also silver. But it was too small, so I couldn't wear it.
d) It is possible that the witness also made a gold monogram for me. This monogram was placed on my riding crop. I believe the monogram was made of part gold and part silver.
e) I don't know whether the witness also received gold from teeth for his work. It may be possible, why not.
f) I often talked to the boy. It is possible he asked about his relatives and that I then told him that he now had easier jobs than his relatives who worked on farms. I have no memory of such a conversation. What I remember is that I repeatedly sent Polish farmer sausages to the young boy and his brothers.
g) It is quite possible that individual Unterführers had gold melted down in order to take it with them on vacation. It is certainly also possible that the Unterführers brought pieces of jewellery that needed to be polished or re-worked. These pieces of jewellery may also have belonged to the dead Jews.
h) As far as the rings are concerned, which were made for the Unterführer's or for the German camp staff, it is correct that the rings were made of silver and the runes were made of gold.

I have no recollection of the fact that civilian items were worked on in the camp's tailor shop, the material for which came from the possessions of the dead inmates. What I can remember is that uniforms, especially trousers were made there. But then the material had to be obtained from the clothing store in Lublin. I had a linen suit made for me myself. That was in the summer of 1942, just before my family came. I had bought the linen from a farmer near the camp. It had been handmade. At that time I didn't have anything to do for my family members.

If the statements made by the witness Cukierman on the Consular record of May 9, 1968, are held up to me, I declare:

I never asked for any clothes that were intended for my family members and that my wife was supposed to take to Germany. It is true that my wife and the two eldest daughters were visiting near Sobibór at that time. I have stated that before.

When it is pointed out to me that I was supposed to prevent in Treblinka, namely the disappearance of valuables, was common practice in Sobibór, I declare: Yes that's pretty much right.

Robert Juhrs

May 23, 1962
Frankfurt-am-Main

When I arrived in Sobibór I was lodged in a one-storey stone building near the entrance. A number of the original staff were still in the camp. Having newly arrived I had no contact with these members of the camp personnel. These so-called 'Oldies' kept away from us and had nothing to do with us. They simply did not notice us. Between us and them there was an unbridgeable chasm.

I was able to move freely throughout the camp, Parts III—extermination camp and IV—munitions store, no longer existed. There everything had been levelled to the ground. I did not see the so-called funnel made of barbed-wire which led from Camp II to Camp III, it had very probably already been removed. Even the inner fence was no longer there—likewise there were no ditches or buildings.

At this time there were still about 30 male worker Jews in the camp who were employed on clearing up operations. One day while I was in Sobibór these roughly 30 Jews were shot in the area of Camp III. I was not present at these executions as at the time I was busy with clearing up duties in Camp I.

The execution detail consisted of the old members of the camp staff and Ukrainian volunteers. During my stay there I only heard shots from the distance. When I left Sobibór a few members of the camp staff were still present. I had to report to T4 in Berlin—there I was detailed by T4 to spend a week clearing up after air-raids.

Arthur Matthes

July 4 1962
Cologne

Following my duties at Treblinka I arrived at the Jewish Extermination Camp in Sobibór in the autumn of 1943. At this point in time Treblinka had terminated its activities and a number of the Treblinka staff were being transferred to Sobibór. I myself was in Sobibór only a short time, namely from the autumn of 1943, until approximately Christmas of that year.

In Sobibór I was made responsible for the so-called estate, this comprised of looking after two cows, four horses, twenty pigs and a number of geese, chickens and rabbits. As assistants I had one Ukrainian man and several women. These were not the so-called worker-Jews. The Ukrainians were all volunteers.

The estate was in Camp II—I was housed in one of the barracks outside the camp. The Officer—in charge of the camp at that time—was *SS-Hauptsturmführer* Gottlieb Hering. I estimate that the then personnel comprised of twenty men and twenty volunteers.

Some of the buildings had already been removed—I went several times into the annihilation camp, Camp III. The aims of the camp were known to me. From the distance I could still see one building. I did not see any ditches or mass graves.

The fencing of the whole camp was still intact as were the minefields which were being cleared by *Wehrmacht* experts. Some days after my arrival in Sobibór some 100 worker-Jews were transferred there from Treblinka, who were employed in the dismantling and clearing up. They were not employed by me. In November or December of that year while I was still there, these 100 Jews were shot. One morning about 7 a.m. I saw these Jews come past, where I was working, being led to Camp III.

They were dressed and lined up in several rows. I did not see who was in charge of the group. A number of the staff and the Ukrainian volunteers were the escorts. I was not required to participate in the executions, but from my place of work I could hear the shots of the execution squad in Camp III. In my opinion these were not salvos but single shots in Camp III. I also heard from colleagues during the meal-time on the same day, that they had shot these 100 Jews that morning. Afterwards the corpses were cremated—I assume that this was done in an open field.

Franz Suchomel

January 24 1962 & November 7, 1962
Alotting

In October 1943, a few days after the uprising in Sobibór I was called to the office in Treblinka. There I was informed by SS-Officer Kurt Franz, the Camp Commandant that I was being transferred to the extermination camp at Sobibór, since a number of personnel there had fallen in the uprising.

The transfer of personnel from Treblinka to Sobibór took place in three separate groups. I was included in the first of these. Two further details arrived later. At this time I was delighted to be leaving Treblinka. My healthy common sense told me that these worker-Jews being employed on the dismantling of the Camp would be liquidated. For understandable reasons I did not want to have anything to do with this. With me to Sobibór came Eduard Pötzinger[510], and Hermann Sydow, and two other people whose names I no longer recall.

We were received in Sobibór by the Camp Commandant Franz Reichleitner and informed of our new duties. He said that the camp was being dismantled and we had to pack the remainders of the Jewish clothes. In this connection I remember that my immediate task was to remove the clothing of the five comrades who had lost their lives. In addition I had to sort out the personal belongings of the dead and prepare these for dispatch to their families. I know for certain that I dealt with the belongings of comrades Rudi Beckmann, and Josef Wolf. I do not remember the names of the three other fallen comrades.

After my arrival in Sobibór I could find no traces of the uprising. Only near the fencing by the rail track was there evidence of damage. Members of the camp staff also showed me the spots where Wolf, Stengelin, and Graetschus had been killed.

---

[510] The correct name was Karl Pötzinger.

I was also glad that when I arrived in Sobibór there were no Jews. Now I must amend this statement, in that there were a few Jews in the camp, perhaps about twenty, who had voluntarily returned after the uprising, or had been in hiding. In this connection I remember clearly that two Jews, a married couple from Holland were found in Camp I, hidden under the floor. By the way of explanation I have to say that the barracks in Sobibór were constructed on top of meter high piles, to avoid the danger of flooding. The Dutch couple had loosened the floorboards and during the day hid in the space below, they were discovered because at night the barrack was used for the preparation of food. These two Jews, like the other Sobibór Jews were killed, with the Treblinka Jews to which matter I will revert in detail.

In the first half of November the remaining Treblinka Jews arrived in Sobibór. I remember exactly that one morning the Treblinka Jews were lined on the barrack square of Camp I, the Jewish chief *Kapo* Karl Blau, who came from Vienna, stepped forward and reported to Gustav Wagner, who was in charge.

Then the Jews were split into groups, probably by Gustav Wagner or Karl Frenzel. Two shoemakers and six or eight tailors were allocated to me. The remaining Jews and Jewesses were put to work on the usual camp duties and on the camp dismantling operations, which were taking place enormously fast.

The Jews had to work very hard, while receiving little sustenance. I know about this because they came to me to complain. At this time it was an almost daily event that the Jews employed by me, came to me and told me, 'Boss, last night another one hanged himself in the sleeping barrack.' When I asked why they had done this, it was explained to me that they had to work hard, received little to eat, and from time to time were also beaten. There existed between me and the Treblinka Jews a certain trust. The Jews also suspected that their final days in Sobibór were at hand.

These suspicions were in fact justified, as one day, in the second half of November, Gustav Wagner announced one morning at 6 a.m. that he had been instructed to report to Lublin that same evening, that the liquidation of the last of the Jews had been carried out. It was noticeable that this angered him. He let it be known that the Jews would have to be worked extra hard on this day, to tire them out and make them unable to offer resistance.

Consequently the Jews on one of the details engaged on work outside the camp were driven especially hard on that day. The unrest among the Jews was palpable. This was particularly the case with the Jews who were working for me in the tailors shop. The chief *Kapo* Karl Blau, also came to me and asked, 'Boss, has the time now come that we must die?' I replied, probably.' Karl Blau then said to me, 'I shall now go to the barrack with my wife to take poison.' He then asked me to bury him and his wife decently. I was deeply shaken and promised to fulfil his last wish. This conversation with Blau took place in the Jewish cookhouse, where he and his wife were working. A short time before the Jews working for me had been collected by Ukrainian volunteers.

On this day the liquidation of the Jews took place in sections. In the course of the morning, the worker Jews, who had been engaged on the camp dismantling operations were taken to be executed. I heard shooting at intervals. As the shots were barely perceptible I assume they were pistol shots. Afterwards the Jews who had been working in the workshops, the kitchens, and the laundry in Camp I, were taken to be executed.

I then went with my comrades Adolf Gentz and Johann Klier to the Jewish sleeping barracks as I thought of Karl Blau's last words and wanted to carry out his wish. There we indeed found the corpses of Blau and his wife, as well as those of another couple, both doctors, who had also swallowed poison. With the help of a handcart we took the corpses to the execution place which was located at the former practice shooting range in the wood outside Camp III. As to the exact location of this shooting range I can say that it was to the south-west of Camp III.

In the course of the morning the news had filtered through that this would be the place for the executions. In any case that is where we saw the corpses of the Treblinka Jews lying on a wooden structure about 15 m long and 2m high made from dry branches and other easily inflammable wood. As we arrived the structure was already alight.

Chapter VII
Testimonies by Former
Trawnikimänner

These are the Testimonies of some of the former *Trawnikimänner*; the Red Army soldiers who had surrendered to the Germans, and who, as Prisoners of War, had volunteered for service in the SS. They had been trained in the *SS-Ausbildungslager* at Trawniki.

During interrogations by the Soviet authorities, they provided very detailed accounts of their training, and eventual deployment to death camps and concentration camps. They provided comprehensive details of the camp's layouts and facilities, and details of both the Germans and their fellow guards. They also covered their responsibilities and the extermination process that they participated in personally, and were eyewitness to. They explained the murderous efficiency of the SS, and their often brutal and callous behaviour.

Mikhail Razgonayev

September 20, 1948
City of Dniepropetrowsk

After I had completed in May 1942, the school of SS Forces at Trawniki and received the title of *Wachmann* (Guard in the SS forces), I was sent for practical work to a special camp that was located in the township of Sobibór. The camp was in an area of Poland, about 50 kilometres from the town of Chelm, and about 100-150 kilometres from the township of Trawniki, where I had undergone training as a *Wachmann*.

The Sobibór camp was located in a forest, on an area that had been specially prepared. Not far from the Sobibór junction were the railway lines that passed the junction of the camp. There were no other residential buildings or populated areas in the proximity of the camp. The camp was located within a forest clearing, in an area from which the trees had been removed. The area of the camp was 2-3 square kilometres.

The whole area of the camp was fenced with one row of barbed-wire to a height of 2 meters—there were no other fences around the camp, beyond the barbed-wire fence was forest. In the barbed-wire fence in the direction of the railway junction, there were two openings: one for the passage of trains, which was closed off with wooden gates, that were opened only when a train was arriving at the camp, and a second entrance—alongside the first, for the passage of staff to the camp and for carts. This entrance was also operated through wooden gates. Both entrances to the camp were carefully guarded by *Wachmänner*, from among the *Volksdeutsche*. By the camp entrances, inside the camp, there was a guard post in which was located the detail of duty guards in charge of the entrances to the camp. There were no other entrances.

Alongside the railway line that was located within the camp, a wooden hut was built that was intended for disembarkation of people from the carriages. The unloading site was separated from the area of the camp by a barbed-wire fence. From the unloading site, a special passageway of barbed-wire fed to an area of the camp. Two wooden huts had been put up in the camp, termed 'dressing rooms.' The 'dressing rooms' were also fenced off with barbed-wire, in which were special passageways from each hut that led to a large stone building that was termed 'bath-house', and it was not possible to see through them what was happening by the 'bath-house.' In the part of the camp where the 'bath-house' was located—a wooden hut had been put up, at which the work detail that was specially allocated for work in the gas chambers stayed.

In the other part of the camp, where the 'dressing rooms' were located a number of wooden huts, cut off from them, were built and used as storerooms, where the effects and clothes of the people who arrived at the camp, were sorted and kept. At the same place there were huts for a second 'work detail' that engaged in the sorting of the clothes of the people who had been exterminated at the camp. Not far from the entrance to the camp were located a number of buildings in which we stayed—we the *Wachmänner*, Germans—among them the 'work detail' in the camp: apart from that there were also other buildings—a dining room, hairdresser, laundry and others. All these buildings were also located within the camp, but not far from the entrance of the camp. The 'work-detail' comprised over 100 people.

I personally arrived for service at the Sobibór camp in May 1942; at that time most of the camp was built and functioning, that is to say—mass exterminations of people had already been implemented there. However, during the period of my service at the Sobibór camp from May 1942, to July 1943,—the construction work at the camp continued. I, among others, took part in the construction of buildings for 'dressing rooms,' and clothes stores, and in July 1943, I was sent from the Sobibór camp to the area of Rawa Ruska, in order to prepare building materials for the camp.

The Commander of the Sobibór death camp was a German officer of the *SS* forces. I do not know his rank or surname. His deputy was *Oberleutnant* Niemann, also an officer in the *SS* forces. All the activity of the camp for mass destruction was performed under their direct command.

The service staff of the camp consisted of German NCO's, the number of whom at the camp was about 30. The camp staff also comprised *Wachmänner* from among the *Volksdeutsche*, whose status at the camp was higher than ours—of the *Wachmänner* and was equivalent to German soldiers. I personally during my service at the camp belonged to a group of *Wachmänner*, comprising 70-80 persons. The group of *Wachmänner* was divided into a number of platoons, about 20 per platoon. Each platoon was headed by a

Wachmann or *Oberwachmann*, from the *Volksdeutsche*, who had a good mastery of German.

At the Sobibór camp there were two 'work-details,' as I have testified above. One detail, comprising 50 people worked in the part of the camp where the building of the gas chamber was built; a second work-detail of 10 people, mostly women, worked at the clothing stores on the sorting of effects and clothes of the people who had been exterminated at the camp.

The work of the two details was commanded by Germans of the rank of NCO's whose surnames I do not recall. Apart from this a service detail of the camp also included a *Kapo*. To the position of *Kapo*, people were appointed from among the civilians arriving at the extermination camp. These were in effect 'policemen' who supervised the work and the order within the work-detail and that was also made up of civilians, who had been brought to the camp for extermination purposes, but were not exterminated, because they were used for work.

In 1943, a group of Russian girls were brought to the Sobibór camp. Soviet citizens, who performed at the camp laundry work and cleaning. They would launder the clothes of the Germans and ourselves—the *Wachmänner*—and cleaned the rooms in which the Germans lived. These girls, of whom there were about 20, also belonged to the service administration of the camp.

Outside the camp, beyond the barbed-wire fence were placed Guard posts—2 *Wachmänner* every 200 meters, such that the whole area of the camp from the outside world was surrounded by *Wachmänner*, who kept between them visual and audio contact. The role of the guards was to carefully supervise, so that none of the foreigners would come close to the camp and also to prevent escape attempts from the camp through the barbed-wire. So that the guarding of the barbed-wire and the camp area would be more effective, permanent Guard Towers were built at the corners of the camp, and there too, *Wachmänner* stood on guard day and night.

In order to go from one part of the camp to the other, one had to cross special passageways, fenced with barbed-wire, that were also carefully guarded by *Wachmänner* and Germans. Apart from the wire fenced passageways, all the buildings within the camp were guarded—the residential huts of the *Wachmänner's* huts, where the work details stayed, and the residential buildings of the Germans and other buildings.

Very rarely were *Wachmänner* sent outside the camp, and then only on the condition that someone from the *Volksdeutsche* accompanied them. With regard to the civilians who were brought to the camp for extermination, no regime was determined with respect to them, for they were not held at the camp, and as a rule, were exterminated on their day of arrival at the camp. Only civilians of Jewish nationality would arrive for extermination at the Sobibór camp; Men, women, old people and children of various ages would arrive.

The unloading of the trains was not undertaken in one go, but in stages. At one time, people were taken out of approximately 10 wagons, and then another 10. The arriving civilians were told they had been brought to a camp, to a transit camp, at which they would undergo sanitary treatment and a medical board, and afterwards they would receive a referral as to exactly where to travel. Soldiers who used to accompany the train with the people were not workers at the Sobibór camp. Therefore, immediately after the unloading of the train, they would depart with empty wagons, to bring new victims. On average, two trains a day would arrive at the camp—approximately 2,000 people, who were exterminated the same day.

Immediately after the people who were brought to the camp, were taken off the train, they were sorted according to the following criteria: all the men who were capable of moving on their own, were referred to a separate hut, that was isolated from the other huts, by a barbed-wire fence..... women with children, who were also capable of moving on their own, were referred to another isolated hut—a 'dressing room.' Earlier in the description of the camp and the buildings that were in the area of the camp, I forgot to mention that ..... at a distance from the huts—'dressing rooms,' there was a small building, that was called the 'clinic.'

During the sorting and separation of the men and women and their referral to the huts, that were cut off from each other, sick and weak persons were found, who were unable to move on their own. People from the 'work-detail' would lead or carry these sick and weak civilians to the 'clinic' where apparently they would receive medical aid—but in fact, they, as the others were exterminated.

It had to be added that the Germans also thought about other details that also served as camouflage for the true reason for which the people were brought to the Sobibór camp. Thus, for example, in the 'dressing room' there were train timetables, all sorts of posters, appealing to people to maintain order. When the people were invited to the 'bath-house,' each one was given a piece of soap. The lie would end only when the people went into the gas-chambers, where they would discover that there was no 'bath-house,' and that they had been taken there to be destroyed.

The people who were brought to the camp were destroyed in two ways: through suffocating gas in special gas chambers and by shooting in the area of the camp itself. The gas chambers, or as they were termed for camouflage—'bath-house,' was a stone building punctiliously isolated by a system of barbed-wire fences from other parts of the camp and hidden by young trees, saplings in particular, from the view of the huts—'dressing rooms,' so that the people who were in the 'dressing rooms,' would not be able to see what was happening by the 'bath-house.' The 'bath-house,' was distant from the 'dressing rooms,' so that the cries emerging from the gas chambers, when the people realized that they had been tricked and were persuaded that they had been brought there not to bathe, but for their destruction, could not be heard.

In the building with gas chambers, there was a wide corridor, on one side of which there were four chambers, the floor, ceiling and walls were of concrete. They had four special shower-heads that were intended not to supply water, but for the entry of exhaust gases through which the people in the chambers were killed.

Each chamber had two doors, internal on the corridor side, through which the people would enter the chamber, and external, that opened outwards, and through which the bodies would be removed. The doors—the internal and external—were closed hermetically and fitted with rubber strips that did not allow the gas to escape from the chamber.

Behind the rear wall of the building was located on a base, under an awning, a strong motor that would begin to work the moment the chambers were full and the doors were closed hermetically. From the motor led a pipe that went through the ceiling of the building corridor with the gas chambers. From the pipe would emerge into each chamber a metal pipe, ending with a showerhead, that was used in the bath-houses for the supply of water. Through this system the exhaust gasses from the motor would be led into the chamber. The 'work-detail' dealt with the clearing of the chambers after the people who had been put in them had been killed and they would bring the bodies to the pits in carts.

Before the arrival of the train, the Germans would hold a briefing for the *Wachmänner,* who participated that day in the guarding of the trains and the barbed-wire fenced passageways in the area of the camp, so as to prevent any act that might disclose the purpose for which the people had been brought to the camp... because among the people, rumours had already spread that the Germans had camps where the extermination of civilians of Jewish nationality was performed. The Germans feared a rebellion on the part of the people who were brought to the camp and they took all measures to prevent this, because in the event of a rebellion, it would be impossible to overcome it, despite all the means of the camp staff.

During the time of my service as a *Wachmann* and afterwards as an *Oberwachmann* at the Sobibór camp I saw the process of extermination of people with my own eyes. In the first stage, the men were exterminated naked. Accompanied by a *Kapo*, completely naked people, about 150-200 were referred through the barbed-wire passageways from the 'dressing rooms' to the gas chambers, without knowing they were going to die. After a certain time, when this group of 150-200 people would enter one of the gas chambers (each chamber contained 200 people), the same *Kapo* would return and accompany a new group of the same number of people, who would be put into a second chamber, and so it would continue until all 4 chambers were full.

When the last chamber was full of people, an engine of great power would be operated and for 15-20 minutes the exhaust fumes were piped into the chambers. This time was sufficient to kill the people who had been put into the chambers. After the chambers were filled with people, a sign would be given by the Germans who serviced the gas chambers, according to which an engine of great power was operated. I cannot see how the engine was built, because I do not know.

After 15-20 minutes, the people in the chambers suffocated, the doors would be opened, the gas from the chambers would leave and the 'work-detail' would start clearing the chambers. The bodies from the chambers were taken by carts to the pits, were thrown into them and, after all the people who had arrived at the camp that day had been exterminated, the pits would be covered by soil.

Those civilians who were unable to move on their own were shot. As a rule, immediately after the unloading of the train, they would be taken by the 'work-detail' to a separate hut, called the 'clinic' and they stayed there until those who could move on their own, had been exterminated in the gas chambers. The number of sick from one train would come to 30-50 people, depending on the number of trains that would arrive in one day. All the sick who had stayed at the 'clinic' were brought by a 'work-detail,' undressed to the pits and were shot by us—*Wachmänner* and the Germans at short range.

Until December 1942, the bodies used to be buried in pits in the area of the camp. From December 1942, they began to burn the bodies in large bonfires, with the help of bulldozers, that began to remove the bodies of those who had been exterminated previously and burn them in bonfires. Members of the 'work-detail' performed this work.

During May-June 1942, I twice took part personally in the shooting of two groups of people. The first time, a group of 50 sick and infirm were shot by the *Wachmänner*, I among them. At the execution by shooting, a group of *Wachmänner* and Germans, about 10 in number, took part. I personally shot with a rifle and killed on this occasion not more than 5 people.

The second time, also in June 1942, I participated in an execution by shooting of a group of civilians that consisted of about 25 persons. I personally killed on that occasion, not more than 3 people.

In June 1942, I was appointed by the camp command to work inside the camp as a carpenter. I built 'dressing rooms,' huts, for the storage of effects and clothes of the people who were being destroyed at the camp. Apart from that, watch-towers around the camp were built with my participation. In December 1942, for my loyal service in the German *SS* forces and for my good work as a carpenter, I was promoted to the rank of *Oberwachmann*.

On average at the Sobibór camp, 1500 innocent civilians were exterminated each day. I served at the Sobibór camp until July 1943, and afterwards I was sent by the camp command to the area of Rawa Ruska for the preparation of building materials for the camp. I injured myself there by chance and in November-December 1942, I was dismissed from service in the *SS*-forces.

The minutes have been read out before me; recorded according to what I said correctly.

Mikhail Razgonyev

Ignat Danilchenko

November 21, 1979
City of Tyumen

I served as an *SS* guard in the Sobibór concentration camp in Poland from March of 1943, through March or April (I cannot now precisely remember) of 1944. The camp was located near a small railroad station called Sobibór, near the edge of a forest and was designed for mass killing of persons of Jewish nationality from the Soviet Union, Poland, Holland and other nations occupied by the Nazis. Jews from Germany were also killed here. The camp covered approximately four square kilometres and was surrounded by four rows of barbed wire 3m high. There were two entrances into the camp which were closed by wooden gates on the side of the wire barrier facing the railroad siding. One gate was designed to admit railroad trains into the camp, while the other was designed for trucks. There was a smaller gate in the second gate through which Germans and guards passed.

A railroad platform was built in the camp, near the railroad siding, on a level with the doors on the freight cars. This was the spot where the people brought to the camp in railroad cars to be killed were unloaded. The platform was separated from the general territory of the camp by a single row of barbed wire. A passage, also surrounded by barbed wire, led from the platform to an area where the prisoners were ordered to leave their belongings. Another passage 30-40 m long, surrounded by barbed wire, led from this spot, the people were led along this passage to so-called 'dressing rooms,' where they were forced to strip naked. The women's hair was also cut off here. The Germans and the guards took valuables (gold rings, earrings, watches etc.) from the prisoners. A passage approximately 3m wide densely surrounded by barbed wire intertwined with twigs and branches led from the dressing rooms.

The naked people were driven along this passage to a large stone building with what was called the 'showers.' Actually, this was a gas chamber where the arriving Jews were killed in six gas chambers (250 persons in each) by exhaust gasses from diesel engines which were located near the gas chamber. I remember hearing from other guards (I cannot remember their names) that there were two such diesels, supposedly from tanks. I did not personally see these engines, and I do not know precisely where they were located in the area of the gas chamber. This final passage was densely surrounded by armed guards on both sides, right up to the very doors of the gas chamber. When the doors of the gas chamber were opened, the people were driven into the chambers by Germans and guards from a special detachment which worked only in this area of the camp.

The guards guarded the prisoners from the moment the freight cars were unloaded right up to the gas chamber in order to prevent attempts to escape and to eliminate panic and disorder which might arise among the prisoners.

With the aid of the guards, when unloading the freight cars the Germans announced to the Jews that they would be disinfected in Sobibór and then sent to work. Therefore in the majority of cases the people walked calmly along the passages, right up to the doors of the gas chamber. Armed guards stood on both sides of the passages, ready to open fire at the slightest sign of resistance among the prisoners. From conversations with the guards I know that after the people were killed in the gas chamber their bodies were loaded on trolleys which ran up to the 'showers' on a railroad branch line and then hauled a short distance from the area of the gas chamber, stacked on a trestle of rails and burned.

A special detachment of 50 men consisting of German Jews who were prisoners in the camp burned the bodies under the supervision of the Germans. The Jews from this detachment lived in a barracks in the area of the gas chamber. The outside of the barracks was guarded round-the-clock.

The gas chamber building and the place where the bodies were burned were carefully camouflaged by the Germans with trees. However, everyone always knew when bodies were being burned, since the flame blazed over the camp, the glow could be seen for several kilometres and the unique stench of burnt flesh could be smelled in the air. I do not know who ran the diesel engines. It is possible that they were guards, but I do not know who specifically they were. As a rule, all Jews brought to the camp were killed on the very same day. Actually, this was a factory for the mass killing of people. For six months after my arrival at the camp, an average of one or two trains delivered prisoners to the camp daily. There were approximately 25 freight cars in each train, more or less. Each car contained roughly 50-60 prisoners. All of the Jews delivered were killed on the very same day, and those who were not healthy enough to walk to the gas chamber themselves were shot in the area of the gas chamber in a so-called 'infirmary.'

Approximately 1500 Jews were killed in the camp each day. It is difficult for me to provide a more precise estimate of the number of prisoners killed each day, but there were at least 1500 of them. These included women, elderly persons and children. In addition, Jews from nearby ghettos were delivered in 5-6 trucks, with 20-25 persons in each. By late 1943 the trains full of prisoners had begun to arrive more rarely, and by the spring of 1944[511] they had completely stopped arriving. During this period Jews who were still being delivered from the ghettos were killed in the camp, but deliveries of prisoners from the ghettos also became more rare.

The superintendent of the camp was a German *SS* officer, whose name and rank I have forgotten. At the time he was 35-40 years old, tall and well-built. I cannot now specify his other features, since so many years have passed since then. There was a company of *SS* guards consisting of approximately 120 men in the camp. The company consisted of four platoons with approximately 30 men in each platoon. The company commander was a

---

[511] Sobibór was liquidated in November 1943, thus the 1944 date is incorrect.

German *SS* officer. The platoon leaders were guards of German nationality. The commander of the 1st platoon in which I served was also of German nationality. I remember that he was either from the Donbas or from Zaporozhe. I do not remember his last name, but he was called Karl. Because he was short, the guards gave him the nickname Karlik. I do not remember the other platoon leaders.

The platoons were formed according to height. Guards at least 180cm tall served in the 1st platoon. At that time I was 184cm tall. Of the guards who served with me in the 1st platoon I remember Ivan Ivchenko, who was our cook and Ivan Demjanjuk. When I arrived at Sobibór, Demjanjuk already served in the camp as a private in the *SS* guards.

I do not know Demjanjuk's patronymic. From conversations with Demjanjuk I do know that he was from Vinnitsa Oblast. He was roughly 2-3 years older than I, had light brown hair with noticeable bald spots at that time, was heavyset, had grey eyes and was slightly taller than I, roughly 186-187cm tall.

I remember Demjanjuk's appearance well, and I could possibly identify him. I do not know directly from where and when precisely Demjanjuk arrived at Sobibór. From what Demjanjuk said I know that like all of us (the guards) who served in Sobibór he had been trained at the *SS* camp in Trawniki. I saw Demjanjuk for the first time when I arrived at Sobibór, he was already there.

Demjanjuk told me that he served in the Soviet Army and had been taken prisoner by the Germans early in the war. I do not know under what circumstances he was taken prisoner. It is possible that Demjanjuk told me about this, but I cannot remember now. I do not know whether he had any wounds. I personally did not see any traces of wounds on Demjanjuk. At Sobibór, Demjanjuk served as a private in the *SS* guard and was dressed in a black *SS* uniform with a grey collar. He was always armed with a loaded rifle.

While standing guard outside the camp Demjanjuk, like the other guards, was issued a sub-machine gun and ammunition.

While at his post he was obligated to make sure that there were no attempts by outside persons to enter the camp or attempted escapes from it. Demjanjuk, like all guards in the camp, participated in the mass killing of Jews. I also participated in this crime and I was convicted and punished for it. While I was at the camp I repeatedly saw Demjanjuk, armed with a rifle, together with other guards and, in many cases, myself, guard prisoners in all areas of the camp, from the unloaded platform to the entrance into the gas chamber. Demjanjuk escorted people until they reached the gas chamber to avoid violations by the prisoners of the 'procedure' in which they were sent to be killed. I cannot specifically say under what circumstances or how many groups of prisoners Demjanjuk escorted to the gas chamber during his service at the camp, since this was constant, daily work.

I did not see whether Demjanjuk shot anyone while they were being sent to the gas chamber. Such cases occurred in the camp if the prisoners showed any kind of resistance. It is difficult for me to say who shot the sick and weak prisoners in the 'infirmary.' It is possible that they were shot by guards on orders from the Germans, but at present I can state nothing specific about this. I do not know whether Demjanjuk participated in the shootings of sick prisoners. Together with Demjanjuk I had to guard the place where the prisoners were unloaded from the railroad cars. I saw Demjanjuk and other guards push the Jews with rifle butts and hit them, this was a common occurrence during unloading. it is therefore difficult to single out the actions of Demjanjuk in treating the prisoners.

Demjanjuk was considered to be an experienced and efficient guard. For example, he was repeatedly assigned by the Germans to get Jews in surrounding ghettos and deliver them in trucks to the camp to be killed.

I did not receive any such assignments, since I did not have sufficient experience. Demjanjuk also guarded the outside of the barracks for the special detachment which serviced the gas chamber. I saw him at this post many times, carrying a rifle. I do not know whether he served guard duty inside the gas chamber zone. As I remember, Demjanjuk was frequently granted leave because he conscientiously carried out all orders from the Germans.

In March or April of 1944, Demjanjuk and I were sent from Sobibór to the city of Flossenburg in Germany, where we guarded an aircraft factory and a concentration camp for political prisoners. In case we were wounded, all of the guards at this camp, including Demjanjuk, were given a tattoo on the inside of the left arm, above the wrist, designating their blood type. I still have this tattoo, the German letter 'B' designating my blood type. I do not know what letter designated Demjanjuk's blood type. In late autumn of 1944, in October or November, Demjanjuk and I (among other guards) were sent to the city of Regensburg, or rather from the concentration camp located 18-29 km from Regensburg. Until April of 1945, we guarded the prisoners in this camp, who did construction work. In April of 1945, due to the approach of the front the entire camp was evacuated and marched toward the city of Nuremburg. I escaped along the way but Demjanjuk continued to accompany the prisoners. I suggested that he escape with me, but he refused. I have never seen Demjanjuk since then and his fate is unknown to me. I also know nothing about the fate of the prisoners who were on that march.

The questioning was completed at 6:15 pm. The questioning was conducted with a rest break. I have read the record and my statements were recorded faithfully into the record from my words. I have no additions or corrections to make.

Signature of Witness: (signature)

Iwan Karakasz

September 1943

Iwan Mikhailovich Karakasz was born in 1922. He was a Communist Youth League member, with a high-school education. He was a Ukraine national and he served in the Red Army. He was captured by the Germans, and was probably trained at the *SS*-Training School at Trawniki, and then posted to the Sobibór death camp near Włodawa, Poland. He served there for twenty-eight days, before deserting to join the Zukhov partisan detachment, on July 19, 1943. He provided this statement during September 1943, a month before the prisoner revolt.

Death Camp Sobibór
Consists of five basic camps: I, II, III, IV, V
Camp I includes:
Guard Compartment
Medical Facility
Canteen for Germans
Restaurant for Germans
House where Germans lived
Armoury
Barracks where Ukrainian police lived
Barrack for the Camp Duty Guard, the club is there too
Canteen for the Ukrainian Police
The number of the Germans in the camp is 27, and the number of the Ukrainians is up to 80 persons.

Armament: All Ukrainians are armed with Russian rifles, there are 120 rifles overall. Germans are armed with two SVT pistols, 3 automatic guns, the rest are Russian rifles. In the armoury there are also 1 machine-gun Degtyarew, 1 RKM, 1 manual, 1 Russian machine, 1 Polish machine, 20 German grenades, approximately 5,000 cartridges.

Camp II includes:
4 Barracks for the housing and working of Jews
1 Barrack where Female Jews live
3 Locksmith and woodwork workshops
3 Sewing, shoe and other workshops

The number of Jews in this camp is about 250 people, who are assigned to work in this camp, these figures do not include Camp III.

Camp III includes:

The camp where they sort Jewish clothes, and they also store clothes there

Camp IV includes:

The Gas Chambers (Banya) where they suffocate Jews. Banya is an old Slavic term that refers to a Steam Bath / Sauna

Barrack where Jewish laborers live, approximately 150 people

Bonfire where they burn Jews

Tea Room and duty room for Germans. There are repair shops nearby

A tower with a machine-gun

Camp V includes:

60 Western Ukrainians sent here supposedly for guarding the construction of a new railroad. They are not connected with the rest of the camp.

Camp's Guard

The guard consists of 27 people. There are two shifts. These are Ukrainians, each shift is 7 hours. There are 7 towers, each is guarded by one person with a rifle and 15 cartridges, only during the daytime. Also each of these five camps is guarded independently. There is also a night guard circulating round the camp during the night time, three persons who are *Volksdeutsche*. There are two Ukrainian and two German guardsmen inside the camp.

Facts:

I hear how a train with a bolt and noise is approaching the camp. I hear gun shots and machine-gun shots. The train stops at the station. At the same time all the guards in the camp are on alert. They are waiting. 8-10 cars are detached from the train and are rolled down to the camp. Jewish laborers open the cars and the people are thrown out of there, some are alive, some are dead. All are thrown onto an embarkment.

I hear groans and cries of people and children. Germans shouting and particularly whips whistling. People are marched from the embankment along a corridor made from wire. Here is the first barrack where they leave all their belongings, blankets, suitcases and bags. On the way out of this barrack they meet a German with a whip who separates men to the left and women to the right.

Women are then marched along within Camp II to the last two barracks where they are undressed until naked, money, watches, gold, silver, diamonds are all taken away. Then men are marched into the barrack where they are also undressed until naked, and then marched along the same corridor to the banya. The banya consists of eight chambers. Each chamber fits up to 500 people. They close the door hermetically, turn a switch, and a gas driven by an engine forcefully rushes into the chamber.

One can hear people's groans, mooing and crying through the chamber's walls. In 5-10 minutes people are not quite dead yet. They are thrown into narrow-gauge railway cars. At the same time guards extract their teeth and pull rings from their fingers. The piles of corpses are rolled down to the bonfire and are thrown on the ground and with extreme speed are thrown on the rails up to 1,000—1,500 people in a group.

Then they make a fire under them and people are burned. A master German is sitting in the restaurant having a glass of rum and commanding, 'Those who are not working well should be shot. Those who are not laughing should be drowned in water. Those who are weak should be hanged.' All that is left from these burned people, who lived just an hour ago, are white bones. They are ground into powder and poured into a pit. And this process continues day and night. People are murdered and the Germans take all their wealth, profit from them. These are our 'defenders and liberators,' presumably from the Soviet regime.

Detailed Description of the Banya—Gas Chamber Building

The Banya is a cement house with a length about 28 meters in width some 10 meters. From the outside it looks like a shop with smooth walls and wide doors which are opened to the outside. There are two entrances. Inside the Banya there is a corridor.

There are four chambers on its left side and four on the right, where people are suffocated by poisonous gas.

The Banya contains pipes directed to each chamber. A chamber looks like a cube with the side length of about 7 meters. Inside a chamber there is an entrance door, on the opposite side there is another door for pulling corpses out. Inside the chamber there are holes for inserting gases and at the top (*illegible*) for the gasses to exit. After the people have been suffocated. Inside there is an electric bulb and a small slit for controlled observation.

On the right and left from the banya, there is a narrow-gauge railway for transporting corpses, pulled out from the chambers, to the bonfire. Each chamber holds 500 people. I guess for masking the true purpose of the banya, it is decorated with flowers and other decorations.

Iwan Karakasz
(Date and Signature: Illegible)[512]

---

[512] Testimony kindly provided by Gary Hochman. Holocaust Historical Society.

Chapter VIII
The Author's Visits to Sobibór

Trip to Poland 2002

During July 2002, members of the ARC Group met up in the home of Michael Peters in Alfstedt, Germany. The group members consisted of Johannes Feuser, Peter Laponder, Michael Peters, William 'Billy' Rutherford, and Chris Webb.

We departed from Alfstedt by taxi to Bremervörde train station, where we took a local train to Hamburg *Hauptbahnhof*. There we caught a train to Berlin, where we boarded an ICE train to Dresden. We then boarded a local train to Pirna, where we visited the former T4 Euthanasia Institute in Pirna-Sonnenstein.

After an overnight stay in the Hotel Gerberhaus in Pirna, on Friday July 19, 2002, we caught a train from Pirna, to Dresden, returning to Berlin, where we caught a train to Warsaw, which arrived at circa 19:00 hours. We then boarded a train from Warsaw, which left at 20:50 hours, arriving in Lublin at circa 23:00 hours, where we were met by Michael Tregenza, our English guide, and our driver Piotr. After a quick bite to eat in the Old Town, we were driven to the Hotel Viktoria.

On Saturday 20 July, we went by our transit van bus from Lublin to the former Bełżec death camp, and onto Zamość where we stayed overnight in the Hotel Renesans. The following morning after breakfast we left Zamość and drove to Trawniki, to see the former *SS* Training Camp, and from there we went to the former Sobibór death camp, which in fact was the first time I had visited the site.

Sunday 21 July 2002–Sobibór

Leaving Trawniki we drove to the site of the former death camp at Sobibór. What struck me as we drove through the dense forest, was just how remote this place was. As we pulled up to the former death camp, we saw the green coloured house where Stangl and Reichleitner, the two camp commandants, lived. We walked along the ramp, opposite the railway station, to the buffer at the end of the line, before continuing onto the Commandant's old house. The railway station was no longer in use, the station had closed in April 2000.

Peter, with his forthcoming Treblinka model in mind, was keen to measure the well in the back garden of Stangl's former dwelling, and we had a look in the odd-shaped concrete structure that might have been near the site of the old armoury, comparing it with photographs from the 1950's; which show a building next to the Commandant's house. Mike Tregenza negotiated with the Forester to allow us to go into the back garden. However, only one person was allowed inside the former Commandant's dwelling, and Billy Rutherford was allowed to go upstairs,—he was photographed looking out of the window. Michael Peters spent a lot of time looking at the detail of the original green paint on the villa, and he observed that under the painting was just rough wood, and that formerly there may have been white paint, as this was the normal custom.

After a tour of the modern looking museum we were led by the local forester who took us deep into the forest, alas not to the Forester's Tower, which dominated the landscape. He showed us the barbed wire attached to the trees and he let me take some. He also showed us some of the foundations in the so-called North Camp (*Nordlager*).

We toured the former camp area, took photographs of the ramp and the buffer. We saw the site of the former gas chambers and Billy found an old spent bullet cartridge, which he handed to Mike Tregenza.

We saw the two monuments, one a reddy-brown figure of what looks like a woman and child and the huge dome-like structure that covered the ash from the murdered victims. We then left the former camp area, wandered over to the railway station and re-crossed the railway tracks and entered the lumber yard with its concrete bunker-like building. Mike Tregenza said this was post-war.[513]

We then left the former death camp and then Piotr drove down some incredibly bumpy back roads to find the main road back to Lublin.

When we returned from Poland, we launched www.deathcamps.org website, which was a name I came up, along with the name 'ARC' (Aktion Reinhard Camps) group, in December 2002.

Trip to Poland 2004

Two years later the ARC Group undertook a second field trip to Poland. This time only Michael Peters and Chris Webb from the original members made the trip, along with invited guests Melvyn Conroy, Paul Denton, Carmelo Lisciotto, Cameron Munro, Larry and Tim Turnquist. Artur Hojan acted as a co-guide along with Chris Webb. We were joined at various places by Lukasz Biedka, and Robert Kuwalek. Our driver was Jozef, who hailed from Nowa Huta.

The trip was extensive it covered Krakow, Plaszow, Auschwitz, Kielce, Radom, Zwolen, Siedlce, Treblinka, Sobibór, Adampol, Włodawa, Lublin, Trawniki, Poniatowa, Izbica, Bełżec, Zamość, Ciechanow, and Jaroslaw. An extract related to the visit to Sobibór follows:

---

[513] Chris Webb, *Journal of the ARC Trip to Poland—2002* and 2004 (Unpublished Work).

July 23, 2004–Sobibór

On July 23, 2004, we drove from the Hotel Lublinianka in Lublin, which during the occupation was the imposing *Deutsches Haus*, and drove to the former site of the death camp at Sobibór, it was a lovely sunny day. We arrived at the site, and parked near the muse[u]m. It was a beautiful warm and sunny day.

We first saw the buffer at the end of the ramp, painted white, and walked along the ramp, to look at the former Commandant's house, which now had a dazzling shiny roof, but this time we did not go into the back garden like last time.

Paul Denton set up his heavy film equipment at the end of the ramp, standing by a railway wagon carrying cut logs, and started to film the general area of the former camp site. Meanwhile Cameron Munro and Chris Webb explored the closed former railway station and the adjacent buildings. The station building had not changed much, although the station sign bearing the name Sobibór above the front door had disappeared.

After this a group of us walked through the former camp site, and another thing had changed, the distinctive Forester's Tower no longer dominated the landscape. Recently the tower had collapsed and all you could see now was the remains of the foundations.

We found the path that was the old 'Tube' and visited the two memorials that I mentioned in the 2002 visit, then we visited the new Chapel that had been built, on the site of the pre-war Catholic Chapel—which had served as *the Lazarett* when the camp was in existence during 1942, and 1943. On September 15, 1984, the first stone was laid for a new Church. The building of a new church, on the site of a former death camp, is a source of some controversary.

We were then joined by Krystof Skwirowski, from the nearby Włodawa Museum, who showed us the site of the log-road which ran through the former *Nordlager*, where captured ammunition was cleaned and stored. Some traces of this log-road was still visible, if you knew where to look. Krystof clutched in his hand the ARC folder on Sobibór, produced by Billy Rutherford and which he had donated to the Sobibór museum during the 2002, visit. Krystof had met Billy during one of his earlier visits to Sobibór and he remembered him with great affection.

We finished our trip with a visit to the small museum, which had a model of the former death camp, some barbed wire, and bricks presumably from the demolished gas chambers and some photographs of some of the *SS* men who served at Sobibór.

My overriding feeling about Sobibór is the sense of foreboding—that hundreds of thousands of people were murdered here, in the dense forests of south-eastern Poland, in the most brutal way, still pervaded the site.

Illustrations and Sources

The bulk of the historical photographs of Sobibór can be found in the recent publication '*Fotos Aus Sobibor*' which was published by Metropol Verlag in 2020. These images are courtesy of the USHMM in Washington DC. A few other historical photographs come from the *Hessisches Hauptstaatsarchiv*, in Wiesbaden, Germany. The trial photographs are courtesy of *Ullstein-Bild Verlag* and the *Süddeutsche Zeitung*.

The modern day photographs come from my private archive, taken during my personal trips to Sobibór between 2002, and 2004, with the ARC Group.

Fig. 1. Main Entrance (USHMM)

Fig. 2. Camp View (USHMM)

Fig. 3 Watchtower (USHMM)

Fig. 4. Altes Kasino (USHMM)

Fig. 5. Erbhof (USHMM)

Fig. 6. Sobibór Station with *Reichsbahn* Personnel (Hessisches Hauptarchiv, Wiesbaden, Germany)

Fig. 7. Borner, Frenzel, Stangl, Bauer and Wagner in the Swallow's Nest with two unknown women. (The Ghetto Fighters' House Museum, Israel/The photo archive)

Fig. 8. Trawnikimänner (USHMM)

Fig. 9. Beckmann, Altes Kasino (USHMM)

Fig. 10. Niemann (USHMM)

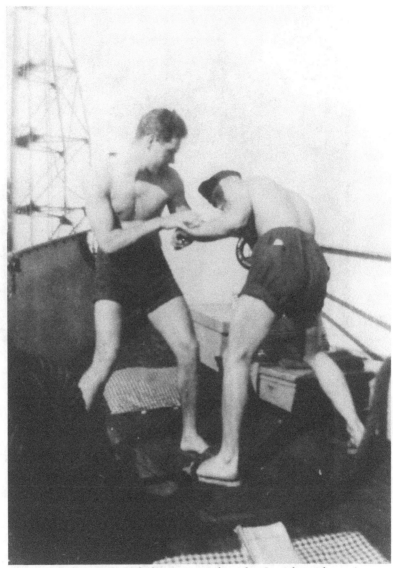

Fig. 11. Hubert Gomerski boxing match with a Jewish worker prisoner, under the shadow of the Forester's Tower (Hessisches Hauptarchiv, Wiesbaden, Abtl. 461, Nr. 36346 Bd. 13, Blatt 2062)

Fig. 12. Gomerski and an unidentified German Officer during the boxing match in Sobibór (Hessisches Hauptarchiv, Wiesbaden, Abtl. 461, Nr. 36346 Bd. 13, Blatt 2062)

Fig. 13. Hubert Gomerski photographed with Jewish prisoners who took part in boxing matches in Sobibór (Hessisches Hauptarchiv, Wiesbaden, Abtl. 461, Nr. 36346 Bd. 13, Blatt 2062)

Fig. 14. Fritz Konrad (USHMM)

Fig. 15. Graetschus (USHMM)

Fig. 16. Niemann, Beckmann, Rost (USHMM)

Fig. 17. Niemann (USHMM)

Fig. 18. Niemann and dogs (USHMM)

Fig. 19. Niemann and Wagner (USHMM)

Fig. 20. Niemann by Sorting Barracks (USHMM)

Fig. 21. Reichleitner and Bauer (USHMM)

Fig. 22. Off Duty (USHMM)

Fig. 23. Rudolf Kamm, Willi Wendland, Heinrich Unverhau, Fritz Konrad and Johann Klier (USHMM)

Fig. 24. Wendland and Kamm

Fig. 25. Lachmann, Gomerski and Beckmann (The Ghetto Fighters' House Museum, Israel/The photo archive)

Fig. 26. Sobibór Ramp—July 2002 (C. W. Private Archive)

Fig. 27. Sobibór Former Commandants Villa—July 2002 (C. W. Private Archive)

Fig. 28. Sobibór Former Commandants Villa – Rear View – July 2002 (C. W. Private Archive)

Fig. 29. Sobibór Armoury—July 2002 (C. W. Private Archive)

Fig. 30. Sobibór Train Station (C. W. Private Archive)

Fig. 31. Sobibór Forester's Tower—July 2002 (C. W. Private Archive)

Fig. 32. Sobibór North Camp—Barbed-Wire Fence—July 2002 (C. W. Private Archive)

Fig. 33. Sobibór North Camp—Bunker Foundations—July 2002 (C. W. Private Archive)

Fig. 34. Sobibór Monument—July 2002 (C. W. Private Archive)

Fig. 35. Sobibór Well—July 2002 (C. W. Private Archive)

Fig. 36. Sobibór Mound of Ashes—July 2004 (C. W. Private Archive)

Fig. 37. Group by a Sobibór Sign—July 2004 (C. W. Private Archive—courtesy of Paul Denton)

Fig. 38. Setting up the Camera—July 2004 (C. W. Private Archive)

Fig. 39. Sobibór 'Tube'—July 2004 (C. W. Private Archive)

Fig. 40. End of the Line—Sobibór Railway Buffer—July 2002 (C. W. Private Archive)

Fig. 41. Chris Webb, Artur Hojan, Krystof Skwrowski—Sobibór—July 2004 (Chris Webb Private Archive—courtesy of Paul Denton)

Fig. 42. Sobibór Railway Building—July 2002 (C. W. Private Archive)

Fig. 43. Sobibór Sign—July 2004 (C. W. Private Archive)

Fig. 44. Lumber Yard—Sobibór—July 2002 (C. W. Private Archive)

Fig. 45. New Church—Sobibór—July 2002 (C. W. Private Archive)

Fig. 46. Sobibór Railway Buffer—July 2002 (C. W. Private Archive)

Fig. 47. General View—Sobibór—July 2002 (C. W. Private Archive)

Fig. 48. Log Road—Sobibór—July 2002 (C. W. Private Archive)

Drawings, Maps and Sources

The drawings of the Sobibór death camp are courtesy of the late William 'Billy' Rutherford, and are held in my private archive. The Deportations to Sobibór was kindly given to me by the late Sir Martin Gilbert, who graciously supported my research efforts.

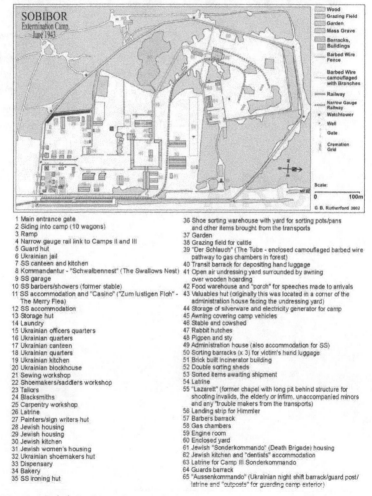

1 Main entrance gate
2 Siding into camp (10 wagons)
3 Ramp
4 Narrow gauge rail link to Camps II and III
5 Guard hut
6 Ukrainian jail
7 SS canteen and kitchen
8 Kommandantur - "Schwalbennest" (The Swallows Nest)
9 SS garage
10 SS barbers/showers (former stable)
11 SS accommodation and "Casino" ("Zum lustigen Floh" - The Merry Flea)
12 SS accommodation
13 Storage hut
14 Laundry
15 Ukrainian officers quarters
16 Ukrainian quarters
17 Ukrainian canteen
18 Ukrainian quarters
19 Ukrainian kitchen
20 Ukrainian blockhouse
21 Sewing workshop
22 Shoemakers/saddlers workshop
23 Tailors
24 Blacksmiths
25 Carpentry workshop
26 Latrine
27 Painters/sign writers hut
28 Jewish housing
29 Jewish housing
30 Jewish kitchen
31 Jewish women's housing
32 Ukrainian shoemakers hut
33 Dispensary
34 Bakery
35 SS ironing hut
36 Shoe sorting warehouse with yard for sorting pots/pans and other items brought from the transports
37 Garden
38 Grazing field for cattle
39 "Der Schlauch" (The Tube - enclosed camouflaged barbed wire pathway to gas chambers in forest)
40 Transit barrack for depositing hand luggage
41 Open air undressing yard surrounded by awning over wooden hoarding
42 Food warehouse and "porch" for speeches made to arrivals
43 Valuables hut (originally this was located in a corner of the administration house facing the undressing yard)
44 Storage of silverware and electricity generator for camp
45 Awning covering camp vehicles
46 Stable and cowshed
47 Rabbit hutches
48 Pigpen and sty
49 Administration house (also accommodation for SS)
50 Sorting barracks (x 3) for victim's hand luggage
51 Brick built incinerator building
52 Double sorting sheds
53 Sorted items awaiting shipment
54 Latrine
55 "Lazarett" (former chapel with long pit behind structure for shooting invalids, the elderly or infirm, unaccompanied minors and any "trouble makers from the transports)
56 Landing strip for Himmler
57 Barbers barrack
58 Gas chambers
59 Engine room
60 Enclosed yard
61 Jewish "Sonderkommando" (Death Brigade) housing
62 Jewish kitchen and "dentists" accommodation
63 Latrine for Camp III Sonderkommando
64 Guards barrack
65 "Aussenkommando" (Ukrainian night shift barrack/guard post/ latrine and "outposts" for guarding camp exterior)

Doc. A   Sobibór Camp Layout June 1943

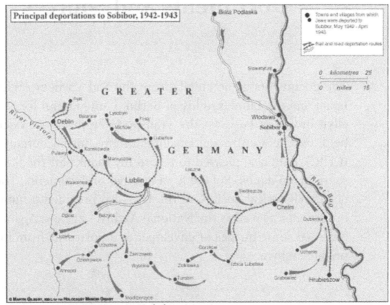

Doc. B. Deportations to Sobibór Map

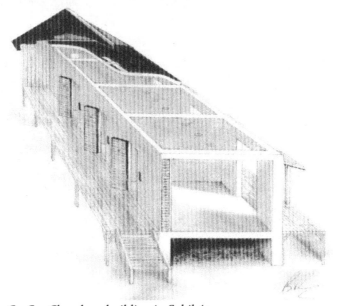

Doc. C. Gas Chambers building in Sobibór

Documents and Sources

The documents come chiefly from the Yad Vashem Archives in Israel and the Bundesarchiv in Berlin. I am grateful for Dr Llewellyn Brown in Paris for the Transports From France document held by the Centre de Documentation Juive Contemporaine (CDJC). I am also pleased to record my thanks for the State Museum in Majdanek, Poland for a number of documents. The Holocaust Historical Society in the UK, also provided a number of documents, as well as the National Archives at Kew. Again I have included some images of envelopes and postcards from my own private archive.

Doc. 1. Sobibór envelope (C. W. Private Archive)

Doc. 2. Jenny Khan Postcard from Krasnystaw (C.W. Private Archive)

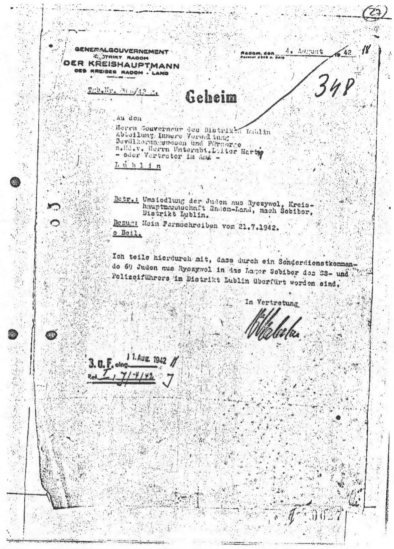

Doc. 3. Sobibór entry 352 (Yad Vashem)

;tstelle Feldpostnummer
- 16 107 A -
.1.-Reiterabteilung III

O.U., den 22. Oktober 1943

An das
SS- Polizei - Regiment 25
in L u b l i n.

Lagebericht!

    Die augenblickliche Lage bestätigt die hiesigen Annahmen, daß ein großer Teil der Juden über den Bug gegangen ist. Ein weiterer Teil der Juden, die noch am 16.10.43 in der Gegend B u k o w a - S a w i n geschlossen gesichtet sein sollen, scheinen sich vollkommen in alle Winde zerstreut zu haben. Aus den verschiedensten Orten laufen nach und nach Meldungen ein, wonach 1,2 oder 3 Juden sich freiwillig eingefunden haben, gefangen oder erschossen wurden (Sobibor, Wolczyny, Uhrusk, Sarwin, Cholm usw.)
    Insgesamt sind es bisher rund 100 von 300, die im Zusammenwirken mit Truppenpolizei, Wehrmacht, Zollgrenzschutz usw. erledigt wurden.
    In dem Gebiet der Planquadrate befinden sich geschlossene Judenmengen von mehr als 3 - 5 Mann auf keinen Fall mehr. Alles weitere muß der Kleinarbeit überlassen bleiben. Größere Einsätze lohnen z.Zeit nicht mehr. Drei Einsätze laufen z.Zeit noch. Ich schlage daher vor, die noch eingesetzten Verbände der Truppenpolizei, Wehrmacht und SS heute abend entlassen zu dürfen und weitere Aufklärung durch 2. Schwadron anzusetzen.

Nachtrag: Am 19.10. wurde das Planquadrat 141,
            am 20.10. wurde das Planquadrat 164 und am 21.10.
            das Planquadrat 171 im Einvernehmen mit 1+18 der
            Sicherheitspolizei Lublin durchkämmt.
Am 19. und am 20.10 wurden je 3 Juden auf der Flucht erschossen.
Am 21.10. wurden 4 Verdächtige festgenommen und der Sicherheitspolizei Cholm übergeben.

Major d. Sch.P.
u. Abt.-Kommandeur

Doc. 4. Sobibór Umsiedlung 352 (Yad Vashem)

**Der Befehlshaber
der Sicherheitspolizei und des SD
in Lothringen-Saarpfalz**
Tgb.-Nr. III/1 669/43 g.

DOCUMENT: XLIX-3

B. d. S. - Paris
Eing. 14 APR 1943
G.B.Nr. 5687
Abt. IV 3 Anl.:

Metz, den 9.4.43

Geheim

An den
Befehlshaber der Sicherheitspolizei und des SD
z.Hd. SS-Standartenführer Dr. K n o c h e n oVIA

Paris

Betrifft: Judentransport vom 23.3.43 von Frankreich nach
Sobibor/Gen.Gouv.

Aus dem Erfahrungsbericht des Leiters des Begleitkommandos der Schutzpolizei dieses Transportes ist ersichtlich, dass die Verpflegungs- und Gepäckwagen nicht plombiert, sondern nur mit einfachem Bindedraht zugebunden waren. Zur ordnungsgemässen Übernahme und Übergabe der Verpflegungs- und Gepäckwagen ist eine Plombierung jedoch unbedingt erforderlich.

Ich gebe hiervon Kenntnis mit der Bitte, die zuständigen Stellen entsprechend anzuweisen.

Im Auftrage:

Doc. 5. Letter to Dr. Helmuth Knochen—Regarding the deportation of Jews from France to Sobibór (CDJC Paris)

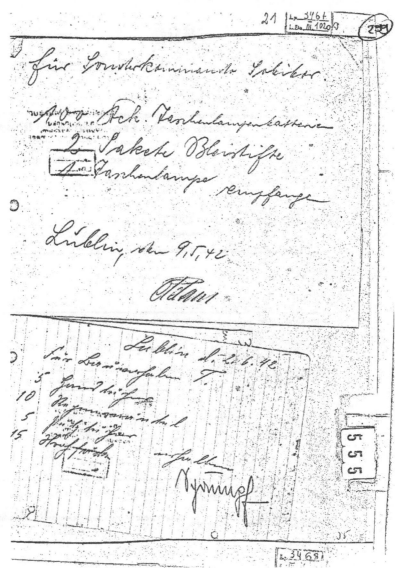

Doc. 6. Handwritten note regarding material for *SS Sonderkommando* Sobibór (Yad Vashem)

Doc. 7. Treblinka—Sobibór Waybill Transfer of prisoners (Yad Vashem)

Gendarmeriezug Cholm   Cholm, den 7. Januar 1943.
Tgb.Nr. 56/43

An
den Kommandeur der Gendarmerie
in L u b l i n
a.d.Dienstwege
nachrichtlich dem Herrn Kreishauptmann in C h o l m

Betrifft: Flucht der beiden Wachmänner (Trawniki-Männer) Viktor
         K i s i l j o w, Kenn-Nr. 1471 und Wasyl Z i s c h e r,
         Kenn-Nr.93.
Bezug: Fernmündliche Meldung vom 26.12.1942 sowie Funkspruch
         Cholm Nr.2 vom 4.1.1943.

      In der Nacht zum 26.12.1942 waren die oben angeführten beiden
Wachmänner Viktor K i s i l j o w, Kenn-Nr.1471 und Wasyl
Z i s c h e r, Kenn-Nr.93, unter Mitnahme zweier russ. Gewehre
und einer größeren Menge Munition aus dem Lager Sobibor, Kreis
Cholm, entwichen. Gleichzeitig waren 5 Juden (Jüdinnen) ent-
wichen. Die sofort eingeleiteten Fahndungen verliefen zunächst
erfolglos.
      In der Nacht zum 1. Januar 1943 erhielt der Postenführer des
poln. Pol.Postens Wierzbica, Gemeinde Olchowiec, poln. Polizei-
Meister Meisnerowiec, von dem V-Mann der Kol. Staszyce (Kozia-
Gora), Gem. Olchowiec, die Meldung, daß um 22 Uhr bei ihm in der
Wohnung zwei Banditen mit einer Frau Unterkunft genommen haben.
Einer der Banditen habe ein Gewehr bei sich. Der Postenkomman-
dant rückte hierauf um 4 Uhr zusammen mit den beiden ihm unter-
stellten poln.Pol.-Hauptw. Franz Piescikowski und Max Kwiatkowski aus, um die Banditen auszuheben. Als sie sich im Morgen-
grauen dem betr. Wohnhause bis auf etwa 40 m genähert hatten,
flüchteten von da plötzlich 2 Männer und eine Frau, nachdem
einer der Flüchtenden einen Schuß auf die angreifenden Pol.-Be-
amten abgegeben hatte, der jedoch fehlging. Durch das sofort
aufgenommene Feuer der Polizisten wurden die 3 Flüchtigen nie-
dergestreckt. Nunmehr stellte es sich heraus, daß es sich bei
den erschossenen vermeintlichen Banditen um die beiden
aus dem Lager Sobibor entwichenen Wachmänner und bei der Frau
um eine Jüdin namens Pesia Liberman, geb.20.11.1916 zu Cholm,
zuletzt ebenda wohnhaft, handelte. Die in den Dienstausweisen
Nr. 1471 und 93 (sie wurden bei den Erschossenen vorgefunden)
enthaltene Personenbeschreibung stimmt mit den Erschossenen
überein. Ein russ. Gewhr mit 93 Schuß Munition, Uniformen, Stie-
fel, Dienstausweise pp. wurden beim Gend.-Zug sichergestellt
und das Lager in Sobibor zwecks Abholung verständigt.

      Daß die beiden entwichenen Wachmänner sich ihrer selbstge-
nommenen Freiheit nicht lange erfreuen und schließlich kein wei-
teres Unglück anrichten konnten, ist allein das Verdienst des
Postenkommandanten und poln. Pol.-Meisters Meisnerowiec. Pflicht-
bewußt und einsatzfreudig wie er ist, hat er sofort nach Erhalt
der Meldung die Aushebung der vermeintlichen Banditen in die We-
ge geleitet. Seine Tatentschlossenheit und Einsatzfreudigkeit
hat dann auch zum vollen Erfolge geführt.

      Diese seine Haltung verdient eine Anerkennung. Ich schlage
daher die Bewilligung einer Geldbelohnung in Höhe von 200,--Zl.

Doc. 8. Report by Police Chief Tischer Cholm—regarding shootout involving Trawnikimänner and a Jewess from Sobibór dated January 7, 1943 (NIOD Amsterdam, Holland)

Dr.-Ing Ganzenmüller
Staatssekretär im Reichsverkehrsministerium
Stellvertretender Generaldirektor
der Deutschen Reichsbahn

Berlin W 8, den 28. Juli 1942
Voßstraße 35
Fernruf 120030

Herrn
SS-Obergruppenführer W o l f
Berlin SW 11
Prinz-Albrecht-Str 8
- Persönlicher Stab des
Reichsführers SS -

Sehr geehrter Pg Wolf!

Unter Bezugnahme auf unser Ferngespräch vom 16. Juli teile ich Ihnen folgende Meldung meiner Generaldirektion der Ostbahnen (Gedob) in Krakau zu Ihrer gefälligen Unterrichtung mit:

"Seit dem 22.7. fährt täglich ein Zug mit je 5 000 Juden von Warschau über Malkinia nach Treblinka, außerdem zweimal wöchentlich ein Zug mit 5 000 Juden von Przemysl nach Belzek. Gedob steht in ständiger Fühlung mit dem Sicherheitsdienst in Krakau. Dieser ist damit einverstanden, daß die Transporte von Warschau über Lublin nach Sobibor (bei Lublin solange ruhen, wie die Umbauarbeiten auf dieser Strecke diese Transporte unmöglich machen (ungefähr Oktober 1942)."

Die Züge wurden mit dem Befehlshaber der Sicherheitspolizei im Generalgouvernement vereinbart. SS- und Polizeiführer des Distrikts Lublin, SS-Brigadeführer Globotschnigg, ist verständigt.

Heil Hitler!
Ihr ergebener

Ganzenmüller

Doc. 9. Letter from Ganzenmüller to Karl Wolf regarding transports (Yad Vashem)

152. Polizeirevier
27/II, Reichsbrückenstraße 46   Wien, den 20. Juni 1942.

Erfahrungsbericht.

Betr.: Transportkommando für den Judentransport
Wien - Aspangbahnhof nach Sobibor am 14.6.1942.
Bezug: Kdo. d. Sch.-1a- 6260/42 v. 20.3. 1942.

Das Transportkommando bestand aus Rev. Lt. d. Sch. Fischmann als Führer, 2 Hauptw.d.Sch. und 13 Wachtm.d.Sch.d.Res.(SS) der 1. Polizei-Reservekompanie Ost. Der Dienst des Transportkommandos wurde am 14.6.1942 um 11,00 Uhr nach vorheriger fernmündlicher Anfrage bei SS-Hauptsturmführer Brunner am Aspangbahnhof angetreten.

1. **Einwaggonierung der Juden.**
Die Einwaggonierung der Juden in den bereitgestellten Sonderzug auf dem Aspangbahnhof begann um 12,00 Uhr unter Leitung und Aufsicht des SS-Hauptsturmführers Brunner und des SS-Hauptscharführers Girzik der Zentralstelle für jüdische Auswanderung und wickelte sich glatt ab. Damit setzte zugleich der Bewachungsdienst des Transportkommandos ein. Insgesamt wurden 1000 Juden abtransportiert. Die listenmäßige Uebernahme der Juden erfolgte um 16,00 Uhr. Das Transportkommando musste sich infolge Waggonmangels an Stelle eines Wagens zweiter Klasse mit einem solchen dritter Klasse begnügen.

2. **Fahrt von Wien nach Sobibor.**
Der Zug Da 38 wurde am 14.6.1942 um 19,08 Uhr von Wien abgefertigt und fuhr über Lundenburg, Brünn, Neisse, Oppeln, Tschenstochau, Kielce, Radom, Deblin, Lublin, Chelm nach Sobibor, nicht wie vorgesehen nach Izbica. Ankunft in Sobibor am 17.6.42 um 08,15 Uhr. In Lublin, Ankunft am 16.6. um 21,00 Uhr, erwartete der SS-Obersturmführer Pohl den Zug am Bahnhof und liess 51 arbeitsfähige Juden im Alter von 15 bis 50 Jahren auswaggonieren und in ein Arbeitslager bringen. Zugleich gab er den Auftrag die übrigen 949 Juden in das Arbeitslager nach Sobibor zu bringen. Die beiden Namensverzeichnisse, drei Gepäckwagen (mit Lebensmittel, sowie 100.000.—Zloty wurden dem SS-Obersturmführer Pohl in Lublin übergeben. Um 23,00 Uhr erfolgte die Abfahrt von Lublin nach Sobibor. Im Judenlager Trawniki, ca 30 km vor Lublin wurden die drei Waggon mit Gepäck und Lebensmittel dem SS-Scharführer Mayerhofer übergeben.

3. **Übergabe der Juden in Sobibor.**
Der Zug fuhr am 17.6. um 08,15 Uhr in das neben dem Bahnhof Sobibor gelegene Arbeitslager, wo vom Lagerkommandanten Oberlt. d.Sch. Stangl die 949 Juden übernommen und sogleich mit der Auswaggonierung begonnen wurde, welche um 09,15 beendet war.

4.) **Fahrt von Sobibor nach Wien.**
Die Abfahrt von Sobibor erfolgte sogleich nach der Beendigung der Aussendung der Juden mit dem Sonderzug um 10,00 Uhr nach Lublin, wo die Ankunft am 18.6. um 02,30 erfolgte. Für diesen Zug wurden keine Fahrspesen bezahlt. Von Lublin aus erfolgte am 18.6. um 08,13 Uhr mit dem fahrplanmäßigen Eilzug die Fahrt nach Krakau, wo um 17,30 Uhr des gleichen Tages die Ankunft erfolgte. In Krakau wurde beim Reserve Polizei Batl.74/3 Komp. genächtigt. Am 19.6. wurden von der genannten Kompanie für 16 Mann je eine Tagesverpflegung an die Männer ausgehändigt. Von Krakau wurde die Weiterreise am 19.6. um 20,08 Uhr ebenfalls mit einem fahrplanmäßigen Eilzug angetreten. Ankunft in Wien Ostbahnhof am

Doc. 10. Wien—Sobibór Transport Report, Part 1 (Yad Vashem)

MOST SECRET.

TO BE KEPT UNDER LOCK AND KEY: NEVER TO BE REMOVED FROM THE OFFICE

message: ZIP/GPD 1956 CC-HH transmitted 15.10.1943

```
DBA de LYPB  1138  BBD SQR Nr. 8  1115   298    DQAA       6890
SS Pol.führer LUBL, SS Brigadeführer GUENTHER. Geheim!
Aus dem Lager SOBIBOR sind circa 700 Juden ausgebrochen. Es
ist anzunehmen, dass dieselben über die Bug-Grenze fliehen
werden. Es wird gebeten, entsprechende Gegenmassnahmen
einzuleiten. SOBIBOR liegt im Distrikt LUBLIN, 5 Km. vom Bug
zwischen CHOLM und WLODAWA.
Von SS Pol.führer LUBLIN.
```

PUBLIC RECORD OFFICE — Ref.: HW 16/38

Doc. 11. Sobibór Revolt—Intercepted German Police Decode 15 October 1943 (National Archives, Kew)

Abschrift!

Beförderungsliste

für Angehörige der SS-Sonderkommandos " Einsatz Reinhard "
auf Befehl des Reichsführers-SS

Es werden vorgeschlagen:

Allgemeine-SS

1.	SS-Hstuf. Pol.Major	Christian	Wirth	SS-Nr.345 464	zum SS-Stubaf.
2.	SS-Ostuf.	Gottlieb	Hering	SS-Nr.--- ---	" SS-Hstuf.
3.	SS-Oscha.	Mariritius	Scha r	SS-Nr.269 394	" SS-Ustuf.
4.	SS-Strm.	Erwin	Fichtner	SS-Nr.206 977	" SS-Uscha.
5.	SS-Oscha.	Willi	Häusler	SS-Nr.187 860	" SS-Hscha.
6.	SS-Uscha.	Franz	Hödl	SS-Nr.302 133	" SS-Scharf.
7.	Pol.Hptmann	Franz	Reichsleitner	" --- ---	" SS-Hstuf.
8.	SS-Mann	Wenzel	Rehwald	SS-Nr.321 745	" SS-Uscha.
9.	SS-Scharf.	Gustav	Wagner	SS-Nr.276 962	" SS-Oscha.
10.	SS-Rttf.	Gustav	Münzberger	SS-Nr.321 758	" SS-Uscha.
11.	SS-Strm.	Karl	Schiffner	SS-Nr.321 225	" SS-Uscha.
12.	SS-Rttf.	Richard	Schuh	SS-Nr. 98 020	" SS-Uscha.
13.	Pol.Oblt. SS-Oscha. und Lagerleiter	Franz	Stangl	SS-Nr.296 569	" SS-Hstuf.

Waffen-SS

1.	SS-Schütze	Hans	Gietzig	zum SS-Rottenf.
2.	SS-Oscha.	Kurt	Franz	zum SS-Ustuf.
3.	SS-Uscha.	Willy	Mätzig	zum SS-Scharf
4.	SS-Hscha.	Johann	Niemann	zum SS-Ustuf.
5.	SS-Hscha.	Jo...	Oberhauser	zum SS-Ustuf.
6.	SS-Hscha.	Gottfried	Schwarz	zum SS-Ustuf.
7.	SS-Oscha.	Lorenz	Hackenholt	zum SS-Hscha.
8.	SS-Oscha.	Fritz	Jirmann	zum SS-Hscha.

Polizei

1.	Pol.Wm.d.R.	Arthur	Dachsel	D-Nr.12003	zum Pol.Owm.d.R.
2.	Pol.Wm.d.R.	Hans	Zänker	" 52	zum Pol.Owm.d.R.
3.	Pol.Rottwm.d.R.	Erich	Dietze	" 12010	zum Pol.Owm.d.R.
4.	Pol.Rottwm.d.R.	Kurt	Vey	" 12012	zum Pol.Owm.d.R.
5.	Pol.Rottwm.d.R.	Willi	Großmann	" 12004	zum Pol.Owm.d.R.
6.	Pol.Rottwm.d.R.	Kurt	Seidel	" 12011	zum Pol.Owm.d.R.

F.d.R.d.A.

SS-Hauptsturmführer

Doc. 12. Einsatz Reinhard—Promotion List (Yad Yashem)

Dr. med. Irmfried Eberl
SS-Untersturmführer
z.Zt. SS-Arbeitslager Sobibor   Sobibor, den 26.4.42.

An die

    Landes-Heil- und Pflegeanstalt Bernburg
    - Verwaltung -
    z.Hd. Fräulein D i t t m a n n

                  B e r n b u r g / S a a l e
                  Postfach 263.

Betrifft: Medikamentenbestellung.

    Sehr geehrtes Fräulein D i t t m a n n !

    In der Anlage übersende ich Ihnen zwei Aufstellungen von Medikamenten und Instrumenten, die ich Sie zu besorgen bitte. Diese Dinge sind für das Lager hier und für mein Lager bestimmt und werden dringenst benötigt. Das für Sobibor bestimmte Paket bitte ich an Herrn Schütt, SS-Oberscharführer, SS-Arbeitslager Sobibor zu schicken; das zweite Paket an mich zu adressieren. Beide Pakete können über Berlin mittels Kurier an uns geschickt werden. Den Paketen bitte ich auch eine Rechnung beizulegen, damit die Kosten verrechnet werden können.

                  H e i l   H i t l e r !

2 Anlagen

Doc. 13. Irmfried Eberl letter from Sobibór, page 1 (Hessisches Hauptarchiv, Wiesbaden, Germany)

Programm

zum Besuch des RF-SS am 18. und 19. Juli 1942

Sonnabend, den 18.7.42:

12.00 bis 14.30 Uhr	Mittagessen und Kaffee im Haus des SS- und Polizeiführers,
	anschließend Fahrt über Parkstrasse, Sachsenstrasse, Warschauerstrasse, Mannschaftshaus,
15.00 bis 17.00 Uhr	Besichtigung des SS-Mannschaftshauses, Rückfahrt Warschauerstrasse, Distriktstrasse zur Julius-Schreck-Kaserne
17.00 bis 18.00 Uhr	Besichtigung der volkspolitischen Dienststellen beim SS- und Polizeiführer
18.00 bis 19.00 Uhr	Besuch der Chopinstrasse 27 und SS-Standortverwaltung
19.30 bis 20.30 Uhr	Abendessen beim SS- und Polizeiführer mit anschließenden Besprechungen

Sonntag, den 19.7.42:

7.30 Uhr	Frühstück im Haus des SS- und Polizeiführers
8.30 Uhr	Abfahrt nach Trawniki
9.00 Uhr	Ankunft und 30 Min. Besichtigung des Lagers Trawniki
10.15 Uhr	Ankunft in Chelm, 1 Std. Besichtigung der 2.SS-R-Reiter-Schwadron mit kleinem Imbiss
11.30 Uhr	Abfahrt vom Bahnhof Chelm nach Sobibor, Fahrt und Besichtigung 1 Std. 45 Min.
13.15 Uhr	Ankunft in Chelm
13.30 bis 14.15 Uhr	Mittagessen bei der 2.SS-Reiter-Schwadron
14.15 bis 15.00 Uhr	Besichtigung des Flüchtlingslagers in Chelm
15.00 Uhr	Abfahrt nach Wysokie
16.15 Uhr	Ankunft in Wysokie
17.15 Uhr	Abfahrt nach Lublin
18.30 Uhr	Ankunft in Lublin, Besichtigung des KGL und der Bekleidungswerke, 1 Std.
20.00 Uhr	Abendessen im Haus des SS- und Polizeiführers.

Gäste:
Reichsführer-SS
SS-Obergruppenführer Pohl
SS-Obergruppenführer Krüger
SS-Oberführer Kassel
SS-Standartenführer Prof. Dr. Wüst
SS-Hauptsturmführer Grothmann
SS-Hauptsturmführer Schmittker
Biermeier

Doc. 14. Heinrich Himmler's Program of Visits—Trawniki and Sobibór July 1942 (Holocaust Historical Society)

Der Beauftragte des RF# f.d.Errichtung der
#- und Polizeistützpunkte im neuen Ostraum.
- Abwicklungsstelle -

Abtlg. IIb/456/42.   Lublin, den 31. Juli 1942.

Betr.: Auflösung des Arbeitsstabes des Beauftragten des RF# f.d.
       Errichtung der #- und Polizeistützpunkte im neuen Ostraum.
Bezug: Erlaß des RF#uChdDtPol.i.RMdI. vom 29.6.42 - O VuR Org. 6 -
       738/42.

An
Abteilung IVb,
Stabskompanie,
Vorläufige Polizei-Kraftfahrzeuginstandsetzungswerkstätten Osten
- Nachschubstelle Lublin -
Polizei-Regiment Lublin,
Ausbildungslager Trawniki,
#- und Polizeiführer im Distrikt Lublin
- #-Mannschaftshaus -
in Lublin.

Gemäß Ziffer 3 des o.a. Bezugserlasses werden die nachstehend auf-
geführten Revier-Offiziere, Meister und Wachtmeister (SB.) d. Sch.
mit Wirkung vom 1.8.1942 dem Polizei-Regiment Lublin zugeteilt und
diesem wirtschaftlich und disziplinell unterstellt:

1.	Rev.Ltn.d.Sch.	Knothe, Georg	P.V. Litzmannstadt	
2.	Mstr.d.Sch.	Schröder, Erwin	" Chemnitz	
3.	Rev.Obw.d.R.	Kögler, Fritz	" Chemnitz	#-u.Pol.Führer
4.	" " "	Kreißig, Erich	" Chemnitz	
5.	" "	Lange, Werner	" Dresden	
6.	" "	Preuninger, Arth.	" Leipzig	
7.	Obw. " "	Schleitt, Walter	" Leipzig	#-u.Pol.Führer
8.	Rev.Obw." "	Natke, Willy	" Leipzig	#-u.Pol.Führer
9.	Obw.d.Sch.	Hohl, Valentin	" Frankfurt/M.	
10.	Mstr.d.Sch.	Drechsel, Albert	" Chemnitz	Trawniki
11.	Wm. d.R.	Heß, Herbert	" Liegnitz	"
12.	" "	Lachmann, Erich	" "	"
13.	" "	Metschke, Arth.	" Görlitz	"
14.	" "	Stiebert, Erwin	" Grünberg	"
15.	Rev.Obw.d.R.	Franz, Otto	" Liegnitz	"
16.	Wm. "	Heidrich, Walter	" Löwenberg	"
17.	Obw. "	Heinze, Rudolf	" Chemnitz	"
18.	Mstr.d.Sch.	Grundmann, Kurt	" Dresden	
19.	Rev.Obw.d.R.	Spallek, Erich	" Berlin	
20.	" " "	Grunwald, Alfred	" Görlitz	
21.	Obw. "	Gantke, Herbert	" Bunzlau	
22.	Rev.Obw. "	Thiel, Willi	" Hirschberg	
23.	Obw. "	Gehrich, Otto	" Glogau	
24.	Rev.Obw. "	Gollik, Gerhard	" Breslau	#-u.Pol.Führer

- 2 -

Doc. 15. Lachmann 436 (Yad Vashem)

INFORMATIEBUREAU VAN
HET NEDERLANDSCHE ROODE KRUIS

GEBOUW PANDER, AFD. J. 'S-GRAVENHAGE, -7 JAN 1949
DOSSIER: 123068 VLAMINGSTRAAT 2
J.M.G./Adm./LA 6347

VERKLARING

De Directeur van het Informatiebureau van het Nederlandsche Roode Kruis verklaart hierbij, dat blijkens de archieven van het aan hoofde genoemde Bureau

Abraham Nol,

geboren 2-11-'19 te Uitgeest,

laatste adres: Linnaeuskade 14 te Amsterdam

op 13-5-'43 in Westerbork kwam en op 18-5-'43 met bestemming Sobibor (Polen) van Westerbork uit werd gedeporteerd.

In aanmerking genomen, dat uit de verklaringen, afgelegd door drie personen, te weten:

Sara Engel-Wijnberg
Chaim Engel } woonachtig te Zwolle, Veemarkt 23

en

Ursula Stern, woonachtig te Utrecht, van Alphenstraat 5,

die van de ruim 33.000 uit Nederland naar Sobibor gedeporteerde personen het langdurig verblijf in dit kamp overleefden, blijkt, dat vrijwel alle personen die naar Sobibor werden gevoerd, onmiddellijk na aankomst door gas werden verstikt en daarna gecremeerd;
voorts, dat van of omtrent gezochte sedert de deportatie niets naders werd vernomen;
kan worden vastgesteld, dat
Abraham Nol voornoemd, op of omstreeks
21-5-'43 aan de gevolgen van gasverstikking is overleden.

De Directeur,

J. van de Vosse.

Doc. 16. Abraham Nol—Dutch Red Cross Notification (Holocaust Historical Society)

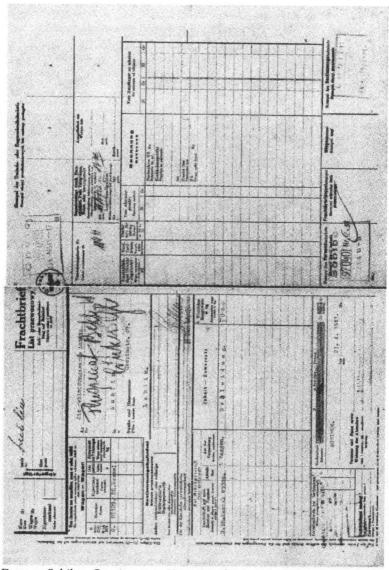

Doc. 17. Sobibor Consignment Note 1943 (Holocaust Historical Society)

Appendix 1

Alphabetical List of Ukrainian Guards—Sobibór

Name	Additional Information
ANTONOV, Wasil	
BAIDIN, Ilya	
BARANDTIMOV, Sabit	
BATARONOV, Aglam	
BELYI, Michail	
BIALOWAS, Jan	
BIELAKOW, B	Sentenced and executed in the USSR
BIELINSKI	From Lvov
BILIK, Ivan	
BODESSA, Iwan	Bauer, in his post-war investigations, referred to Bodessa as Paetesser, but corrected himself
BOGUNOV, Dimitrij	
BRANDECKI, Felix	
BUSINNIJ, Prokofi	
CHABIBULIN, Achmed	
CHROMENKO, Chariton	
DABIZJA	Looked after the stable, where the Commandant's horses were kept.
DALKE, Henrich	*Volksdeutscher*
DANILCHENKO, Ignat	Sentenced and imprisoned in the USSR
DEMJANJUK, Ivan	Tried in Israel for War Crimes committed in the Treblinka death camp. Accused of being Ivan the Terrible. Found guilty then released following an appeal. Re-tried in Bonn, Germany for War Crimes committed in Sobibór. Sentenced in Germany to five years imprisonment. He died pending an appeal on March 17, 2012.
DEPTYAREV, Vasili	
DIMIDA, Konstantinl	
DOMERATZKI, Jakob	

DUDA, Michal	
DZIRKAL, Karl	*Oberwachtmeister*
ENGELHARDT, Jakub	A *Volksdeutsche*. In charge of a 12 man unit which protected the camp's construction site in the early phase of the camps existence
FEDORENKO, Ivan	
FLUNT, Miron	
FROLOV, Gennardi	
GEUSLER	An interpreter
GONCHARENKO, Anatoli	
GONCHARENKO, Nikolai	
GONCHAROW, Efim	
GORDIENNKO, Nikolai	
GORLOV, Fedor	
HETMANIEC, Wasil	Dismantling Commando. Killed *SS*-NCO Erich Floss in Zawadowka, near Chelm on October 22, 1943
HOTOROWICZ, Jan	
INDYUKOV, Ivan	
ISAENKO, Aleksei	
IVCHENKO, Ivan	Served as a cook
IWASHENKO, Piotr	
JARYNIUK, Ivan	
JAWOROW, Fiodor	Highly respected *Wachmann*. Served at Belzec, Sobibór and Treblinka
JECHAI, Iosof	
JEFIMOV, Wasili	
JERMOLDAYEV, Ivan	
JUDIN, Nikolai	
KABRIOV, Nurgali	
KAISER, Aleksy	*Volksdeutscher*—Served in Italy. Photographed with Hödl and Gomerski
KAKORACH, Ivan	
KARAKASZ, Iwan	Deserted from Sobibór after only 28 days service there. He testified about his time in the death camp
KARAS, Pavel	
KARIMOV, Fetich	
KARPENKO, Alexander	
KASZEWACKI	Came from Kiev. Often visited the kitchen, and spoke to Hershel Cukierman. He deserted from Sobibór.
KISLEW, Viktor	Deserted from the camp on December 25, 1942, along with 2 Jewish men and one Jewish woman. Killed in a shoot-out with 3 Polish policemen in the village of Kozia Gorka

KLATT, Ivan	*Volksdeutscher*—Killed in the revolt on October 14, 1943.
KOSCHEKUK, Piotr	
KOSCHEMYKIN, Jakov	
KOSZEWADZKI, Volodia	Deserted from Sobibór
KOSTENKO, Emil	Operated the Gas Chamber in *Lager III*
KOZACZUK, Piotr	
KOZLOWSKI, Iwan	
KRAWCHENKO, Filip	
KRUPKA	
KRUPINEWICH, Mikolaii	
KUDIN, Pavel	
KURAKOV, Leonid	
KUSEVANOV, Michail	
LIBODENKO	Went to Italy, according to Hödl
LORENZ, Friderich	*Volksdeutscher—Oberwachmann*
LYACHOV, Gregorli	
LYACHOV, Ivan	
MALINOWSKI	
MAKARENKO, Pawel	
MARTYNOW, Nikolai	
MARTYNOW, Terentij	
MASHENKO, Andrei	
MATWIEJENKOW, M.	Sentenced and executed in the USSR
MAUER	*Volksdeutscher*
MEDVEDEV, Nikolai	
MIKOLAYENKO, Semion	
MORDWINICHEV, Pavel	
NABIYEW, Bari	
NAGORNYI, Andrej	
NIJKO, Wasily	
NIKOFOROW, Ivan	Sentenced and executed in the USSR
OLEXENKO, Anatoli	
PANSHUK, Ivan	
PANKOW, Anatoli	
PANKOW, Vassily	
PAULENKO	Mentioned in the *KdO* Report October 12, 1943
PAWLI, Nikolai	Also served at Bełżec
PICHEROV, Dimitrii	
PODIENKO, W.	Sentenced and executed in the USSR
RAZGONAYEV, Mikhail	
RESCHETNIKOV, Michail	
REZERCHY, Igor	
RIMKUS, Tadas	*Volksdeutscher—Oberwachmann*

ROIL	Mentioned in post-war investigations by Erich Bauer
ROKTSUK	
RUDENKO, Piotr	
RYABEKA, Fyodor Yakolev	Transferred from Treblinka Death Camp to Sobibór in March 1943
RYSCHKOV, Vasily	
SABIROV, Chares	
SBESNIKOV, Petro	
SCHEVCHENKO, Dimitrii	
SCHIRPEV, Kamil	
SCHRIBER, Klaus	*Volksdeutscher*—Killed in the revolt on October 14, 1943
SCHULTZ, Emanuel	Also served in Treblinka. Aka Emanuel Szulc
SELEZNEV, Mikolaj	
SENJONOW	Mentioned in the *KdO* Report October 12, 1943
SERGIENKO, Grigorij	
SERIK, Dimitrij	
SHICHAVIN, Pavel	
SHUKOW, Ivan	
SIRENKO, Maxim	
SIROTENKO, Vladmir	
SOKOREV, Semion	
SOKUR, Kuzma	
SZILPNY, Heinrich	*Volksdeutscher*
TARASKOV	Recalled by Dov Freiburg in his memoirs
TASS	
TICHONOWSKI, Fedor	Sentenced and executed in the USSR
TISCHENKO, Ivan	
USTINNOKOV, Ivan	
VAKUTENKO, Ivan	
VASKIN, Kuzma	
VOLYNIETS, Efim	
WASEM, Yakob	*Gruppenwachmann*
WEDENKO, Fiodor	
YASKO, Alexsander	
ZABERTNEV, Konstantin	
ZAJCEW, J	Sentenced and executed in the USSR
ZISCHER, Emil	*Volksdeutscher*. Deserted from the camp on December 25, 1942, along with 2 Jewish men and one Jewish woman. Killed in a shoot-out with 3 Polish policemen in the village of Kozia Gorka.

Appendix 2

Glossary of Nazi Terms

Abteilung: A branch, section or sub-section of a main department or office (*Hauptamt, Amstgruppe* or *Amt*, q.v) Also a military or para-military unit of up to battalion strength, i.e. approximately 700 men.

Allgemeine-SS: General body of the SS consisting of full-time, part-time and inactive or honorary members, as distinct from the *Waffen-SS* (see entry for *Waffen-SS*).

Amt: A directorate or an office of a ministry.

Amstgruppe: A branch of a *Hauptamt*.

Anschluss: Annexation of Austria to the German Reich in March 1938.

Arbeitslager: Labor/Work Camp.

Aussenstelle/Aussendientstelle: Out-station of an office, agency or ministry.

Gau: One of 42 main territorial divisions of the Nazi Party.

Gauleiter: The highest ranking Party Official in a *Gau*, responsible for all political and economic activity, mobilization of labor and civil defense.

Geheime Staatspolizei (Gestapo): Secret State Police which became *Amt* IV of the RSHA in September 1939. Headed by *SS-Obergruppenführer* Heinrich Müller.

Generalgouvernement: German-occupied Poland administered by Hans Frank from his headquarters in Krakau.

Hauptamt: A main or central office.

Höhere SS- und Polizeiführer: Higher SS and Police Leader. Himmler's personal representative in each Military Region. Also established in the occupied territories. Nominally the commander of all SS and Police units in his area, as well as acting as a liaison officer with the military and senior regional authorities.

Judenrat: Jewish Councils established by the Nazis for Jewish self-administration, in all its various facets; food, housing, labor allocation, welfare, police, economic, and social etc.

Kapo: A prisoner—functionary in the Nazi camps who was assigned by the SS camp staff to supervise labor brigades, maintain discipline, or fulfil administrative tasks.

Kommando: A brigade, squad or detail.

Kommissariat: A Regional HQ of the Police; also a political administration in the occupied eastern territories (e.g. *Reichskommissariat* Ukraine).

Kreishauptmann: The principal district official in the *Generalgouvernement* and occupied territories.

Kriminalpolizei (Kripo): Criminal Police, the plainclothes detective squads which together with the *Gestapo* formed *the Sicherheitspolizei*. In 1939 the *Kripo* became *Amt V* of the *Reichssicherheitshauptamt (RSHA)*. Headed by *Reichskriminaldirektor* Arthur Nebe.

Lagerälteste: Camp Elder, the senior prisoner in a Nazi camp.

Leitstelle: A Regional HQ of the *Gestapo* or *Kripo* established at the HQ of a Military District or capital of a county.

Oberkapo: Senior *Kapo* in a Nazi camp.

Oberzugführer: Senior platoon leader; in charge of the platoon leaders.

Ordnungspolizei (Orpo): Order Police. The regular uniformed police, comprising the *Schutzpolizei (Schupo)*, *Gendarmerie* (rural constabulary), and *Feuerschutzpolizei* (Fire Fighting Police), together with certain technical and auxiliary services.

Organisation Todt: A para-military government organization used mainly for the construction of strategic highways and military installations. Named after Fritz Todt, Reichsminister for Armaments and Ammunition, who died on February 8, 1942, when his aircraft crashed.

Reichsgau: One of eleven regions formed from territories annexed to the Reich.

Reichskanzlei: Chancellery of the Reich directed by Hans Lammers.

Referat: A sub-section within a *Gruppe*.

Referent: The official in charge of a *Referat*.

Reichsführer-SS: Reich Leader of the *SS*. Heinrich Himmler's SS-title from June 1936.

Reichskriminalpolizeiamt (RKPA): Berlin HQ of the *Kriminalpolizei (Kripo)* which in September 1939 became *Amt V* of the *Reichssicherheitshauptamt (RSHA)*.

Reichssicherheitshauptamt (RSHA): Reich Security Main Office, formed in September 1939 and combined the *Sicherheitspolizei* and the *Sicherheitsdienst (SD)*. It was both an *SS-Hauptamt* and a branch of the Reich Ministry of the Interior.

Schutzpolizei (Schupo): Protection Police. The regular uniformed municipal constabulary forming the bulk of the *Ordnungspolizei*.

Sicherheitsdienst (SD): Security Service. The intelligence branch of the *SS* headed by Reinhard Heydrich.

Sicherheitspolizei (Sipo): Security Police, comprising the *Kripo* and *Gestapo*, headed by Reinhard Heydrich.

Sonderkommando: A special unit of the *SS* employed for police and political tasks in occupied territories. Also used to denote the special brigades of prisoners in the Auschwitz—Birkenau concentration camps who dealt with the intended victims and the corpses.

SS-Leibstandarte 'Adolf Hitler': Hitler's bodyguard regiment. The oldest of the *SS*-militarized formations, formed in 1933. Commanded by Joseph 'Sepp' Dietrich.

SS- und Polizeiführer: *SS* and Police Leader. In command of a District in the eastern occupied territories, subordinate to a *Höhere SS- und Polizeiführer*.

Standarte: *SS* or *SA* formation equivalent to a regiment, i.e. approximately 3,000 men.

Sturmabteilung (SA): Storm Detachment, also called the 'Brown Shirts' after their uniform. The original Nazi para-military organization founded in 1921.

Sturmbann: An *SA* or *SS* unit, equivalent to a battalion, i.e. 750-1,000 men.

SS-Totenkopfverbände: *SS*-Death's Head units which guarded the concentration camps. In 1939 they formed the nucleus of the *SS-Totenkopf* Division, one of the first field formations of the *Waffen-SS*.

SS-Verfügungstruppen: The pre-war militarized formations of the *SS*, renamed the *Waffen-SS* in 1939.

Volksdeutsche: Ethnic Germans.

Vorarbeiter: Foreman of a team of workers.

Waffen-SS: Fully militarized SS formations. Initially composed of the *SS-Verfügungstruppen* and the *SS-Totenkopf* units. During the Second World War it comprised of 40 Divisions, both German and non-German units.

Wehrkreis: Military Region, usually indicated on maps by a Roman numeral.

Wehrmacht: The German Armed Forces, i.e. the army, air force and navy.

Wirtschafts- und Verwaltungshauptamt (WVHA): Administration and Economic Main Office of the *SS*, formed from the *SS-Hauptamt Haushalt und Bauten* in 1940. Headed by Oswald

Pohl, the *WVHA* supervised the *SS* economic enterprises and administered the concentration camps.

Zugführer: Military term for platoon leader.

Appendix 3

Table of Equivalent Ranks

SS-Reichsführer	Reichs Leader
SS-Oberstgruppenführer	General
SS-Obergruppenführer	Lieutenant-General
SS-Gruppenführer	Major-General
SS-Brigadeführer	Brigader-General
SS-Oberführer	Senior-Colonel
SS-Standartenführer	Colonel
SS-Obersturmbannführer	Lieutenant-Colonel
SS-Sturmbannführer	Major
SS-Hauptsturmführer	Captain
SS-Obersturmführer	First-Lieutenant
SS-Untersturmführer	Second-Lieutenant
SS-Sturmscharführer	Sergeant-Major
SS-Hauptscharführer	Master-Sergeant
SS-Oberscharführer	Sergeant First Class
SS-Scharführer	Staff Sergeant
SS-Unterscharführer	Sergeant
SS-Rottenführer	Corporal
SS-Sturmmann	Acting Corporal
SS-Oberschütze	Private First Class
SS-Schütze	Private

Appendix 4

Transports from Holland

This chapter is from dedicated to Lea de Jongh, who was born on February 16, 1919 in Amsterdam, and who perished in Sobibór:

Lea de Jongh was born on February 16, 1919 in Amsterdam. She worked as a nurse in the Central Jewish Lunatic Asylum in Apeldorn Bos. She was murdered in Sobibór on July 16, 1943. Although already mentioned in the Jewish Roll of Remembrance, this Appendix offers the opportunity to provide more background details on the tragic fate of Dutch Jews and their often deadly connection to Sobibór.

She was just one of the countless Dutch victims who lost their lives in Sobibór. The photograph is courtesy of Benny Yacobi, and I thank him very much.

During 1939, the Dutch authorities established a camp in Westerbork, a town in the north-eastern part of Holland, to house German Jews fleeing from the Nazi regime in Germany. Another camp was established in Vught, located in the south of the country. This camp was for Jewish citizens.

In early January 1942, Jewish citizens were expelled from the provinces and were concentrated mainly in Amsterdam. From April 1943, onwards, the Jews were only allowed to live in the Amsterdam Jewish Quarter, in the camp at Westerbork, or in the camp at Vught.

The place where Jews were gathered in Amsterdam, and then transported to Westerbork Camp, was the *Hollandsche Schouwburg* (Dutch Theatre), which was located in the Jewish Quarter in Amsterdam. Westerbork eventually became the main transit camp in the Netherlands.

The commandants of Westerbork were; Erich Deppner, succeeded by Josef Dichner, the final commandant was *SS-Obersturmführer* Albert Gemmeker. Gemmeker was born on September 27, 1907, in Düsseldorf. He was appointed to the post on October 12, 1942, which he held until 1944. He was the commandant responsible for the transports that went to Sobibór.

A total of nineteen transports left Westerbork Camp in Holland for Sobibór. Commencing on March 2, 1943; the final one departed on July 20, 1943. These transports carried 34,313 Jews in a mixture of passenger cars and freight wagons.

One of the nineteen transports left on Tuesday 1, June 1943. This was witnessed and recorded by Philip Mechanicus in his diary. Philip lost his life in Auschwitz on October 12, 1944. His detailed and descriptive account of the transport, which Jules Schelvis and his wife Rachel were on, deserves to be included in this chapter:

Tuesday June 1. The transports are as loathsome as ever. The wagons used were originally intended for carrying horses. The deportees no longer lie on the straw, but on the bare floor in the midst of their food supplies and small baggage, and this applies even to the invalids who only last week got a mattress.

They are assembled at the hut exits at about seven o'clock by OD men, the Camp Security Police, and are taken to the trains in lines of three, to the Boulevard des Miseres in the middle of the camp. The train is like a long mangy snake, dividing the camp in two and made up filthy old wagons. The Boulevard is a desolate spot, barred by OD men to keep away interested members of the public. The exiles have a bag of bread which is tied to their shoulder with a tape and dangles over their hips, and a rolled up blanket fastened to the other shoulder with string and hanging down their backs.

Shabby emigrants who own nothing more than what they have on and what is hanging from them. Quiet men with tense faces and women bursting into frequent sobs. Elderly folk, hobbling along, stumbling over the poor road surface under their load and sometimes going through pools of muddy water. Invalids on stretchers carried by OD men.

On the platform the Commandant with his retinue, the 'Green Police,' Dr Spanier, the Medical Superintendent, in a plain grey civilian suit, bareheaded and very dark, with his retinue, Kurt Schlesinger, the head of the Registration Department, in riding breeches and jackboots, a nasty face and straw-coloured hair with a flat cap on it. Alongside the train doctors holding themselves in readiness in case the invalids need assistance.

The deportees approaching the train in batches are surrounded by OD men standing there in readiness (now NB men also, i.e. men from the Emergency Squad), to prevent any escapes. They are counted off a list brought from the hut and go straight into the train. Any who dawdle or hesitate are assisted. They are driven into the train, or pushed, or struck, or pummelled or persuaded with a boot, and kicked on board, both by the 'Green Police' who are escorting the train and by OD men.

Noise and nervous outbursts are not allowed, but they do occur. Short work is made of such behaviour—a few clips suffice. The OD men base their uncouth behaviour on that of their German colleagues who are lavish in the use of their fists and inflict quick, hard punishment with their boots. The Jews in the camp refer to them as the Jewish *SS*. They are hated like the plague and people would gladly flay many of them alive if they dared.

Men and women, old and young, sick and healthy, together with children and babies, are all packed together into the same wagon. Healthy men and women are put in amongst others who suffer from complaints associated with old age and are in need of constant care, men and women who have lost control over certain primary physical functions, cripples, the old, the blind, folk with stomach disorders, imbeciles, lunatics. They all go on the bare floor, in amongst the baggage and on it, crammed tightly together. There is a barrel, just one barrel for all these people, in the corner of the wagon where they can relieve themselves publicly. One small barrel not large enough for so many people. With a bag of sand next to it, from which each person can pick up a handful to cover the excrement. In another corner there is a can of water with a tap for those who want to quench their thirst.

When the wagons are full and the prescribed quota of deportees has been delivered, they are closed up. The Commandant gives the signal for departure—with a wave of his hand. The whistle shrills, usually at about eleven o'clock, and the sound goes right through everyone in the camp, to the very core of their being.

So the mangy looking-snake crawls away with its full load. Schlesinger and his retinue jump up on the footboard and ride along for a little bit for the sake of convenience, otherwise they would have to walk back. That would wear out their soles. The Commandant saunters contentedly away. Dr Spanier, his hands behind his back and his head bent forward in worried concentration, walks back to his consulting room.[514]

Jules Schelvis recounts what happened to this transport on its arrival at the Sobibór death camp on June 4, 1943—thus providing the reader with a description of both the start of the journey East, and its tragic conclusion for most of the Jewish deportees:

---

[514] Deborah Slier and Ian Shine, *Hidden Letters*, Star Bright Books, New York 2008, pp. 146-147.

The Jews of the *Bahnhofskommando* were very heavy-handed getting us off the train onto the platform. They let on they were Jewish by speaking Yiddish, the language of the Eastern European Jews. The SS men standing behind them were shouting, '*Schneller, schneller*' (Faster, faster) and lashed out at people once they were lined up on the platform. Yet the first impression of the camp itself aroused no suspicion, because the barracks looked rather like little Tyrolean cottages, with their curtains and geraniums on the window sills.

But this was no time to dawdle. We made our way outside as quickly as possible. Rachel and I, and the rest of our family, fortunately had no difficulty in swiftly making our way onto the platform, which had been built up of sand and earth. Behind us we heard the agonized cries of those who could not get up quickly enough, as their legs had stiffened as a result of sitting in an awkward position for too long, severely affecting their circulation. But no one cared. One of the first things that occurred to me was how lucky we were to be all together, and that the secret of our destination would now finally be revealed. The events so far did not hold out much promise though, and we understood that this was only the beginning.

Jules Schelvis explained what happened next:

It was obvious we had arrived at our final destination: a place to work, as they had told us in Holland. A place where the many who had gone before us should now also be working. Our presence must be of quite some importance; why else would the Germans have bothered to bring us all the way here, travelling for three days and nights, covering a distance of two thousand kilometres? Yet the Germans were using whips, lashing out at us and driving us on from behind. My father-in-law, walking beside me, was struck for no reason. He shrank back in pain only for a moment, not wanting anyone to see. Rachel and I firmly gripped each other's hand, desperate not to get separated in this hellish situation. We were driven along a path lined with barbed wire towards some large barracks and dared not look round to see what was happening behind us.

We wondered what had happened to the baby in our wagon, and to the people unable to walk: and what about the sick and the handicapped? But we were given no time to dwell on these things, and, besides, we were too preoccupied with ourselves. 'What shall I do with my gold watch?' Rachel said. 'They will take it from me in a minute.' I replied, 'Bury it, because it could be worth a lot of money later.' As she was walking, she noticed a little hole in the sand, and quickly threw the watch down, using her foot to cover it up. 'Remember,' she said, 'where I have buried it. We can try digging it up later, when we have a little more time.'

Like cattle, we were herded through a shed that had doors on either side, both wide open. We were ordered to throw down all our luggage and keep moving. Our bread and backpacks, with our name, date of birth and the word 'Holland' written on them, ended up on top of the huge piles, as did my guitar, which I had naively brought and carefully guarded all the way. Quickly glancing around, I saw how it ended up underneath more luggage. It dawned on me then that there was worse to come. Robbed of everything we had once spent so much care and time in acquiring, we left the shed through the door opposite.

I was so taken aback and distracted by having had all our possessions taken from us, that although I had seen an *SS* man at some point, I never noticed, until it was too late, that the women had been sent in a different direction. Suddenly Rachel was no longer walking beside me. It happened so quickly that I had not been able to kiss her or call out to her. Trying to look around to see if I could spot her somewhere, an *SS* man snapped at me to look straight ahead and to keep my '*Maul* (gob) shut.'

Rachel Schelvis had been separated with the women and sent to the gas chambers, Jules recalled what happened next:

Along with the men around me, I was driven on at a slightly slower pace to a point just past an opening in a fence, where yet another *SS* man was posted. He looked the younger men up and down fleetingly, seeming to have no interest in the older ones. With a quick nudge of his whip, he motioned some of them to line up separately by the edge of the field. Directly in front of me, my brother-in-law Ab was directed to join this growing group. My father-in-law, David, and Herman, my thirteen-year old brother-in-law, were completely ignored. My father-in-law was too old, Herman too young. Glancing at me for a moment, he let me pass as well. He needed to select only eighty healthy-looking men.

> Those who had not been selected had to move along into the field and sit down. That Friday, 4 June 1943, the Sobibór sun beat down on our heads. It was midday and very hot already. There we were, defenceless, powerless, exhausted, at the mercy of the Germans, and completely isolated from the rest of the world. No one could help us out here. The SS held us captive and were free to do as they pleased.
>
> The rows of men out on the field were getting bigger as those from the other wagons joined us. While we were waiting, I had a little time to collect my thoughts. Our harsh treatment seemed to be in conflict with the image of the Tryolean cottage-like barracks with their bright little curtains and geraniums on the windowsills. They had had such a friendly and calming effect on me after all the tensions of the proceeding days. The camp had seemed devoid of any other people, apart from the Germans and the Jews who had welcomed us on the platform.
>
> As I sat there, I noticed a few Dutch prisoners had approached from the other side of the barbed wire fence and were trying to make contact with us. I recognized Moos van Kleef, the owner of the fish shop on the corner of the Weesperstraat. My arms gestured a question: how are things here, what can we expect? To assuage us, he yelled out to us that it was alright here, no reason to be concerned. I heard him say, 'We have a job here, everything is new or has to be built.' My mind was ticking over faster. I thought, this must be the new camp for which they will require some sort of order service police. That must be why they need those young men. My intuition told me I would want to be a part of that group. Not so much for the order service, but to be with my brother-in-law, whom I could still see in the distance.

Jules Schelvis then made a life-saving decision:

> The field had become quite crowded, and I had already come to terms with the idea of working in the camp when I saw the same SS man approaching. With his hands behind his back he ambled past the rows of men quite smugly, seeming quite pleased with himself. As he came closer, I suddenly remembered the order service. He had almost passed when I jumped up and put up my hand. I asked permission to ask him a question. Glancing back at me quite affably, he hesitated briefly and then nodded his approval. I requested in my best German, to join the other group.

He stared into the distance, tapping his whip against his boot a few times. He turned around and asked: 'How old are you?' I replied, '*Twenty-two, Herr Offizier.*' 'Healthy?' '*Jawohl, Herr Offizier*'—I had no idea what his rank was. 'Can you speak German?' '*Jawohl Herr Offizier.*'

Not altogether disinterested, he searched me with his eyes for a moment, apparently lost in thought. Then, nodding his head in the direction of the group, he said, '*Na Los.*' I quickly ran towards it. The young men, relieved at finally being able to release some of the tension built up over the past few days, were chatting to an almost amiable SS man there. To my joy, my best friend Leo de Vries was also among them. The German looked surprised when I joined them, because he believed the eighty-strong group to be complete. A little incredulously he asked, 'They sent you here as well? So now we have eighty-one, one too many, because to my knowledge there should only be eighty.'

After standing around and exchanging thoughts for a while, we were cut off abruptly by the SS man, who suddenly in quite a different tone of voice, told us to shut up. He continued: 'My colleague has selected you to work at another camp not far from here. You will return to Sobibór every evening so you can meet and enjoy yourselves with your family and friends.' Pointing towards the field, he carried on: 'They are going to have a bath now. This is why the men have been separated from the women, because they obviously cannot bathe together. All the others who arrived today will stay here.' As he spoke, I also saw the SS man addressing the men out on the field, though I could not quite hear his exact words. Obviously they were being told to undress, because I saw them starting to take off their clothes.

By the time 'our' SS man had lined us up in rows of five, all those out on the field had already removed their shoes and vests. Urged on by his loud *Eins-zwo-drei-vier* cadence, he tried to get us to march smartly and in step towards the camp exit. He could not imagine how miserable we were after being scrunched up for days inside the cattle wagons.

On our way to the train I must have passed the spot where Rachel had buried her watch. I could not remember it. But I thought I might remember again in a few hours' time, when on my return, I would be headed in the same direction as when we arrived.

Two wagons and an engine stood ready for departure. All traces of turmoil had been erased from the platform, as though it had never happened. The train arrived in Trawniki on the very same day, 4 June 1943. The group had to walk the remaining five kilometres from there to Dorohucza.[515]

Ilana Safran testified:

> At Vught there were many Jewish families and many children. Later we were transferred to Westerbork, the place where Dutch Jews were concentrated and we remained there for one week. In April 1943, we left for Poland. The journey to Poland was dreadful, the prisoners from Western countries believed they were going to Labor Camps.
>
> When we reached Sobibór, a selection took place—young girls were placed on one side, the others including children went to the gas chambers. We were given postcards, 'Write to your families, that you have arrived safely.' I wrote a card to some Dutch friends, it reached its destination and I found it after the war.[516]

Dov Freiberg described the arrival of a transport that was a hospital, complete with doctors, nurses and patients:

> I remember the arrival of a hospital from Holland. The patients were carried on stretchers, and the whole hospital team accompanied them. A table was put on the square, and a doctor, perhaps the director of the hospital was sitting there. Doctors and nurses went around, checked the patients, gave injections, served water and pills.
>
> The doctor was busy writing and giving some notes to the nurses. There was an impression that the whole area had turned into a hospital. After a few hours there were no more patients or hospital personnel.[517]

Selma Wijnberg arrived in Sobibór on April 9, 1943, from Westerbork. She described the event:

---

[515] J. Schelvis, *Sobibór*, Berg-Oxford, New York, 2007, pp. 76-78.
[516] Miriam Novitch, *Sobibór*, Holocaust Library, New York, 1980, p. 87.
[517] Y. Arad, *Belzec, Sobibór, Treblinka*, Indiana University Press, Bloomington and Indianapolis, 1987, p. 149.

The men had been separated from the women, 30 young women and 70 men were selected to work in *Lager II*. The others from the transport, in groups of 500 or 600, were led into *Lager II*, where *Oberscharführer* Michel said they needed to be deloused before being sent on to Ukraine.

The women had to undress in a shed, and the men out in the open. Not knowing what to expect, they were taken with their children to the gas chambers in *Lager III*. That same evening Frenzel ordered me to dance, while someone played the accordion. I had not realized that Sobibór was a camp where people were gassed.[518]

Alex Cohen was transported from Westerbork to Sobibór on March 17, 1943. He was one of the lucky ones who survived the war. He recalled his arrival:

> We arrived close to midnight on the Friday. It was obviously dark. The first we heard was all the shouting by the *Moffen*—a derogatory Dutch term for the Germans. We had to go along a path and stop by a reed fence. The women and children had to move on and disappeared through a gate.
>
> We could hear the carts, the sick people were being thrown into; and a lot of crying and screaming. The men were still lined up in front of the fence and, once the train was empty, a German asked whether there were any doctors or nurses among us.
>
> They had to step forward. I considered pretending to be a medic, but decided against it. About ten people stepped forward. Then he asked for workers up to 35 years of age. As there were too few of these, he increased the age limit to 40. I joined the queue, and as we were standing there, he asked us what our trades was. I told him I was a metal worker and was made to stand apart from the rest along with a few others. We had to leave our luggage and get back onto the same train on which we had only just arrived. About 35 to 40, of us, as well as the doctors and medics were sent on a transport to Lublin.[519]

Thomas 'Toivi' Blatt in his memoirs mentioned a transport from Holland, arriving in Sobibór on May 7, 1943. He mentioned two

---

[518] J. Schelvis, *Sobibór*, Berg-Oxford, New York, 2007, p. 75.
[519] Ibid, p.74.

German twin girls, one who was called Inge, but he never mentioned the other twin's name, nor sadly their surname.

According to Blatt the family originally from Germany, emigrated to Holland, when the Nazis came to power and settled in Scheveningen. The father was a high official in the German Justice Department and the mother divorced the father, soon after coming to Holland. As well as the twin girls, her father and only brother all arrived in Sobibór, on the same transport.

Myself and other people have tried to find out more information about this family, but sadly we have to admit defeat on this. What happened to the twins and the rest of the family is unclear.

Record of Transports from Westerbork to Sobibór

March 2nd 1943 – July 20th 1943

Date of Deportation	Number of People Deported	Number of Survivors
March 2	1105	
March 10	1105	13
March 17	964	1
March 23	1250	
March 30	1255	
April 6	2020	2
April 13	1204	
April 20	1166	
April 27	1204	
May 4	1187	
May 11	1446	1
May 18	2511	
May 25	2862	
June 1	3006	1
June 8	3017	
June 29	2397	
July 6	2417	
July 13	1988	
July 20	2209	
Totals	34,313	18

Source: Jules Schelvis, *Sobibór*, p.203.

677

Appendix 5

Transports from Slovakia

The deportation of Slovakian Jews commenced on March 25, 1942, when 1,000 young women from Poprad, and another 1,000 from Bratislava were sent to Auschwitz-Birkenau. Following a selection, 331 Slovakian Jews were the first *RSHA transport* to be gassed in the converted farmhouse in Birkenau, known in the camp as the 'Red House.'

By June 26, 1942, some 53,000 out of a total population of 89,000 had been deported to the East. One survivor of the transports from Sabinov was deported to Poland on May 21, 1942, among a transport numbering 1,000. In 1943, he wrote down what he experienced, but for his own safety, he did not divulge his name. His comprehensive account deserves to be recorded in full:

> On May 27, 1942, our transport of around a thousand Jews went from Sabinov, via Zilna and Cadoa straight to Poland. At the border we had to line up at the station to be counted by the German *Sicherheitsdienst (SD)*. The women were counted inside the wagons. We continued our journey for two or three days, until we arrived at Rejowiec-Lubelski in the Lublin district, where we had to get out of the wagons. We were dying of thirst throughout the journey. Twice we were given water, but no food at all. But we had taken adequate provisions.
>
> In Rejowiec we were received by Engineer Holzheimer from the water company at Chelm and the *SA Kreishauptmann*. Nine members of the Jewish Order Service *(OD)* were also there at Rejowiec, and their Commandant Kessler from Brno, who was very helpful to us.
>
> The next day, two transports the same size as ours arrived from Stropkov, followed by one from Humenne, so then there were

3,000 of us Slovakian Jews gathered there. The Jews at Rejowiec had been resettled during the immediate days of Passover, so that there were only 300 of the original population left by the time we arrived at the ghetto. There were another 60 Jews from the Protectorate, and a few women from Nitra.

We were allocated a share of what had previously been Jewish houses, but there was very little space, which meant we had to share a room of 3 by 4 meters with 20 to 25 people. For eight days no one paid any attention to us. There was no supervision, it was a terrible chaos. No food was provided. The provisions given to us at Zilna, were stored in the school building, after we had to relinquish the valuable foods to the men of the *SA*. We only got them back after fifteen days, all inedible.

After a while, the 3,000 Slovakian Jews were called upon to volunteer for work, on draining the swamps. Only young, strong men were considered for these jobs. Fathers heading a family of more than three children were refused. In total 450 men were put to work. Each day they received 250 grams of bread, a watery soup in the afternoon, and black coffee in the evening.

Another 500 or 600 young people, irrespective of their family commitments, were taken to other camps in the area, such as Sawin, Sajozice, and the *SA* squadron at Chelm. They were selected for the Jewish Order Service, who accepted bribes and were corruptible. It should be noted here that the Jewish Council, which was still functioning, contained various elements. A special mention should go to the self-sacrificing help given by the women from Nitra. The same could not be said of others. No one else ever cared about the remaining 2,000 Jews from Slovakia.

After three or four weeks the Jewish Council at Chelm opened a community kitchen, where for 50 *Groschen* you could get a bowl of soup. A respected man named Fraenkel was in charge, he was later shot along with all his family. The scarcity of food and appalling sanitary conditions caused many cases of typhoid, diarrhoea and other ailments. Many elderly people died.

One evening a drunken Polish policeman appeared on the doorstep of the physician Doctor Grossman from Sabinov, who had just returned from a housecall. The policeman ordered the doctor to hand over his wristwatch, and they started arguing. The policeman threatened the doctor with his weapon, and the doctor defended himself, and they ended up fighting. The Jewish OD and the Jews from the surrounding houses were called into help. When the policeman got his gun back, he fired three shots into the air. Immediately after that, the Polish police turned up and arrested everyone in Doctor Grossman's house, as well as another 24 inhabitants from neighbouring houses, including five men of the OD. Grossman himself, tried to get away, but was fatally wounded. The 24 who were arrested were executed the next day for instigating a Communist uprising. Five members of the OD from Brno were among them.

On August 9, 1942, the Gendarmerie suddenly ordered the entire Jewish population from the ghetto and the Labor Camp—about 2,700 people—to assemble in the square in front of the school. Those who were too ill, or weak to comply, were shot inside their homes. The patients of the 'Jewish Hospital' suffered the same fate, including Doctor Sebok from Sabinov, who had been struck down by typhoid. At about 10 a.m. the elderly who had sat down on top of their luggage, because they were getting tired, were shot in the neck by the SS. And so 30 or 40 people died.

Then we got our marching orders, women in front, the men following behind. Doctor Borkenfeld was the last one. I advised him to walk up front, because the back rows were too dangerous. He replied it was his duty as a physician. After only 30 or 40 meters, they started firing at us from the left with rifles and machine pistols. The group thinned out dramatically. Later in Krychow I was told by a one-time member of the Jewish Council of Rejowiec, a Polish Jew by the name of Holzblatt that 700 Jews had been killed in this incident. In Rejowiec only a few stayed behind to work at the nearby sugar factory. Later I heard that they were taken to Trawniki to dig peat (Dorohucza).

At Rejowiec station we were received by the so-called 'Black Ukrainians.' We were pushed inside cattle wagons, 120 to 130 of us to a wagon, without any kind of registration. The doors were closed. We stood there until 8 p.m. Twenty-five men were taken out again to collect the luggage that had been left behind and load it into the wagons. While they were doing this, the 'Black Ukrainians' were harassing and assaulting them. It was unbearably hot in the wagon—it was August—we were given no water, we were gasping for air. The women were ripping their clothes off. We were like sardines, even the slightest movement was impossible.

One hundred and fifty people died of suffocation, twenty in my wagon, young strong people among them.

At about half past midnight, we arrived at Sobibór, where we were received by the SS with whips. We were finally given a little water, but still no food. We were taken to a fir-lined path, where the women had to go to the right and the men to the left. Twenty-five men were selected to remove the dead and the luggage from the train. We never saw them again.

The next morning we saw most of the women walking in rows of four to a place farther away from us. At eight o'clock an SS Lieutenant appeared and ordered everyone who had previously done any drainage work to step forward. To the 100 men and 50 women who volunteered he said cryptically, 'You are born again.' From the remaining group, technicians, blacksmiths, and watchmakers were selected, while the rest of the transport had to join the women in the field.

We left for Osowa and stayed the night there. The 500 German and Czech Jews made us very welcome and fed us. The next morning we went to Krychow, escorted by Jewish policemen. We went past the Hansk country estate and met about a hundred Jewish girls who were busy threshing. They were in relatively good shape. Krychow is a penal camp in a swamp area, established by the previous Polish government. The area has now been considerably drained by the Jews. When we arrived there were about 1,200 people, including 400 Czechs, 200 Slovakians and all the rest Poles. Living conditions were incredibly bad. Two hundred of us were put up in barracks measuring 60 by 4 meters.

There was neither straw nor blankets and no place to wash, everything was really dirty and bugs everywhere. We were so riddled with lice they literally covered our bodies. We had nothing to help us against them. Our rations consisted of 150 grams of bread, one serving of soup made from cabbage leaves, without fat or salt. And black coffee. We knew from experience that one could die of starvation within six weeks on that kind of diet. Most people ended up with swollen feet and cheeks, and typhoid and dysentery were also rife. Most of us had typhoid. We counted at least twelve dead each day. Out of the 155 people, 60 died.

The work itself was not demanding, but we were too weak to cope with it. The physician was not allowed to say we were ill. Even with a fever of 39 degrees C, one still had to work. And if one did end up in hospital after all, the only treatment was being able to lie down. There was no medication, no special food. If you survived—fine, if you did not—fine as well. You could buy medicine for a lot of money, but most people lacked the means.

On October 16, 1942, we were told that some of our group would be sent on to the *'Judenstaat'* Włodawa on the River Bug, 25 kilometres from Kychow. The elderly and sick who could hardly work were picked for resettlement. The hospital was also cleared out, and all patients sent to Włodawa. Those people were sent off without shoes, without luggage, because the rubber boots worn whilst at work were camp property, and they were not allowed to collect their own shoes. Four days later the entire Wlodawa population was deported to Sobibór.

At some stage, prisoners from the camps at Ujazdow, and Hansk were transferred to ours for the winter. This made living conditions worse, unbearable even. On December 9, it was suddenly announced that a 'complete resettlement' would take place. Apart from 100 people, who were selected to stay, to whom another 10 were added, all the rest were taken away. Some women and girls from Nitra and some other Czech women and girls stayed behind. As for the men, I was the only Slovakian, and there were two others from Bohemia. The rest were all Polish Jews. The group owes a lot to Piroska Taussig from Nitra, who had earned herself a special position in the office and helped us wherever possible. We owe it to her that so many girls escaped further deportation.

In the spring of 1943, more people arrived at the camp, Polish Jews this time. In June 1943, the camps at Osowa, Sawin, Sajozice and Luta were liquidated and the rest were sent to us, increasing our number to 533. In Hansk there were still 100-110 women and 5 men.

The situation at Krychow improved considerably from the start of 1943. After December 9, 1942, we received a daily bread ration of 400 or 500 grams, and thick potato soup for a midday meal. We were given decent iron beds: the sanitary facilities improved and we could wash ourselves. The health situation improved as well; after this we had only three deaths among the 110 originally held back. Three further people who were sick, were shot at the behest of the Deputy Commandant while the Camp Commandant was on leave. In March, when the camp got fuller again, the food situation got worse. Bread rations went back down to 150 grams per day; our midday meal went back to vegetable soup without any fat.

In April 1943, rumours were going around that the Dutch and Belgian Jews would be arriving and this was confirmed by the camp leadership. But they never came. A railway worker told me what happened to them. The transports from Holland and Belgium arrived in very good shape. Unlike us they had been transported in second-class passenger wagons, and were given food and white bread at larger stations. But they were all taken to Sobibór.

A few elderly and weak people were sent back to their country with the message that only those fit to work were required. That would suppress the Dutch and Belgian population's resistance against deportations, because the Jews were supposedly put to work. To begin with some of the Jews were actually put to work, as were Jews from other countries, but the *SD* would not have it. At Sobibór they were all put to death.

In the neighbourhood of Sobibór at night, one can always see fire and smell the stench from burning hair for miles around. There are indications—and people are saying it anyhow—that the buildings having been killed by electricity and gas and later buried, are now being dug up and burnt to remove all traces.

If anyone managed to escape back in 1942, those who were left behind were severely punished. Most of the escapees were Polish Jews who were familiar with local conditions. They formed groups in the forest and survived by robbing. Later on, the only ones who were punished after an escape attempt, were those who had actually tried to escape, if they were recaptured.

Doctor Sobel from Pecovska Nova Ves and Feinerl both escaped from Sawin, when there was still a camp there. Both were recaptured. Sobel was executed and the other taken back to Sawin, but escaped again. He has not been heard of since. Lajos Klein from Michalowce escaped too. His fate is also unknown. To my knowledge about 8,000 Jews in their striped outfits, were working on drainage and construction projects at Lublin.

The following *SS* and *SA* officials were particularly ruthless towards the Jews: *SS-Scharführer* Raschendorf in Chelm,[520] *SA-Scharführer* Johann Loffler in Krychow came from somewhere near Chemnitz,[521] *SA-Scharführer* Hilvert in Osowa, *SA-Scharführer* Bayko in Osowa, *SA-Scharführer* Ondyke in Sawin, who had been a butcher, Holzheimer, an engineer in charge of the Water Board at Chelm was particularly responsible.

Slovakia
17 August 1943[522]

---

[520] Listed in the report as Haschendorf.
[521] Listed in the report as Lofflerin.
[522] J. Schelvis, *Sobibór*, Berg-Oxford, New York, 2007, pp. 211-215.

Appendix 6

Transports from the Greater German Reich

The transports from the Greater German Reich to Sobibór were much more complicated than say, the transports from Holland, which went from Westerbork transit camp direct to Sobibór—a journey that usually lasted three days.

There were direct transports from large cities such as Berlin, Frankfurt and Vienna, and direct transports from other locations such as Kassel and Koblenz. There were also a number of transports to the so-called Transit Ghettos in Poland, such as Izbica, Piaski, and Rejowiec, and to *Theresienstadt*, near Prague.

The length of stay in the Transit Ghettos varied, some were deported onto the death camps immediately, while some deportees stayed a long time. What did not differ was the poor quality of food and appalling sanitary conditions. Whether they perished in the Transit Ghettos or one of the three *Aktion Reinhardt* death camps of Bełżec, Sobibór or Treblinka, is difficult to be completely precise.

In the case of *Theresienstadt*, the Nazis established a ghetto which acted as a transit camp, in the fortress town of Terezin, renamed *Theresienstadt*, some 40 miles from Prague, in Northwestern Czechoslovakia (now the Czech Republic). Here they interned the Jews of Bohemia and Moravia, and elderly Jews from the Greater German Reich. Some of these Jews had served the *Kaiser* during the First World War, and some of those had been decorated.

Transports from *Theresienstadt* went directly to Sobibór and Treblinka, as well as to aforementioned Transit Ghettos located in Poland, and ghettos in the Lublin district such as Lublin itself, Krasnystaw, Włodawa, and Zamość. From these locations the deportees ended up sharing the same awful fate as those who made the journey directly to the death camps.

The Transit Ghettos such as Izbica, Piaski, and Rejowiec were subjected to clearing '*Aktions*', where the Polish Jews were sent to the death camps and their vacated dwellings were taken over by Jews brought there from other countries. On occasions, the arriving Jews were simply sent straight to the deadly gas chambers in the camps, whilst at other times the Jews were incarcerated into the Transit Ghettos. Sometimes the Germans created Jewish Order Service (*OD*) from young, fit, heathy men, from say Slovakia, to oversee the Polish Jews, thus sowing the seeds of division.

One of those Jews deported from the Greater German Reich to Piaski was Hermann Mayer, who was born on October 6, 1878, in Bingen. A resident of Worms, he was deported from Mainz-Darmstadt on March 25, 1942, to Piaski. He sent a postcard back to the *Reich*, and its message read, 'We hope and pray with unswerving faith in God that, in time the Almighty will rectify things.' Hermann Mayer was deported from Piaski to the Bełżec death camp in 1942, where he perished.

Also deported to Piaski on the same transport of March 25, 1942, was Herta Hertha Mansbacher, the fifty-seven year old teacher, who was born on January 7, 1885, in Darmstadt, she had courageously sought to prevent the burning down of the synagogue in Worms in November 1938. The night was infamously known as '*Kristallnacht*'. On the same transport were sixteen Jews who had been wounded and decorated in the First World War—three of these German army veterans were; Julius Neumann, who was born on December 22, 1890, in Rauenthal and lived in Worms; Manuel Katz, who was born on April 20, 1878, in Erdmannrode / Hunfeld, who also resided in Worms; and the aforementioned Hermann Mayer. All these people shared the same fate and were murdered in the Bełżec extermination camp, via the Piaski Transit Ghetto.[523]

Zygmunt Klukowski, a Polish doctor who lived near Izbica in Szczebrzeszyn, kept a diary and his entry for March 26, 1942, read:

> There is great unhappiness and fear among the Jews. From everywhere comes news about the incredible violence against the Jews. They are bringing trainloads of Jews from Czechoslovakia, Germany, and even from Belgium. They are also resettling the Jews from various towns and villages and taking them somewhere to Bełżec. Today I heard a story about what they did to the Jews of Lublin. It is difficult to believe it is true. Today they deported the Jews from Izbica—they were also taken to Bełżec, where there is supposed to be some monstrous camp.[524]

For a great number of victims, we know they were deported from the Greater German Reich to one of the Transit Ghettos in Poland, and for some the trial ends there. As for the others, whether they perished in our, or in Sobibór, which the late Robert Kuwalek told me was considered an 'overflow camp' for Bełżec, will probably never be known.

The BBC program, 'My Family, the Holocaust and Me,' presented by the Judge Robert Rinder (who stars in his own TV Program) in 2019, recounted the story of Sabina Federmann, formerly Jakubowicz, who was born on June 14, 1892, in Zdunska Wola, Poland. She was married to Salomon Federmann, who was incarcerated in Buchenwald Concentration Camp, but who survived the Holocaust and settled in the United Kingdom, and was Robert Rinder's grandfather.

Sabina was a resident of Frankfurt-am-Main who was deported from Frankfurt on June 11, 1942, and she was forced to pay her own fare of *RM* 50, for the transportation costs. She was deported from the *Grossmarkthalle* eastern cellar that the *Gestapo* rented. From the cellar the deportees were driven to the *Grossmarkthalle*

---

[523] M. Gilbert, *The Holocaust—The Jewish Tragedy*, William Collins and Son, London, 1986, pp. 307-308.
[524] Ibid. p. 308.

railway station next to the hall. During the deportations the market carried on trading as normal, so the traders and customers were not spared the sight of the deportations.

What is interesting is that the *Bundesarchiv* online resource, the *Gedenkbuch*, lists Sabina Federmann as having been deported on May 24, 1942, from Frankfurt to Izbica. I took this up with the people who made the program and they were adamant that Sabina was murdered in Sobibór, and that she was deported on June 11, 1942.

During 1942, as the following table will demonstrate, the Nazis transported vast numbers of Jewish people from within the Greater German Reich to the East, and the vast majority of these would perish in the deadly gas chambers built by the Nazis, in the three death camps.

This table is taken from the online resource, the Bundesarchiv *Memorial Book—Chronology of Deportations from the Greater German Reich*:

Date	Deported From	Deported To	Number of People
1942			
22 March	Koblenz	Izbica	1,000
24 March	Nurnberg	Izbica	1,000
25 March	Mainz-Darmstadt	Piaski	1,000
28 March	Berlin	Piaski	985
1 April	Theresienstadt	Piaski	1,000
3 April	Munich	Piaski	989
9 April	Vienna	Izbica	998
13 April	Breslau	Izbica	1,000
18 April	Theresienstadt	Rejowiec	1,000
22 April	Düsseldorf	Izbica	942
23 April	Theresienstadt	Piaski	1,000
25 April	Wurzburg	Krasnystaw	955
26 April	Stuttgart	Izbica	1,000
27 April	Theresienstadt	Izbica	1,000
27 April	Vienna	Wlodawa	998
28 April	Theresienstadt	Zamość	1,000
30 April	Dortmund	Zamość	791
30 April	Koblenz	Krasniczyn	1,000
30 April	Theresienstadt	Zamość	1,000
3 May	Breslau	Lublin	1,000

8 May	Frankfurt	Izbica	938
9 May	Theresienstadt	Sobibór	1,000
12 May	Vienna	Izbica	1,001
15 May	Vienna	Izbica	1,006
17 May	Theresienstadt	Lublin	1,000
24 May	Frankfurt	Izbica	957
25 May	Theresienstadt	Lublin	1,000
1 June	Kassel	Izbica/Sobibór	1,000
5 June	Vienna	Sobibór	1,001
11 June	Frankfurt	Sobibór	1,253
12 June	Theresienstadt	Sobibór	1,000
13 June	Theresienstadt	Sobibór	1,000
13 June	Berlin	Sobibór	1,030
14 June	Vienna	Sobibór	996
15 June	Koblenz, Cologne, Düsseldorf	Sobibór	1,003

Appendix 7

The Sobibór Area Labor Camps

This chapter is dedicated to my to friend the late Robert Kuwalek, Polish Historian, who died far too young. He helped write this account with me, and I thank him for that.

In accordance with the German plans at the very beginning of the occupation, the Lublin district was intended to become the pillar of the *Generalgouvernement*'s agricultural policy. In order to modernise the agriculture in this region, the German authorities wanted to regulate the small rivers and to improve the meadows. Therefore the *Wasserwirtscharftsinspektion* (Inspection for the Water Economy) in the Lublin district installed a network of small work camps during 1940. Jewish and Polish prisoners worked there. Chelm County became one of several centres for these camps. The Sobibór death camp was built in this district in early 1942.

In 1940, Jews mainly from the Lublin and Warsaw districts were sent to these work camps. They received an official salary of 96 *zloty* per month, but this amount was poor reward for the extremely hard work in often very difficult conditions. These forced labor camps were set up in the swampy surroundings of Sobibór. They were located at Adampol, Czerniejow, Dorohusk Kamien, Krychow, Luta, Nowosiolki, Osowa, Ruda Opalin, Sawin, Siedliszcze, Sobibór village, Staw-Sajczyce, Tomaszowka, Ujazdow, Włodawa and Zmudz.

In some places the camps were located in school buildings, abandoned farms, or industrial buildings. Except for the camp at Krychow, the prisoners lived in barns on private farms, or in a mill, in the case of Staw-Sajczyce. The camps were under the supervision of the German civil administration, but the prisoners were guarded by *Trawnikimänner* or by Jewish Police in Osowa. In the camp at Sawin, the Jewish prisoners were also supervised by Jewish Police and Polish Guardsmen, who worked for the *Wasserwirtscharftsinspektion*.

The prisoners were forced to work 8-10 hours daily, most of the time they stood in water in wet clothes, without the opportunity to change them. Food was also a major problem. Only those who came from towns close to the camps had the opportunity of obtaining some food from home. The Jews taken from the Warsaw Ghetto or the Warsaw district depended on the camp's kitchens. If they had some money they could buy bread from the local peasants. In some camps like Krychow, the prisoners were killed when camp commandant Adolf Loeffler discovered they had made contact with local Poles. The Polish farmers accused of selling food to the prisoners were beaten. In Osowa these contacts were not so strictly forbidden. Because they had no money, the Jews exchanged their clothes for food.

In 1941, alone, 2,500 out of 8,700 Jews from the Warsaw Ghetto had to be released from the camps because of sickness. Many Jews died of starvation, typhus epidemics and the harsh working conditions. In several camps such as Osowa or Sawin they were shot in mass executions. In the autumn of 1941, in Osowa, the last remaining group of 58 Jewish prisoners were executed close to the camp. Two of them survived and became functionaries in the next period between 1942, and 1943.

In 1941, approximately 2,200 Jews from the Warsaw Ghetto were sent to Krychow, Osowa, Sawin, and Staw-Sajczyce. The number of people who were released from these camps during June and July 1941, when almost all of the large buildings were taken over by the German *Wehrmacht* at the beginning of the war against the Soviet Union, is not known. In Osowa the average number of prisoners was 400-500 people. In Siedliszcze, approximately 2,000 and in Sawin 700-800.

Krychow was the largest camp within the network, located south-west of Sobibór, close to Hansk village. It was built before the Second World War as a detention camp for Polish criminals. Even then the prisoners had to regulate the rivers of this region. In 1940, the Hansk local administration received an order from the German civil administration to prepare buildings of the former camp for transports of Gypsies. These were Gypsies from the Gypsy camp in Bełżec. The whole group of Gypsies has been estimated to have between 1,000 and 1,500 people. According to the statements by Polish witnesses from Hansk, the Gypsies in Krychow were not guarded and not forced to work. Most of them could not speak Polish. They exchanged their clothes for food and begged for money. In the autumn of 1940, they were deported from Krychow. Some of them were sent to Siedlce Ghetto.

Between the end of 1940, and early 1941, most of the prisoners in Krychow were Jews from the Warsaw Ghetto and local Polish and Ukrainian farmers, arrested for not having paid their quotas. Around 1,500 prisoners in Krychow, according to witnesses in Hansk, were beaten by the guards and suffered from starvation and illness. 150 Jews worked as manual workers. Many Jews had to work in fields that belonged to the German 'Colonists' or at the manors taken over by the Germans. Even women and children between eight and twelve years old, had to work there. With the beginning of *Aktion Reinhardt* all of these forced labor camps were reserved for Jews only. After their families had paid sums of money for their release, they were set free at the beginning of 1942.

The Jews arrived from the liquidated ghettos in the surroundings of Sobibór, Rejowiec, Siedliszcze, Sawin, Włodawa, and Chelm, or were sent after selection to the Sobibór death camp: the transports from abroad were subjected to selections. People from Slovakia, Holland, Germany and Austria did not realize or could not believe that their relatives and friends were being led away to be murdered in the gas chambers. Sobibór was almost unique in selecting large groups of prisoners to work in other camps. It is unknown how many people were selected at Sobibór for work in the local forced labor camps.

Franz Stangl, the commandant of Sobibór recalled, in an interview with Gitta Sereny, his visit with *Baurat* Bruno Moser to the Krychow Labor Camp, during April 1942:

> *Baurat* Moser suggested we make a round of the camps he supplied in the district. The first camp I saw was about half-way between Chelm and Sobibór, a farm called Krychow. It employed two to three hundred Jewish women, mostly German, or at least German speaking. I went in there to look around. There was nothing—you know—sinister about it; they were quite free, if you like it was just a farm where the women worked under the supervision of Jewish guards. Well I suppose you could call them Jewish Police. As I say, I looked around and the women seemed quite cheerful—they seemed healthy. They were just working, you know. They were armed with *weissen Schlagmitteln* (white implements for beating).[525]

Aside from the difficult conditions of life and work, in spring and summer, mosquitoes were a big problem and selections in the camps were regularly organized. Sick people and children were sent by horse-drawn carts or by foot to the Sobibór death camp. In the camps located very close to Sobibór, the inmates knew about the death camp. This psychological pressure shattered their will to resist and survive. In many Polish testimonies, the witnesses mentioned the passivity of the prisoners. In Osowa village, seven kilometres away from Sobibór and surrounded by a vast forest, no prisoners escaped from the camp, although some Poles attempted to help them.

SS-Arbeitslager Dorohucza, which was located halfway between Lublin and Chelm, some five kilometres from Trawniki, became operational in late February, and early March 1943. Here prisoners were forced to dig peat, in very harsh conditions. Out of the 500 Jews, about half of them were Dutch Jews selected on the ramp at the Sobibór death camp.

---

[525] Sereny, *Into That Darkness*....., op.cit., p.107.

The Commandant of Dorohucza was *SS-Hauptscharführer* Gottfried Schwarz, who had served with distinction at the Bełżec death camp. According to other SS Officers, Robert Juhrs and Ernst Zierke, who also served at Bełżec and Sobibór death camps, it was confirmed that the last commandant of Dorohucza, was Fritz Tauscher, who had also served at the Bełżec death camp.

Dorohucza camp was liquidated during the *Aktion Erntefest* massacre in November 1943, when the Jewish prisoners in most of the Jewish Labor Camps in the Lublin district were brutally murdered. Robert Juhrs recalled the events of November 3, 1943:

> I know I celebrated my birthday on 17, October 1943, at Dorohucza. One morning soon after, we were completely surprised to find our camp surrounded by a police unit. I remember clearly that it was a misty morning. Our guards had detected silhouettes in the mist and sounded the alarm, as they expected a partisan attack. Shortly after an officer in police uniform entered our camp. He was accompanied by one other man, who might have been from the *SD*. I cannot be sure, however. As far as I recall, the police officer may have had the rank of *Oberleutnant,* because I think he had at least one star on his epaulettes.
>
> The police officer commanded all the Germans to step forward and lay down their weapons, and the watchmen had to do the same. We were forced to follow his orders. After this, all the Jews had to get out of their barracks and step forward. I still remember our cook—a Jewess from Leipzig, whose name I have forgotten—asking me what it was all about. I told her I did not know, and it was a surprise to me as well. At the same time, I got the impression that the Jews knew from experience what the purpose of this action was.
>
> After the Jews had vacated their barracks, their quarters were searched. Then the Jews guarded by the police unit left in the direction of Trawniki. I found out later that all the Jews from this commando were shot near the trenches within the Trawniki command area. Unfortunately I cannot tell you who ordered this operation, and I never found out who the police officer was. In answer to the question, I am convinced that my comrades were also

completely taken by surprise. A few days after the operation, we received orders from Lublin to go to Sobibór.[526]

Only during the final liquidation of the Adampol Labor Camp near Włodawa on August 13, 1943, did some of the prisoners, who were in contact with the partisans, try to organize any resistance and fight against the police. It is important to mention that most of the inmates in Adampol were Polish Jews who knew their fate.

During the liquidation of the camp, 475 Jewish prisoners were executed on the spot. Most of the foreign Jews had no possibility of escaping because they did not know the language, the region or the people.

In Sawin, successful escapes by two Czech Jews are known, one of those who escaped lost his mother during a selection in Sawin, and only found out after the war that Sawin was not far away from the Sobibór death camp. In other camps the biggest group of prisoners were Jews from outside of Poland. Polish witnesses often mention their frequent close contact with Czech Jews. Polish farmers realized that among the deportees were Jews who had converted to Christianity. For example in Sawin, a dentist from Czechoslovakia was a member of the church choir, and her son played the violin during mass. Christian Jews from Czechoslovakia were also in Krychow.

Zygmunt Leszczynski from Hansk stated:

> Among the Jews who were in the camp in Krychow, there were also Catholics. I saw how, during the transport to Krychow some of them stopped before the cross which was close to the street and they crossed themselves and prayed. I saw also that some of them wore small crosses on the chest.
>
> In the summer and autumn of 1943, most of these Labor Camps were liquidated and their inmates were sent to the Sobibór death camp. From Krychow the prisoners were taken on horse-drawn

---

[526] J. Schelvis, *Sobibor*, Berg-Oxford, New York, 2007, p. 127.

wagons. From Sawin they had to walk and many of them were killed on the way to the death camp.[527]

Henryk Stankeiwicz from Sawin, made a statement:

> I remember we were together with my father in front of our house 5-8 meters away from the street. Suddenly we saw the *Kalmuk*—probably a Ukrainian guard—and behind him several hundred marching people in a column. They walked very slowly and looked starved and dirty. Several of them took off their hats and told us words of farewell, 'Goodbye Mr Stankeiwicz, we are going to the fire'.[528]

After the selections in the Labor Camps and during their final liquidations the Germans forced the Polish farmers to use their horse-drawn wagons to transport the old people and the invalids. In front of the main gate of the death camp in Sobibór, the Poles had to abandon the wagons and Ukrainian guards from the camp drove the wagons through the gate. Then the Poles heard the victims screaming and after one or two hours the wagons were brought back to them.

Probably the last camp to be liquidated was in Luta village. The camp existed, according to the testimonies of local inhabitants, until the Sobibór revolt on October 14, 1943. The inmates from Luta observed a group of prisoners from the Sobibór death who tried to escape to the nearby forest. After the revolt the Jews from Luta were taken to the death camp and murdered.

In Osowa, a small cemetery can be seen with graves of the prisoners who died in the camp. It is very difficult to say how many people passed through the Sobibór area work camps, or perished there.

In an interview with Stephan Stelmaszuk during 1983, he gave an account of what happened to at the Osowa Jewish Labor Camp:

---

[527] Robert Kuwalek in correspondence with the author.
[528] Ibid.

Was there a Jewish camp in Osowa, where you lived?

There was a Jewish camp. The people who left for the Soviet Union left their homes. Not just their homes, also the barns and sheds. They built onto that. The camp was at the centre of the village. They built more houses there. They fenced it off with barbed wire.

The guards were Jewish. They wouldn't escape anyway. As far as I know only two did. Then a German from Chelm was shot dead. He was visiting the commander of the Jewish camp in Osowa. They shot him through the window. Germans from Chelm came. They wanted to murder ten families, who lived there, because a German had been killed. Five families on the one side of the camp, and five on the other side.

But that didn't happen. There was an observation tower for the Germans. The people were already digging graves, but someone thought of something and ran to the observation tower. He said they wanted to shoot people and graves were being dug. The Germans from the observation tower were with the Wehrmacht. They didn't concern themselves with politics. They went there to stop the execution. They weren't allowed to do it, or they'd have them to deal with. It became a heated dispute. The Germans from the tower wanted to protect them.

These Germans just walked around the village, no one bothered them. They didn't have to be afraid of the people. On the contrary they even did some trading. They traded thread with butter. The Germans sent butter to their families. The Poles had good contacts with the Germans in the observation tower. And the Germans saved the families that were going to be killed.

The two Jews probably killed that German man. They had managed to get a gun from somewhere. The commanders house was close to the barbed wire. There was a road near this barbed wire and a pavement a few meters away. It was dark, the light was on. They had that gun. The two Jews had escaped from the camp. Half of the prisoners could have escaped. There was only one German commander and the guards were Jewish.

They were a bit older. Anyone who wanted to escape could. But not many people did. Only a few escaped. After that German was killed, the Jews from Osowa, were deported straight away. They were taken to Sobibór in cars. Normally they had to walk. Many Jews walked past our village. As I told you before, on the way, eight or ten Jews, I'm not sure, I didn't count them, a few people were killed on the way to Sobibór.

You didn't always smell it in our village. You could smell it when the ovens were on. And if the wind blew towards Osowa, then you could really smell the stench. But it was still four kilometres away. If the wind went in the other direction then the smell would too.[529]

---

[529] Stephan Stelmaszuk Interview 1983—www.sobiborinterviews.nl—online resource.

Selected Bibliography

ARAD, Yitzhak: *Belzec, Sobibor, Treblinka—The Aktion Reinhard Death Camps,* Indiana University Press, Bloomington and Indianapolis 1987.

BEM, Marek, *Sobibor Extermination Camp 1942-1943,* Stichting Sobibor, Amsterdam 2015.

BERGER, Sara: *Experten der Vernichtung: Das T4-Reinhardt-Netzwerk in den Lagern Belzec, Sobibor und Treblinka,* Hamburger Institut für Sozialforschung, Hamburg 2013.

BIALOWTZ, Philip, *A Promise at Sobibor,* The University of Wisconsin Press, Madison Wisconsin, 2010.

BLATT, Thomas (Toivi): *Sobibor: The Forgotten Revolt,* H.E.P, Issaquah 1988.

BLATT, Thomas (Toivi): *From the Ashes of Sobibor,* Northwestern University Press, Evanston Illinois 1997.

BÖHM, Dr Boris: *Nationalsozialistische Euthanasie-Verbrechen in Sachsen,* Kuratorium Gedenkstätte Sonnenstein, Dresden /Pirna 1996.

BÖHM, Dr Boris: *Sonnenstein Heft 3,* Kuratorium Gedenkstätte Sonnenstein/Pirna 2001.

COWDERY, Ray & VODENKA, Peter: *Reinhard Heydrich: Assassination,* USM Inc, Lakeville 1994.

CZECH, Danuta: *Auschwitz Chronicle,* Henry Holt, New York 1989.

ENCYKLOPDIE CESKY KRUMLOV. History of Photography in Cesky Krumlov.

FREIBERG, Dov, *To Survive Sobibor*, Gefen Publishing House, Jerusalem 2007.

GILBERT, Martin: *Final Journey*, George Allen & Unwin Ltd, London 1979.

GILBERT, Martin: *The Holocaust—The Jewish Tragedy*, William Collins, London 1987.

GRABITZ, Helge and SCHEFFLER, Wolfgang: *Letzte Spuren*, Hentrich Edition, Berlin 1993.

HILBERG, Raul: *Die Vernichtung der europäischen Juden, Band 2*, Fischer Taschenbuch Verlag, Frankfurt am Main 1990.

HILBERG, Raul: *The Destruction Of The European Jews*, Holmes & Meier, New York & London 1985.

HINZ-WESSELS, Annette. *Tiergartenstrasse 4. Schaltstelle der nationalsozialistischen "Euthanasie"-Morde*, Ch. Links Verlag, Berlin 2015.

HOFFMANN, Dr Ute and SCHULZE, Dietmar: *"...wird heute in eine andere Anstalt verlegt". Nationalsozialistische Zwangssterilisation und "Euthanasie" in der Landes-Heil- und Pflegeanstalt Bernburg. Eine Dokumentation*, Dessau 1997.

JORGENSEN, Torben: *Stiftelsen-Bolerne fra Aktion Reinhardt*, Gyldenals, Bogklubber, Gylling 2003.

KEPLINGER, Brigitte, MARCKGOTT, Gerhart, REESE, Hartmut: *Tötungsanstalt Hartheim*, Oberösterreichisches Landesarchiv, 3rd edition, Linz 2013.

KLEE, Ernst: *Das Kulturlexikon zum Dritten Reich*, S. Fischer Verlag GmbH, Frankfurt am Main 2007.

KLEE, Ernst: *Was sie Taten—Was sie Wurden*, S. Fischer Verlag GmbH, Frankfurt am Main 1986.

KLEE, Ernst, DRESSEN, Willi, RIESS, Volker: *The Good Old Days*, Hamish Hamilton, London 1991.

KRANZ, Tomasz: *Extermination of Jews at the Majdanek Concentration Camp*, Panstwowe Muzeum na Majdanka, Lublin 2007.

KUWALEK, Robert: *From Lublin to Bełżec*, Ad Rem, Lublin 2006.

LANZMANN, Claude: *Shoah*, Pantheon Books, New York 1985.

LONGERICH, Peter: *The Unwritten Order—Hitler's Role in the Final Solution*, Tempus, Stroud 2001.

MACLEAN, French L.: *The Camp Men*, Schiffer Military History, Atglen PA 1999.

MARES, Jan: *Josef Wolf (Senior) Potvrzeni ze se zivnost opovedela*, South Bohemian Scientific Library in Ceske Budejovice, Budweis 2021.

MARSALEK, Jozef: *Majdanek*, Interpress, Warsaw 1986.

NOVITCH, Miriam: *Sobibor Martyrdom and Revolt*, Holocaust Library, New York 1980.

POPRZECZNY, Joseph: *Hitler's Man in the East Odilo Globocnik*, McFarland and Company, Jefferson and London 2004.

RASHKE, Richard: *Escape From Sobibor*, Michael Joseph, London 1982.

REITLINGER, Gerald: *The Final Solution*, Vallentine, Mitchell, London 1953.

SCHELVIS, Jules: *Sobibor A History of a Nazi Death Camp*, Berg, Oxford and New York 2007.

SCHMIDT, Amy, LOEHRER, Gudrun. *The Mauthausen Concentration Camp Complex. World War II and Postwar Records*, Reference Information Paper 115. National Archives and Records Administration NARA, Washington DC 2008.

SCHOENBERNER, Gerhard: *The Yellow Star*, Corgi Books, London 1978.

SAIDEL, Rochelle: *Mielec, Poland*, Geffen Publishing House, Jerusalem 2012.

SERENY, Gitta: *Into That Darkness—From Mercy Killing To Mass Murder*, Pimlico, London 1974.

SLIER, Deborah and SHINE, Ian: *Hidden Letters*, Star Bright Books, New York 2008.

TREGENZA, Michael: *Christian Wirth and the First Phase of Einsatz Reinhard*, Zeszyty Majdanka Vol XIV, Panstwowe Muzeum na Majdanka, Lublin 1992.

TREGENZA, Michael: *Christian Wirth: Inspekteur des SS-Sonderkommando Aktion Reinhard*, Zeszyty Majdanka Vol Xv, Panstwowe Muzeum na Majdanka, Lublin 1993.

TRIALS OF WAR CRIMINALS before the Nuernberg Military Tribunals under Control Council Law No 10, Volume 1, The Medical Case, Nurnberg October 1946—April 1949, Library of Congress, Washington DC.

VARIOUS AUTHORS: *Fotos Aus Sobibor: Die Niemann-Sammlung zu Holocaust und Nationalsozialismus*, Metropol-Verlag, Berlin 2020.

ZEMAN, Pavel. *Tam byl ten krejci z Cech—Nacisticky program euthanazie a Nemci z Ceskeho Krumlova*, in pamet a dejiny, vol 1/2013, Prague.

Other Publications

Einsatz Reinhardt—Varia—The Extermination of Jews in the *Generalgouvernement*—majdanek. Eu, Lublin 2022
GILBERT, Sir Martin: Maps of *Aktion Reinhardt*

Unpublished:
TREGENZA, Michael: Private Report, Allötting Germany 1972

TREGENZA, Michael: Christian Wirth The Exemplary Officer

TREGENZA, Michael: Only the Dead—Christian Wirth and *SS Sonderkommando* Bełżec, 1988

WEBB, Chris: The ARC Trips to Poland 2002 and 2004 (Holocaust Historical Society)

Paper Correspondence

BIEMANN, Georg Private correspondence with the author 2020-2021

BLATT, Thomas Toivi Private correspondence with the author

KUWALEK, Robert Private correspondence with the author

RUTHERFORD, William: Private correspondence with the author 2003-2005

SCHELVIS, Jules Private correspondence with the author

TREGENZA, Michael: Private correspondence with author

Archival Sources

Bundesarchiv, Berlin

Bundesarchiv Koblenz, *Aussenstelle* Ludwigsburg (formerly the Zentrale Stelle der Landesjustizverwaltungen, Ludwigsburg).

Bundesarchiv Koblenz, *Aussenstelle* Berlin-Lichterfelde (formerly the Berlin Document Centre).

Centre de documentation Juive Contemporaine, Paris, France

Chris Webb Private Archive, Whitehill, UK

Digital Archives of the State Regional Archives, Trebon, Czech Republic

Ghetto Fighters House, Israel

Holocaust Historical Society, UK

Majdanek Museum, Lublin, Poland

Michael Tregenza Archive, Lublin, Poland

National Archives Kew, London, UK

National Archives, Washington DC, USA

NIOD Instituut voor Oorlogs, Holocaust en Genocidestudies (Institute for War, Holocaust and Genocide Studies), Amsterdam, The Netherlands

Sobibor Muzeum (Włodawa)

Staatsarchiv München, Germany

Süddeutsche Zeitung

Tall Trees Archive UK

Ullstein Bild, Germany

United States Holocaust Memorial Museum (USHMM), Washington DC, USA

Wiener Library, London, UK

Yad Vashem, Jerusalem, Israel

Zentrale Stelle der Landesjustizverwaltungen Ludwigsburg, Germany

Websites

Action Reinhard Camps (ARC)—www.deathcamps.org
Archives.gov
archivesportaleuropre.net
bundesarchiv.de/gedenkbuch—Memorial Book
digi.ceskearchiv.cz
Guardian online
Holocaust Education & Archive Research Team (H.E.A.R.T)
Holocaust.cz
Holocaust Historical Society (HHS)
Jewish Gen
Joods Monument
Kohoutikriz.org
Loc.gov

Niod.nl
Nizkor—Adolf Eichmann Complete Trial Transcripts
Sobiborinterviews.nl
The Nizkor Project–Shofar FTP Archive File
Ustrcr.cz
Yad Vashem Central Database of Shoah Victims Names

Acknowledgements

ABDO, Alexander, (Hessisches Hauptstaatsarchiv Wiesbaden, Germany)

ABUYS, Guido (Kamp Westerbork, Holland)

ARORA, Surinder

BACCA Sonia (Wiener Library, London)

BALSAM, Robert (Bundesarchiv Berlin)

BEIER, Undine (Bundesarchiv Germany)

BIEDKA, Lukasz

BIELECKI, P

BIEMANN, Georg, (Osnabrück, Germany)

BIERSCHNEIDER, Robert (Staatsarchiv München)

BLATT, Thomas ((Toivi), Sobibor Survivor)

BOHM, Dr. Boris (Sonnenstein/Pirna Memorial)

BORGERT, Dr Heinz-Ludger (Hauptarchiv Ludwigsburg, Germany)

BROWN, Dr. Llewellyn (Paris, France)

BUCH, Karin (Ullstein Bild)

COCHOLATY, Michal (Czech Author and Historian)

CÜPPERS, Martin (Ludwigsburg)

DÄVERS, Jana (ibidem-Verlag, Hannover)

DE LESTRE, Howard

EIGELSBERGER, Peter (Schloss Hartheim, Austria)

ENGELKING, Barbara (Warsaw)

FALKSOHN, Howard (Wiener Library, London)
FELDMAN, Claire (Back Cover Photograph)
FELDMAN, Professor Matthew (York)
FERRERO, Shaul (Yad Vashem)
GILBERT, Sir Martin (Author and Historian)
GOHLE, Dr Peter (Ludwigsburg)
GRABHER, Michael (Author)
GROSMAN, Judy (Ghetto Fighters House, Israel)
HANEJKO, Eugenius (Director of Regional Museum Tomaszow Lubelski, Poland)
HANEJKO, Tomasz (Director Bełżec Memorial Museum, Poland)
HEIDEWEG, Hans
HOJAN, Artur (T4 Association, Berlin, Germany)
HOPPITT, Anne-Marie (Editor)
ITZKOVICH, Dafna (Ghetto Fighters House, Israel)
KATZ, Lilli-Mai
KROSEN, Peter (Stadarchief, Amsterdam, Netherlands)
KUKAWSKI, Lukasz (Sobibor Museum, Wlodawa)
KUWALEK, Robert (Former Bełżec Museum Director)
LISCIOTTO, Carmelo (H.E.A.R.T)
MOLL, Franziska (Bundesarchiv Berlin)
MORROW, Kevin (Researcher, USA)
MOSCOVITZ, Emmanuelle (Yad Vashem, Jerusalem, Israel)
MUNRO, Cameron (T4 Association, Berlin, Germany)
OLEKSY-ZBOROWSKI, Tomasz
O'NEIL, Dr Robin (Author and Historian)
OREN, Zvi (Ghetto Fighters House, Israel)
PARZER, Robert
PENNEWAARD, Aline
PETERS, Michael
POTTKAMP, Rene (NIOD Amsterdam)
POPRZECZNY, Joe (Perth, Australia)

PRIWTZER, Sebastian (Gedenkstätte Grafeneck, Germany)
RUTHERFORD, William (Billy)
SCHARNETZKY, Julius
SCHWANINGER, Florian (Schloss Hartheim, Austria)
SCHELVIS, Jules
SCOLARO, Peggy
SPYRAKIS, Heather
SPYRAKIS, Mark (Technical Support)
SPYRAKIS, Nikky
STADLER, Harry
STEINBERG, Jerry (Foreword)
STRAUS, Susan
TARKOWSKI, Krzych, (Majdanek Museum, Lublin)
TELEZYNSKA, Ewa (Warsaw)
TREGENZA, Michael (Author and Historian)
TYAS, Stephen
VAN LIEMPT, Martin
WEBB, Frederick John
WEBB, Shirley
WITTE, Peter (Historian and Author, Germany)
YACOBI, Benny
ZIEMER, Daniel (Sonnenstein Memorial, Germany)
ZOODSMA, Marieke (NIOD Amsterdam, Holland)

Index of Names

A

Aalst-Prins, Van, Emma 212
Abele, Berta (formerly Westerfeld) 263
Abeles, Renate (formerly Kahn) 263
Abraham, Emanuel 263
Abraham, Mathilde (formerly Mayer) 263
Abt, Bessy 263
Ackermann, Hedwig (formerly Lorig) 263
Ackermann, Klara (formerly Schaffer) 264
Ackermann, Lana 264
Adejes, Albert 336
Adler-Heymann, Sophie 212
Adler-Enoch, Emmy 212
Adler, Adelheid (formerly Gollisch) 264
Adler, Bertha (formerly Oppenheim) 264
Adler, Clothilde (formerly Nassauer) 264
Adler, Ida 264
Adler, Max 212
Ahronson, Klara (formerly Blumenthal) 264
Alexander, Luise 264
Alster, Sholmo 111, 142, 167, 195
  Biography 167
Altheimer, Kathinka 264
Antonov, Wasil 661, 662
Appel, Jenny (formerly Schwab) 264

Appel, Sofia 265
Apt, Benjamin 265
Apt, Berta (formerly Rosenberg) 265
Arad, Yitzhak (Historian) 25, 26, 27
Arm, Erna (formerly Munz) 265
Arm, Rosel 265
Arnholz, Bertha (formerly Lewin) 265
Aron, Sitta 265
Aronsohn, Fanny (formerly Rosenthal) 265
Asser, Israel 213
Asser, Mathilde 213
Asser-Vet, Eva 213
Atzel, Fanny (formerly Tannenberg) 266

B

Bacarach, Abraham 266
Bacharach, Betty (formerly Muller) 266
Bacharach, Frieda, Friederike 266
Bacharach, Grete 266
Bacharach, Klara (formerly Lazarus 266
Bacharach, Meta (formerly Spier) 266
Bacharach, Sophie 266
Bachenheimer, Hildegard 267
Bachenheimer, Paul 267
Bachmann, Hilde (formerly Cohen) 267

Bachrach-Schwarzenberger, Lina 213
Bachrach, Klara 213
Baer, Chana 267
Baer, Clementine 267
Baer, Gunther 267
Baer, Irma (formerly Ullmann) 267
Baer, Paula (formerly Bermann) 267
Baer, Sofie 267
Bahir, Moshe 53, 57, 69, 79, 126, 130, 140, 201, 205, 375
   Biography 167
Baidin, Ilya 661
Bajrach, Abram 'Fibs' 58
   Biography 196
Bajrach, Max
   Biography 196
Barandtimov, Sabit 661
Barbl, Heinrich 41, 441, 445, 452, 506
   Biography 378
Bardach, Antonius 167
Bataronov, Aglam 661
Bauch, Ernst 486, 504, 516, 532
   Biography 378
Bauchwitz, Kurt 268
Bauchwitz, Regina (formerly Meyer) 268
Bauer, Erich 36, 38, 41, 42, 48, 50, 67, 95, 98, 115, 118, 120, 122, 129, 137, 179, 186, 198, 216, 378, 387, 389, 392, 395, 396, 400, 406, 409, 415, 419, 427, 428, 432, 435, 438, 441, 442, 451, 452, 453, 455, 460, 472, 473, 474, 475, 476, 477, 478, 479, 480, 481, 482, 486, 500, 514, 516, 540, 541, 542, 551, 554, 557, 561, 562, 565, 661, 664
   Biography 378
   Testimony 426–82
Bauer, Rickchen (formerly Strauss) 268
Baum, Josef 268
Baum, Lieb 196
Baum, Toni (formerly Bierig) 268
Becher, Werner 429, 447, 549
   Biography 379
Beck, Rosa 268
Becker, Gertrude (formerly Brodreich) 268
Beckmann, Rudolf 16, 69, 87, 90, 100, 103, 137, 143, 171, 172, 206, 354, 379, 429, 430, 441, 444, 447, 448, 454, 455, 456, 463, 466, 468, 478, 480, 486, 541, 555, 557, 564, 565, 580
   Biography 379
Beer, de, Cacille 268
Belyi, Michail 661
Benda, Adalbert 114, 115
Benedick, Flora (formerly Scheuer) 268
Benedick, Lothar 269
Benedict, Amalie 269
Berandecki, Felix 661
Berney, Rosalie (formerly Katz) 269
Bernstein, Eva 269
Bernstein, Eva, Mirjam 269
Bernstein, Jutta (formerly Fleischmann) 269
Bernstein, Lotte 269
Beulich, Max 549
   Biography 380
Beverstein, Adele 269
Bialowas, Jan 661
Bialowitz, Philip 77, 91, 92, 129, 145, 152, 168, 189
   Biography 167
Bialowitz, Symcha 91, 152, 168, 186
Bickhardt, Edith 269

Bielakow, B 126, 661
Bielinski *Trawnikimann* 661
Bierman, Falk 213
Bierman, Helene 213
Bilik, Ivan 661
Binamowitsch, Liba 270
Biow, Alice 270
Biow, Hedwig 270
Biskubicz, Jakub 88, 95, 101, 126, 151
   Biography 168
Blatt, Leon 197
Blatt, Thomas (Toivi) 5, 17, 46, 75, 95, 96, 98, 113, 131, 132, 135, 143, 147, 150, 153, 155, 158, 160, 162, 165, 169, 178, 182, 185, 188, 189, 193, 196, 197, 198, 201, 203, 206, 379
   Biography 168
Blau, Adele 582
   Biography 197
Blau, Karl 116, 117, 581, 582
   Biography 197
Blaurock, Emil 429, 486, 541, 549
   Biography 380
Bleich, Erna 270
Bleich, Ita (formerly Sturm) 270
Bleich, Ruth 270
Bloch-Wertheimer, Melanie Erika 214
Bloch, Friederike (formerly Levi) 270
Bloch, Ilse 270
Bloch, Lina (formerly Kleinstrass) 270
Bloch, Siegmund *b.1861* 270
Bloch, Siegmund *b.1878* 271
Blok-Elias, Minna 214
Bluhm, Lotte (formerly Weisfeldt) 271
Blum, Arthur 271

Blum, Caroline (formerly Weinberger) 271
Blum, Hanna 271
Blum, Ida (formerly Braumann) 271
Blum, Leontine (formerly Lorch) 271
Blum, Martha 271
Blumberg, Meta (formerly Lewald) 272
Blumenfeld, Georg 272
Blumenthal, Adolf 272
Blumenthal, Bernhard 272
Blumenthal, Else 272
Blumenthal, Hilde (formerly Schwarz) 272
Blumenthal, Mathilde (formerly Kahn) 272
Blutstein, Fanny 272
Bodenheimer, Martha (formerly Ermann) 272
Bodenheimer, Siegfried 273
Bodessa, Iwan 48, 117, 118, 434, 444, 461, 661
Bogunov, Dimitrij 661
Bohm, Ernst 198, 273
Bojarski, *Farmer* 113, 178, 193
Bolender, Kurt 37, 41, 50, 51, 59, 68, 118, 125, 134, 137, 138, 139, 140, 144, 380, 390, 429, 436, 443, 447, 450, 453, 457, 459, 460, 461, 466, 467, 472, 473, 478, 480, 481, 482, 487, 497, 499, 506, 511, 512, 513, 516, 519, 541, 554, 560, 571, 572
   Biography 380
Borger, Rosa (formerly Melamed) 273
Borner, Gerhard 36
   Biography 381
Bornstein, Moshe 169
Borzkowski-Stroz, Gitla 214

Borzkowski, Hermann 214
Borzykowski, David 214
Brachold, Gisela (formerly Burstin) 273
Brand, Berek 198
Brand, Hanka 198
Brasch, Clotilde (formerly Frank) 273
Braunsberg, Emile (formerly Stern) 273
Braunsberg, Viktor 273
Bredow, Paul 35, 53, 69, 137, 208, 429, 445, 446, 447, 458, 487, 516, 531, 541, 554
   Biography 381
Bree, Max 103, 429, 560
   Biography 381
Bresler, Dr. Szulim 198
Bresler, Jozek 198
Briefwechsler, Paula (formerly Blumenthal) 274
Brinker, Motel 198
Bronne, Emma (formerly Beisinger) 274
Bronne, Gertrud 274
Bronne, Ruth 274
Bruck-Falkenberg, Herta 215
Bruck, Van Family 215
Bruckmann, Hulda 274
Bucheim, Johanna (formerly Simon) 274
Bucheim, Riga 274
Bucksteeg, Josef
   Biography 424
Buhler Brothers 366
Bühler, Josef (Dr.) 20
Businnij, Prokofi 661
Butwies, Cornelie 274

C

Cahn, Berta (formerly Jacobi) 274

Cahn, Erich 274
Cahn, Hedwig (formerly Ferse) 275
Cahn, Selma 275
Cahn, Toni 275
Cats, Minny, Hanny 188, 192
   Biography 215
Chabibulin, Achmed 661
Chromenko, Chariton 661
Cohen, Alex 336
Cohn, Hannacha 275
Cohn, Recha (formerly Grunspan) 275
Cohn, Thekla (formerly Kaufmann) 275
Cowdery, Ray 19
Cuckierman, Josef 148
   Biography 169
Cukierman, Hershel 75, 148, 156, 169, 201, 662
   Biography 169
Cybulski, Boris 103, 184, 422
Czapnik, Zina 339
   Biography 337
Czarlinski, Johanna 275
Czepik, (Forename unknown) 198

D

Dabizja *Trawnikimann* 134, 661
Dachsel, Arthur 160, 161, 381, 433, 487, 541, 560
   Biography 381
Dalberg-Nussbaum, Bella 216
Dalberg, Julius, Jonas 215
Dalke, Henrich 661
Dam, Max, van 78
   Biography 216
Danilchenko, Ignat 661
   Testimony 594–99
Dannenberg, Emmy (formerly Wolfes) 275

Dannenburg, Ruth 276
Danzig, Mina 276
David (Surname unknown) 95
David, Hilda 276
David, Klara (formerly Kahn) 276
David, Magarethe (formerly Heymann) 276
Decker, Getta (formerly Frank) 276
Deen, Helga 217
Deen, Klaus Gottfried 217
Deen, Willy 217
Deen-Wolf, Kathe 217
Demjanjuk, Ivan 26, 28, 126, 127, 597, 598, 599, 661
Deptyarev, Vasili 661
Dietze, Erich 549
   Biograpy 382
Dimida, Konstantinl 661
Dizirkal, Karl 662
Doenberg, Henny (formerly Goldmann) 276
Dollefeld, Clara (formerly Wallach) 276
Dollefeld, Mathilde 276
Domeratski, Jakob 661
Dresden-Polak, Anna 218
Dresden, Eva 218
Drezler, Josef 170
Drieduite, Alexander 218
Drieduite, Celine 218
Drieduite, David 218
Drucker, Aron 277
Drucker, Martin, Samuel 218, 219
Drucker, Rosa 277
Drucker, Ruth 219
Drucker-Ehrenfreund, Gitla 219
Dubois, Werner 98, 100, 122, 124, 162, 198, 382, 400, 437, 456, 463, 464, 484, 497, 554, 561, 564, 571, 574
   Biography 382

Duda, Michal 662
Duniec, Josef 70, 71, 167
   Biography 170

E

Eberl, Irmfried (Dr.) 27, 28, 63, 373, 374, 383, 384, 388, 391
   Biography 383
Eckmann, Emma (formerly Sulzbacher) 277
Ehlbaum, Hanni 277
Ehlbaum, Perla (fromerly Bernstein) 277
Ehrenfreund, Leo, Leib 219
Ehrenfreund, Martha (formerly Rosenstein) 219
Ehrlich, Anita 277
Ehrlich, Ella (formerly Berlin) 277
Ehrlich, Frieda 277
Ehrlich, Hermann 278
Ehrlich, Kathinka (formerly Simon) 278
Ehrmann, Henny (formerly Hahn) 278
Ehrmann, Leopol 278
Ehrmann, Rosa 278
Eichmann, Adolf 20, 416
Eichorn, Irma (formerly Pfifferling) 278
Eisenberger, Karoline (formerly Worms) 278
Eisenstadt, Heinz 278
Eisenstadt, Henriette (formerly Lewkowitz) 278
Eisenstadt, Herta 279
Eisenstadt, Marta 279
Eisenstadt, Rosa 279
Eisenstadt, Willi 279
Elbert, Hugo 199
Elias-Frank, Bertha (formerly Frank) 220

Elias, Bella (formerly Weinstein) 279
Elias, Frieda 219
Elias, Helen 220
Elias, Julie (formerly Pohly) 279
Elias, Moritz 219, 220
Eliazer, Judith 337, 340
Ellinger, Martha (formerly Birnzweig) 279
Elshoffer, Wilhelm 280
Elsoffer, Selma (formerly Lichtenstein) 279
Eltbogen, Blanka 280
Eltbogen, Gertrud 280
Eltbogen, Katherina 280
Eltbogen, Phillipp 280
   Biography 280
Emmerich, Ile (Ilse) 220
Engel, (Forename Unknown)- 'Engel the Locksmith'
   Biography 199
Engel, Alexander 280
Engel, Chaim 90, 91, 103, 133, 154, 171, 172, 206, 379, 415
   Biography 170
Engel, Selma 61, 62, 72, 73, 90, 91, 154, 171, 172, 210
   Biography 171
Engelbert, Wilhelmine (formerly Lipp) 280
Engelhardt, Jakub 662
Ensel, Bertha 337, 340
Epstein, Sara (formerly Wechsler) 281
Erbsen, Lina 281
Ermann, Alfred 281
Ermann, Hilde 281
Ermann, Ruth 281
Ernst, Emil 220
Eschwege, Felix 281
Eschwege, Gabriel 281
Eschwege, Regina (formerly Michel) 282
Ettling, Marie 282

F

Fajgenbaum, Jakub 172
Falkenstein, Frieda 282
Falkenstein, Margarete 282
Farntrog, Betty 282
Federmann, Sabina (formerly Jakubowicz) 282
Fedorenko, Ivan 662
Feilchenfeld, Meta (formerly Kohler) 282
Feilchenfeld, Ruth 283
Feinberg, Sophie 283
Feiwel-Nussbaum, Fanny 220, 221
Feiwel, Jozef, Chaim, Benjamin 220
Feiwel, Norbert 220, 221
Feldman, Else 283
Feldman, Regina 149, 183, 186
   Biography 195
Felenbaum-Weiss, Hella 173
Felhendler, Leon 76, 82, 84, 85, 86, 94, 145, 157, 158, 161, 173, 184, 208
   Biography 172
Fiebelmann, Elsie 283
Fischelberg, Genia (formerly Spatz) 283
Fischelberg, Mira 283
Flajszhakier, Shaul 'Negro' 147
   Biography 199
Flamm, Efraim 283
Flamm, Hermine (formerly Fleischer) 283
Fledel, Ruth 284
Fledel, Selma (formerly Lauh) 284
Fleischer, Leibl 200
Fleischmann, Otto 284

Fleischmann, Rosa (formerly Friedmann) 284
Florsheimer, Gertrude 284
Floss, Erich Herbert 41, 51, 53, 98, 116, 385, 409, 430, 487, 497, 528, 532, 541, 551, 554, 662
  Biography 384
Flunt, Miron 662
Forker, Alfred
  Biography 385
Frank-Rosenbusch, Elsa 221
Frank, Dora 284
Frank, Ernst 284
Frank, Eva 284
Frank, Federik 221
Frank, Hans 221
Frank, Helena (formerly Zeilberger) 284
Frank, Irene (formerly Schonfeld) 285
Frank, Johanna (formerly Sender) 285
Frank, Melitta (formerly Kern) 285
Frank, Sara. 285
Frankenberg, Brunhilde 285
Frankenberg, Else (formerly Rose) 285
Frankl, Elli (formerly Schachtel) 285
Franz, *Kapo* 200
Franz, Kurt 28, 351, 385, 386, 387, 401, 407, 410, 430, 580
  Biography 385
Freiberg, Dov 43, 44, 45, 66, 67, 74, 78, 87, 94, 100, 101, 112, 126, 133, 134, 151, 152, 153, 156, 174, 206, 369, 413, 679
  Aunt-Esther 43, 44
  Biography 174
  Cousin-Mirale 43, 44
  Uncle-Micheal 43, 44
Freiberman, Szama 181, 182
  Biography 175
Frenzel, Karl 28, 35, 38, 41, 61, 70, 75, 77, 78, 79, 80, 83, 85, 92, 97, 98, 100, 118, 120, 122, 124, 129, 130, 135, 137, 146, 148, 155, 156, 158, 159, 169, 175, 177, 187, 192, 206, 207, 208, 216, 325, 378, 380, 381, 387, 388, 418, 419, 428, 437, 439, 441, 443, 450, 453, 454, 455, 456, 457, 459, 460, 461, 462, 463, 466, 468, 475, 479, 481, 487, 493, 495, 506, 512, 514, 516, 522, 531, 541, 551, 552, 554, 556, 557, 558, 561, 562, 565, 581, 680
  Biography 387
Freudenberger, Minna (formerly Stern) 285
Freudenthal, Berta (formerly Buchheim) 285
Fried, Marrianne 285
Fried, Moritz 286
Fried, Selma 286
Friedberg, Hans 200
Friedlander, Minna (formerly Mayer) 286
Friedman, Beate 286
Friedman, Betti (formerly Goldschmidt) 286
Friedmann, Benno 221
Friedmann, Edith 286
Friedmann, Jakob, Salomon 221, 222
Friedmann, Judith 286
Friedmann, Lina 286
Friedmann, Margarete (formerly Schwabach) 286
Friedmann, Margot 287
Friedmann, Susi 287
Friedmann-Sonnenberg, Liebe, Rachela 222
Friesem, Ruth (formerly Liebmann) 287

Frolov, Gennardi 662
Fruchter, Gisela (formerly Braun) 287
Fruchter, Mendel 287
Fuchs, Erich 41, 48, 49, 124, 378, 388, 389, 413, 436, 437, 439, 441, 445, 451, 452, 453, 456, 457, 462, 470, 568
  Biography 388
Fuld, Bertha (formerly Joseph) 287
Fuld, Erna (formerly Junghaus) 287
Furth, Marie (formerly Amann) 287

G

Gabčík, Jozef 19
Gans, Elfriede (formerly Meyer) 287
Gans, Else 288
Gans, Judis 288
Gans, Rosa 288
Ganss, Martha (formerly Altmann) 288
Gaulstich, Friedrich 91, 103, 178, 253, 430, 487
  Biography 389
Geiss, Franziska (formerly Levi) 288
Geniek (Forename unknown) *Kapo* 86
  Biography 200
Gentz, Adolf 582
  Biography 390
Gernsheimer, Hans 288
Gernsheimer, Lothar 288
Gernsheimer, Ludwig 288
Gernsheimer, Therese (formerly Levi) 288
Gerson-Riese, Toni 222
Gerson, Max 222

Getzinger, Anton 'Toni' 35, 48, 80, 81, 137, 151, 390, 430, 444, 445, 447, 452, 453, 458, 467, 500, 511, 512, 526, 537, 541, 542
  Biography 390
Geusler *Trawnikimann* 662
Gezang-Goudeket, Florence 222
Gezang-Huib, Koenrad 222
Gisela (Surname unknown) 67, 449, 461, 462
  Biography 201, 207
Globocnik, Odilo 19, 20, 21, 22, 25, 26, 27, 28, 31, 39, 40, 60, 62, 63, 64, 73, 74, 106, 107, 108, 119, 121, 355, 356, 357, 358, 359, 360, 361, 362, 363, 365, 369, 370, 373, 384, 386, 387, 388, 393, 416, 427, 441, 501, 507, 567, 571
  Biography 355
Glogowski, Gertrud (formerly Lewinberg) 289
Gluckauf, Friedericke (formerly Reiss) 289
Goberman, Moshe 201
Godfried-Nussbaum, Margarete Flora 223
Gokkes, Catharina, (Kathy) 180, 188
  Biography 175
Goldberg, Frieda (formerly Lowenstein) 289
Goldberg, Lothar 289
Goldfarb, Moshe 180, 182
  Biography 175
Goldmann, Anna (formerly Seligmann) 289
Goldmann, Hugo 289
Goldmeier, Karohne (formerly Muller) 290
Goldmeier, Louis 290
Goldmeier, Meta (formerly Goldwein) 290

Goldmeier, Nathan 290
Goldschmidt, Charlotte 290
Goldschmidt, Felix 290
Goldschmidt, Freda (formerly Lowenstein) 290
Goldschmidt, Freda (formerly Strauss) 290
Goldschmidt, Gottfried 291
Goldschmidt, Helene (formerly Borchert) 291
Goldschmidt, Helene (formerly Muller) 291
Goldschmidt, Henry 291
Goldschmidt, Hilda (formerly Reiss) 291
Goldschmidt, Hilda (formerly Stern) 291
Goldschmidt, Ilse 291
Goldschmidt, Isidor 291
Goldschmidt, Jenny (formerly Hamburger) 292
Goldschmidt, Johanna (formerly Lowenberg) 292
Goldschmidt, Johanna (formerly Rosenbach) 292
Goldschmidt, Juda 292
Goldschmidt, Julius 292
Goldschmidt, Karl 292
Goldschmidt, Lina (formerly Birk) 292
Goldschmidt, Lothar 292
Goldschmidt, Markus 293
Goldschmidt, Minna 293
Goldschmidt, Regina (formerly Nordhauser) 293
Goldschmidt, Regina (formerly Wikowsky) 293
Goldschmidt, Selma (formerly Gutmann) 293
Goldschmidt, Sigmund 293
Goldschmidt, Simon b.1876 293
Goldschmidt, Simon b.1884 293

Goldstein, Betty 294
Goldstein, Cacilie (formerly Keins) 294
Goldstein, Nora 294
Goldstein, Schlomo 201
Goldstern, Eugenie 294
Gomerski, Hubert 35, 37, 52, 59, 68, 81, 82, 88, 121, 137, 151, 158, 167, 184, 380, 390, 391, 418, 428, 436, 441, 450, 453, 473, 477, 479, 480, 482, 485, 486, 493, 494, 497, 499, 506, 511, 512, 513, 514, 516, 542, 554, 557, 562, 565, 662
  Biography 390
  Testimony 520–33
Gompertz, Klaartje (Clara) 338
Goncharenko, Anatoli 662
Goncharenko, Nikolai 662
Goncharow, Efim 662
Gordiennko, Nikolai 662
Gork, Betty (formerly Scheige) 289
Gorlov, Fedor 662
Göth, Amon 22, 27, 362, 363, 364
  Biography 362
Gottlieb, Josef 294
Gottlieb, Karoline 294
Gottlieb, Lina 294
Gottschalk, Alice (formerly Ullmann) 294
Gottschalk, Jochanan 295
Graetschus, Siegfried 36, 46, 66, 89, 90, 103, 137, 145, 179, 194, 431, 463, 466, 531, 542, 580
  Biography 391
Grinbaum, Esther 86, 203
  Biography 201
Griner, Chaim 201
Grisha (Soviet POW) 201
Gromer, Siegfried 392, 430, 447, 453, 457, 518, 561
  Biography 392

known as 'Red Cake' 59, 64
Gross, Eva (formerly Grossmann) 295
Gross, Josef 295
Groth, Paul 35, 53, 67, 134, 137, 140, 141, 174, 181, 207, 392, 430, 444, 447, 460, 481, 487, 542, 554
  Biography 392
Grumbacher, Emilie (formerly Grunbaum) 295
Grunblatt, Olga (formerly Pakula) 295
Grunebaum, Bella 295
Grunebaum, Bella (formerly Strauss) 295
Grunebaum, Blanka 295
Grunewald, Franziska 295
Grunewald, Ida (formerly Lazarus) 296
Grunfeld, Margot 296
Grunfeld, Rosa (formerly Hecht) 296
Gunther, Wilhelm 104, 418
Gunzenhauser, Betty 296
Guthmann, Frieda (formerly Gerson) 296
Gutmann, Franziska 296
Guttkind, Annemarie 296
Guttsmann, Walter Johann 296
Gutwirth, Fanny (formerly Bruder) 297

H

Haas, Eugenie 297
Haas, Karoline 297
Haas, Recha (formerly Moller) 297
Haberman-Jungenwirt, Chaja, Malka 223
Haberman, Abraham 223
Haberman, Mina 223

Hackenholt, Lorenz 65, 393, 394, 395, 396, 401, 512, 547, 554, 561, 565
  Biography 393
Haendel, Else (formerly Loser) 297
Hahn, Augusta 223
Hahn, Cacille *b.1877* 297
Hahn, Cacille *b.1900* 297
Hahn, Franziska (formerly Levi) 297
Hahn, Frieda 297
Hahn, Johanna (formerly Strahlheim) 297
Hahn, Lenni 298
Hahn, Leonore 298
Hain, Paula (formerly Marx) 298
Hakel, Emil
  Biography 392
Halberstadt, Leon 146
  Biography 202
Hamber, Amalie (formerly Mayer) 298
Hamberg, Betty (formerly Pulver) 298
Hamberg, Hermann 298
Hamberg, Moritz 298
Hamberg, Susanne 298
Hamburger-Korn, Bertha 224
Hamburger-Schlachter, Bertha 223
Hamburger, Heinrich 299
Hamburger, Jessie 223
Hamburger, Levie 223, 224
Hamburger, Samuel 224
Hamme, Joel 224
Hamme, Marcus 224
Hammerschlag, Mirjam (formerly Lillenfeld) 299
Hammerschlag, Sophie 224
Hammerschmidt, Cilla 299
Hammerschmidt, Rosa 299

Hana (Surname unknown) 299
Hanau, Leonie (formerly Mayer) 299
Hanff, Hans 299
Hanff, Irmgard (formerly Openheimer) 300
Hannel, Salomea 176
Hase, Karl 300
Hase, Rolf 300
Hase, Selma (formerly Jakob) 300
Hasenkopf, Reisel (formerly Birnbach) 300
Hecht, Else (formerly Bar) 300
Hecht, Gitta (formerly Goldschmidt) 300
Hecht, Goldina 300
Hecht, Ida 301
Hecht, Jakob 301
Hecht, Jettchen 301
Hecht, Jettchl (formerly Plaut) 301
Hecht, Lothar 301
Hecht, Ludwig 301
Hecht, Meier 301
Hecht, Sophie 301
Hecht, Steffi 301
Heilberg, Meta (formerly Falkenstein) 302
Heilberg, Selma 302
Heilbronn, Julius 302
Heilbrunn, Frieda (formerly Eisemann) 302
Heilbrunn, Gertrud (formerly Strauss) 302
Heilbrunn, Jettchen 302
Heilbrunn, Maya 302
Heilbrunn, Meta 302
Heimenrath, Hedwig 303
Helft, Kuno 303
Helft, Lucie (formerly Heinemann) 303
Hene, Dora (formerly Nebel) 303

Henlein, Martha (formerly Albert) 303
Hering, Gottlieb 28, 103, 116, 377, 460, 484, 491, 578
　Biography 376
Herszmann, Josef 176
Herz, Irma (formerly Fuld) 303
Herz, Kiewe 146
　Biography 202
Herzberg, Bronja (formerly Wajuryb) 303
Herzberg, Fabisch 303
Hes, Bernard 303
Hes, Fanny (formerly Idstein) 304
Hes, Nathan 304
Hes, Paula 304
Hes, Recha 304
Hes, Rose (formerly Blumenfeld) 304
Hesdorfer, Johanna (formerly Joseph) 304
Hess, Frieda 304
Hess, Lilly (formerly Suser) 304
Hess, Martha (formerly Weil) 305
Hess, Selma (formerly Simons) 305
Hess, Thekla (formerly Buchheim) 305
Hetmaniac, Wasil 116, 385, 662
Heydrich, Reinhard 19, 20
Heymann, Anna (formerly Lerner) 305
Heyum, Johanna (formerly Israel) 305
Hiller, Richard
　Biography 396
Himmler, Heinrich 20, 21, 23, 26, 63, 68, 69, 70, 73, 74, 107, 108, 116, 322, 355, 356, 357, 358, 361, 362, 369, 407, 418, 471, 502, 503, 515, 524, 527, 530, 666, 667

719

Hirsch, Adele (formerly Simon) 305
Hirsch, Alfred 305
Hirsch, Auguste 305
Hirsch, Charleska (formerly Neuhaus) 305
Hirsch, Else (formerly Stock) 305
Hirsch, Emma (formerly Bach) 306
Hirsch, Emma (formerly Katz) 306
Hirsch, Frieda (formerly Lowenthal) 306
Hirsch, Henriette (formerly Scharff) 306
Hirsch, Ilse 306
Hirsch, Mirjam 306
Hirsch, Rosa (formerly Seufert) 306
Hirschberg, Alice 306
Hirschberg, Rose 306
Hirschberg, Selma 307
Hirschberger, Betty 307
Hirschbrandt, Helga 307
Hirschbrandt, Ida (formerly Strauss) 307
Hirschbrandt, Otto 307
Hirschmann, Kurt 307
Hirschmann, Salomon 307
Hirschmann, Sara (formerly Rosenberg) 307
Hirtreiter, Josef 'Sepp' 121, 396, 397, 416, 494, 542
  Biography 396
Hitler, Adolf 21, 355, 387
Hochmann, Moshe 89
  Biography 176
Hoddis, Jakob van (Davidsohn, Hans) 308
Hödl, Franz 48, 65, 118, 397, 444, 445, 447, 453, 458, 505, 561, 662, 663
  Biography 397

Hoff, Martha (formerly Frankel) 308
Hoffman, Otto 20
Höfle, Hermann Julius 22, 27, 28, 103, 119, 120, 121, 357, 358, 360, 361, 362, 363, 427
  Biography 357
Hoflich, Gerda 308
Hoflich, Hilde (formerly Rothschild) 308
Hofmann, Selma (formerly Lowenberg) 308
Hohenberg, Ella (formerly Levi) 308
Hollander, Elvira (formerly Troplowitz) 308
Holzheimer, Franz 33
Holzmann, Erna 309
Holzmann, Martha (formerly Ackermann) 309
Honigman, Zyndel 176
Hormann, Bella 309
Horn, Frieda (formerly Kerzner) 309
Hotorowicz, Jan 662
Hoxter, Erika 309
Hoxter, Ilse 309
Hoxter, Rosa (formerly Nussbaum) 309
Huisman, Sophia 338, 340

I

Idstein, Therese 309
Ikenberg, Isaak 225
Immergluck, Lotte (formerly Goldstein) 309
Indyukov, Ivan 662
Isaacson, Anna (formerly Sondheim) 310
Isaak, Beate 310
Isaak, Betty 310

Isaak, Billa 310
Isaak, Edith 310
Isaak, Elfriede 310
Isaak, Leopold 310
Isaak, Lina (formerly Liebermann) 310
Isaak, Max 310
Isaak, Moritz 311
Isaak, Rahel 311
Isaak, Rosa 311
Isaak, Selma (formerly Wallach) 311
Isaak, Theodor 311
Isaenko, Aleksei 662
Isenberg, Berta 311
Isenberg, Emilie 311
Isenberg, Selma 311
Israel, Ada (formerly Robert) 312
Israel, Amalie (formerly Falkenberg) 312
Israel, Bernhard 312
Israel, Dina (formerly Falkenstein) 312
Israel, Hedwig (formerly Hallgarten) 312
Israel, Herta 312
Israel, Isaak 225
Israel, Margot 312
Israel, Rosa (formerly Kaufmann) 312
Israel, Rosel 313
Ittner, Alfred 41, 51, 53, 124, 437, 450, 453, 456, 457, 466, 467, 487, 516, 519, 552, 553, 554
  as Paul 430, 542
  Biography 397
Itzkovich, Michael 110
  Biography 177
Itzkowitz, Hilda (formerly Strauss) 313
Ivchenko, Ivan 597, 662
Iwashenko, Piotr 662

J

Jacob, Karl 313
Jacob, Klarchen 313
Jacob, Louis 313
Jacob, Rolf 313
Jacobs-Lazarus, Julie 225
Jacobs, Charlotte (formerly Rosenbaum) 313
Jacobs, Jacob b. *Jan 1886* 225
Jacobs, Jacob b. *May 1886* 225
Jacobs, Jacob b. *1859* 225
Jacobs, Jacob b. *1895* 225
Jacobs, Jozeph 225
Jacobsohn, Hedwig (formerly Cohn) 313
Jacobson, Mariana 226
Jahl, Karla 314
Jakob, Hedwig (formerly Lowenthal) 314
Jarynuik, Ivan 662
Jaworow, Fiodor 662
Jechai, Iosef 662
Jefimov, Wasili 662
Jeret, Etta (formerly Kronfeld) 314
Jermoldayev, Ivan 662
Jesse, Rosalie (formerly Philipp) 314
Jonas, Kurt 314
Jonassohn, Hans 314
Jongh, de Lea 671
  Biography 226
Jordan, Hedwig (formerly Examus) 314
Jordan, Hedwig (formerly Mendel) 314
Joseph, Helene (formerly Buchheim) 314
Jourdan, Elisabeth 314
Jourgrau-Friedmann, Lea 226
Juda, Berta (formerly Simon) 314

Judel, Flora (formerly Susskind) 315
Judin, Nikolai 662
Juhrs, Robert 118, 125, 398, 423, 437, 456, 698
   Biography 398
   Testimony 577–78
Junghaus, Rosa (formerly Lyon) 315
Jungheim, Aron 315
Jungheim, Julchen (formerly Plaut) 315

K

Kabriov, Nurgali 662
Kaempfer, Georg 315
Kaempfer, Herta (formerly Bergheim) 315
Kaempfer, Irmgard 315
Kaempfer, Marion 315
Kahn, Berta 315
Kahn, Betti (formerly Nusbaum) 316
Kahn, Edgar 202
Kahn, Erna 316
Kahn, Fanny (formerly Katz) 316
Kahn, Frieda 316
Kahn, Frieda (formerly Kahn) 316
Kahn, Frieda (formerly Strauss) b. 1881 316
Kahn, Frieda (formerly Strauss) b. 1897 316
Kahn, Gertrud 316
Kahn, Henriette (formerly Weiss) 316
Kahn, Ida (formerly Simon) 317
Kahn, Ilse 317
Kahn, Irma 317
Kahn, Jakob 317
Kahn, Jenny (formerly Klein) 317
Kahn, Johanna (formerly Levi) 317

Kahn, Lore 317
Kahn, Melitta (formerly Dreyfus) 317
Kahn, Selma 317
Kahn, Toni 318
Kahn, Werner 318
Kaiser, Alexsy 117, 118, 431, 542, 562, 662
Kaiser, Emilie (formerly Guggenheimer) 318
Kaiser, Frieda (formerly Schonfrank) 318
Kaiser, Sara (formerly Heiser) 318
Kakorach, Ivan 662
Kamm, Emil 318
Kamm, Rosa (formerly Kamm) 318
Kamm, Rudolf 395, 399, 431, 561, 562
   Biography 398
Kamm, Ruth 318
Kann, Ellen (formerly Kahn) 319
Kanter, Kantel 319
Kanter, Karoline (fomerly Weinberg) 319
Kanter, Ludwig 319
Kanthal, Baruch 319
Kanthal, Bertha (formerly Summer) 319
Kaplan, Hans 319
Kaplan, Helga 319
Kapper, Anna (Annie) 226
Kar, Abraham, van de 226
Kar, Anna, van de 226
Kar, David van de 227
Kar, van de, Betje (formerly Wurms) 227
Kar, van de, Jacob 227
Karakasz, Iwan 662
   Testimony 599–603
Karas, Pavel 662
Karimov, Fetich 662

Karle, Olga (formerly Grunstein) 320
Karlebach, Sophie 320
Karolek 147
   Biography 203
Karpenko, Alexander 662
Kaschmann, Rosi 320
Kaszewacki *Trawnikimann* 662
Katz, Benjamin, 'Bunio' 80, 88, 131, 203, 216, 325
   Biography 203
Katz, Berta (formerly Katz) 320
Katz, Berta b.*1887* 320
Katz, Edith 320
Katz, Emilie (formerly Lowenstein) 320
Katz, Frieda 320
Katz, Gertrud 320
Katz, Hedwig (formerly Plaut) 321
Katz, Irma 321
Katz, Johanna (formerly Rosenbaum) 321
Katz, Lina (formerly David) 321
Katz, Martha 321
Katz, Recha (formerly Kahn) 321
Katz, Sally 321
Katz, Salomon 321
Katz, Selma (formerly Steinberger) 321
Katz, Serka 177
Katz, Siegfried 321
Katzenheim, Alfred 322
Katzenstein-Rosenblatt, Sophie 227
Katzenstein, Abraham 322
Keezer, Elsa, Virginie 227
Keizer-Haas, Rebekka 227
Keizer, Louis 227, 228
Kempner, Friedrich-Wilhelm 322
Kindler-Kornfeld, Ides 228
Kindler, Adolf 228
Kindler, Gitta Bronia 228

Kindler, Herz 228
Kisilew, Viktor 67, 180, 662
Klatt, Ivan 58, 89, 90, 103, 115, 179, 182, 194, 463, 488, 542, 663
Kleerekoper-Ossedrijver, Kaatje 228
Kleerekoper, Elisabeth 228
Kleerekoper, Gerrit 228
Klier, Johann 36, 118, 121, 148, 399, 456, 582
   Biography 399
   Testimony 520–33
Kloot-Nordheim, Helena 229
   Biography 229
Kloot, Abraham 229
Kloot, Jacob 229
Kloot, Rebecca 229
Klos, Walter 549
   Biography 400
Koch, Johanna 70
   Biography 322
Kohn, Abram 177
Kon-Dydakov, Chana 230
   Biography 230
Kon, Mosiek, Markus 230
   Biography 229
Kon, Szymon 229
Kon, Wolf, Majlech 230
Konrad, Fritz 91, 99, 103, 419, 420, 431, 466, 488, 542
   Biography 400
Koopman-Vogel, Deborah 230
   Biography 230
Koopman-Porcelijn, Clara 230
Koopman, Levie 230
   Biography 230
Kopf, Joseph 75, 185
   Biography 177
Korenfeld, Chaim 178
Kornfeld, Josef 230
Koschekuk, Piotr 663
Koschemykin, Jakov 663
Koslowski, Iwan 663

Kostenko, Emil *Trawnikimann* 50, 129, 663
Kostmann, Fredek 113, 178, 193
  Biography 178
Koszewadski, Volodia 150, 156, 157
Kozaczuk, Piotr 663
Kozewadzski, Volodia 663
Krawchenko, Filip 663
Krawczak, Z 33
Krüger, Wilhelm Friedrich 20, 365
Krupinewich, Mikolaii 663
Krupka *Trawnikimann* 148, 663
Kubiš, Jan 19
Kudin, Pavel 663
Kugelmann, Siegfried 322
Kuptshin, Sasha 203
Kurakov, Pavel 663
Kusevanov, Michail 663
Kwiatkowski 67, 180

L

Lachmann, Erich 41, 124, 149, 150, 392, 400, 431, 434, 437, 447, 453, 456, 460, 464, 465, 466, 478, 488, 536, 537, 545
  Biography 400
  Testimony 533–46
Lambert, Erwin Herman 23, 39, 65, 118, 125, 370, 394, 401, 437, 456, 506
  Biography 400
  Testimony 547–48
Lampie-Polak, Mina 231
Lampie, Alida 230
Lampie, Maurits 231
Lampie, Max 231
Lampie, Miep 231
Leeda-van de KAR, Celina 231
Leitman, Shlomo 109
Leitman, Szlomo 83, 84, 91, 97, 103, 192, 389
  Biography 178
Lejst, Chaim 179
Lerch, Ernst 22, 28, 116, 359, 360, 362
  Biography 359
Lerer, Samuel 122, 134, 186, 378, 574
  Biography 179
Lerner, Yehuda 88, 89, 90, 103, 175, 194, 305, 392
  Biography 179
Leszczynski, Zygmunt 699
Levi, Erich 231
Levi, Rika 231
Levi, Sally 231
Levy-Moses, Hedwig 232
Lewandowski-Mecca, Karoline 232
Liberman, Pesia 67, 180, 471
  Biography 180
Libodenko *Trawnikimann* 663
Licht, Aron 180
Lichtman, Berek 147
  Biography 203
Lichtman, Eda 35, 61, 78, 86, 96, 149, 150, 155, 175, 177, 188, 189, 198, 199, 200, 201, 203, 204, 205, 206, 207, 208, 209, 210, 215, 299, 400, 537
  Biography 180
Lichtman, Itzhak 146
  Biography 181
Lillenthal, Fritz 232
Litwinowski, Yefim 181
Loewenstein, Frieda (formerly Schwarzchild) 322
Loewenstein, Friederike 323
Loewenstein, Gustav 323
Loewenstein, Henriette 323
Loewenstein, Julie 323
Loewenstein, Lilli, Lilly 323
Loewenstein, Mathilde, Mathilda (formerly Rosenthal) 323

Loewenstein, Minna (formerly Cohen) 323
Loewenstein, Mirjam 323
Loewenstein, Paula (formerly Gottschalk) 323
Loewenstein, Rudolf 324
Loewenstein, Selma 324
Loewenstein, Selma (formerly Vogel) 324
Loewenstein, Wilhelm 324
Loffler, Alfred 416
Longerich, Peter 20
Lorenz Fredrich 663
Lowenstein, Else (formerly Goldberg) 232
Lowenstein, Hannelore 232
Lowenstein, Ilse 323
Lowenstein, Inge 232
Lowenstein, Kurt 339
Lubartowska, Helka 87
  Biography 203
Ludwig, Karl 62, 68, 402, 431, 447, 448, 449, 461, 488, 562
  Biography 401
Lustbader-Presser, Leja 232
Lutomirski, Isidor 233
Lutomirski, Martha 233
Lychov, Grigorli 663
Lychov, Ivan 663

M

Machles, Szmul 175, 182
  Biography 181
Makarenko, Pawel 663
Malinowski *Trawnikimann* 149, 663
Manuskowski, Wolf 233
Mar, De La Graanboom, Esther 233
Marchenko, Ivan Ivanovich (Ivan the Terrible) 26

Margulies, Abraham 88, 148
  Biography 181
Martynow, Nikolai 663
Martynow, Terentji 663
Marum, Eva Brigitte 204
Marx, Bettina, Babette 324
Marx, Elfriede 324
Marx, Ella (formerly Strauss) 324
Marx, Emil 324
Marx, Emilie 325
Marx, Emilie (formerly Ackerman) 324
Marx, Erich 233
Marx, Sara (formerly Barmann) 325
Marx, Solly, Samuel 325
Mashenko, Andrei 663
Matthes, Heinrich 28, 351, 402, 403, 406, 416
  Biography 402
  Testimony 578–79
Matwiejenkow, M. 126, 663
Matys, (Forename unknown) 175, 181
  Biography 182
Matzig, Willy 403
  Biography 403
Mauer, *Trawnikimann* 663
  as Maurer 484, 562
Mausberger, Werner 549
  Biography 404
Mazurkiewitch, Semion 110
  Biography 182
Mechanicus, Marianne 233
Medvedev, Nikolai 663
Menche, Chaskiel 80, 89, 103, 185
  Biography 182
Mendel
  Biography 182
Mendels, Heijman Sallij 339
Mentz, Willy 28, 405, 433
  Biography 404
Merenstein, Mosek 183

Metz, Zelda 74, 157, 186, 400
  Biography 183
Meyer-Stern, Sophie 234
Meyer, Berta 233
Meyer, Levi 234
Michalsen, Georg (Michalczyk, Georg) 22, 358, 361, 362
  Biography 103, 360
Michel, Hermann 35, 41, 42, 50, 137, 149, 405, 430, 431, 444, 516, 517
  Biography 405
Miete, August 28
Mikolayenko, Semion 663
Mileczina, Raja 337
  Biography 339
Misnerowiec 67, 180
Moniek (Surname unknown) 88
  Biography 204
Montezinos, Salomon Levie 340
Mordwinichev, Pavel 663
Morgensztern, Rabbi Mendel 204
Morpurgo-Morpurgo, Sara 234
Morpurgo, David 234
Moser, Bruno *Baurat* 32, 62, 424, 449, 554, 697
  Biography 424
Muller-Lindeman, Sophia 234
Muller, Adolf 36
  Biography 405
Muller, David 234
Müller, Heinrich (Gestapo) 20
Muller, Izaak 234
Mundek (Surname unknown)
  Biography 205
Munzberger, Gustav 406, 434, 549
  Biography 406
Mussenfeld, Muniek 205

N

Nabiyew, Bari 663

Naftanial, Herbert *'Berliner'* 80, 206, 253, 325
  Biography 325
Nagornyi, Andrej 663
Neuhaus-Seligman, Helene 235
Neuhaus, David, Peter 234
Neuhaus, Justin, Jacob 235
Niemann, Johann 15, 88, 89, 103, 155, 170, 176, 189, 201, 205, 208, 388, 407, 410, 428, 430, 448, 453, 463, 468, 486, 488, 497, 498, 511, 514, 528, 531, 532, 543, 554, 565, 587
  Biography 407
Nijko, Wasily 663
Nikoforow, Ivan 663
Nol, Abraham 235
Nol, Mozes, Richard 235
Noord, Elisabeth 236
Noord, Esther 236
Nord, Joseph 236
Nord, Mozes 236
Nord, Rachel 236
Norden, Alexander 236
Norden, Betsy 236
Norden, Hartog 237
Norden, Henni Sophia 237
Nowak, Anton 36, 103, 431, 543, 549
  Biography 407
Nowak, Walter 408, 549
  Biography 407
Nunez-Vas, Jacob 237
Nunez-Vas, Philip 237
Nunez-Vas, Samuel 237
Nunez-Vaz-Cohen, Betje 238
Nussbaum, Benjamin 238
Nussbaum, Hulda 238

O

Oberhauser, Josef 24, 42, 64, 68, 434, 554
Olexenko, Anatoli 663
Oppenheimer, Inge 238
Orgelist-de Leeuwe 238
Orgelist, Leentje 238
Orgelist, Roosje 238
Ossedrijver-Winkel, Anna 239
Ossedrijver, Dora 239
Ossedrijver, Jacques 239
    Biography 239
Oster-Windmuller, Rosalia, Rosalie 239
Oster, Else 326
Oster, Julie 326
Oster, Raphael, Rafael 239

P

Pankow, Anatoli 663
Pankow, Vassily 663
Panshuk, Ivan 663
Parijs-Vieijra, Rosa 239
Parijs, David 239
Parijs, Samuel 239
Parkola, Franciszek 108
Paulenko *Trawnikimann* 663
Pawali, Nikolai 663
Pechersky, Alexander 'Sasha' 74, 82, 83, 84, 85, 88, 90, 92, 94, 95, 97, 98, 109, 111, 126, 159, 173, 182, 184, 185, 186, 187, 189, 194, 202, 203, 241
    Biography 183
Pelc, Josel 155, 184
    Biography 184
Penha, de, la, David 240
Penha, de, la, Judith 240
Penha, de, la, Leah 240
Penha, Elias 340
    Biography 240
Penha-Blits, Mirjam 240
    Biography 340
Peperwortel, Nathan 341
Philips, Meijer 341
Picherov, Dimitrii 663
Piescikowski 67, 180
Pines, Joseph 69
    Biography 205
Piwonski, Jan 32, 33, 34, 47, 117
Platnicki, Naum 184
Plaut-Mainzer, Bertha 240
Plotnikow, Chaim 185
Podchlebnik, Szlomo 75, 177, 182
    Biography 185
Podienko, W. *Trawnikimann* 126, 663
Pohl, Oswald 28, 60, 73, 74, 669
Polak, Cato 340, 341
Polak, Surry 340, 343
    Biography 342
Polak, Suze 340, 342
    Biography 343
Polak, Wolf 240
Polisecki, Mandel 205
Polisecki, Mania 205
Polisecki, Rozalia 206
Poppert, Walter, Michel 80
    Biography 241
Poppert, Erich, Karl 241
Poppert-Schonborn, Gertrud (formerly Schonborn) 241
Post, Philip 416
    Biography 408
Pötzinger, Karl 408, 431, 447, 488, 543, 580
    Biography 408
Powroznik, Haim (Pozner, Herman) 185
Pozycki, Hersz 90, 91, 103, 171, 172, 185, 415
    Biography 206

Pozycki, Symon *Kapo* 80, 91, 185, 253
  Biography 206
Pozycki, Yankel 185
Praag-Hollander, Celina van 241
Praag, van, Benjamin 241
Preger, Annie 242
Presser, Kitty 242
Presser, Simon 242
Prins, Eduard 242

R

Raab, Estera 122, 154, 179, 183, 378, 407
  Biography 186
Rabinowitz, Shimon 206
Railing, Hugo 326
Razgonayev, Mikhail 663
  Testimony 585–93
Reichleitner, Franz 25, 27, 28, 63, 64, 65, 69, 88, 106, 107, 130, 131, 145, 354, 375, 376, 388, 392, 397, 400, 427, 428, 429, 446, 448, 453, 454, 465, 484, 485, 486, 488, 491, 498, 499, 504, 506, 507, 508, 511, 512, 513, 522, 526, 531, 543, 547, 555, 557, 580, 606
  Biography 375
Reisner-Bialowitz, Lea 186
Reiter, Frieda (formerly Keh) 242
  Biography 242
Reiter, Moritz, Moses 242
  Biography 242
Reitlinger, Gerald 19
Reschetnikov, Michail 663
Rewald, Wenzel (Fritz) 98, 395, 432, 441, 488, 543, 549
  Biography 409
Rezerchy, Igor 663
Richter, Kurt 36, 98, 137, 432, 444, 543, 549
  Biography 409
Rimkus, Tadus 663
Roet, Rachel 243
Roil *Trawnikimann* 434, 664
Roksuk, *Trawnikimann* 664
Root, Juda 243
Rosen-Susskind, Margarete, Marianne
  Biography 243
Rosen, Hella, Emmi 243
  Biography 243
Rosen, Jacob, Jakob 326
Rosen, Kate, Kathe (formerly Neumann) 326
Rosenfeld, Semion 92
  Biography 186
Rosenstiel-Oppenheimer, Irma 243
Rosenstiel, Albert 243
Rosenstiel, Liselotte, Karoline (Luka) 17, 84, 109, 187, 244
  Biography 187
Rosenstiel, Wilhelm 243
Rosenthal, Calman, Carl 243
Rosenthal, Edith 326
Rosenthal, Else 326
Rosenthal, Ernst, Samuel 326
Rosenthal, Friederike (formerly Lob) 327
Rosenthal, Georg 327
Rosenthal, Gerda 327
Rosenthal, Hans, Albert 327
Rosenthal, Hedwig 207
Rosenthal, Hertha 327
Rosenthal, Ilse 327
Rosenthal, Karl 327
Rosenthal, Kathe, Minna 327
Rosenthal, Mina (formerly Heilbronn) 327
Rosenthal, Minna (formerly Gutheim) 328

Rosenthal, Minna (formerly
    Wertheim) 327
Rosenthal, Rosalie (formerly
    Hecht) 328
Rosenthal, Selma (formerly
    Sondheimer) 328
Rost, Paul 407, 408, 410, 434, 464,
    488, 522, 528, 543, 562
    Biography 409
    Testimony 548–50
Rotenberg, Aizik 187
Rotenberg, Azik 112
Roth, Auguste (formerly
    Rosenblatt) 328
Roth, Emil 328
Roth, Emilie (formerly Becker)
    328
Roth, Erna (formerly Grunpeter)
    328
Roth, Hanna, Anna 328
Roth, Heinrich 328
Roth, Inge, Inga 328
Rotter, Jankiel (Jankus) 101, 137,
    138, 191, 207, 209
    Biography 207
Rudenko, Piotr 664
Rum, Franz 434
    Biography 410
Ruth (Surname unknown) 67, 201,
    449, 461, 462
    Biography 207
Rutherford, William 'Billy'
    (Historian) 605, 606, 609, 638
Ryabeka, Fyodor Yakovel 664
Ryba, Walter 94, 103, 199, 410, 432,
    489, 543
Ryschkov, Vasily 664

S

Sabirov, Chares 664
Salomonson-Philips, Esther 244
Salomonson, Rosalie, Johanna 244
Salz, Sala 87
    Biography 207
Sanger, Betty (formerly Bloch) 329
Sanger, Flora 329
Sanger, Frieda 329
Sanger, Friedrich 329
Sbesnikov, Petro 664
Schafer, Herbert 434, 464, 466,
    544
    Biography 411
Scharfe, Herbert 460, 549
    Biography 411
Schelvis-Borzykowski, Rachel 17,
    344
    Biography 244
Schelvis, Jules 5, 17, 165, 190, 241,
    244, 344
    Biography 344
Schelvis, Marie 244
Schelvis, Rebecca 244
Schelvis, Salomon 344
Schevchenko, Dimitrii 664
Schiffner, Karl 411, 412, 432, 489,
    543
    Biography 411
Schlosser-van Dam, Judic 245
Schlosser, Ernst 329
Schlosser, Gompert 245
Schlosser, Levi 245
Schlosser, Miechel 245
Schlosser, Simon 245
Schmidt, Fritz
    Biography 412
Schmidt, Salomon 245
Schreiber, Klaus 96, 103, 664
Schrijver-Okker, Clara 246
    Biography 247
Schrijver-Mendels, Flora 247
Schrijver-Wolff, Mariana 247
Schrijver, Abraham 246
Schrijver, Betje 246

Schrijver, Hermanus 246
Schrijver, Joseph, Nardus 247
  Biography 246
Schrijver, Philip 246
Schrijver, Salomon B.1885 246
Schrijver, Salomon B.1917 246
Schripev, Kamil 664
Schultz, Emanuel
  Szulc, Emanuel 126, 664
Schulz, Anna (formerly Haas) 247
Schulz, Emil 247
Schulze, Erich 562
  Biography 412
Schutt, Hans-Heinz 550–54
Schutt, Hans-Heinz 36, 51, 52, 124, 201, 413, 424, 432, 435, 437, 438, 450, 453, 456, 461, 462, 466, 467, 470, 493, 516, 536, 543, 569
  Biography 413
Schwartz (Firstname unknown) 413
Schwarz-Rosenbaum, Mathilde 248
Schwarz, Clementine (formerly Hanau) 329
Schwarz, Elizabeth (formerly Backhaus) 329
Schwarz, Fanny (formerly Kowler) 330
Schwarz, Gottfried
  Biography 413
Schwarz, Harry 330
Schwarz, Helene (formerly Birnzweig) 330
Schwarz, Herbert 247
Schwarz, Irmgard (formerly Lillenfeld) 330
Schwarz, Leo B.1897 330
Schwarz, Leopold, Leo B.1916 330
Schwarz, Levi 247
Schwarz, Lili (formerly Forst) 330
Schwarz, Lina 330

Schwarz, Lina (formerly Kahn 330
Schwarz, Moritz 330
Schwarz, Walter
  Biography 188
Seleznev, Mikolaj 664
Seligmann, Jacob Moritz 248
Sender (Forename unknown) 98
  Biography 189
Senjonow *Trawnikimann* 664
Sereny, Gitta (Author) 39, 40, 43, 62, 63, 123, 197, 356, 402, 697
Sergienko, Grigorij 664
Serik, Dimitrij 664
Shalayev, Nikolay 26
Shichavin, Pavel 664
Shubayev, Alexander 'Kalimali' 88, 103, 109, 110, 111, 184, 205, 407
  Biography 83, 189
Shukow, Ivan 664
Sickel, Kurt (Dr.) 22
Siefert, Rudolf
  Biography 414
Siegel, Herbert '*Rajowiecer*' 325
  Biography 207
Siegel, Jossel 146
  Biography 189
Simons-a Cohen, Rebecca 248
Simons, Hans 331
Simons, Ilse (formerly Albesheim) 331
Simons, Louis 248
Simons, Salomon 248
Simons, Simon 248
Sirenko, Maxim 664
Sirotenko, Vladmir 664
Slier-Salomonson, Saline, Rozette 250
Slier-Vleeschhouwer, Catharina 250
Slier, Eliazar
  Biography 248
Slier, Elisabeth, Anna 248

Slier, Henri 249
Slier, Joseph 250
  Biography 249
Slier, Leentje 249
Slier, Meijer 249
Slier, Mozes 249
Slier, Philip 248
  Biography 249, 250
Slier, Plas, Anna 249
Sluijzer- Finsi, Serline 250
  Biography 250
Sluijzer, Levie 250
  Biography 250
Smeer-Zwaab, Dora 251
Smeer, Elisabeth
  Biography 251
Smeer, Jacob 251
Smeer, Jacob Philip 251
  Biography 251
Smit, Engeline (formerly de-Vries) 251, 252
Smit, Leopold 252
Sobelman, Cvi 189
Sobol, Bajle 189
Sokorev, Semion 664
Sokur, Kuzma 664
Sommer-Strauss, Lina 252
Sommer, Bruno 252
Sommer, Julius 252
Spitz, Siegfried 80, 91, 325
  Biography 252
Sporrenberg, Jakob 103, 106, 107, 108
Srulek (Forename unknown) 208
Stangl, Franz 16, 25, 28, 39, 40, 41, 42, 60, 62, 63, 64, 68, 79, 120, 123, 136, 137, 141, 197, 354, 356, 368, 369, 372, 373, 374, 375, 376, 380, 381, 404, 405, 424, 427, 428, 429, 430, 437, 439, 441, 443, 444, 448, 450, 453, 454, 455, 459, 460, 461, 462, 468, 478, 480,

489, 499, 506, 508, 513, 516, 517, 519, 537, 543, 554, 606, 697
  'Trottel' 64
  Biography 372
  Testimony 566–77
  Wife, Theresa 62, 64
Stankeiwicz, Henryk 700
Stark, Shaul 208
Steffl, Thomas 91, 100, 103, 171, 172, 354, 414, 415, 421, 422, 432, 561, 562, 565
  Biography 414
Steinberg-Hertz, Selma 253
Steinberg, Salomon 253
  Biography 253
Stelmaszuk, Stephan 47, 48, 700, 702
Stengelin, Erwin 103, 580
  Biography 415
Stern, Maier 253
Stern, Ursula (b. Ilona Safran) 77, 175, 180, 187
Steubl, Karl 35, 68, 137, 174, 415, 432, 441, 446, 450, 461, 489, 491, 506, 511, 512, 543, 557
  Biography 415
Stodel-Borzykowski, Chaja 345
  Biography 254
Stodel-Konig, Martha 254
Stodel, Abraham 254
  Biography 345
Stodel, Albert, Leopold, Clement 254
  Biography 253
Stodel, Leo
  Biography 254
Stodel, Levie 254
Stodel, Lola Ronny 253
  Biography 254
Stodel-Katz, Martha 254
Straten, Van, Rosette 190
Straten, Van, Serline 190

Straus-Kuperschmid, Ester, Chaje 255
Strauss, Abraham 255
Strauss, Adelheid (formerly Braunschwiger) 331
Strauss, Anna (formely Rosenberger) 331
Strauss, Anneliese 331
Strauss, Berta 331
Strauss, Bertha (formerly Strauss) 331
Strauss, Berthold b.1923 331
Strauss, Berthold b.1927 331
Strauss, Else b.1897 332
Strauss, Else b.1920 332
Strauss, Emma (formerly Nussbaum) 332
Strauss, Fanny 332
Strauss, Grete 332
Strauss, Gretel 332
Strauss, Hannchen (formerly Lorge) 332
Strauss, Hanni b.1907 332
Strauss, Hanni b.1920 332
Strauss, Hulda (formerly Eichberg) 333
Strauss, Irma 333
Strauss, Isaak 333
Strauss, Karl 333
Strauss, Liebmann 333
Strauss, Lucie 333
Strauss, Margarete 333
Strauss, Marie (formerly Eisenger) 333
Strauss, Marie (formerly Glass) 333
Strauss, Martha (formerly Meyer) 333
Strauss, Meier 334
Strauss, Minna (formerly Plant) 334
Strauss, Rosa 334

Strauss, Rosa (formerly Jacob) 334
Strauss, Rosa (formerly Katz-Stiefel) 334
Strauss, Sally 334
Strauss, Selma (formerly Strauss) 334
Strauss, Siegfried 334, 345
Streibel, Kurt 67
Sturm, Moshe *'Govenor'* 79, 80, 196, 203, 207, 208, 325
Suchomel, Franz 24, 399, 416, 421, 453, 562
 Biography 416
 Testimony 580–83
Syczuk, Tadeus 48
Sydow, Hermann 416, 580
 Biography 416
Szilpny, Heinrich 664
Szmais, Abraham 190
Szmajzner, Josel 208
Szmajzner, Mosze 101, 136, 191
 Biography 191
Szmajzner, Nojech 56, 101, 191, 207
 Biography 209
Szmajzner, Posel 209
Szmajzner, Ryrka 209
Szmajzner, Stanislaw 56, 57, 58, 59, 64, 80, 81, 92, 94, 98, 101, 123, 136, 137, 140, 141, 142, 144, 161, 162, 170, 190, 192, 200, 208, 209, 576
 Biography 191
 known as Sholmo 54
Szpiro, Mira 209
Szymiel, Leon 192

T

Taraskov, *Trawnikimann* 664
Tass, *Trawnikimann* 664
Teitelbaum, Israel Isi 255
Themans, Bernard, Salomon

Biography 255
Themans, Bernard, Salomon 255
Themans, Judik (formerly Simons) 255
   Biography 255
Themans, Leon 255
Themans, Sonja 255, 256
Thomalla, Richard 16, 24, 32, 33, 365, 448, 450, 497
   Biography 364
Thomas, Kurt 101, 134, 145, 175, 189, 192, 200, 202, 215
Thomas, Martin
   Biography 417
Tichonowski, Fedor 126, 664
Tischenko, Ivan 664
Tonninge, Mozes 256
Trager, Chaim 193
Tregenza, Michael 25
Trootswijk-Hijmans, Annie 256
   Biography 345
Trootswijk, Menno 345
   Biography 256
Tsibulsky, Boris 83, 85, 88, 109, 110
Tuchman, Zygmund 210
Turtelaub, Meier 256

U

Unger-Schumir, Erna 256
Unger, Chaim 256
Unger, Jakob, Wolf 256
Unverhau, Heinrich 36, 118, 125, 399, 417, 432, 435, 438, 456, 466, 489, 494, 506, 543, 555, 557, 563
   Biography 417
Ustinnokov, Ivan 664

V

Vaispapir *See* Wajspapier
Vaksin, Kuzma 664

Vakutenko, Ivan 664
Valk-Emmerich, Selma 257
Valk, Magdalena 257
Vallaster, Josef 36, 37, 48, 49, 91, 103, 137, 203, 390, 429, 430, 441, 444, 445, 447, 450, 452, 453, 457, 459, 467, 477, 489, 522, 523, 526, 544
   Biography 417
Vallaster, Jozef 28
Van Kleef-Van Damm, Saartje 257
   Biography 257
Van Kleef, Salomon 257
van Liempt, Martin 212
van Staden, Li *See* van Straten, Serline
Velde, David Juda Van Der 257
Verduin, Lena 346
Verduin, Sophia 346
Verstandig, Erna 257
Veterman, Jetje 340, 347
Veterman, Sientje 340, 347
Viool, Betje, Judik 257
Viool, Raphael 77, 78
   Biography 258
Visjager-Peters, Rebecca 258
Visser, Israel, Bernard 258
Visser, Kurt Alfred 348
Vodenka, Peter 19
Volyniets, Efim 664

W

Wacjen, Szmul 113, 147, 178, 195
   Biography 193
Wagner, Gustav 28, 35, 41, 57, 58, 68, 78, 80, 88, 117, 118, 120, 136, 137, 138, 139, 141, 142, 146, 148, 150, 152, 154, 155, 159, 161, 163, 168, 179, 185, 191, 192, 196, 199, 207, 208, 209, 325, 387, 418, 419, 433, 437, 439, 441, 443, 444, 446,

448, 450, 453, 454, 456, 463,
465, 468, 472, 473, 478, 480,
486, 489, 491, 493, 504, 506, 511,
512, 514, 516, 531, 544, 552, 556,
558, 561, 562, 563, 581
Biography 418
Wagner, Ilse 258
Wahrhaftig, Abraham 258
Wahrhaftig, Adolf, Adi 258
Waizen, Aleksej 193
Wajspapier, Arkady 89, 103, 109,
110, 179
Biography 194
Waks, Berl 194
Walter, Arthur
Biography 419
Wang, Abraham 194
Wasem, Yakob *Trawnikiman* 664
Weber-Brasch, Irma 258
Wedenko, Fiodor 664
Weijl, Jules, Jacob 258
Weisbecker, Otto 81
Weiss, Bertha (formerly Levy) 335
Weiss, Bruno 41, 206, 433
Biography 419
Weiss, Charlotte (formerly Hirsch) 335
Weiss, Erich 335
Weiss, Frieda (formerly Friedman) 335
Weiss, Grete (formerly Hendler) 335
Weiss, Mina (formerly Sonnenberg) 335
Weiss, Rita 259
Weiss, Theodor 335
Weissberg, Dr. Leon 210
Weissberg, Susel 210
Wendland, Willi 98, 99, 100, 400,
419, 420, 435, 557, 559, 560, 563,
564, 565
Biography 419

Werwyk, Kalman 75, 76, 142, 143, 167
Biography 195
Wieszubski
Biography 210
Winnik, Elisabeth 259
Winnik, Keetje 259
Wins, Jozef 348
Wirth, Christian 23, 25, 27, 40, 41,
42, 63, 65, 67, 68, 103, 115, 122,
354, 366, 367, 368, 369, 370, 371,
373, 377, 388, 392, 394, 395, 396,
403, 433, 450, 453, 463, 469, 472,
484, 491, 496, 498, 505, 506,
507, 508, 512, 521, 522, 523, 526,
527, 532, 547, 548, 554, 567, 568,
569, 570, 571, 573
Biography 366
Wolf brothers 36, 354, 400, 415,
421, 422, 433, 438, 456, 490, 494,
506
Wolf, Franz 98, 99, 124, 400, 419,
421, 438, 562
Biography 420
Testimony 555–66
Wolf, Josef 16, 91, 92, 99, 103, 135,
400, 419, 421, 422, 563
Biography 420
Wolf, Joseph 580
Wolf-Nussbaum, Maier 259
Wulbrandt, Erich 104

Y

Yanek, the carpenter 97
Yasko, Alexsander 664

Z

Zabertnev, Konstantin 664
Zajcew, J. *Trawnikimann* 126, 664
Zak, David, Jacob (Dedi) 259

Zander, Clara 260
Zanker, Hans
  Biography 422
Zaspel, Fritz 549
  Biography 422
Zeehandelaar, Abraham 260
Zeehandelaar, Mozes, Gerrit 260
Zeeman, Joseph 260
Zierke, Ernst 125, 544, 559, 563, 698
  Biography 422
Zijtenfeld, Jacob 260
Zijtenfeld, Moniek 260
Zischer, Emil 67, 180, 664
Ziss, Meier 147
  Biography 195
Zucker, Chana (formerly Sockel) 335
Zucker, Sara 335
Zwartverwer- Spier, Tilly 260

ibidem.eu